AF764250

A Practical Guide to International Philanthropy

This book is a practical guide to the issues faced by philanthropists seeking to engage in international charitable activities and offers alternative approaches to traditional U.S.-based foundations. A significant portion of the regulatory burdens facing U.S. private foundations derives from tax benefits available to donors under U.S. law. A charitable organization must initially qualify and then be maintained under a complex regulatory regime. If some or all of these tax benefits are either unavailable or not needed, or if the tax advantages are outweighed by the burdens of regulatory compliance, foundations can be established in foreign jurisdictions. Charitable activities can then be operated flexibly and privately outside the constraints of the U.S. regulatory regime. For existing private foundations, this book suggests strategies designed to hedge against ever-increasing and intrusive regulation.

Jonathon R. Moore, an internationally recognized expert on the legal aspects of philanthropy, is a partner with the law firm of Moore & Bruce, LLP, in Washington, D.C., and London, England. His practice focuses on planning and compliance matters for exempt organizations and for non-U.S. and U.S. corporate and individual clients interested in establishing charitable organizations. He is a member of the District of Columbia and New York bars, the Committee on Exempt Organizations of the American Bar Association's Section on Taxation, the Philanthropic Advisors Network of the Council on Foundations, and the District of Columbia Estate Planning Council.

A Practical Guide to International Philanthropy

Jonathon R. Moore
Moore & Bruce, LLP

CAMBRIDGE
UNIVERSITY PRESS

CAMBRIDGE UNIVERSITY PRESS
Cambridge, New York, Melbourne, Madrid, Cape Town, Singapore,
São Paulo, Delhi, Dubai, Tokyo

Cambridge University Press
32 Avenue of the Americas, New York, NY 10013-2473, USA

www.cambridge.org
Information on this title: www.cambridge.org/9780521116411

© Jonathon R. Moore 2010

This publication is in copyright. Subject to statutory exception
and to the provisions of relevant collective licensing agreements,
no reproduction of any part may take place without the written
permission of Cambridge University Press.

First published 2010

Printed in the United States of America

A catalog record for this publication is available from the British Library.

Library of Congress Cataloging in Publication data

Moore, Jonathon R.
A practical guide to international philanthropy / Jonathon R. Moore.
p. cm.
Includes bibliographical references and index.
ISBN 978-0-521-11641-1 (hardback)
1. Charitable uses, trusts, and foundations – United States. 2. Nonprofit organizations – Law and legislation – United States.
3. Charities – United States. I. Title.
KF740.M66 2009
346.73′064 – dc22 2009022608

ISBN 978-0-521-11641-1 Hardback

Cambridge University Press has no responsibility for the persistence or
accuracy of URLs for external or third-party Internet Web sites referred to in
this publication and does not guarantee that any content on such Web sites is,
or will remain, accurate or appropriate.

Disclaimer

This book is not a comprehensive treatment of all the legal, tax, and accounting issues surrounding international philanthropy. It is intended rather as a practical guide and as a review of the major topics associated with international philanthropic endeavors. It is hoped that it will prove especially helpful to individuals and families wishing to establish a structure dedicated to international philanthropy, individuals currently working with U.S. or other national charitable foundations, and persons who advise or otherwise deal with these people and groups.

Jonathon R. Moore is the author of this book. The author and his law firm, Moore & Bruce, LLP, expressly disclaim any liability to any person in respect of anything done or omitted in reliance on anything contained herein. The information contained in this book is not intended and should not be construed as any form of legal advice. Nor is the provision of this information intended to create an attorney-client relationship between the author or Moore & Bruce, LLP, and the reader. No person should act or refrain from acting on the basis of any matter contained herein without seeking appropriate legal or other professional advice.

This book is based on materials available as of August 1, 2009. The information contained herein is subject to change.

Readers' comments and corrections would be greatly appreciated. Please send these to jmoore@mooreandbruce.com. Updates to topics covered in this work are posted at http://www.mooreandbruce.com.

Contents

Preface

There have been many developments in the law and regulation of international charities since the author's previous work on the subject, *International Charitable Foundations: An Introduction*, which was published in 2002 by Richmond Law & Tax Ltd. and Transnational Publishers Inc. Although that work is now out of print and seriously out of date, this book borrows liberally from it, not only in terms of organization and approach but also with respect to topics and areas of the law that are fundamentally unchanged.

Since the publication of the prior work, three watershed events have occurred that compel the pages that follow.

First, the September 11, 2001, terrorist attacks are unquestionably one of those historical markers against which ideas, practices, and laws are measured by before-and-after comparisons. The revelation that international terrorists utilized charitable structures as covert financing vehicles as well as instrumentalities of political patronage precipitated scrutiny of all international charitable activities from the Internal Revenue Service as well as the U.S. Treasury Department's other agencies charged with the detection and prosecution of international financial crimes. The most tangible manifestation of this enhanced scrutiny has been the Treasury Department's issuance of a series of guidelines of recommended best practices for U.S. charities involved in international activities. These guidelines are discussed in detail and constitute an evolving area of law that will require future monitoring by all who work in this area.

Second, the well-publicized decision by the American entrepreneur Warren Buffet to donate more than $30 billion to the Bill and Melinda Gates Foundation will resonate throughout the regulatory regimes governing private foundations for years to come. The gift created a philanthropic behemoth with more than $60 billion in assets, and in one act of generosity, rendered the Gates Foundation nearly six times the size of the next largest private foundation, the Ford Foundation. By comparison, a single private charity will now command assets exceeding the annual gross domestic product of more than fifty countries, including oil-rich Kuwait, and will have assets comparable to or exceeding those of numerous Fortune 500 corporations, including Boeing, Disney, and Home Depot. So much wealth in the hands of so few individuals, whether dedicated to public purposes – here, improving education and health care – or otherwise, will inevitably precipitate calls for greater transparency, which will then be followed by new standards of regulation from those members of Congress and other branches of government who unabashedly will take the view that the Gates Foundation is not spending its philanthropic dollars wisely or appropriately.

Third, the trend toward enhanced regulation of all U.S.-based charities, public and private, in the name of reform has continued unabated. Major new legislation regulating charities was enacted in August 2006, and additional legislative initiatives are sure to follow, at both the federal and the state levels. Occasional abuses by well-known public charities – for example, the grants of excessive tax benefits to wealthy insiders in the Nature Conservancy relating to environmental easements – have unleashed congressional calls for new levels of regulation. Broadly speaking, the direction of these proposals is to extend the Sarbanes-Oxley "reforms" in corporate governance to the charitable arena. Driven by inherent congressional distrust of private wealth and of charitable vehicles created by the wealthy, increased levels of regulation are to be expected in the future.

The long-term implications of each of these trends for practitioners of international philanthropy are addressed in this book.

"Give, and it shall be given unto you; good measure, pressed down, and shaken together, and running over, shall men give unto your bosom. For with the same measure that ye mete withal shall it be measured to you again."

Luke 6:38

"And besides this, giving all diligence, add to your faith virtue; and to virtue knowledge; And to knowledge temperance; and to temperance patience; and to patience godliness; And to godliness brotherly kindness; and to brotherly kindness charity."

2 Peter 1:5–7

Who should read this book

You are successful and affluent. Perhaps you have become wealthy as an entrepreneur who has formed and grown a successful business. Perhaps you have achieved success as an investor by multiplying the capital you have accumulated from the sale of a business. Perhaps you have recently received a sizable inheritance. Now what?

Presumably the material wealth you now possess will be sufficient to maintain the standard of living you have set for yourself and your family so that you no longer need to "make a living." So now is the time to ask yourself, What is my passion? For many, it will be golf, sailing, or travel. But for many others, such pursuits by themselves would not be fulfilling. For these persons, a wider cause – whether promoting education, alleviating poverty, promoting peace and understanding among nations, enhancing protection of the environment, or advancing science – beckons. Having spent much of your adult life pursuing financial security, success now accords the freedom to pursue goals that will benefit some segment of humankind. Just as your endeavors in business or investing have been notable, your philanthropic goals will likely target something significant.

This book is written for those families and individuals who are ready to pursue charitable goals seriously, as well as those who are already doing so. Its principles also apply to businesses seeking to set aside some portion of their potential or accumulated profits to devote to such pursuits. They also apply to existing U.S. foundations considering expansion of their scope and perhaps adoption of a hedging strategy in the event trends toward overreaching government regulation continue.

The pages that follow will examine factors and decisions that are inherently private. As will be explained in detail, U.S. tax disincentives drive numerous charitable organizations to operate as public charities. Public charities, however, usually expend a sizable portion of the gifts they receive each year for their charitable purposes and then each year again seek to raise additional resources to replenish those grants. If you contemplate funding an organization with a single or series of large gifts and wish to avoid raising new funding from outside sources on a continuing basis, you will not be interested in establishing a new public charity. Fundamentally, you will want to control the direction in operations of the philanthropic endeavors to be pursued.

In evaluating whether to establish a private foundation, it is assumed that the purposes of the foundation will be innovative and uniquely responsive to a set of perceived problems – and perhaps controversial. Of course, if your philanthropic interests are addressed by an existing public charity, you may wish to devote your resources to furthering that entity's goals. In that case, join the organization, support it, and perhaps become a member of its board. If you can find such an organization, so that your charitable goals can be realized by piggybacking on an existing organizational and legal infrastructure created and maintained by a public charity, you can stop reading now.

To the extent, however, that existing charities may not fulfill your sense of what can or should be accomplished in any particular field of charitable endeavor – and in particular, your potential for leadership – this book will provide guidance on alternatives to pursuing your vision. Your efforts have generated the resources; it is your prerogative to pursue and advance your values and philanthropic goals. The vehicle for doing so will allow you to instill in your children or other family members or friends the values you are articulating and pursuing and attract a group of individuals that share these values and will help you implement them. Moreover, it will allow you to pass your unique charitable values on to succeeding generations and serve as a uniting force for your family and/or close circle of friends.

So how do you set up a foundation? What type of legal structure do you use and where do you establish it? Most individuals in the United States, that is, U.S. citizens and residents for tax purposes (so-called green-card holders), pursuing philanthropic goals will either participate in existing entities or establish private foundations under the law of a particular state. Frequently, decisions on structure will be driven by tax considerations as to the deductibility from federal and state income taxes or estate taxes and exclusion from gift taxes. Indeed, most of the current structure of regulation of U.S. charitable organizations derives from the tax benefits granted to donors and the exemption from taxation to the organizations themselves.

This book discusses the legal framework and mechanics of establishing a charitable entity that qualifies for tax benefits available under U.S. law. Those benefits, however, come with strings attached in the form of a complex regulatory regime, under which the charitable organization must initially qualify and then be operated and maintained. Moreover, in the wake of the September 11, 2001, terrorist attacks and the Enron-era corporate scandals, Congress, the Internal Revenue Service, and state legislatures are all actively looking for new ways to regulate charities. Stricter, and therefore more intrusive, regulation in some form or another will surely be a permanent part of the regulatory framework under which U.S.-based charities must operate in the future.

Where the tax benefits available under U.S. law are of minimal value because of the donor's individual tax circumstances, are not necessarily needed, or can be deliberately forgone, this book argues that foreign jurisdictions should be considered as the situs for the charity. In foreign jurisdictions, the charity can be operated flexibly – and privately – outside of the constraints of the U.S. regulatory regime governing private foundations. This book provides a road map for establishing a charity in a foreign jurisdiction and describes the advantages and disadvantages of utilizing foreign charitable structures for U.S. citizens and residents.

For some individuals, the U.S. tax advantages available are more than outweighed by the burdens and constraints of regulatory compliance. For others, their charitable purposes are impossible to achieve under current U.S. regulations. For example, anonymity of gifts is virtually impossible from a U.S. private foundation. Likewise, devoting all of the profits from an ongoing business enterprise toward charitable purposes is prohibited by the U.S. private foundation regulatory regime. Such individuals may deliberately choose to forgo short-term tax benefits in favor of longer-term freedom accorded from a foreign foundation structure.

The ideas in this work may also appeal to families and individuals who are already operating private foundations in the United States and are concerned with the growing intrusiveness of government regulation of their charitable endeavors. For this group, the possibility of cloning the charitable organization outside of the United States represents a hedging strategy, so that if expanding regulation should become too burdensome, the charitable structure will already be in place for continuing philanthropic activities outside of the United States without interruption. In the interim, the foreign charitable structure can be test-driven. Just as investors employ multiple strategies to buffer risks inherent in any specific investment sector, establishment of a foreign private foundation can provide an alternative approach to pursuing charitable goals unconstrained by the burdens of multiple layers of government regulation in the United States.

This book is written for American philanthropists – current and potential. Although its author is a lawyer and the legal topography to be navigated in order to have a basic understanding of the area is complex, the approach of this book is practical and hands-on. The usual law review or legal textbook formats and their emphasis on footnoted minutiae are avoided. Although lawyers not expert in the area of exempt organizations may find the topics covered useful as a general overview of applicable law, this book does not hold itself out to be a comprehensive legal treatise. It is written for laypeople making decisions to create charitable organizations and for their advisers. Nevertheless, primary authorities and references are cited.

False charity

Many of the ideas in this book are controversial. Its subtitle could well be "Living with Anachronistic Internal Revenue Code Provisions Governing International Charitable Activities." The observations herein and the possible alternative charitable structures described are most decidedly not mainstream thinking, and indeed may be perceived as dangerous, overly aggressive, or subversive by legislative and executive branch individuals charged with implementing, overseeing, and perhaps expanding the existing regimes regulating private foundations, particularly in the post–September 11 world.

None of the suggestions offered, however, should be understood to provide a road map to those who would subvert charitable or philanthropic enterprises for illegitimate purposes. Much has been written after September 11, 2001, about certain so-called Islamic charities. Although having names suggesting that their purposes, for example, are to alleviate poverty and hunger among children, some of these entities in fact have served as conduits for supporting terrorism. The subversion or perversion of charitable organizations for evil purposes should not be permitted to constrain the vast array of legitimate philanthropic organizations that are working creatively to address numerous problems of the world, which are not or cannot be remedied by governments or private enterprise.

Stated differently, none of the comments or suggestions in this book should be viewed as a guide to gaming the system or an invitation to subterfuge.

A Practical Guide to International Philanthropy

CHAPTER ONE

Introduction

Charitable giving as an American value

Before delving into the details of international philanthropic endeavors, a brief digression is in order. In dealing with the international work of various charities, it is impossible to overlook how so many charitable activities are predominantly American in concept and implementation. Indeed, in surveying the landscape of international charitable endeavors, one is struck by the relatively small contribution made by individuals of other countries. It is difficult not to conclude that there is something uniquely American about the culture that creates such a strong desire to help others or to work for causes for the general betterment of mankind.

As a legal practitioner, I work frequently with individuals from other countries. When I describe my work on behalf of American charities, clients are often puzzled. In their cultures, family wealth is to be zealously preserved, so it can be passed on to future generations. By contrast, many Americans fundamentally believe that large amounts of wealth in the hands of the young will result in no good whatsoever and, in fact, will be likely to inure to their long-term detriment. After all, self-reliance and hard work are the main values to be passed to the next generation, and many believe that it is important to give back to society generally some measure of individual success and affluence.

Another quintessentially American attitude is that it is up to individuals rather than the government to ameliorate poverty, malnutrition, and disease and to improve education. In most of the countries in Europe, by contrast, individuals do not feel that they need to contribute in these fields, perhaps because the government implements recognized and established minimum standards in a number of basic areas.[1] The concept of the welfare state has developed over the course of centuries in Europe; it has never been generally accepted in the United States. By contrast, the problems and outright failures of government programs are acknowledged and well documented in America. Indeed, a number of U.S. presidents have devoted

1 "This is how Europe's welfare state works: Taxes are so high that private citizens have come to believe it is only the state's duty to support cultural institutions and public welfare. The ambit for private giving shrinks." "The Charity Revolt," *Wall Street Journal*, editorial, March 10, 2009.

considerable efforts to encouraging private charities to step in and address the perceived social welfare shortcomings of government.

Add to this the prominence and importance of religion in many American lives, and we have at least a partial explanation of why charitable giving is so central to American cultural values. From the mid-1800s and Washington Gladden's social gospelism to numerous social activist churches in contemporary America, churches have played a prominent role in charitable activities. But so do churchgoers. A recent Social Capital Community Benchmark survey indicated that Americans who attend services weekly are 25 percent more likely to give to charity than are people who rarely or never go to church. In terms of dollars given, American churchgoers give nearly four times as much annually as do their secular counterparts and volunteer, on average, twice as frequently.

Charitable giving in America today

Charitable organizations as a group are often referred to as the third sector or the independent sector. Those individuals unfamiliar with the scope of charitable endeavors may think this designation a misnomer, as the size of the charitable sector is often perceived as minuscule when compared with that of the government or private enterprise. While the charitable sector is unquestionably the smallest of the three sectors, the number and diversity of U.S. charities are truly astounding.

Magnitude

Organizations

There are currently approximately 1.8 million organizations in the United States that are recognized as exempt from taxation by the Internal Revenue Service.[2] Chart A, which is taken from the Internal Revenue Service's *Data Book 2007*, from the most recent year for which such data are available, lists various types of exempt organizations by statutory category. According to data compiled by the National Center for Charitable Statistics, a project of the Center on Nonprofits and Philanthropy at the Urban Institute, such entities accounted for approximately $1.4 trillion in revenue and $3 trillion dollars in assets in 2004.[3] If the nonprofit sector were a country, it would have the seventh-largest economy in the world.[4] A recent survey of the nonprofit sector published in *The Chronicle of Philanthropy* indicates that, in 2005, the sector employed 12.9 million people, who earned 8.1 percent of the nation's total wages.[5] Moreover, the workforce of the charitable nonprofit sector represents 10.5 percent of the country's total workforce.[6]

2 Internal Revenue Service, *Data Book 2007*, table 25.
3 www.urban.org/uploadedpdf/311373_nonprofit_sector.pdf.
4 www.ncna.org/index.cfm?fuseaction=Page.viewPage&pageId=734.
5 "The Nonprofit World: Its Size and Scope," *Chronicle of Philanthropy*, May 15, 2008, 32.
6 Lester M. Salamon and S. Wojciech, *Employment in America's Charities: A Profile* (Johns Hopkins Center for Civil Society Studies, 2006). Copies of this report are available at the Center for Civil Society Studies Web site, at http://www.jhu.edu/ccss.

Chart A. *Tax-exempt organizations and nonexempt charitable trusts, fiscal years 2004–2007*

Type of organization, Internal Revenue Code section	2004 (1)	2005 (2)	2006 (3)	2007 (4)
Tax-exempt organizations and other entities, total	**1,680,061**	**1,709,205**	**1,726,491**	**1,789,554**
Section 501(c) by subsection, total	**1,540,554**	**1,570,023**	**1,585,479**	**1,648,306**
(1) Corporations organized under act of Congress	116	123	126	134
(2) Title-holding corporations	7,144	7,116	7,120	7,136
(3) Religious, charitable, and similar organizations[a]	1,010,365	1,045,979	1,064,191	1,128,367
(4) Social welfare organizations	138,193	136,060	135,155	134,843
(5) Labor and agriculture organizations	62,561	61,075	60,932	60,634
(6) Business leagues	86,054	86,485	86,563	88,071
(7) Social and recreation clubs	70,422	70,399	70,569	71,092
(8) Fraternal beneficiary societies	69,798	67,391	65,752	64,216
(9) Voluntary employees' beneficiary associations	12,866	12,567	12,206	12,128
(10) Domestic fraternal beneficiary societies	21,328	21,091	21,385	20,390
(12) Benevolent life insurance associations	6,716	6,718	6,738	6,793
(13) Cemetery companies	10,728	10,819	10,879	11,098
(14) State-chartered credit unions	4,289	4,083	3,976	3,860
(15) Mutual insurance companies	1,988	2,127	2,126	2,073
(17) Supplemental unemployment benefit trusts	462	448	438	434
(19) War veterans' organizations	36,141	36,166	35,982	35,702
(25) Holding companies for pensions and other entities	1,285	1,274	1,238	1,234
Other 501(c) subsections[b]	98	102	103	101
Section 501(d) Religious and apostolic associations	**141**	**146**	**162**	**162**
Section 501(e) Cooperative hospital service organizations	**38**	**37**	**37**	**37**
Section 501(f) Cooperative service organizations of operating educational organizations	**1**	**1**	**1**	**1**
Section 501(k) Child care organizations	**3**	**2**	**6**	**15**

(*continued*)

Chart A (*continued*)

Type of organization, Internal Revenue Code section	2004 (1)	2005 (2)	2006 (3)	2007 (4)
Section 501(n) Charitable risk pools	**1**	**2**	**2**	**1**
Nonexempt charitable trusts	**139,323**	**138,994**	**140,804**	**141,032**

[a] Includes private foundations. Not all section 501(c)(3) organizations are required to apply for recognition of tax exemption, including churches, integrated auxiliaries, subordinate units, and conventions or associations of churches.

[b] Includes teachers' retirement funds [section 501(c)(11)]; corporations to finance crop operations [section 501(c)(16)]; employee-funded pension trusts [section 501(c)(18)]; black-lung trusts [section 501(c)(21)]; multiemployer pension plans [section 501(c)(22)]; veterans' associations founded prior to 1880 [section 501(c)(23)]; trusts described in section 4049 of the Employee Security Act of 1974 (ERISA) [section 501(c)(24)]; state-sponsored high-risk health insurance organizations [section 501(c)(26)]; and state-sponsored workers' compensation reinsurance organizations [section 501(c)(27)].

Source: Tax Exempt and Government Entities SE:T:BSP.

Although it is already large, the sector is growing rapidly. In 2007, more than eighty-five thousand new charitable organizations sought recognition of tax-exempt status under section 501(c)(3) from the Internal Revenue Service.[7] Moreover, the ten-year snapshot of the nonprofit sector by the Urban Institute published in *Chronicle of Philanthropy* indicates that the sector is growing more rapidly than the overall economy.[8] For example, while the economy grew approximately 35 percent for the years 1995 through 2005, the revenue of nonprofit groups increased nearly 55 percent, and their total assets grew by 77 percent in the same period.

Donors

Although there is no single methodology or data source by which donations to charities can be quantified, reasonable estimates confirm that charitable giving in America is indeed substantial. A well-publicized annual survey by the Giving USA Foundation estimated that charitable giving in the United States exceeded $305 billion in 2007.[9] The survey began with annual Internal Revenue Service data compilations of itemized charitable deductions. Because most higher-income taxpayers itemize their deductions, and because general information is available concerning the relative proportionate shares of contributions made by different income groups, the survey applies that methodology to derive an overall estimate

7 IRS *Data Book 2007*, table 24.
8 "The Nonprofit World: Its Size and Scope," *Chronicle of Philanthropy* (May 15, 2008), 32.
9 *Giving USA 2008*. The report is researched and written by the Center on Philanthropy at Indiana University.

of annual individual donations to include the two-thirds of taxpayers who do not itemize deductions. To these estimates are added corporate contributions. These figures are then corroborated against data obtained from most larger charitable organizations themselves, to confirm the accuracy of the donor figures.

Not surprisingly, a high concentration of wealthy families contributed substantially to the overall total. In a recent profile of major donors in 2008 by *Chronicle of Philanthropy*, the fifty largest donors are documented as having given or pledged $15.5 billion in 2008. To make the top 50 list, donors had to commit at least $30.5 million. The top two gifts were $5.2 billion and $4.5 billion.[10]

Scope

The focus of this book is on charitable organizations. In the broad classifications of exempt organizations, charities fall under section 501(c)(3), which covers "religious, scientific, educational and charitable organizations." The term "charitable" is not defined in the statute, and the regulations, while listing numerous types of charitable endeavors, expressly decline to limit the type of activities that are considered charitable under the law.[11]

A sense of the broad scope of charitable endeavors can be seen in Chart B, which was compiled by the Foundation Center. It gives an excellent overview of grant making by category of charitable use. The chart not only is useful in illustrating broad categories of charitable endeavors (e.g., arts, culture, education, environment, human services, science) but also breaks down the broad categories into typical activities.[12]

The analysis of charitable giving conducted by the Foundation Center indicates that more than $42.9 billion in charitable grants were made in 2007 by various types of foundations (independent foundations, corporate foundations, and community foundations), in addition to grants made by so-called public charities.[13] The 2007 giving figures represent a nearly 10 percent increase from 2006.[14] These include, for example, more than $710 million to museums, nearly $1.2 billion for medical research, and more than $700 million for community improvement. Within each of these categories and subcategories, numerous creative, innovative, and visionary grants were made.

The foregoing statistics include only foundations and other tax-exempt organizations operating in the United States or reporting information to the Internal Revenue Service. Internationally, the levels of charitable activities without a doubt

10 Maria Di Mento and Caroline Preston, "A Year of Big Bequests," *Chronicle of Philanthropy*, January 29, 2009, 6.

11 Regulations section 1.501(c)(3)-1(d)(2).

12 An even more comprehensive list of the types of activities considered to be charitable has been developed by the National Center for Charitable Statistics. Its "National Taxonomy of Exempt Entities" breaks down the categories listed in Chart B into numerous additional subcategories. The system is accessible on the Internet at http://nccs2.urban.org/ntee-cc/.

13 www.foundationcenter.org/gainknowledge/research/pdf/fgge08.pdf.

14 www.foundationcenter.org/gainknowledge/research/pdf/fgge08.pdf.

Chart B. *Distribution of foundation grants by subject categories, circa 2006*

	Dollar value of grants		No. of grants	
Subject	Amount ($)	%	No.	%
Arts and Culture				
Policy, management, and information[a]	21,931	0.1	208	0.1
Arts, multipurpose	213,693	1.1	2,527	1.8
Media and communications	176,517	0.9	1,594	1.1
Visual arts/architecture	167,566	0.9	886	0.6
Museums	710,863	3.7	4,196	3.0
Performing arts	807,724	4.2	8,264	5.9
Humanities	90,941	0.5	782	0.6
Historic preservation	112,057	0.6	1,309	0.9
Other	28,416	0.1	329	0.2
Total arts and culture	$2,329,708	12.2	20,095	14.3
Education				
Policy, management, and information[a]	$68,457	0.4	384	0.3
Elementary and secondary	1,360,743	7.1	10,295	7.3
Vocational and technical	13,221	0.1	224	0.2
Higher education	1,652,129	8.6	9,008	6.4
Graduate and professional	439,777	2.3	2,458	1.7
Adult and continuing	32,016	0.2	502	0.4
Library science and libraries	254,211	1.3	1,241	0.9
Student services	160,088	0.8	997	0.7
Educational services	325,448	1.7	3,412	2.4
Total education	$4,306,090	22.5	28,521	20.3
Environment and animals				
Environment	$923,541	4.8	6,978	5.0
Animals and wildlife	221,559	1.2	1,655	1.2
Total environment and animals	$1,145,100	6.0	8,633	6.1
Health				
General and rehabilitative				
Policy, management, and information[a]	$138,076	0.7	585	0.4
Hospitals and medical care	922,943	4.8	5,979	4.3
Reproductive health care	254,227	1.3	1,006	0.7
Public health	923,379	4.8	1,915	1.4
Other	147,118	0.8	917	0.7
Specific diseases	651,358	3.4	3,402	2.4
Medical research	1,160,460	6.1	2,071	1.5
Mental health	196,901	1.0	2,385	1.7
Total health	$4,394,462	23.0	18,260	13.0
Human services				
Crime, justice, and legal services	191,525	1.0	2,593	1.8
Employment	135,041	0.7	1,850	1.3
Food, nutrition, and agriculture	184,147	1.0	2,015	1.4
Housing and shelter	246,343	1.3	3,952	2.8

(continued)

Subject	Dollar value of grants		No. of grants	
	Amount ($)	%	No.	%
Safety and disaster relief	116,484	0.6	854	0.6
Recreation and sports	318,672	1.7	2,752	1.9
Youth development	328,119	1.7	5,179	3.7
Human services, multipurpose	1,125,563	5.9	16,822	12.0
Total human services	$2,645,895	13.8	36,047	25.7
Information affairs, development, peace, and human rights	$1,091,730	5.3	3,703	2.7
Public affairs/society benefit				
Civil rights and social action	218,562	1.1	2,250	1.6
Community improvement and development	700.123	3.7	6,364	4.5
Philanthropy and voluntarism[sic]	753,510	3.9	5,134	3.7
Public affairs	370,296	1.9	3,059	2.2
Total public affairs/society benefit	$2,042,490	10.7	16,807	12.0
Science and technology				
Policy, management, and information	$21,132	0.1	148	0.1
General science	225,419	1.2	678	0.5
Physical science	116,901	0.6	706	0.5
Technology	88,447	0.4	508	0.3
Life science	98,291	0.5	381	0.3
Other	400	0.0	1	0.0
Total science and technology	$550,591	2.9	2,422	1.7
Social science				
Social sciences and economics	$86,237	0.5	649	0.5
Interdisciplinary/other	172,855	0.9	679	0.5
Total social sciences	$259,092	1.4	1,328	0.9
Religion	$412,355	2.2	4,485	3.2
Other	$16,512	0.1	122	0.1
Total grant dollars	$19,123,033	100.0	140,484	100.0

Notes: Dollar figures in thousands; due to rounding, figures may not add up. Based on all grants of $10,000 or more awarded by a national sample of 1,263 larger U.S. foundations (including 800 of the 1,000 largest ranked by total giving). For community foundations, only discretionary grants are included. Grants to individuals are not included in the file.

[a] Includes a broad range of supporting activities or organizations identified by eighteen common codes.

Source: The Foundation Center, 2008. Copyright © 2008, The Foundation Center. All rights reserved. Permission to use, copy, and/or distribute this document in whole or in part for internal, noncommercial purposes without fee is hereby granted provided that this notice and appropriate credit to the Foundation Center is included in all copies. All references to data contained in this document must also credit the Foundation Center No other reproduction, republishing, or dissemination in any manner or form is permitted without prior written consent from the Foundation Center. Requests for written consent should be submitted to the Foundation Center's Research Department. The Foundation Center's Statistical Information Service, http://foundationcenter.org/findfunders/statistics/.

are certain to be broader, if not significantly so, and therefore represent a significant contribution to the well-being of the world.

The dramatic expansion of international charitable giving is the topic of a 2008 study prepared by the Foundation Center in cooperation with the Council on Foundations: *International Grantmaking IV, an Update on US Foundation Trends.* The study verifies that international grant making grew at a far faster rate than overall giving from 2002 to 2007. The study points out that increasingly the problems facing the world transcend political borders, such as global climate change, and accordingly are receiving ever-increasing attention from philanthropists. While a large portion of the increase in international grant making derives from the Gates Foundation, even without its substantial contribution, the growth in international grant making is outpacing overall charitable giving in the United States.

The study utilizes the same classification system set forth in Chart B in quantifying the levels and distribution of international grant making. Chart C compares the distribution of grants by category between U.S.-based and overseas recipients. Although the Gates Foundation is responsible for extraordinary levels of grants for health-care initiatives outside of the United States, significant distribution internationally among broad categories is noteworthy, particularly in the categories of international development and environmental, including climate change issues.

Causes

Manifestly, there is no shortage of problems in the world that are not being adequately addressed by governments or private enterprise. The breadth and imagination of charitable endeavors therefore should come as no surprise. Often, these endeavors are as highly focused, if not as quirky,[15] as the business enterprises that gave rise to the charitable resources in the first instance. For example:

- Gordon Moore, founder of Intel, through the Gordon and Betty Moore Foundation, has funded efforts to protect global biodiversity through Conservation International. Through a series of grants totaling $261 million over ten years, it has helped create an alliance of conservation partners that hopes to leverage $4.5 billion to acquire large parcels of land in twenty-five so-called biodiversity hot spots. Although the areas represent just 1.4 percent of the earth's land surface, they are said to claim more than

15 See John Elkington and Pamela Hartigan's recent book, *The Power of Unreasonable People: How Social Entrepreneurs Create Markets That Change the World* (Harvard Business School Press, 2008). The book cites examples of social entrepreneurs creating dramatic goals and results, such as Sir Richard Branson's Virgin Earth Challenge, which seeks to find a commercially viable technology that will remove 1 billion metric tons of carbon dioxide from the atmosphere each year for ten years. The book also identifies ten "opportunity spaces" where social entrepreneurs can step in and solve present and future challenges, including an expanding world population, nutrition and natural resource shortages, educational disparities, and environmental concerns. See also Edward Humes, *Eco Barons: The Dreamers, Schemers, and Millionaires Who Are Saving Our Planet* (Ecco/HarperCollins, 2009).

Chart C. *Distribution of international grants to United States–based vs. overseas recipients by major program area, 2006*

	U.S.-based recipients				Overseas recipients			
Program Area	Amount	%	No.	%	Amount	%	No.	%
Health	$762,780,210	32.8	852	10.2	$1,033,581,395	54.7	752	15.8
Health care, general	31,420,786	1.4	311	3.7	52,054,924	2.8	140	2.9
Medical research	374,764,862	16.1	58	0.7	113,395,132	6.0	97	2.0
Mental health	1,012,485	0.0	22	0.3	1,925,440	0.1	30	0.6
Public health	92,352,768	4.0	118	1.4	584,588,526	30.9	94	2.0
Reproductive health care	61,795, 782	2.7	160	1.9	116,365,426	6.2	161	3.4
Specific diseases	201,433,527	8.7	183	2.2	165,251,947	8.7	230	4.8
International development, relief	542,385,058	23.4	2,438	29.2	341,887,061	18.1	1,004	21.1
Agricultural development	82,913,939	3.6	124	1.5	219,063,140	11.6	179	3.8
Community/economic development	95,659,188	4.1	425	5.1	56,537,094	3.5	303	6.4
Development/relief, general	200,687,130	8.6	767	9.2	11,839,677	0.6	65	1.4
Human services	45,283,032	1.9	448	5.4	25,338,954	1.3	369	7.8
Relief/humanitarian aid	117,841,769	5.1	674	8.1	19,108,196	1.0	88	1.8
Environment	256,749,170	11.1	880	10.5	71,620,973	3.8	555	11.7
Animals and wildlife	33,364,579	1.4	183	2.2	8,844,323	0.5	55	1.2
Conservation, other	5,120,891	0.2	57	0.7	5,261,678	0.3	66	1.4
Natural resources	172,112,125	7.4	502	6.0	52,011,636	2.8	386	8.1
Pollution control	46,151,575	2.0	138	1.7	5,503,336	0.3	48	1.0
International affairs	233,017,944	10.0	1,176	14.1	14,579,719	0.8	71	1.5
Foreign policy	27,279,672	1.2	148	1.8	3,570,000	0.2	14	0.3
International affairs, research/policy	12,661,798	0.5	31	0.4	175,000	0.0	5	0.1

(*continued*)

Chart C (*continued*)

	U.S.-based recipients				Overseas recipients			
Program Area	Amount	%	No.	%	Amount	%	No.	%
Peace and security	107,174,916	4.6	471	5.6	10,569,250	0.6	45	0.9
Promoting international understanding	61,524,617	2.6	370	4.4	248,618	0.0	6	0.1
International affairs, other	24,376,941	1.0	156	1.9	16,851	0.0	1	0.0
Education	123,238,777	5.3	684	8.2	121.386,370	6.4	699	14.7
Adult and continuing	180,184	0.0	8	0.1	629,798	0.0	5	0.1
Elementary and secondary	19,921,247	0.9	184	2.2	12,855,897	0.7	190	4.0
Graduate and professional	30,707,758	1.3	133	1.6	15,721,759	0.8	102	2.1
Higher education	42,799,258	1.8	213	2.6	55,764,519	2.9	194	4.1
Libraries	2,437,122	0.1	26	0.3	23,144,305	1.2	32	0.7
Education, other	27,193,208	1.2	120	1.4	13,270,092	0.7	176	3.7
Public affairs/society benefit[a]	83,591,954	3.6	367	4.4	79,697,172	4.2	333	7.0
Civil society/democracy, other	15,882,582	0.7	83	1.0	26,086,848	1.4	124	2.6
Philanthropy and voluntarism [sic]	25,578,337	1.1	171	2.0	37,963,264	2.0	133	2.8
Public affairs/government	42,131,035	1.8	113	1.4	15,647,060	0.8	76	1.6
Arts and culture	78,447,492	3.4	644	7.7	78,606,687	4.2	354	7.4
Arts, multidisciplinary	3,951,616	0.2	59	0.7	9,235,511	0.5	65	1.4
Historic preservation	2,521,323	0.1	51	0.6	8,263,019	0.4	20	0.4
Humanities	18,991,250	0.8	107	1.3	6,797,213	0.4	37	0.8
Media and communications	15,852,157	0.7	83	1.0	6,148,148	0.3	45	0.9
Museums/visual arts	22,714,339	1.0	153	1.8	34,434,524	1.8	111	2.3
Performing arts	11,145,486	0.5	99	1.2	13,421,222	0.7	71	1.5
Arts, other	3,271,321	0.1	92	1.1	307,050	0.0	5	0.1

Social sciences	117,575,173	5.1	345	4.1	29,601,681	1.6	155	3.3
Economics	3,870,399	0.2	22	0.3	5,065,400	0.3	14	0.3
International law/law	7,277,520	0.3	20	0.2	2,232,281	0.1	12	0.3
International area studies	85,063,704	3.7	206	2.5	3,333,826	0.2	22	0.5
Population studies	12,537,620	0.5	28	0.3	6,923,649	0.4	22	0.5
Women's studies	1,211,500	0.1	8	0.1	1,697,700	0.1	7	0.1
Interdisciplinary research, other	5,590,930	0.2	42	0.5	4,496,013	0.2	39	0.8
Social sciences, other	2,023,500	0.1	19	0.2	5,852,812	0.3	39	0.8
Human rights/civil liberties	71,107,248	3.1	532	6.4	70,789,546	3.7	367	7.7
Civil liberties, legal services	12,369,878	0.5	146	1.7	31,313,160	1.7	188	3.9
Human rights	48,830,117	2.1	314	3.8	24,818,353	1.3	152	3.2
Migration, refugee issues	9,907,253	0.4	72	0.9	14,658,033	0.8	27	0.6
Religion	28,793,241	1.2	317	3.8	30,770,544	1.6	342	7.2
Science and technology	24,951,496	1.1	116	1.4	17,352,085	0.9	111	2.3
Biological science	6,230,847	0.3	22	0.3	2,987,880	0.2	24	0.5
General science	12,148,890	0.5	30	0.4	8, 556, 011	0.5	35	0.7
Science, other	6,571,759	0.3	64	0.8	5,808,194	0.3	52	1.1
Other	0	0.0	0	0.0	838,204	0.0	18	0.4
Total	$2,322,637,763	100.0	8,351	100.0	$1,890,711,437	100.0	4,761	100.0

Notes: Based on all grants of $10,000 or more from a sample of 1,263 foundations.

[a] The "public affairs/society benefit" category includes grants for public affairs, philanthropy, and general grants to promote civil society. Civil society grants are also found in other categories, such as human rights and international development.

Source: The Foundation Center, *International Grantmaking IV*, 2008.

60 percent of all plant and animal species.[16] With an endowment of approximately $6 billion, the Gordon and Betty Moore Foundation focuses on environmental conservation, science, and the San Francisco Bay Area. In 2007, the foundation awarded 134 grants totaling $230 million.[17]

- Richard C. Blum, a San Francisco investment banker, founded the American Himalayan Foundation following his visit to Nepal twenty-eight years ago.[18] The foundation supports the construction of schools, retirement homes, and health clinics as well as the restoration of cultural landmarks in rural areas of Nepal, Tibet, Bhutan, and Pakistan. Its annual budget of approximately $2.5 million helps to support about seventy-five projects.[19]
- Sir John Templeton, founder of the Templeton family of mutual funds, which were sold to Franklin Resources in 1992 for $913 million, established the $1 million Templeton Prize, which recognizes "progress toward a research or discoveries about spiritual realities." Its first recipient was Mother Teresa. Templeton's foundations annually make grants in excess of $20 million. Among the stated purposes in the governing documents are the following: "The major intentions of the Founder are: (i) to encourage new spiritual information and spiritual research to increase as rapidly as medical information did in the 20th century; (ii) to encourage the world to spend at least one tenth as much resources on research for new spiritual information as the world spends on science research."[20]
- Jim Barksdale, founder of Netscape, established the Barksdale Reading Institute in Oxford, Mississippi, to address illiteracy in his home state.[21] In 2000, he contributed $100 million to this project. Last year, the institute delivered reading programs to students in twelve Mississippi schools.[22]

As the foregoing individuals have demonstrated, meaningful progress on significant problems is achievable in each potential philanthropist's field of interest. The challenge is to identify a problem that can be remedied or mitigated given the level of human and economic resources available. Virtually any cause that will benefit humankind generally can be pursued.

Motivation

The magnitude and scope of charitable giving in contemporary America are manifestly obvious; the reasons for giving are less so. Over the past few years, leading

16 Paul Rogers, "Another Record Gift by Intel Co-Founder," *San Jose Mercury News*, December 9, 2001; Conservation International Press Release, December 9, 2001.

17 www.moore.org/.

18 *Chronicle of Philanthropy*, March 7, 2002, 5.

19 Additional examples of the imagination and vision of philanthropists are found among the recipients of the Daily Points of Light Award, at www.pointsoflight.org., an organization inspired to promote philanthropy following the use of the phrase "a thousand points of light" in several speechs by President H. W. Bush, including a State of the Union Address.

20 A lengthy article on Sir John Templeton's efforts to ensure that his foundations continue to pursue his goals after his death appears in "A Donor's Divine Intervention," *Chronicle of Philanthropy*, June 12, 2003, 7.

21 Aline Sullivan, "Investing in Philanthropy," *Barron's*, December 17, 2001, at 30.

22 www.msreads.org/schools/all.html.

financial service providers hoping to expand their business in the charitable sector have commissioned surveys seeking to learn more about why affluent donors give to charity. A November 1998 survey by U.S. Trust quantified various motivations for giving as follows:

- Desire to support worthwhile causes, 79 percent
- Responsibility to share good fortune, 69 percent
- To meet communities' critical needs, 63 percent
- Help organization that has benefited family or a friend, 50 percent
- Set example for children, 46 percent
- Fill gaps left by government cutbacks, 29 percent
- Tax benefits, 11 percent
- Respect and recognition, 4 percent
- Pressure from acquaintances, 2 percent

As will be seen in the topics discussed in this work, two of these results are notable. The relatively low score for the "respect and recognition" factor suggests that privacy, if not anonymity, in charitable matters may be more important to donors than public policy makers have acknowledged.[23] More surprising still is the relatively low ranking of tax benefits as a motivating factor.

This latter issue was the subject of considerably greater scrutiny in a recent survey conducted by Bank of America and the Center on Philanthropy at Indiana University.[24] When asked how donors would change giving if the estate tax were repealed, 54 percent replied that it would stay the same, 24.6 percent indicated that it might increase somewhat, and 11.5 percent stated that it would "dramatically increase." Only 7.8 percent responded that giving would "somewhat decrease," and 2.1 percent responded that giving would "dramatically decrease." A follow-up question asked how donors would change giving if no deductions from income taxes were available for charitable gifts. Surprisingly, 51.7 percent of the respondents indicated that giving would remain the same, while 37 percent indicated that giving would decrease somewhat. Only 10 percent of the respondents indicated that giving would decrease "dramatically."

As this work goes to press, President Obama has proposed capping the tax deduction available to upper-income taxpayers, in part to finance the health care and climate change initiatives proposed by his administration. As initially proposed, the top-two marginal tax brackets, currently 33 percent and 35 percent – but expected to rise to 36 percent and 39 percent respectively at the end of 2009, would be permitted to claim charitable deductions only at the rate of the next-lower tax bracket, currently 28 percent. The effect of this for the top income bracket would be

23 The Center on Philanthropy at Indiana University survey sponsored by Bank of America found that 20.9 percent of respondents indicated that they would be inclined to give more to charity if their names would not be made public, www.philanthropy.iupui.edu/research/portraits-donors-report-dec-2007.pdf.

24 Caroline Preston, "Donations and Deductions: Half of Wealthy Americans Say They Would Give Even If They Got No Federal Tax Break," *Chronicle of Philanthropy*, March 12, 2009, 7.

to limit charitable deductions to $0.28 on the dollar rather than $0.35 on the dollar. Coming at a time of the decreasing ability of wealthy Americans to fund charitable activities in the recessionary downturn, charities have begun lobbying against this proposal.[25] If the proposal becomes law, future data may become available to further evaluate the extent to which tax benefits motivate charitable giving.

As discussed in greater detail herein, the extensive regulation of private foundations is premised on the income tax deductibility of charitable contributions. Where the tax benefit of a charitable deduction is insignificant or can be forgone, charitable structures can be established and operated outside the United States without being subject to the private foundation regulatory regime. If in fact the tax deduction is irrelevant in terms of charitable motivation in nearly half of the potential donors surveyed, the alternatives to establishing a United States–based charity discussed in this book may be of considerably broader interest than is generally recognized.

25 See Suzanne Perry and Caroline Preston, "A Taxing Proposition: Nonprofit Leaders Come Out Divided on President Obama's Plans," *Chronicle of Philanthropy*, March 12, 2009, 6, and Suzanne Perry, "Economists Try to Calculate the Impact of Tax Changes on Charitable Giving," *Chronicle of Philanthropy*, March 12, 2009, 8.

CHAPTER TWO

Fundamental concepts relating to charitable organizations

Before describing the legal framework governing charitable giving and charitable organizations in the United States, it is appropriate to discuss some fundamental concepts. These concepts not only pervade U.S. laws regulating both donors and donees but also frequently appear in foreign laws regarding the formation and functioning of charitable organizations.

Private inurement

The key provision of the Internal Revenue Code granting tax exemption to U.S. charitable organizations, Section 501(c)(3), includes the phrase: “no part of the net earnings [shall] inure . . . to the benefit of any private shareholder or individual.” When considering whether to form a charitable organization, the basic concept of private inurement must be kept in mind.

The concept relates as much to the distinction between charitable endeavors and commerce as it does to the difference between for-profit entities and nonprofit entities. A for-profit entity, whether constituted as a corporation, partnership, limited liability company, or sole proprietorship, has owners for whose benefit the enterprise is operated. As shareholders, partners, or interest holders, those owners have a right to receive a share of profits or dividends and are entitled to receive any equity capital left in the business venture on its termination, dissolution, or liquidation. Nonprofit entities, by contrast, are not operated for the benefit of any founder, shareholder, executive, or employee. Although under the laws of some states nonprofit corporations, for example, might issue stock to the founders for control purposes, such stock ownership does not entitle the individual to share in the profits or in the value of the assets on dissolution.

Of course, the difference between for-profit enterprises and nonprofit organizations pertains fundamentally to purpose. Businesses are formed to make money; charities exist to provide some form of public benefit. It is important to note in this regard that the specific charitable purposes are expressly not for the benefit of any specific individuals. Accordingly, as a general rule, the founders, their families, and associates may not receive economic benefit from the charity.[1] The violation of this fundamental principle will not only contravene the tax laws granting benefits to the contributors and the charitable organizations but also may risk intervention by applicable regulatory authorities, such as the corporation commissioner, the secretary of state, or the state's attorney general. Although the level of supervision is frequently less strict in foreign jurisdictions, the same risk of legal exposure for utilizing charitable contributions and assets for private inurement can arise. Nothing said in this book concerning the relative advantages or disadvantages of operating a charitable organization in a foreign jurisdiction should be construed to imply that any aspect of the charitable endeavors may inure to private individuals at any time.

Invariably, issues of private inurement involve insiders of the charity, whether the founders, board members, trustees, large donors, or managers. Inherent in the analysis of whether an inappropriate economic benefit has inured to an individual is the notion of control over decision making within the organization by the insider. Frequently, the "insider" designation is also attributed to family members, including spouses and children, or to other entities, such as corporations, limited liability companies, trusts, or partnerships, which are controlled by the insider.

Federal rules governing private foundations in United States have strict prohibitions against any dealings between designated insiders, called "disqualified persons," and the foundation (see Chapter 4). Prohibited transactions include sales or exchanges of property or services and borrowing or lending funds. Even if the proposed transaction is demonstrably fair and reasonable, it is generally off-limits under these rules. These concepts apply as well to the regulation of public charities. Economic benefits received by insiders of public charities also receive special scrutiny, with the charity potentially exposed to penalties targeting so-called excess benefit transactions.

Public benefit versus private benefit

A related concept is that of private benefit. Charitable organizations must be dedicated to some form of public benefits, however broadly or narrowly defined. Use of the charity's assets for a private benefit – that is, to benefit a specific individual – therefore violates the fundamental charitable purpose. Unlike a private inurement, which typically benefits an insider of the charity, such as a significant contributor, an officer, or a board member, a private benefit occurs when the individual receiving benefits is not within the class of beneficiaries for which the charity is established.

This is not to say that individuals cannot properly receive the benefits of charity; rather, for an individual properly to receive a charitable benefit, he or she must fall

1 An important exception is that such individuals may receive reasonable compensation for services rendered to or on behalf of the charity, where "reasonable" is determined by comparison with what other charities of comparable size pay their employees to perform similar duties.

within the charitable class for which the charity is operated to benefit. Thus, if a charity is founded to alleviate hunger among indigent children, the charity might, for example, define the charitable class as including anyone whose family of four earns less than $20,000 per year.[2] Gifts to such individuals would not be construed as rendering a private benefit.

A number of areas of charitable endeavor are perpetually fraught with difficulties in defining the reach of public versus private benefits. For example, in awarding scholarships to individuals for university-level study, in advance of any scholarship grants, private foundations in the United States are required to develop an objective and nondiscriminatory plan for the final recipients of scholarships and to have it approved by the Internal Revenue Service. This practice developed in response to numerous abuses where the class eligible to receive scholarship benefits was perceived as rigged to benefit insiders, their families, and friends. The Internal Revenue Service prefers that private foundations in the United States give resources targeted for scholarship aid directly to the universities themselves, so that the universities may distribute the scholarship aid in accordance with their own presumptively objective selection criteria.

As with the private inurement doctrine, a charitable organization risks sanctions if it confers a private benefit. In essence, to do so likely would violate its charitable purposes. Intervention by regulatory authorities, state and federal, can follow. Potential sanctions can range from fines in the form of excise taxes on taxable distributions to the loss of tax-exempt status.

Public charities versus private foundations

Another fundamental distinction in the laws and regulations governing charitable organizations pertains to public charities versus private foundations. Although the term "foundation" is sometimes used by entities that draw support from a wide cross-section of the public, for the purposes of this book, the term refers to an independent entity funded by an individual, his or her family, or a single corporation or business enterprise.

It is important to point out that in the United States, the term "foundation" connotes a charitable purpose, but from a legal standpoint, the term is not necessarily so restricted. Thus, an entity utilizing "foundation" in its name is not necessarily a charity or indeed even a nonprofit organization. As will be outlined in this book, the entity can be recognized as a tax-exempt charity only by establishing to the Internal Revenue Service that it is organized and operated for charitable purposes. Significantly, under the laws of many foreign countries, the term "foundation"

2 It was these distinctions that engendered controversy in the wake of September 11. Both established charitable organizations and those created in response to the tragedies were confronted with difficult issues on defining the charitable class (e.g., where to draw the line) in disbursing millions of dollars among the families of the victims.

does not have a charitable connotation. For example, private foundations under Panamanian or Liechtenstein law are more akin to trusts under U.S. law, typically established for the benefit of individual family members, though they frequently also provide a vehicle for a family's charitable causes. Such foundations are expressly established to provide private inurements and private benefits and therefore could not gain recognition as a charity under U.S. law. Nevertheless, for the purposes of this book, we will use the term to refer to a charitable entity typically established by individuals, families, and corporations.

The major difference between a public charity and a private foundation is that a public charity typically raises funds from a broad segment of the public on a continuous or repetitive basis, usually to meet its operating needs and charitable purposes, whereas a private foundation is funded by a small number of individuals, in a single gift or a series of reasonably large gifts that then form an endowment. Income from the endowment is then used to fund charitable activities, consistent with the private foundation's charitable purposes. Moreover, control of a private foundation usually remains with the donors, whereas a public charity is frequently governed by a more diverse board of directors or trustees, some of whom may be elected by members. Participation in a public charity – as a member or otherwise – is usually open to anyone contributing financial or other support.

As discussed in Chapter 3, the characterization of an entity as a public charity gives rise to numerous tax benefits, both for the donors and for the entity itself. In contrast, characterization as a private foundation triggers multiple layers of regulation in the form of excise taxes and penalties, and it triggers more restrictive rules as to income tax deductibility for donors, as described more fully in Chapter 4. It is necessary to discuss public charities, because in the typical legalese of the Internal Revenue Code, an entity is deemed to be a foundation only if it is not a public charity. As a matter of public policy in the United States, public charities are the favored vehicle and are viewed by Congress as somewhat more capable of self-governance and less susceptible to control (and therefore abuse) by the founder and his or her family and friends. By contrast, based on well-publicized abuses by a few wealthy families in the 1960s, the laws governing private foundations provide for closer scrutiny and are enforced by escalating levels of penalties in the form of excise taxes, both against the foundation and against any individuals responsible for contravening the regulatory regime.[3]

The manner in which the Internal Revenue Code defines private foundations by means of various exceptions, which are generally referred to as "public charities,"

3 Ironically, over the years, certain aspects of the regulatory regime governing private foundations have, to a lesser extent, been extended to public charities as well. This trend is expected to continue. For example, Senator Charles Grassley, the ranking Republican on the Senate Finance Committee, and its former chair, has proposed requiring universities to spend at least 5 percent of their endowments annually or face punitive taxes. This mirrors the minimum expenditure requirements applicable to private foundations that have been in the law since 1969. See Colin Levy, "The Taxman Cometh," *Wall Street Journal*, May 9, 2008, at W11.

is illustrated in Chart D.[4] If the organization is described under one of the boxes numbered 1 through 4, it is regarded as a public charity and is not subject to the complex regulatory regime applicable to private foundations described in Chapter 4.

It is assumed for purposes of this book that the reader may be interested in establishing a private foundation rather than a public charity. Accordingly, mention of public charities generally is limited to the extent needed to define private foundations for purposes of the U.S. legal regime.

Nonprofit versus tax exempt versus charitable

For the sake of clarity, brief mention is appropriate as to the distinction among nonprofit, tax-exempt, and charitable types of entities. Although all charitable institutions must be nonprofit, not all nonprofit entities are eligible to be tax exempt. Section 501(c) of the Internal Revenue Code enumerates some twenty-seven categories of organizations that can qualify for tax-exempt status. While broad, the categories are nevertheless specific and do not encompass the full range of nonprofit entities. Chart A, taken from the Internal Revenue Service Data Bank and reprinted in Chapter 1, shows the range and usage of the various categories of exempt organizations, from business leagues to pension funds and veterans associations.

The tax-exemption process requires the nonprofit entity to apply to the Internal Revenue Service for recognition of exempt status, which will be granted on showing that the organization is formed and operated for an exempt purpose. The process for qualifying charitable organizations as tax exempt is described in Chapter 3. Similar procedures apply to the other categories of exempt organizations.

As can be readily seen from the categories of exempt organizations shown in Chart A, charitable organizations are but one of many types of exempt organizations. Traditional charities include such organizations as schools, universities, community chests, and churches.[5] Nevertheless, as pointed out previously, neither the statute nor the regulations specifically limit the use of the term "charitable," and as a matter of practice, it has been broadly interpreted so as to allow a full range of activities generally devoted to public betterment, as distinguished from private benefits or private inurements.

The distinction between charitable, exempt, and nonprofit can have enormous legal consequences, both under the laws of the United States and under the laws of other jurisdictions. For example, tax-exempt status in United States is not available for political campaigns or funding for political advocacy. Nevertheless, organizations interested in various aspects of public policy that may, from time to time, take

4 Chart D is based on a chart from J. Edie, *First Steps in Starting a Foundation*, 4th ed. (Council on Foundations, 1997), at 7.

5 Section 170(b)(i)(A).

Chart D Legal Definition of Private Foundations

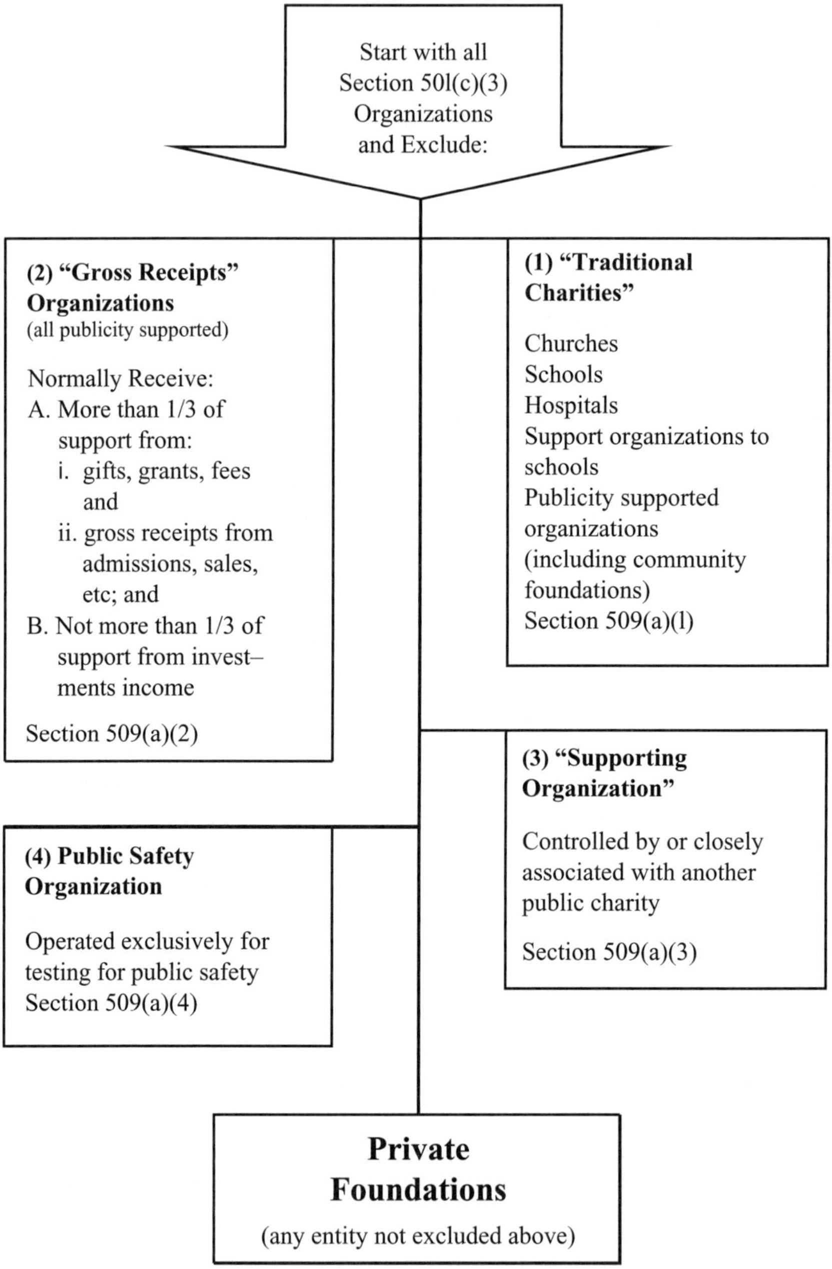

positions on matters of public policy may, or may not, qualify as exempt, depending on the type of activities in which the organizations engage. If such organizations are primarily engaged in scholarly research, they may qualify as tax-exempt educational organizations. As the results of the research are used to shape public policy debate, at some point the line may be crossed to political activities, thus raising a red flag in terms of the entity obtaining or maintaining tax-exempt status.

As a matter of U.S. law, such issues can be extremely complex.[6] Under the laws of other jurisdictions, however, where an entity's purposes are described as public, as opposed to private or business, the entity may be specifically sanctioned by law.[7] Accordingly, the distinctions between nonprofit and tax exempt and philanthropic or charitable may well have different implications under the laws of non-U.S. jurisdictions, which may become highly relevant to philanthropists seeking to establish an organization that may not qualify as tax exempt under U.S. law.

6 The intersection of the regulation of political activities, particularly lobbying and fund-raising, with the First Amendment's guarantees of free speech has always been controversial. When tax policy issues are overlaid, the complexity is enhanced. An examination of the legal issues involved in exempt organizations that engage in various forms of political activities is beyond the scope of this book. A good overview of the subject may be found in J. Blazek, *Tax Planning and Compliance for Tax-Exempt Organizations*, 4th ed. (Wiley, 2004), at 611.

7 See discussion of Bermuda purpose trusts in Chapter 9.

CHAPTER THREE

U.S. legal framework governing charitable organizations

Legal structures

In the United States, charitable organizations are usually organized as trusts or as nonprofit corporations. Although a number of states have now enacted comprehensive statutes governing trust law based on the Uniform Trust Code,[1] in many state jurisdictions, common law continues to govern trusts. The laws regulating nonprofit corporations are typically a subset of state corporation laws. Because corporations are juridical creatures of state law, there are no federal corporation laws as such, although the regulatory regimes that govern the grant and operation of exemption from federal taxation may be viewed as an additional overlay on applicable state law. A charity may also take the form of an unincorporated association and, in some jurisdictions, a limited liability company (LLC).

Nonprofit corporations

Nonprofit corporations are by far the preferred vehicle for charitable organizations in the United States.[2] There are two principal reasons for this. First, a corporation is a limited liability entity, so that founders are insulated from any liabilities that may be incurred by the charity. Second, the corporate governance structure – a board of directors overseeing officers who are charged with the daily operations of the organization – is familiar to most participants in charitable endeavors.

Because charities are not engaged in business as such, in theory, isolating the founders against claims would not seem to be essential. Nevertheless, in the current litigious environment of the United States, a corporate structure is viewed by many potential donors as indispensable, as they do not want their charitable activities

1 The Uniform Trust Code is a model statute drafted by the National Conference of Commissioners on Uniform State Laws. As of this writing, it has been enacted in whole or in part by fifteen states. In numerous subject areas, there are substantial derogations from common law in the Uniform Trust Code.

2 Most states have specific nonprofit or not-for-profit corporation statutes, although there are many variations. Virginia, for example, has a "Nonstock" Corporation Act, sections 13.1–801 *et seq.*, Virginia Code (2008), which although not limited to nonprofit entities is generally utilized by them.

to give rise to legal exposure. Moreover, under the corporate laws of most states, a nonprofit corporation can provide for broad indemnity for its officers and directors. As a practical matter, unless the officers or directors are engaged in fraud or criminal activities, the indemnification provided by the charity should accord them sufficient protection.[3]

Charitable entities organized as nonprofit corporations are usually governed by a board of directors. The board appoints and supervises officers in charge of the charity's operations. The board can be self-perpetuating, with the founders appointing the initial board, and the board itself filling any vacancies in directorships that may occur. Where charities have a large membership base, some portion of the board can be selected by the membership at large, and different seats on the board can be reserved for specific classes of members, for example, depending on the size of donations.

Where a charity organized as a nonprofit corporation operates in a state or in multiple jurisdictions other than the one where it is incorporated, it will be required to apply for a certificate of authority to conduct its operations in the "foreign" state. This allows charities to avail themselves of better corporate law in one state, even though they operate in another. For example, Delaware corporate law is universally recognized as preferable.[4] This is because it is complete, well thought through, and flexible. Of equal significance, the state bureaucracy that implements and interprets the law, the office of the Delaware secretary of state, has a well-deserved reputation for efficiency and responsiveness.[5] Accordingly, many charities are incorporated in Delaware and then qualify as foreign corporations in the state where they will actually operate.[6]

3 In addition, directors' and officers' liability insurance, so-called errors and omissions policies, is generally available for nonprofit corporations. Moreover, the cost of such insurance is usually significantly less for charities and nonprofit organizations than for business enterprises.

4 Delaware General Corporation Law, title 8, chapter 1, Delaware Code of 1953, as amended. Delaware is one of the few states that does not have a separate section of laws devoted exclusively to nonprofit corporations. Therefore, a charitable entity incorporating in Delaware would be a regular corporation, but it might, for example, state in its charter that it does not issue stock. Even though Delaware does not have a nonprofit corporation law, when a Delaware corporation must qualify in a foreign jurisdiction because it is operating there, it would typically obtain a certificate of authority under the local jurisdiction's nonprofit corporation law.

5 Unlike the secretary of state or corporation commission bureaucracies of many states, which pride themselves on strictly enforcing all requirements, down to the color of the ink used to sign documents filed, the Delaware secretary of state has a number of troubleshooters readily available to work with nonprofit entities and their counsel to draft whatever filings are needed to carry out a specific transaction. Rather than having a filing rejected, counsel might receive a telephone call from the Delaware secretary of state's office, and any difficulty or deficiency can be quickly resolved or corrected. Corrected amendments can be filed via facsimile and paid for by credit card. This contrasts sharply with practices in other jurisdictions, which all too frequently appear to be designed to demonstrate the authority of low-level clerks to reject filings, unnecessarily adding to administrative costs and discouraging legitimate charitable activities.

6 In certain states, the corporation is also required to register, often for the purpose of regulating charitable solicitations. For example, the New York office of the attorney general requires registration with the Charities Bureau. See www.oag.state.ny.us/charities/charities.html.

Trusts

Generally speaking, trusts are creatures of common law and are validly created under state laws in the United States and in foreign jurisdictions that derive their law from the laws of England,[7] such as Bermuda, the Isle of Man, and the Cayman Islands.[8] In addition, a number of non–common law jurisdictions, such as Switzerland, Liechtenstein, and the Netherlands Antilles, authorize by statute the creation of trusts.

An increasing number of states have undertaken legislative initiatives to improve on the common law of trusts as interpreted and implemented in their jurisdiction. In these instances, common law may be significantly altered by statutory law regulating trusts. A good example is Delaware. Recent amendments to the Delaware trust law permit the person creating the trust, called the "grantor" or "settlor," to establish governance regimes separate and apart from the trustee for managing assets and for making distributions, which in the case of charitable trusts could cover all grant-making activities. In this way, for example, the grantor may choose to remain involved in managing trust assets, without the trustee incurring liability in the event of investment losses. Likewise, the grantor or his or her family members may choose to serve on a committee controlling charitable grants, again without any duty on the part of the trustee to supervise the authorized grant-making activities of the committee. In this manner, the trustee's discretion and authority are limited to providing directed trustee services, that is, to serving as bare legal trustee while reserving fundamental functions relating to the operation of the trust to the philanthropist grantor or members of his or her family. Common law would not permit such delegation of authority but would expose the trustee to liability for losses to the trust assets or unauthorized grants. These improvements on the common law of trusts are creating the possibility for creative new forms of charitable trusts.

Unlike nonprofit corporations, charitable trusts usually do not need to obtain any kind of government approval to operate in any particular jurisdiction in the United States. (If it is raising funds from the public, however, it will likely need to register with the applicable state authority that regulates such fund-raising.)

Normally grantors of charitable trusts should not be expected to be exposed to liability for claims against the trust, although trustees might be. Because trustees owe a fiduciary duty to the beneficiaries of the trust, for any claims against the trust or the trustee to be successful, in theory they need to be based on an alleged

7 Trusts as a legal structure derive from the distinction in English common law between the beneficial ownership or use of property and its legal ownership. The legal ownership and title to property in trust is held by a trustee, whereas use, or beneficial ownership, runs to the beneficiaries of the trust. The origins date to feudal times when the king was the legal owner of all land but granted the right to use the land to his lords.

8 Other common law jurisdictions include the Bahamas, Barbados, Nevis, Gibraltar, and the Channel Islands.

breach of fiduciary duty. Professional fiduciaries, such as financial institutions, trust companies, and lawyers, are well aware of this exposure and accept it as part of serving in a trustee capacity. Of course, most professional trustees maintain liability insurance and also require the trust to indemnify them against such claims. As is the case with indemnification of corporate officers and directors, standard indemnification clauses would not shield trustees in the event that they were to engage in fraudulent or criminal activities.

Although most persons considering the establishment of charitable organizations in United States regard a corporate governance structure as preferable to a trust structure, this most certainly is a misperception. It is possible to have multiple trustees or a board of trustees. As with a corporate board of directors, cotrustees or a board of trustees can appoint managers to run the charitable entity's operations. The grantor may expressly give power to remove trustee(s) to so-called trust protectors or to a committee of trust advisers.[9] Moreover, certain functions, such as advising on how the endowment fund is to be invested or how grants are to be made, can be delegated to individuals or committees other than the trustee(s). As discussed previously, the law of certain states, such as that of Delaware, will permit such delegation in the trust instrument itself, so that the trustee will not be viewed as in breach of its fiduciary responsibilities, for example, if the designated investment adviser makes imprudent investments.

Generally speaking, trusts are viewed as a less flexible vehicle than corporations, which can amend their charters or bylaws, but again, this is a misperception. It all depends on the declaration of trust or the trust agreement. Use of a discretionary trust, with power given to the trustee to amend the trust document, perhaps subject to consent of the trust protectors or a committee of trust advisers, accords the trust the ultimate flexibility in adapting to changing circumstances over time. Indeed, a trust can even migrate to a new jurisdiction, including a foreign jurisdiction, so that it can be governed by an entirely different set of laws.[10]

In comparing the relative advantages of operating a charity as a nonprofit corporation or a trust, the charitable donor must first become comfortable with the concept of a trustee controlling the entity. To overcome this hurdle, there is no substitute for an in-depth interview of the persons or institutions under consideration

9 See Chapter 8, in this volume.

10 By contrast, a corporation usually may not migrate to a new jurisdiction because it is a creation of statutory law of a particular state. Although a corporation can be moved to a new jurisdiction, the steps to do so are complex. Typically reincorporation or redomiciling a corporation requires liquidation of the old corporation and the formation of a new corporation in the new jurisdiction or the formation of a new corporation in a new jurisdiction and merging of the old corporation into it, so that the new corporation is the surviving entity. As suggested by the foregoing description, such transactions are time consuming and expensive, both in terms of legal costs and in terms of filing fees. Migrating a trust, however, can be as simple as having the trustee declare that the law of a new jurisdiction shall govern the situs and administration of the trust.

for serving as trustees. Once a sufficient comfort level is attained, the potential grantor may recognize that there can be far greater flexibility and control in utilizing a trust as the vehicle for the charity than he or she may have imagined.

Unincorporated associations

A short word is also appropriate regarding unincorporated associations, which can also serve as charitable vehicles. As with a corporate charter and bylaws, an unincorporated association will need a governing document, such as a constitution. Of course, any governance structure imaginable can be created, including one where authority over different aspects of the entity's work and administration can be delegated to various committees. These governance structures can be created at little or no cost, as lawyers would not necessarily be required to draft legal papers, and in many jurisdictions, unincorporated associations are not required to register with any state or local regulatory body.[11]

The major downside in utilizing an unincorporated association is the potential for personal liability to the individuals involved in the work on behalf of the charity. For this reason alone, nonprofit corporations or trusts are usually preferred over unincorporated associations.

Limited liability companies

Limited liability companies (LLCs) are a relatively new form of legal organization that seek to combine the limited liability benefits of operating as a corporation with the more flexible mechanisms for allocating profits, losses, and capital requirements among the principals, as can be done with partnerships.[12] Although the law of many states limits the use of the LLC vehicle to for-profit enterprises,[13] certain states, including Delaware, permit LLCs to be used for nonprofit purposes.[14]

Rather than use bylaws to govern the structure of the organization, as would a corporation, LLCs use an operating agreement, under which the controlling parties typically delegate the authority to operate the organization to a manager or group of managers. The operating agreement can also provide for the LLC to be managed by officers, like a corporation, and for the officers to be appointed and managed by a board of directors or executive committee. The operating agreement is a flexible mechanism and can provide for whatever form of administrative structure is required, including provisions governing the succession of management. As with the other forms of legal structures described here, the operating agreement could provide mechanisms for delegating authority or management control over grant making and/or investment decisions.

11 At least on formation – again, some form of registration may be required under state or local law if the charitable association will solicit donations from the public.
12 Another variant of this theme is the limited liability partnership.
13 For example, California, the District of Columbia, New York, and Virginia.
14 Carolyn Klamp and David R. Heinen, *State Law Survey, Delaware Law Concerning Exempt Organizations*, Tax Analysts Electronic Citation: 2002 TNT 48–53, November 1, 2001.

Presumably one of the major advantages for utilizing an LLC structure for a charitable organization, as with a business organization, is a simplified management structure. Whereas a corporation must have directors and officers, an LLC need have only a manager. All of the management functions and responsibilities could thus be placed in the hands of a single individual.

Because LLCs are not commonly used for charitable organizations, and the laws of relatively few states appear to permit such use, it is simply noted that this form continues to evolve and may become more commonly used for charitable structures in the future.

U.S. taxation

Among the core issues that any potential philanthropist must address are the U.S. tax aspects of the gifts used to establish the charity and the tax status of the entity to be created. Depending on the type of property used to create a charitable entity, the timing of the gift, and the charitable purposes of the proposed entity, different planning conclusions will follow an application of relevant tax rules. Accordingly, it is necessary to devote considerable detail to the U.S. tax regime governing charitable giving and charitable enterprises organized in the United States and outside of it.

Unfortunately, this area is fraught with complexity, particularly where some aspect of the operations or the origins of the charity are to take place outside of the United States. At the conclusion of perhaps the most comprehensive survey and evaluation written of the current U.S. tax laws on this subject, Professor Harvey Dale, of New York University Law School and founder of the National Center on Philanthropy and the Law, observed: "It is impossible to justify the incredible complexity, inconsistency, and impenetrability of the relevant statutory, regulatory, and other authorities bearing on foreign charities. There can be no reason – and there certainly is no rhyme – to the current pattern."[15] Nevertheless, an understanding of the basic structure governing U.S. taxation of charitable institutions is indispensable for proper planning.

U.S. federal charitable income tax deduction

Any discussion of the tax deductibility of charitable donations should be prefaced by noting that there is nothing in the U.S. Constitution or in common law that inherently grants a tax benefit to donors of charitable gifts or guarantees charities an exemption from taxation. These features have been a part of the landscape for so long that it is easy to overlook the fact that Congress came close to not granting special tax benefits to charities when it initially adopted the income tax. Thus, it is important to remember that tax benefits accorded to various aspects of charitable endeavors are entirely a matter of statute, which can be amended by the U.S. Congress at any time. Stated differently, charities do not possess any

15 Harvey Dale, "Foreign Charities," 48 *Tax Lawyer* 657 (1995).

inherent rights to tax exemptions – a basic fact that congressional reformers inject into the continuing political dialogue surrounding proposals to expand regulation of charities and other exempt organizations.

1 Individual donors

General rules

Generally speaking, section 170(a) of the Internal Revenue Code grants individuals a deduction for gifts to charitable organizations. Different limitations on the extent of the deductibility apply depending on whether the charitable organization is a public charity or a private foundation. Generally speaking, cash gifts to public charities are deductible up to 50 percent of adjusted gross income per year, whereas cash gifts to private foundations are limited to 30 percent of adjusted gross income. To the extent that these limits are exceeded, a carry-forward for up to five future tax years is permitted.

As mentioned previously, as this work goes to press, President Obama has proposed capping the tax deduction available to upper-income taxpayers, in part to finance the health-care and climate-change initiatives that have been proposed by his administration. As initially proposed, the top two marginal tax brackets, currently 33 percent and 35 percent, but scheduled to rise to 36 percent and 39.6 percent, respectively, at the end of 2010, would be permitted to claim charitable deductions only at the rate of the next lower tax bracket, currently 28 percent, but scheduled to rise to 31 percent at the end of 2010. The effect of this for the top income bracket would be to limit future charitable deductions to $0.31 on the dollar rather than $0.396 on the dollar.

The tax benefit resulting from the deductibility of significant gifts can be diminished by the alternative minimum tax (AMT). Its impact will differ among taxpayers depending on the level of tax preference items on the donor's individual return in the year a large charitable gift is made. Even though charitable deductions are not tax preference items for AMT purposes, the AMT frequently diminishes the posttax value of deductions, and thus the tax benefit of the gift, because the AMT tax rate is typically lower than the donor's regular marginal rate.

Reform of the AMT is perennially on the list of matters to be addressed by the tax-writing committees of the U.S. Congress. Because the AMT as currently enacted does not provide for any adjustment for inflation, more and more taxpayers are caught annually by the AMT, particularly in those jurisdictions with high levels of state income and property taxes, such as New York, California, and the District of Columbia. Congressional efforts to address the perceived unfairness of the AMT thus far have primarily resulted in short-term fixes, sometimes in effect for only brief periods. The legislative landscape of AMT is expected to shift in the near term, and therefore any analysis of the AMT's impact on charitable giving should be expected to be obsolete in short order. Nevertheless, the issue bears mentioning, as for certain taxpayers, the AMT may play an important role in determining whether for particular taxpayers a non-U.S. structure for establishing a charitable organization is more attractive.

Different rules also apply to gifts of appreciated property, depending on whether the donee organization is a public charity or a private foundation. The limitation on the deductibility of gifts of appreciated property to public charities is 30 percent of the taxpayer's adjusted gross income, as compared with 20 percent for gifts to private foundations. In addition, gifts of such property to public charities are deductible to the extent of their fair market value, whereas the value of gifts of appreciated property to private foundations is deductible only to the extent of the donor's adjusted basis (costs plus improvements) to the property.[16]

Nondeductibility of gifts to foreign charities

Significantly, section 170(c)(2) of the Internal Revenue Code limits the deductibility of charitable contributions for U.S. federal income tax purposes to contributions to or for the use of "a corporation, trust, community chest, fund or foundation" that is "created or organized in the United States, or in any possession thereof, or under the law of the United States, any State, the District of Columbia, or any possession of the United States." Therefore, contributions to foreign charitable organizations are not deductible. Moreover contributions to U.S. organizations that merely act as conduits for foreign charitable organizations are also not deductible for U.S. income tax purposes.[17] Impermissible conduits have been found to exist where the U.S. charity conducts fund-raising for the foreign organization, where it is contractually bound to forward funds raised, net of administrative expenses, to the foreign charity, or where the funds raised are specifically earmarked for the foreign charity.

The geographical limitation on the deductibility of charitable gifts has been part of the U.S. tax law since 1938 and was not an inadvertent decision on the part of the Congress. Enacted near the zenith of isolationist sentiment in the United States, this limitation is explained in the legislative history:

> [T]he bill provides that the deduction . . . be also restricted to contributions made to domestic institutions. The exemption from taxation of money or property devoted to charitable and other purposes is based upon the theory that the Government is compensated for the loss of revenue by its relief from financial burden which would otherwise have to be made by appropriations from public funds, and by the benefits resulting from the promotion of the general welfare. The United States derives no such

16 Section 170(b).

17 See generally Rev. Rul. 63-252, 1963-2 C.B. 101. Conduit status may be avoided if a U.S. charity is considered the actual recipient and does not act merely as a fund-raising mechanism for the foreign charity. The test is whether the U.S. charity has control over the donated funds and discretion as to their use so as to ensure that the funds will be used to carry out the U.S. charity's purposes. See also Chapter 5 in this volume, Rev. Rul. 66-79, 1966-1 C.B. 48, and Rev. Rul. 76-1957, 1976-1 C.B. 61.

benefit from gifts to foreign institutions, and the proposed limitation is consistent with the above theory. If the recipient, however, is a domestic organization, the fact that some portion of its funds is used in other countries for charitable and other purposes (such as missionary and educational purposes) will not affect the deductibility of the gift.[18]

Significantly, however, the geographic limitation on deductibility based on the U.S. situs of the donee organization does not carry over to bar U.S. charitable organizations from using their charitable resources outside of the United States. Rather, charitable grants outside the United States by both public charities and private foundations are subject to considerable regulation by the Internal Revenue Service, as described in Chapter 5.

> The nondeductibility for U.S. federal income tax purposes of individual gifts to foreign charities is the single most important element of the tax legislative landscape relating to topics discussed in this book. The various mechanisms that U.S. persons and charitable entities have created to deal with this critical provision, so that charitable giving can be conducted on an international basis, is the primary focus of this work.

Even if the foregoing rationale were valid in 1938 (it has been extensively criticized in numerous law review articles over the years), the policy behind the nondeductibility of gifts to foreign charities is dubious in the twenty-first century. In today's world of multibillion-dollar foreign aid from the U.S. government, the legislative history's assertion that the United States derives no benefit from direct gifts to foreign institutions from its citizens is seriously outdated. But more fundamentally, the world today is a much smaller place than it was seven decades ago. Protection of the environment outside of the United States benefits the United States and its citizens as well. Climate change is not a problem susceptible of national solution. Alleviation of poverty and illiteracy outside the United States furthers overall U.S. foreign policy, for example, by addressing the root causes of hopelessness that have led to the formation of terrorist organizations, including various radical Islamic movements. Periodic threats of global pandemics suggest that is inappropriate and shortsighted to limit efforts to alleviate disease to within the borders of the United States.

However anachronistic the prohibition on deductibility of gifts to foreign charities may be, there currently is no reasonable prospect that this aspect of U.S. tax law will be changed. Any enlargement of charitable gift deductibility should be expected to be opposed by those in Congress seeking to protect tax revenues. Moreover, the lack of any domestic political constituency to advocate and support such a change

18 House Report No. 1860, 75th Congress, 3d Session 19–20 (1938).

will likely keep any initiative to permit the deductibility of gifts to foreign charities off of the legislative calendar. Finally, as indicated previously, the trend in the law post–September 11 terrorist attacks is to dramatically expand the regulation of U.S. charitable activities, including, in particular, activities of U.S. charitable organizations outside the United States. Indeed, it is reasonable to conclude that any initiative to revisit the obviously anachronistic rationale for limiting direct charitable contributions to foreign organizations, a fixture in U.S. law since 1938, would be trumped by the perceived need to expand U.S. government regulation and supervision of foreign charitable activities in the post–September 11 world. Liberalized deductibility of gifts to foreign charitable organizations therefore should not be seen as a realistic legislative prospect.[19]

Treaty overrides

The general rule disallowing an income tax deduction for donations to foreign charitable organizations is overridden by bilateral income tax treaties between the United States and other countries, but in only three instances:

1. *Mexico.* Under article 22(2) of the U.S.-Mexico tax treaty, U.S. individuals are granted deductions for direct gifts to Mexican charities, as defined in Mexican law, provided that the Mexican standards are "essentially equivalent" to U.S. law regulating charitable organizations.
2. *Canada.* Under certain circumstances, U.S. individuals are eligible for tax deductions for direct gifts to Canadian charities under article 21(5). Significantly, U.S. standards for determining deductibility rather than Canadian ones apply.
3. *Israel.* The most recent amendments to the U.S.-Israel tax treaty added article 15A, which permits U.S. individuals to deduct direct contributions to charities organized in Israel. As with the Canadian treaty, U.S. standards apply.

In each instance, however, special rules may limit further the utility of these deductions in particular circumstances.[20]

With the willingness of certain European countries to permit income tax deductions for cross-border gifts, including gifts to U.S. charities in some cases, it is possible that additional treaty benefits may become available in the near future that would permit limited deductibility of direct gifts to foreign charities. This will be a slow process, as the forum for considering such rules will be bilateral income tax

19 Europe has moved more rapidly toward permitting cross-border charitable giving. This trend recently received a huge boost when the European Court of Justice (ECJ) ruled that gifts made by a taxpayer to charitable institutions in another member state must generally be deductible under national law of the donor's country. See *Persche*, ECJ, C-316/07, January 27, 2009, http://curia.europa.eu. In that case, a German national claimed a tax deduction for a gift in kind to a Portuguese charity. The ECJ referred to treaty provisions establishing the European Union, which prohibits restrictions on the movement of capital as mandating Germany's allowance of the claimed deduction.

20 For example, under the Canadian Treaty, the applicable percentage limitations are further qualified by reference to Canadian source income. Thus, a U.S. citizen without Canadian source income is not eligible to deduct gifts to Canadian charities.

treaty negotiations, which do not necessarily occur periodically or even at regular intervals. As indicated in the previous section, as an overall policy matter, these limited and highly qualified exceptions are not likely to erode to any significant extent the general rule against deductibility of direct gifts to foreign charitable organizations.

Practical considerations

If the individual considering establishing a charitable entity requires the donation establishing the entity to be tax deductible, use of a charitable organization either formed in the United States or in a treaty-exemption country is mandated.

In contrast, there are a number of circumstances in which a current charitable deduction from income tax may not be needed or available in any event. For example:

- If an entrepreneur wishes to establish a charitable organization with 10 percent of the stock of a closely held corporation, for which there is no public market, an income tax deduction might have little value and therefore might not be required.
- If the potential donor wishes only to establish the entity during his or her lifetime, and intends to defer funding of the charity until his or her death, there may be no current need for the deduction from federal income taxes.
- If a high-net-worth individual in a particular tax year has relatively low income, perhaps because an investment strategy emphasizes capital appreciation over current income, so that a significant gift to establish a new charitable organization would exceed the limitations for tax deductibility in the current year and perhaps not be recoverable even in future carry-forward years, then establishing a foreign charity might be considered.
- If an entrepreneur wishes to dedicate all of the profits of a new business venture to charity, the enterprise could be set up outside of the United States and owned by a foreign charity. Because the premise of the business is unproven and the venture unfunded, no charitable deduction would be available.

2 Corporate donors

As in the case of individual donors, the general rule of section 170, which allows a deduction from gross income subject to the federal corporate income tax, also applies to gifts from corporations to charities. As with individuals, gifts to qualified charities are deductible from corporate taxable income if the charity is created or organized domestically. There is one additional qualifier, however: "a contribution or gift by a corporation to a *trust, community chest, fund or foundation* shall be deductible by reason of this paragraph only if it is to be used within the United States" (section 170(c)(2), emphasis added). This qualification does not apply to gifts to charitable organizations organized as corporations.

This additional condition appears to have been left over from legislation enacted in 1935, which was amended in 1938. Whether attributable to sloppy legislative drafting or to the nature of the legislative process, which pejoratively has been analogized to making sausage, the language remains. As a result, U.S. corporate donors have good reason to prefer charities that are in corporate form. Such entities may utilize gifts for charitable purposes outside of the United States without jeopardizing the tax deductibility of the contribution from the corporate donor.

As with charitable gifts from individuals, a cap is imposed on the amount of the deduction. For corporations, the limitation is 10 percent of its taxable income, and any excess contributions may be carried forward for five years.[21] As with individuals, the AMT can have an impact on tax benefit to be derived from corporate gifts to charity.

3 Trusts and estates

As separate taxable entities, trusts and estates are subject to income tax. Therefore, the question arises as to how they handle contributions to charitable organizations. In general, rules applicable to trusts also apply to estates. But as we will see, not all trusts are treated alike.

Section 642(c) provides a special rule for amounts paid or permanently set aside for a charitable purpose. An estate or trust, but only a complex trust, not a simple trust, is allowed a deduction against taxable income in lieu of the section 170(c) deduction, for any amount paid for a purpose specified in section 170(c) (determined without regard to that provision of section 170(c) that requires that for a charitable contribution to a corporation, community chest, and so on, to qualify, the recipient must be "created or organized in the United States or in any possession thereof, or under the law of the United States, any State, the District of Columbia, or any possession of the United States"[22]). "Thus, an amount paid to a corporation, trust, or community chest, fund, or foundation otherwise described in Section 170(c)(2) shall be considered paid for a purpose specified in Section 170(c) even though the corporation, trust, or community chest, fund, or foundation is not created or organized in the United States, any State, the District of Columbia, or any possession of the United States."[23]

It is clear that this result was intended. The legislative history of the provisions, dating back to 1919,[24] when there was no geographic restriction imposed on the charitable deduction for either individuals or trusts and estates, and including 1938,[25] when the restriction sprang up for individuals and corporations, but was not – one can only assume deliberately – placed on trusts and estates, demonstrates

21 Taxable income is computed without regard for the deduction for charitable contributions, the deductions for dividends received, and any net operating loss and capital loss carrybacks. See section 170(b)(2) of the Internal Revenue Code and Treasury Regulation section 1.170–11(a).

22 A complex trust, in brief, is a nongrantor trust (i.e., not subject to the special rules in sections 671–79). Also, it is not a trust that, by its terms, is required to distribute all its income on a current basis and not to pay, set aside, or use income for charitable purposes. Complex trusts and their beneficiaries are defined and taxed under sections 661–63. Simple trusts – those that must distribute all their income on a current basis and not pay, set aside, and so on, income for charitable purposes – are dealt with in section 651.

23 Regs. Section 1.642(c)-1(a)(2).

24 Revenue Act of 1918, Pub. L. No. 65-254, § 219(b), 40 Stat. 1057, 1071 (1919).

25 Revenue Act of 1938, Pub. L. No. 75-554 (1938).

the point. The U.S. Tax Court has confirmed the allowance of the deduction for trusts and estates regardless of geography, and the Internal Revenue Service has acquiesced in the Tax Court judgment.[26]

The outcome seems odd; two different results for two similarly situated taxpayers. But it has been argued that it makes sense. The thinking is that, because a U.S. individual could make a gift (nondeductible) to a foreign charity, which invests the funds tax free in the United States and earns, say, portfolio interest or capital gains, another individual should be able to make a gift to a U.S. trust (again, no deduction at this point), which invests the funds in the United States and then makes gifts each year to a foreign charity and takes the deduction. In both cases, the U.S. donor is not receiving a deduction, and in both, the income is, when all is said and done, not taxed, either because it is earned by the non-U.S. charity or because the donor trust offsets income with the deduction. In a different light, the rule still looks odd. How is it even handed for an individual, who earns money however he or she earns money, to be denied a deduction to a foreign charity and a trust, which earns money by investing in a portfolio, to be allowed the deduction? In any event, note that the allowance of the deduction to the trust is not a direct, simple-minded path to avoiding the geographic restriction.

It was necessary to protect the prohibition on deductible gifts to a foreign charity from one form of end run. Section 681 disallows deductions otherwise allowable under section 642(c) "with respect to income of the taxable year which is allocable to its [the trust's] unrelated business income for such year."[27] If this provision were not installed, taxpayers would simply put regular business under a charitable entity, let the charitable entity earn unrelated business taxable income (UBIT), let the charitable entity deduct the contribution to the foreign business, and thus obtain the economic benefit of the deduction. Although one might think that transferring regular businesses to putative charitable organizations is far fetched, there is a history of attempts to do just this; and the complicated and ever-evolving UBIT provisions are designed to squelch this.[28]

U.S. federal estate and gift tax deductions

1 Federal estate tax charitable deduction

Under existing U.S. tax law, an estate tax deduction is generally allowed for "all bequests, legacies, devises, or transfers," in unlimited amounts, to or for the use of certain qualified charities. A qualified charity is described broadly as any entity organized and operated exclusively for "religious, charitable, scientific, literary, or educational purposes," in the same manner as the entities eligible to receive gifts that are deductible for income tax purposes. Significantly, unlike the deductibility

26 *Estate of Tait v. Commissioner*, 11 T.C. 731, 736-37 (1948), acq. 1950–1 C.B. 5.
27 Section 681.
28 Section 513.

for income tax purposes, the deduction for estate tax purposes is not premised on the donee charitable organization being organized in the United States or the funds being utilized in the United States.[29]

There are numerous differences in the language describing gifts that are eligible for deductions from the income tax and the estate tax. These differences have been described by commentators as "inexplicable," "maddening," and "bizarre"; but there is no question that the blanket prohibition on deductibility of gifts to non-U.S. charities that applies to income tax deductions does not apply to estate tax deductions. Nevertheless, other rules operate to limit the deductibility of testamentary gifts to foreign private foundations, unless such organizations receive more than 85 percent of their support from sources outside of the United States.[30] Therefore, as a practical matter, any U.S. individual desiring to fund a foreign private foundation in large or substantial measure by testamentary gift, must qualify the foreign foundation as tax exempt. Section 2055(e)(1) of the Internal Revenue Code disallows estate tax deductions to foreign private foundations unless the foreign private foundation has qualified as tax exempt under section 501(c)(3).

The availability of an estate tax deduction for gifts to non-U.S. charities in unlimited amounts is among the most significant features of the applicable U.S. tax regime. While lifetime gifts to charities remain subject to both the percentage limitations (generally speaking, 50 percent of adjusted gross income for gifts to public charities and 30 percent for gifts to private foundations) and the alternative minimum tax, testamentary gifts are not so limited. Accordingly, the establishment of private foundations, which will be funded in substantial or large measure on the donor's death, are increasingly attractive.

2 Federal gift tax charitable deduction

Rules that are similar to the U.S. federal estate tax deduction rules also allow a charitable contributions deduction for U.S. gift tax purposes.[31] Again, there are inconsistencies in the applicable statutory language, but such inconsistencies do not qualify the conclusion that gifts to non-U.S. charities generally qualify for exclusion from the gift tax.

As with the estate tax, however, deductions from amounts subject to the gift tax are disallowed for gifts to foreign private foundations unless such entities receive more than 85 percent of their support from outside the United States,[32] or unless the foreign private foundation has been recognized by the IRS as tax exempt under

29 Section 2055(a)(2); Treas. Reg. Section 20.2055–1(a).

30 Section 4948(b).

31 Compare the text of the Internal Revenue Code at section 2522(a)(2) with sections 170(c)(2) and 2055(a)(2).

32 The annual gift tax exclusion, currently $13,000 per donor per donee per year, plus the lifetime gift exclusion of $1 million would have to be exceeded for the gift to be taxable. The split gift rules would also apply, so that if the donor is married and his or her spouse has his or her full lifetime gift tax exclusion available, up to $2 million could potentially be excluded from gift tax for a gift to a foreign charitable organization that is classifiable as a private foundation.

section 501(c)(3). As a practical matter, therefore, philanthropists wishing to make substantial lifetime gifts to foreign charitable organizations will want to ensure that the donee is qualified as tax exempt.

Although understandable in terms of symmetry with the trust and estate rules, the nondeductibility of gifts to foreign private foundations operates as a significant constraint on establishment of foreign charitable structures by U.S. donors. It is one thing to forgo an income tax deduction on gifts to foreign charities, but it is quite another matter to be subject to a gift tax if the foreign charity is classifiable as a foreign private foundation under U.S. rules.[33] While the current $1 million lifetime exemption applicable to gifts, as well as the annual exempt amount, currently $13,000 per donor per donee, or $26,000 per married couple for so-called split gifts, could mitigate or eliminate any gift tax liability, as a practical matter, many potential charitable donors are reluctant to utilize their exemptions in this manner, as doing so will likely trigger higher estate taxes in the future.[34] Accordingly, as is discussed in greater detail in this book, strategies to establish foreign private foundations must necessarily focus closely on the valuation of any gifts utilized to establish the charitable structure. Otherwise, exposure to U.S. gift taxes can be an unintended result.

Exempt status

Under applicable U.S. tax laws, a charitable corporation or trust that is qualified as exempt from taxation derives two primary benefits. First, all income earned on its investments and all donations received are exempt from income tax. Second, fund-raising is facilitated, as the charitable corporation or trust can inform potential donors that their contributions will be deductible, subject to the percentage limitations described previously. Tax-exempt status, however, does not come automatically from establishing an organization whose purposes fit the statutory categories of being organized and operated exclusively for "religious, charitable, scientific, literary, or educational purposes." Rather, the organization must apply to the Internal Revenue Service to be recognized as tax exempt, the status of which is then reviewed periodically for compliance with the applicable rules.[35]

For public charities and private foundations, the application for tax-exempt status is made on Form 1023, a copy of which, together with the instructions, is

33 If the annual exclusion is exceeded, the value of any gift would first be applied against the donor's unified (lifetime) credit, currently $1 million, before any gift tax would be payable. The U.S. gift taxes are imposed at rates beginning at 18 percent and increasing to 35 percent of the value of the gift (section 2502).

34 Even though under current law, at least through December 31, 2009, the amounts excludable from federal estate taxes are greater than the lifetime gift tax exclusion, the gift tax and estate tax credits are referred to as "unified credits," in that utilizing any part of one's $1 million lifetime gift tax exclusion is taken into account dollar for dollar in reducing the available amount exempt from estate taxes.

35 Among the purposes behind the large quantity of information required by Form 990-PF, Appendix 5, is the monitoring of the organization's tax-exempt status.

found in Appendix 1.[36] The current version of Form 1023 is significantly longer and more detailed than the version utilized until recently, and it reflects growing scrutiny by the Internal Revenue Service of all charitable organizations, a continuing trend that is one of the important underpinnings of the subjects covered by this book. The new version of Form 1023 is significantly more intrusive into relationships and potential transactions between the organization and so-called disqualified persons than the previous version, and it is a harbinger of the type of regulation the entity will face annually in completing its tax and information returns. The level of effort required to complete the application for exempt status is indicated in the instructions, which set forth the estimated time to compile the records needed to complete the form, become familiar with the form and applicable law, prepare the form, and send it in.[37] The estimated time required in connection with completion of the basic form exceeds one hundred hours, and this does not include any time that will be required in connection with one or more of the various schedules, some of which can require ten additional hours of work.

The incrementally longer, more detailed and more intrusive Form 1023 has been accompanied by closer scrutiny being brought to bear by the Internal Revenue Service on approvals of exempt status. In recent years, the IRS bureaucracy charged with reviewing Form 1023 appears to be operating under an administrative mandate to ensure that organizations applying for exempt status in fact meet all of the requirements. Applicants should expect to have at least one inquiry from the reviewing official as to the nature and scope of the purported charitable activities to be undertaken before approval is granted. Stated differently, IRS review is rigorous; application approvals are not rubber stamped.

Generally speaking, newly formed charitable organizations seek to obtain exempt status contemporaneously with being formed. Because qualification depends on being both organized and operated for exempt purposes, and the organization will not have had much in the way of operating experience at the time it applies, the application places considerable emphasis on the organizational documents. Accordingly, particular care must be taken in drafting the corporate charter and bylaws, if applicable, or the trust agreement, to make clear the organization's charitable purposes.

The organizational documents should recite and restate the applicable provisions of law that form the basis for the tax exemption. Examples of forms of organizational documents that have been approved by the Internal Revenue Service are included

36 Organizations qualifying for exempt status under section 501(c)(3) utilize Form 1023; organizations qualifying under the other provisions of section 501(c) (see Chart A in Chapter 1) utilize Form 1024. Form 1024 asks for similar information but has specific sections tailored to the bases for exempt status in the subsections of section 501(c) other than those in subsection (3).

37 These estimates are required by the Federal Paperwork Reduction Act, which, while designed to compel the federal government to reduce paperwork required in connection with compliance with U.S. law, highlights the onerous burdens presented. Apparently, the Paperwork Reduction Act did not deter the Internal Revenue Service from vastly broadening and enlarging the scope of the information required to qualify for recognition of tax-exempt status.

in Appendix 2 for a private foundation and in Appendix 3 for a public charity.[38] Numerous provisions are included in the corporate charter that are required by the IRS before approval can be granted. These include statements regarding prohibitions on private inurements and directors to distribute any assets remaining on dissolution or liquidation in accordance with the organization's charitable purposes or to other qualified charities.

Under the law, the statement of purposes in the organizational documents can be quite broad (e.g., educational, charitable). Nevertheless, the Internal Revenue Service requires a reasonable level of specificity in answering questions regarding the organization's purposes. To that end, the Form 1023 application process requires a detailed narrative regarding specific activities in which the organization proposes to engage.[39] Not surprisingly, these narratives are frequently the source of follow-up questions that the IRS requires to be answered prior to granting the application.

Where the organization will not qualify as a public charity because it will not rely on broad public support, the organizational documents will also be required to spell out the entity's intended compliance with the various regulatory constraints governing private foundations. These are described in Chapter 4. Thus, additional "magic" language needs to be included in the organizational documents, typically the corporate charter, where the organization will be classified as a private foundation and therefore subject to additional levels of regulation.[40]

In addition to providing organizational documents to the Internal Revenue Service, the application for recognition of exempt status must be supported by financial projections, which can be time consuming and costly to prepare. Nevertheless, in the event that the actual financial results differ significantly from the pro forma information provided on Form 1023, the organization's exempt status is not subject to challenge. Applicants must also obtain a taxpayer identification number and pay a user fee in connection with the application. Currently, for exempt organizations that have had or expect to have annual gross receipts of less than $10,000 annually for a four-year period, the user fee is $300. Above this threshold, the user fee is $750.[41]

Termination of exempt status

Once a foundation has received a determination letter recognizing its status as an exempt organization, it must be operated in accordance with the charitable purposes set forth in its organizational documents, as represented to the Internal Revenue Service in obtaining exempt status. Failure to do so can trigger in the imposition of penalties in the form of excise taxes, as summarized in Chapter 4.

38 These templates are discussed in detail in Chapter 9.
39 See Appendix 1, part IV.
40 See Appendix 2.
41 Applicants use Form 8718 to claim the lower user fee.

Repeated or flagrant disregard of applicable standards can result in the Internal Revenue Service revoking the organization's exempt status.

If the charitable organization decides to terminate its exempt status itself, it must formally notify the Internal Revenue Service.[42] The procedures to be followed in terminating exempt status are governed by a series of special rules, but usually this is accomplished by transferring all of the assets of the exempt entity to an existing public charity. The failure to do so triggers a penalty tax equal to the lesser amount of the aggregate tax benefits the organization has received as a result of its exempt status or the value of its net assets.[43] Stated differently, if the organization seeks to terminate its exempt status, potentially all of its assets are subject to forfeiture to the U.S. Treasury Department.

42 Section 507(a)(1).
43 Section 507(c).

CHAPTER FOUR

U.S. legal constraints

Private foundation rules

Incremental regulatory initiatives

1 Tax Reform Act of 1969

Following public hearings that highlighted abuses by private foundations established by wealthy U.S. individuals, Congress enacted a comprehensive series of rules governing private foundations as part of the Tax Reform Act of 1969. As a result, any charitable organization that does not meet the legal definition of a public charity must be operated in compliance with a complex regulatory regime administered by the Internal Revenue Service if it is to maintain its tax-exempt status.

Prior to the enactment of these measures, the propriety of various transactions and practices was judged by an arm's-length standard – that is, whether the transaction or practice at issue was reasonable and fair when judged from the perspective of how unrelated parties might have acted. After focusing on several highly publicized cases involving wealthy families, Congress determined that objective tests should be substituted for the inherently subjective, "all facts and circumstances" evaluations of such practices, which had been the standard under existing law.

During the hearings, which culminated in the enactment of the Tax Reform Act of 1969, Congress criticized previous Internal Revenue Service enforcement efforts as ineffective. It found that the difficulty in proving a violation of law under the arm's-length standard tended to discourage the IRS from enforcing the law. Because the only sanction then available was to revoke the organization's tax-exempt status – tantamount to capital punishment for the charitable organization – as a practical matter, both the IRS and the courts were reluctant to pursue less-than-egregious practices.

The congressional solution was to impose a series of penalties, in the form of excise taxes, which could be graduated and targeted, not only against the exempt organization but against responsible foundation managers as well. These excise taxes are imposed in the context of a regulatory regime that substitutes bright-line tests of behavior for the subjective, arm's-length standard under prior law.

As is so often the case with efforts to reform perceived bad practices legislatively, Congress undertook a number of broad initiatives, some of which represent reasonable, commonsense practices that might form the basis for a charitable organization's policy, while others have proved overreaching. The particulars of the regulatory regime enacted follow here, as it is important for anyone considering the establishment of a charitable organization in the United States to have a sense of how burdensome the regulatory environment is likely to be. Indeed, many professionals working in the charitable-giving sector counsel against forming a private foundation, unless the donor is able to establish the foundation with a minimum of \$500,000 to \$1 million. Otherwise, the costs of regulatory compliance will likely outweigh the charitable benefits that the organization will be able to provide.[1] Although your author does not agree with this view, it is clear that for a significant number of regulatory-adverse philanthropists, the growing regulatory burden has the potential to diminish or discourage altogether charitable initiatives they otherwise might wish to undertake.

2 Recent "reform" initiatives

Notwithstanding the broad reach of the 1969 reforms, in recent years, Congress has perennially revisited the rules governing private foundations, public charities, and nonprofits more generally. The obligatory political theatrics invariably include public hearings highlighting abuses. The abusers subpoenaed by congressional tax-writing committees have engaged in practices that obviously should have been the subject of Internal Revenue Service audits and penalties, sometimes so egregious as to merit criminal prosecution. Reforms are then proposed, targeting not only the obvious questionable practices but other areas of congressional interest as well. Often the abuses targeted, while perhaps egregious, nevertheless occur with infrequency and could be sanctioned under existing law. Instead, Congress enacts a complex rifle-shot provision, usually coupled to multiple new disclosure requirements, the cumulative effect of which is to significantly increase the administrative burdens of compliance.

1 One of the by-products of the regulatory burdens on private foundations has been the growth of so-called donor-advised mutual funds. The program established by the Vanguard Group, for example, requires donors to commit to making donations of a minimum of \$25,000. These will allow the donor to "create a lasting philanthropic legacy without incurring the high costs and administrative requirements of a private foundation." See generally www.vanguardcharitable.org/ProgramOverview. Such entities are, in essence, pass-though vehicles for donations to public charities, which accord donors considerable flexibility in timing their donations. Because the charitable gift (to the mutual fund) is irrevocable, the donor obtains the tax deduction benefit in the year the donation is made, even if the gifts to charities do not occur until subsequent years. In the interim, the mutual funds are pleased to invest the endowment fund for a management fee. Vanguard's Charitable Endowment Program held nearly \$1.7 billion in charitable assets in 2007, representing nearly 6,300 individuals and families, who distributed more than \$370 million to charities in 2007. *Chronicle of Philanthropy*, May 29, 2008, at 15. Similar programs have been established by a number of major mutual fund families, including Fidelity, T. Rowe Price, and the Calvert Group. The Calvert Group offers donors the opportunity to invest in its Social Investment Portfolio and its Community Investment Pool.

The Pension Protection Act of 2006 fits this pattern. Among the abuses targeted in televised hearings and well-circulated sound bites was the practice of wealthy individuals donating taxidermy (e.g., stuffed or mounted animal heads) to charity and deducting the full costs of the safari or expedition during which the animal was killed. Final legislation included eighteen separate so-called reforms, including provisions relating to "rules relating to charitable contributions of taxidermy." While in the process of enacting the various reforms targeting taxidermy abuses, Congress used the occasion to the double most of the excise taxes used to enforce behavior of private foundations described in detail below that were imposed by the Tax Reform Act of 1969. In addition, the 2006 act expanded regulation of donor-advised funds and significantly tightened rules relating to so-called supporting organizations, which typically operate in close connection with other charitable organizations.

Likewise, the oxymoronic Tax Increase Prevention and Reconciliation Act of 2005 (TIPRA) included new excise taxes and disclosure rules targeting abusive tax-shelter transactions involving exempt organizations.[2] Among the abusive tax shelters cited in the legislative history are foreign currency transactions in which the exempt organization is an assignee of offsetting foreign currency puts and calls, which has the effect of generating artificial losses for the nonexempt assignor. Broad – and somewhat uncertain[3] – amendments to the tax law, coupled with corresponding new disclosure requirements, require foundation managers to be familiar with a new series of complex requirements if they are to ensure their organizations' compliance with applicable rules.

3 Future trends

Creeping Sarbanes-Oxley

Congress should be expected to continue to propose additional legislation regulating private foundations. Whether one should appropriately view initiatives in this area as part of the overall class warfare that comprises much of the political rhetoric on any form of tax legislation, it is clear that a majority of the members of the tax-writing committees view the large accumulations of private wealth vested in foundations with suspicion and distrust. Ominously, the current ranking member and former chair of the Senate Finance Committee, Charles E. Grassley, regards

2 TIPRA creates a new section 4965 of the code and amends sections 6033(a)(2), 6011(g), and 6652(c)(3).

3 See Comments of the New York State Bar Association on Section 4965, dated August 25, 2006, which was submitted in response to Notice 2006–65, July 11, 2006: "Many observers have criticized the new law as overbroad. As first proposed in Congress, the provision was aimed at tax-shelter transactions that a tax-exempt entity knowingly entered into. However, as enacted, the provisions apparently apply to most tax shelter-type transactions that the IRS has deemed to be *potentially* abusive, whether or not a tax-exempt knew (or had reason to know) that the transaction was within the scope of the statute, and without regard to whether the transaction generates any tax or other benefits to the tax-exempt participant or involves the tax-exempt entity acting as an accommodation party."

the charitable sector with particular suspicion and places a high priority on new regulatory initiatives.

Warren Buffet's recent gift of nearly $30 billion to the Bill and Melinda Gates Foundation is sure to present numerous opportunities for congressional intervention. Whatever grant-making decisions are made by the Gates Foundation, they cannot be expected to please everyone or to be vanilla neutral or noncontroversial. There will always be members of Congress ready to challenge the priorities set by the Gates Foundation or the manner in which the funds are spent. The magnitude of the wealth to be distributed is simply too great for Congress not to take an active interest or attempt to play a role in its spending decisions.[4] Whether scrutiny, initially in the form of oversight hearings and subsequently in the form of proposed legislation, takes two years or five to occur, it is virtually inevitable. An unfortunate by-product of this intervention will be enhanced scrutiny of the entire private foundation sector.

In addition to the fundamental distrust and suspicion with which congressional lawmakers regard accumulations of private wealth, the much-heralded reforms to corporate accountability and governance embodied in the Sarbanes-Oxley Act are finding their way into new proposals to regulate private foundations.[5] No matter that the purpose of Sarbanes-Oxley was to address abuses by public companies in the wake of securities and accounting frauds at Enron, MCI WorldCom, and Tyco Industries by adding new requirements and heightened penalties to the securities laws regulating public companies, as well as enhanced notions of regulation over accounting disclosures and the manner in which corporate entities are governed. The same approaches are permeating proposals to regulate the nonprofit sector.

In June 2004, the Senate Finance Committee released a "staff discussion draft" that outlined a number of possible reforms in the regulation of charities and other tax-exempt organizations. A number of these proposals were enacted into law in TIPRA and the Pension Protection Act of 2006; a number remain on the table for future consideration.[6]

Administrative initiatives

In addition to implementing the foregoing regulatory initiatives mandated by Congress in recent legislation, the Internal Revenue Service on its own administratively has been ratcheting up regulatory oversight of private foundations and public charities. Premised on the assertion that "good governance is a leading indicator

4 Revealing, perhaps, are the comments of Congressman Xavier Becerra (D-Calif.) who characterized the tax exemption granted to charitable organizations as a "$32 billion earmark." He explained: "I have an obligation to make sure that those $32 billion that *would have gone to the federal government* are used for a . . . public good" (emphasis added.) These comments were cited in the *Wall Street Journal* editorial "Congress Targets Philanthropy," December 24, 2008, at A10.

5 Public Law No. 107-204, 116 Stat. 745 (2002).

6 See also Guide to Nonprofit Corporate Governance in the Wake of Sarbanes-Oxley by the ABA Coordinating Committee on Nonprofit Governance (2005).

of good tax compliance,"[7] and consistent with the previously described Sarbanes-Oxley policy underpinnings, the Internal Revenue Service has increasingly been prescribing standards of corporate governance for charities. For example:

- On February 2, 2007, the IRS circulated a "discussion draft of preliminary guidelines" designed to help charitable boards of directors promote good governance practices. The draft covers a variety of topics, from suggesting a clearly articulated mission statement to publishing a code of ethics and whistle-blower policies for each charity. The paper further suggests a variety of transparency initiatives on everything from financial audits to compensation practices and document retention policies. Although this discussion draft does not carry the force of law, it is reasonable to assume that it accurately states the IRS's position on a number of governance issues, which any charity under audit might be well advised to adopt and follow.
- The current instructions to Form 1023 virtually mandate applicants adopt a conflict of interest policy. Lest there be any confusion on what policy would be acceptable to IRS reviewers, a suggested text to be adopted by the organization is provided (see Appendix 4). Presumably, answering no to the question in Form 1023 as to whether the organization applying for recognition of tax-exempt status has adopted a conflict of interest policy would result in either a denial of the application or a telephone call from the IRS reviewing agent asking why such a policy has not been adopted.[8] Never mind that there is no legal requirement that tax-exempt organizations enact a conflict of interest policy or follow one with a different formulation. Accordingly, it is recommended that a conflict of interest policy utilizing the IRS format be adopted prior to filing Form 1023.
- In the current Treasury Department Anti-Terrorist Financing Guidelines, discussed in detail subsequently, a section on recommended governance practices strongly recommends that charities at a minimum have three members of their boards of directors or have three trustees, if organized as a trust.
- In 2008, the IRS completed a significant makeover of Form 990, the information return required of public charities. Under the banner of transparency, the IRS proposed new levels of reporting for the purpose of providing information to the public regarding each charity's efficiency in utilizing its resources to achieve its charitable purposes. The proposal called for inclusion of so-called efficiency indicators on the first page or summary sheet of each Form 990, disclosing fund-raising expenses as a percentage of total contributions, compensation of top officials as a percentage of total contributions, total expenses as a percentage of net assets, and the percentage of gross receipts received after professional fund-raisers had been paid. The proposal was withdrawn "in the face of strong criticism," according to Steven T. Miller, commissioner of exempt organizations.[9] Nevertheless, the proposals had the strong support of the IRS and might reasonably be expected to be proposed again in the future.

7 Remarks of Steven T. Miller, commissioner of tax-exempt and government entities, before the Georgetown Law Center Seminar on Representing and Managing Tax-Exempt Organizations, April 24, 2008.

8 Part V, question 5a.

9 "Putting Charity to the Test," *Chronicle of Philanthropy*, May 15, 2008, at 29.

Although IRS administrative initiatives appear to be most visible in the area of corporate governance, the IRS appears to be willing to undertake preemptive initiatives in circumstances where Congress might otherwise step in with new legislation. For example, the IRS has recently revived a seldom-used regulatory approach referred to as the "commensurate test," which evaluates whether exempt organizations are spending their funds on their charitable purposes commensurate with their financial resources.[10] It would appear that the IRS could utilize this test to revoke the exempt status of public charities that utilize a disproportionate amount of resources for fund-raising or executive compensation. The approach was the subject immediately to criticism by attorneys practicing before the Exempt Organizations Division as so inherently vague as to invite arbitrary actions on the part of the IRS.

Many IRS administrative initiatives are driven by congressional oversight or the threat of oversight hearings. For example, the Internal Revenue Service recently announced that it would be sending extensive questionnaires to four hundred colleges and universities seeking information "to disclose intimate financial details, including spending on perks like housekeeping services for executives, and their income and losses on business activities like learning and travel tours."[11] These initiatives follow closely on highly publicized criticism of certain medical school faculty members at universities in Wisconsin and Georgia, by Senator Grassley's office. The targeted individuals, who were also well-respected medical practitioners, were chastised for failing to disclose ties to pharmaceutical and medical device manufacturers. The medical schools were criticized for being unaware of conflicts of interests and for having no procedures in place for disclosing them. Contemporaneous with the announcement of the university questionnaires, the deputy IRS commissioner in charge of exempt organizations told the national meeting of the National Association of State Charity Officials to expect greater scrutiny of charities from the IRS.[12] With the liberal wing of the Democratic Party now firmly in control of both Congress and the executive branch, enhanced administrative scrutiny should be expected for the foreseeable future.

State legislative initiatives

Notwithstanding increasing Internal Revenue Service regulation of charities, a number of state legislatures have also undertaken new regulatory initiatives. Perhaps the most notorious of these was California Assembly Bill 624 in the 2007–8 legislative session, the Foundation Diversity and Transparency Act. The bill proposed requiring that foundations having more than $250 million in assets report the racial, gender, and sexual orientation of their board members, staff, and grantees. Within a year, similar bills were introduced in New York, Florida, Pennsylvania, and New

10 "New IRS Rules Help Donors Vet Charities," *Wall Street Journal*, May 29, 2008, at D1.
11 "IRS Asks Colleges to Disclose New Details," *Chronicle of Philanthropy*, October 16, 2008, at 37.
12 *Chronicle of Philanthropy*, October 16, 2008, at A33.

Jersey by activist legislators seeking to channel private foundation resources to advance a variety of social and political goals.[13]

While the California bill was withdrawn as a result of a political compromise,[14] the initiative may be seen as a typical rekindling of interest in regulation of charities at the state level following a long period of inactivity and inattention. Traditionally, with the exception of New York and California, state corporation enforcement officials have deferred to the Internal Revenue Service in regulating charities. Ironically, many observers have noted that the Internal Revenue Service became involved in the regulation of charities only because of inaction and neglect on the part of state regulators. In effect, the IRS filled a void using the granting of tax-exempt status as the basis for regulating the charitable sector. Increased interest on the part of legislatures at the state level in charitable matters may signal a growing interest in regulation at the state level, in addition to the growing level that is to be expected at the federal level.

Self-appointed watchdogs

Perhaps following Ralph Nader's model for public interest law firms, self-appointed watchdogs monitoring U.S. charities have proliferated in recent years. The most well-known of these are the American Institute of Philanthropy, the Better Business Bureau Wise Giving Alliance, Charity Navigator, and Wall Watchers' Ministry Watch.[15] Most of these organizations reportedly have annual budgets exceeding $500,000 and employ up to ten full-time staff members.

These organizations are enabled by the ready availability of information on public charities and private foundations on the Internet, a significant portion of which is derived from the Forms 990 and 990-PF, which the Internal Revenue Service makes public. Each purports to evaluate charities and nonprofit groups based on an unbiased ratings system, applied uniformly.[16]

They also contribute to the public policy debate before the Congress, state legislatures, and state attorney general's offices, and thus may be seen to be a further impetus for increased regulation. In addition to contributing opinion pieces to newspapers, they provide running commentary in the blogosphere. Needless to say, philanthropists cherishing privacy and anonymity are likely to be highly discouraged by the approach taken by these self-appointed watchdogs.

13 See Riley, "Philanthropy and Its Enemies," *Wall Street Journal*, March 3, 2009, at A13.

14 "Shaking Down Philanthropies," *Wall Street Journal*, lead editorial, July 26, 2008, at A8. See also "The Philanthropy Shakedown," a follow-up editorial on December 30, 2008, at A10.

15 "Organizations That Monitor Nonprofit Groups Are Growing in Popularity," *Chronicle of Philanthropy*, November 28, 2002, at 22.

16 Here is a representative sample from a report of the Better Business Bureau Wise Governing Alliance published in the regular column, *Watchdog Watch*, in the June 29, 2006, issue of *Chronicle of Philanthropy:* "Dream Factory . . . does not meet the standards calling for a charitable organization to have a minimum of three evenly spaced meetings per year of the full governing body; and does not have a board policy for assessing, at least every two years, the organization's performance and effectiveness for determining actions to achieve its mission."

Taking all of the foregoing recent developments into account, uncertainty as to the direction and scope of future regulation should form an important part of the factors to be considered in forming a U.S. private foundation. The only certainty is that Congress, the Internal Revenue Service, and the states will continue to look closely at tax-exempt organizations and will increase the compliance and excise tax burdens faced by U.S.-based private foundations.[17]

The purpose of this book is to help potential donors considering formation of charitable organizations evaluate whether an entity should be formed in the United States or outside of it. An understanding of the existing regulatory framework applicable to charitable foundations organized under U.S. law is central to this evaluation, and therefore a summary of the principal features of the Internal Revenue Service's regulation of private foundations follows here.

Excise tax on investment income

The general rule is that the interest, dividends, and net realized capital gains of private foundations are subject to a 2 percent excise tax, according to section 4940 of the Internal Revenue Code.[18] The primary justification given for this provision in the legislative history of the Tax Reform Act was the following: "The Congress has concluded that private foundations should share some of the burden of paying the cost of government, especially for more extensive and vigorous enforcement of the tax laws relating to exempt organizations."[19]

On the basis of this rationale, this excise tax was initially set at 4 percent. After several years, the Council on Foundations petitioned Congress to revisit the tax, given that it was generating several multiples of revenue in excess of the annual budget of the Exempt Organizations Branch of the Internal Revenue Service. As a result, the tax was more recently recharacterized, at least by the council, as a user fee. In addition, the law was amended so that in certain instances where a specific threshold of giving is exceeded, the excise tax called for by this section can be reduced to 1 percent. Even so, the complexity of establishing eligibility for the lower rate has resulted in relatively few private foundations claiming the lower rate.

Self-dealing

Section 4941 imposes strict rules against self-dealing between private foundations and their insiders. To enforce the prohibitions against self-dealing, the law created a

17 See generally "The Coming Charity Crackdown," *Forbes*, August 15, 2005, at 67.

18 For foreign private foundations, the tax is 4 percent, but only as to U.S. source interest and dividends (see section 4948(a)).

19 General Explanation of the Tax Reform Act of 1969, H.R. 13270, 91st Congress, 1st Session, Pub. Law No. 91-172 at 29 (1970) (hereafter, the General Explanation). The original proposal as reported by the Committee on Ways and Means of the House of Representatives provided for a 7.5 percent excise tax on investment income of foundations. House Report No. 91-413 (Part 1), 91st Congress, 1st Session, at 19 (1969).

new category of disqualified persons, which is defined to include trustees; directors; foundation managers; substantial contributors to the foundation; certain family members of the foregoing (including spouses and children); and corporations, partnerships, and other business entities related to or controlled by these individuals. A "substantial contributor" for these purposes is an individual, corporation, or other entity that has contributed in the aggregate more than 2 percent of the total contributions to the foundation. As a practical matter, all founders of private foundations typically fall within this definition and therefore are "disqualified persons" for purposes of the private foundation regulatory regime.

The following transactions between private foundations and any disqualified person are prohibited: (1) the sale, exchange, or leasing of property; (2) the lending of money or other extension of credit; (3) the furnishing of goods, services, or facilities; (4) the payment of compensation or expenses by the foundation to a disqualified person; and (5) the transfer to or use by or for the benefit of a disqualified person of the foundation's income or assets. Violations of the rules against self-dealing trigger a series of escalating penalties, in the form of excise taxes, against both the foundation and the person responsible for the defined self-dealing. The excise taxes are designed to discourage defined self-dealing and to force the private foundation to unwind the prohibited transaction by imposing prohibitively high excise taxes until the act of self-dealing is corrected.

For purposes of interpreting these rules, it does not matter that the transaction may be beneficial to the foundation. For example, the sale or leasing of real property to a foundation by a founder or other disqualified person at below-market rates would fall within the purview of the prohibitions even if it were to save the foundation substantial resources from having to purchase or lease property on the open market. Nevertheless, it is clear that Congress perceived that nothing less than the integrity of private foundations itself was at stake when it substituted objective, bright-line tests for existing arm's-length standards.[20]

The Pension Protection Act of 2006 doubled the excise taxes on self-dealing. Beginning for tax years commencing after August 2006, the initial tax of 5 percent of the amount involved in the act of self-dealing doubles to 10 percent. The initial tax is imposed on the disqualified person involved in the act of self-dealing; the foundation manager involved becomes liable for the payment of an excise tax of half the amount imposed on the disqualified person, previously 2.5 percent but increased to 5 percent.[21] The initial taxes are imposed for each year beginning in the year the act of self-dealing occurs and ends on the notice of the assessment or the notice of deficiency. If the act of self-dealing is not corrected, an additional tax of 200 percent of the amount involved is imposed on the disqualified person and a tax of 50 percent of the amount involved is imposed on the foundation manager refusing to agree to corrective action.

20 General Explanation, at 30.

21 If the participation by the foundation manager or director was not willful and was due to reasonable cause, the excise tax is limited to $10,000 per act under the old law and $20,000 per act under the Pension Protection Act of 2006.

The excise tax on self-dealing, as well as the other categories of punitive, behavior-modifying excise taxes described herein, is enforced in connection with representations that the exempt organization must make in connection with filing its annual tax return on Form 990-PF (see Appendix 5). Part VII-B of the form asks a series of difficult questions for the purpose of identifying those exempt organizations that are subject to the penalty excise taxes. It is imperative for foundation managers to become familiar with the complexities of the private foundation regulatory regime so that each of the potential trip-wire questions can confidently be answered in the negative. Although answering these questions can be burdensome, the burden pales in comparison with the effort that must be undertaken in the event that, for example, a prohibited transaction with a disqualified person must be identified. In that event, the exempt organization must also file Form 4720, the Return of Certain Excise Taxes on Charities (see Appendix 6), which then requires the exempt organization to disclose the particulars of any transaction giving rise to excise taxes, so that the appropriate tax can be applied.[22]

Minimum distributions

Among the evils Congress sought to remedy by the 1969 Act was the use of tax-exempt private foundations to accumulate and hold large amounts of capital resources. In its current form, section 4942 requires foundations to pay out in "qualifying distributions" a minimum of 5 percent of the market value of their assets each year. Until the Pension Protection Act of 2006, failure to do so triggered an initial penalty tax of 15 percent of the shortfall. The initial tax has now doubled to 30 percent. If the foundation fails to make the necessary qualifying distributions by the end of the next tax year, an additional tax of 100 percent is imposed on any undistributed amounts. The foundation's choice therefore is a simple one: make the qualifying distributions to charitable purposes or have the amounts forfeited to the government.

Qualifying distributions include eligible grants to other charitable organizations, activities in furtherance of the foundation's exempt purposes, expenditures for assets acquired by the foundation for the conduct of its functions, and reasonable and necessary administrative expenses.[23] There are complex rules for the calculation and timing of the required minimum payouts.[24]

22 As burdensome as Form 990-PF is, Form 4720 is even more so. According to the public notice required by the Paperwork Reduction Act, which requires the government to estimate how much time is required to complete any particular government-mandated form, the time needed to complete and file Form 4720 is "49 hours, 55 minutes for record-keeping, 16 hours, 30 minutes to learn about the law or the form, 23 hours, 22 minutes to prepare the form and 1 hour, 36 minutes to copy assemble and send the form to the IRS."

23 Because a significant number of the members of the congressional tax-writing committees believe that administrative expenses should not qualify for inclusion in foundation expenditures constituting the minimum annual distributions, proposals to eliminate, cap, or qualify the extent to which administrative expenses are deemed to be qualifying distributions are among the "reforms" to the private foundation regulatory regime that are introduced perennially as proposed legislation.

24 See the instructions to Form 990-PF, Appendix 5.

As a practical matter, unless the foundation's investments are yielding a minimum of 5 percent per year, which, at least in several recent years of declining stock market values, has been a challenge to achieve, the foundation in essence must move toward spending itself out of existence each year to comply with this rule. As a result, private foundations that are begun with modest gifts may not let their endowment fund accumulate, so that more ambitious charitable goals might be accomplished in the future. Moreover, the diminution of capital forced by this rule in the long run can impede the ability of the foundation to accomplish its charitable goals. The impact of this rule in the recent recessionary downturn, where a number of private foundations have endured declines in the value of their investment portfolios in the range of 25 percent to 50 percent, has been particularly harsh.

The Pension Protection Act of 2006 has for the first time extended the minimum distribution rules to donor-advised funds. The congressional consideration of this provision revealed a strong bias against continued accumulation of wealth in tax-exempt structures, including private foundations. The notion that the government should, by regulation, help private foundations spend themselves out of existence is a recurring theme for a number of reform-minded legislators. The current legislative debates strongly suggest that there will be pressure in the future to increase the mandatory minimum distributions.[25] The extension of this rule to public charities in the near future is also possible, if not probable.

Excess business holdings

In the legislative history of the Tax Reform Act, Congress cited numerous instances where wealthy families utilized private foundations to acquire and aggregate large numbers of related (and sometimes unrelated) businesses. Even though all of the dividends and capital appreciation from such businesses were dedicated to charitable purposes (presumably regular corporate income taxes were paid on unrelated business activities), Congress denounced these activities as inappropriate and as inherently unfair competition to for-profit enterprises.[26] Like the rationale given by Congress for the adoption of the minimum distributions rules, Congress viewed the accumulation of capital in business enterprises owned by tax-exempt organizations suspiciously.

As a result, section 4943 requires that foundations and their disqualified persons together may not own more than 20 percent of the voting stock of business corporations or equivalent interests in business partnerships. This threshold is increased to 35 percent if effective control of a corporation's holdings in question are held by one or more persons who are not disqualified persons, as would likely be the case with most publicly held companies. If the foundation itself owns less than

25 Recent policy debates have suggested extending minimum distribution rules to public charities. For example, increasingly, highly endowed private universities have been criticized for annually raising tuition and room and board charges while their endowments accumulate to staggering levels.

26 General Explanation, at 40.

2 percent of the corporate holdings under scrutiny, it does not matter what percentage is owned by disqualified persons. Similar rules apply to foundation holdings in partnerships and other unincorporated enterprises; private foundations are not permitted to have holdings in a proprietorship.

The value of defined "excess holdings" had been subject to an annual excise tax of 5 percent, but as with a number of the other excise taxes applicable to private foundations, the Pension Protection Act of 2006 doubled the excise tax to 10 percent. In addition, divestiture of defined excess holdings must follow if the foundation is to avoid additional penalty taxes. Generally, private foundations have a five-year period to divest themselves of defined excess business holdings, although this may be extended an additional five years in certain circumstances.

Of all of the "reforms" introduced by the Tax Reform Act of 1969, the policies behind the provisions relating to excess business holdings are the most questionable, if not dubious. Why shouldn't a philanthropist be able to dedicate all of the profits of an enterprise to charitable goals? There would be no inherent competitive advantage for such an enterprise, as suggested by the legislative history of section 4943, as the business would not be able to achieve its purposes if it were not run profitably. Indeed, such enterprises should be encouraged, rather than prohibited.

It should be noted that the excess business holdings rules present difficult problems for highly successful entrepreneurial families seeking to devote a substantial portion of their wealth to charity. For example, the Walton family, founders of Wal-Mart, have engaged in highly publicized efforts to modify this legislation, though unsuccessfully to date. These rules also present difficulties to highly successful owners of closely held enterprises.

> Stated bluntly, Congress has determined that for-profit enterprises cannot be solely dedicated to charitable purposes. This restriction is one of the most significant aspects of the private foundation regulatory change driving U.S. philanthropists to establish new charities outside of the United States. Most foreign jurisdictions do not prohibit charities from owning significant stakes in private enterprises. As a result, numerous entrepreneurs have established non-U.S. businesses to fund charitable interests that, because of the excess business holdings private foundation rules, must be established and operated outside of the United States.

Jeopardizing investments

Notwithstanding fiduciary standards applicable to trustees and directors of foundations, section 4944 imposes penalties for speculative investments by private foundations. The applicable standard is "ordinary business care and prudence" based on all relevant facts and circumstances prevailing at the time the investment is made and on the short- and long-term financial needs of the foundation to carry out its exempt purposes.[27] No categories of investment are deemed per se violations, but the regulations indicate that margin trading, commodity futures trading, investments in oil and gas interests, puts, calls, straddles, warrants, and short selling should all be viewed as red flags. Although the applicable regulations predate the growth in hedge funds, presumably most strategies employed by hedge funds would be sufficiently risky to fall within the purview of the section 4944 prohibitions.

Indeed, among the most shocking revelations surrounding the Bernard Madoff fraud was that numerous private foundations and charities had invested substantial portions of their endowments in Madoff-managed funds, including a number of prominent Jewish philanthropies. As of the date of publication of this book, it was believed that investors had lost approximately $65 billion in a series of hedge funds managed by Madoff in what has been described as the largest Ponzi scheme in history. Almost immediately a number of commentators pointed out in interviews with leading newspapers that the officers, directors, and managers of charities responsible for selecting the Madoff funds faced personal exposure under the jeopardy investments rules. A Senate Finance Committee staffer, Theresa Pattara, stated in an interview in *The Chronicle of Philanthropy*: "I'd be curious to know if any of those foundations considered the impact of [section] 4944 before they made those investments.... [I]t would be fair to ask for board minutes, the thought processes and the decision-making they went through before putting all their money at risk."[28]

When investments are found to have jeopardized a foundation's purposes, penalty taxes, measured as a percentage of the amounts improperly invested, may be imposed on both the foundation and the managers responsible for the questionable investments. All of the penalties and disincentives relating to these prohibitions were doubled by the Pension Protection Act of 2006. The model used follows the approach seen previously: an initial tax of 10 percent (previously 5 percent) is imposed on the foundation and on foundation managers participating in the investment decision, knowing that it jeopardized the carrying out of the foundation's exempt purposes. The initial tax on foundation managers previously may not exceed $10,000 (previously $5,000) per investment. If the jeopardizing investment is not redeployed to a more appropriate investment or sold or otherwise disposed of, an additional tax of 50 percent (previously 25 percent) of the amount of the investment is imposed on the foundation and an additional tax of 10 percent (previously 5 percent) of the amount of the investment is imposed on the foundation manager who refused to agree to removing the investment from jeopardy. The additional tax on foundation managers is linited to $20,000 per investment (previously $10,000).

27 Regulation 53.4944-1 (a)(2)(i).

28 January 15, 2009, at 37. The article also lists a number of private foundations and charities that invested with Madoff funds, topped by the Picower Foundation with $958 million invested and the Chais Family Foundation with $178 million invested.

The Madoff scandal underscores the public policy rationale for this provision. Several prominent foundations, some of which have been operating for decades, have had to shut down their operations and dissolve or drastically reduce the services they provide as the result of investment losses with Madoff funds.

Taxable expenditures

The hearings leading to the 1969 legislation identified a number of abuses in grant making by private foundations. Congress addressed these in section 4945. Unconvinced that disincentives to engage in such abusive activities were sufficiently large, in enacting the Pension Protection Act of 2006, Congress doubled all of the relevant penalties. Accordingly, a penalty tax, initially 20 percent of the amount involved, against the foundation, and 5 percent against the foundation's managers, up to $10,000, was imposed on several targeted activities as follows:

- *Lobbying.* Expenditures to attempt to influence legislation are prohibited.
- *Electioneering and voter registration.* Expenditures to attempt to influence the outcome of any public election or to support voter registration drives are prohibited.
- *Grants to individuals.* Travel, study, and similar grants to individuals are prohibited.
- *Noncharities.* Qualified public charities alone are eligible to receive grants from private foundations, unless they are for charitable purposes and the foundation is willing to exercise so-called expenditure responsibility, as described in greater detail herein.

If the expenditure is not corrected, an additional tax of 100 percent is imposed on the foundation, and a tax of 50 percent of the expenditure (up to $20,000) is also imposed on any foundation manager who agreed to making a taxable expenditure knowing that it was a taxable expenditure.

The foregoing is a general summary of the prohibitions on disbursements in the foregoing areas. In many cases, giving for related activities is possible but subject to extensive and detailed qualifications.[29] As a result, most private foundations make

29 An excellent example of the type of difficulties that charities encounter is found in the uproar that followed the revelation that the Red Cross had distributed but a small portion of the hundreds of millions of dollars it collected on behalf of the victims of September 11, 2001. In an op-ed column by Daniel Henninger on November 16, 2001, in the *Wall Street Journal*, titled "Charity Begins at Home, Ends Up Nowhere," he stated: "there were something over 5000 victims of 9/11. . . . We know their names and where their families live. So what's the problem with letting Americans everywhere help them financially? The problem is that the U.S. tax code forbids it. . . . Seriously. Steven Miller of the Internal Revenue Service explained the relevant tax law to Congress last week: 'an affected individual generally is not entitled to charitable funds without a showing of need.' If a tax-exempt charity gives money to a person whose income is above a certain level, that charity could lose its tax-exempt status. Bureaucracy and formal procedures allow a complex society to function with a needed degree of predictability and, in theory, efficiency. . . . We've arrived at the point where our most important institutions must carry the cumulative burden of doing not only what they were created to do, but also making sure they never fail in any one decision to conform to our obsessions with fairness, inclusiveness and social rectitude. . . . It says something about the American people, all for the good, that when the call went out to help the September 11 families, they answered, thinking the monetary and moral transmission here should be as straightforward as anything ever gets. Well it's not. A simple act of charity has also become complicated."

it a practice to steer clear of giving in these areas, if only to avoid complex and time-consuming compliance and oversight.

Reporting requirements

The 1969 amendments also added extensive reporting requirements for private foundations.[30] These reports are filed on Form 990-PF (a copy of which is found in Appendix 5, together with the instructions). This information return is used by the Internal Revenue Service to gather extensive information on all aspects of a foundation's activities, compelled by the need to determine whether and to what extent any of the excise taxes described previously may be payable.

The information required by Form 990-PF is extensive, including gross income and expenses, balance sheet, grants for exempt purposes, and total contributions and gifts, including the names and addresses of all "substantial contributors."[31] The various excise taxes under sections 4940 through 4945, described earlier, are imposed by the schedules to Form 990-PF, some of which involve considerable complexity, and as discussed earlier, the necessity for filing Form 4720.

These returns are available for inspection and copying by the public and must be made available for public inspection at the foundation's offices on request. Numerous self-appointed watchdog entities have standing Freedom of Information Act requests on file with the Internal Revenue Service, so that, as a practical matter, all information submitted with a foundation's Form 990-PF will be found on the Internet within a matter of weeks after it is filed. For example, GuideStar, a service of Philanthropic Research Inc., takes all raw data received by the IRS on Forms 990 and 990-PF and posts the information on its Web site (www.guidestar.org). The basic information is readily available to anyone utilizing a search engine, although for an annual subscription, many such philanthropic monitoring Web sites will provide an analysis of data comparing various foundations with one another.

Congress frequently imposes policies of transparency or full disclosure, where perceived evils can be eliminated or mitigated. The oft-cited policy justification for this approach is that sunshine is the best disinfectant. While this approach may constitute effective public policy in such areas as regulation of securities offerings and political campaign financing, many question whether the extension of such an approach to private philanthropy is appropriate. Many regard charitable giving as a private matter. Anonymity can be seen to be a virtue in philanthropy but is not possible if a private foundation is to be the donor. Moreover, it is far from clear that the abuses identified by Congress justify the level of disclosures required of private foundations. While full disclosure may be as American as apple pie, many donors are significantly constrained, if not offended, at having their eleemosynary objects subject to public scrutiny, and their foundation tax and information returns readily

30 Section 6033.
31 Defined as contributing more than 2 percent of the organization's funding.

disseminated to anyone who types in their name on an Internet search engine. Indeed, a recent survey revealed that 20.9 percent of respondents indicated that they would be inclined to increase charitable gifts if such gifts could be made anonymously.[32]

'A little-known characteristic of donor-advised funds underscores the importance a number of substantial donors place on anonymity. Some of the largest account holders with donor-advised funds are individuals and families who also have substantial private foundations. The reason they contribute to donor-advised funds is to maintain anonymity for certain gifts. Donor-advised funds do not file Form 990-PF, and donor-advised funds maintain the confidentiality of names of their account holders and the amount held in each account. Typically, however, donor-advised funds permit only their account holders to make donations to public charities. Accordingly, substantial donors seeking to maintain anonymity in their gifts can only do so for grants to public charities. The extent to which transparency rules governing private foundations constrain other types of charitable giving is not known and cannot be quantified. Nevertheless, the conclusion is inescapable that the rules actively discourage some forms of charitable giving.

Any doubt as to the comprehensiveness of the regulatory environment governing private foundations in the United States is quickly dispelled by reviewing the information required of private foundations on Form 990-PF. If the thirty-one pages of instructions were not daunting enough, the disclosures as to the estimated average time to prepare the form, as required by the Paperwork Reduction Act,[33] surely are:

- Recordkeeping, 140 hours and 37 minutes
- Learning about the law or the form, 28 hours and 15 minutes
- Preparing the form, 33 hours and 39 minutes
- Copying and sending to the IRS, 32 minutes

Honest philanthropists have the right to ask whether the thirty-year-old U.S. regulatory scheme continues to be appropriate.[34] Many view the Internal Revenue Service's expansion into a number of the areas covered by the regulatory regime described previously as overreaching.[35] As with many areas of government

32 Bank of America and Center on Philanthropy at Indiana University survey published in *Chronicle of Philanthropy*, November 9, 2006, at 16.
33 Instructions to Form 999-PF at 28, Appendix 4.
34 See "The Ironies of Foundation Regulation," an opinion piece by Peter Frumkin, in *Chronicle of Philanthropy*, February 5, 2004, at 31. The article gives thought to how the law of unintended consequences has played out in the regulation of charities called for by the Tax Reform Act of 1969.
35 Part of the problem is that charitable organizations are creatures of state law and should be overseen and regulated by the states in which they are formed or incorporated. Few states, with the notable exceptions of New York and California, however, devote much in the way of enforcement resources to policing charitable organizations. Nevertheless, in being called on to enforce the statutory scheme created by Congress in 1969, the Internal Revenue Service is required to work in areas far beyond its usual tax-collecting function.

regulation, once Congress decides to intervene to remedy an abuse, invariably the form of regulation goes further than was required to remedy the perceived problem. Nevertheless, potential philanthropists should not lose sight of the basic fact that acceptance of the regulatory regime is the price of income tax deductibility for gifts to private foundations. If this deductibility is not needed – or can be forgone – viable alternatives in the form of foreign foundations can be utilized to undertake desired charitable purposes.

CHAPTER FIVE

Constraints on cross-border philanthropy

As noted in Chapter 3, the Internal Revenue Code draws numerous distinctions between charitable endeavors inside and outside of the United States. Sometimes the distinctions are fine lines, and sometimes they are bright lines. The distinctions frequently are arbitrary and for no apparent reason. As a matter of policy, there should be little difference between a charitable dollar spent to feed a hungry child in Alabama versus one spent to feed a hungry child in Azerbaijan. As a legal matter, however, there is.

At the time most of the provisions relating to the deductibility of charitable contributions from income, estate, and gift taxes were enacted into law, the world was a much larger place. Today, however, with fast, convenient, and relatively inexpensive air transportation available to virtually every part of the world – together with the ability to communicate instantly, whether by landline or wireless telephone, facsimile, the Internet, or video conferencing – the objects of philanthropy know no boundaries. Nevertheless, U.S. law represents a significant constraint on borderless philanthropy.

Of course, the fundamental prohibition against deductibility of donations to charities not organized in the United States has not barred the door to U.S.-raised charitable dollars supporting foreign charitable endeavors. Rather than a Berlin Wall, the prohibition in practice has been a kind of Maginot Line that cross-border philanthropy must circumvent. This chapter examines the legal regimes regulating foreign grant making by U.S. charities (labeled for convenience as "outbound charities") and the practice of foreign charities establishing U.S.-based charities, frequently referred to as "American friends of..." organizations (labeled for convenience as "inbound charities") to raise money from U.S. donors.

Outbound charities

As discussed in Chapter 4, unless a private foundation makes gifts to public charities, it runs the risk of incurring excise taxes for failing to meet its minimum distribution requirements under section 4542. Moreover, if the gift is not a defined "qualifying distribution," it may also be deemed a taxable expenditure, which would potentially be subject to additional excise taxes. From a definitional standpoint, for a private foundation safely to make a gift to a public charity, that entity must be qualified as tax exempt under section 501(c)(3). Although this is basic to U.S. public charities, many foreign charities will not have so qualified, and therefore gifts to such foreign charities do not automatically pass muster under the regulatory regime governing private foundations. For this reason, most U.S. private foundations make their gifts to U.S. public charities, following the path of least resistance. If, however, a charitable donor's interests lie in areas that are partially or wholly outside the United States, an additional set of regulatory constraints must be understood and mastered to accomplish the intended charitable purposes.[1]

Equivalency determinations

Because payments from a U.S. private foundation to a U.S. public charity by definition are qualifying distributions, the IRS has established a procedure whereby grantors can make a "reasonable judgment" and "good faith determination" that the gift to the foreign entity has all of the indicia of a gift to a U.S. public charity, and therefore should be accorded the same legal status as a gift to a U.S. public charity.[2] Revenue Procedure 92–94, a copy of which is found in Appendix 7, in essence spells out safe-harbor rules for having a grant to a foreign entity be deemed the legal equivalent of a grant to a U.S. public charity.

The good-faith determination may be based on an affidavit of the grantee or on an opinion of counsel of the grantor or the grantee. The form of the affidavit is set forth in Revenue Procedure 92-94, and its elements track essentially the same subjects as Form 1023, the Application for Recognition of Exempt Status under section 501(c)(3) (see Appendix 1). In summary, the affidavit must include the following:

- The purposes for which the grantee was organized
- A description of the grantee's past, current, and future activities and operations
- A copy of the grantee's organizational and governing documents
- A statement that none of the grantee's income and assets confers an improper private benefit
- A statement that no person has a proprietary interest in the income or assets of the grantee
- A copy of the relevant statutory law or prohibition in the grantee's governing instruments controlling the distribution of the grantee's assets on dissolution
- A statement that the grantee is not engaged, except to an insubstantial extent, in activities that further nonexempt purposes or influence legislation
- A statement that the grantee does not engage in political or campaign activities on behalf of candidates for public office

1 An excellent resource for this subject is the Web site United States International Grantmaking, developed jointly by the Council on Foundations and the International Center for Not-for-Profit Law, located at www.usig.org. Additional articles, analyses, and forms relating to the subjects of this chapter can be found at the Web site.

2 See Regulations 53.4945–6(c)(2)(ii), 53.4942(a)–3(a)(6), and 53.4945–5(a)(5).

- A statement indicating whether the grantee is controlled by another organization, and if so, the name of that organization
- A statement of what type of publicly supported charity the grantee is (such as a school, hospital, church)
- If the grantee claims to be publicly supported, a schedule of financial support for the four most recently completed taxable years.

If, instead of offering an affidavit, an opinion of counsel is to be substituted, counsel must have reviewed a sufficient number of facts concerning the grantee's operations and support to enable the IRS to reach a conclusion that the grantee would be characterized as a public charity under the code. In other words, any counsel rendering an opinion based on anything less than a review of all the foregoing listed factors will leave his or her client on thin ice.

Notwithstanding laudable efforts on the part of the IRS to simplify and streamline the process of grant making to foreign charities, the equivalency determination process remains complex, time-consuming, and costly,[3] if not mission impossible. Compliance frequently involves translating organizational documents and foreign laws into English, examining years of financial records, and attempting to reconcile differences between U.S. GAAP and foreign accounting methods. In addition, cultural differences can impede the ability of U.S. grantors to obtain all of the information necessary to make the equivalency determination.

As a practical matter, organizations seeking to employ the equivalency determination methodology frequently hit the proverbial brick wall when trying to verify the areas of operations that are governed by the typical boilerplate that the IRS requires U.S. organizations to include in their charter or constitution to be recognized as tax exempt. For example, the IRS requires language prohibiting private inurnments to be included in corporate charters.[4] Without inclusion of such a prohibition in the foreign entity's organizational documents – and there is no reason a foreign organization would include such language – it is difficult for the lawyer to opine that the foreign organization would be accorded tax-exempt status under U.S. law. Frequently such organizations are reluctant to amend their organizational documents to include such language, and therefore the equivalency determination criteria cannot be met.

The typical organizational boilerplate required by the IRS is but one example of the impediments faced by counsel asked to opine that a foreign charity would be recognized as tax exempt in the United States. The recently expanded and enhanced Form 1023 contains a numerous examples of areas of potential pitfalls. Bluntly stated, the unique qualifications that the IRS now includes on Form 1023 – "wrong"

3 The experience of one private foundation: "When the Kunstadter Foundation made its first international grant of $2,500 to a project in China, . . . it sent the paperwork to its lawyer for review. A bill for $3,000 accompanied the lawyer's [equivalency determination] letter." "Family Foundations Discuss How Small Grants Can Make a Difference," *Chronicle of Philanthropy*, February 21, 2002, at 16.

4 For example, see Appendix 2, article 10, for typical language.

answers to which can be a trip wire for the IRS to reject an application for recognition of exempt status – are unlikely to be found in organizational or operational documents of any foreign charity.

In short, even though well-articulated safe harbors are prescribed in Revenue Procedure 92-94 to allow grants to foreign charities, numerous technical barriers to compliance frequently inhibit U.S. foundations from qualifying to make foreign grants on the basis of an equivalency determination.

Expenditure responsibility

Where an equivalency determination affidavit or opinion of counsel cannot be obtained, it is still possible for U.S. foundations to make a qualifying distribution grant to a foreign grantee. These are the same procedures that apply where grants are made to U.S.-based recipients that are not public charities. The so-called expenditure responsibility rules are designed to ensure that the grantee is utilizing the grant in the same manner and for analogous purposes as would a public charity. The following subsections summarize the major elements of expenditure responsibility.

Pre-grant inquiry

The private foundation must be satisfied that the grant will be used for proper, charitable purposes. Accordingly, the foundation will typically review the grantee's history, experience, and practices. Since the grantee will be the best source of this information, the foundation will typically have a questionnaire or interview script it will follow at the initial stages of its grant-making process.

Written agreement

Where the grantee is not a public charity, the terms of the grant must be memorialized in a written contract.[5] The regulations are quite specific as to the elements that must be included in such agreements. In addition to basic identifying information, including the purposes of the grant, the grantee must make the following commitments in writing:

- To repay any portion of the grant that is not used for the stated purposes
- To submit thorough periodic or annual reports on the manner in which the funds were expended and the progress the grantee has made toward achieving the purposes or goals set forth in the grant
- To maintain receipts and records of all expenditures, which may be made available to the grantor at any time
- Not to use any of the grant for noncharitable, lobbying, or campaign activities[6]

5 Sample forms that any exempt organization might use as models for grant agreements may be found in John A. Edie, *Expenditure Responsibility Step by Step*, 3rd ed. (Council on Foundations, 2002).

6 See the discussion of taxable expenditures under section 4945, in Chapter 4, *supra*.

Reports

The grantee must provide regular reports to the grantor on the progress and fulfillment of the grant.

Reports to the IRS

Form 990-PF requires that the grantee add a schedule to its return on Form 990-PF providing a summary paragraph on each expenditure responsibility grant's status.

Financial accounts

If the grantee is a private foundation itself, it must be able to prove that all of the grant funds have been expended and not retained as part of its endowment fund. These so-called out-of-corpus rules are administered in tandem with the minimum distribution rules described previously, so that private foundations may not circumvent the minimum distribution rules by making grants to other private foundations, which themselves might hold the funds and not distribute them for charitable purposes. Any private foundation receiving a grant from another private foundation therefore must establish that the funds were expended on a timely basis for the purposes of the grant. If the grantee is not a private foundation, the grantee must agree to segregate the grant in a separate bank account until all of the funds have been expended.

Until recently, the extent to which the equivalency determination and expenditure responsibility rules overlap or provided a hierarchy for foreign giving was not entirely clear. In 2001, the Council on Foundations secured an information letter from the IRS affirming that U.S. private foundations could invoke the expenditure responsibility rules for foreign grant making without first attempting to obtain an equivalency determination affidavit.[7] In other words, even though the grant was made to a foreign public charity, the U.S. foundation could dispense with the cumbersome equivalency determination rules and instead be in compliance with the qualifying distribution rules by following the expenditure responsibility procedures.

Treasury Department Anti-Terrorist Financing Guidelines

Two days after September 11, 2001, President Bush issued Executive Order No. 13224,[8] which directed the U.S. Treasury Department to work with other elements of the federal government and the international community to develop a comprehensive and sustained campaign against the sources and conduits of terrorist financing. Within several months, Congress enacted the USA PATRIOT Act

7 The April 18, 2001, letter from the IRS to John A. Edie, Esq., senior vice president and general counsel, Council on Foundations, can be downloaded from the council's Web site at www.cof.org/government/index.htm.

8 66 *Fed. Reg.* 49079, September 25, 2001.

(Uniting and Strengthening America by Providing Appropriate Tools Required to Intercept and Obstruct Terrorism). Investigations following September 11 revealed that charities were the second most important source of financing for terrorist organizations.[9] In short order, the U.S. government froze the assets of four U.S.-based charitable organizations and identified several dozen additional foreign-based charities that were involved in channeling funds to organizations involved in terrorist activities.

In response, in part, to concerns raised by Arab American and American Muslim communities, which had experienced a sharp drop in support for constituent charitable organizations, the Treasury Department issued the Anti-Terrorist Financing Guidelines: Voluntary Best Practices for U.S.-Based Charities (hereafter, the Treasury Guidelines) in November, 2002. Although the suggested guidelines, for the most part, constituted a restatement of the obvious for private foundation managers well versed in the subjects described previously and for practitioners experienced in regulation of cross-border charitable transactions more generally, they served as a highly visible notice that the stakes involved in cross-border philanthropy had permanently changed after September 11.

The initial Treasury Guidelines invited public comment, which proved quite animated. The Treasury Guidelines were criticized as:

- Duplicative
- Burdensome, in that the costs of compliance depleted resources available for charitable purposes
- Overreaching, in that abuses from U.S.-based charities were minimal
- Counterproductive, in that numerous international programs in dealing with the root causes of terrorism, poverty, hunger, and lack of educational opportunities would be curtailed or discouraged as a result of the Treasury Guidelines
- Creating a chilling effect on international charitable grant making
- Most significant, dangerous, in that they gave rise to the inference that U.S. charities owed a duty to the U.S. government to report questionable foreign practices.

In response to the wave of harsh criticism, revised Treasury Guidelines were issued on December 5, 2005. As with the initial version, the revised Treasury Guidelines also requested public comment. In response, criticism of the Treasury Guidelines continued unabated, with numerous commentators calling for their withdrawal.[10]

After considering the second round of comments, the Treasury Department published what appears to be the final version of the Treasury Guidelines on October 31, 2006 (found here in Appendix 8). The final version did make a number

9 Remarks of David Aufhauser, general counsel, U.S. Treasury Department, before the American Bar Association Section of Taxation's Committee on Exempt Organizations, May 9, 2003.

10 In an unusual response, both the Council on Foundations and the American Bar Association proposed an alternative approach, a carefully crafted substitute brochure titled "Principles of International Charity," a copy of which is available from the director of international programs at the Council on Foundations.

of substantive changes in response to the comments received. The Treasury Department's comments on the responses received may be found on its Web site (www.treasury.gov/offices/enforcement/key-issues/protecting/charities-intro.shtml). Even though no further comments were invited, one of the primary groups actively opposing the Treasury Guidelines, the Council on Foundations, reiterated its objections to the Treasury Guidelines. It renewed its suggestions to adopt the more general and flexible Principles of International Charity, which had been drafted by a private-sector group of interested trade associations and professionals.[11] As the Treasury's initiatives addressing charitable abuses appear to have concluded, the Council on Foundations' letter may appropriately be viewed as agreeing to disagree.

One commentator uncharitably but not inaccurately characterized the Treasury Guidelines as "expenditure responsibility on steroids." The Treasury Guidelines are important in highlighting the attention that foundation managers must pay to a number of post–September 11 antiterrorist legislative and regulatory initiatives. Among the additional due diligence measures that foundation managers must now follow is to ensure that grantees are not included on the master list of specially designated nationals maintained by the Office of Foreign Assets Control (OFAC) of the Treasury Department (for the list, see www.treasury.gov/offices/enforcement/ofac/sdn). The OFAC Web site also includes useful information on the sanctions regimes it enforces against global terrorism, foreign terrorist organizations, and foreign governments involved in terrorist activities.[12]

Failure to impose the controls necessary to ensure that charitable grants do not find their way into the hands of terrorist organizations risks criminal prosecution, as well as the reputation and future of the charitable organization, which could face a loss of exempt status or a blocking of its assets. Accordingly, the Treasury Guidelines form an important part of the framework for running a private foundation seeking to carry out its charitable purposes outside the United States. It must be emphasized that whether or not the private foundation is based inside or outside the United States, these concerns must be kept in mind. Of course, U.S. citizens participating in the foreign activities of foreign private foundations are still subject to U.S. criminal prosecution for violations of the Patriot Act. Equally important, most countries in which foreign charities might be based have enacted and vigorously enforce measures to combat money laundering, drug trafficking, and the diversion of resources to terrorist organizations. Therefore, an enhanced level of scrutiny is required in administering foreign charitable grants.

The U.S. Treasury Department continues to emphasize that the Treasury Guidelines are voluntary. Even so, IRS agents performing audits of charities have been known to cite to the Treasury Guidelines, thereby suggesting, if not coercively,

11 Letter from Steve Gunderson, president and chief executive officer, Council on Foundations, December 18, 2006.

12 31 Code of Federal Regulations sections 594–97.

that Treasury's guidance should be followed.[13] Moreover, apparently, charities not abiding by the Treasury Guidelines were excluded from participation in the recent Combined Federal Campaign, which solicits contributions directly from federal employees. Regardless, the Treasury Guidelines are a stern warning from the U.S. government that charities engaging in international grant making must play close attention to avoiding the diversion of charitable resources toward terrorist interests.[14]

Inbound charities

Numerous foreign charities, from universities to relief organizations to museums to medical and scientific research organizations, benefit from significant support in the United States. As indicated in Chapter 3, however, a distinguishing element of U.S. income tax laws is the nondeductibility of direct gifts to foreign charities. Viewing the potential for fund-raising in the United States from abroad, these organizations have looked for ways to exploit this potential donor base. Because many donors require tax deductibility for their contributions, and in any event, the availability of deductibility facilitates fund-raising, the solution to the nondeductibility problem is for the foreign organizations to establish U.S.-organized entities, duly recognized as tax exempt by the IRS.

Consistent with the axiom that the law will not permit a person to do indirectly what is prohibited from being done directly, the IRS has ruled that where donors earmark a gift to a U.S. charity for transfer to or use by a foreign charity, the U.S. charity will be seen to be an "agent for, or a channel of, a foreign charitable organization," and the charitable deduction will be disallowed.[15] Nevertheless, given the obvious merit of foreign charities being able to raise funds in the United States, the IRS has qualified the so-called conduit rule: disallowing the deductibility of such donations where gifts to the U.S. entity are not earmarked for foreign use, the governing board of the U.S. charity maintains discretion and control over all donations, and all gifts to foreign donees are consistent with the stated charitable purposes of the exempt organization.

These organizations are typically referred to as "American friends of..." organizations. For example, the American Friends of Oxford University has raised significant funds in the United States over the years from Oxford alumni, including

13 Likewise, language suggesting that the Treasury Guidelines are mandatory apparently is used in the standard scripts that IRS reviewing agents use in scrutinizing applications for the recognition of tax-exempt status.

14 An excellent discussion of the practical aspects of additional scrutiny of risks required of U.S. charities engaged in international grant making may be found in the comments prepared by the Committee on Exempt Organizations of the American Bar Association Section of Taxation in response to IRS Announcement 2003–29, which is published in *The Tax Lawyer*, 57 (2003): 195. In particular, the comments outline various suggested best practices for establishing a know-your-grantee process.

15 See Revenue Ruling 63–252, 1963–2 C.B. 101, and Rev. Rul. 66-79, 1966-1 C.B. 48.

generations of Rhodes Scholars who have been privileged to study at Oxford. In soliciting donations to Oxford, however, the American Friends of Oxford University is careful to indicate to potential donees that their contributions are to the U.S. charity, which will maintain discretion over their use. The fact that virtually all funds raised by the organization have found their way to Oxford University in England does not necessarily contravene applicable IRS rules. Presumably, the board of directors of the organization meets periodically to discuss resources raised and potential grants. After full discussion of the merits and relative priorities for grant making, the board will exercise its discretion to make specific gifts for specific purposes to Oxford University, all consistent with its own charitable purposes, in the same manner as other organizations.

The administration of "American Friends of..." organizations is one of the few areas of tax practice where form prevails over substance. Readers considering the establishment of such organizations should clearly understand that obtaining and maintaining tax deductibility for the U.S. donor base is more than a wink and nod on the part of the IRS; therefore, considerable attention must be paid to the required legal structure employed. In the first instance, the corporate charter must contain ample focus on U.S. qualified charitable activities and not merely recite a purpose of supporting a foreign charity. Appendix 3 contains a template corporate charter that has been approved on numerous occasions by the IRS for use by "American Friends of..." organizations. It is recommended that references to U.S.-based charitable purposes and activities be included in the corporate charter. As a practical matter, this approach usually does not create any problems, as most foreign charities looking to establish "American Friends of..." organizations already have sizable interests or activities in the United States, whether taking the form of alumni organizations or sponsoring research, exhibitions, or performances.

Next, in organizing and qualifying the "American Friends of..." organization for tax-exempt status, care must be taken in organizing the governing board so that the foreign charity is not overly represented and certainly does not control governance. There is certainly no prohibition, either in legal authorities or in practice, against some representation on the governing board by the foreign charity, including persons outside of the United States. Nevertheless, it must be clear from all the facts and circumstances that the governing body of the U.S. charity is independent and fully capable of exercising unfettered discretion. Accordingly, substantially overlapping board membership with the governing body of the foreign charity should be avoided. One or two interlocking board members, who serve on both the foreign and the "American Friends of..." organization, is an acceptable practice.

In its fund-raising activities, the "American Friends of..." organization should emphasize its own independent charitable purposes and avoid obligating itself to support any specific foreign project or organization. Indeed, it should reject any gifts that are earmarked for foreign use or are conditional on a specific foreign use. Solicitation materials should emphasize that all contributions are subject to control of the U.S. entity. The return of any funds to donors insisting on specific foreign uses would underscore the governing body's independence and that the U.S. entity is not acting as a mere conduit.

Decisions of the governing body should be memorialized in written minutes, taking care to describe the discussion as to grant making and the positions expressed by various members of the governing body. Accordingly, the discretion being exercised will be demonstrable and readily transparent in the event the IRS questions the operations of the section 501(c)(3) entity.

Once the "American Friends of..." organization is established, administration of the organization must be on the same basis as any section 501(c)(3) exempt organization engaged in grant making outside of the United States. As indicated previously, this means complying with applicable practices and procedures regarding equivalency determinations or expenditure responsibility. Because most "American Friends of..." organizations are by name linked to well-known public charities outside the United States, frequently compliance with the equivalency determination procedures can prove relatively straightforward. Where an equivalency determination is not readily forthcoming, however, expenditure responsibility will be required. This would include written agreements with the foreign donee charity, together with follow-up on accounting and financial matters relating to the grant, including proof that funds were expended consistent with the U.S. organization's charitable purposes.

CHAPTER SIX

Why create a foreign charity?

The bias in U.S. law against private foundations

As has been suggested herein, once a potential philanthropist sets out to establish a charitable organization, he or she will quickly learn that it will be far easier to create a public charity rather than face the regulatory burdens and constraints of creating and maintaining a private foundation. Fundamentally, the entire private foundation regulatory regime can be avoided by broadening support for the organization so that at least 35 percent of the support each year comes from the general public. Moreover, founders frequently come quickly to the conclusion that the compliance efforts that are entailed in equivalency determinations and expenditure responsibility on grants to nonpublic charities can be avoided by funding grantees that are already qualified as public charities.

The burdens and complexities of the U.S. regulatory regime governing private foundations have had the predictable effect of discouraging philanthropists from establishing private foundations.[1] Among the more visible manifestations of this effect is the rise of donor-advised funds. According to its recent survey of donor-advised funds,[2] *The Chronicle of Philanthropy* found that the assets of 103 of the largest such funds grew by 25 percent in 2007, reaching a staggering $23.3 billion. The amount of money distributed to charities from donor-advised mutual funds also jumped significantly, increasing 24 percent to $4.2 billion in 2007.

Sooner or later, all of the gifts transferred to such funds will flow to public charities.[3] Therefore, it is the public charities and not organizations directly

1 In some instances, private foundations that have been established for decades have determined to convert to public charity status by broadening their fund-raising efforts. The most notable example is the Pew Charitable Trusts, which announced that, effective January 1, 2008, it would change its tax status to be a public charity. The primary reason for this was to avoid the absolute bar on private foundations engaging in lobbying activities.

2 *Chronicle of Philanthropy*, May 29, 2008, at 15.

3 There is no legal requirement that grants from donor-advised funds be restricted to public charities. As a practical matter, most donor-advised funds so require, primarily because they are administered by large mutual fund companies, who, as indicated earlier, are primarily interested in managing investments rather than in charitable activities per se. If a donor-advised fund were to make a grant to a private foundation, it would have to exercise expenditure responsibility, which most donor-advised-fund administrators are ill equipped to do. Accordingly, the typical agreement that

overseen by the donors themselves that will utilize the charitable resources. From a public policy standpoint, it is appropriate to ask how much of the creative spirit of charitable giving is lost by channeling these funds to existing public charities. Stated differently, had these donors, many of whom are giving substantial amounts, not been encumbered by regulatory burdens – whether actual or perceived – might not new and innovative solutions for the various problems facing our society have been devised?[4]

It is impossible to measure the extent to which the regulatory burdens imposed by the Internal Revenue Code on private foundations have discouraged the establishment of charitable endeavors. Many potential philanthropists who have accumulated sufficient wealth to consider endowing a charitable fund have mastered the hypertechnical legal and accounting expertise necessary to succeed in the current business regulatory environment. For those who have achieved fluency in complex legal or accounting matters, compliance with the regulatory regime governing private foundations may not be particularly burdensome. For others, however, perhaps more skeptical of intrusive government, the regulatory landscape will first invoke fear, then avoidance.

Increased regulatory intrusiveness is to be expected

As indicated in Chapter 4, a number of legislative and administrative initiatives hold the potential for vastly increased regulation of charitable activities in the United States. These initiatives are taking place on a number of different fronts, at both the state and the federal levels. While it cannot be predicted with certainty which of the initiatives will be enacted or implemented, there can be little doubt that increased government scrutiny of the charitable sector will result in additional regulatory burdens in the future.

An example of this increase may be seen in revisions to Form 1023, Appendix 1, within the past three years. The form itself has grown from nine pages having four parts to twelve pages having nine parts, not counting schedules applicable to specific categories of organizations. The instructions have increased to twenty-four pages from seven pages. The Paperwork Reduction Act estimates of time required to complete Form 1023 have ballooned from an already-staggering 64 hours to nearly 105 hours, not including the time required to fill out any of the schedules, several

a donor-advised fund will enter into with its donors requires that grants be limited to public charities.

4 One by-product of the legal and regulatory landscape favoring public charities has been the significant expansion of large public charities. This expansion has been accomplished by an ever-growing charitable infrastructure, which some observers have characterized as the bureaucratization of American philanthropy. The recent criticism of the American Red Cross began when it was revealed that the Red Cross planned to hold back an astronomical sum from the funds raised in the name of helping the victims of the September 11, 2001, terrorist attacks to fund other Red Cross programs and expenses. After its chair resigned and the organization came under a barrage of criticism, it announced that every dollar collected in the name of addressing September 11 would be disbursed to the victims.

of which exceed 15 hours apiece. Much of the expanded Form 1023 implements the creeping Sarbanes-Oxley tendencies of the IRS, as broad inquiries are made into any number of discrete areas that the IRS believes could be problematic, such as executive compensation.

While the effort required to apply for exempt status has significantly increased, the likelihood of being required to supply additional information and documentation before being granted approval has also increased. The IRS has responded to congressional scrutiny of private foundations by raising the bar for approval administratively. Where an application for exempt status is identified for closer scrutiny, the applicant can often expect multiple pages of additional questions – akin to interrogatories a litigant might receive. In short, the administrative approval process is anything but the proverbial rubber stamp, and frequently significant efforts are required beyond completing Form 1023.

Corresponding changes have recently been implemented by the Internal Revenue Service for Form 990, the information reporting form for public charities. The increase in scope, particularly in the manner in which suspected problematic practices are treated, is analogous to the enhanced Form 990-PF. Although the core form is only eleven pages, there is a significant increase in the number of disclosures that are required. To keep the core form manageable, the IRS utilizes a trip-wire approach whereby certain answers on the core form trigger the requirement of filing one or more of sixteen supporting schedules. The schedules probe the details of many potentially problematic areas, including lobbying, transactions with insiders, and significantly, international activities. The new Form 990 reporting requirements are being phased in over three years, so that for the 2008 tax year, only organizations with $1 million or more in gross receipts or more than $2.5 million in assets must file. By 2010, these thresholds decrease to $200,000 in gross receipts and $500,000 in assets. Simultaneously, new registration requirements for public charities that are below these thresholds have been implemented. GuideStar estimates that up to a half million public charities, which formerly were not subject to any reporting requirements, could lose their tax exemptions as a result of the broadened requirements.[5]

Perhaps because "reform" of charities is an easy political target, legislators are expected to continue to expand the regulatory agenda governing U.S. charities. Accordingly, qualified U.S. charitable organizations are certain to face growing regulatory burdens and constraints of unknown scope and complexity in the future.

Advantages of a foreign charitable organization

Avoiding the U.S. private foundation regulatory regime

Fortunately, a potential philanthropist need not choose either burdensome regulation or a pass-through vehicle, such as a donor-advised mutual fund. Instead, a

5 Suzanne Coffman, "Half A Million Nonprofits Could Lose Their Tax Exemptions," GuideStar Newsletter 9, no. 1, January 2009, at www.guidestar.org.

charitable organization can be established in a foreign jurisdiction, outside of the constraints applicable to private foundations organized in the United States.

Perhaps the perspective brought to philanthropy through use of a foreign entity may be best understood by way of an example. Charles F. Feeney was a successful businessman who developed a chain of duty-free shops at international airports around the world. As his business grew, he decided to devote an increasing share of the profits to philanthropy. He established the Atlantic Foundation and the Atlantic Trust under Bermuda law and contributed a substantial portion of his stock holdings in his businesses to these charitable entities.

Feeney was particularly interested in providing increased educational opportunities in poor communities in the United States and Ireland. Feeney, however, was a strong believer in anonymity. Accordingly, among the conditions attached to the grants that his foundations made were that the source of his gifts would remain anonymous.

The foundations continued their generous support of education in this manner for more than a decade, extending grants in excess of $600 million. The source of the gifts came to light when Feeney's business agreed to be acquired by a publicly traded corporation, and applicable securities laws required disclosure of the ownership of its shares. It was then revealed that the subject shares were owned by Bermuda charitable trusts. Shortly thereafter, Feeney agreed to be interviewed by the *New York Times*, and the full scope of his charitable work came to light.[6] Today, the Bermuda charitable trusts established by Feeney are estimated to have between $4 billion and $10 billion in assets.

Feeney's charitable objectives could never have been achieved if his foundations had been organized under U.S. law. As discussed in Chapter 4, section 4943 would have prohibited the foundations from owning more than 20 percent of the stock of Feeney's enterprises. Had they done so, the value of the holdings would have been subject to excise taxes, and the foundations would have been required to divest a sufficient number of shares to be in compliance. Of equal significance from Feeney's perspective, the gifts he made could not have been on an anonymous basis. Private foundations recognized as tax exempt by the Internal Revenue Service must file Form 990-PF annually, the schedules of which are required to disclose most substantial gifts. Although he might have requested the donees to show the gifts as anonymous, surely the magnitude of the gifts would have caught the attention of people reviewing the public records, either directly or over Web sites publicizing IRS data, who would have revealed their sources.

Of course, establishing a private foundation in a foreign jurisdiction is not appropriate in all circumstances. If a deduction from federal income tax is a fundamental consideration for establishing the foundation, there is little choice but to establish it

6 Now that the silence has been broken, Feeney's charities have become more visible and are seeking to broaden their grant-making activities. To this end, charities have established a Web site, www.atlanticphilanthropies.org.

in the United States and abide by the private foundation rules. After all, regulation and scrutiny is the price exacted for tax deductibility. Nevertheless, there are a number of situations where the potential philanthropist may not require tax deductibility. For example:

- Where a foundation can be established by early contribution of founders' shares in a start-up company, the shares of which have little or no value, little or no tax benefit will be derived from the contribution.
- Where the foundation will be funded principally from testamentary gifts, potential donors may be less motivated by incentives accorded by *income* tax deductibility.
- If the donor has significant assets but these generate little or no income, the ceiling on deductibility may render any deduction from income taxes relatively insignificant.

Different aspects of the U.S. regulatory regime governing private foundations will have different levels of significance for different donors. For Feeney, the excess holdings and disclosure requirements of U.S. law were apparently undesirable. For others, the mandatory annual minimum distributions might be a significant impediment. For others, the strict rules against dealings between the foundation and disqualified persons might be offensive. (Presumably, the propriety or legality of such dealings under the laws of foreign jurisdictions might more typically be governed by the type of arm's-length standards that were applied in the United States prior to the adoption of the private foundation excise tax rules in 1969.)

> In conclusion, where income tax deductibility has little or no value or can be foregone, the formation of a charitable organization under the laws of foreign jurisdiction can accord potential philanthropists the opportunity to conduct their charitable activities outside of the constraints of the U.S. regulatory framework applicable to private foundations.

Hedging against future U.S. government intrusiveness

The increased regulation of U.S. charitable organizations is evident at all levels. Detailed examples have been provided here. Both the federal and state governments have undertaken increased regulatory initiatives against the charitable sector. Growing intrusiveness occurs administratively as well as at the behest of Congress and state legislatures. It is an unfortunate phenomenon that when perceived abuses are identified, a new round of legislative "reforms" is advocated, notwithstanding the fact that the targeted practice might have been illegal under existing law.

In this environment, a legitimate concern of existing philanthropists, those who perhaps already have established a private foundation under U.S. law, might be whether increasing government intrusiveness will reach a tipping point. For these individuals and families, the establishment of a mirror-image foundation in a foreign jurisdiction might be an appropriate strategy. Whatever the charitable purposes of the existing U.S. organization might be, these could be cloned in a foreign structure. The foreign structure could be funded by donations from the existing U.S. private foundation, which would have to disclose the grants on Form 990-PF, and would have to satisfy the equivalency determination or expenditure responsibility requirements applicable to any grant to a foreign private foundation. Particular attention would be to be paid to the out-of-corpus rules, which would require grant money to be expended in accordance with the timetable in the grant and not be accumulated as an endowment.

Just as high-net-worth investors engage in multiple strategies to diversify a portfolio, some of which might involve alternative investments such as private equity, real estate, commodities, and hedge funds, the establishment of a foreign clone of a U.S. private foundation might be viewed as an appropriate hedging strategy against possible future overreaching by federal and state regulators.

CHAPTER SEVEN

Picking a jurisdiction

From the perspective of advising U.S. persons on the formation of charitable organizations, the fundamental distinction is between the laws of the United States and the laws of other, non-U.S. jurisdictions. The United States represents but one of several dozen "good" jurisdictions where a philanthropist might confidently form a charitable organization. Unless the potential founder of a charitable organization is familiar with a specific foreign jurisdiction, however, the notion of entrusting significant charitable operations or a substantial endowment to unfamiliar persons or institutions in an unfamiliar setting can be daunting. This chapter analyzes the factors to be taken into consideration when choosing a foreign jurisdiction in which to locate a charitable organization.

The search for an appropriate jurisdiction should be undertaken without haste and with the objective of finding a comfort level in dealing with individuals and organizations in the foreign jurisdiction that is, in every respect, equivalent to the level of trust and comfort the founder currently has with his or her own professional advisers in the home jurisdiction. If that comfort level is not reached, the search should be abandoned and more familiar alternatives – making direct gifts to U.S. public charities, establishing a U.S. private foundation, or donating to a donor-advised mutual fund – should be pursued.

Over years of experience in working with individuals, families, and companies, we have often been surprised at the speed with which persons evaluating foreign jurisdictions have become comfortable, even where they may have initially begun the exercise with skepticism. The sophistication and experience of many foreign professionals sometimes comes as a surprise to U.S. persons. This experience is not universal, however. Unless and until an appropriate comfort level is reached with the jurisdiction being evaluated, a final decision should be deferred and additional jurisdictions should be considered and evaluated.

This chapter discusses, and in no particular order or level of significance, the primary considerations in selecting a foreign jurisdiction for the establishment of a charitable organization. Before doing so, however, a few words are appropriate on recent changes to the law that potentially blur the distinction between traditional notions of U.S. and foreign.

What is foreign anyway?

Domestic or *foreign*; *U.S.* or *non-U.S.*; *onshore* or *offshore*. Although we have noted the dispositive significance of the physical or juridical location of a charitable entity from the standpoint of qualifying a donation for deductibility from income tax, when it comes to deciding on a jurisdiction in which to form a charity, lines blur and the concept of foreign may not necessarily need to imply being across any border. This is because amendments to the Internal Revenue Code by the Small Business Tax Act of 1996 made it possible to have a trust validly formed under the laws of one of the fifty states and administered domestically but nevertheless be treated as a foreign trust for U.S. tax purposes.

Prior to the 1996 amendments, whether a trust was viewed for U.S. tax purposes as domestic or foreign turned on a number of uncertain and potentially ambiguous tests. The drafters of the 1996 amendments saw utility in fashioning a bright-line test for categorizing a trust as domestic or foreign. The legislative history states that the purpose of the amendments was to level the playing field competitively so that U.S. banks and trust companies could compete with foreign or multinational financial institutions for trust business for wealthy foreign families. Indeed, if wealthy foreign families could confidently use U.S.-based banks and trust companies without exposing trust assets to U.S. taxation, employment in the U.S. financial services sector would be enhanced.

Under the 1996 amendments, implementing regulations to which were promulgated in final form on February 1, 1999, it is possible to add certain elements to a trust declaration or agreement that will, in essence, disqualify the trust from being treated as a domestic trust so that it is categorized as a foreign trust for U.S. tax purposes. For example, the inclusion of so-called flight provisions, which trigger automatic migration of the trust to a new jurisdiction in the event of war, civil unrest, or widespread confiscation or nationalization of property, will cause a trust to be classified as a foreign trust.[1] Trust companies in a number of jurisdictions, Delaware in particular, now actively market their ability to create so-called hybrid trusts for individuals and families seeking categorization of trusts as foreign, while keeping administration in the United States and using the amended and improved Delaware trust law.

On this basis, a philanthropist seeking to establish a foreign charitable trust, not qualified as tax exempt under section 501(c)(3) and therefore outside of the private foundation regulatory regime described in the preceding chapters, could do so in a U.S. jurisdiction such as Delaware. Nevertheless, most U.S. philanthropists seeking to establish foreign charities will do outside of the United States.

The subsequent sections cover factors that philanthropists will want to evaluate in selecting a jurisdiction in which they may consider establishing a charity.

1 Charles M. Bruce, *United States Taxation of Foreign Trusts* (Kluwer Law International, 2000) at 36–42.

Law

Sometimes U.S. persons are not fully aware of the extent to which they desire and rely on a fully developed legal system until they encounter one which is not. Although culturally one of the distinguishing factors of contemporary life in the United States is the overemphasis on law and legal process (and therefore, collaterally, lawyers), a careful review of the foreign law and legal system that will become the basis for the formation and operation of a foreign charity is critical. The primary areas for evaluation are corporate or trust law, the regulations and institutions governing charitable organizations, and the procedures governing access to the courts. The evaluation may also want to consider the legal oversight mechanisms and the enforcement policy of the government agency or bureau charged with regulating charities.

Not surprisingly, there is enormous variation in the comprehensiveness of governing statutes and the quality of decisional law among jurisdictions. Jurisdictions such as Bermuda and the Channel Islands, which have relied heavily on offshore corporate, insurance, and trust businesses, have well-developed laws and legal infrastructure. The sheer volume of transactions in such jurisdictions makes it far more likely that any particular problem that might arise will be governed by a specific statute or will have decisional law that provides the necessary guidance.[2]

Fundamentally, the type of structure envisioned by the charitable donor – a corporation or a trust – will come into play. If the donor is looking to establish a trust, he or she will want a common law jurisdiction, such as England, Bermuda, the Cayman Islands, the Bahamas, Isle of Man, the Channel Islands, and so on, and not a jurisdiction having a civil code.[3] Nevertheless, a number of jurisdictions have actively sought to improve and enhance their trust laws by new legislation. For example, in a number of jurisdictions, so-called purpose trust legislation has been enacted to permit trust vehicles to be used for a broad variety of purposes, some of them charitable. For example, under the laws of Bermuda, purpose trusts are useful for carrying out broad charitable purposes, as traditional trusts must have ascertainable beneficiaries.

If a corporate form will be used, the evaluation may well find that the corporate law of particular jurisdictions under review is significantly more developed. In most of the primary offshore jurisdictions, the corporate law is derived from British company law and is quite similar from jurisdiction to jurisdiction. Even so, a number of the jurisdictions have worked on their business laws to keep them current and to provide a competitive edge to their service sector. Many such jurisdictions have corporate regulatory regimes that seek to bolster the jurisdiction as a corporate domicile for corporations that have international operations, which is defined as

2 By analogy, New York or Delaware corporate law is far more developed (and, therefore, usually "better") than the corporate law of Vermont or the District of Columbia.

3 Switzerland has enacted trust statutes, even though it is a civil code jurisdiction. Nevertheless, charitable donors considering the use of trust structures should look to the various jurisdictions whose laws are derived from laws of England.

having no active trade or business in the jurisdiction of incorporation. The status then confers an exemption from taxation. Some of the regimes may be of potential utility to philanthropist seeking to establish charitable vehicles.

An additional aspect of the legal topography bears mentioning: government rules and enforcement practices concerning compliance with anti-money-laundering and proceeds-of-crime statutes. Virtually every jurisdiction now has such rules – the Patriot Act in the United States is a significant enhancement of such laws enacted prior to September 11, 2001. As will be seen in the subsequent sections, vigorous enforcement of such statutes is manifested in government approvals, which in some jurisdictions may be necessary to form a corporation, and which exist in virtually all jurisdictions in connection with opening a bank account. In each instance, the operative compliance regime calls for know-your-customer (KYC) due diligence on the part of the corporate service provider or financial institution. Depending on the levels of KYC required, substantially higher costs can result.

Financial services infrastructure

The foreign charity will require banking services. If organized as a trust, it may also choose to utilize the trust services of a financial institution. If organized as a corporation, requirements of local law may mandate that the charity engage local officers or directors. In such cases, it may be customary practice to utilize nominee officers, directors, or stockholders. For all these reasons, the financial strength and professional reputations of financial services firms should form an important part of evaluating a foreign jurisdiction.

In most jurisdictions, it is possible to engage a brand-name bank or trust company, as many worldwide financial services institutions have headquarters, for example, in New York, London, Zurich, or Toronto, and often have branch offices in such jurisdictions as Bermuda. This is not to suggest that a local bank or trust company would not provide better services. Indeed, some of the preeminent private banks and trust companies in the world operate in only a single jurisdiction or a few.

The selection process for choosing an international financial services provider will be no different than the process for selecting banking relationships in the United States. Not only will financial stability be essential, but also reputation and service are important factors to consider. The potential philanthropist's existing banking relationships or professional advisers may be used to gain introductions to appropriate candidates. Due diligence will likely also require a personal visit by the potential philanthropist to the offices where the services will be provided.

Professional infrastructure

Ultimately, the security and soundness of a particular jurisdiction can depend on the quality of the legal and accounting professionals that are available. Few jurisdictions have the scale and scope of legal and accounting firms that are common in the United States. Many so-called final-four accounting firms have branches or affiliated offices in many of the jurisdictions that one might typically consider. It is less common for large U.S. law firms to have branch offices in such jurisdictions, although increasingly, large firms in major offshore jurisdictions have engaged in cross-border mergers with firms in other offshore jurisdictions to create sizable law firms able to provide sophisticated advice on the relative merits of locating in jurisdictions where they practice.[4]

Foreign law firms should be evaluated much in the same way as U.S. law firms. The Martindale Hubbell law directory and Web site lists law firms in virtually all jurisdictions.[5] The same format is followed for law firms in Barbados as in the United States, listing bar admissions, educational background, and professional memberships. A review of the Martindale Hubbell listings can identify those law firms with attorneys, solicitors, or barristers who have been trained in the United States or abroad or have been affiliated with law firms in larger jurisdictions.[6] More important, potential donors should utilize their own professional advisers to network in order to locate appropriate candidates for assistance.[7] In many foreign jurisdictions, law firms or departments in law firms specialize in so-called private client practice, which usually encompasses the types of services that philanthropic enterprises need.[8] The strength and depth of a particular law firm's private client practice department is probably as important a consideration as the overall reputation of that firm.

While prospective new counsel or accountants can be interviewed by telephone, there is no substitute for a personal interview. Again, unless the professional under consideration inspires confidence, the potential philanthropist should keep looking. Such interviews are best conducted at the home offices of the firms that will provide the services. Accordingly, even if the professional adviser under consideration is planning a trip to the United States on other business or will be visiting the United States on a promotional trip, the prospective philanthropist will gain a more accurate view of the professional by interviewing them on their home turf.

Proximity or access to the United States

Although the world is a much smaller place than it was a decade or two ago, certain jurisdictions are far more convenient to deal with and travel to than others.

4 E.g., Appleby, based in Bermuda, and Ogier, based in the Cayman Islands.

5 See www.martindale.com.

6 Martindale Hubbell, however, does not rate foreign law firms and lawyers as it does in the United States.

7 Increasingly, U.S. law firms participate in international affiliations of law firms in multiple jurisdictions, such as Lex Mundi.

8 These firms often have captive trust companies that are available to serve a fiduciary role in the charitable entity to be established. For example, the law firm of Conyers, Dill & Pearman, based in Bermuda, has established the affiliated trust company Codan Trust Company Limited, which has branches in a number of jurisdictions. A number of other Bermuda law firms have done the same.

The popularity and extensive use of Bermuda and the Bahamas derive in large measure from their proximity to the United States. There are daily flights to Bermuda from New York; Philadelphia; Baltimore; and Charlotte, North Carolina. Each day there are multiple flights to the Bahamas from New York, Miami, and Atlanta. This is in stark contrast to jurisdictions like the Isle of Man or the Channel Islands, where a transatlantic flight must be followed by poor connections on small aircraft.

In this day and age, most of the jurisdictions under consideration will have state-of-the-art telecommunications services for both voice and data. This is not always the case, however. If a jurisdiction such as Barbados, for example, is under consideration, additional investigation should be made into telecommunications capabilities to ensure that proper communications can be maintained with local professionals and service providers.

Any difference in time zones should also be considered. Most jurisdictions in Europe are five or six time zones away. As a practical matter, conducting business or relying on professionals in the Channel Islands or Gibraltar, for example, of necessity is limited to the morning hours in the United States, which, depending on the level of activities, can be difficult or constraining.

Reputation

Unfortunately, lax law enforcement and laissez-faire bank regulators in a number of jurisdictions opened the way for money laundering by drug traffickers, terrorists, and other international criminals. The tightening of regulation that followed revelations of some of these practices in some jurisdictions did not come soon enough to salvage the jurisdiction's reputation. Once lost, reputations are difficult to regain. Thus, potential philanthropists seeking to evaluate foreign jurisdictions should play close attention to the general reputation of the jurisdiction.

Even jurisdictions that have worked very hard to regulate banking activities and corporate formations closely have, from time to time, been tainted by scandal. For example, in Jersey, several highly publicized incidents demonstrated that the highest level of scrutiny is required to protect the reputation of the jurisdiction.

Operating in a jurisdiction that maintains stricter controls, however, often results in higher costs, both in setting up the entity and in maintaining it. One way these jurisdictions screen out undesirable business and ensure that such business will go elsewhere is by requiring relatively high filing fees and annual maintenance or franchise tax assessments. For example, the high filing fees applicable to forming corporations in Bermuda and Jersey often result in the corporations being formed in lower-cost jurisdictions such as the British Virgin Islands.[9]

9 Higher costs in Bermuda relate directly to the requirements of the Bermuda Monetary Authority, which strictly scrutinizes applications for new corporations and often requires financial intermediaries to conduct additional due diligence of new clients.

Increasingly, another mechanism that certain jurisdictions use to scrutinize new entities is the requirement of a review by a government agency of the principals seeking to establish a new entity there. This review would be in addition to the almost universal KYC requirements implemented by most financial services institutions.[10] For example, the Bermuda Monetary Authority requires persons forming a new corporation in Bermuda to answer a lengthy questionnaire and submit extensive supporting documentation, which goes well beyond the typical financial institution KYC requirements. This review is far more than a rubber stamp, and not infrequently, it results in denying the applicant the authorization to form a new corporation in Bermuda.

Language

The ability to conduct business in a particular jurisdiction in English can be important to potential philanthropists. Although English has become the universal business language, not all jurisdictions have uniformly high-quality English-speaking professionals. The good news is that many of the more favored foreign jurisdictions in which to locate a private foundation are former British colonies or remain so-called crown dependencies, and therefore English remains the dominant language, if not the official one.

Political risks

Although most jurisdictions that philanthropists might consider would scarcely be viewed as presenting any kind of risk of political instability, this factor should not be overlooked. Particularly since the end of the Cold War, the world has been a relatively calm place. In the United States, we tend to ignore or discount the possibility of political risk, largely because the United States is such a stable political environment. Nevertheless, the relative stability of governments and the emphasis on the rule of law should be reviewed.

Political risk, however slight, can be mitigated by any number of preemptive measures, including the following:

- If the charity is to be formed as a trust, flight provisions should be included whereby an emergency trustee in another jurisdiction would automatically be installed if various enumerated events of duress were to occur, including war, civil insurrection, and so on.
- Charitable assets might be held in another jurisdiction through custodial arrangements, with investments predominantly in low-risk jurisdictions, such as the United States or the EU.

10 Typically, the KYC requirements of most financial institutions in non-U.S. jurisdictions (and increasingly in U.S. jurisdictions as well, at least as pertains to non-U.S. persons) include a review of passports and require reference letters from another financial institution with which the customer has maintained relationship for at least five years, and from professionals, such as a law or accounting firm.

- Charitable assets might be under the control of an investment adviser in another jurisdiction.
- Hybrid trust vehicles might be considered, so that situs and administration remain in the United States.

Costs

Most, but not all, of the foregoing factors will have an impact on the total costs of establishing a charitable entity in a foreign jurisdiction. As with any cost-benefit analysis, intangibles will often come into play and may, in fact, be the determining factor. Nevertheless, all the relative costs of the different components need to be balanced in reaching a final decision on an appropriate jurisdiction.

CHAPTER EIGHT

Establishing a foreign charitable foundation

You have made the major decisions. After having lengthy discussions with your advisers and making due diligence visits to various fiduciaries and professionals, you have chosen a foreign jurisdiction. You have also decided to form a trust or a new corporation. You have selected a trustee or a registered agent and perhaps nominee officers or directors. Now what?

U.S. tax considerations

As already stated, because your organization will be formed in a foreign jurisdiction, any donations used to establish it will not be deductible for federal income tax purposes.[1] Nevertheless, any future gifts or testamentary bequests can be fully deductible, without limitation, from both U.S. estate[2] and gift[3] taxes.

If a corporate vehicle is utilized, the transfer of funds or property to form the entity should not subject either the donor or the corporation to income taxation. Nor will the transfer cause any gain to be recognized in the case of the transfer of appreciated property.[4] Assuming that the laws of the foreign jurisdiction make clear that a charitable organization has no shareholders as such, the entity, though labeled a "corporation," should not run afoul of the U.S. Subpart F rules applicable to controlled foreign corporations.[5]

If a trust is utilized, presumably it will be an irrevocable trust, and the trust agreement or declaration of trust will provide the trustee with specific guidance as to the types and purposes of charitable endeavors that the entity will pursue.

1 Section 170(c)(2). See also Chapter 3 in this volume.
2 Section 2055(a).
3 Section 2522 (a) (2).
4 Section 351.
5 The U.S. shareholders of a controlled foreign corporation (CFC) are taxed, generally speaking, on all the income of the CFC except active business income. "Controlled foreign corporation" means, briefly, any foreign corporation of which more than 50 percent of either the total combined voting power of all classes of stock of the corporation entitled to vote or the total value of the stock of the corporation is owned, directly or indirectly, by U.S. shareholders. A U.S. shareholder is any person owning 10 percent or more of the total combined voting power of all classes of stock of the corporation. See sections 957 and 951(b).

The trust should be a nongrantor trust, so that income earned by the trust is not taxable to the U.S. settlor.[6] It should be noted that there are a few special rules in the Internal Revenue Code governing transfers to foreign trusts, which, on their face, appear to complicate the establishment of a foreign charitable trust:

- Section 684 triggers the recognition of gain on transfers of appreciated property to foreign trusts.
- Section 679 deems any foreign trust having U.S. beneficiaries to be a grantor trust, so that income of the foreign trust is treated as income to the U.S. grantor.

Fortunately, the Internal Revenue Service by rulemaking has clarified that these constraints do not apply to foreign trusts that are established for charitable purposes as described in section 501(c)(3).[7] Significantly, the foreign trust need not obtain a determination letter from the IRS recognizing its tax-exempt status to qualify for exclusion from these rules.[8]

If a trust is utilized, the U.S. person creating the trust will need to file Form 3520, Annual Return to Report Transactions with Foreign Trusts (see Appendix 9), with his or her annual income tax return in the year in which the trust is formed unless the trust has obtained a determination letter from the Internal Revenue Service. To address concerns about the increasing use of offshore accounts by U.S. persons to avoid declaring taxable income, in 1996, Congress amended the Internal Revenue Code to impose significant penalties for failure to report creation of foreign trusts. No exception to these reporting rules applies to a foreign trust created for charitable purposes where the trust has not obtained a determination letter.

In completing Form 3520, the settlor should name a U.S. agent for the foreign trust. The agent can be the settlor, a family member, or an unrelated party, but the agreement to serve as U.S. agent for the foreign charitable trust must be in writing. Where no U.S. agent is named, the Internal Revenue Service is given a high degree

6 Under the rules governing grantor trusts in sections 671 through 679, if the settlor, for example, retains the right to amend the trust, change the beneficiaries, or revoke the trust, the trust assets are deemed to have remained the taxpayer's property for tax purposes notwithstanding the transfer of legal title to the trustee, and the taxpayer remains taxable on any income or capital gains earned by the trust. See generally Charles M. Bruce, *United States Taxation of Foreign Trusts* (Kluwer, 2000), at 106–15.

7 The exception to the tax imposed by section 684 is set forth in section 1.684-3(b) of the regulations. The exception to treatment as a grantor trust under section 679 is set forth at section 1.679-4(a)(3). When both of these regulations were proposed, no exemption for foreign charitable trusts was included. The explanation for the change given by the Internal Revenue Service is set forth at T.D. 8956 (July 20, 2001) and T.D. 8955 (July 20, 2001).

8 If the foreign charitable organization wishes to make grants for charitable endeavors inside the United States, particular care will need to be given to the drafting of the trust instrument, so that the trust will be viewed as "described in Section 501(c)(3)," and grantor trust status can be avoided. For example, all of the language the Internal Revenue Service normally requires, for example, with respect to charitable purposes, avoidance of private inurements, and contribution to charitable purposes on dissolution, should be included even if the settlor does not intend to apply for recognition of tax-exempt status in the United States.

of discretion to determine the tax consequences of any transactions involving the foreign trust,[9] and therefore a U.S. agent should in all instances be named.

Distributions to U.S. grantees from the foreign charitable organization will be taxable to the U.S. grantees or not depending on the nature of the grantee and the use to which the grant will be put. Of course, if the grantee is tax exempt under section 501(c)(3), it will not be taxed on the distribution. Grants to foreign entities or persons generally should not be taxed by the United States.

Should the foreign entity apply for exempt status in the United States?

Foreign charitable organizations frequently apply for and obtain exempt status. Eligibility for tax-exempt status under section 501(c)(3) is based on charitable purposes and not limited geographically to entities formed in the United States.[10] The IRS's policy on qualifying foreign charities under section 501(c)(3) is clear: "The fact that an organization has been formed under foreign law will not preclude its qualification under Section 501(c) . . . if it meets the test of exemption."[11]

The Internal Revenue Service generally applies the same standards to foreign charities as it would to U.S. entities seeking exempt status.[12] Thus, to qualify, the foreign private foundation must be both organized and operated for charitable purposes, must not be operated for private benefit or inurement, and may not engage in lobbying or political activities. Whether the foreign private foundation should seek exempt status under U.S. tax rules, however, involves evaluating a number of factors, pro and con.

Section 501(c)(3) notice requirements

All newly formed section 501(c)(3) domestic organizations are required to notify the IRS that they are applying for tax-exempt status. The normal rule is that this must be done within fifteen months of formation, although a twelve-month grace period automatically permits the application to be made within twenty-seven months of formation. As described in Chapter 3, Form 1023 (see Appendix 1) is used to give the requisite statutory notice and apply for exempt status. Domestic

9 See Instructions for Form 3520, in Appendix 9, at 4, and Charles M. Bruce, *United States Taxation of Foreign Trusts* (Kluwer, 2000), at 205.

10 By contrast, sections 501(c)(1), (19), (21), and (22) do contain geographic limitations. Under section 509(a), all private foundations, both domestic and foreign, are described under section 501(c)(3).

11 Revenue Ruling 66-177, 1966–1 C.B. 13.

12 Professor Dale discusses the problem foreign entities typically have in meeting IRS standards in "Foreign Charities," 48 *Tax Lawyer* 657 (1995). This can be particularly problematic for foreign educational institutions with respect to meeting standards of nondiscrimination for private universities and schools in the wake of *Bob Jones University v. United States*, 461 U.S. 574 (1983).

charitable organizations failing to apply or that have their applications rejected will be taxable as regular corporations or trusts.

Certain foreign charities are exempted by statute from the notice and filing requirements applicable to domestic private foundations. Section 4948(b) and the regulations issued thereunder state that the requirements do not apply to foreign charities that receive at least 85 percent of their support from non-U.S. sources.[13] Thus, if more than 15 percent of the support for a foreign charity will come from U.S. sources, the entity by law is required to apply for exempt status. Failure to do so will result in characterization of the foreign charity as a foreign corporation or a foreign trust for U.S. tax purposes.

Tax implications of exempt status for foreign private foundations

There are four primary aspects of U.S. law that should be evaluated before determining whether a foreign foundation established by a U.S. person should seek exempt status under U.S. law.

1 Deductibility of lifetime gifts and testamentary bequests of U.S. donors

The nondeductibility of gifts to foreign charities for U.S. federal income tax purposes is a fundamental part of the legal landscape.[14] The ban on deductibility applies to both foreign public charities and foreign private foundations. As discussed previously, this statutory restriction dates from isolationist sentiments in Congress in the 1930s and remains a central part of U.S. tax law governing charitable structures. Although this restriction does not on its face apply in the context of estate and gift taxes, the private foundation notice requirements operate to bar estate and gift tax deductions for lifetime gifts and testamentary bequests to foreign private foundations, where the foreign private foundation has not qualified for tax-exempt status under section 501(c)(3).[15] Accordingly, this rule is among the most basic considerations in determining whether to seek exempt status in the United States for foreign private foundations.

As discussed already, mandatory notice provisions applicable to private foundations apply to both foreign and domestic private foundations. Section 508(a) states that, unless a private foundation has given notice to the IRS and has been recognized as exempt, it "shall not be treated as a organization described in

13 Such entities are deemed to be tax exempt for U.S. tax purposes without so qualifying. They are expressly exempted from the excise tax regulatory regime in chapter 42 applicable to private foundations. Nevertheless, section 4648(c) further provides that any such organization that engages in any acts or practices that would result in the imposition of excise taxes under the private foundation rules applicable to U.S. private foundations shall not be accorded exempt status, and, where it has been notified by the Internal Revenue Service of such disqualification, deductions for any donations to it are disallowed.

14 See Chapter 3 in this volume.

15 See Internal Revenue Code sections 2055(e)(1) and 508(d)(2)(B). If a foreign private foundation does not obtain exempt status pursuant to the notice requirements of section 508(a), it is regarded as a taxable private foundation. Nevertheless, donations to foreign public charities are fully deductible for estate and gift tax purposes. See, e.g., PLR 9853037.

section 501(c)(3)." The effect of this provision is to render the entity taxable for U.S. purposes. Section 508(d)(2)(B) disallows the deductibility of gifts to "taxable private foundations" under both the estate tax and the gift tax provisions. Accordingly, if the donor is establishing a foreign private foundation with a relatively small initial gift, with the expectation that the foundation will be largely funded on his or her death, the foreign private foundation should be qualified as tax exempt. Likewise, if the donor wishes to immediately fund the foreign private foundation with a gift of greater than $1 million or his or her remaining lifetime gift tax exemption, the foreign private foundation should apply for recognition of tax-exempt status, so that the donor can avoid gift tax liability.[16]

Estate tax deductibility

The need to qualify a foreign private foundation as tax exempt for the purpose of claiming an estate tax deduction will turn on many factors, some of which will likely remain subject to a high level of uncertainty in the foreseeable future. We are currently in the final years of estate tax relief under the Economic Growth and Tax Relief Reconciliation Act of 2001. This act has phased down the highest marginal estate tax rate from 55 percent to 45 percent through December 31, 2009. In 2009, the final year of the staged increases in the amounts exempt from estate tax, the exempt amount is $3.5 million. Unless Congress acts to amend the law, there will be no estate tax in 2010, but on January 1, 2011, the rate and exemption structure of prior law will be reinstated, so that only $1 million will be exempt from estate tax and a top marginal rate of 55 percent will apply.

To date, Congress has been unable to reach a political compromise on avoiding a return to lower exemption amounts and higher marginal rates. During the 2008 presidential campaign, Barack Obama stated that he favored a continuation of the higher exempt amounts and the lower rates set forth in the act as fully phased-in – that is, an exemption of $3.5 million per person from federal estate taxes with marginal rates of 45 percent imposed on taxable amounts. It is not known, however, whether escalating federal budget deficits resulting from the various bailout measures to confront the deep economic recession of 2008–9 will change President Obama's views on estate taxes. Moreover, the strong Democratic majorities in both houses of Congress may advocate lower exemptions and higher marginal rates. Significantly, failure to act under the current regime will result in reinstatement of prior law with significantly higher marginal rates and lower lifetime exemptions, so that political inertia might well result in significantly higher estate taxes in the future.

In this uncertain environment, most potential philanthropists looking to fund a foreign private foundation through a testamentary gift will want that gift to qualify for the estate tax charitable deduction. This may not invariably be the case, and

16 This threshold for avoiding gift taxation would be as high as $2 million if the donor is married and his or her spouse agrees to characterize the contribution as a split gift.

depending on, among other things, the size of the testamentary gift, the testator's dispositive plan, and the extent to which other gifts to family members may be taxable, the potential donor may elect not to seek a determination letter.

Gift tax deductibility

The fact that lifetime gifts to establish foreign private foundations are not exempt from gift tax unless and until the foreign private foundation obtains a determination letter is a substantial, if not the substantial, impediment to establishing a foreign charity outside of the private foundation regulatory regime. Standard wisdom among estate planners is to avoid paying gift taxes. Under the current gift tax regime, each individual is granted a lifetime exemption from the gift tax of $1 million and an unlimited number of annual exempt gifts, currently in the amount of $13,000 per donee.[17] If the individual is married, split gifting doubles these amounts where the spouse consents to the use of his or her exemptions. The gift tax regime is unified with the estate tax regime to the extent that lifetime gifts utilizing the lifetime exemption reduce the individual's estate tax exemption dollar for dollar. All said, however, most advisers believe it imprudent to be making gifts that trigger any gift taxes – after all, the estate tax regime is likely to be significantly amended in the near term, and under current law, death in 2010 would be free of estate taxes altogether.

Notwithstanding the foregoing, numerous philanthropists seeking to develop their charitable visions anonymously and without the constraints of the private foundation regulatory regime will fund foreign private foundations with lifetime gifts subject to the gift tax. Those doing so must report the gift on Form 706, the Annual Gift Tax Return, and to the extent lifetime and annual exclusions are unavailable, pay gift tax on the transfer. Because most potential philanthropists do not want a portion of their philanthropic endowment to be transferred to the U.S. government, as a practical matter, the foregoing gift tax consequences limit significant new gifts to establish foreign private foundations. In many instances, funding up to or below the lifetime exclusion amounts are made, with the hope that the endowment can be invested well and grow significantly.

Of course, if the foreign private foundation does not apply for recognition of tax exemption, it would not be constrained by the private foundation regulatory regime. In one case, a client aggressively invested the endowment in a hedge fund. In another instance, a client funded a non-U.S.-business venture, the profits from which were dedicated to the foundation's charitable purposes. Neither of these activities could have been undertaken had the founding philanthropists decided to bring their founding gifts within the exemption to gift taxes by obtaining a determination letter from the Internal Revenue Service, as prohibitions on jeopardy investments and excess business holdings, described in Chapter 4, would have prohibited such activities.

17 The annual exclusion amount is indexed for inflation but can change only in increments of $1,000.

2 Excise and income taxes

If the foreign private foundation is regarded as a foreign corporation or a foreign trust (since it would not have qualified as tax exempt for U.S. purposes), only its U.S. source dividends, interest, and similar passive income generally will be subject to U.S. taxation. Generally speaking, this will subject the foreign entity to the statutory withholding rate of 30 percent for U.S. source interest, dividends, rent, salaries, wages, premiums, annuities, compensations, remunerations, emoluments, or other fixed or determinable annual or periodical gains, profits, and similar income (known as "FDAP income"), unless a lower tax treaty rate applies,[18] or unless the foreign private foundation applies for withholding at a rate of 4 percent, as is detailed subsequently. This type of income is from U.S. sources if it is paid by domestic U.S. corporations, U.S. citizens or resident aliens, or entities formed under the laws of the United States or a U.S. state. Income is also from U.S. sources if the property that produces the income is located in the United States or if services for which the income is paid were performed in the United States. By structuring investments to be in securities and property outside of the United States, the foreign entity may avoid U.S. taxation altogether.

For a foreign private foundation that has qualified as tax exempt under section 501(c)(3), its U.S. source interest and dividends would also be taxable but under a special rule in section 4948(a), which substitutes a 4 percent excise tax on such income for the 2 percent excise tax on defined net investment income, which is applicable to domestic private foundations under section 4940. The difference in the tax base applicable to foreign versus domestic private foundations is that net capital gains are taxed to domestic entities but are not taxed to foreign entities. This mirrors the tax rules applicable to non-tax-exempt persons and entities. Treaty rules may also apply to reduce the usual rate of withholding on U.S. source dividends and interest earned by foreign private foundations.[19] Of course, as with non-tax-exempt foreign private foundations, the 4 percent excise tax in section 4648(a) can be avoided entirely by investing the foreign private foundation's endowment in non-U.S. securities.

Withholding at the lower rate is claimed by filing Form W-8EXP, whether or not the foreign private foundation has obtained recognition of tax exempt status from the IRS. If the foreign foundation has not received a determination letter from the IRS, it may claim the lower rate by supporting the Form W-8EXP by an opinion of counsel that the foundation is "described in Section 501(c)." In rendering such

18 See sections 1441 and 1442. There are currently sixty-four bilateral income tax treaties in effect. The treaty between the United States and Switzerland, for example, provides for withholding at the rate of zero on interest and as low as 5 percent on dividends.

19 For example, the treaty rate with Barbados applicable to interest payments is 5 percent. See Protocol Amending the Convention between the United States and Barbados for the Avoidance of Double Taxation and the Prevention of Fiscal Evasion with Respect to Taxes on Income (signed December 18, 1991).

an opinion, counsel will necessarily have to review the organizational documents of the foreign entity, together with the manner in which it operates, to ensure that its organization and operations are "exclusively for religious, charitable, scientific, testing for public safety, literary, or educational purposes" (see Appendix 10 for a copy of Form W-8EXP, together with instructions).[20] Significantly, this is one area where the benefits of lower tax rates apply regardless of whether the foreign private foundation has qualified as a tax-exempt organization under U.S. law.[21]

The problem of obtaining an opinion of U.S. counsel that the foreign organization is "described in Section 501(c)(3)" is the same problem that international grant makers confront in attempting to comply with the equivalency determination rules.[22] Unless the foreign charity includes the required Internal Revenue Service boilerplate, counsel may be reluctant to issue the requested ruling, in which case the foreign charity faces choosing between a higher rate of withholding, up to 30 percent, on U.S. FDAP income or moving investments offshore to avoid U.S. taxation altogether.

3 Complying with (or avoiding altogether) the private foundation regulatory regime

The most significant difference between qualifying a foreign private foundation as tax exempt under section 501(c)(3) and not doing so is that entities so qualified are brought within the excise tax regulatory regime of chapter 42 applicable to private foundations, as described previously.[23] Thus, for example, the foreign private foundation would be subject to the minimum distribution requirements of section 4942, the penalties applicable to excess business holdings under section 4943, and the prohibitions on self-dealing in section 4941. This curious extraterritorial reach of the private foundation regulatory provisions derives from the definition of "private foundation" to include "a domestic or foreign organization" in section 509(a). But before the foreign private foundation ever files its first Form 990-PF, the IRS extends the regulatory regime to foreign private foundations by requiring the organizational documents (e.g., memorandum and articles of association, bylaws, trust agreement) of the entity applying for exempt status to include provisions that require compliance with the regulatory regime as a precondition to approval of exempt status.[24]

20 In rendering such an opinion, the methodology set forth in the rules regarding equivalency determinations is useful to follow.

21 Technically speaking, the basis for the assessment is different depending on whether the foreign private foundation has obtained tax-exempt status from the Internal Revenue Service. If it has, the 4 percent excise tax under section 4948(a) applies in place of the 2 percent excise tax on investment income under section 4940(a), whereas the nonqualified foreign private foundation having U.S. source dividend, interest, and other FDAP income is subject to a withholding tax of 4 percent.

22 See Chapter 5 in this volume.

23 Sections 4940 through 4948, described in Chapter 4.

24 See section 508(e). An example of documentation required is found in Appendix 3, which is discussed in Chapter 9 in this volume.

In addition to bringing the foreign foundation within the chapter 42 regime, once the foundation receives a determination letter, it must comply with all rules and pay all required excise taxes and penalties. Failure to do so or taking action to withdraw from exempt status will trigger special rules governing termination of exempt status.[25] In summary, any foundation withdrawing from exempt status must transfer all of its assets to public charities or pay a tax equal to the lesser of the net assets of the foundation or the aggregate tax benefits the organization has received from its inception as a result of its exemption from tax.

4 Grant-making and fund-raising activities

If the foreign charitable organization intends to engage in collaborative efforts with U.S. private foundations or public charities, or will itself from time to time seek grants from U.S. charitable entities, it may want to qualify as exempt under U.S. law so as to minimize the compliance actions required by the U.S. grant-making entities. Having a determination letter, the foreign charitable organization will be far more attractive to potentially collaborating U.S. charities. As discussed in Chapter 4, if a foreign charitable entity is qualified as tax exempt under U.S. law, no equivalency determination would need to be undertaken by the U.S. donor. Moreover, expenditure responsibility becomes somewhat less burdensome for the U.S. grant-making entity where the grantee has qualified as tax exempt under section 501(c)(3).[26]

An additional benefit of obtaining a determination letter is that it may be useful at some point to certify to a foreign government or person that the foundation is exempt under U.S. law. One reason for doing so might be to claim reduced withholding under the laws of the foreign jurisdiction. This can be done using Form 6166.[27]

Governance issues

The overwhelming majority of the legal documents used to create a trust or corporation will be legal boilerplate and will take relatively little time to draft, as compared to the efforts that potential philanthropists would typically go through to determine what kind of structure they will utilize and what jurisdiction they will choose. Invariably, however, a significant amount of customization will be required to establish the mechanism for managing and overseeing the organization and providing for an orderly succession of powers following the demise of the founder.

Often, families seeking to establish an independent private foundation do so to provide a structure for implementing the family's charitable values. Indeed,

25 These are set forth in section 507 of the Internal Revenue Code and are summarized in Chapter 3.
26 For example, the grantee would not be required to maintain a separate bank account for the grant. Rather, the out-of-corpus rules would apply. See Chapter 4 in this volume.
27 See IRS Publication 686 (Certification for Reduced Tax Rates in Tax Treaty Countries).

founders frequently are looking to involve family members in the grant-making process. Part of this involvement will be a form of training younger generation(s) to carry on the charitable work and values of the family after the demise of the founding members.[28] Succession issues therefore are central to the family's efforts to establish – and perpetuate – its charitable vision.

Fundamentally, governance issues must address the basic need of the enterprise for guidance, both in investment decisions and in grant making. The mechanisms decided on must also ensure the safety and security of the endowment, considerations that have added significance when dealing with trustees or corporate board members and officers in foreign jurisdictions.

Board of directors or trustees

The basic repository of management power of the entity will be the board of directors, if the entity is organized as a corporation, or the trustee(s), if organized as a trust. Applicable foreign law may require at least one member of the board or one trustee, and perhaps a majority, to be a citizen of the country where the entity is organized. If a corporation, the founding family invariably will want to have one or more of its members on the board. If a trust, the family may want a member to serve as cotrustee with a local bank, trust company, or attorney. Alternatively, the perception of distance and independence for the trustee or cotrustees can be achieved by use of a trust protector or a committee of trustee advisers, described subsequently.

Compensation of professional fiduciaries is typically established by standard, published fee schedules if a bank or trust company is selected to serve. There is usually room for negotiating such fee schedules, at least in the short term. Negotiating fees with potential fiduciaries is always a worthwhile exercise. Even if it does not yield a reduction in administrative costs, negotiations frequently reveal institutional biases. For example, it is better to know up front whether the institution you are engaging fundamentally is not interested in your business, whether because of the size of the initial gift or because of differences in style or culture.[29] After all, costs will be lower in the long term, and service will be better, if the initial relationship can be maintained over the years.

Family members serving on boards or as trustees can be compensated, notwithstanding the self-dealing prohibitions applicable to defined "disqualified persons" under section 4942. Likewise, expenses for attending board or trustee meetings can

28 For additional information on establishing and running a family foundation, the Council on Foundations publishes a four-volume series covering such issues as governance, grant making, and management (www.cof.org).

29 In recent years, a number of brand-name fiduciaries have sought to pare down client lists to those with relatively significant endowments. This is frequently accomplished by manifestly noncompetitive fee schedules, designed to drive lower-net-worth individuals and families elsewhere. It seems that 80–20 or 90–10 management theories are now even being extended to private banking ("80 percent of revenues derive from 20 percent of the business," or the corollary "80 percent of the headaches are caused by 20 percent of the clients").

be reimbursed. Care should be taken to follow established guidelines of reasonableness, so that neither the compensation nor the expenses are deemed to be excessive, thereby trigging penalties.

The Council on Foundations publishes an annual survey on standards and practices for such compensation.[30] Fundamentally, whether compensation is reasonable or excessive will be based on all relevant factors, which will include a review of the scope of the duties being performed; the size of the foundation, both in terms of its endowment and number of employees; and the experience and professional qualifications of the person being compensated.

At the end of the day, common sense should prevail (or its alternative, the "smell test"). It will always be inappropriate to place the founder's twenty-three-year-old son on the board and pay him a $200,000 per-year salary where the foundation makes only minimal grants annually to public charities. Likewise, it will be hard to justify reimbursement of expenses for annual board meetings in the South of France in August, with a suite at the Grand-Hotel du Cap-Ferrat, where the foundation is formed in Bermuda and all of its grant-making activities and all of its members live in the Western Hemisphere.

Compensation issues are usually less problematic for foundations established by corporations. It is usually possible to staff the foundation, including the board, officers, and key committees, with employees of the donor corporation. Frequently, such employees will work part-time for the foundation and part-time for the corporate donor, and their remuneration from the foundation may reflect the relative portion of time devoted to foundation matters.

Committees

Depending on the basic management structure, use of committees can be a convenient way to segregate or delegate discrete functions to those family members or trusted colleagues with expertise in a particular area. If the entity is organized as a corporation, this might typically be done as a committee of the board. Alternatively, the committee members might have consulting agreements with the foundation. If organized as a trust, the committee might be one or more of the trustees, or it might be entirely made up of nontrustees who have been engaged in consulting capacities. Thus, use of committees might permit the family to engage a member in grant-making decisions without involving him or her in the charity's other management decisions.

The two most common areas for utilizing committees are to oversee or manage investment of the endowment fund and to recommend grant making. Depending on the size and scope of the endowment fund or the grant-making activities, this

30 See www.cof.org. On the Council on Foundations' home page, go to "Learn" and click on "Learn more about research and download files" to access the current year's Salary and Benefits Report Summary. Alternatively, use the search function for the Salary and Benefits Report.

mechanism can be a convenient and flexible one for involving family members, utilizing their particular interests, skills, and experience, and for formalizing communications regarding the desires and goals of the founding family to the trustees or the board.

A structure involving committees also works well with corporate foundations. The donor corporation can provide highly qualified members to particular committees based on the employee's expertise or professional training. The board of directors can authorize specific committees in the charitable organization's bylaws. Alternatively, corporate foundations can turn to outsiders – nondirectors, who may or may not also be officers, directors, or employees of the sponsoring corporation on advisory boards.

Control

Unlike an ordinary business corporation set up to earn a profit, a foundation organized as a corporation would not usually have voting stock. Accordingly, the usual control by stockholders over the board (and thus, indirectly, over the officers and employees) is not typically present. Control over the board, therefore, which includes power to hire and fire outside directors, may be maintained in the family by means of the initial structure. To do so, the bylaws or memorandum of association should be drafted to provide a mechanism for succession that will ensure that future generations of the family will control the charity.

Such mechanisms are invariably customized and drafted to accommodate family idiosyncrasies. It would be inappropriate to describe a typical arrangement, because so many different approaches are used. Suffice it to say that the arrangement must be specific but flexible. Like a good estate plan, it must contemplate different orders for the deaths of principal family members, as well as potential incapacities and the possibility that "the plane might go down," so to speak, on the way to the family reunion, simultaneously creating multiple vacancies on the governing body.

With trusts, a committee of trust advisers can be used. If the trust is to be characterized for U.S. tax purposes as a foreign nongrantor trust, so that the gift establishing the charity is complete and the charitable endowment no longer is deemed to be part of the settlor's property for U.S. income and estate tax purposes, the settlor must have parted with most, if not all, incidents of control over the trust, such as the ability to revoke or amend the trust agreement.

If a trust document granting broad discretionary powers to the trustees is to be used, a committee of trust advisers might be given the responsibility to advise, but not direct, the trustees on appropriate investment of the funds. The trustees, in keeping with their fiduciary responsibilities, will receive the advice of the committee but will retain the discretion as to whether to follow that advice. Nevertheless, the committee will also be granted the power to terminate any trustee, in accordance with ascertainable standards, such as a conflict of interest or breach of fiduciary responsibility, or otherwise. A typical mechanism utilizing a committee of trust advisers may be found in Appendix 11, which shows a Bermuda charitable trust.[31]

31 Clause 26. The power to hire and fire trustees may also be exercised by a so-called trust protector. As with a committee of trust advisers, the protector's powers, responsibilities, and activities may be broad or narrow, depending on the perceived need for controls over the trustees, but great care should be exercised not, in effect, to negate the creation of the trust by not letting go of the property being transferred, or not really putting the trustee in actual possession of the property, behaving as if the trust did not exist, or behaving as though the committee or the protector were in fact a cotrustee with all the fiduciary duties that befall a trustee. See Charles M. Bruce, *United States Taxation of Foreign Trusts* (Kluwer, 2000), chap. 3 (Definitions of Trust and Foreign Trust), and discussion of incomplete transfers and sham trusts therein. The use of a protector should be avoided, as this formulation has a history of abuse, which can be seen in a host of cases involving abusive trusts.

CHAPTER NINE

Representative structures

This chapter describes a few typical organizational structures for establishing charitable organizations, both domestically and in foreign jurisdictions. Forms for each of the representative vehicles are included as appendices to this book. The subsequent text describes a number of the salient features of each template.

Private foundation organized as a Delaware corporation

As discussed in Chapter 3, Delaware law is universally recognized as having among the most user-friendly corporation statutes. The Delaware General Corporation Law is updated and improved on an annual basis, and it is administered in a timely and and efficient manner and at low cost. Delaware does not have separate nonprofit corporate statutes, and therefore charities simply use the Delaware General Corporation Law and form a corporation without any stock.

The template at Appendix 2 includes standard Delaware boilerplate, adding specific language tailored to qualify the entity as tax exempt under section 501(c)(3), first to qualify the entity as tax exempt and then to fit the private foundation regulatory requirements. In using the template, the incorporator may want to insert one or more specific charitable purposes in article 3. The language immediately after the specific purposes is a prerequisite for qualifying for tax-exempt status, expressly mentioning tax-exempt purposes. The numbered paragraphs that follow track the private foundation rules and are required by the Internal Revenue Service of all new entities that will be classified as private foundations. Note that these provisions must be expressly cross-referenced in Form 1023 (see Appendix 1, part III).

Additional conforming language required by the Internal Revenue Service is also set forth in articles 10 and 11. These provisions set forth prohibitions on private inurements and include specific directions as to the disposition of assets for charitable purposes on dissolution of the corporation. These provisions also must be cross-referenced expressly in Form 1023.

Note that Delaware law permits incorporation of entities having the word "foundation" in their name with no further qualification. The template adds "Inc.," which should be included if the entity contemplates applying for a certificate of authority to transact business in another jurisdiction as a nonprofit entity. Most states require a designation of limited liability to be included in the name of any corporation before it can be authorized to conduct business in the state. For most U.S. jurisdictions, this would include such suffixes as "Inc.," "Incorporated," "Corp.," "Corporation," "Limited," and so on. Accordingly, if operations in other states are contemplated, it is recommended that such a designation be included in the official name on file with the Delaware secretary of state. It is a good practice to clear and reserve the full name of the corporation, including the suffix, in the intended additional jurisdiction prior to incorporating in Delaware, to avoid any possible issues with the name on qualifying in the other jurisdiction.[1]

"American friends of . . ." organized as a Delaware corporation

Whereas the template previously discussed includes the necessary bells and whistles to gain the recognition of a private foundation as tax exempt, because most "American Friends of . . . " organizations are public charities, this template (Appendix 3) includes only the language needed for tax-exempt status as a public charity. It is recommended that the specific purposes clauses in article 3 include the language "in the United States and other countries of the world." This then leaves the applicant ample authority to argue that the charitable purposes of the entity include qualified U.S. charitable activities. If the board of directors of the corporation, in keeping with the exercise of its discretion, votes to make a grant to a public charity outside the United States, the broad purposes language should ensure that the grant is within the purview of the stated charitable purposes of the corporation.

Bermuda charitable trust

As a common-law jurisdiction, Bermuda has well-established laws regarding trusts. Where the common law has needed improvement to facilitate new types of family and business transactions, the Bermuda legislature has passed a series of statutes, which have permitted Bermuda to stay at the forefront of preferred offshore jurisdictions. Trusts are a common vehicle for achieving charitable purposes in Bermuda, and if the new charity will not solicit charitable contributions in Bermuda, no registration of the charity is required. Likewise, unlike the United States, the charity need not apply to the tax authorities for recognition of exempt status, as no income taxes or taxes on earnings or capital gains are levied by the Bermuda government.

A representative Bermuda charitable trust template is attached as Appendix 11.[2] It is a fairly straightforward declaration of trust that takes the form of a

1 Administration of these laws from state to state is often inconsistent and at times quirky. For example, even though most states allow the suffix "Limited" or "Ltd.," Florida currently does not. This would mean that any corporation wanting to qualify in Florida would need to use a different suffix, which can be confusing in practice.

2 Appendix 11 is based on a template provided by Michael J. Mello, QC, JP, of Mello Jones & Martin, Thistle House, 4 Burnaby Street, Hamilton, Bermuda.

discretionary trust, the major portions of which are standard boilerplate administrative provisions. The identity of the grantor does not appear in the document, as the trust is established by the trustee's declaration rather than in the form of an agreement between the settlor and the trustee. Except for several references to Bermuda law, and specifically to the Charities Act of 1978, the trust instrument could serve as a template declaration of trust in a number of common law jurisdictions.

Among the significant provisions of the template in Appendix 11 are the recitals of the objects of charitable purposes in article 3. The template presented makes none of the recitals required of organizational documents for entities that will be qualified in the United States as tax exempt under section 501(c)(3), as it is intended that such a charity would not apply to the Internal Revenue Service for exempt status. Nevertheless, multiple provisions are added to make it clear that the trust is to be regarded as a nongrantor trust for U.S. tax purposes and is described in section 501(c)(3).[3]

The governance procedures vest control in a committee of trust advisers in article 26. The committee is given the power to appoint or replace the trustee in article 7.[4] Although it is a committee, article 26.4 empowers the first chair to act for the committee, thereby vesting all powers of the committee in the initial chair. The initial chair is appointed by the trustee by a separate deed appended to the declaration of trust.

One difference between charitable trusts and regular trusts under Bermuda law is that the rule against perpetuities does not apply to charitable trusts. Accordingly, the language typically seen in a Bermuda trust to ensure compliance with the rule against perpetuities is omitted.

Generic foreign charitable trust agreement

The trust template attached as Appendix 12 differs in approach from the template under Bermuda law previously discussed. In terms of form, this document is a trust agreement, joined in by the settlor, rather than a declaration of trust, executed only by the trustee. More significant, this template includes all of the necessary recitals that the Internal Revenue Service requires in organizational documents of charitable organizations seeking tax-exempt status.[5] These recitals are woven throughout the document, but in particular, article 6 tracks the regulatory regime governing private foundations operating as section 501(c)(3) entities.

It should be noted that specific charitable purposes are not enumerated; rather, the trustees are given the discretion to distribute income and principal of the

3 See part 1, articles 3.1(c), 7.1, and 14.

4 A committee of trust advisers is an excellent alternative to a so-called protector, which, depending on the powers given to the protector, can call into question the validity of the trust.

5 Section 508(e).

trust fund for general charitable purposes. As indicated in Chapter 3, the Internal Revenue Service requires more specificity before a determination letter can be issued. Descriptions of specific projects and purposes should therefore be set forth in responses to Form 1023 (see Appendix 1, part IV). The Internal Revenue Service has issued a determination letter to a charitable entity that used a trust agreement based on this template.

A generic template is provided (see Appendix 12). Except for customized language that might reference local law regulating charities and provide the appropriate clause addressing the applicable rule against perpetuities, the language provided should be able to be used in any number of common law jurisdictions, including the Bahamas, Barbados, the Cayman Islands, Gibraltar, Guernsey, Jersey, the Isle of Man, and Nevis. Service providers in each of these jurisdictions should be able to provide sufficient guidance to tailor the document to local use. In each instance, local counsel may have further suggestions on appropriate modifications to comply with local law.

Bermuda purpose trust

Bermuda, as well as a number of other jurisdictions,[6] has enacted legislation permitting the creation of so-called purpose trusts. In Bermuda, the concept was developed because charitable trusts under Bermuda law had been construed restrictively to require a public purpose, so that a number of philanthropic trusts failed to meet the required test and became void. Moreover, traditional trusts, formed under common law, had been ruled invalid unless specific beneficiaries – persons or organizations – were named. Under the new statutory authorization of the Trusts (Special Provisions) Act of 1989, purpose trusts need not benefit a specified class of beneficiaries but rather can be devoted to a general purpose. Accordingly, they are excellent vehicles for carrying out charitable goals.

In addition, purpose trusts can be a useful vehicle for accomplishing broad, public interest or policy purposes, which, because of the proscriptions in U.S. law against lobbying and political activities, might not qualify for tax-exempt status under U.S. law. For example, if a philanthropist wished to promote controversial ideas regarding limiting or ameliorating air pollution, with the intention that his or her ideas be implemented into law, a purpose trust might be considered.[7]

The template at Appendix 13 was drafted to create a vehicle authorized by the Trusts (Special Provisions) Act of 1989. The purposes, which need not necessarily

6 Significantly, Delaware has recently enacted purpose trust legislation. As discussed in Chapter 7, inclusion of flight provisions, for example, in a trust formed and administered under Delaware law would render the trust classifiable as a foreign trust for U.S. tax purposes. Although a number of major trust companies in Delaware have been actively been promoting so-called hybrid trusts (i.e., Delaware trusts classifiable as foreign trusts for U.S. tax purposes), none has yet published preferred templates for hybrid purpose trusts.

7 Because lobbying by U.S. private foundations is prohibited, such an entity could not qualify as tax exempt in the United States.

fit the definition of "charitable" for purposes of U.S. law, are to be enumerated in paragraph 4. Unlike some charitable trust declarations or agreements, which merely grant discretion to the trustee to distribute funds for charitable purposes, specific purposes should be included. (Under Bermuda law, the uses of purpose trusts are not confined to public, quasi-charitable, or philanthropic endeavors; they may be used for specific business transactions, such as holding shares of a company pending fulfillment of particular conditions, much like an escrow or custody arrangement under U.S. law.)

Accordingly, because the purposes may not be "charitable" within the meaning of section 501(c)(3), such that the exception to the grantor trust rules for organizations "described in Section 501(c)(3)" is inapplicable, numerous provisions are included to ensure categorization as a nongrantor trust for U.S. tax purposes. In that regard, a belt-and-suspenders approach is followed, preferring redundancy to sparsely crafted drafting.

Bermuda law requires the inclusion of a number of specific provisions. For example, an enforcer must be named in the trust deed, which should provide for the appointment of a successor. By law, the trustee is required to notify the attorney general of Bermuda in the event that the enforcer is unable to act, after which the attorney general may apply to the courts for the appointment of a successor. The template cross-references the duties of the enforcer to the statute in part 2, paragraph 28.

The template includes a committee of trust advisers, as in the other foreign trust templates discussed previously. In addition, the template provides for a grant advisory committee, which typically might include members of the founder's family.[8] As discussed in Chapter 8, such a mechanism is an excellent way to institutionalize participation by family members in grant making and to instill family charitable values.

Another difference under Bermuda law between a charitable trust and a purpose trust is that the purpose trust is subject to the rule against perpetuities, which, by statute, permits purpose trusts to remain in existence for up to one hundred years. Compliance with Bermuda's Perpetuities and Accumulations Act of 1989 is covered in the definitional provisions of the template.

8 Part 2, clause 28.

CHAPTER TEN

Further resources

Additional resources and guidance pertaining to many of the subjects discussed in this book are readily available on the Internet. The best sources of information on establishing and maintaining private foundations are the following:

- Council on Foundations (2121 Crystal Drive, Suite 700, Arlington, Virginia 22202; Web address: www.cof.org). Although it is a member organization, the council's Web site is an extraordinary resource for anyone working with private foundations. Most of the publications from previous issues of the council's periodicals can be readily downloaded, and helpful leads to additional resources are easily accessible. The council provides valuable guidance to the entire charitable sector in publishing surveys of compensation for officers and directors of private foundations, information that is not available from any other sources. It is also an excellent source for a number of topical publications on all aspects of organizing and administering private foundations.
- Internal Revenue Service (Web address: www.irs.gov/charities/index.html). A Web site for charities and other nonprofits. Ready access can be gained to the current versions of all official IRS publications and forms, as well as general guidance on forming and maintaining a tax-exempt charity.
- GuideStar (4801 Courthouse Street, Williamsburg, VA 23188; Web address: http://www.guidestar.org). This organization has created a database using all of the information provided by the Internal Revenue Service on Forms 990, 990-PF, and 990-EZ. Any member of the public can access data on any tax-exempt organization from the Web site. Subscribers can create customized reports on specific exempt sectors.
- The Foundation Center (79 Fifth Avenue/16th Street, New York, NY 10003 and 1627 K Street, NW, Washington, D.C. 20036; Web address: /www.foundationcenter.org). The Foundation Center compiles a significant amount of data on the nonprofit sector, which is made available on its Web site. According to a center publication, it "maintains the most comprehensive database on U.S. grantmakers and their grants – a robust, accessible knowledge bank for the sector. It also operates research, education, and training programs designed to advance philanthropy at every level."
- National Center on Philanthropy and the Law, New York University Law School (110 West Third Street, Room 205, New York, NY 10012-1074; Web address: www.law.nyu.edu/ncpl/). This organization maintains a comprehensive bibliography of all English-language resources pertaining to the law of nonprofit organizations.

- United States International Grantmaking (Web address: http://www.usig.org). This is a joint venture project of the Council on Foundations with the International Center for Not-For-Profit Law. The Web site contains valuable information on numerous international issues and focuses on legal issues of interest to U.S. charities engaged in international grant making.
- National Center for Charitable Statistics, a project of the Center on Nonprofits and Philanthropy at the Urban Institute (2100 M Street, NW, Washington, D.C. 20037; Web address: http://nccs.urban.org/). The center takes raw data from the information returns filed by public charities and foundations with the Internal Revenue Service and generates a broad range of statistics that show the extent and scope of charitable and nonprofit endeavors in the United States.
- Foundation Source (55 Walls Drive, Fairfield, Connecticut 06824; Web address: www.foundationsource.com). A leading provider of outsourced administrative services to foundations. The organization can provide back-office resources and management to smaller private foundations with insufficient resources to justify administrative staffing.

All of the foregoing Web sites contain numerous links to other organizations offering additional resources on charitable activities on the Web.

Glossary of terms

Additional Tax – Under the regulatory regime applicable to private foundations, excise taxes are initially assessed on the foundation and its managers. If the infraction that gave rise to the initial penalty is not corrected, additional excise taxes, sometimes called "second-tier taxes," are imposed.

Alternative Minimum Tax, or AMT – A stand-alone, separate income tax computation applicable to both individuals and corporations, which can have the effect of diminishing the value of all deductions, including charitable donations.

Annual Information Return – Required of all tax-exempt entities. Form 990 is required for public charities.

Articles of Organization – The documents used to create a foundation; they are called "articles of incorporation" or "certificate of incorporation" for a domestic corporation; "memorandum and articles of association" for a corporation organized in the United Kingdom, crown dependencies and former British colonies; and a "trust agreement," "deed of settlement," or "declaration of trust" for a trust.

Board of Directors – The governing body of a corporation.

Bylaws – The rules governing the operation of a corporation or nonprofit corporation, covering such items as the selection of directors, establishment of committees, conduct of meetings, and administration of the entity.

Declaration of Trust – A form of trust established by the trustee only. It may be contrasted with a deed of settlement or trust agreement, where both settlor and trustee execute the trust instrument.

Determination Letter – Evidence issued by the Internal Revenue Service that the charitable organization is recognized as tax exempt.

Disqualified Person – A person who is a trustee, director, or officer of or a substantial contributor to a private foundation, as well as members of that individual's family.

Electioneering – Participating in a campaign for the election of a candidate for public office.

Enforcer – An individual charged with overseeing the actions of a trustee of a purpose trust to ensure that the trustee is administering the trust in accordance with its purposes.

Generally Accepted Accounting Principles, or GAAP – The standards applied by licensed certified public accountants in the United States, and by licensed accountants or chartered accountants in other jurisdictions.

Generation-Skipping Transfer Tax, or GST Tax, or GSTT – Part of the U.S. federal estate tax regime, which imposes an additional tax on bequests that skip a generation, for example, testamentary gifts from a grandparent to grandchildren when their parents are surviving.

Grantor – A person establishing a trust by a gift of property. Sometimes also called a "settlor."

Grantor Trust – Under U.S. tax laws, a grantor trust is the characterization of assets and income of a trust as remaining with the grantor for income and/or estate tax purposes even though legal ownership of the trust property has been vested with a trustee.

Intermediate Sanctions – Penalty taxes applied to disqualified persons of public charities that receive an excessive benefit from financial transactions with the charity. For example, overcompensation of a public charity's executive is characterized as an excessive benefit transaction and can trigger intermediate sanctions.

Internal Revenue Code, or IRC – Federal tax law in the United States, formally referred to as the Internal Revenue Code of 1986, as amended.

Internal Revenue Service, or IRS – The agency of the U.S. federal government charged with tax collection and enforcement, including regulation of tax-exempt organizations. The IRS is a branch of the Department of the Treasury.

"Know your customer," or KYC – Due diligence requirements imposed on banks, trust companies, and other financial institutions with respect to customers and prospective customers under the Patriot Act in the United States and other anti-money-laundering, antiterrorism, and anti-proceeds-of-crime legal regimes in the United States and elsewhere.

Limited Liability Company, or LLC – A business enterprise created under the laws of most states that insulates its owners, called "members" or "interest holders," from liability to third parties beyond capital contributed to the LLC. Unlike a corporation, which must divide profits and ownership rights proportionally to ownership, LLCs, like partnerships, can apportion participation in profits, losses, management, and ownership on any basis agreed to by the members.

Lobbying – Political activities for the purpose of influencing pending legislation or executive branch decision making.

Operating Foundation – A private foundation that uses a substantial portion of its income to provide charitable services or administer charitable programs on its own. Private foundations qualifying as operating foundations are not subject to a number of restrictions applicable to private foundations.

Protector – A person (other than a trustee) whose consent is required for the exercise of powers conferred on the trustees or who may have power to appoint or remove trustees.

Rule against Perpetuities – A common-law doctrine, frequently modified by statute (or eliminated altogether by statute) limiting the duration of time that property may remain in trust. Historically, this time period was set at the lives in being (at the time the trust was created) plus twenty-one years. Many modern statutes simply set the perpetuity period at a specific number of years, for example, one hundred, or have eliminated it altogether.

Settlement – A document that creates a trust in circumstances where a person known as a settlor transfers his or her property to a trustee to be held in trust in accordance with the arrangements set out in the settlement. Also called a "trust agreement."

Settlor – A person establishing a trust by a gift of property. Sometimes also referred to as a "grantor."

Template – A form of legal document that can be modified or customized in accordance with specified purposes.

Trust – A legal relationship in which a person (known as the "trustee") holds the legal title to property (of which he or she is not the owner in his or her own right) for the benefit of any person (known as a "beneficiary") or purpose that is not solely for the benefit of the trustee.

Trustee – A person or trust company that holds trust property for beneficiaries of a trust and is responsible for the administration of a trust.

Appendices

Department of the Treasury
Internal Revenue Service

Notice 1382

(January 2009)

Changes for Form 1023:

- Mailing address
- Parts IX and X

Changes for Form 1023, Application for Recognition of Exemption Under Section 501(c)(3) of the Internal Revenue Code

Change of Mailing Address

The mailing address shown on Form 1023 Checklist, page 28, the first address under the last checkbox; and in the Instructions for Form 1023, page 4 under *Where to File,* has been changed to:

Internal Revenue Service
P.O. Box 12192
Covington, KY 41012-0192

Changes for Parts IX and X

Changes to Parts IX and X are necessary to comply with new regulations that eliminated the advance ruling process. Until Form 1023 is revised to reflect this change, please follow the directions on this notice when completing Part IX and Part X of Form 1023. For more information about the elimination of the advance ruling process, visit us at *www.irs.gov* and click on *CHARITIES & NON-PROFITS.*

Part IX. Financial Data

The instructions at the top of Part IX on page 9 of Form 1023 are now as follows. For purposes of this schedule, years in existence refer to completed tax years.

1. If in existence less than 5 years, complete the statement for each year in existence and provide projections of your likely revenues and expenses based on a reasonable and good faith estimate of your future finances for a total of:

   a. Three years of financial information if you have not completed one tax year, or

   b. Four years of financial information if you have completed one tax year.

2. If in existence 5 or more years, complete the schedule for the most recent 5 tax years. You will need to provide a separate statement that includes information about the most recent 5 tax years because the data table in Part IX, has not been updated to provide for a 5th year.

Part X. Public Charity Status

Do not complete line 6a on page 11 of Form 1023, and **do not sign** the form under the heading "Consent Fixing Period of Limitations Upon Assessment of Tax Under Section 4940 of the Internal Revenue Code."

Only complete line 6b and line 7 on page 11 of Form 1023, if in existence 5 or more tax years.

Notice **1382** (1-2009)
Cat. No. 52336F

Form **1023** (Rev. June 2006) Department of the Treasury Internal Revenue Service

Application for Recognition of Exemption Under Section 501(c)(3) of the Internal Revenue Code

OMB No. 1545-0056

Note: *If exempt status is approved, this application will be open for public inspection.*

*Use the instructions to complete this application and for a definition of all **bold** items.* For additional help, call IRS Exempt Organizations Customer Account Services toll-free at 1-877-829-5500. Visit our website at **www.irs.gov** for forms and publications. If the required information and documents are not submitted with payment of the appropriate user fee, the application may be returned to you.

Attach additional sheets to this application if you need more space to answer fully. Put your name and EIN on each sheet and identify each answer by Part and line number. Complete Parts I - XI of Form 1023 and submit only those Schedules (A through H) that apply to you.

Part I **Identification of Applicant**

1 Full name of organization (exactly as it appears in your **organizing document**)		**2** c/o Name (if applicable)
3 **Mailing address** (Number and street) (see instructions)	Room/Suite	**4** Employer Identification Number (EIN)
City or town, state or country, and ZIP + 4		**5** Month the annual accounting period ends (01 – 12)
6 Primary contact (officer, director, trustee, or **authorized representative**) a Name:		**b** Phone:
		c Fax: (optional)

7 Are you represented by an authorized representative, such as an attorney or accountant? If "Yes," provide the authorized representative's name, and the name and address of the authorized representative's firm. Include a completed Form 2848, *Power of Attorney and Declaration of Representative,* with your application if you would like us to communicate with your representative. ☐ **Yes** ☐ **No**

8 Was a person who is not one of your officers, directors, trustees, employees, or an authorized representative listed in line 7, paid, or promised payment, to help plan, manage, or advise you about the structure or activities of your organization, or about your financial or tax matters? If "Yes," provide the person's name, the name and address of the person's firm, the amounts paid or promised to be paid, and describe that person's role. ☐ **Yes** ☐ **No**

9a Organization's website:

b Organization's email: (optional)

10 Certain organizations are not required to file an information return (Form 990 or Form 990-EZ). If you are granted tax-exemption, are you claiming to be excused from filing Form 990 or Form 990-EZ? If "Yes," explain. See the instructions for a description of organizations not required to file Form 990 or Form 990-EZ. ☐ **Yes** ☐ **No**

11 Date incorporated if a corporation, or formed, if other than a corporation. (MM/DD/YYYY) / /

12 Were you formed under the laws of a **foreign country?** If "Yes," state the country. ☐ **Yes** ☐ **No**

For Paperwork Reduction Act Notice, see page 24 of the instructions. Cat. No. 17133K Form **1023** (Rev. 6-2006)

Form 1023 (Rev. 6-2006) Name: EIN: – Page **2**

Part II Organizational Structure

You must be a corporation (including a limited liability company), an unincorporated association, or a trust to be tax exempt. (See instructions.) **DO NOT file this form unless you can check "Yes" on lines 1, 2, 3, or 4.**

1 Are you a **corporation**? If "Yes," attach a copy of your articles of incorporation showing **certification of filing** with the appropriate state agency. Include copies of any amendments to your articles and be sure they also show state filing certification. ☐ **Yes** ☐ **No**

2 Are you a **limited liability company (LLC)**? If "Yes," attach a copy of your articles of organization showing certification of filing with the appropriate state agency. Also, if you adopted an operating agreement, attach a copy. Include copies of any amendments to your articles and be sure they show state filing certification. Refer to the instructions for circumstances when an LLC should not file its own exemption application. ☐ **Yes** ☐ **No**

3 Are you an **unincorporated association**? If "Yes," attach a copy of your articles of association, constitution, or other similar organizing document that is dated and includes at least two signatures. Include signed and dated copies of any amendments. ☐ **Yes** ☐ **No**

4a Are you a **trust**? If "Yes," attach a signed and dated copy of your trust agreement. Include signed and dated copies of any amendments. ☐ **Yes** ☐ **No**

b Have you been funded? If "No," explain how you are formed without anything of value placed in trust. ☐ **Yes** ☐ **No**

5 Have you adopted **bylaws**? If "Yes," attach a current copy showing date of adoption. If "No," explain how your officers, directors, or trustees are selected. ☐ **Yes** ☐ **No**

Part III Required Provisions in Your Organizing Document

The following questions are designed to ensure that when you file this application, your organizing document contains the required provisions to meet the organizational test under section 501(c)(3). Unless you can check the boxes in both lines 1 and 2, your organizing document does not meet the organizational test. **DO NOT file this application until you have amended your organizing document.** Submit your original and amended organizing documents (showing state filing certification if you are a corporation or an LLC) with your application.

1 Section 501(c)(3) requires that your organizing document state your exempt purpose(s), such as charitable, religious, educational, and/or scientific purposes. Check the box to confirm that your organizing document meets this requirement. Describe specifically where your organizing document meets this requirement, such as a reference to a particular article or section in your organizing document. Refer to the instructions for exempt purpose language. Location of Purpose Clause (Page, Article, and Paragraph): ____________ ☐

2a Section 501(c)(3) requires that upon dissolution of your organization, your remaining assets must be used exclusively for exempt purposes, such as charitable, religious, educational, and/or scientific purposes. Check the box on line 2a to confirm that your organizing document meets this requirement by express provision for the distribution of assets upon dissolution. If you rely on state law for your dissolution provision, do not check the box on line 2a and go to line 2c. ☐

2b If you checked the box on line 2a, specify the location of your dissolution clause (Page, Article, and Paragraph). Do not complete line 2c if you checked box 2a. ____________

2c See the instructions for information about the operation of state law in your particular state. Check this box if you rely on operation of state law for your dissolution provision and indicate the state: ____________ ☐

Part IV Narrative Description of Your Activities

Using an attachment, describe your *past, present,* and *planned* activities in a narrative. If you believe that you have already provided some of this information in response to other parts of this application, you may summarize that information here and refer to the specific parts of the application for supporting details. You may also attach representative copies of newsletters, brochures, or similar documents for supporting details to this narrative. Remember that if this application is approved, it will be open for public inspection. Therefore, your narrative description of activities should be thorough and accurate. Refer to the instructions for information that must be included in your description.

Part V Compensation and Other Financial Arrangements With Your Officers, Directors, Trustees, Employees, and Independent Contractors

1a List the names, titles, and mailing addresses of all of your officers, directors, and trustees. For each person listed, state their total annual **compensation**, or proposed compensation, for all services to the organization, whether as an officer, employee, or other position. Use actual figures, if available. Enter "none" if no compensation is or will be paid. If additional space is needed, attach a separate sheet. Refer to the instructions for information on what to include as compensation.

Name	Title	Mailing address	Compensation amount (annual actual or estimated)

Form **1023** (Rev. 6-2006)

Part V Compensation and Other Financial Arrangements With Your Officers, Directors, Trustees, Employees, and Independent Contractors *(Continued)*

b List the names, titles, and mailing addresses of each of your five highest compensated employees who receive or will receive compensation of more than $50,000 per year. Use the actual figure, if available. Refer to the instructions for information on what to include as compensation. Do not include officers, directors, or trustees listed in line 1a.

Name	Title	Mailing address	Compensation amount (annual actual or estimated)

c List the names, names of businesses, and mailing addresses of your five highest compensated **independent contractors** that receive or will receive compensation of more than $50,000 per year. Use the actual figure, if available. Refer to the instructions for information on what to include as compensation.

Name	Title	Mailing address	Compensation amount (annual actual or estimated)

The following "Yes" or "No" questions relate to *past, present, or planned* relationships, transactions, or agreements with your officers, directors, trustees, highest compensated employees, and highest compensated independent contractors listed in lines 1a, 1b, and 1c.

2a Are any of your officers, directors, or trustees **related** to each other through **family** or **business relationships**? If "Yes," identify the individuals and explain the relationship. ☐ **Yes** ☐ **No**

b Do you have a business relationship with any of your officers, directors, or trustees other than through their position as an officer, director, or trustee? If "Yes," identify the individuals and describe the business relationship with each of your officers, directors, or trustees. ☐ **Yes** ☐ **No**

c Are any of your officers, directors, or trustees related to your highest compensated employees or highest compensated independent contractors listed on lines 1b or 1c through family or business relationships? If "Yes," identify the individuals and explain the relationship. ☐ **Yes** ☐ **No**

3a For each of your officers, directors, trustees, highest compensated employees, and highest compensated independent contractors listed on lines 1a, 1b, or 1c, attach a list showing their name, qualifications, average hours worked, and duties.

b Do any of your officers, directors, trustees, highest compensated employees, and highest compensated independent contractors listed on lines 1a, 1b, or 1c receive compensation from any other organizations, whether tax exempt or taxable, that are related to you through **common control**? If "Yes," identify the individuals, explain the relationship between you and the other organization, and describe the compensation arrangement. ☐ **Yes** ☐ **No**

4 In establishing the compensation for your officers, directors, trustees, highest compensated employees, and highest compensated independent contractors listed on lines 1a, 1b, and 1c, the following practices are recommended, although they are not required to obtain exemption. Answer "Yes" to all the practices you use.

a Do you or will the individuals that approve compensation arrangements follow a conflict of interest policy? ☐ **Yes** ☐ **No**
b Do you or will you approve compensation arrangements in advance of paying compensation? ☐ **Yes** ☐ **No**
c Do you or will you document in writing the date and terms of approved compensation arrangements? ☐ **Yes** ☐ **No**

Form 1023 (Rev. 6-2006) Name: EIN: – Page **4**

Part V **Compensation and Other Financial Arrangements With Your Officers, Directors, Trustees, Employees, and Independent Contractors** *(Continued)*

d Do you or will you record in writing the decision made by each individual who decided or voted on compensation arrangements? ☐ **Yes** ☐ **No**

e Do you or will you approve compensation arrangements based on information about compensation paid by **similarly situated** taxable or tax-exempt organizations for similar services, current compensation surveys compiled by independent firms, or actual written offers from similarly situated organizations? Refer to the instructions for Part V, lines 1a, 1b, and 1c, for information on what to include as compensation. ☐ **Yes** ☐ **No**

f Do you or will you record in writing both the information on which you relied to base your decision and its source? ☐ **Yes** ☐ **No**

g If you answered "No" to any item on lines 4a through 4f, describe how you set compensation that is **reasonable** for your officers, directors, trustees, highest compensated employees, and highest compensated independent contractors listed in Part V, lines 1a, 1b, and 1c.

5a Have you adopted a **conflict of interest policy** consistent with the sample conflict of interest policy in Appendix A to the instructions? If "Yes," provide a copy of the policy and explain how the policy has been adopted, such as by resolution of your governing board. If "No," answer lines 5b and 5c. ☐ **Yes** ☐ **No**

b What procedures will you follow to assure that persons who have a conflict of interest will not have influence over you for setting their own compensation?

c What procedures will you follow to assure that persons who have a conflict of interest will not have influence over you regarding business deals with themselves?

Note: A conflict of interest policy is recommended though it is not required to obtain exemption. Hospitals, see Schedule C, Section I, line 14.

6a Do you or will you compensate any of your officers, directors, trustees, highest compensated employees, and highest compensated independent contractors listed in lines 1a, 1b, or 1c through **non-fixed payments**, such as discretionary bonuses or revenue-based payments? If "Yes," describe all non-fixed compensation arrangements, including how the amounts are determined, who is eligible for such arrangements, whether you place a limitation on total compensation, and how you determine or will determine that you pay no more than reasonable compensation for services. Refer to the instructions for Part V, lines 1a, 1b, and 1c, for information on what to include as compensation. ☐ **Yes** ☐ **No**

b Do you or will you compensate any of your employees, other than your officers, directors, trustees, or your five highest compensated employees who receive or will receive compensation of more than $50,000 per year, through non-fixed payments, such as discretionary bonuses or revenue-based payments? If "Yes," describe all non-fixed compensation arrangements, including how the amounts are or will be determined, who is or will be eligible for such arrangements, whether you place or will place a limitation on total compensation, and how you determine or will determine that you pay no more than reasonable compensation for services. Refer to the instructions for Part V, lines 1a, 1b, and 1c, for information on what to include as compensation. ☐ **Yes** ☐ **No**

7a Do you or will you purchase any goods, services, or assets from any of your officers, directors, trustees, highest compensated employees, or highest compensated independent contractors listed in lines 1a, 1b, or 1c? If "Yes," describe any such purchase that you made or intend to make, from whom you make or will make such purchases, how the terms are or will be negotiated at **arm's length**, and explain how you determine or will determine that you pay no more than **fair market value**. Attach copies of any written contracts or other agreements relating to such purchases. ☐ **Yes** ☐ **No**

b Do you or will you sell any goods, services, or assets to any of your officers, directors, trustees, highest compensated employees, or highest compensated independent contractors listed in lines 1a, 1b, or 1c? If "Yes," describe any such sales that you made or intend to make, to whom you make or will make such sales, how the terms are or will be negotiated at arm's length, and explain how you determine or will determine you are or will be paid at least fair market value. Attach copies of any written contracts or other agreements relating to such sales. ☐ **Yes** ☐ **No**

8a Do you or will you have any leases, contracts, loans, or other agreements with your officers, directors, trustees, highest compensated employees, or highest compensated independent contractors listed in lines 1a, 1b, or 1c? If "Yes," provide the information requested in lines 8b through 8f. ☐ **Yes** ☐ **No**

b Describe any written or oral arrangements that you made or intend to make.

c Identify with whom you have or will have such arrangements.

d Explain how the terms are or will be negotiated at arm's length.

e Explain how you determine you pay no more than fair market value or you are paid at least fair market value.

f Attach copies of any signed leases, contracts, loans, or other agreements relating to such arrangements.

9a Do you or will you have any leases, contracts, loans, or other agreements with any organization in which any of your officers, directors, or trustees are also officers, directors, or trustees, or in which any individual officer, director, or trustee owns more than a 35% interest? If "Yes," provide the information requested in lines 9b through 9f. ☐ **Yes** ☐ **No**

Part V Compensation and Other Financial Arrangements With Your Officers, Directors, Trustees, Employees, and Independent Contractors *(Continued)*

b Describe any written or oral arrangements you made or intend to make.

c Identify with whom you have or will have such arrangements.

d Explain how the terms are or will be negotiated at arm's length.

e Explain how you determine or will determine you pay no more than fair market value or that you are paid at least fair market value.

f Attach a copy of any signed leases, contracts, loans, or other agreements relating to such arrangements.

Part VI Your Members and Other Individuals and Organizations That Receive Benefits From You

The following "Yes" or "No" questions relate to goods, services, and funds you provide to individuals and organizations as part of your activities. Your answers should pertain to *past, present,* and *planned* activities. (See instructions.)

1a In carrying out your exempt purposes, do you provide goods, services, or funds to individuals? If "Yes," describe each program that provides goods, services, or funds to individuals. ☐ **Yes** ☐ **No**

b In carrying out your exempt purposes, do you provide goods, services, or funds to organizations? If "Yes," describe each program that provides goods, services, or funds to organizations. ☐ **Yes** ☐ **No**

2 Do any of your programs limit the provision of goods, services, or funds to a specific individual or group of specific individuals? For example, answer "Yes," if goods, services, or funds are provided only for a particular individual, your members, individuals who work for a particular employer, or graduates of a particular school. If "Yes," explain the limitation and how recipients are selected for each program. ☐ **Yes** ☐ **No**

3 Do any individuals who receive goods, services, or funds through your programs have a family or business relationship with any officer, director, trustee, or with any of your highest compensated employees or highest compensated independent contractors listed in Part V, lines 1a, 1b, and 1c? If "Yes," explain how these related individuals are eligible for goods, services, or funds. ☐ **Yes** ☐ **No**

Part VII Your History

The following "Yes" or "No" questions relate to your history. (See instructions.)

1 Are you a **successor** to another organization? Answer "Yes," if you have taken or will take over the activities of another organization; you took over 25% or more of the fair market value of the net assets of another organization; or you were established upon the conversion of an organization from for-profit to non-profit status. If "Yes," complete Schedule G. ☐ **Yes** ☐ **No**

2 Are you submitting this application more than 27 months after the end of the month in which you were legally formed? If "Yes," complete Schedule E. ☐ **Yes** ☐ **No**

Part VIII Your Specific Activities

The following "Yes" or "No" questions relate to specific activities that you may conduct. Check the appropriate box. Your answers should pertain to *past, present,* and *planned* activities. (See instructions.)

1 Do you support or oppose candidates in **political campaigns** in any way? If "Yes," explain. ☐ **Yes** ☐ **No**

2a Do you attempt to **influence legislation**? If "Yes," explain how you attempt to influence legislation and complete line 2b. If "No," go to line 3a. ☐ **Yes** ☐ **No**

b Have you made or are you making an **election** to have your legislative activities measured by expenditures by filing Form 5768? If "Yes," attach a copy of the Form 5768 that was already filed or attach a completed Form 5768 that you are filing with this application. If "No," describe whether your attempts to influence legislation are a substantial part of your activities. Include the time and money spent on your attempts to influence legislation as compared to your total activities. ☐ **Yes** ☐ **No**

3a Do you or will you operate bingo or **gaming** activities? If "Yes," describe who conducts them, and list all revenue received or expected to be received and expenses paid or expected to be paid in operating these activities. **Revenue and expenses** should be provided for the time periods specified in Part IX, Financial Data. ☐ **Yes** ☐ **No**

b Do you or will you enter into contracts or other agreements with individuals or organizations to conduct bingo or gaming for you? If "Yes," describe any written or oral arrangements that you made or intend to make, identify with whom you have or will have such arrangements, explain how the terms are or will be negotiated at arm's length, and explain how you determine or will determine you pay no more than fair market value or you will be paid at least fair market value. Attach copies or any written contracts or other agreements relating to such arrangements. ☐ **Yes** ☐ **No**

c List the states and local jurisdictions, including Indian Reservations, in which you conduct or will conduct gaming or bingo.

Form 1023 (Rev. 6-2006) Name: EIN: – Page **6**

Part VIII Your Specific Activities *(Continued)*

4a Do you or will you undertake **fundraising**? If "Yes," check all the fundraising programs you do or will conduct. (See instructions.) ☐ **Yes** ☐ **No**

☐ mail solicitations
☐ email solicitations
☐ personal solicitations
☐ vehicle, boat, plane, or similar donations
☐ foundation grant solicitations
☐ phone solicitations
☐ accept donations on your website
☐ receive donations from another organization's website
☐ government grant solicitations
☐ Other

Attach a description of each fundraising program.

b Do you or will you have written or oral contracts with any individuals or organizations to raise funds for you? If "Yes," describe these activities. Include all revenue and expenses from these activities and state who conducts them. Revenue and expenses should be provided for the time periods specified in Part IX, Financial Data. Also, attach a copy of any contracts or agreements. ☐ **Yes** ☐ **No**

c Do you or will you engage in fundraising activities for other organizations? If "Yes," describe these arrangements. Include a description of the organizations for which you raise funds and attach copies of all contracts or agreements. ☐ **Yes** ☐ **No**

d List all states and local jurisdictions in which you conduct fundraising. For each state or local jurisdiction listed, specify whether you fundraise for your own organization, you fundraise for another organization, or another organization fundraises for you.

e Do you or will you maintain separate accounts for any contributor under which the contributor has the right to advise on the use or distribution of funds? Answer "Yes" if the donor may provide advice on the types of investments, distributions from the types of investments, or the distribution from the donor's contribution account. If "Yes," describe this program, including the type of advice that may be provided and submit copies of any written materials provided to donors. ☐ **Yes** ☐ **No**

5 Are you **affiliated** with a governmental unit? If "Yes," explain. ☐ **Yes** ☐ **No**

6a Do you or will you engage in **economic development**? If "Yes," describe your program. ☐ **Yes** ☐ **No**

b Describe in full who benefits from your economic development activities and how the activities promote exempt purposes.

7a Do or will persons other than your employees or volunteers **develop** your facilities? If "Yes," describe each facility, the role of the developer, and any business or family relationship(s) between the developer and your officers, directors, or trustees. ☐ **Yes** ☐ **No**

b Do or will persons other than your employees or volunteers **manage** your activities or facilities? If "Yes," describe each activity and facility, the role of the manager, and any business or family relationship(s) between the manager and your officers, directors, or trustees. ☐ **Yes** ☐ **No**

c If there is a business or family relationship between any manager or developer and your officers, directors, or trustees, identify the individuals, explain the relationship, describe how contracts are negotiated at arm's length so that you pay no more than fair market value, and submit a copy of any contracts or other agreements.

8 Do you or will you enter into **joint ventures**, including partnerships or **limited liability companies** treated as partnerships, in which you share profits and losses with partners other than section 501(c)(3) organizations? If "Yes," describe the activities of these joint ventures in which you participate. ☐ **Yes** ☐ **No**

9a Are you applying for exemption as a childcare organization under section 501(k)? If "Yes," answer lines 9b through 9d. If "No," go to line 10. ☐ **Yes** ☐ **No**

b Do you provide child care so that parents or caretakers of children you care for can be **gainfully employed** (see instructions)? If "No," explain how you qualify as a childcare organization described in section 501(k). ☐ **Yes** ☐ **No**

c Of the children for whom you provide child care, are 85% or more of them cared for by you to enable their parents or caretakers to be gainfully employed (see instructions)? If "No," explain how you qualify as a childcare organization described in section 501(k). ☐ **Yes** ☐ **No**

d Are your services available to the general public? If "No," describe the specific group of people for whom your activities are available. Also, see the instructions and explain how you qualify as a childcare organization described in section 501(k). ☐ **Yes** ☐ **No**

10 Do you or will you publish, own, or have rights in music, literature, tapes, artworks, choreography, scientific discoveries, or other **intellectual property**? If "Yes," explain. Describe who owns or will own any copyrights, patents, or trademarks, whether fees are or will be charged, how the fees are determined, and how any items are or will be produced, distributed, and marketed. ☐ **Yes** ☐ **No**

Form **1023** (Rev. 6-2006)

Part VIII Your Specific Activities *(Continued)*

11 Do you or will you accept contributions of: real property; conservation easements; closely held securities; intellectual property such as patents, trademarks, and copyrights; works of music or art; licenses; royalties; automobiles, boats, planes, or other vehicles; or collectibles of any type? If "Yes," describe each type of contribution, any conditions imposed by the donor on the contribution, and any agreements with the donor regarding the contribution. ☐ **Yes** ☐ **No**

12a Do you or will you operate in a **foreign country** or **countries?** If "Yes," answer lines 12b through 12d. If "No," go to line 13a. ☐ **Yes** ☐ **No**

b Name the foreign countries and regions within the countries in which you operate.

c Describe your operations in each country and region in which you operate.

d Describe how your operations in each country and region further your exempt purposes.

13a Do you or will you make grants, loans, or other distributions to organization(s)? If "Yes," answer lines 13b through 13g. If "No," go to line 14a. ☐ **Yes** ☐ **No**

b Describe how your grants, loans, or other distributions to organizations further your exempt purposes.

c Do you have written contracts with each of these organizations? If "Yes," attach a copy of each contract. ☐ **Yes** ☐ **No**

d Identify each recipient organization and any **relationship** between you and the recipient organization.

e Describe the records you keep with respect to the grants, loans, or other distributions you make.

f Describe your selection process, including whether you do any of the following:

(i) Do you require an application form? If "Yes," attach a copy of the form. ☐ **Yes** ☐ **No**

(ii) Do you require a grant proposal? If "Yes," describe whether the grant proposal specifies your responsibilities and those of the grantee, obligates the grantee to use the grant funds only for the purposes for which the grant was made, provides for periodic written reports concerning the use of grant funds, requires a final written report and an accounting of how grant funds were used, and acknowledges your authority to withhold and/or recover grant funds in case such funds are, or appear to be, misused. ☐ **Yes** ☐ **No**

g Describe your procedures for oversight of distributions that assure you the resources are used to further your exempt purposes, including whether you require periodic and final reports on the use of resources.

14a Do you or will you make grants, loans, or other distributions to foreign organizations? If "Yes," answer lines 14b through 14f. If "No," go to line 15. ☐ **Yes** ☐ **No**

b Provide the name of each foreign organization, the country and regions within a country in which each foreign organization operates, and describe any relationship you have with each foreign organization.

c Does any foreign organization listed in line 14b accept contributions earmarked for a specific country or specific organization? If "Yes," list all earmarked organizations or countries. ☐ **Yes** ☐ **No**

d Do your contributors know that you have ultimate authority to use contributions made to you at your discretion for purposes consistent with your exempt purposes? If "Yes," describe how you relay this information to contributors. ☐ **Yes** ☐ **No**

e Do you or will you make pre-grant inquiries about the recipient organization? If "Yes," describe these inquiries, including whether you inquire about the recipient's financial status, its tax-exempt status under the Internal Revenue Code, its ability to accomplish the purpose for which the resources are provided, and other relevant information. ☐ **Yes** ☐ **No**

f Do you or will you use any additional procedures to ensure that your distributions to foreign organizations are used in furtherance of your exempt purposes? If "Yes," describe these procedures, including site visits by your employees or compliance checks by impartial experts, to verify that grant funds are being used appropriately. ☐ **Yes** ☐ **No**

Part VIII Your Specific Activities *(Continued)*

15	Do you have a **close connection** with any organizations? If "Yes," explain.	☐ **Yes**	☐ **No**
16	Are you applying for exemption as a **cooperative hospital service organization** under section 501(e)? If "Yes," explain.	☐ **Yes**	☐ **No**
17	Are you applying for exemption as a **cooperative service organization of operating educational organizations** under section 501(f)? If "Yes," explain.	☐ **Yes**	☐ **No**
18	Are you applying for exemption as a **charitable risk pool** under section 501(n)? If "Yes," explain.	☐ **Yes**	☐ **No**
19	Do you or will you operate a **school**? If "Yes," complete Schedule B. Answer "Yes," whether you operate a school as your main function or as a secondary activity.	☐ **Yes**	☐ **No**
20	Is your main function to provide **hospital** or **medical care**? If "Yes," complete Schedule C.	☐ **Yes**	☐ **No**
21	Do you or will you provide **low-income housing** or housing for the **elderly** or **handicapped**? If "Yes," complete Schedule F.	☐ **Yes**	☐ **No**
22	Do you or will you provide scholarships, fellowships, educational loans, or other educational grants to individuals, including grants for travel, study, or other similar purposes? If "Yes," complete Schedule H. **Note: Private foundations** may use Schedule H to request advance approval of individual grant procedures.	☐ **Yes**	☐ **No**

Form 1023 (Rev. 6-2006) Name: EIN: – Page **9**

Part IX Financial Data

For purposes of this schedule, years in existence refer to completed tax years. If in existence 4 or more years, complete the schedule for the most recent 4 tax years. If in existence more than 1 year but less than 4 years, complete the statements for each year in existence and provide projections of your likely revenues and expenses based on a reasonable and good faith estimate of your future finances for a total of 3 years of financial information. If in existence less than 1 year, provide projections of your likely revenues and expenses for the current year and the 2 following years, based on a reasonable and good faith estimate of your future finances for a total of 3 years of financial information. (See instructions.)

A. Statement of Revenues and Expenses

		Type of revenue or expense	Current tax year	3 prior tax years or 2 succeeding tax years			
			(a) From .... To	(b) From .... To	(c) From .... To	(d) From .... To	(e) Provide Total for (a) through (d)
Revenues	1	Gifts, grants, and contributions received (do not include unusual grants)					
	2	Membership fees received					
	3	Gross investment income					
	4	Net unrelated business income					
	5	Taxes levied for your benefit					
	6	Value of services or facilities furnished by a governmental unit without charge (not including the value of services generally furnished to the public without charge)					
	7	Any revenue not otherwise listed above or in lines 9–12 below (attach an itemized list)					
	8	Total of lines 1 through 7					
	9	Gross receipts from admissions, merchandise sold or services performed, or furnishing of facilities in any activity that is related to your exempt purposes (attach itemized list)					
	10	Total of lines 8 and 9					
	11	Net gain or loss on sale of capital assets (attach schedule and see instructions)					
	12	**Unusual grants**					
	13	Total Revenue Add lines 10 through 12					
Expenses	14	Fundraising expenses					
	15	Contributions, gifts, grants, and similar amounts paid out (attach an itemized list)					
	16	Disbursements to or for the benefit of members (attach an itemized list)					
	17	Compensation of officers, directors, and trustees					
	18	Other salaries and wages					
	19	Interest expense					
	20	Occupancy (rent, utilities, etc.)					
	21	Depreciation and depletion					
	22	Professional fees					
	23	Any expense not otherwise classified, such as program services (attach itemized list)					
	24	Total Expenses Add lines 14 through 23					

Form **1023** (Rev. 6-2006)

Form 1023 (Rev. 6-2006) Name: EIN: – Page **10**

Part IX **Financial Data** *(Continued)*

B. Balance Sheet (for your most recently completed tax year)		**Year End:**
Assets		(Whole dollars)
1 Cash	1	
2 Accounts receivable, net	2	
3 Inventories	3	
4 Bonds and notes receivable (attach an itemized list)	4	
5 Corporate stocks (attach an itemized list)	5	
6 Loans receivable (attach an itemized list)	6	
7 Other investments (attach an itemized list)	7	
8 Depreciable and depletable assets (attach an itemized list)	8	
9 Land	9	
10 Other assets (attach an itemized list)	10	
11 Total Assets (add lines 1 through 10)	11	
Liabilities		
12 Accounts payable	12	
13 Contributions, gifts, grants, etc. payable	13	
14 Mortgages and notes payable (attach an itemized list)	14	
15 Other liabilities (attach an itemized list)	15	
16 Total Liabilities (add lines 12 through 15)	16	
Fund Balances or Net Assets		
17 Total fund balances or net assets	17	
18 Total Liabilities and Fund Balances or Net Assets (add lines 16 and 17)	18	

19 Have there been any substantial changes in your assets or liabilities since the end of the period shown above? If "Yes," explain. ☐ **Yes** ☐ **No**

Part X **Public Charity Status**

Part X is designed to classify you as an organization that is either a **private foundation** or a **public charity**. Public charity status is a more favorable tax status than private foundation status. If you are a private foundation, Part X is designed to further determine whether you are a **private operating foundation**. (See instructions.)

1a Are you a private foundation? If "Yes," go to line 1b. If "No," go to line 5 and proceed as instructed. If you are unsure, see the instructions. ☐ **Yes** ☐ **No**

b As a private foundation, section 508(e) requires special provisions in your organizing document in addition to those that apply to all organizations described in section 501(c)(3). Check the box to confirm that your organizing document meets this requirement, whether by express provision or by reliance on operation of state law. Attach a statement that describes specifically where your organizing document meets this requirement, such as a reference to a particular article or section in your organizing document or by operation of state law. See the instructions, including Appendix B, for information about the special provisions that need to be contained in your organizing document. Go to line 2. ☐

2 Are you a private operating foundation? To be a private operating foundation you must engage directly in the active conduct of charitable, religious, educational, and similar activities, as opposed to indirectly carrying out these activities by providing grants to individuals or other organizations. If "Yes," go to line 3. If "No," go to the signature section of Part XI. ☐ **Yes** ☐ **No**

3 Have you existed for one or more years? If "Yes," attach financial information showing that you are a private operating foundation; go to the signature section of Part XI. If "No," continue to line 4. ☐ **Yes** ☐ **No**

4 Have you attached either (1) an affidavit or opinion of counsel, (including a written affidavit or opinion from a certified public accountant or accounting firm with expertise regarding this tax law matter), that sets forth facts concerning your operations and support to demonstrate that you are likely to satisfy the requirements to be classified as a private operating foundation; or (2) a statement describing your proposed operations as a private operating foundation? ☐ **Yes** ☐ **No**

5 If you answered "No" to line 1a, indicate the type of public charity status you are requesting by checking one of the choices below. You may check only one box.

The organization is not a private foundation because it is:

a 509(a)(1) and 170(b)(1)(A)(i)—a church or a convention or association of churches. Complete and attach Schedule A. ☐

b 509(a)(1) and 170(b)(1)(A)(ii)—a **school**. Complete and attach Schedule B. ☐

c 509(a)(1) and 170(b)(1)(A)(iii)—a **hospital**, a cooperative hospital service organization, or a medical research organization operated in conjunction with a hospital. Complete and attach Schedule C. ☐

d 509(a)(3)—an organization supporting either one or more organizations described in line 5a through c, f, g, or h or a publicly supported section 501(c)(4), (5), or (6) organization. Complete and attach Schedule D. ☐

Form 1023 (Rev. 6-2006) Name: EIN: – Page **11**

Part X Public Charity Status *(Continued)*

e 509(a)(4)—an organization organized and operated exclusively for testing for public safety. ☐

f 509(a)(1) and 170(b)(1)(A)(iv)—an organization operated for the benefit of a college or university that is owned or operated by a governmental unit. ☐

g 509(a)(1) and 170(b)(1)(A)(vi)—an organization that receives a substantial part of its financial support in the form of contributions from publicly supported organizations, from a governmental unit, or from the general public. ☐

h 509(a)(2)—an organization that normally receives not more than one-third of its financial support from gross **investment income** and receives more than one third of its financial support from contributions, membership fees, and gross receipts from activities related to its exempt functions (subject to certain exceptions). ☐

i A publicly supported organization, but unsure if it is described in 5g or 5h. The organization would like the IRS to decide the correct status. ☐

6 If you checked box g, h, or i in question 5 above, you must request either an **advance** or a **definitive ruling** by selecting one of the boxes below. Refer to the instructions to determine which type of ruling you are eligible to receive.

a **Request for Advance Ruling:** By checking this box and signing the consent, pursuant to section 6501(c)(4) of the Code you request an advance ruling and agree to extend the statute of limitations on the assessment of excise tax under section 4940 of the Code. The tax will apply only if you do not establish public support status at the end of the 5-year advance ruling period. The assessment period will be extended for the 5 advance ruling years to 8 years, 4 months, and 15 days beyond the end of the first year. You have the right to refuse or limit the extension to a mutually agreed-upon period of time or issue(s). Publication 1035, *Extending the Tax Assessment Period,* provides a more detailed explanation of your rights and the consequences of the choices you make. You may obtain Publication 1035 free of charge from the IRS web site at *www.irs.gov* or by calling toll-free 1-800-829-3676. Signing this consent will not deprive you of any appeal rights to which you would otherwise be entitled. If you decide not to extend the statute of limitations, you are not eligible for an advance ruling. ☐

Consent Fixing Period of Limitations Upon Assessment of Tax Under Section 4940 of the Internal Revenue Code

For Organization

(Signature of Officer, Director, Trustee, or other authorized official) (Type or print name of signer) (Date)

(Type or print title or authority of signer)

For IRS Use Only

IRS Director, Exempt Organizations (Date)

b **Request for Definitive Ruling:** Check this box if you have completed one tax year of at least 8 full months and you are requesting a definitive ruling. To confirm your public support status, answer line 6b(i) if you checked box g in line 5 above. Answer line 6b(ii) if you checked box h in line 5 above. If you checked box i in line 5 above, answer both lines 6b(i) and (ii). ☐

(i) **(a)** Enter 2% of line 8, column (e) on Part IX-A. Statement of Revenues and Expenses. ________

(b) Attach a list showing the name and amount contributed by each person, company, or organization whose gifts totaled more than the 2% amount. If the answer is "None," check this box. ☐

(ii) **(a)** For each year amounts are included on lines 1, 2, and 9 of Part IX-A. Statement of Revenues and Expenses, attach a list showing the name of and amount received from each **disqualified person.** If the answer is "None," check this box. ☐

(b) For each year amounts are included on line 9 of Part IX-A. Statement of Revenues and Expenses, attach a list showing the name of and amount received from each payer, other than a disqualified person, whose payments were more than the larger of (1) 1% of line 10, Part IX-A. Statement of Revenues and Expenses, or (2) $5,000. If the answer is "None," check this box. ☐

7 Did you receive any unusual grants during any of the years shown on Part IX-A. Statement of Revenues and Expenses? If "Yes," attach a list including the name of the contributor, the date and amount of the grant, a brief description of the grant, and explain why it is unusual. ☐ **Yes** ☐ **No**

Form 1023 (Rev. 6-2006) Name: EIN: – Page **12**

Part XI User Fee Information

You must include a user fee payment with this application. It will not be processed without your paid user fee. If your average annual gross receipts have exceeded or will exceed $10,000 annually over a 4-year period, you must submit payment of $750. If your gross receipts have not exceeded or will not exceed $10,000 annually over a 4-year period, the required user fee payment is $300. See instructions for Part XI, for a definition of **gross receipts** over a 4-year period. Your check or money order must be made payable to the United States Treasury. *User fees are subject to change. Check our website at www.irs.gov and type "User Fee" in the keyword box, or call Customer Account Services at 1-877-829-5500 for current information.*

1	Have your annual gross receipts averaged or are they expected to average not more than $10,000? If "Yes," check the box on line 2 and enclose a user fee payment of $300 (Subject to change—see above). If "No," check the box on line 3 and enclose a user fee payment of $750 (Subject to change—see above).	☐ **Yes** ☐ **No**
2	Check the box if you have enclosed the reduced user fee payment of $300 (Subject to change).	☐
3	Check the box if you have enclosed the user fee payment of $750 (Subject to change).	☐

I declare under the penalties of perjury that I am authorized to sign this application on behalf of the above organization and that I have examined this application, including the accompanying schedules and attachments, and to the best of my knowledge it is true, correct, and complete.

Please Sign Here

(Signature of Officer, Director, Trustee, or other authorized official) (Type or print name of signer) (Date)

(Type or print title or authority of signer)

Reminder: Send the completed Form 1023 Checklist with your filled-in-application. Form **1023** (Rev. 6-2006)

Form 1023 (Rev. 6-2006) Name: EIN: – Page **13**

Schedule A. Churches

1a	Do you have a written creed, statement of faith, or summary of beliefs? If "Yes," attach copies of relevant documents.	☐ **Yes**	☐ **No**
b	Do you have a form of worship? If "Yes," describe your form of worship.	☐ **Yes**	☐ **No**
2a	Do you have a formal code of doctrine and discipline? If "Yes," describe your code of doctrine and discipline.	☐ **Yes**	☐ **No**
b	Do you have a distinct religious history? If "Yes," describe your religious history.	☐ **Yes**	☐ **No**
c	Do you have a literature of your own? If "Yes," describe your literature.	☐ **Yes**	☐ **No**
3	Describe the organization's religious hierarchy or ecclesiastical government.		
4a	Do you have regularly scheduled religious services? If "Yes," describe the nature of the services and provide representative copies of relevant literature such as church bulletins.	☐ **Yes**	☐ **No**
b	What is the average attendance at your regularly scheduled religious services?	______	
5a	Do you have an established place of worship? If "Yes," refer to the instructions for the information required.	☐ **Yes**	☐ **No**
b	Do you own the property where you have an established place of worship?	☐ **Yes**	☐ **No**
6	Do you have an established congregation or other regular membership group? If "No," refer to the instructions.	☐ **Yes**	☐ **No**
7	How many members do you have?	______	
8a	Do you have a process by which an individual becomes a member? If "Yes," describe the process and complete lines 8b–8d, below.	☐ **Yes**	☐ **No**
b	If you have members, do your members have voting rights, rights to participate in religious functions, or other rights? If "Yes," describe the rights your members have.	☐ **Yes**	☐ **No**
c	May your members be associated with another denomination or church?	☐ **Yes**	☐ **No**
d	Are all of your members part of the same **family**?	☐ **Yes**	☐ **No**
9	Do you conduct baptisms, weddings, funerals, etc.?	☐ **Yes**	☐ **No**
10	Do you have a school for the religious instruction of the young?	☐ **Yes**	☐ **No**
11a	Do you have a minister or religious leader? If "Yes," describe this person's role and explain whether the minister or religious leader was ordained, commissioned, or licensed after a prescribed course of study.	☐ **Yes**	☐ **No**
b	Do you have schools for the preparation of your ordained ministers or religious leaders?	☐ **Yes**	☐ **No**
12	Is your minister or religious leader also one of your officers, directors, or trustees?	☐ **Yes**	☐ **No**
13	Do you ordain, commission, or license ministers or religious leaders? If "Yes," describe the requirements for ordination, commission, or licensure.	☐ **Yes**	☐ **No**
14	Are you part of a group of churches with similar beliefs and structures? If "Yes," explain. Include the name of the group of churches.	☐ **Yes**	☐ **No**
15	Do you issue church charters? If "Yes," describe the requirements for issuing a charter.	☐ **Yes**	☐ **No**
16	Did you pay a fee for a church charter? If "Yes," attach a copy of the charter.	☐ **Yes**	☐ **No**
17	Do you have other information you believe should be considered regarding your status as a church? If "Yes," explain.	☐ **Yes**	☐ **No**

Form **1023** (Rev. 6-2006)

Schedule B. Schools, Colleges, and Universities

If you operate a school as an activity, complete Schedule B

Section I Operational Information

1a Do you normally have a regularly scheduled curriculum, a regular faculty of qualified teachers, a regularly enrolled student body, and facilities where your educational activities are regularly carried on? If "No," do not complete the remainder of Schedule B. ☐ **Yes** ☐ **No**

b Is the primary function of your school the presentation of formal instruction? If "Yes," describe your school in terms of whether it is an elementary, secondary, college, technical, or other type of school. If "No," do not complete the remainder of Schedule B. ☐ **Yes** ☐ **No**

2a Are you a public school because you are operated by a state or subdivision of a state? If "Yes," explain how you are operated by a state or subdivision of a state. Do not complete the remainder of Schedule B. ☐ **Yes** ☐ **No**

b Are you a public school because you are operated wholly or predominantly from government funds or property? If "Yes," explain how you are operated wholly or predominantly from government funds or property. Submit a copy of your funding agreement regarding government funding. Do not complete the remainder of Schedule B. ☐ **Yes** ☐ **No**

3 In what public school district, county, and state are you located?

4 Were you formed or substantially expanded at the time of public school desegregation in the above school district or county? ☐ **Yes** ☐ **No**

5 Has a state or federal administrative agency or judicial body ever determined that you are racially discriminatory? If "Yes," explain. ☐ **Yes** ☐ **No**

6 Has your right to receive financial aid or assistance from a governmental agency ever been revoked or suspended? If "Yes," explain. ☐ **Yes** ☐ **No**

7 Do you or will you contract with another organization to develop, build, market, or finance your facilities? If "Yes," explain how that entity is selected, explain how the terms of any contracts or other agreements are negotiated at arm's length, and explain how you determine that you will pay no more than fair market value for services. ☐ **Yes** ☐ **No**

Note. Make sure your answer is consistent with the information provided in Part VIII, line 7a.

8 Do you or will you manage your activities or facilities through your own employees or volunteers? If "No," attach a statement describing the activities that will be managed by others, the names of the persons or organizations that manage or will manage your activities or facilities, and how these managers were or will be selected. Also, submit copies of any contracts, proposed contracts, or other agreements regarding the provision of management services for your activities or facilities. Explain how the terms of any contracts or other agreements were or will be negotiated, and explain how you determine you will pay no more than fair market value for services. ☐ **Yes** ☐ **No**

Note. Answer "Yes" if you manage or intend to manage your programs through your own employees or by using volunteers. Answer "No" if you engage or intend to engage a separate organization or independent contractor. Make sure your answer is consistent with the information provided in Part VIII, line 7b.

Section II Establishment of Racially Nondiscriminatory Policy

Information required by **Revenue Procedure 75-50.**

1 Have you adopted a racially nondiscriminatory policy as to students in your organizing document, bylaws, or by resolution of your governing body? If "Yes," state where the policy can be found or supply a copy of the policy. If "No," you must adopt a nondiscriminatory policy as to students before submitting this application. See Publication 557. ☐ **Yes** ☐ **No**

2 Do your brochures, application forms, advertisements, and catalogues dealing with student admissions, programs, and scholarships contain a statement of your racially nondiscriminatory policy? ☐ **Yes** ☐ **No**

a If "Yes," attach a representative sample of each document.

b If "No," by checking the box to the right you agree that all future printed materials, including website content, will contain the required nondiscriminatory policy statement. ► ☐

3 Have you published a notice of your nondiscriminatory policy in a newspaper of general circulation that serves all racial segments of the community? (See the instructions for specific requirements.) If "No," explain. ☐ **Yes** ☐ **No**

4 Does or will the organization (or any department or division within it) discriminate in any way on the basis of race with respect to admissions; use of facilities or exercise of student privileges; faculty or administrative staff; or scholarship or loan programs? If "Yes," for any of the above, explain fully. ☐ **Yes** ☐ **No**

Schedule B. Schools, Colleges, and Universities *(Continued)*

5 Complete the table below to show the racial composition for the current academic year and projected for the next academic year, of: (a) the student body, (b) the faculty, and (c) the administrative staff. Provide actual numbers rather than percentages for each racial category.

If you are not operational, submit an estimate based on the best information available (such as the racial composition of the community served).

Racial Category	(a) Student Body		(b) Faculty		(c) Administrative Staff	
	Current Year	Next Year	Current Year	Next Year	Current Year	Next Year
Total						

6 In the table below, provide the number and amount of loans and scholarships awarded to students enrolled by racial categories.

Racial Category	Number of Loans		Amount of Loans		Number of Scholarships		Amount of Scholarships	
	Current Year	Next Year	Current Year	Next Year	Current Year	Next Year	Current Year	Next Year
Total								

7a Attach a list of your incorporators, founders, board members, and donors of land or buildings, whether individuals or organizations.

b Do any of these individuals or organizations have an objective to maintain segregated public or private school education? If "Yes," explain. ☐ **Yes** ☐ **No**

8 Will you maintain records according to the non-discrimination provisions contained in Revenue Procedure 75-50? If "No," explain. (See instructions.) ☐ **Yes** ☐ **No**

Form 1023 (Rev. 6-2006) Name: EIN: – Page **16**

Schedule C. Hospitals and Medical Research Organizations

Check the box if you are a **hospital**. See the instructions for a definition of the term "hospital," which includes an organization whose principal purpose or function is providing **hospital** or **medical care**. Complete Section I below. ☐

Check the box if you are a **medical research organization** operated in conjunction with a hospital. See the instructions for a definition of the term "medical research organization," which refers to an organization whose principal purpose or function is medical research and which is directly engaged in the continuous active conduct of medical research in conjunction with a hospital. Complete Section II. ☐

Section I Hospitals

1a Are all the doctors in the community eligible for staff privileges? If "No," give the reasons why and explain how the medical staff is selected. ☐ **Yes** ☐ **No**

2a Do you or will you provide medical services to all individuals in your community who can pay for themselves or have private health insurance? If "No," explain. ☐ **Yes** ☐ **No**

b Do you or will you provide medical services to all individuals in your community who participate in Medicare? If "No," explain. ☐ **Yes** ☐ **No**

c Do you or will you provide medical services to all individuals in your community who participate in Medicaid? If "No," explain. ☐ **Yes** ☐ **No**

3a Do you or will you require persons covered by Medicare or Medicaid to pay a deposit before receiving services? If "Yes," explain. ☐ **Yes** ☐ **No**

b Does the same deposit requirement, if any, apply to all other patients? If "No," explain. ☐ **Yes** ☐ **No**

4a Do you or will you maintain a full-time emergency room? If "No," explain why you do not maintain a full-time emergency room. Also, describe any emergency services that you provide. ☐ **Yes** ☐ **No**

b Do you have a policy on providing emergency services to persons without apparent means to pay? If "Yes," provide a copy of the policy. ☐ **Yes** ☐ **No**

c Do you have any arrangements with police, fire, and voluntary ambulance services for the delivery or admission of emergency cases? If "Yes," describe the arrangements, including whether they are written or oral agreements. If written, submit copies of all such agreements. ☐ **Yes** ☐ **No**

5a Do you provide for a portion of your services and facilities to be used for charity patients? If "Yes," answer 5b through 5e. ☐ **Yes** ☐ **No**

b Explain your policy regarding charity cases, including how you distinguish between charity care and bad debts. Submit a copy of your written policy.

c Provide data on your past experience in admitting charity patients, including amounts you expend for treating charity care patients and types of services you provide to charity care patients.

d Describe any arrangements you have with federal, state, or local governments or government agencies for paying for the cost of treating charity care patients. Submit copies of any written agreements.

e Do you provide services on a sliding fee schedule depending on financial ability to pay? If "Yes," submit your sliding fee schedule. ☐ **Yes** ☐ **No**

6a Do you or will you carry on a formal program of medical training or medical research? If "Yes," describe such programs, including the type of programs offered, the scope of such programs, and affiliations with other hospitals or medical care providers with which you carry on the medical training or research programs. ☐ **Yes** ☐ **No**

b Do you or will you carry on a formal program of community education? If "Yes," describe such programs, including the type of programs offered, the scope of such programs, and affiliation with other hospitals or medical care providers with which you offer community education programs. ☐ **Yes** ☐ **No**

7 Do you or will you provide office space to physicians carrying on their own medical practices? If "Yes," describe the criteria for who may use the space, explain the means used to determine that you are paid at least fair market value, and submit representative lease agreements. ☐ **Yes** ☐ **No**

8 Is your board of directors comprised of a majority of individuals who are representative of the community you serve? Include a list of each board member's name and business, financial, or professional relationship with the hospital. Also, identify each board member who is representative of the community and describe how that individual is a community representative. ☐ **Yes** ☐ **No**

9 Do you participate in any joint ventures? If "Yes," state your ownership percentage in each joint venture, list your investment in each joint venture, describe the tax status of other participants in each joint venture (including whether they are section 501(c)(3) organizations), describe the activities of each joint venture, describe how you exercise control over the activities of each joint venture, and describe how each joint venture furthers your exempt purposes. Also, submit copies of all agreements.
Note. Make sure your answer is consistent with the information provided in Part VIII, line 8. ☐ **Yes** ☐ **No**

Form 1023 (Rev. 6-2006) Name: EIN: – Page **17**

Schedule C. Hospitals and Medical Research Organizations *(Continued)*

Section I Hospitals *(Continued)*

10	Do you or will you manage your activities or facilities through your own employees or volunteers? If "No," attach a statement describing the activities that will be managed by others, the names of the persons or organizations that manage or will manage your activities or facilities, and how these managers were or will be selected. Also, submit copies of any contracts, proposed contracts, or other agreements regarding the provision of management services for your activities or facilities. Explain how the terms of any contracts or other agreements were or will be negotiated, and explain how you determine you will pay no more than fair market value for services. **Note.** Answer "Yes" if you do manage or intend to manage your programs through your own employees or by using volunteers. Answer "No" if you engage or intend to engage a separate organization or independent contractor. Make sure your answer is consistent with the information provided in Part VIII, line 7b.	☐ **Yes**	☐ **No**
11	Do you or will you offer recruitment incentives to physicians? If "Yes," describe your recruitment incentives and attach copies of all written recruitment incentive policies.	☐ **Yes**	☐ **No**
12	Do you or will you lease equipment, assets, or office space from physicians who have a financial or professional relationship with you? If "Yes," explain how you establish a fair market value for the lease.	☐ **Yes**	☐ **No**
13	Have you purchased medical practices, ambulatory surgery centers, or other business assets from physicians or other persons with whom you have a business relationship, aside from the purchase? If "Yes," submit a copy of each purchase and sales contract and describe how you arrived at fair market value, including copies of appraisals.	☐ **Yes**	☐ **No**
14	Have you adopted a **conflict of interest policy** consistent with the sample health care organization conflict of interest policy in Appendix A of the instructions? If "Yes," submit a copy of the policy and explain how the policy has been adopted, such as by resolution of your governing board. If "No," explain how you will avoid any conflicts of interest in your business dealings.	☐ **Yes**	☐ **No**

Section II Medical Research Organizations

1 Name the hospitals with which you have a relationship and describe the relationship. Attach copies of written agreements with each hospital that demonstrate continuing relationships between you and the hospital(s).

2 Attach a schedule describing your present and proposed activities for the direct conduct of medical research; describe the nature of the activities, and the amount of money that has been or will be spent in carrying them out.

3 Attach a schedule of assets showing their fair market value and the portion of your assets directly devoted to medical research.

Schedule D. Section 509(a)(3) Supporting Organizations

Section I Identifying Information About the Supported Organization(s)

1 State the names, addresses, and EINs of the supported organizations. If additional space is needed, attach a separate sheet.

Name	Address	EIN
		–
		–

2 Are all supported organizations listed in line 1 public charities under section 509(a)(1) or (2)? If "Yes," go to Section II. If "No," go to line 3. ☐ **Yes** ☐ **No**

3 Do the supported organizations have tax-exempt status under section 501(c)(4), 501(c)(5), or 501(c)(6)? ☐ **Yes** ☐ **No**

If "Yes," for each 501(c)(4), (5), or (6) organization supported, provide the following financial information:

- Part IX-A. Statement of Revenues and Expenses, lines 1–13 and
- Part X, lines 6b(ii)(a), 6b(ii)(b), and 7.

If "No," attach a statement describing how each organization you support is a public charity under section 509(a)(1) or (2).

Section II Relationship with Supported Organization(s)—Three Tests

To be classified as a supporting organization, an organization must meet one of three relationship tests:

Test 1: "Operated, supervised, or controlled by" one or more publicly supported organizations, or
Test 2: "Supervised or controlled in connection with" one or more publicly supported organizations, or
Test 3: "Operated in connection with" one or more publicly supported organizations.

1 Information to establish the "operated, supervised, or controlled by" relationship (Test 1)
Is a majority of your governing board or officers elected or appointed by the supported organization(s)? If "Yes," describe the process by which your governing board is appointed and elected; go to Section III. If "No," continue to line 2. ☐ **Yes** ☐ **No**

2 Information to establish the "supervised or controlled in connection with" relationship (Test 2)
Does a majority of your governing board consist of individuals who also serve on the governing board of the supported organization(s)? If "Yes," describe the process by which your governing board is appointed and elected; go to Section III. If "No," go to line 3. ☐ **Yes** ☐ **No**

3 Information to establish the "operated in connection with" responsiveness test (Test 3)
Are you a trust from which the named supported organization(s) can enforce and compel an accounting under state law? If "Yes," explain whether you advised the supported organization(s) in writing of these rights and provide a copy of the written communication documenting this; go to Section II, line 5. If "No," go to line 4a. ☐ **Yes** ☐ **No**

4 Information to establish the alternative "operated in connection with" responsiveness test (Test 3)

a Do the officers, directors, trustees, or members of the supported organization(s) elect or appoint one or more of your officers, directors, or trustees? If "Yes," explain and provide documentation; go to line 4d, below. If "No," go to line 4b. ☐ **Yes** ☐ **No**

b Do one or more members of the governing body of the supported organization(s) also serve as your officers, directors, or trustees or hold other important offices with respect to you? If "Yes," explain and provide documentation; go to line 4d, below. If "No," go to line 4c. ☐ **Yes** ☐ **No**

c Do your officers, directors, or trustees maintain a close and continuous working relationship with the officers, directors, or trustees of the supported organization(s)? If "Yes," explain and provide documentation. ☐ **Yes** ☐ **No**

d Do the supported organization(s) have a significant voice in your investment policies, in the making and timing of grants, and in otherwise directing the use of your income or assets? If "Yes," explain and provide documentation. ☐ **Yes** ☐ **No**

e Describe and provide copies of written communications documenting how you made the supported organization(s) aware of your supporting activities.

Schedule D. Section 509(a)(3) Supporting Organizations *(Continued)*

Section II **Relationship with Supported Organization(s)—Three Tests** *(Continued)*

5 Information to establish the "operated in connection with" integral part test (Test 3)
Do you conduct activities that would otherwise be carried out by the supported organization(s)? If "Yes," explain and go to Section III. If "No," continue to line 6a. ☐ **Yes** ☐ **No**

6 Information to establish the alternative "operated in connection with" integral part test (Test 3)

a Do you distribute at least 85% of your annual **net income** to the supported organization(s)? If "Yes," go to line 6b. (See instructions.) ☐ **Yes** ☐ **No**

If "No," state the percentage of your income that you distribute to each supported organization. Also explain how you ensure that the supported organization(s) are attentive to your operations.

b How much do you contribute annually to each supported organization? Attach a schedule.

c What is the total annual revenue of each supported organization? If you need additional space, attach a list.

d Do you or the supported organization(s) **earmark** your funds for support of a particular program or activity? If "Yes," explain. ☐ **Yes** ☐ **No**

7a Does your organizing document specify the supported organization(s) by name? If "Yes," state the article and paragraph number and go to Section III. If "No," answer line 7b. ☐ **Yes** ☐ **No**

b Attach a statement describing whether there has been an historic and continuing relationship between you and the supported organization(s).

Section III **Organizational Test**

1a If you met relationship Test 1 or Test 2 in Section II, your organizing document must specify the supported organization(s) by name, or by naming a similar purpose or charitable class of beneficiaries. If your organizing document complies with this requirement, answer "Yes." If your organizing document does not comply with this requirement, answer "No," and see the instructions. ☐ **Yes** ☐ **No**

b If you met relationship Test 3 in Section II, your organizing document must generally specify the supported organization(s) by name. If your organizing document complies with this requirement, answer "Yes," and go to Section IV. If your organizing document does not comply with this requirement, answer "No," and see the instructions. ☐ **Yes** ☐ **No**

Section IV **Disqualified Person Test**

You do not qualify as a supporting organization if you are **controlled** directly or indirectly by one or more **disqualified persons** (as defined in section 4946) other than **foundation managers** or one or more organizations that you support. Foundation managers who are also disqualified persons for another reason are disqualified persons with respect to you.

1a Do any persons who are disqualified persons with respect to you, (except individuals who are disqualified persons only because they are foundation managers), appoint any of your foundation managers? If "Yes," (1) describe the process by which disqualified persons appoint any of your foundation managers, (2) provide the names of these disqualified persons and the foundation managers they appoint, and (3) explain how control is vested over your operations (including assets and activities) by persons other than disqualified persons. ☐ **Yes** ☐ **No**

b Do any persons who have a family or business relationship with any disqualified persons with respect to you, (except individuals who are disqualified persons only because they are foundation managers), appoint any of your foundation managers? If "Yes," (1) describe the process by which individuals with a family or business relationship with disqualified persons appoint any of your foundation managers, (2) provide the names of these disqualified persons, the individuals with a family or business relationship with disqualified persons, and the foundation managers appointed, and (3) explain how control is vested over your operations (including assets and activities) in individuals other than disqualified persons. ☐ **Yes** ☐ **No**

c Do any persons who are disqualified persons, (except individuals who are disqualified persons only because they are foundation managers), have any influence regarding your operations, including your assets or activities? If "Yes," (1) provide the names of these disqualified persons, (2) explain how influence is exerted over your operations (including assets and activities), and (3) explain how control is vested over your operations (including assets and activities) by individuals other than disqualified persons. ☐ **Yes** ☐ **No**

Schedule E. Organizations Not Filing Form 1023 Within 27 Months of Formation

Schedule E is intended to determine whether you are eligible for tax exemption under section 501(c)(3) from the postmark date of your application or from your date of incorporation or formation, whichever is earlier. If you are not eligible for tax exemption under section 501(c)(3) from your date of incorporation or formation, Schedule E is also intended to determine whether you are eligible for tax exemption under section 501(c)(4) for the period between your date of incorporation or formation and the postmark date of your application.

1	Are you a church, association of churches, or integrated auxiliary of a church? If "Yes," complete Schedule A and stop here. Do not complete the remainder of Schedule E.	☐ **Yes**	☐ **No**
2a	Are you a public charity with annual **gross receipts** that are normally $5,000 or less? If "Yes," stop here. Answer "No" if you are a private foundation, regardless of your gross receipts.	☐ **Yes**	☐ **No**
b	If your gross receipts were normally more than $5,000, are you filing this application within 90 days from the end of the tax year in which your gross receipts were normally more than $5,000? If "Yes," stop here.	☐ **Yes**	☐ **No**
3a	Were you included as a subordinate in a group exemption application or letter? If "No," go to line 4.	☐ **Yes**	☐ **No**
b	If you were included as a subordinate in a group exemption letter, are you filing this application within 27 months from the date you were notified by the organization holding the group exemption letter or the Internal Revenue Service that you cease to be covered by the group exemption letter? If "Yes," stop here.	☐ **Yes**	☐ **No**
c	If you were included as a subordinate in a timely filed group exemption request that was denied, are you filing this application within 27 months from the postmark date of the Internal Revenue Service final adverse ruling letter? If "Yes," stop here.	☐ **Yes**	☐ **No**
4	Were you created on or before October 9, 1969? If "Yes," stop here. Do not complete the remainder of this schedule.	☐ **Yes**	☐ **No**
5	If you answered "No" to lines 1 through 4, we cannot recognize you as tax exempt from your date of formation unless you qualify for an extension of time to apply for exemption. Do you wish to request an extension of time to apply to be recognized as exempt from the date you were formed? If "Yes," attach a statement explaining why you did not file this application within the 27-month period. Do not answer lines 6, 7, or 8. If "No," go to line 6a.	☐ **Yes**	☐ **No**
6a	If you answered "No" to line 5, you can only be exempt under section 501(c)(3) from the postmark date of this application. Therefore, do you want us to treat this application as a request for tax exemption from the postmark date? If "Yes," you are eligible for an advance ruling. Complete Part X, line 6a. If "No," you will be treated as a private foundation.	☐ **Yes**	☐ **No**
	Note. Be sure your ruling eligibility agrees with your answer to Part X, line 6.		
b	Do you anticipate significant changes in your sources of support in the future? If "Yes," complete line 7 below.	☐ **Yes**	☐ **No**

Form 1023 (Rev. 6-2006) Name: EIN: – Page **21**

Schedule E. Organizations Not Filing Form 1023 Within 27 Months of Formation *(Continued)*

7 Complete this item only if you answered "Yes" to line 6b. Include projected revenue for the first two full years following the current tax year.

Type of Revenue	Projected revenue for 2 years following current tax year		
	(a) From .... To	**(b)** From .... To	**(c)** Total
1 Gifts, grants, and contributions received (do not include unusual grants)			
2 Membership fees received			
3 Gross investment income			
4 Net unrelated business income			
5 Taxes levied for your benefit			
6 Value of services or facilities furnished by a governmental unit without charge (not including the value of services generally furnished to the public without charge)			
7 Any revenue not otherwise listed above or in lines 9–12 below (attach an itemized list)			
8 Total of lines 1 through 7			
9 Gross receipts from admissions, merchandise sold, or services performed, or furnishing of facilities in any activity that is related to your exempt purposes (attach itemized list)			
10 Total of lines 8 and 9			
11 Net gain or loss on sale of capital assets (attach an itemized list)			
12 Unusual grants			
13 Total revenue. Add lines 10 through 12			

8 According to your answers, you are only eligible for tax exemption under section 501(c)(3) from the postmark date of your application. However, you may be eligible for tax exemption under section 501(c)(4) from your date of formation to the postmark date of the Form 1023. Tax exemption under section 501(c)(4) allows exemption from federal income tax, but generally not deductibility of contributions under Code section 170. Check the box at right if you want us to treat this as a request for exemption under 501(c)(4) from your date of formation to the postmark date. ▶ ☐

Attach a completed Page 1 of Form 1024, Application for Recognition of Exemption Under Section 501(a), to this application.

Form **1023** (Rev. 6-2006)

Form 1023 (Rev. 6-2006) Name: EIN: – Page 22

Schedule F. Homes for the Elderly or Handicapped and Low-Income Housing

Section I General Information About Your Housing

1 Describe the type of housing you provide.

2 Provide copies of any application forms you use for admission.

3 Explain how the public is made aware of your facility.

4a Provide a description of each facility.
b What is the total number of residents each facility can accommodate?
c What is your current number of residents in each facility?
d Describe each facility in terms of whether residents rent or purchase housing from you.

5 Attach a sample copy of your residency or homeownership contract or agreement.

6 Do you participate in any joint ventures? If "Yes," state your ownership percentage in each joint venture, list your investment in each joint venture, describe the tax status of other participants in each joint venture (including whether they are section 501(c)(3) organizations), describe the activities of each joint venture, describe how you exercise control over the activities of each joint venture, and describe how each joint venture furthers your exempt purposes. Also, submit copies of all joint venture agreements. ☐ Yes ☐ No

Note. Make sure your answer is consistent with the information provided in Part VIII, line 8.

7 Do you or will you contract with another organization to develop, build, market, or finance your housing? If "Yes," explain how that entity is selected, explain how the terms of any contract(s) are negotiated at arm's length, and explain how you determine you will pay no more than fair market value for services. ☐ Yes ☐ No

Note. Make sure your answer is consistent with the information provided in Part VIII, line 7a.

8 Do you or will you manage your activities or facilities through your own employees or volunteers? If "No," attach a statement describing the activities that will be managed by others, the names of the persons or organizations that manage or will manage your activities or facilities, and how these managers were or will be selected. Also, submit copies of any contracts, proposed contracts, or other agreements regarding the provision of management services for your activities or facilities. Explain how the terms of any contracts or other agreements were or will be negotiated, and explain how you determine you will pay no more than fair market value for services. ☐ Yes ☐ No

Note. Answer "Yes" if you do manage or intend to manage your programs through your own employees or by using volunteers. Answer "No" if you engage or intend to engage a separate organization or independent contractor. Make sure your answer is consistent with the information provided in Part VIII, line 7b.

9 Do you participate in any government housing programs? If "Yes," describe these programs. ☐ Yes ☐ No

10a Do you own the facility? If "No," describe any enforceable rights you possess to purchase the facility in the future; go to line 10c. If "Yes," answer line 10b. ☐ Yes ☐ No

b How did you acquire the facility? For example, did you develop it yourself, purchase a project, etc. Attach all contracts, transfer agreements, or other documents connected with the acquisition of the facility.

c Do you lease the facility or the land on which it is located? If "Yes," describe the parties to the lease(s) and provide copies of all leases. ☐ Yes ☐ No

Form **1023** (Rev. 6-2006)

Form 1023 (Rev. 6-2006) Name: EIN: – Page **23**

Schedule F. Homes for the Elderly or Handicapped and Low-Income Housing *(Continued)*

Section II Homes for the Elderly or Handicapped

1a Do you provide housing for the elderly? If "Yes," describe who qualifies for your housing in terms of age, infirmity, or other criteria and explain how you select persons for your housing. ☐ **Yes** ☐ **No**

b Do you provide housing for the handicapped? If "Yes," describe who qualifies for your housing in terms of disability, income levels, or other criteria and explain how you select persons for your housing. ☐ **Yes** ☐ **No**

2a Do you charge an entrance or founder's fee? If "Yes," describe what this charge covers, whether it is a one-time fee, how the fee is determined, whether it is payable in a lump sum or on an installment basis, whether it is refundable, and the circumstances, if any, under which it may be waived. ☐ **Yes** ☐ **No**

b Do you charge periodic fees or maintenance charges? If "Yes," describe what these charges cover and how they are determined. ☐ **Yes** ☐ **No**

c Is your housing affordable to a significant segment of the elderly or handicapped persons in the community? Identify your **community**. Also, if "Yes," explain how you determine your housing is affordable. ☐ **Yes** ☐ **No**

3a Do you have an established policy concerning residents who become unable to pay their regular charges? If "Yes," describe your established policy. ☐ **Yes** ☐ **No**

b Do you have any arrangements with government welfare agencies or others to absorb all or part of the cost of maintaining residents who become unable to pay their regular charges? If "Yes," describe these arrangements. ☐ **Yes** ☐ **No**

4 Do you have arrangements for the healthcare needs of your residents? If "Yes," describe these arrangements. ☐ **Yes** ☐ **No**

5 Are your facilities designed to meet the physical, emotional, recreational, social, religious, and/or other similar needs of the elderly or handicapped? If "Yes," describe these design features. ☐ **Yes** ☐ **No**

Section III Low-Income Housing

1 Do you provide low-income housing? If "Yes," describe who qualifies for your housing in terms of income levels or other criteria, and describe how you select persons for your housing. ☐ **Yes** ☐ **No**

2 In addition to rent or mortgage payments, do residents pay periodic fees or maintenance charges? If "Yes," describe what these charges cover and how they are determined. ☐ **Yes** ☐ **No**

3a Is your housing affordable to low income residents? If "Yes," describe how your housing is made affordable to low-income residents. ☐ **Yes** ☐ **No**

Note. Revenue Procedure 96-32, 1996-1 C.B. 717, provides guidelines for providing low-income housing that will be treated as charitable. (At least 75% of the units are occupied by low-income tenants or 40% are occupied by tenants earning not more than 120% of the very low-income levels for the area.)

b Do you impose any restrictions to make sure that your housing remains affordable to low-income residents? If "Yes," describe these restrictions. ☐ **Yes** ☐ **No**

4 Do you provide social services to residents? If "Yes," describe these services. ☐ **Yes** ☐ **No**

Form **1023** (Rev. 6-2006)

Form 1023 (Rev. 6-2006) Name: EIN: – Page **24**

Schedule G. Successors to Other Organizations

1a Are you a **successor** to a **for-profit organization**? If "Yes," explain the relationship with the **predecessor** organization that resulted in your creation and complete line 1b. ☐ **Yes** ☐ **No**

b Explain why you took over the activities or assets of a for-profit organization or converted from for-profit to nonprofit status.

2a Are you a successor to an organization other than a for-profit organization? Answer "Yes" if you have taken or will take over the activities of another organization; or you have taken or will take over 25% or more of the fair market value of the net assets of another organization. If "Yes," explain the relationship with the other organzation that resulted in your creation. ☐ **Yes** ☐ **No**

b Provide the tax status of the predecessor organization.

c Did you or did an organization to which you are a successor previously apply for tax exemption under section 501(c)(3) or any other section of the Code? If "Yes," explain how the application was resolved. ☐ **Yes** ☐ **No**

d Was your prior tax exemption or the tax exemption of an organization to which you are a successor revoked or suspended? If "Yes," explain. Include a description of the corrections you made to re-establish tax exemption. ☐ **Yes** ☐ **No**

e Explain why you took over the activities or assets of another organization.

3 Provide the name, last address, and EIN of the predecessor organization and describe its activities.

Name: ______________________ **EIN:** ___–___

Address: ______________________

4 List the owners, partners, principal stockholders, officers, and governing board members of the predecessor organization. Attach a separate sheet if additional space is needed.

Name	Address	Share/Interest (If a for-profit)

5 Do or will any of the persons listed in line 4, maintain a working relationship with you? If "Yes," describe the relationship in detail and include copies of any agreements with any of these persons or with any for-profit organizations in which these persons own more than a 35% interest. ☐ **Yes** ☐ **No**

6a Were any assets transferred, whether by gift or sale, from the predecessor organization to you? ☐ **Yes** ☐ **No**
If "Yes," provide a list of assets, indicate the value of each asset, explain how the value was determined, and attach an appraisal, if available. For each asset listed, also explain if the transfer was by gift, sale, or combination thereof.

b Were any restrictions placed on the use or sale of the assets? If "Yes," explain the restrictions. ☐ **Yes** ☐ **No**

c Provide a copy of the agreement(s) of sale or transfer.

7 Were any debts or liabilities transferred from the predecessor for-profit organization to you? ☐ **Yes** ☐ **No**
If "Yes," provide a list of the debts or liabilities that were transferred to you, indicating the amount of each, how the amount was determined, and the name of the person to whom the debt or liability is owed.

8 Will you lease or rent any property or equipment previously owned or used by the predecessor for-profit organization, or from persons listed in line 4, or from for-profit organizations in which these persons own more than a 35% interest? If "Yes," submit a copy of the lease or rental agreement(s). Indicate how the lease or rental value of the property or equipment was determined. ☐ **Yes** ☐ **No**

9 Will you lease or rent property or equipment to persons listed in line 4, or to for-profit organizations in which these persons own more than a 35% interest? If "Yes," attach a list of the property or equipment, provide a copy of the lease or rental agreement(s), and indicate how the lease or rental value of the property or equipment was determined. ☐ **Yes** ☐ **No**

Form **1023** (Rev. 6-2006)

Schedule H. Organizations Providing Scholarships, Fellowships, Educational Loans, or Other Educational Grants to Individuals and Private Foundations Requesting Advance Approval of Individual Grant Procedures

Section I ***Names of individual recipients are not required to be listed in Schedule H.***
Public charities and private foundations complete lines 1a through 7 of this section. See the instructions to Part X if you are not sure whether you are a public charity or a private foundation.

1a Describe the types of educational grants you provide to individuals, such as scholarships, fellowships, loans, etc.
b Describe the purpose and amount of your scholarships, fellowships, and other educational grants and loans that you award.
c If you award educational loans, explain the terms of the loans (interest rate, length, forgiveness, etc.).
d Specify how your program is publicized.
e Provide copies of any solicitation or announcement materials.
f Provide a sample copy of the application used.

2 Do you maintain case histories showing recipients of your scholarships, fellowships, educational loans, or other educational grants, including names, addresses, purposes of awards, amount of each grant, manner of selection, and relationship (if any) to officers, trustees, or donors of funds to you? If "No," refer to the instructions. ☐ Yes ☐ No

3 Describe the specific criteria you use to determine who is eligible for your program. (For example, eligibility selection criteria could consist of graduating high school students from a particular high school who will attend college, writers of scholarly works about American history, etc.)

4a Describe the specific criteria you use to select recipients. (For example, specific selection criteria could consist of prior academic performance, financial need, etc.)
b Describe how you determine the number of grants that will be made annually.
c Describe how you determine the amount of each of your grants.
d Describe any requirement or condition that you impose on recipients to obtain, maintain, or qualify for renewal of a grant. (For example, specific requirements or conditions could consist of attendance at a four-year college, maintaining a certain grade point average, teaching in public school after graduation from college, etc.)

5 Describe your procedures for supervising the scholarships, fellowships, educational loans, or other educational grants. Describe whether you obtain reports and grade transcripts from recipients, or you pay grants directly to a school under an arrangement whereby the school will apply the grant funds only for enrolled students who are in good standing. Also, describe your procedures for taking action if the terms of the award are violated.

6 Who is on the selection committee for the awards made under your program, including names of current committee members, criteria for committee membership, and the method of replacing committee members?

7 Are relatives of members of the selection committee, or of your officers, directors, or **substantial contributors** eligible for awards made under your program? If "Yes," what measures are taken to ensure unbiased selections? ☐ Yes ☐ No

Note. If you are a private foundation, you are not permitted to provide educational grants to **disqualified persons**. Disqualified persons include your substantial contributors and foundation managers and certain family members of disqualified persons.

Section II **Private foundations complete lines 1a through 4f of this section. Public charities do not complete this section.**

1a If we determine that you are a private foundation, do you want this application to be considered as a request for advance approval of grant making procedures? ☐ Yes ☐ No ☐ N/A
b For which section(s) do you wish to be considered?
- 4945(g)(1)—Scholarship or fellowship grant to an individual for study at an educational institution ☐
- 4945(g)(3)—Other grants, including loans, to an individual for travel, study, or other similar purposes, to enhance a particular skill of the grantee or to produce a specific product ☐

2 Do you represent that you will (1) arrange to receive and review grantee reports annually and upon completion of the purpose for which the grant was awarded, (2) investigate diversions of funds from their intended purposes, and (3) take all reasonable and appropriate steps to recover diverted funds, ensure other grant funds held by a grantee are used for their intended purposes, and withhold further payments to grantees until you obtain grantees' assurances that future diversions will not occur and that grantees will take extraordinary precautions to prevent future diversions from occurring? ☐ Yes ☐ No

3 Do you represent that you will maintain all records relating to individual grants, including information obtained to evaluate grantees, identify whether a grantee is a disqualified person, establish the amount and purpose of each grant, and establish that you undertook the supervision and investigation of grants described in line 2? ☐ Yes ☐ No

Form 1023 (Rev. 6-2006) Name: EIN: – Page **26**

Schedule H. Organizations Providing Scholarships, Fellowships, Educational Loans, or Other Educational Grants to Individuals and Private Foundations Requesting Advance Approval of Individual Grant Procedures *(Continued)*

Section II **Private foundations complete lines 1a through 4f of this section. Public charities do not complete this section.** *(Continued)*

4a Do you or will you award scholarships, fellowships, and educational loans to attend an educational institution based on the status of an individual being an *employee of a particular employer?* If "Yes," complete lines 4b through 4f. ☐ **Yes** ☐ **No**

b Will you comply with the seven conditions and either the percentage tests or facts and circumstances test for scholarships, fellowships, and educational loans to attend an educational institution as set forth in Revenue Procedures 76-47, 1976-2 C.B. 670, and 80-39, 1980-2 C.B. 772, which apply to inducement, selection committee, eligibility requirements, objective basis of selection, employment, course of study, and other objectives? (See lines 4c, 4d, and 4e, regarding the percentage tests.) ☐ **Yes** ☐ **No**

c Do you or will you provide scholarships, fellowships, or educational loans to attend an educational institution to employees of a particular employer? ☐ **Yes** ☐ **No** ☐ **N/A**

If "Yes," will you award grants to 10% or fewer of the eligible applicants who were actually considered by the selection committee in selecting recipients of grants in that year as provided by Revenue Procedures 76-47 and 80-39? ☐ **Yes** ☐ **No**

d Do you provide scholarships, fellowships, or educational loans to attend an educational institution to children of employees of a particular employer? ☐ **Yes** ☐ **No** ☐ **N/A**

If "Yes," will you award grants to 25% or fewer of the eligible applicants who were actually considered by the selection committee in selecting recipients of grants in that year as provided by Revenue Procedures 76-47 and 80-39? If "No," go to line 4e. ☐ **Yes** ☐ **No**

e If you provide scholarships, fellowships, or educational loans to attend an educational institution to children of employees of a particular employer, will you award grants to 10% or fewer of the number of employees' children who can be shown to be eligible for grants (whether or not they submitted an application) in that year, as provided by Revenue Procedures 76-47 and 80-39? ☐ **Yes** ☐ **No** ☐ **N/A**

If "Yes," describe how you will determine who can be shown to be eligible for grants without submitting an application, such as by obtaining written statements or other information about the expectations of employees' children to attend an educational institution. If "No," go to line 4f.

Note. Statistical or sampling techniques are not acceptable. See Revenue Procedure 85-51, 1985-2 C.B. 717, for additional information.

f If you provide scholarships, fellowships, or educational loans to attend an educational institution to *children of employees of a particular employer* without regard to either the 25% limitation described in line 4d, or the 10% limitation described in line 4e, will you award grants based on facts and circumstances that demonstrate that the grants will not be considered compensation for past, present, or future services or otherwise provide a significant benefit to the particular employer? If "Yes," describe the facts and circumstances that you believe will demonstrate that the grants are neither compensatory nor a significant benefit to the particular employer. In your explanation, describe why you cannot satisfy either the 25% test described in line 4d or the 10% test described in line 4e. ☐ **Yes** ☐ **No**

Form **1023** (Rev. 6-2006)

Form 1023 Checklist

(Revised June 2006)

Application for Recognition of Exemption under Section 501(c)(3) of the Internal Revenue Code

Note. *Retain a copy of the completed Form 1023 in your permanent records. Refer to the General Instructions regarding Public Inspection of approved applications.*

Check each box to finish your application (Form 1023). Send this completed Checklist with your filled-in application. If you have not answered all the items below, your application may be returned to you as incomplete.

☐ Assemble the application and materials in this order:
- Form 1023 Checklist
- Form 2848, *Power of Attorney and Declaration of Representative* (if filing)
- Form 8821, *Tax Information Authorization* (if filing)
- Expedite request (if requesting)
- Application (Form 1023 and Schedules A through H, as required)
- Articles of organization
- Amendments to articles of organization in chronological order
- Bylaws or other rules of operation and amendments
- Documentation of nondiscriminatory policy for schools, as required by Schedule B
- Form 5768, Election/Revocation of Election by an Eligible Section 501(c)(3) Organization To Make Expenditures To Influence Legislation (if filing)
- All other attachments, including explanations, financial data, and printed materials or publications. Label each page with name and EIN.

☐ User fee payment placed in envelope on top of checklist. DO NOT STAPLE or otherwise attach your check or money order to your application. Instead, just place it in the envelope.

☐ Employer Identification Number (EIN)

☐ Completed Parts I through XI of the application, including any requested information and any required Schedules A through H.
- You must provide specific details about your past, present, and planned activities.
- Generalizations or failure to answer questions in the Form 1023 application will prevent us from recognizing you as tax exempt.
- Describe your purposes and proposed activities in specific easily understood terms.
- Financial information should correspond with proposed activities.

☐ Schedules. Submit only those schedules that apply to you and check either "Yes" or "No" below.

Schedule A	Yes ___	No ___	Schedule E	Yes ___	No ___
Schedule B	Yes ___	No ___	Schedule F	Yes ___	No ___
Schedule C	Yes ___	No ___	Schedule G	Yes ___	No ___
Schedule D	Yes ___	No ___	Schedule H	Yes ___	No ___

☐ An exact copy of your complete articles of organization (creating document). Absence of the proper purpose and dissolution clauses is the number one reason for delays in the issuance of determination letters.

- Location of Purpose Clause from Part III, line 1 (Page, Article and Paragraph Number) ________
- Location of Dissolution Clause from Part III, line 2b or 2c (Page, Article and Paragraph Number) or by operation of state law ________

☐ Signature of an officer, director, trustee, or other official who is authorized to sign the application.

- Signature at Part XI of Form 1023.

☐ Your name on the application must be the same as your legal name as it appears in your articles of organization.

Send completed Form 1023, user fee payment, and all other required information, to:

Internal Revenue Service
P.O. Box 192
Covington, KY 41012-0192

If you are using express mail or a delivery service, send Form 1023, user fee payment, and attachments to:

Internal Revenue Service
201 West Rivercenter Blvd.
Attn: Extracting Stop 312
Covington, KY 41011

Printed on recycled paper

Instructions for Form 1023

Department of the Treasury
Internal Revenue Service

(Rev. June 2006)

Application for Recognition of Exemption Under Section 501(c)(3) of the Internal Revenue Code

Section references are to the Internal Revenue Code unless otherwise noted.

Contents **Page**

Contents **Page**

What's New

The user fee for the initial application for recognition of exemption under IRC Section 501(c)(3) has been increased. Part XI of Form 1023 has been revised to reflect the new fee. See Rev. Proc. 2006-8, 2006-1 I.R.B. 245 for more information about user fees that may be applicable to tax-exempt organizations.

How To Get Forms and Publications

Personal Computer

You can access the IRS website 24 hours a day, 7 days a week at www.irs.gov to:

- Order IRS products online.
- Download forms, instructions, and publications.
- Get answers to frequently asked tax questions.
- Search publications online by topic or keyword.
- Send us comments or request help by email.
- Sign up to receive local and national tax news by email.

CD-ROM

You can order Publication 1796, IRS Tax Products CD, and obtain:

- Current-year forms, instructions, and publications.
- Prior-year forms, instructions, and publications.
- Bonus: Historical Tax Products DVD — Ships with the final release.
- Tax Map: an electronic research tool and finding aid.
- Tax Law frequently asked questions (FAQs).
- Tax Topics from the IRS telephone response system.
- Fill-in, print, and save features for most tax forms.
- Internal Revenue Bulletins.
- Toll-free and email technical support.
- The CD is released twice during the year.
  - o The first release will ship the beginning of January 2007.
  - o The final release will ship the beginning of March 2007.

Purchase the CD from National Technical Information Service at www.irs.gov/cdorders $25 (no handling fee) or call 1-877-CDFORMS (1-877-233-6767) toll-free to buy the CD for $25 (plus a $5 handling fee). Price is subject to change.

By Phone and In Person

You can order forms and publications by calling **1-800-TAX-FORM** (1-800-829-3676). You can also get most forms and publications at your local IRS office.

Overview of Section 501(c)(3) Organizations

Who Is Eligible for Section 501(c)(3) Status?

Organizations organized and operated exclusively for religious, charitable, scientific, testing for public safety, literary, or educational purposes, or to foster national or international amateur sports competition, or for the prevention of cruelty to children or animals are eligible to file Form 1023 to obtain recognition of exemption from federal income tax under section 501(c)(3) of the Internal Revenue Code.

Form 1023 not necessary. The following types of organizations may be considered tax exempt under section 501(c)(3) even if they do not file Form 1023.

- Churches, including synagogues, temples, and mosques.
- Integrated auxiliaries of churches and conventions or associations of churches.
- Any organization that has gross receipts in each taxable year of normally not more than $5,000.

Even though the above organizations are not required to file Form 1023 to be tax exempt, these organizations may choose to file Form 1023 in order to receive a determination letter that recognizes their section 501(c)(3) status and specifies whether contributions to them are tax deductible.

Qualification of a Section 501(c)(3) Organization

There are two key requirements for an organization to be exempt from federal income tax under section 501(c)(3). A 501(c)(3) organization must be organized and operated exclusively for one or more exempt purposes.

Organized. An organization must be organized as a corporation (including a limited liability company), trust, or unincorporated association. The organizing document (articles of incorporation if you are a corporation, articles of organization if you are a limited liability company, articles of association or constitution if you are an association, or trust agreement or declaration of trust if you are a trust) must limit the organization's purpose(s) and permanently dedicate its assets to exempt purposes.

Operated. An organization must be operated to further one or more of the exempt purposes stated in its organizing document. Certain other activities are prohibited or restricted, including, but not limited to, the following activities. A 501(c)(3) organization must:

a. Absolutely refrain from participating in the political campaigns of candidates for local, state, or federal office.
b. Absolutely ensure that its assets and earnings do not unjustly enrich board members, officers, key management employees, or other insiders.
c. Not further non-exempt purposes (such as purposes that benefit private interests) more than insubstantially.
d. Not operate for the primary purpose of conducting a trade or business that is not related to its exempt purpose(s).
e. Not engage in activities that are illegal or violate fundamental public policy.
f. Restrict its legislative activities.

Legislative activity. An organization does not qualify for section 501(c)(3) status if a substantial part of its activities is attempting to influence legislation.

Form 5768. Most public charities are eligible to elect to make expenditures to influence legislation by filing Form 5768, Election/Revocation of Election by an Eligible Section 501(c)(3) Organization To Make Expenditures To Influence Legislation. By filing Form 5768, an eligible organization's legislative activities will be measured solely by an expenditure limit rather than by the "no substantial amount" limit. For additional information on the expenditure limit or the no substantial amount limit, see Publication 557, Tax-Exempt Status for Your Organization.

For this purpose, "legislation" includes action by Congress, a state legislature, a local council, or a similar governing body, with respect to acts, bills, resolutions or similar items (such as legislative confirmation of appointive offices). Legislation also includes action by the public in a referendum, ballot initiative, constitutional amendment, or similar procedure. Legislation generally does not include actions by executive, judicial, or administrative bodies.

Organizations may involve themselves in issues of public policy without being engaged in legislative activity. For example, organizations may conduct educational meetings, prepare and distribute educational materials, or otherwise consider public policy issues. Similarly, an organization may appear before a governmental body to offer testimony about a decision that may affect the organization's existence.

TIP A private foundation is not allowed to influence legislation.

Political campaign intervention. All 501(c)(3) organizations are absolutely prohibited from directly or indirectly participating or intervening in any political campaign on behalf of (or in opposition to) any candidate for elective public office. Non-partisan voter education activities (including public forums and voter education guides) are permitted. Similarly, non-partisan activities to encourage people to participate in the electoral process, such as voter registration and get-out-the-vote drives, are not prohibited political campaign activity. However, voter education or registration activities that (a) favor one candidate over another, (b) oppose a candidate in some manner, or (c) favor a group of candidates, are prohibited.

Public Charities and Private Foundations

Every organization that qualifies for tax-exempt status under section 501(c)(3) is further classified as either a public charity or a private foundation. For some organizations, the primary distinction between a public charity and a private foundation is an organization's source of financial support.

A public charity has a broad base of support, while a private foundation receives its support from a small number of donors. This classification is important because different tax rules apply to the operations of each entity.

Deductibility of contributions to a private foundation is more limited than contributions to a public charity. See Publication 526, Charitable Contributions, for more information on the deductibility of contributions. In addition, private foundations are subject to excise taxes that are not imposed on public charities.

Public charities. The following 501(c)(3) organizations are classified as public charities.

- Churches.
- Schools.
- Hospitals, medical research organizations, and cooperative hospital service organizations.
- Organizations that receive substantial support from grants, governmental units, and/or contributions from the general public.
- Organizations that normally receive more than one-third of their support from contributions, membership fees, and gross receipts from activities related to their exempt functions, and not more than one-third of their support from gross investment income and net unrelated business income.
- Organizations that support other public charities.

If an organization requests public charity classification based on receiving substantial public support, it must continue to seek significant and diversified public support contributions in later years. A new organization that cannot show it will receive enough public support may request an advance ruling of its status. After 5 years, it must file Form 8734, Support Schedule for Advance Ruling Period, showing its sources of support during the advance ruling period. If the organization does not meet the public support requirements during the 5-year advance ruling period, it could be reclassified as a private foundation.

Private foundation. A 501(c)(3) organization that cannot meet one of the specific exceptions to be classified as a public charity is a private foundation.

TIP Classification as a private foundation has nothing to do with the name of the organization. There are many organizations that include the word foundation in their names that are **not** private foundations for tax purposes.

Private operating foundations. A private foundation that lacks general public support but actively conducts exempt programs (as opposed to making grants to other organizations to conduct exempt activities) may be treated as a private operating foundation. Private operating foundations are subject to more favorable rules than other private foundations in terms of charitable contribution deductions and attracting grants from private foundations. In order to be classified as a private operating foundation, an organization must meet certain support tests.

State Registration Requirements

Tax exemption under section 501(c)(3) is a matter of federal law. After receiving federal tax exemption, you may also be required to register with one or more states to solicit for contributions or to obtain exemption from state taxes. The National Association of State Charity Officials (NASCO) maintains a website that provides informational links to the various states for these purposes. It can be accessed at www.nasconet.org.

General Instructions

Section references are to the Internal Revenue Code unless otherwise noted.

"You" and "Us". Throughout these instructions and Form 1023, the terms "you" and "your" refer to the organization that is applying for tax-exempt status. The terms "us" and "we" refer to the Internal Revenue Service.

Definitions. Terms in bold type in Form 1023 are defined throughout these instructions and in Appendix C.

Answers

Answer items completely. Where a "Yes" or "No" reply is not requested, you may answer "Not Applicable" where appropriate. If you believe you have previously answered the item, you may refer to your previous answer.

CAUTION Your answers must provide sufficient detail about your past, present, and planned activities to prove that you are an exempt organization. We will not be able to recognize you as tax exempt based on generalizations. Therefore, we need to understand the specific activities you will undertake to reach your charitable goals.

Financial data. Form 1023 asks you to answer a series of questions and provide information to assist us in determining if you meet the requirements for tax exemption under section 501(c)(3). One of the key pieces of information requested is financial data. This data, whether budgeted or actual, should be consistent with other information presented in the application.

For example, if you are requesting public charity status under one of the public support tests, the financial data should show contributions from the public or receipts from providing exempt services. Budgeted financial data should be prepared based upon your current plans. We recognize that the organization's actual financial results may vary from the budgeted amounts.

Past, present, and planned activities. Many items on Form 1023 are written in the present tense; however, your answers should be based on your past, present, and planned activities.

Language and currency requirements. Prepare Form 1023 and attachments in English. Provide an English translation if the articles of organization or bylaws are in any other language.

We may ask you to provide English translations of foreign language publications you submit with your Form 1023.

Report financial information in U.S. dollars (specify the conversion rate used). Combine amounts from within and outside the United States and report the total for each line on the financial statements.

Purpose of Form

Completed Form 1023 required for section 501(c)(3) exemption. Form 1023 is filed by organizations to apply for recognition of exemption from federal income tax under section 501(c)(3). Upon approval, we will issue a determination letter that provides written assurance about the organization's tax-exempt status, and its qualification to receive tax-deductible charitable contributions. Every organization qualifying for exemption under section 501(c)(3) will also be classified as either a "public charity" or a "private foundation."

Other organizations that may file Form 1023. Other organizations that apply for tax-exempt status under section 501(c)(3) by filing Form 1023 include section 501(e) and (f) cooperative service organizations, section 501(k) childcare organizations, and section 501(n) charitable risk pools.

Obtaining Tax-Exempt Status

To apply for tax-exempt status, file Form 1023 and pay the appropriate user fee.

Expedite Requests

We will only approve expedited processing of an application where a request is made in writing and contains a compelling reason for processing the application ahead of others. Circumstances generally warranting expedited processing include:

- A grant to the applicant is pending and the failure to secure the grant may have an adverse impact on the organization's ability to continue operations.
- The purpose of the newly created organization is to provide disaster relief to victims of emergencies such as flood and hurricane.
- There have been undue delays in issuing a letter caused by problems within the IRS.

User Fee

The law requires payment of a user fee with each application. Submit the appropriate user fee based on your average annual gross receipts as indicated on Form 1023. Enclose payment with your application. DO NOT STAPLE or otherwise attach your check or money order to your application.

You may pay your user fee with a personal or certified check, bank check, or cashier's check. Processing your application will not be delayed by the form of payment unless your check is returned to us for insufficient funds.

Generally, a user fee will be refunded only if we decline to issue a determination. Additional guidance regarding user fees is available in Rev. Proc. 2006-8, 2006-1 I.R.B. 245, or later revision (revised in the first Internal Revenue Bulletin (I.R.B.) issued each year).

For additional information on the user fee, see Part XI.

Group Exemption

Form 1023 is not used to apply for a group exemption. A group exemption is issued to a central organization that recognizes on a group basis the exemption of subordinate organizations on whose behalf the central organization has applied. See Publication 557 for information on how to apply for a group exemption.

Leaving a group exemption. If a subordinate organization in an existing group exemption wishes to apply for an individual exemption, it should notify its parent organization of its intention to leave the group ruling before filing Form 1023.

What to File

All applicants, unless otherwise noted, must complete Parts I through XI of Form 1023, plus any required schedules and attachments.

The following organizations must complete additional schedules to Form 1023.

IF your organization is a(n) . . .	THEN you must file Schedule . . .
Church	A
School, College, or University	B
Hospital or Medical Research Organization . .	C
Section 509(a) Supporting Organization	D
Organization Not Filing Form 1023 Within 27 Months of Formation	E
Home for the Elderly or Handicapped and Low-Income Housing	F
Successor to Other Organizations	G
Organization Providing Scholarships, Fellowships, Educational Loans, or Other Educational Grants to Individuals and Private Foundations Requesting Approval of Individual Grant Procedures	H

Assembly of Application Package

To assist us in processing the application, documents should be submitted in the following order.

- User fee enclosed but not attached to the application form.
- Form 1023 Checklist.
- Form 2848, Power of Attorney and Declaration of Representative (if needed).

• Form 8821, Tax Information Authorization (if needed).
• Expedite request (if needed).
• Application (Form 1023, Checklist, and Schedules A through H, as required).
• Organizing document.
• Amendments to organizing document in chronological order.
• Bylaws or other rules of operation and amendments.
• Documentation of nondiscriminatory policy for schools, as required by Schedule B.
• Form 5768, Election/Revocation of Election by an Eligible Section 501(c)(3) Organization To Make Expenditures To Influence Legislation (if filing).
• All other attachments, including explanations, financial data, and printed materials or publications.

Attachments

Use an attachment where there is insufficient space on the form for you to legibly and accurately respond to a question. For any attachments submitted with your Form 1023:
• Use 8½ x 11 inch paper.
• Provide your name and Employer Identification Number (EIN) at the top of each page.
• Identify the Part and line number to which the attachment relates.

Include any court decisions, rulings, opinions, or any other documents that will assist us in processing your Form 1023.

Generally, attachments in the form of tape, recordings or other electronic media are not acceptable unless accompanied by a transcript.

Attachments must be in English.

When to File

If you file Form 1023 within 27 months after the end of the month in which you were legally formed, and we approve the application, the legal date of formation will be the effective date of your exempt status.

If you do not file Form 1023 within 27 months of formation, you may not qualify for exempt status before the date we receive Form 1023. The date considered to be the date we receive Form 1023 is generally the postmark date. For exceptions and special rules, including automatic extensions, see Schedule E of Form 1023.

Where To File

Send the completed Form 1023 application, with all required information, and the applicable user fee to:

Internal Revenue Service
P.O. Box 192
Covington, KY 41012-0192

If you are using express mail or a delivery service, send the completed Form 1023 application, with all required information and user fee to:

Internal Revenue Service
201 West Rivercenter Blvd.
Attn: Extracting Stop 312
Covington, KY 41011

Private Delivery Services

In addition to the United States mail, you can use certain private delivery services designated by the IRS to meet the "timely mailing as timely filing/paying" rule for tax returns and payments. The most recent list of designated private delivery services includes only the following:
• DHL Express (DHL): DHL "Same Day" Service; DHL Next Day 10:30 AM; DHL Next Day 12:00 PM; DHL Next Day 3:00 PM; and DHL 2nd Day Service.
• Federal Express (FedEx): FedEx Priority Overnight, FedEx Standard Overnight, FedEx 2Day, FedEx International Priority, and FedEx International First.
• United Parcel Service (UPS): UPS Next Day Air, UPS Next Day Air Saver, UPS 2nd Day Air, UPS 2nd Day Air A.M., UPS Worldwide Express Plus, and UPS Worldwide Express.

The private delivery service can tell you how to get written proof of the mailing date.

Filing Assistance

For help in completing this form or general questions relating to an exempt organization, call the Exempt Organization Customer Account Services toll free at 1-877-829-5500. You may also access information on our website at www.irs.gov/eo.

Listed below are a number of publications that may be helpful to your organization.

• Publication 517, Social Security and Other Information for Members of the Clergy and Religious Workers
• Publication 526, Charitable Contributions
• Publication 557, Tax-Exempt Status for Your Organization
• Publication 598, Tax on Unrelated Business Income of Exempt Organizations
• Publication 1771, Charitable Contributions Substantiation and Disclosure Requirements
• Publication 1828, Tax Guide for Churches and Religious Organizations
• Publication 3079, Gaming Publication for Tax-Exempt Organizations
• Publication 3833, Disaster Relief: Providing Assistance through Charitable Organizations
• Publication 4220, Applying for 501(c)(3) Tax-Exempt Status
• Publication 4221, Compliance Guide for 501(c)(3) Tax-Exempt Organizations
• Publication 78, Cumulative List of Organizations Described in Section 170(c) of the Internal Revenue Code of 1986 (searchable online at www.irs.gov/eo)

Philanthropic Research, Inc., aka GuideStar, a 501(c)(3) nonprofit organization, maintains information about specific section 501(c)(3) organizations (searchable online at www.guidestar.org).

Signature Requirements

An officer, director, trustee, or other official who is authorized to sign for the organization must sign Form 1023 at the end of Part XI. The signature must be accompanied by the title or authority of the signer and the date. Please clearly print the accompanying information.

Figure 1. Table of Annual Returns

Type of Annual Return	Who Should File
Form 990, Return of Organization Exempt from Income Tax	Section 501(c)(3) public charities
Form 990-EZ, Short Form Return of Organization Exempt from Income Tax	Section 501(c)(3) public charities whose gross receipts during the year were less than $100,000 and total assets at the end of the year were less than $250,000
Schedule A (Form 990 or 990-EZ), Organization Exempt under Section 501(c)(3)	Section 501(c)(3) public charities
Schedule B (Form 990, 990-EZ, or 990-PF), Schedule of Contributors	All section 501(c)(3) organizations
Form 990-PF, Return of Private Foundation	Private foundations, including private operating foundations
Form 990-T, Exempt Organization Business Income Tax Return	Public charities and private foundations that have gross unrelated business income of $1,000 or more

Representation

Form 2848. Attach a completed Form 2848 if you want to authorize a representative to represent you regarding your application. An individual authorized by Form 2848 may not sign the application unless that person is also an officer, director, trustee, or other official who is authorized to sign the application.

CAUTION A centralized authorization file (CAF) number is not required to be listed on Form 2848.

Form 8821. Form 8821 authorizes us to discuss your application with the person you have appointed.

Form 8821 does not authorize your appointee to advocate your position with respect to the Federal tax laws; to execute waivers, consents, or closing agreements; or to otherwise represent you before the IRS. If you want to authorize an individual to represent you, use Form 2848.

After You Submit Form 1023

We will acknowledge receiving your application in writing. You may expect to receive this notice within 21 days of the postmark date of the Form 1023. Read the notice thoroughly because it will provide further information about the processing of your Form 1023.

No additional information needed. If our initial review shows that you qualify, we will send you a letter stating that you are exempt under section 501(c)(3) and whether you are a public charity or a private foundation.

Additional information needed. If the initial review shows that we need additional information or changes, we will assign Form 1023 to a specialist who will call or write you. Generally, we assign applications in the order we receive them. Unless the application is approved for expedited processing, it will be worked in the order received.

If the additional information indicates that you qualify, we will send you a letter stating that you are exempt under section 501(c)(3) and whether you are a public charity or a private foundation. If we conclude that you do not qualify for exemption, we will send you a letter that explains our position and your appeal rights.

Annual Filing Requirements

If an annual information return or tax return is due while the Form 1023 is pending, complete the return, mark "Application Pending" in the heading, and send the return to the address indicated in the instructions.

Information on return filing requirements and exceptions may be found in Publications 557 and 598 and in the instructions to the annual returns listed in Figure 1.

TIP You may also be required to file other returns, such as employment tax returns or benefit plan returns, which are not discussed here.

Public Inspection

Information available for public inspection. If we approve exempt status under section 501(c)(3), the following information will be open for public inspection.

- Your complete Form 1023 and any supporting documents.
- All correspondence between you and the IRS concerning Form 1023, including Form 2848.
- The letter we issue approving your exemption.
- Annual information returns (Forms 990, 990-EZ, or 990-PF).
- Schedule A, included with Forms 990 or 990-EZ.
- Schedule B, included with Forms 990 or 990-EZ, except the names and addresses of contributors and other identifying information about contributors.
- Schedule B, included with Form 990-PF, including names, addresses and other identifying information about contributors.

Information not available for public inspection. The following items will not be open for public inspection.

- Any information relating to a trade secret, patent, style of work, or apparatus that, if released, would adversely affect you. (We must approve withholding this information.)
- Any other information that would adversely affect the national defense. (We must approve withholding this information.)
- User fee check.
- Information only applications from the United States Virgin Islands, Bureau of Internal Revenue (BIR) and related supporting documents.
- Contributors' names and addresses and identifying information about contributors included with Forms 990 or 990-EZ and the Schedule B, filed with these forms.
- Form 990-T, Exempt Organization Business Income Tax Return.

When applying for tax-exempt status, you must clearly identify any information that is not open for public inspection by separately marking it as "NOT SUBJECT TO PUBLIC INSPECTION" and attaching an explanation of why you are asking for the information to be withheld. We will decide whether to withhold the identified information from public inspection.

Making documents available for public inspection. Both you and the IRS must make the information that is subject to disclosure available for public inspection. The public may contact us toll-free at 1-877-829-5500 to request public inspection or copies of the information. The public may also request inspection of the information or a copy of the information directly from you.

An exempt organization may post the documents required to be available for public inspection on its own website. The information return and exemption application materials must be posted exactly as filed with the IRS. Only the information that is not open for public inspection may be deleted.

If an exempt organization posts the documents on its website, it must provide notice of the website address where the documents may be found, but it need not provide copies of the information. However, documents posted on an organization's website must still be made available for public inspection without charge at its main office during regular business hours.

Documents are not considered available for public inspection on a website if the otherwise disclosable information is edited or subject to editing by a third party when posted. To date, the IRS has not approved any third party websites for posting.

See Publication 557 for additional guidance on public inspection.

Foreign Organizations in General

Foreign organizations are those that were created in countries other than the United States, its territories, or its possessions. Foreign organizations may apply for tax-exempt status on income earned in the United States in the same way that domestic organizations apply for exempt status. See, Language and currency requirements.

A foreign organization applying for exempt status should complete all required parts of Form 1023. There are, however, special rules below for some Canadian organizations.

TIP Contributions by U.S. residents to foreign organizations generally are not deductible. Tax treaties between the U.S. and certain foreign countries provide specific limited exceptions.

Annual returns for foreign organizations. A foreign organization that obtains exemption as a public charity must file an information return annually (Form 990 or Form 990-EZ). A foreign organization that is a private foundation must file Form 990-PF annually. However, a foreign organization, other than a private foundation, may be relieved from filing Form 990 or Form 990-EZ in any year in which it has gross receipts from U.S. source income of $25,000 or less and has not conducted significant activity in the United States. See the Instructions for Form 990 and Form 990-EZ, and the Instructions for Form 990-PF for further information. A foreign organization that is subject to unrelated business income tax must file Form 990-T.

Canadian Organizations

Canadian organizations that have received a Notification of Registration from the Canada Customs and Revenue Agency (formerly, Revenue Canada), and whose registrations have not been revoked ("Canadian registered charities"), are automatically recognized as section 501(c)(3) organizations and are not required to file Form 1023. Canadian registered charities are also presumed to be private foundations. A Canadian registered charity may complete certain portions of the Form 1023 in order to be listed as a section 501(c)(3) organization in IRS Publication 78, or to request classification as a public charity, rather than a private foundation. A Canadian registered charity should only complete and submit the following documents.

- Copy of its Notification of Registration.
- Part I of Form 1023.
- Part X of Form 1023 (if requesting public charity classification).
- Signature line in Part XI of Form 1023.
- Form 8833, Treaty-Based Return Position Disclosure Under Section 6114 or 7701(b).
- No user fee is required.

Organizations Created in United States Territories and Possessions

Organizations created in possessions and territories of the United States are generally treated as domestic organizations. These organizations complete all required parts of Form 1023 to apply for exempt status under section 501(c)(3). Special rules, discussed below, apply to some Virgin Islands organizations.

Charitable contributions to organizations created in United States possessions and territories are deductible by the donors if the organization qualifies for exempt status under section 501(c)(3).

Virgin Islands Organizations

The United States Virgin Islands, Bureau of Internal Revenue (BIR) may request an information only letter concerning the exempt status under section 501(c)(3) of an organization formed in the Virgin Islands. The organization itself does not seek U.S. recognition of exempt status. The information only procedure requires the BIR to complete Form 1023 and supporting documents for the organization, but does not require a user fee payment. The application and supporting documents are not open for public inspection (see Public Inspection, for more information).

All other Virgin Islands organizations that seek U.S. recognition of exempt status under section 501(c)(3) must follow the normal application process.

Specific Instructions

Part I. Identification of Applicant

Line 1. Full name of organization. Enter your complete name exactly as it appears in your organizing document, including amendments.

Line 2. c/o Name. If you have an "in care of" name, enter it here.

Line 3. Mailing address. Enter your complete address where all correspondence will be sent. If mail is not delivered to the street address and you have a P.O. Box, show the box number instead of the street address.

For a foreign address, enter the information in the following order: city, province or state, and country. Follow the country's practice in placing the postal code in the address. Do not abbreviate the country name.

Line 4. Employer Identification Number (EIN). Enter the nine-digit EIN assigned to you.

CAUTION Do not submit this application until you have obtained an EIN.

An EIN is your account number with us and is required regardless of whether you have employees. If you need an EIN, you can apply for one by:

1. Calling 1-800-829-4933.
2. Calling 1-215-516-6999, if you are located outside the United States.
3. Mailing Form SS-4 to the IRS.
4. Faxing Form SS-4 to a location provided in the Instructions for Form SS-4.

You can get Form SS-4 online at www.irs.gov, or by calling 1-800-829-3676, to order IRS tax forms and publications.

If you previously applied for an EIN and have not yet received it, or you are unsure whether you have an EIN, please call our toll-free customer account services number, 1-877-829-5500, for assistance.

Line 5. Month the annual accounting period ends (01-12). Enter the month that your annual accounting period ends, using a two-digit number format. For example, if your annual accounting period ends December 31, enter "12." Your annual accounting period is the 12-month period on which your annual financial records are based. Your first tax year could be less than 12 months.

Check your bylaws or other rules of operation for consistency with the annual accounting period entered in line 5.

Line 6a. Primary contact. Your primary contact person may be an officer, director, trustee, or other individual who is permitted to speak with us according to your bylaws or other rules of operation. Your primary contact person may also be an "authorized representative," such as an attorney or certified public accountant for whom you have submitted a completed Form 2848, with the Form 1023.

Line 7. If you wish to be represented by an authorized representative, a completed Form 2848 must be attached to the Form 1023.

Line 8. Provide information about persons, other than your officers, directors, trustees, employees, or authorized representative(s), whom you paid, or promised to pay, to assist you in establishing your organization, developing programs to solicit funds, or otherwise advising you about organizational, financial, or tax matters.

For example, provide information about a paid consultant who advised you about obtaining tax exemption.

Line 9a. Organization's website. Enter your complete website address if you have one. Also, list any websites maintained on your behalf. The information on your website should be consistent with the information in your Form 1023.

Line 9b. Email (optional). Enter your email address to receive educational information from us in the future. Because of security concerns, we cannot send confidential information via email. However, we can use a fax to contact you.

Line 10. Generally, organizations not required to file Form 990 (or Form 990-EZ) include churches, certain church affiliated organizations, certain affiliates of a governmental unit, and organizations with annual gross receipts normally not more than $25,000. For more information, see the Instructions for Form 990 and Form 990-EZ.

TIP Private foundations must file Form 990-PF regardless of the amount of their gross receipts.

Line 11. List the date you were legally created by month, day, and year (for example, 02/01/2004). The date should be consistent with your organizing document described in Part II.

Line 12. For purposes of completing this application, you are formed under the laws of a foreign country if you are not formed under the laws of (1) the United States, its territories and possessions, (2) federally recognized Indian tribal or Alaska Native governments, or (3) the District of Columbia.

Part II. Organizational Structure

Only trusts, unincorporated associations, or corporations (including limited liability companies) are eligible for tax-exempt status under section 501(c)(3) of the Code. Sole proprietorships, partnerships, or loosely affiliated groups of individuals are not eligible.

To qualify for tax-exempt status, you must check "Yes" on either line 1, 2, 3, or

4 and submit a copy of your organizing document.

Line 1. A "corporation" is an entity organized under a Federal or state statute, or a statute of a federally recognized Indian tribal or Alaskan native government. A corporation's organizing document is its "articles of incorporation."

Certification of filing. If formed under state statute, your articles of incorporation must show certification of filing. This means your articles show evidence that on a specific date they were filed with and approved by an appropriate state authority. The document must be an exact copy of what is on file with your state.

If you do not have a copy of your articles of incorporation showing evidence of having been filed and approved by an appropriate state official, you may submit a substitute copy of your articles of incorporation. This substitute copy may be handwritten, typed, printed, or otherwise reproduced. It must be accompanied by a declaration, signed by an officer authorized to sign for you, that it is a complete and correct copy of the articles of incorporation and that it contains all the powers, principles, purposes, functions, and other provisions by which you currently govern yourself.

Line 2. A "limited liability company (LLC)" that files its own exemption application is treated as a corporation rather than a partnership. Instead of articles of incorporation, an LLC's organizing document is its state-approved "articles of organization." If it has adopted an "operating agreement," then this document is also part of its organizing document.

An LLC may only have 501(c)(3) member(s) to qualify for an exemption. An LLC should not file an exemption application if it wants to be treated as a disregarded entity by its tax-exempt member.

Line 3. An "unincorporated association" formed under state law must have at least two members who have signed a written document for a specifically defined purpose.

The articles of organization of an unincorporated association must include the name of your organization, your purpose, the date the document was adopted, and the signatures of at least two individuals. If your copy does not contain the proper signatures and date of adoption, you may submit a written declaration that states your copy is a complete and accurate copy of the signed and dated original. Your declaration should clearly indicate the original date of adoption.

TIP Bylaws may be considered an organizing document only if they are properly structured (includes name, purpose, signatures, and intent to form an organization).

Line 4a. A trust may be formed by a trust agreement or declaration of trust. A trust may also be formed through a will.

If your trust agreement copy does not contain the proper signatures, you may submit a written declaration that states your copy is a complete and accurate copy of the signed and dated original. Your declaration should clearly indicate the original date that it was signed.

Trust created by a will. For trusts created by a will, include a copy of the death certificate or a statement indicating the date of death, and a copy of the relevant portions of the will.

Trust agreement and non-charitable interests. If your trust agreement provided for distributions for non-charitable interests, indicate the date on which these interests expired. If your trust agreement continues to provide for these interests, you will not qualify for tax-exempt status.

Line 4b. Generally, a trust must be funded with property, such as money, real estate, or personal property to be legally created.

Line 5. "Bylaws" are generally the internal rules and regulations of an organization. If you have bylaws, you should submit a current copy.

Bylaws do not need to be signed unless they are the organizing document as described in line 3 above.

Part III. Required Provisions in Your Organizing Document

Line 1. Purpose clause. Your organizing document must limit your purposes to those described in section 501(c)(3). Those purposes are: charitable, religious, educational, scientific, literary, testing for public safety, fostering national or international amateur sports competition, and preventing cruelty to children or animals.

The generally accepted legal definition of "charitable" includes relief of the poor, the distressed, or the underprivileged; advancement of religion; advancement of education or science; erecting or maintaining public buildings, monuments, or works; lessening the burdens of government; lessening neighborhood tensions; eliminating prejudice and discrimination; defending human and civil rights secured by law; and combating community deterioration and juvenile delinquency. Therefore, the phrase "relief of the poor" in your organizing document properly limits your purposes.

If your purposes are limited in some way by referring to section 501(c)(3), your organizing document also properly limits your purposes. For example, the phrase "relief of the elderly within the meaning of section 501(c)(3)" in your organizing document also properly limits your purposes.

However, if the purposes listed in your organizing document are broader than those listed in section 501(c)(3), you should amend your organizing document before applying. A reference to section 501(c)(3) will not ensure that your purposes are limited to those described in section 501(c)(3). All of the language in your organizing document must be considered. The following is an example of an acceptable purpose clause:

> The organization is organized exclusively for charitable, religious, educational, and scientific purposes under section 501(c)(3) of the Internal Revenue Code, or corresponding section of any future federal tax code.

See Publication 557 for further information and examples of how to limit your purposes.

Any amendment to your articles of organization you submit should show evidence that it was signed, dated, and certified as described in Part II.

Line 2a. Dissolution clause. Your organizing document must permanently dedicate your assets for a section 501(c)(3) purpose. This means that if you dissolve your organization in the future, your assets must be distributed for an exempt purpose described in section 501(c)(3), or to the federal government, or to a state or local government for a public purpose.

If your organizing document states that your assets would be distributed to members or private individuals or for any purpose other than those provided in section 501(c)(3), you must amend your organizing document to remove such statements.

If multiple amendments are required, they may be done at the same time. For example, if you are a corporation and are required to amend both your purpose and dissolution clauses, you may file a single amending document with your appropriate government authority.

The following is an example of an acceptable dissolution clause:

> Upon the dissolution of this organization, assets shall be distributed for one or more exempt purposes within the meaning of section 501(c)(3) of the Internal Revenue Code, or corresponding section of any future federal tax code, or shall be distributed to the federal government, or to a state or local government, for a public purpose.

Naming a specific organization to receive your assets upon dissolution will only be acceptable if your articles state that the specific organization must be exempt under section 501(c)(3) at the time your dissolution takes place and your articles provide for an acceptable alternative if the specific organization is not exempt. See Publication 557 for further information and examples of acceptable language for dedication of assets in your organizing document.

Line 2c. Operation of state law. If you are a corporation formed in the following states, then you do not need a specific provision in your articles of incorporation providing for the distribution of assets upon dissolution.

Arkansas	Minnesota
California	Missouri
Louisiana	Ohio
Massachusetts	Oklahoma

If you are a testamentary charitable trust formed in the following states, then you do not need a specific provision in your trust agreement or declaration of trust providing for the distribution of assets upon dissolution.

Alabama	South Dakota
Louisiana	Virginia
Pennsylvania	

If you are a testamentary charitable trust formed in the states listed below and the language of your trust instrument provides for a general intent to benefit charity, then you do not need a specific provision in your trust agreement or declaration of trust providing for the distribution of assets upon dissolution.

Arkansas	Minnesota
California	Mississippi
Colorado	Missouri
Connecticut	Nebraska
Delaware	New Hampshire
District of Columbia	New Jersey
Florida	North Carolina
Georgia	Ohio
Illinois	Oklahoma
Indiana	Oregon
Iowa	Rhode Island
Kansas	Tennessee
Kentucky	Texas
Maine	Vermont
Maryland	Washington
Massachusetts	Wisconsin
Michigan	

Operation of state law is based on Rev. Proc. 82-2, 1982-1 C.B. 367.

Foreign organizations. Foreign organizations may be able to rely upon the applicable laws of their jurisdiction in a similar manner. You must provide a copy of the applicable law with an English translation.

Part IV. Narrative Description of Your Activities

Describe completely and in detail your past, present, and planned activities. Do not refer to or repeat the purposes in your organizing document. You may refer to other parts of the application rather than repeat information provided elsewhere.

For each past, present, or planned activity, include information that answers the following questions.

- What is the activity?
- Who conducts the activity?
- When is the activity conducted?
- Where is the activity conducted (for example: Los Angeles and San Francisco, California)?
- How does the activity further your exempt purposes?
- What percentage of your total time is allocated to the activity?
- How is the activity funded? (This should agree with the financial data in Part IX.)
- List any alternate names under which you operate, including any "aka" (also known as) or "dba" (doing business as) names.

If you have a website, you may attach a paper copy to support your narrative description of activities.

Part V. Compensation and Other Financial Arrangements With Your Officers, Directors, Trustees, Employees, and Independent Contractors

Compensation. For purposes of Part V, compensation includes salary or wages, deferred compensation, retirement benefits, whether in the form of a qualified or non-qualified employee plan (pensions or annuities), fringe benefits (personal vehicle, meals, lodging, personal and family educational benefits, low interest loans, payment of personal travel, entertainment, or other expenses, athletic or country club membership, and personal use of your property), and bonuses.

Example. Assume an organization compensates its director as follows:

Wages	
Director Compensation	$ 2,500
Salary as Chief Executive Officer	40,000
Deferred retirement	2,000
Health insurance policy	5,000
Use of a vehicle	5,000
Total Compensation	$ 54,500

Information in Part V must be consistent with the information provided in Part IX. Financial Data.

Line 1a. For each person listed, state their total annual compensation, or proposed compensation, for all services to the organization, whether as an officer, employee, or other position. Use actual figures, if available. Officers, directors, and trustees may use the organization's address for mailing.

Line 1b. Employees may use the organization's address for mailing. Report total compensation. For employees who are also officers, directors, or trustees, their compensation as employees and for all other services should be reported in line 1a.

Line 1c. "Independent contractors" are persons who are not treated as employees for employment tax purposes. For information on determining if an individual is an employee or an independent contractor, see Publication 15-A, Employer's Supplemental Tax Guide.

Line 2a. Describe family or business relationships between your officers, directors, or trustees. "Related" refers to both family and business relationships.

- "Family relationships" include the individual's spouse, ancestors, children, grandchildren, great grandchildren, siblings (whether by whole or half blood), and the spouses of children, grandchildren, great grandchildren, and siblings.
- "Business relationships" include employment and contractual relationships, and common ownership of a business where any officers, directors, or trustees, individually or together, possess more than a 35% ownership interest in common. "Ownership" means voting power in a corporation, profits interest in a partnership, or beneficial interest in a trust.

Line 2b. Describe family or business relationships between you and any of your officers, directors, or trustees other than their position with you as an officer, director, or trustee.

Line 2c. Describe family or business relationships between your officers, directors, or trustees and your five highest compensated employees or five highest compensated independent contractors who will receive more than $50,000 in taxable or non-taxable compensation per year.

Line 3b. "Common control" means that you and one or more other organizations have (1) a majority of your governing boards or officers appointed or elected by the same organization(s), or (2) a majority of your governing boards or officers consist of the same individuals. Common control also occurs when you and one or more commonly controlled organizations have a majority ownership interest in a corporation, partnership, or trust. See the instructions for line 2a, above, for a definition of ownership.

Line 4. By adopting these recommended compensation-setting practices, such as by resolution of your governing board, you will be establishing procedures aimed at helping to prevent your top officials from receiving excess compensation benefits.

Line 4e. "Similarly situated organizations" means tax-exempt or taxable organizations of a comparable size, purpose, and resources. Adjustments due to geographic area, and other specific conditions are appropriate, but should be documented. The source(s) of comparable compensation data, both taxable and non-taxable, should be documented and copies retained in your permanent records.

Line 4g. "Reasonable compensation" is the amount that would ordinarily be paid for like services by like organizations under like circumstances as of the date the compensation arrangement is made. Establishing and documenting reasonable compensation is important because excessive compensation may result in excise taxes on both the individual and the organization. In addition, this may jeopardize the organization's tax exemption.

Line 5a. A "conflict of interest" arises when a person in a position of authority over an organization, such as a director, officer, or manager, may benefit personally from a decision he or she could make. A Sample Conflict of Interest Policy is included as Appendix A.

Adoption of a conflict of interest policy is not required to obtain tax-exempt status. However, by adopting the sample policy or a similar policy, you will be choosing to put in place procedures that will help you avoid the possibility that those in positions of authority over you may receive an inappropriate benefit.

Line 6a. A "fixed payment" means a payment that is either a set dollar amount or fixed through a specific formula where the amount does not depend on discretion. For example, a base salary of $200,000 that is adjusted annually based on the increase in the Consumer Price Index is a fixed payment.

A "non-fixed payment" means a payment that depends on discretion. For example, a bonus of up to $100,000 that is based on an evaluation of performance by the governing board is a non-fixed payment because the governing body has discretion over whether the bonus is paid and the amount of the bonus.

Line 7a. Do not include purchases of goods and services in your normal course of operations that are available to the general public under similar terms and conditions.

Arm's length. An arm's length standard exists where the parties have an adverse (or opposing) interest. For example, a seller wants to sell his goods at the highest possible price, while a buyer wants to buy at the lowest possible price. These are adverse interests.

In negotiating with a person, an adverse interest is assumed if that person is otherwise unrelated to you in the sense of not being in a position to exercise substantial influence over you or your affairs. If the person is in a position to exercise substantial influence over your affairs, then an arm's length standard requires additional precautions to eliminate the effect of the relationship.

Using a conflict of interest policy, information about comparable transactions between unrelated parties, and reliable methods for evaluating the transaction, are examples of precautions that would help make the negotiation process equivalent to one between unrelated persons.

Fair market value. This is the price at which property or the right to use property would change hands between a willing buyer and a willing seller, neither being under any compulsion to buy, sell, or transfer property or the right to use property, and both having reasonable knowledge of relevant facts.

Line 7b. Do not include sales of goods and services in your normal course of operations that are available to the general public under similar terms and conditions.

Line 9a. Answer "Yes" if any of your officers, directors, or trustees:

- Is an officer, director, or trustee in another organization (other than a section 501(c)(3) organization) that has a lease, contract, loan, or other agreement with you.
- Possess more than a 35% ownership interest in any organization that has a lease, contract, loan, or other agreement with you. For example, you would answer "Yes" if one of your directors were an officer for a section 501(c)(4) organization with whom you had a lease for office space. You would also answer "Yes" if one of your directors owns more than 35% of the voting stock of a corporation to which you made a loan.

Part VI. Your Members and Other Individuals, and Organizations That Receive Benefits From You

Line 1a. Benefits to individuals. Describe any programs where you provide goods, services, or funds to individuals. For example, describe programs by which you provide food to the homeless, employment counseling to senior citizens, or grants to victims of a disaster.

Line 1b. Benefits to organizations. Describe any programs where you provide goods, services, or funds to organizations. For example, programs where you provide equipment, accounting assistance, or grants to other organizations.

Line 2. For programs that are available only for members, include a sample membership application and a schedule of membership dues. Also, describe any different membership levels and the benefits each membership level receives.

Line 3. Describe any business or family relationship between individuals who receive goods, services, or funds through your programs with any officer, director, trustee, or with any of the five-highest compensated employees or independent contractors listed in Part V, lines 1a, 1b, or 1c.

Part VII. Your History

Line 1. You are a "successor" if you have:

- Substantially taken over all of the assets or activities of another organization,
- Been converted or merged from another organization, or
- Installed the same officers, directors, or trustees as another organization that no longer exists and that had purpose(s) similar to your purpose(s).

TIP The predecessor organization may be or may not have been a tax-exempt or non-exempt organization.

Part VIII. Your Specific Activities

Line 1. You participate in a political campaign if you promote or oppose the candidacy of an individual for public office. Your explanation should include representative copies of your political literature, brochures, pamphlets, etc. Candidate debates and nonpartisan voter education are permitted.

TIP Organizations described in section 501(c)(3) are prohibited from supporting or opposing candidates for public office in any political campaign. If you answer "Yes," you are not qualified for tax exemption under section 501(c)(3) and should reconsider whether the filing of application Form 1023 is appropriate for your organization. See Publication 557 for a description of other Internal Revenue Code sections under which you may qualify.

Line 2a. You are attempting to "influence legislation" if you directly contact or urge the public to contact members of a legislative body for the purpose of proposing, supporting, or opposing legislation. You are also attempting to influence legislation if you advocate the adoption or rejection of legislation. If you answer "Yes," your explanation should include the percentage of your total time and total funds spent on such legislative activities. Also, submit representative copies of your legislative literature, brochures, pamphlets, etc.

Organizations described in section 501(c)(3) are prohibited from engaging in a substantial amount of legislative activities. Whether you are engaged in substantial legislative activities depends on all of the facts and circumstances.

Line 2b. By filing Form 5768 your legislative activities will be measured solely by expenditure limits under section 501(h) rather than by whether legislative activity is considered substantial. Form 5768 is included in Package 1023 for your convenience. It describes the types of organizations that are eligible to make an election. For a discussion of the requirements of section 501(h), see Publication 557. If you are an organization that elects to use expenditure limits in influencing legislation:

- Attach a copy of Form 5768 that has already been separately filed with us, or
- Provide a completed Form 5768 with your exemption application.

Churches and private foundations are not eligible to make this election.

Line 3a. For purposes of this application, "bingo" is a game of chance played with cards that are generally printed with 5 rows of 5 squares each on which participants place markers to form a preselected pattern to win the game. Other gaming activities include pull-tabs, raffles, keno, split-the-pot, and other games of chance.

Describe these activities, including how often your bingo or other gaming activities are conducted, where they are conducted, and who conducts them. Also describe whether your workers are compensated. If workers are compensated, describe who receives compensation and how the amount is determined.

Revenue associated with these activities means gross revenue amounts.

Expenses associated with these activities means direct and indirect expenses. The dollar value of prizes should be included in expenses.

Gaming may be subject to unrelated business income tax. See Publication 3079 for further information about gaming.

Line 3c. Local jurisdictions include cities, counties, towns, municipalities, and similar government jurisdictions within a state. A local jurisdiction also includes an Indian Reservation.

Line 4a. "Fundraising" includes efforts to raise funds through appeals for financial support. Fundraising may be conducted by your employees or volunteers, through an agent, or through an independent contractor. If you answer "Yes," check all the boxes that apply and complete lines 4b through 4e.

Line 4d. Local jurisdictions include cities, counties, towns, municipalities, and similar government jurisdictions within a state. A local jurisdiction also includes an Indian Reservation.

Line 4e. This line is intended to obtain information from you regarding donor-advised funds that you may maintain. A "donor-advised fund" is maintained if you establish separate accounts for a donor whereby the donor may exercise a right to make a recommendation on either uses of the account, such as providing advice about how to invest, or distributions from the account, such as providing advice about how to make expenditures.

Line 5. You are "affiliated" with a governmental unit if you were created by, controlled by, or closely related to a governmental unit. Identify each governmental unit and describe your relationship with it. Include details of any financial reports or audits required by the governmental unit. Also, describe any power or authority given to you by the governmental unit.

For purposes of this question, a "governmental unit" includes a State, a possession of the United States, or any political subdivision of a State or a possession of the United States, or the United States, or the District of Columbia.

A governmental unit would generally not qualify for exemption under section 501(c)(3). Also, if you can exercise certain sovereign powers, such as the power to tax or police powers, you would generally not qualify for exemption under section 501(c)(3).

Line 6a. "Economic development" organizations are generally formed to combat community deterioration by assisting businesses located in a particular geographic area whose economy is economically depressed or deteriorating. Their varieties of activities include grants, loans, provision of information and expertise, or creation of industrial parks. Economic development organizations may also be formed to eliminate prejudice and discrimination or lessen the burdens of government through involvement with business development.

If your exempt purpose is to combat community deterioration, describe whether the area or areas in which you will operate have been declared blighted or economically depressed by a government finding. If the area has not been declared blighted or economically depressed, a more suitable exemption may be under sections 501(c)(4) or 501(c)(6). See Publication 557 for more information.

If your exempt purpose is to eliminate prejudice and discrimination, describe how your activities further this purpose.

If your exempt purpose is to lessen the burdens of government, describe whether the government has recognized your activities as those for which it would otherwise be responsible, and any involvement you have with governmental entities that demonstrates that you are actually lessening governmental burdens.

Line 7a. "Develop" means the planning, financing, construction, or provision of similar services involved in the acquisition of real property, such as land or a building. For example, you should provide information regarding the services of a consultant who puts together an arrangement for you to acquire a nursing home through the issuance of tax-exempt bonds.

Line 7b. "Manage" means to direct or administer. For example, you would provide information about an organization hired to administer a museum gift shop. See the instructions for Part V, line 2a, for a description of the term business or family relationships.

Line 7c. See the instructions for Part V, line 2a, for a description of the term business or family relationships. See the instructions for Part V, line 7a, for a description of the term arm's length.

Line 8. A "joint venture" is a legal agreement in which the persons jointly undertake a transaction for mutual profit. Generally, each person contributes assets and shares risks. Like a partnership, joint ventures can involve any type of business transaction and the persons involved can be individuals, groups of individuals, companies, or corporations.

Line 9a. Childcare services provide care for children away from their homes. An organization providing childcare services may qualify for tax-exempt status as either a:

- School under IRC 170(b)(1)(A)(ii).
- Childcare organization under IRC 501(k).

Refer to the instructions for Part VII, line 19, to determine if you qualify as a school.

A childcare organization qualifies under IRC 501(k) if it provides care for children away from their homes; substantially all of the childcare enables individuals to be gainfully employed; and the services provided by the organization are available to the general public.

Line 9b. "Gainfully employed" includes enabling individuals to work or to seek work.

Line 9c. Section 501(k) states that to qualify as a childcare organization, substantially all of the care you provide should be to permit individuals to be gainfully employed. If less than 85% of your services are for children of working parents or caretakers:

- Describe the percentage of the children for whom you provide services to permit parents or caretakers to work, and
- Describe any efforts you are taking to increase the percentage of the children for whom you provide services to permit parents or caretakers to work.

Line 9d. Describe any eligibility requirements, such as employment with a particular employer.

Line 10. " Intellectual property" includes:

- Patents (for inventions).
- Copyrights (for literary and artistic works such as novels, poems, plays, films, musical works, drawings, paintings, photographs, sculptures, architectural designs, performances, recordings, film, and radio or television programs).
- Trade names, trade marks, and service marks (for symbols, names, images, and designs).
- Formulas, know-how, and trade secrets.

Line 12a. A "foreign country" is a country other than the United States, its territories and possessions, and the District of Columbia.

Line 13d. A "relationship" between you and the recipient organization includes the following situations:

• You control the recipient organization or it controls you through common officers, directors, or trustees, or through authority to approve budgets or expenditures.
• You and the recipient organization were created at approximately the same time and by the same persons.
• You and the recipient organization operate in a coordinated manner with respect to facilities, programs, employees, or other activities.
• Persons who exercise substantial influence over you also exercise substantial influence over the other organization.

Line 14a. Answer "Yes" if you make grants, loans, or other distributions, such as goods, to a foreign organization. For purposes of completing this application, a domestic organization is one that is formed under the laws of the United States, its territories and possessions, federally recognized Indian Tribal and Alaska Native governments (including political subdivisions), or the District of Columbia. A "foreign organization" is one that is not a domestic organization.

A list of federally recognized Indian tribes is provided in Rev. Proc. 2002-64, 2002-2 C.B. 717. A list of entities that are treated as political subdivisions of Indian tribal governments is provided in Rev. Proc. 86-17, 1986-1 C.B. 550 and Rev. Proc. 84-36, 1984-1 C.B. 510.

Line 15. A "close connection" between you and another organization includes the following situations:
• You control the organization or it controls you through common officers, directors, or trustees, or through authority to approve budgets or expenditures.
• You and the organization were created at approximately the same time and by the same persons.
For example, you were formed within months of the time that a social welfare organization and a political action committee were established by the same persons who were instrumental in your formation.
• You and the organization operate in a coordinated manner with respect to facilities, programs, employees, or other activities.
For example, you share rental expenses for office space and employees with a for-profit corporation.
• Persons who exercise substantial influence over you also exercise substantial influence over the other organization and (1) you either conduct activities in common or (2) have a financial relationship.
For example, a voting member of your governing body is also a voting member of the governing body of a business league with which you intend to cooperate in planning an advertising campaign that will inform the public about the benefits of a particular program.
For example, a voting member of your governing body is also a voting member of the governing body of a business league that has made a loan to you.

Line 16. A "cooperative hospital service organization" described in section 501(e) is organized and operated on a cooperative basis to provide its section 501(c)(3) hospital members one or more of the following activities.
• Data processing.
• Purchasing (including purchasing insurance on a group basis).
• Warehousing.
• Billing and collection (including purchasing patron accounts receivable on a recourse basis).
• Food.
• Clinical.
• Industrial engineering.
• Laboratory.
• Printing.
• Communications.
• Record center.
• Personnel (including selecting, testing, training, and educating personnel) services.

A cooperative hospital service organization must also meet certain other requirements specified in section 501(e). For additional information, see Publication 557.

Line 17. A cooperative service organization of operating educational organizations described in section 501(f) is organized and operated to provide investment services to its members. Those members must be organizations described in section 170(b)(1)(A)(ii) or (iv), and either tax exempt under section 501(a) or whose income is excluded from taxation under section 115(a).

See Publication 557 for additional information.

Line 18. A "charitable risk pool" described in section 501(n) is organized and operated to pool insurable risks of its section 501(c)(3) members (other than risks related to medical malpractice). A section 501(n) organization must be organized under state law provisions authorizing risk pooling arrangements for charitable organizations and also meet certain other requirements provided by section 501(n).

See Publication 557 for additional information.

Line 19. "A school" is an educational organization whose primary function is the presentation of formal instruction and which normally maintains a regular faculty and curriculum and normally has a regularly enrolled body of pupils or students in attendance at the place where its educational activities are regularly carried on. A school may include a:
• Primary, secondary, preparatory, or high school.
• College or university.
• Trade or technical school.
• Nursery or pre-school.
• School that you operate as an activity, such as a school that is operated as an activity of a museum, historical society, or church.

If you are a nursery or pre-school that meets the description of a school, you would answer "Yes" to line 19 and complete Schedule B. You would also answer "No" to Part VIII, line 9a.

If you are a nursery or pre-school that does not meet the description of a school, you would answer "No" to line 19. You would answer "Yes" to Part VIII, line 9a, if you are applying for exemption as a childcare organization.

See Publication 557 for additional information.

Line 20. "Hospital or medical care" includes the treatment of any physical or mental disability or condition, whether as an inpatient or outpatient. A hospital includes:
• Hospitals and rehabilitation institutions, outpatient clinics, or community mental health or drug treatment centers if the principal purpose or function is the providing of medical or hospital care or medical education or research.
• Medical research organizations, if the principal purpose or function is the continuous active conduct of medical research in conjunction with a hospital.

See Publication 557 for additional information.

Line 21. "Low-income housing" refers to rental or ownership housing provided to persons based on financial need. "Elderly housing" refers to rental or ownership housing provided to persons based on age, including retirement, assisted-living, independent living, continuous care, and life care arrangements. "Handicapped housing" refers to rental or ownership housing provided to persons based on physical or mental disabilities, including nursing homes.

If you are a skilled nursing facility, you should also complete Schedule C.

Line 22. Answer "Yes" if you pay monies to an individual as a scholarship, fellowship, or educational loan, for travel, study, or other similar purposes. Also answer "Yes" if you pay such amounts on behalf of an individual to a school or a tuition or educational savings program.

Travel, study, or other similar purposes include payments made to enhance a literary, artistic, musical, scientific, teaching or other similar capacity, skill, or talent of the individual recipient. For example amounts paid to:
• Vocational high school students to be used to purchase basic tools.
• Teachers to induce them to teach in an economically depressed, public school system.
• A scientific researcher to underwrite that individual's research project.

Educational grants do not include amounts you pay to an individual as compensation, such as payments made to a consultant for personal services or to produce a report for you.

Educational grants do not include amounts paid to another organization that distributes your funds as a scholarship to an individual if you have no role in the selection process.

If you are a "private foundation" as described in Part X, you can request advance approval of your grant-making procedures by completing Schedule H and avoid the possible imposition of excise taxes under section 4945.

Part IX. Financial Data

A. Statement of Revenues and Expenses

Existed 4 years or more. If you have been in existence for 4 or more years, complete the A. Statement of Revenues and Expenses for your most recently completed year and each of the three years immediately before it for a total of four years of financial information. Place financial information for your most recently completed year in the column marked Current tax year.

CAUTION: We may request financial information for more than four years if necessary.

Existed more than one year, less than 4 years. If you have been in existence for more than 1 year and less than 4 years, provide your actual income and expenses for each completed year you have existed and projections of your likely income and expenses based on a reasonable and good faith estimate of your future finances for your current year and each year you have not existed for a total of 3 years of financial information. Place financial information for the year you are filing this application in the column marked Current tax year.

Existed less than 1 year. If you have existed for less than 1 year, you must provide projections of your likely income and expenses for your current year and projections of your likely income and expenses for the next 2 years based on a reasonable and good faith estimate of your future finances. Place financial information for the year you are filing this application in the column marked Current tax year.

Preparing the statement. Prepare the statements using the method of accounting you use in keeping your books and records. If you use a method other than the cash receipts and disbursements method, attach a statement explaining the method used. For example, state whether you used the accrual method of accounting to prepare the financial statements included with this application.

Prepare the statements using the accounting period entered on Part I, line 5. Financial information should reflect projected activities reported elsewhere in this application.

Line 1. Include funds or other items of value that you receive as gifts, grants, or contributions. For example, if one of your activities is a food drive, the value of the donated food must be included on this line. Also include on this line payments a governmental unit makes to enable you to both:

- Accomplish your exempt purpose(s), and
- Provide a service or facility directly to the general public.

See the instructions to line 9 if you are uncertain whether revenue should be included as a grant in line 1 or as gross receipts in line 9. Unusual grants are not included on this line, but are included on line 12.

Examples

1. A city pays the symphony orchestra to provide free music programs in the public schools. The programs are open to the public. This income received from a governmental unit accomplishes the orchestra's exempt purpose and directly provides a service to the general public. The income is a grant to the symphony orchestra that should be listed on line 1.

2. The symphony orchestra sells tickets to the public for its fall season. Such income is gross receipts received from the general public in performance of the orchestra's exempt function and should be listed on line 9.

3. The public school system pays the symphony orchestra to create several musical pieces suitable for the school system's elementary music curriculum. This payment by a governmental unit for the music compositions is primarily for its (the school system's) own use, not for the direct benefit of the public. Therefore, this income is gross receipts received from a governmental unit in performance of the orchestra's exempt function that should be listed on line 9.

Line 2. Include amounts received from members to provide support to the organization. Do not include payments from members or on behalf of members to purchase admissions, merchandise, services, or use of facilities.

Line 3. Include gross income from dividends, interest, payments received on securities, loans, rents, and royalties that are held for investment purposes.

Line 4. Net income from unrelated business activities generally includes income from any trade or business activity that is regularly carried on, not conducted with substantially all (at least 85%) volunteer labor, and not related to your exempt purposes. (This amount can be taken from Form 990-T, if filed.)

Report on line 9 income from activities that are not related to the accomplishment of your exempt purposes, but are not considered unrelated business activities. For example, income from the sale of merchandise by volunteers that is not treated as an unrelated trade or business is reported on line 9.

See Publication 598 for additional information regarding unrelated business income.

Line 5. Include the amount collected by any local tax authority from the public on your behalf.

Line 6. To determine the value of services or facilities furnished by a governmental unit, use the fair market value of the services or facilities furnished to you. Do not include the value of services or facilities generally provided to the public without charge.

Line 7. Enter the total income from all sources not reported on lines 1 through 6, or lines 9, 11, and 13. Submit an itemized list showing each type and amount of income included on this line. Also, briefly describe each type of income.

Line 8. Add lines 1 through 7 and enter the amount.

Line 9. "Gross receipts" is income from activities that you conduct to further your exempt purposes (excluding amounts listed on other lines). It includes payments by a governmental unit that may be called a "grant," but that is actually payment for a service or facility for the use of the government payer, rather than for the direct benefit of the public.

Figure 2. Part IX–A. Statement of Revenues and Expenses Line 11. Net Gain or (Loss)

	Categories		
	(A) Real Estate	(B) Securities	(C) Other
1. Gross sales price of assets (other than inventory) by category.			
2. **Less:** Cost or other basis and sales expenses.			
3. Gain or (loss). Subtract line 2 from line 1.			
4. Net gain or (loss) – Add line 3 of columns (A), (B), and (C). Enter here and on Form 1023, Part IX - A. Statement of Revenues and Expenses, line 11.			

Example: The state government gives a conservation group a grant to study the consequences to an ecologically significant woodland area of a new sewage treatment plan. Although the payment is called a grant, it is actually gross receipts that should be included on line 9. The payment is by a governmental unit (state) for a study for its own use, not for the direct benefit of the general public. The study could have been done by a for-profit consulting company rather than by the tax-exempt conservation group.

Submit an itemized list of payments by any governmental units showing:

- Payer (governmental unit or bureau).
- Purpose of payment.
- Amount.

Include as gross receipts the income from activity conducted:

- Intermittently (not regularly carried on), such as an occasional auction.
- With substantially all (at least 85%) volunteer labor, such as a car wash.
- For the convenience of members, students, patients, officers, or employees, such as a parking lot for a school's students and employees.
- With substantially all contributed merchandise, such as a thrift store.

See Publication 598 for additional information regarding income that is not from an unrelated trade or business.

Line 10. Add lines 8 and 9 and enter the amount.

Line 11. Attach a schedule with total amounts entered (rather than each individual transaction) for each category using the format in Figure 2.

Line 12. "Unusual grants" generally are substantial contributions and bequests from disinterested persons that by their size adversely affect classification as a public charity. They are unusual, unexpected, and received from an unrelated party.

You must fully describe your unusual grants in Part X, line 7. For additional information about unusual grants and a description of public charity classification see Publication 557.

Line 13. Add lines 10 through 12 and enter the amount.

Line 14. Fundraising expenses include the total expenses incurred by you for soliciting gifts, grants, and contributions included on line 1. Where you allocate a portion of your other expenses to fundraising, submit an itemized list describing the amounts allocated. Include fees paid to professional fundraisers for soliciting gifts, grants, and contributions.

Line 15. If distributions have been made, submit an itemized list showing the name of each recipient, a brief description of the purposes or conditions of payment, and the amount paid.

Colleges, universities, and other educational institutions and agencies subject to the Family Educational Rights and Privacy Act (20 U.S.C. 1232g) need not list the names of individuals who were provided scholarships or other financial assistance where such disclosure would violate the privacy provisions of the law. Instead, such organizations should group each type of financial aid provided, indicate the number of individuals who received the aid, and specify the aggregate dollar amount.

Line 16. If payments have been made, submit an itemized list showing the name of each recipient, a brief description of the purposes or condition of payment, and amount paid. Do not include any amounts on line 15.

Line 17. Enter the total amount of compensation. Be consistent with information provided in Part V, lines 1a, 1b, and 1c.

Line 18. Enter the total amount of employees' salaries and wages not reported on line 17, above.

Line 19. Enter the total interest expense for the year, excluding mortgage interest treated as an occupancy expense on line 20.

Line 20. Enter the amount paid for the use of office space or other facilities, heat, light, power, and other utilities, outside janitorial services, mortgage interest, real estate taxes, and similar expenses.

Line 21. If you record depreciation, depletion, and similar expenses, enter the total amount.

Line 22. Professional fees are those charged by individuals and entities that are not your employees. They include fees for professional fundraisers (other than fees listed on line 14, above), accounting services, legal counsel, consulting services, contract management, or any independent contractors.

Line 23. Submit an itemized list showing the type and amount of each significant expense for which a separate line is not provided.

Line 24. Add lines 14 through 23 and enter the amount on line 24.

B. Balance Sheet

Complete the following for your most recently completed tax year. If you have not completed a full tax year, use the most current information available. Be sure to enter the year-end date for the information provided and not the date the form is prepared.

Line 1. Enter the total cash in checking and savings accounts, temporary cash investments (money market funds, CDs, treasury bills, or other obligations that mature in less than one year), and petty cash funds.

Line 2. Enter the total accounts receivable that arose from the sale of goods and/or performance of services, less any reserve for bad debt.

Line 3. Enter the amount of materials, goods, and supplies you purchased or manufactured and held to be sold or used in some future period.

Line 4. Enter the total amount of bonds or notes that you issued that will be repaid to you. Submit an itemized list that shows the name of each borrower, a brief description of the obligation, the rate of return, the due date, and the amount due.

Line 5. Enter the total fair market value (FMV) of corporate stocks you hold. Submit an itemized list of your corporate stock holdings. For stock of closely held corporations, the statement should show the name of the corporation, a brief summary of the corporation's capital structure, the number of shares held, and their value as carried on your books. If such valuation does not reflect current fair market value, also include fair market value.

For stock traded on an organized exchange or in substantial quantities over the counter, the statement should show the name of the corporation, a description of the stock and the principal exchange on which it is traded, the number of shares held, and their value as carried on your books and their fair market value.

Line 6. Enter the total amount of loans (personal and mortgage loans) receivable. Submit an itemized list that shows each borrower's name, purpose of loan, repayment terms, interest rate, and original amount of loan. Report each loan separately, even if more than one loan was made to the same person.

Line 7. Enter the total book value of other investments. Include the total book value of government securities (federal, state, or municipal), and buildings and equipment held for investment purposes. Submit an itemized list identifying and reporting the book value of each building/item of equipment held for investment purposes.

Line 8. Enter the total book value of buildings and equipment not held for investment. This includes facilities you own and equipment you use in conducting your exempt activities. Submit an itemized list of these assets held at the end of the current tax year/period, including the cost or other basis.

Line 9. Enter the total book value of land not held for investment.

Line 10. Enter the total book value of any other category of assets not reported on lines 1 through 9. For example, you would include patents, copyrights, or other intangible assets. Submit an itemized list of each asset.

Line 11. Add lines 1 through 10 and enter the amount.

Line 12. Enter the total amount of accounts payable to suppliers and others, such as salaries payable, accrued payroll taxes, and interest payable.

Line 13. Enter the total unpaid portion of grants and contributions you have committed to pay to other organizations or individuals.

Line 14. Enter the total of mortgages and other notes payable outstanding at the end of the current tax year/period. Submit an itemized list that shows each note separately, including the lender's name, purpose of loan, repayment terms, interest rate, and original amount.

Line 15. Enter the total amount of any other liabilities not reported on lines 12 through 14. Submit an itemized list of these liabilities, including the amounts owed.

Line 16. Add lines 12 through 15 and enter the amount.

Line 17. Under fund accounting, an organization segregates its assets, liabilities, and net assets into separate funds according to restrictions on the use of certain assets. Each fund is like a separate entity in that it has a self-balancing set of accounts showing assets, liabilities, equity (fund balance), income, and expenses. If you do not use fund accounting, report only the "net assets" account balances, which include capital stock, paid-in capital, retained earnings or accumulated income, and endowment funds.

Line 18. Add lines 16 and 17 and enter the amount.

Line 19. If you answer "Yes," describe the change and explain what caused it.

Part X. Public Charity Status

Line 1a. Organizations that are exempt under section 501(c)(3) are private foundations unless they are:

- Churches, schools, hospitals, governmental units, entities that undertake testing for public safety; organizations that have broad financial support from the general public; or
- Organizations that support one or more other organization(s) that are themselves classified as public charities.

Section 501(c)(3) organizations excepted from private foundation status are public charities. See the instructions for Part X, lines 5a through 5i for a more detailed description of public charities.

Unless you meet one of the exceptions above, you are a private foundation and must answer, "Yes," on line 1a.

Line 1b. Section 508(e) provides that a private foundation is not tax exempt unless its organizing document contains specific provisions. These specific provisions require that you operate to avoid liability for excise taxes under sections 4941(d), 4942, 4943(c), 4944, and 4945(d). You can also meet these provisions by reliance on state law.

See Publication 557, Chapter 3, Section 501(c)(3) Organizations: Private Foundations, for samples of provisions that will meet section 508(e). Also, see Appendix B. for a list of states that have enacted statutory provisions that satisfy the requirements of section 508(e), subject to notations. Appendix B. is based on Revenue Ruling 75-38, 1975-1 C.B. 161.

Line 2. Some private foundations are private operating foundations. These are types of private foundations that lack general public support, but make qualifying distributions directly for the active conduct of their educational, charitable, and religious purposes. "Directly for the active conduct" means that the distributions are used by the foundation itself to carry out the programs for which it is organized and operated. Grants made to assist other organizations or individuals are normally considered indirect.

For additional information about private operating foundations, log on to www.irs.gov/charities/foundations/article/0,,id=136358,00.html.

Line 3. If you have existed for one year or more, you must provide financial information that demonstrates you meet the requirements to be classified as a private operating foundation.

Line 4. If you have existed for less than one year, you must ordinarily provide an affidavit or opinion of counsel that sets forth facts concerning your operations and projected support to demonstrate that you are likely to satisfy the requirements to be classified as a private operating foundation. If you have not provided an affidavit or opinion of counsel, you may provide a narrative statement that provides sufficient information to demonstrate that you are likely to satisfy the requirements to be classified as a private operating foundation.

Line 5a. Check this box if your primary purpose is operating a church or a convention or association of churches. The term "church" includes mosques, temples, synagogues, etc. If you select this box, complete and submit Schedule A.

Line 5b. Check this box if your primary purpose is operating a school. If you select this box, complete and submit Schedule B.

If you operate a school but it is not your primary purpose, do not check this box. However, you must still complete and submit Schedule B.

Be sure your response is consistent with Part VIII, line 19.

Line 5c. Check this box if your primary purpose is providing medical or hospital care, or medical education or research (performed in association with a hospital). If you select this box, complete and submit Schedule C.

A hospital includes a rehabilitation institution, outpatient clinic, community mental health clinic, drug treatment center, or skilled nursing facility.

A hospital does not include convalescent homes, homes for children or the aged, or institutions whose principal purpose or function is to train handicapped individuals to pursue some vocation.

Cooperative hospital service organizations described in section 501(e) should also check this box, but do not complete Schedule C.

Line 5d. Check this box if you are organized and operated to support organizations described in lines 5a through 5c, 5f, 5g, or 5h, or an organization that is tax exempt under section 501(c)(4), (5), or (6). If you select this box, complete and submit Schedule D.

The organization(s) you support should have a significant influence over your operations.

Line 5e. Check this box if your primary purpose is to test products to determine their acceptability for use by the general public.

Contributions to organizations of this type are not deductible under section 170(c). Also, organizations that primarily test for specific manufacturers do not qualify for exemption under section 501(c)(3).

Line 5f. Check this box if you are organized and operated exclusively to benefit a college or university owned or operated by a governmental unit. You must also normally receive a substantial part of your support from a governmental unit or from contributions from the general public.

Organizations that qualify under this category would generally also qualify under section 509(a)(3), line 5d, which would be an easier public charity status to maintain.

Line 5g. Check this box if you normally receive a substantial part of your support from grants from governmental units or from contributions from the general public, or a combination of these sources. Typically, a substantial part of your income would be shown on Part IX-A. Statement of Revenues and Expenses, lines 1 and 2.

CAUTION If you select this public charity status, you must request either an advance ruling or a definitive ruling by completing Part X. line 6.

Under this public charity status, you must meet the one-third public support test or the 10% facts and circumstances test.

Public support test. An organization must receive either (1) at least one-third of its total support from governmental agencies, contributions from the general public, and contributions or grants from other public charities, or (2) at least 10% of its total support from governmental agencies, contributions from the general public, and contributions or grants from other public charities and also satisfy a facts and circumstances test.

Facts and circumstances test. Facts and circumstances include (1) the amount of support you received from the general public, governmental units, or public charities, (2) whether you have a continuous and bona fide program for solicitation of funds from the general public, governmental units, or public charities, and (3) all other facts and circumstances, including the public nature of your governing board, the extent to which your facilities or programs are publicly available, the extent to which your dues encourage membership, and whether your activities are likely to appeal to persons having a broad common interest or purpose. For additional information about the 10% facts and circumstances test, see Publication 557 and Treas. Regs. section 1.170A-9(e)(3).

Line 5h. Check this box if you normally receive more than one-third of your support from contributions, membership fees, and gross receipts from activities related to your exempt functions, or a combination of these sources, and not more than one-third of your support from gross investment income and net unrelated business income. Typically, a substantial part of your income would be shown on Part IX-A. Statement of Revenues and Expenses, lines 1, 2, and 9.

Under this public charity status, you must meet both the "one-third public support test" and the "not-more-than-one-third investment income and net unrelated business income test". Before checking this box, consider the types of income you listed on Part IX-A. Statement of Revenues and Expenses, lines 1 through 13. If you select this public charity status, you must request either an advance ruling or a definitive ruling by completing Part X, line 6. See Publication 557 for additional information about these tests.

Line 5i. Check this box if you are unsure whether you are better described in box 5g or 5h. By checking this box, you agree to let us choose the best public charity status for you.

Request For Advance Ruling Or Definitive Ruling

If you checked the box for line 5g, 5h, or 5i, you must check either line 6a or 6b. Your request for an "advance ruling" or a "definitive ruling" depends on the following factors:

- The date you were formed or other date that your exemption would be effective;
- Whether you have completed at least one tax year (consisting of at least 8 full months) from the date you were formed or other date that your exemption would be effective; and
- The amount and type of income you have received.

Line 6a. Request for Advance Ruling. By checking the box on line 6a, you are requesting an advance ruling for your public charity status. The advance ruling gives you a 5-year period in which you can get the financial support needed to meet one of the public support tests described in line 5g or 5h. Generally, the financial information for the 5-year period is submitted at the end of your advance ruling period and a final determination is made as to whether you are a public charity or a private foundation.

When your advance ruling period ends in 5 years, we will ask that you provide updated information about your public support by completing Form 8734.

Statute extension. To receive an advance ruling, you must agree to extend the statute of limitations for any of the 5 tax years in the advance ruling period. This agreement allows us additional time to assess federal taxes under section 4940 if you do not qualify as a public charity for any of the 5 tax years in the advance ruling period. You are not required to agree to the extension requested. However, in this situation, we will not be able to issue an advance ruling. If you agree to the extension, the statute will extend 8 years, 4 months, and 15 days beyond the end of your first tax year. By signing the consent, you are agreeing to the statute extension. If, at the end of your 5-year advance ruling period, we determine that you do not meet the public support tests and you are a private foundation, we will assess the tax under section 4940 for that 5-year period.

If you requested an advance ruling, we will return a copy of Part X of your application with your signed consent, also signed by an IRS official. Keep this signed document in your permanent records.

First tax year not completed. If you have not yet completed your first tax year consisting of at least 8 full months, you must check the box for line 6a to request an advance ruling. For example, if you were formed on May 15, 2003, with an accounting period that ends December 31, and you submitted your application on August 15, 2004, you must request an advance ruling since your first tax year consisted of only 7½ months and you have not completed your second tax year.

Completed first tax year. If you have completed your first tax year consisting of at least 8 full months but cannot currently meet one of the required public charity supports tests, you may still wish to request an advance ruling. This request should only be made if you reasonably expect to meet the required public charity support tests within the 5-year advance ruling period.

Completed more than 5 tax years. If you have completed more than 5 tax years from the date your exemption would be effective, do not request an advance ruling.

Line 6b. Request for Definitive Ruling. By checking line 6b, you are requesting a definitive ruling for your public charity status. The definitive ruling is given to you when you apply if you have existed at least one tax year of 8 months or more, and meet one of the public support tests described in these instructions and Publication 557.

A definitive ruling must be based on your public support computed on the cash method of accounting. Therefore, if you use the accrual method of accounting, please use a worksheet to convert your revenue accounts from the accrual to the cash basis. Such a worksheet is provided in Instructions for Schedule A (Form 990 or 990-EZ), Part IV-A. Support Schedule.

If you have completed your first tax year consisting of at least 8 full months and can meet one of the required public charity support tests, you should check the box for line 6b.

To show that you meet one of the required public charity support tests, complete lines 6b(i) and/or 6b(ii).

Line 6b(i)(a). From Part IX-A. Statement of Revenues and Expenses, add the line 8 amounts from completed tax years only. Multiply the total by 2% (0.02) and enter the amount in the space provided.

Line 6b(ii)(b). The required list for this line should include the name of and amounts paid by each individual or organization included on line 9, Part IX-A. Statement of Revenues and Expenses, that were greater than the larger of 1% of line 10, of the Part IX-A. Statement of Revenues and Expenses or $5,000 for any completed tax year. Your list for each payer must show a year-by-year breakdown of the amounts reported for completed tax years on Part IX-A. Statement of Revenues and Expenses, line 9.

Do not include disqualified persons in this list. Disqualified persons should be listed in line 6b(ii)(a).

If you did not receive such payments, check the box for this line.

For purposes of this application, a "disqualified person" is any individual or organization that is:

1. A "substantial contributor" to you (defined below).
2. An officer, director, trustee, or any other individual who has similar powers or responsibilities.
3. An individual who owns more than 20% of the total combined voting power of a corporation that is a substantial contributor.
4. An individual who owns more than 20% of the profits interest of a partnership that is a substantial contributor.
5. An individual who owns more than 20% of the beneficial interest of a trust or estate that is a substantial contributor.
6. A member of the family of any individual described in 1, 2, 3, 4, or 5 above.
7. A corporation in which any individuals described in 1, 2, 3, 4, 5, or 6 above, hold more than 35% of the total combined voting power.
8. A trust or estate in which any individuals described in 1, 2, 3, 4, 5, or 6 above, hold more than 35% of the beneficial interests.
9. A partnership in which any individuals described in 1, 2, 3, 4, 5, or 6

above, hold more than 35% of the profits interest.

Substantial contributor. A "substantial contributor" is any individual or organization that gave more than $5,000 to you from the date you were formed or other date that your exemption would be effective, to the end of the year in which the contributions were received. This total amount contributed must also be more than 2% of all the contributions you received. A creator of a trust is treated as a substantial contributor regardless of the amount contributed.

For more information regarding substantial contributors, log on to the IRS website at www.irs.gov/charities/foundations/article/0,,id=136935,00.html.

Family members. A "member of the family" includes the spouse, ancestors, children, grandchildren, great grandchildren, and their spouses.

For additional information concerning members of the family, go to www.irs.gov/charities/foundations/article/0,,id=136955,00.html.

Further information about disqualified persons, can be obtained at www.irs.gov/charities/foundations/article/0,,id=136927,00.html.

Line 7. "Unusual grants" generally are substantial contributions and bequests from disinterested persons that by reason of their size adversely affect classification as a public charity. They are unusual, unexpected, and received from an unrelated party. If you answer "Yes" to line 7, submit a statement for each grant. The statement should include the name of the contributor, the date and amount of the grant, a brief description of the grant, and an explanation of why it is unusual. You should include details of any additional funds you expect to receive from the contributors listed. If they qualify for unusual grant treatment, these amounts should be reported on Part IX-A. Statement of Revenues and Expenses, line 12.

See Publication 557 for additional information about unusual grants.

Part XI. User Fee Information

CAUTION Your application will not be processed without payment of the proper user fee.

Your user fee may be paid by a personal or certified check, bank check, or cashier's check. Your check should be made payable to the United States Treasury.

Gross receipts. The total amount listed on Part IX-A. Statement of Revenues and Expenses, line 10 is your gross receipts for purposes of determining your user fee.

Line 1. Compute the average of your gross receipts for a 4-year period based on either (1) the gross receipts you expect to receive over your first four years if you have not completed a 4-year period, or (2) the gross receipts you actually received for the immediately preceding 4 years if you have completed a 4-year period.

Schedule A. Churches

General Information:

There is no single definition of the word "church" for tax purposes. When determining whether a section 501(c)(3) religious organization is also a church, we will consider characteristics generally attributed to churches and the facts and circumstances of each organization applying for public charity status as a church.

The characteristics generally attributed to churches are as follows.

- A distinct legal existence.
- A recognized creed and form of worship.
- A definite and distinct ecclesiastical government.
- A formal code of doctrine and discipline.
- A distinct religious history.
- A membership not associated with any other church or denomination.
- Ordained ministers ministering to the congregation.
- Ordained ministers selected after completing prescribed courses of study.
- A literature of its own.
- Established places of worship.
- Regular congregations.
- Regular religious services.
- Sunday schools for the religious instruction of the young.
- Schools for the preparation of ministers.

Although it is not necessary that each of the above criteria be met, a congregation or other religious membership group is generally required. A church includes mosques, temples, synagogues, and other forms of religious organizations. For more information, see Publication 1828.

The practices and rituals associated with your religious beliefs or creed must not be illegal or contrary to clearly defined public policy.

Specific Line Items

Line 1a. Provide a copy of your written creed, statement of faith, or summary of beliefs.

Line 1b. A "form of worship" refers to religious practices that express your devotion to your creed, faith, or beliefs.

Line 2a. A "code of doctrine and discipline" refers to a body of laws or rules that govern behavior.

Line 2b. Your "religious history" includes the story of your establishment and major events in your past.

Line 2c. Your literature includes any writings about your beliefs, rules, or history.

Line 3. A "religious hierarchy or ecclesiastical government" refers to people or institutions that exercise significant influence or authority over you.

Line 4a. Indicate the regular days and times of your religious services. Describe the order of events during your regular worship service and explain how the activities conducted as part of your services further your religious purposes. Also include sample copies of church bulletins, pamphlets, or flyers that are distributed to your members or the general public.

Line 4b. Enter on the line provided, the average number of members and non-members who attend your regularly scheduled religious services.

Line 5a. An "established place of worship" is a place where you hold regularly scheduled religious services. It may be a place that you own, rent, or which is provided freely for your use. If you answer "Yes," go to line 5b. If you answer "No," describe where you meet to hold regularly scheduled religious services.

Line 6. An "established congregation" or "other religious membership group" includes individuals who regularly attend and take part in the religious services of your organization at an established location. An established congregation generally does not include members of only one family. If you answer "No" because you do not have an established congregation or other religious membership, you may be a religious organization that does not qualify as a church. If you do not qualify as a church, you will need to go back to Part X, line 5, to reconsider your public charity status.

TIP You may request classification as a church at a later date after you establish a congregation or other religious membership group. For information about this option, contact our customer account service representatives at 1-877-829-5500 (toll-free).

Line 7. Enter the total number of your current members in the line provided. If you have no members, enter zero.

Line 8a. Answer "Yes" if you have a prescribed way to become a member. Answer "Yes" even if you just keep records of who is currently a member. Describe any actions required for individuals to become members. Submit copies of any application forms used.

Line 8b. Describe any rights and benefits of members. You should include details of any levels of membership and the rights and/or benefits associated with each level.

Line 8c. If your members may be associated with another denomination or church, describe the circumstances in which your members would be members of your church and another church.

Line 8d. See Glossary, Appendix C, for a description of the word "family."

Line 9. Answer "Yes" if you conduct baptisms, weddings, funerals, or other religious rites.

Line 10. A school for the religious instruction of the young refers to any regularly scheduled religious, educational activities for youth, such as a "Sunday school."

Line 11a. A "prescribed course of study" refers to formal or informal training. It does not include self-ordination or paying a fee for an ordination certificate without completing a course of study. Describe the course of study completed by your religious leader.

Line 12. Answer "Yes" if your religious leader is listed in Part V, line 1a.

Line 14. Answer "Yes" if you are part of a group of churches with similar beliefs and structures, such as a convention, association, or union of churches.

Line 16. If you answer "Yes," submit a copy of your church charter. Identify the organization that issued the charter and describe the requirements you met to receive it. Do not describe organizational charters you received from your state's Secretary of State, Franchise Tax Board, or similar administrative office.

Line 17. Attach any additional information you would like us to consider that would help us classify you as a church.

Schedule B. Schools, Colleges, and Universities

General Information:

An organization is a school if it:
- Presents formal instruction as its primary function.
- Has a regularly scheduled curriculum.
- Has a regular faculty of qualified teachers.
- Has a regularly enrolled student body.
- Has a place where educational activities are regularly carried on.

The term "school" includes primary, secondary, preparatory, high schools, colleges, and universities. It does not include organizations engaged in both educational and non-educational activities, unless the latter are merely incidental to the educational activities. Non-traditional schools such as an outdoor survival school or a yoga school may qualify.

The term "school" does not include home schools.

Section I. Operational Information

Line 1a. Answer "Yes" if you have a regularly scheduled curriculum, a regular faculty of qualified teachers, a regularly enrolled student body, and facilities where your educational activities are regularly carried on. Submit evidence establishing that you meet these factors, as described below:
- Evidence that you have a regularly scheduled curriculum includes a list of required courses of study, dates and times courses are offered, and other information about how to complete required courses.
- Evidence that you have a regular faculty of qualified teachers, includes certifications by the appropriate state authority or successful completion of required training.
- Evidence of a regularly enrolled student body includes records of regular attendance by students at your facility.
- Evidence of a place where your exclusively educational activities are regularly carried on includes a lease agreement or deed for your facility.

If you answer "No," do not complete Schedule B. You do not meet the requirements of a school and you will need to go back to Part X, line 5, to reconsider your public charity status.

Line 1b. Answer "Yes" if your primary function is the presentation of formal instruction. If you answer "No," do not complete Schedule B. You do not meet the requirements of a school and you will need to go back to Part X, line 5, to reconsider your public charity status.

Line 2a. Answer "Yes" if you are a public school. Submit documentation of your status as a public school. If you answer "Yes," do not complete the remainder of Schedule B.

Line 2b. Answer "Yes" if you have a signed contract or agreement with a state or local government under which you operate and receive funding. Submit a signed and dated copy of your contract or agreement. If you answer "Yes," do not complete the remainder of Schedule B.

Line 3. Enter the name of the public school district and county where you operate.

Line 4. Answer "Yes" if you were formed or substantially expanded during a period of time when public schools in your district or county were desegregated by court order.

CAUTION If you are unsure whether to answer "Yes," contact an appropriate public school official.

Line 5. Answer "Yes" if a state or federal administrative agency or judicial body ever determined your organization to be racially discriminatory. Identify the parties involved and the forum in which the case was presented. Explain the reason for the action, the decision reached, and provide legal citations (if any) for the decision. Also, explain in detail any changes made in response to the action against your organization or the decision reached.

Line 7. In responding to this line, you may reference information previously provided in response to Part VIII, line 7a, 7b, or 7c, along with any additional information to fully respond.

Line 8. Answer "Yes" if you manage or intend to manage your programs through your own employees or by using volunteers. Answer "No" if you engage or intend to engage a separate organization or independent contractor. Make sure your answer is consistent with the information provided in Part VIII, line 7b. In responding to this line, you may reference information previously provided in response to Part VIII, line 7a, 7b, or 7c, along with any additional information to fully respond.

Section II. Establishment of Racially Nondiscriminatory Policy

A section 501(c)(3) organization that is a school must publish a notice of its racially nondiscriminatory policy as to students as follows.

> The M school admits students of any race, color, national origin, and ethnic origin to all the rights, privileges, programs, and activities generally accorded or made available to students at the school. It does not discriminate on the basis of race, color, national origin, and ethnic origin in administration of its educational policies, admission policies, scholarship and loan programs, and athletic and other school-administered programs.

Every private school is subject to the provisions of Revenue Procedure 75-50, 1975-2 C.B. 587 (Rev. Proc. 75-50). See Publication 557, which sets forth the requirements of Rev. Proc. 75-50 under the section for Private Schools.

A private school must also certify annually that it meets the requirements of Rev. Proc. 75-50. This can be accomplished by filing Schedule A (Form 990, Form 990-EZ) Organization Exempt Under Section 501(c)(3).

Schools that do not file Form 990 must file Form 5578, Annual Certification of Racial Nondiscrimination for a Private School Exempt From Federal Income Tax.

Line 1. Answer "Yes" if your organizing document or bylaws contain a nondiscriminatory statement as to students similar to the one shown above.

Answer "No" if the nondiscrimination statement is not included. If the statement is not included in your organizing document or bylaws, you may submit a copy of your signed and dated resolution that was adopted according to your internal rules or regulations. Your resolution should approve a nondiscriminatory policy similar to the one shown above.

Line 2. Answer "Yes" if your brochures, application forms, advertisements, and catalogues dealing with student admissions, programs, and scholarships contain a statement similar to the following.

> The M school admits students of any race, color, and national or ethnic origin.

Submit representative copies of each document.

If you answer "No," to line 2, but checked the box on line 2b, you are agreeing that all future printed materials, including Internet content, will contain a statement of nondiscriminatory policy as to students similar to the one provided above.

Line 3. You must demonstrate that you have made your nondiscriminatory policy known to all segments of the general community served by the school. One way of meeting this requirement is to publish the school's nondiscriminatory policy annually. If you have already published your notice, submit the actual page of the newspaper on which the notice appears. We cannot accept a photocopy, other electronic reproduction, or partial page of the newspaper.

Answer "No," if you have not attached your notice and describe how you meet the publicity requirement of Rev. Proc. 75-50.

See Publication 557 or Rev. Proc. 75-50 for guidance on the format and content of the required notice and whether any exceptions may apply to you.

TIP A notice published in the legal notices section or classified advertisements of your local newspaper is generally not acceptable.

Line 5. Enter the racial composition of your student body, faculty, and administrative staff in the spaces provided. Enter actual numbers, rather than percentages, for the current year and projected numbers for the next academic year. If the number is zero, then enter "0."

CAUTION Do not identify students, faculty, and staff by name.

If you are completing the table based on estimates, submit documentation that supports how you arrived at the estimated numbers. For example, if your estimates are based on the racial composition of the community in which you operate, submit current census data of the racial composition for the area. If your numbers and the census numbers differ greatly, explain why.

Line 6. Enter the racial composition of students to whom you award loans and scholarships in the spaces provided. Enter actual numbers, rather than percentages, for the current year and projected numbers for the next academic year. If the number is zero, then enter "0."

CAUTION Do not identify students by name.

Line 7a. Submit a list that identifies each individual or organization by name. Your list must include your incorporators, founders, board members, donors of land, and donors of buildings.

Line 7b. Answer "Yes" if any individuals or organizations on your list have an objective to keep public or private school education segregated by race. Explain how these individuals or organizations promote segregation in public or private schools.

Line 8. Answer "Yes" if on a continuing basis, you will maintain for a minimum period of three years the following records.

- Your racial composition (similar to the information requested in Schedule B, Section II, line 5).
- Evidence that your scholarships and loans are awarded on a racially nondiscriminatory basis (similar to the information requested in Schedule B, Section II, line 6).
- Copies of all materials used by you or on your behalf to solicit contributions.
- Copies of brochures, application forms, advertisements, and catalogues dealing with student admissions, programs, and financial aid.

Answer "No" if you do not maintain records and explain how you meet the recordkeeping requirements under Rev. Proc. 75-50.

CAUTION Failure to maintain these records or produce them upon the proper request, will create a presumption that you have not complied with the requirements of Rev. Proc. 75-50.

Schedule C. Hospitals and Medical Research Organizations

General Information:

An organization qualifies as a hospital if it is a:

- Hospital.
- Cooperative hospital service organization (Schedule C not required).
- Medical research organization operated in conjunction with a hospital.

Hospital. An organization is a "hospital" if its principal purpose or function is providing medical or hospital care or medical education or research. Medical care includes treatment of any physical or mental disability or condition, on an inpatient or outpatient basis. Thus, if an organization is a rehabilitation institution, outpatient clinic, or community mental health or drug treatment center, it is a hospital if its principal function is providing treatment services as described above.

A hospital does not include convalescent homes, homes for children or the aged, or institutions whose principal purpose or function is to train handicapped individuals to pursue a vocation.

Medical research organization. An organization is a "medical research organization" if its principal purpose or function is the direct, continuous, and active conduct of medical research in conjunction with a hospital. The hospital with which the organization is affiliated must be described in section 501(c)(3), a federal hospital, or an instrumentality of a governmental unit, such as a municipal hospital.

"Medical research" means investigations, experiments, and studies to discover, develop, or verify knowledge relating to the causes, diagnosis, treatment, prevention, or control of human physical or mental diseases and impairments. For more information, see Treas. Regs. section 1.170A-9(c)(2).

If you are a hospital, check the first box on Schedule C and complete Section I.

If you are a medical research organization, check the second box on Schedule C and complete Section II.

Section I. Hospitals

Line 1. Answer "Yes" if all doctors in your community are eligible for staff privileges at your facility. You may answer "Yes" if staff privileges at your facility are limited by capacity.

Answer "No" if all doctors in your community are not eligible for staff privileges at your facility.

If you answer "No," describe in detail how you limit eligibility for staff privileges at your facility. Include details of your eligibility criteria and selection procedures for your courtesy staff of doctors.

Line 2a. Answer "Yes" if you admit all patients in your community who can pay for themselves or through private health insurance.

Answer "No" if you limit admission for these individuals in any way. If you answer "No," describe your admission policy in detail. You should explain how and why you restrict patient admission.

Line 2b. Answer "Yes" if you admit all patients in your community who participate in Medicare.

Answer "No" if you limit admission in any way for these individuals. If you answer "No," describe your admission policy in detail. You should explain how and why you restrict patient admission to exclude persons who participate in Medicare.

Line 2c. Answer "Yes" if you admit all patients in your community who participate in Medicaid.

Answer "No" if you limit admission in any way for these individuals. If you answer "No," describe your admission policy in detail. You should explain how and why you restrict patient admission to exclude persons who participate in Medicaid.

Line 3a. Answer "Yes" if you require a deposit from Medicare and/or Medicaid patients before admission. If you answer "Yes," describe in detail how you determined the amount required and explain why a deposit is needed.

Line 3b. Answer "Yes" if you require a deposit for other patients before admission and the requirement is the same as for Medicare and/or Medicaid patients.

Answer "No" if you require a deposit, but deposits for Medicare/Medicaid patients and other patients differ as to: (1) the way the amount is determined, or (2) the reason for the deposit. If you answer "No," describe the differences in detail.

Line 4a. Answer "Yes" if you offer emergency medical or hospital care at your facility on a 24-hour basis, seven days a week. If "No," explain why you do not offer an emergency room. For example, emergency care may be inappropriate for the type of services you provide. Also, describe any emergency services that you provide.

Line 4b. Answer "Yes" if you have a specific written plan or policy to accept all patients in need of emergency care without considering their ability to pay.

If you answer "Yes," submit a copy of your plan or policy.

Line 4c. Answer "Yes" if you have specific arrangements with any police, fire, or ambulance service providers to bring emergency cases to your facility.

If you answer "Yes," describe each specific agreement. For written agreements, you may submit a copy of each agreement. If it is oral, explain fully the agreement. For any oral agreements, include details of how and when the agreement was arranged.

Line 5a. Answer "Yes" if you provide free or low cost medical or hospital care services to the poor. If you answer "Yes," answer lines 5b through 5e. Do not answer 5b through 5e if you answer "No."

Line 5b. Submit a copy of your written policy or explain fully the understanding under which you operate regarding the admission and/or treatment of charity cases. Explain how you distinguish between charity care and bad debts.

TIP Include details of how you inform the general public about your policy. Submit copies of any documents or agreements you require charity patients to sign before being admitted and/or treated.

Line 5c. Submit information that shows the amounts you expend for treating charity care patients and the types of services you provide. Include an explanation that distinguishes charity care patient expenditures from uncollected bad debts.

Line 5d. Submit copies of any written agreements you have with municipalities or government agencies to subsidize the cost of admitting or treating charity patients.

Line 5e. A sliding fee scale establishes payments depending on financial ability to pay.

Line 6a. Answer "Yes" if you have a formal program of medical training and research. If you answer "Yes," describe your program in detail, including its length and criteria for acceptance into your program.

Line 6b. Answer "Yes" if you have a formal program of community educational programs. If you answer "Yes," describe your program in detail.

Line 7. Answer "Yes" if you provide office space to physicians conducting their own medical practices.

Line 8. Answer "Yes" if you have a board of directors that is representative of the community you serve. Include a list of each board member with the individual's name and employment affiliation. Also, for each board member, describe how that individual represents the community. Generally, hospital employees and staff physicians are not individuals considered to be community representatives.

TIP Answer "Yes" if an organization described in section 501(c)(3) with a community board exercises rights or powers over you, such as the right to appoint members to your governing board of directors and the power to approve certain transactions. Describe these rights and powers. In addition, describe how each of that organization's board of directors represents the community.

Answer "Yes" if you are subject to a state corporate practice of medicine law that requires your governing board to be composed solely of physicians licensed to practice medicine in the state. If you answer "Yes" on this basis, also provide the following information.

- Describe whether a hospital described in section 501(c)(3) exercises any rights or powers over you.
- Identify the corporate practice of medicine law under which you operate.
- Explain how the section 501(c)(3) hospital exercises any rights or powers over you, such as the right to appoint members to your governing board of directors and the right to approve certain transactions.
- Explain what services you provide to the section 501(c)(3) hospital.

Line 10. Answer "Yes" if you manage or intend to manage your programs through your own employees or by using volunteers. Answer "No" if you engage or intend to engage a separate organization or independent contractor. Make sure your answer is consistent with the information provided in Part VIII, line 7b.

Line 11. Recruitment incentives may be offered to attract or retain physicians as employees or to serve the community in which the hospital is located. Such incentives are generally offered when there is an acute shortage of such physicians in your hospital or within the community.

Line 12. Physicians who have a financial or professional relationship with you include physicians with whom you have a business relationship, such as employees, staff physicians, participants in joint ventures, or physicians with whom you contract for services.

Line 13. A business relationship includes employment, contractual relationship, or status as a member of your board of directors.

Line 14. Answer "Yes" if you have adopted a conflict of interest policy consistent with the sample conflict of interest policy provided in these instructions or you are subject to similar conflict of interest policies under state law. Provide copies of the policies to which you are subject. Although a conflict of interest policy is not required as a matter of tax law, we encourage adoption of a substantive conflict of interest policy because it makes it more likely that you will operate for the benefit of the community and not for private interests.

An example of a substantive conflict of interest policy is available in Appendix A. in these instructions.

Answer "No" if you have not adopted a conflict of interest policy or you are not subject to conflict of interest policies under state law.

Section II. Medical Research Organizations

Line 1. Attach a list of hospitals with which you have relationships relating to the conduct of medical research. Describe in detail the relationship you have with each hospital. Submit copies of any written agreements.

Line 2. Describe in detail all activities that directly accomplish your conduct of medical research.

Making grants to other organizations does not directly accomplish the conduct of medical research.

Line 3. Your schedule should explain how you determine the fair market value of your assets.

Schedule D. Section 509(a)(3) Supporting Organizations

General Information:

A section 509(a)(3) organization is commonly referred to as a "supporting organization." An organization that a supporting organization benefits is commonly referred to as a "supported organization." A supporting organization may support more than one supported organization.

An organization qualifies for public charity status as a supporting organization under section 509(a)(3) if:

- It is organized and at all times thereafter is operated exclusively for the benefit of, to perform the functions of, or to carry out the purposes of one or more public charities described in section 509(a)(1) or 509(a)(2);
- It meets one of three required relationship tests with the supported organization(s); and
- It is not controlled directly or indirectly by "disqualified persons." See specific instructions for Part X, line 6b(ii)(b), for a definition of a "disqualified persons."

A supporting organization can also support the charitable purposes of organizations that are exempt under sections 501(c)(4), (5), or (6).

Section I. Identifying Information About Supported Organization(s)

Line 1. Enter the name, address, and EIN of each organization you support.

Line 2. Answer "Yes" if each supported organization has received a letter from the IRS recognizing it as a public charity under section 509(a)(1) or 509(a)(2). Then, go to Section II, line 1.

Answer "No" if any supported organization has not received a letter from us recognizing it as a public charity under section 509(a)(1) or 509(a)(2). Then, go to line 3.

Line 3. Answer "Yes" if any supported organization you listed in line 1 received a letter from us stating that it is exempt under section 501(c)(4), (5), or (6). Also, to show how the organization meets the public support test, submit the amounts and sources of revenue for the last four completed tax years for the supported organization(s). You should provide the requested financial data in the format shown on Part IX-A. Statement of Revenues and Expenses, for each supported organization. You must then submit the lists requested by Part X, line 6b(ii), which is applicable to the public support test under section 509(a)(2).

Answer "No" if no supported organization listed in line 1 has been recognized as tax-exempt under section 501(c)(4), (5), or (6).

CAUTION If any organization you intend to support has not received a letter from us recognizing it as a public charity under section 509(a)(1) or 509(a)(2), or has not received a determination recognizing that it is tax-exempt under section 501(c)(4), (5), or (6), you must demonstrate, in writing, that each organization you support is described in section 509(a)(1) or 509(a)(2). For example, if you support a church or foreign organization, you should describe how this organization qualifies as a public charity under section 509(a)(1) or 509(a)(2).

Section II. Relationship with Supported Organization(s) – Three Tests

To qualify under section 509(a)(3), you must show that you meet one of three relationship tests with the supported organization(s).

- Test I. Operated, supervised, or controlled by (comparable to a parent-subsidiary relationship);
- Test 2. Supervised or controlled in connection with (comparable to a brother-sister relationship); or
- Test 3. Operated in connection with (responsive to the needs or demands of, and having significant involvement in the affairs of, the supported organization(s)).

Line 1. Answer "Yes" if your governing document, bylaws, or other internal rules and regulations show that the majority of your governing board or officers is elected or appointed by the supported organization(s). Then, go to Section III.

Answer "No" if your governing document, bylaws, or other internal rules and regulations do not show that the majority of your governing board or officers is elected or appointed by the supported organization(s). If you answer "No" but still believe you satisfy this test, explain and go to Section III. Otherwise, go to line 2 because you do not meet the "operated, supervised, or controlled by" relationship test.

Line 2. Answer "Yes" if your governing document, bylaws, or other internal rules and regulations show that a majority of your governing board consists of individuals who also serve on the governing board of the supported organization(s). Then, go to Section III.

Answer "No" if your governing document, bylaws, or other internal rules and regulations do not show that a majority of your governing board consists of individuals who also serve on the governing board of the supported organization(s). If you answer "No" but still believe you satisfy this test, explain and go to Section III. Otherwise, go to line 3 because you do not meet the "supervised or controlled in connection with" relationship test.

Line 3. Answer "Yes" if you are a charitable trust under state law, you name each specified publicly supported organization as a beneficiary in your trust agreement, and each beneficiary organization has the power to enforce the trust and compel an accounting under state law. Then, go to Section II, line 5.

Line 4a. Answer "Yes" if the officers, directors, trustees, or members of the supported organization(s) elect or appoint any of your officers, directors, or trustees. If your governing document, bylaws, or other internal rules and regulations do not provide for this, explain how your officers, directors, or trustees are elected or appointed. Then, go to line 4d.

Line 4b. Answer "Yes" if any members of the governing body of the supported organization(s) also serve as your officers, directors, trustees, or hold another important office for your organization. Describe the position held and whether the position is ongoing. Then, go to line 4d.

Line 4c. Answer "Yes" if your officers, directors, or trustees maintain a close and continuous working relationship with the officers, directors, or trustees of the supported organization(s). Explain the continuous relationship in detail. Then, go to line 4d.

TIP If you answer "No," on line 4c and your answer to lines 3, 4a, and 4b were "No," you do not meet the "operated in connection with" relationship test. You must establish a different relationship with the supported organization or go back to Part X, to reconsider your public charity status.

Line 4d. Answer "Yes" if the supported organization has a significant involvement in your investment policies, making and timing of grants, and directing the use of your income and assets. Explain how the supported organization is involved in these matters.

Line 5. An applicant for tax exemption as a supporting organization under the "operated in connection with" relationship must satisfy either the integral part test or the alternative integral part test. If you are requesting supporting organization status by meeting the "operated in connection with" relationship, you must satisfy either the integral part test or the alternative integral part test. If you satisfy the integral part test described in line 5, then you do not have to complete line 6.

Answer "Yes" if you conduct activities that the supported organization would otherwise conduct. Describe the activities that you conduct, other than distributing funds. Then, go to Section III.

Line 6a. To satisfy the alternative integral part test as a supporting organization, you must distribute at least 85% of your annual "net income" to the organization(s) you support. See the Glossary for a description of "net income" to be used in calculating whether you meet the 85% distribution threshold.

Answer "Yes" if you distribute at least 85% of your net income to the supported organization(s). For purposes of this schedule, "net income" has the same meaning as the term "adjusted net income," which is applicable to private operating foundations.

In general, "adjusted net income" is the excess of gross income, including gross income from any unrelated trade or business, determined with certain modifications, reduced by total deductions. Gross income does not include gifts, grants, or contributions.

If you answer line 6a "No," and your answer to line 5 was "No," unless you establish that the supported organization(s) will be attentive to your operations, you do not meet the "operated in connection with" relationship test. Go back to Part X, to reconsider your public charity status.

Line 6b. Submit a list that shows the total amount distributed annually to each supported organization. Also, indicate how each amount will vary from year to year.

Line 6c. Submit a list that shows the total annual income for each supported organization.

Line 6d. Answer "Yes" if your funds are "earmarked" for a particular program or activity.

If you distribute your income to, or for the use of, a particular department or program of an organization, list the total annual revenue of the supported department or program in line 6c.

Line 7a. The "operated in connection with" test requires that you specify the supported organization(s) by name in your organizing document unless there has been an historic and continuing relationship between you and the supported organization(s).

Line 7b. An historic and continuing relationship depends on all the facts and circumstances that would demonstrate a substantial identity of interests between you and the supported organization.

If you answer "No" to lines 7a and 7b, you may consider amending your organizing document to specify the supported organization(s) by name so you can answer "Yes" to line 7a. Otherwise, you will need to go back to Part X to reconsider your public charity status.

Section III. Organizational Test

Line 1a. If you answered "No" to line 1a, you must amend your organizing document to specify the supported organization(s) by name, purpose, or class. Otherwise, you will not meet the operational test under section 509(a)(3) and you will need to go back to Part X to reconsider your public charity status.

Line 1b. If you answered "No" to line 1b, you must amend your organizing document to specify the supported organization(s) by name. Otherwise you will not meet the operational test under section 509(a)(3) and you will need to go back to Part X to reconsider your public charity status.

Section IV. Disqualified Person Test

Control. As a section 509(a)(3) supporting organization, you may not be controlled directly or indirectly by disqualified persons. You are controlled if disqualified persons can exercise 50% or more of the total voting power of your governing body. You are also controlled if disqualified persons have authority to affect significant decisions, such as power over your investment decisions, or power over your charitable disbursement decisions. You are also controlled if disqualified persons can exercise veto power. Although control is generally demonstrated where disqualified persons have the authority over your governing body to require you to take an action or refrain from taking an action, indirect control by disqualified persons will also disqualify you as a supporting organization.

See the instructions for Part X, line 6b for a description of the term "disqualified person."

A public charity is not a disqualified person.

A "foundation manager" means your:
- Officers, directors, or trustees, or
- An individual having powers or responsibilities similar to those of your officers, directors, or trustees.

Line 1b. See the instructions for Part V, line 2a, for a description of the terms "family or business relationship."

Schedule E. Organizations Not Filing Form 1023 Within 27 Months of Formation

General Information:

The questions in this schedule will help us determine the effective date of exemption for an organization that filed its application more than 27 months after the end of the month in which it was legally formed.
- If you meet exceptions for late filing, your exemption under section 501(c)(3) will be effective from the date you were legally formed.
- If you do not meet any exceptions, your exemption under section 501(c)(3) will be effective from the date you filed your application.
- Although you do not meet any exceptions, you may, nevertheless, qualify for tax exemption as an organization described in section 501(c)(4) for the period beginning with the date you were legally formed and ending with the date you are recognized under section 501(c)(3). Generally, contributions made to a section 501(c)(4) organization are not tax deductible.

Line 1. Answer "Yes" if you are a church or an association of churches. You should have also checked Part X, line 5a, and completed Schedule A. If you qualify as a church or an association of churches, your exemption will be effective from the date of your legal formation.

Answer "Yes" if you are an integrated auxiliary of a church. If you qualify as an integrated auxiliary of a church, your exemption will be effective from the date of your legal formation.

An "integrated auxiliary of a church" refers to a class of organizations that are related to a church or convention or association of churches, but are not such organizations themselves. In general, you must:
- Be described as both tax exempt under section 501(c)(3) and a public charity described in sections 509(a)(1), (2), or (3); and
- Receive financial support primarily from internal church sources as opposed to public or governmental sources.

Men's and women's organizations, seminaries, mission societies, and youth groups that satisfy the above referenced sections 501(c)(3) and 509(a)(1), (2), or (3) requirements are considered integrated auxiliaries whether or not they meet the internal support requirements. More guidance as to the types of organizations that qualify as integrated auxiliaries can be found in Treas. Regs. section 1.6033-2(h).

Line 2a. Answer "Yes" if you are a public charity and your annual gross receipts are normally $5,000 or less. For information about whether your annual gross receipts are normally $5,000 or less, see Publication 557. If you qualify as an organization with annual gross receipts of normally $5,000 or less, your exemption would be effective from the date of your legal formation.

Answer "No" if you are a private foundation, regardless of your gross receipts.

Line 2b. Answer "Yes" if:
- Your gross receipts were normally less than $5,000 for years before your last completed tax year,
- Your gross receipts normally exceeded $5,000 for your last completed tax year, and
- You filed this application within 90 days from the end of your last completed tax year.

Line 3. Lines 3a, 3b, and 3c are applicable to subordinates included in a group exemption application. See Publication 557 for information regarding group exemptions. If you were a subordinate of a group exemption that was timely filed and you are filing for exemption within 27 months from the date you were notified by the organization holding the group exemption letter that either (1) you are no longer covered by the group exemption letter, or (2) the group exemption request was denied, answer "Yes" and do not complete the remainder of this schedule.

Line 4. Answer "Yes" if you were formed on or before October 9, 1969. If you are a corporation, your formation date is the date your articles of incorporation were filed with and approved by your state officials. If you are an association, your formation date is the date you adopted your organizing document. If you are a trust, your formation date is generally the date your trust was both adopted and funded.

CAUTION If you answer "Yes," do not complete the rest of this schedule. As an organization formed on or before October 9, 1969, your exemption would be effective from the date of your legal formation. Answer "No" if you were formed after October 9, 1969.

Line 5. You may receive an extension of time to file Form 1023 beyond the 27-month period if you can establish that you acted reasonably and in good faith, and that granting an extension will not prejudice the interests of the government.
- You filed Form 1023 before we discovered your failure to file.
- You failed to file because of intervening events beyond your control.
- You exercised reasonable diligence but you were not aware of the filing requirements. (The complexity of your filing and experience in these matters is taken into consideration.)
- You reasonably relied on written advice from us.
- You reasonably relied on the advice of a qualified tax professional who failed to file or advise you to file Form 1023.

Answer "Yes" if you wish to request an extension of time to file under these provisions. If you answer "Yes," describe in detail the reasons for filing late based on the factors listed above. Do not complete the rest of this schedule.

Answer "No" if you do not wish to request an extension under these provisions and go to line 6a.

Line 6a. By checking "Yes," and completing Part X, line 6a, you are eligible for an advance ruling to be classified as a public charity from the postmark date of your application.

Do not complete line 6a, 6b, or 7 if you checked the boxes in Part X, lines 5a, 5b, 5c, 5d, or 5e.

Line 6b. If you anticipate significant changes in your sources of support in the future, answer "Yes," and we will base your qualification for an advance ruling on the financial information you provide in line 7. If you check "Yes," complete the financial information requested in line 7 of Schedule E.

If you answer "No," we will base your qualification for an advance ruling on the financial information you provided in Part IX. If you answer "No," do not complete line 7 of Schedule E.

Line 7. Complete projected budgets of income for the first two full tax years after the date you mailed your Form 1023. See the specific instructions for Part IX-A. Statement of Revenues and Expenses, lines 1 through 13, if you need guidance on what to include in the various categories.

Line 8. Check the box if you wish to request exemption under section 501(c)(4) for the period before the postmark date of your Form 1023. If you check the box, attach page 1 of Form 1024. Form 1024 is available on the IRS website at www.irs.gov or by calling 1-800-829-3676.

If you qualify for exemption under section 501(c)(4), you will not be liable for income tax returns as a taxable entity, but you will need to file any exempt organization returns for which you may be responsible. Contributions to section 501(c)(4) organizations are generally not deductible by donors.

Do not check the box if you do not wish to be tax exempt under section 501(c)(4) for the period before the postmark date of your Form 1023. If you do not request and obtain exemption under section 501(c)(4) for the period before the postmark date of your Form 1023, you may be liable for income tax returns as a taxable entity for that time period.

Schedule F. Homes for the Elderly or Handicapped and Low-Income Housing

General Information:

Homes for the elderly or handicapped are eligible for tax exemption as charitable organizations only if they meet the special needs of the elderly or handicapped for residential facilities designed to meet their physical, social, recreation, health care, and transportation needs. Homes for the elderly or handicapped must also be within the financial reach of a significant segment of the elderly or handicapped in the community. Once admitted to the elderly or handicapped housing facility, the organization must have an established policy to maintain them as residents, to the extent possible, even if the residents subsequently become unable to pay the monthly charges.

Low-income housing must provide affordable housing for a significant segment of individuals in your community with low incomes. Your housing may serve a combination of purposes, such as for poor, frail, and elderly persons.

Section I. General Information about Your Housing

Line 1. The type of housing you provide should include both a description of the type of facility provided, such as apartment complex, condominium, cooperative, or private residence, and the nature of your facility, such as assisted-living facility, continuing-care facility, nursing home, low-income facility, etc.

Line 7. See the instructions for Part V, line 7a, for a description of the terms arm's length and fair market value.

Line 8. Answer "Yes" if you manage or intend to manage your programs through your own employees or by using volunteers. Answer "No" if you engage or intend to engage a separate organization or independent contractor. Make sure your answer is consistent with the information provided in Part VIII, line 7b.

Line 9. Government programs include federal, state, or local government programs.

Section II. Homes for the Elderly or Handicapped

Line 2a. Answer "Yes" if you charge a one-time fee for admission to your facility.

Line 2b. Answer "Yes" if you charge daily, weekly, monthly, or annual fees or maintenance charges.

Line 2c. A "community" refers to the area that will be served by your facility. For example, a community may be a local area or a region.

Line 3a. Describe what happens to individuals if they become unable to pay your regular charges. For example, you may have a policy whereby you have a reserve fund for maintaining residents who are having trouble in paying their regular charges. You may also have a policy of keeping residents who are having trouble in paying their regular charges in place for a period of time to permit them to find alternative housing. Include a copy of any printed materials that informs the public about your policy.

Line 3b. Describe any arrangements you have or expect to have with welfare agencies, sponsoring organizations, or others to assist residents who become unable to afford to remain residents.

Line 4. Describe how you provide for the health care needs of residents, including the services provided. This can include providing for the activities of daily living of residents at your facilities and transporting residents to other facilities for medical services.

Line 5. Describe how living units and common areas are designed to meet the physical needs of residents (such as grab bars in bathrooms, wide doorways and hallways, design of kitchens and bathrooms, etc.). Also, include information about facilities and programs designed to meet some combination of physical, emotional, recreational, social, religious, and similar needs of residents.

Section III. Low-Income Housing

Line 2. Answer "Yes" if you charge daily, weekly, monthly, or annual fees or maintenance charges.

Schedule G. Successors to Other Organizations

General Information:

You should complete this schedule as a successor organization if any of the following situations pertain to you.

- You have taken or will take over the activities that were previously conducted by another.
- You have taken or will take over 25 percent or more of the fair market value of the net assets of another organization.
- You were established upon the conversion of an organization from for-profit to non-profit status.

The other organization is the predecessor organization. You should complete this schedule regardless of whether the predecessor (other organization) was exempt or not exempt from federal income tax.

Line 1a. For purposes of this schedule, a "for-profit" organization is one in which persons are permitted to have an ownership or partnership interest, such as corporate stock. It includes sole proprietorships, corporations, and other entities that provide for ownership interests.

Schedule H. Organizations Providing Scholarships, Fellowships, Educational Loans, or Other Educational Grants to Individuals and Private Foundations Requesting Advance Approval of Individual Grant Procedures

General Information:

Complete this schedule if you provide scholarships, fellowships, grants, loans, or other distributions to individuals for educational purposes. When answering the questions on this schedule, you should demonstrate how these distributions further your exempt purposes.

Generally, distributions made to individuals may advance educational purposes if selection is made:

- In a non-discriminatory fashion in terms of racial preference,
- Based on need and/or merit, and
- To a charitable class in terms of being available to an open-ended group, rather than to pre-selected individuals.

A scholarship or fellowship is tax free to the recipient only if he or she is:

- A candidate for a degree at an eligible educational institution; and
- Uses the scholarship or fellowship to pay qualified education expenses.

Qualified education expenses include tuition and fees; and course-related expenses such as books, supplies, and equipment. Room and board, travel, research, clerical help, and non-required equipment are not qualified education expenses. See Publication 970, Tax Benefits for Education, for additional information.

Selection of individuals using a lottery system generally has not been approved by the IRS.

Section I

Line 1b. If you have different grant programs, describe the purpose and amount of each program.

Line 1c. If you award educational loans, describe the terms of the loan (for example, interest rate, duration, forgiveness provision, etc.). Also, describe how any other loan institutions are involved in your program.

Line 1d. Explain how you will publicize your program and whether you publicize to the general public or to another group of possible recipients. Include specific information about the geographic area in which your program will be publicized and the means you will use, such as through newspaper advertisements, school district announcements, or community groups.

Line 1e. Submit sample copies of your solicitation material for applicants or materials announcing the awards. If solicitation is done orally through school counselors or others, explain fully.

Line 2. Organizations that make grants to individuals must maintain adequate records and case histories showing the name and address of each recipient pursuant to Revenue Ruling 56-304, 1956-2 C.B. 306. If you answer "No," explain how you will be able to demonstrate that your distributions serve exempt purposes.

Section II

Line 1a. Only complete lines 1a through 4 if you are a private foundation based on your answers to Part X, line 1a. Answer "Yes" if you are a private foundation and you are requesting advance approval of your grant-making procedures under section 4945(g). Answer "No" if you are a private foundation but do not wish to request advance approval of your grant-making procedures under section 4945(g). If you answer "No," the amounts you distribute as educational grants provided to individuals may be considered taxable expenditures under section 4945.

Answer "N/A" if you are requesting public charity status in Part X.

For more information about advance approval of grant-making procedures of a private foundation, log on to www.irs.gov/charities/foundations/article/0,,id=137397,00.html.

Line 1b. Check the box for section "4945(g)(1)" if your award qualifies as a scholarship or fellowship grant that is awarded on an objective and nondiscriminatory basis and is used for study at a school (see the Schedule B, General Information for what is considered a school).

Check the box for section "4945(g)(3)" if the purpose of your award is to achieve a specific objective, produce a report or other similar product, or improve or enhance a literary, artistic, musical, scientific, teaching, or other similar capacity, skill, or talent of the recipient. Include your educational loan program under this section. You may check more than one box.

If your award qualifies as a prize or award that is subject to the provisions of section 74(b) and your recipient is selected from the general public, you do not have to request advance approval of your grant-making procedures since a prize or award is not subject to the advance approval procedure requirements because it is not a grant for travel, study, or other similar purposes. See Revenue Rulings 77-380, 1977-2 C.B. 419; 76-460, 1976-2 C.B. 371, and 75-393, 1975-2 C.B. 451.

Line 4. For additional information regarding private foundations requesting advance approval of individual grant procedures, go to www.irs.gov/charities/foundations/article/0,,id=137396,00.html.

Line 4a Answer "Yes" if you award scholarships on a preferential basis because you require, as an initial qualification, that the individual be an employee or be related to an employee of a particular employer.

Line 4c. Answer "N/A" if you do not provide scholarships, fellowships, or educational loans to employees of a particular employer.

Line 4d. Answer "N/A" if you do not provide scholarships, fellowships, or educational loans to children of employees of a particular employer.

Line 4e. Answer "N/A" if your answer to line 4d is "N/A."

TIP For purposes of this schedule, a program for children of employees of a particular employer includes children and family members of employees.

Paperwork Reduction Act Notice. We ask for the information on this form to carry out the Internal Revenue laws of the United States. If you want your organization to be recognized as tax exempt by the IRS, you are required to give us this information. We need it to determine whether the organization meets the legal requirements for tax-exempt status.

The organization is not required to provide the information requested on a form that is subject to the Paperwork Reduction Act unless the form displays a valid OMB control number. Books or records relating to a form or its instructions must be retained as long as their contents may become material in the administration of any Internal Revenue law. The rules governing the confidentiality of the Form 1023 application are covered in Code section 6104.

The time needed to complete and file these forms will vary depending on individual circumstances. The estimated average times are:

	Recordkeeping	**Learning about the law or the form**	**Preparing the form**	**Copying, assembling, and sending the form to the IRS**
Parts I to XI	89 hrs. 26 mins.	5 hrs. 10 mins.	9hrs. 39 mins.	48 mins.
1023 Sch. A	10 hrs. 2 mins.	6 mins.	16 mins.	—
1023 Sch. B	15 hrs. 18 mins.	12 mins.	27 mins.	—
1023 Sch. C	11 hrs. 14 mins.	12 mins.	23 mins.	—
1023 Sch. D	9 hrs. 48 mins.	42 mins.	53 mins.	—
1023 Sch. E	14 hrs. 35 mins.	1 hrs. 9 mins.	2 hrs. 22 mins.	16 mins.
1023 Sch. F	11 hrs. 28 mins.	12 mins.	23 mins.	—
1023 Sch. G	6 hrs. 42 mins.	6 mins.	12 mins.	—
1023 Sch. H	7 hrs. 53 mins.	42 mins.	51 mins.	—

If you have comments concerning the accuracy of these time estimates or suggestions for making these forms simpler, we would be happy to hear from you. You can write to the Internal Revenue Service, Tax Products Coordinating Committee, SE:W:CAR:MP:T:T:SP, 1111 Constitution Avenue, NW, IR-6406 Washington, DC 20224.

DO NOT send the application to this address. Instead, see Where to File on page 4.

Appendix A: Sample Conflict of Interest Policy

Note: Items marked **Hospital insert – for hospitals that complete Schedule C** are intended to be adopted by hospitals.

Article I
Purpose

The purpose of the conflict of interest policy is to protect this tax-exempt organization's (Organization) interest when it is contemplating entering into a transaction or arrangement that might benefit the private interest of an officer or director of the Organization or might result in a possible excess benefit transaction. This policy is intended to supplement but not replace any applicable state and federal laws governing conflict of interest applicable to nonprofit and charitable organizations.

Article II
Definitions

1. **Interested Person**
Any director, principal officer, or member of a committee with governing board delegated powers, who has a direct or indirect financial interest, as defined below, is an interested person.

[Hospital Insert – for hospitals that complete Schedule C
If a person is an interested person with respect to any entity in the health care system of which the organization is a part, he or she is an interested person with respect to all entities in the health care system.]

2. **Financial Interest**
A person has a financial interest if the person has, directly or indirectly, through business, investment, or family:
  a. An ownership or investment interest in any entity with which the Organization has a transaction or arrangement,
  b. A compensation arrangement with the Organization or with any entity or individual with which the Organization has a transaction or arrangement, or
  c. A potential ownership or investment interest in, or compensation arrangement with, any entity or individual with which the Organization is negotiating a transaction or arrangement.

Compensation includes direct and indirect remuneration as well as gifts or favors that are not insubstantial.

A financial interest is not necessarily a conflict of interest. Under Article III, Section 2, a person who has a financial interest may have a conflict of interest only if the appropriate governing board or committee decides that a conflict of interest exists.

Article III
Procedures

1. **Duty to Disclose**
In connection with any actual or possible conflict of interest, an interested person must disclose the existence of the financial interest and be given the opportunity to disclose all material facts to the directors and members of committees with governing board delegated powers considering the proposed transaction or arrangement.

2. **Determining Whether a Conflict of Interest Exists**
After disclosure of the financial interest and all material facts, and after any discussion with the interested person, he/she shall leave the governing board or committee meeting while the determination of a conflict of interest is discussed and voted upon. The remaining board or committee members shall decide if a conflict of interest exists.

3. **Procedures for Addressing the Conflict of Interest**
  a. An interested person may make a presentation at the governing board or committee meeting, but after the presentation, he/she shall leave the meeting during the discussion of, and the vote on, the transaction or arrangement involving the possible conflict of interest.
  b. The chairperson of the governing board or committee shall, if appropriate, appoint a disinterested person or committee to investigate alternatives to the proposed transaction or arrangement.
  c. After exercising due diligence, the governing board or committee shall determine whether the Organization can obtain with reasonable efforts a more advantageous transaction or arrangement from a person or entity that would not give rise to a conflict of interest.
  d. If a more advantageous transaction or arrangement is not reasonably possible under circumstances not producing a conflict of interest, the governing board or committee shall determine by a majority vote of the disinterested directors whether the transaction or arrangement is in the Organization's best interest, for its own benefit, and whether it is fair and reasonable. In conformity with the above determination it shall make its decision as to whether to enter into the transaction or arrangement.

4. **Violations of the Conflicts of Interest Policy**

a. If the governing board or committee has reasonable cause to believe a member has failed to disclose actual or possible conflicts of interest, it shall inform the member of the basis for such belief and afford the member an opportunity to explain the alleged failure to disclose.

b. If, after hearing the member's response and after making further investigation as warranted by the circumstances, the governing board or committee determines the member has failed to disclose an actual or possible conflict of interest, it shall take appropriate disciplinary and corrective action.

Article IV
Records of Proceedings

The minutes of the governing board and all committees with board delegated powers shall contain:

a. The names of the persons who disclosed or otherwise were found to have a financial interest in connection with an actual or possible conflict of interest, the nature of the financial interest, any action taken to determine whether a conflict of interest was present, and the governing board's or committee's decision as to whether a conflict of interest in fact existed.

b. The names of the persons who were present for discussions and votes relating to the transaction or arrangement, the content of the discussion, including any alternatives to the proposed transaction or arrangement, and a record of any votes taken in connection with the proceedings.

Article V
Compensation

a. A voting member of the governing board who receives compensation, directly or indirectly, from the Organization for services is precluded from voting on matters pertaining to that member's compensation.

b. A voting member of any committee whose jurisdiction includes compensation matters and who receives compensation, directly or indirectly, from the Organization for services is precluded from voting on matters pertaining to that member's compensation.

c. No voting member of the governing board or any committee whose jurisdiction includes compensation matters and who receives compensation, directly or indirectly, from the Organization, either individually or collectively, is prohibited from providing information to any committee regarding compensation.

[**Hospital Insert – for hospitals that complete Schedule C**
d. Physicians who receive compensation from the Organization, whether directly or indirectly or as employees or independent contractors, are precluded from membership on any committee whose jurisdiction includes compensation matters. No physician, either individually or collectively, is prohibited from providing information to any committee regarding physician compensation.]

Article VI
Annual Statements

Each director, principal officer and member of a committee with governing board delegated powers shall annually sign a statement which affirms such person:

a. Has received a copy of the conflicts of interest policy,

b. Has read and understands the policy,

c. Has agreed to comply with the policy, and

d. Understands the Organization is charitable and in order to maintain its federal tax exemption it must engage primarily in activities which accomplish one or more of its tax-exempt purposes.

Article VII
Periodic Reviews

To ensure the Organization operates in a manner consistent with charitable purposes and does not engage in activities that could jeopardize its tax-exempt status, periodic reviews shall be conducted. The periodic reviews shall, at a minimum, include the following subjects:

a. Whether compensation arrangements and benefits are reasonable, based on competent survey information, and the result of arm's length bargaining.

b. Whether partnerships, joint ventures, and arrangements with management organizations conform to the Organization's written policies, are properly recorded, reflect reasonable investment or payments for goods and services, further charitable purposes and do not result in inurement, impermissible private benefit or in an excess benefit transaction.

Article VIII
Use of Outside Experts

When conducting the periodic reviews as provided for in Article VII, the Organization may, but need not, use outside advisors. If outside experts are used, their use shall not relieve the governing board of its responsibility for ensuring periodic reviews are conducted.

Appendix B: States with Statutory Provisions Satisfying the Requirements of Internal Revenue Code Section 508(e)

The following states have adopted legislation satisfying the requirements of section 508(e) relating to private foundation governing instruments. Information derived from Revenue Ruling 75-38, 1975-1 C.B. 161.

ALABAMA — except where otherwise provided by a decree of a court of competent jurisdiction or by a provision in the private foundation's governing instrument which in either case has been entered or made after October 1, 1971, and expressly limits the applicability of State law.

ALASKA — except for such private foundations which expressly provide in their governing instruments that the applicable sections of Alaska law do not apply to them.

ARKANSAS — except for such private foundations which expressly provide in their governing instruments that the applicable sections of Arkansas law do not apply to them and except in the case of trusts where otherwise provided by decree of a court of competent jurisdiction.

CALIFORNIA — except where otherwise provided by a court of competent jurisdiction.

COLORADO — with respect to trusts that are private foundations except where otherwise provided by a court of competent jurisdiction.

CONNECTICUT — except where otherwise provided by a court of competent jurisdiction.

DELAWARE — except for such private foundations which expressly provide in their governing instruments that the applicable sections of Delaware law do not apply to them.

DISTRICT OF COLUMBIA — except for such corporations which expressly provide in their governing instruments that the applicable sections of District of Columbia law do not apply to them and except in the case of trusts where otherwise provided by a court of competent jurisdiction. (For purposes of this statute, corporations include corporations organized under any Act of Congress applicable to the District of Columbia as well as corporations organized under the laws of the District of Columbia.)

FLORIDA — except for such trusts which file a proper election not to be subject to the applicable provisions of Florida law and for such corporations as to which a court of competent jurisdiction has otherwise determined.

GEORGIA — except for such private foundations which file a proper election not to be subject to such law.

HAWAII — no exceptions.

IDAHO — except for such private foundations which expressly provide in their governing instruments that the applicable sections of Idaho law do not apply to them.

ILLINOIS — except for such corporations which have express provisions to the contrary in their articles of incorporation and except for trusts where it is otherwise provided by a court of competent jurisdiction.

INDIANA — except where otherwise determined by a court of competent jurisdiction with respect to private foundations organized before January 1, 1970.

IOWA — except for such private foundations which expressly provide in their governing instruments that the applicable sections of Iowa law do not apply to them.

KANSAS — except where otherwise provided by a court of competent jurisdiction.

KENTUCKY — except, with respect to corporations in existence on July 1, 1972, to the extent that such a corporation provides to the contrary by amendment to its articles of incorporation adopted after July 1, 1972, and, with respect to trusts in existence on July 1, 1972, where action is properly commenced on or before December 31, 1972, in a court of competent jurisdiction to excuse the trust from compliance with the requirements of section 508(e) of the Code.

LOUISIANA — except for such private foundations which expressly provide in their governing instruments that the applicable sections of Louisiana law do not apply to them.

MAINE — except where otherwise provided by a court of competent jurisdiction.

MARYLAND — except where otherwise provided by a court of competent jurisdiction.

MASSACHUSETTS — except where otherwise provided by a court of competent jurisdiction.

MICHIGAN — with respect to trusts that are private foundations except for such private foundations which file a notice of inconsistency under Michigan law.

MINNESOTA — except for private foundations that have been held by a court of competent jurisdiction not to be affected by such State statute.

MISSISSIPPI — except where otherwise provided by a court of competent jurisdiction.

MISSOURI — except for private foundations that have been held by a court of competent jurisdiction not to be affected by such State statute.

MONTANA — except in the case of trusts where otherwise provided by court decree entered after March 28, 1974, and except in the case of a corporation which has an express provision to the contrary in its articles of incorporation.

NEBRASKA — except for such trusts which effectively elect to be excluded from the applicable sections of Nebraska law, for such corporations which have governing instruments expressly providing to the contrary, and except as a court of competent jurisdiction has otherwise determined in any given case.

NEVADA — no exceptions.

NEW HAMPSHIRE — except where it is otherwise provided by a court of competent jurisdiction.

NEW JERSEY — except for such private foundations which expressly provide in their governing instruments that the applicable sections of New Jersey law do not apply to them.

NEW YORK — except where such law conflicts with any mandatory direction of an instrument by which assets were transferred prior to June 1, 1971, and such conflicting direction has not been removed legally.

NORTH CAROLINA — except for such private foundations which expressly provide in their governing instruments that the applicable sections of North Carolina law do not apply to them and except for trusts that have their governing instruments reformed by a decree of the Superior Court of North Carolina.

NORTH DAKOTA — with respect to trusts that are private foundations except where otherwise provided by a court of competent jurisdiction.

OHIO — except in the case of trusts where it is provided otherwise by a court of competent jurisdiction and except in the case of corporations in existence on September 17, 1971, which expressly adopt contrary provisions in their governing instruments after September 17, 1971.

OKLAHOMA — except for such private foundations which file a proper election not to be subject to such law.

OREGON — no exceptions.

PENNSYLVANIA — except where otherwise provided by a court of competent jurisdiction.

RHODE ISLAND — except where otherwise provided by a court of competent jurisdiction.

SOUTH CAROLINA — except for private foundations which expressly provide in their governing instruments that the applicable sections of South Carolina law do not apply to them.

SOUTH DAKOTA — except where otherwise provided by a court of competent jurisdiction.

TENNESSEE — except where otherwise provided by a court of competent jurisdiction.

TEXAS — except for such private foundations which file a proper election not to be subject to such law.

UTAH — with respect to trusts that are private foundations except where otherwise provided by a court of competent jurisdiction.

VERMONT — except where otherwise provided by a court of competent jurisdiction.

VIRGINIA — except for private foundations whose governing instruments contain express provisions to the contrary or which have filed a proper election not to be subject to such law.

WASHINGTON — except for such private foundations which expressly provide in their governing instruments that the applicable sections of Washington law do not apply to them.

WEST VIRGINIA — with respect to trusts that are private foundations except for such trusts which provide in their governing instruments that the applicable sections of West Virginia law do not apply to them.

WISCONSIN — except as may otherwise be provided by decree of a court of competent jurisdiction.

WYOMING — except where otherwise provided by a court of competent jurisdiction.

Appendix C: Glossary of Terms

Adjusted net income (for Schedule D)

Adjusted net income includes: gross income from any unrelated trade or business; gross income from functionally related businesses; interest payments received on loans; amounts received or accrued as repayments of amounts taken as qualifying distributions for any tax year; amounts received or accrued from the sale or other disposition of property to the extent acquisition of the property was treated as a qualifying distribution for any tax year; any amounts set aside for a specific project to the extent the full set aside was not necessary for the project; interest on government obligations normally excluded under section 103 of the Code; net short-term capital gains on sale or other disposition of property; and income received from an estate if the estate is considered terminated for income tax purposes because of a prolonged administration period.

It does not include: gifts, grants, and contributions received; long-term capital gains or losses; net section 1231 gains; capital gain dividends; the excess of fair market value over adjusted basis of property distributed to the U.S. or a possession or political subdivision, a state or its political subdivision, a charitable trust or corporation for public purposes, or income received from an estate during the administration period.

In computing adjusted net income, deduct the following: ordinary and necessary expenses paid or incurred for the production or collection of gross income, or for the management, conservation, or collection of gross income (includes operating expenses such as compensation of officers, employee wages and salaries, interest, rent, and taxes); straight-line depreciation and depletion (not percentage depletion); and expenses and interest paid or incurred to carry tax-exempt obligations. Do not deduct net short-term capital losses for the year in which they occur (these losses cannot be carried back or carried over to earlier or later tax years); the excess of expenses for property used for exempt purposes over the income received from the property; charitable contributions made by you; net operating losses; and special deductions for corporations.

Advance ruling

A written determination by us on your public charity status that treats you as a publicly supported organization during a 5-year period beginning, generally, from the date of your formation. At the end of the 5-year period, you will qualify for a definitive ruling (defined below) if you were publicly supported based on the support you received during the 5-year period.

Affiliated

Created by, controlled by, or closely related to a governmental unit, including a State, a possession of the United States, or any political subdivision of a State or a possession of the United States, or the United States, or the District of Columbia.

Arm's length

A transaction between parties having adverse (or opposing) interests; where none of the participants are in a position to exercise substantial influence over the transaction because of business or family relationship(s) with more than one of the parties.

Authorized representative

By submitting Form 2848, an attorney or certified public accountant who is permitted to represent you before us regarding your application for tax-exempt status.

Bingo

A game of chance played with cards that are generally printed with 5 rows of 5 squares each, on which participants place markers to form a pre-selected pattern to win the game. Bingo is gambling.

Business relationships

Employment and contractual relationships, and common ownership of a business where any officers, directors, or trustees, individually or together, possess more than a 35% ownership interest in common. Ownership means voting power in a corporation, profits interest in a partnership, or beneficial interest in a trust.

Bylaws

The internal rules and regulations of an organization.

Certification of filing

Articles of incorporation for your organization showing evidence that on a specific date they were filed with and approved by an appropriate state authority.

Charitable risk pool

An organization described in section 501(n), which is organized and operated to pool insurable risks (other than medical malpractice) of its section 501(c)(3) members.

Close connection

A relationship between organizations that may include: control of one organization by another through common governance or through authority to approve budgets or expenditures; coordination of operations as to facilities, programs, employees, or other activities; or common persons exercising substantial influence over all of the organizations.

Common control

You and one or more other organizations have (1) a majority of your governing boards or officers appointed or elected by the same organization(s), or (2) a majority of your governing boards or officers consist of the same individuals. Common control also occurs when you and one or more commonly controlled organizations have a majority ownership interest in a corporation, partnership, or trust. Ownership means voting power in a corporation, profits interest in a partnership, or beneficial interest in a trust.

Community

The local or regional geographic area to be served by an organization.

Compensation

All forms of income from working, including salary or wages; deferred compensation; retirement benefits, whether in the form of a qualified or non-qualified employee plan (for example: pensions or annuities); fringe benefits (for example: personal vehicle, meals, lodging, personal and family educational benefits, low interest loans, payment of personal travel, entertainment, or other expenses, athletic or country club membership, and personal use of your property); and bonuses.

Conflict of interest policy

A conflict of interest arises when a person in a position of authority over an organization, such as a director, officer, or manager, may benefit personally from a decision he or she could make. A conflict of interest policy consists of a set of procedures to follow to avoid the possibility that those in positions of authority over an organization may receive an inappropriate benefit.

Controlled by disqualified persons

As a section 509(a)(3) supporting organization, you may not be controlled directly or indirectly by disqualified persons. You are controlled if disqualified persons can exercise 50% or more of the total voting power of your governing body. You are also controlled if disqualified persons have authority to affect significant decisions, such as power over your investment decisions, or power over your charitable disbursement decisions. You are also controlled if disqualified persons can exercise veto power. Although control is generally demonstrated where disqualified persons have the authority over your governing body to require you to take an action or refrain from taking an action, indirect control by disqualified persons will also disqualify you as a supporting organization.

Cooperative hospital service organization

An organization described in section 501(e) is organized and operated on a cooperative basis to provide its section 501(c)(3) hospital members one or more of the following activities: data processing, purchasing (including purchasing insurance on a group basis), warehousing, billing and collection (including purchasing patron accounts receivable on a recourse basis), food, clinical, industrial engineering, laboratory, printing, communications, record center, and personnel (including selecting, testing, training, and educating personnel) services.

Cooperative service organization of operating educational organizations

An organization described in section 501(f) is organized and operated to provide investment services to its members. Those members must be organizations described in section 170(b)(1)(A)(ii) or (iv), and either tax exempt under section 501(a) or whose income is excluded from taxation under section 115(a).

Corporation

An entity organized under a Federal or state statute, or a statute of a federally recognized Indian tribal or Alaskan native government.

Definitive ruling

A written determination by us on your public charity status that classifies you as a publicly supported organization if you have completed your first tax year, consisting of at least 8 full months, and you meet one of the public support tests. A definitive ruling may also be issued at the end of your 5-year advance ruling period if you were issued an advance ruling and you meet one of the public support tests.

Develop

Develop means the planning, financing, construction, or provision of similar services involved in the acquisition of real property, such as land or a building.

Disqualified person

Any individual or organization that is:

a. A substantial contributor to you (see substantial contributor).

b. An officer, director, trustee, or any other individual who has similar powers or responsibilities.

c. An individual who owns more than 20% of the total combined voting power of a corporation that is a substantial contributor to you.

d. An individual who owns more than 20% of the profits interest of a partnership that is a substantial contributor to you.

e. An individual who owns more than 20% of the beneficial interest of a trust or estate that is a substantial contributor to you.

f. A member of the family of any individual described in a, b, c, d, or e above;

g. A corporation in which any individuals described in a, b, c, d, e, or f above hold more than 35% of the total combined voting power;

h. A trust or estate in which any individuals described in a, b, c, d, e, or f above hold more than 35% of the beneficial interests; and

i. A partnership in which any individuals described a, b, c, d, e, or f above hold more than 35% of the profits interest.

Earmark

Donations or other contributions given to you to assist particular individuals or specific identified groups.

Economic development

Organizations formed to combat community deterioration by assisting businesses located in a particular geographic area whose economy is economically depressed or deteriorating. Economic development activities include grants, loans, provision of information and expertise, or creation of industrial parks. Economic development organizations may also be formed to eliminate prejudice and discrimination or lessen the burdens of government through involvement with business development.

Elderly housing	Generally, the primary beneficiaries of the tax-exempt housing are age 62 and older. The elderly are treated as appropriate charitable beneficiaries for certain purposes regardless of socio-economic status because, as a group, they face many barriers to their basic needs as they age. The elderly, as a class, face forms of distress other than financial, such as the need for suitable housing, physical and mental health care, civic, cultural, and recreational activities, and an overall environment conducive to dignity and independence.
Expenses	Financial burdens or outlays; costs (of doing business); business outlays chargeable against revenues. For purposes of this form, expenses mean direct and indirect expenses.
Fair market value	The price at which property or the right to use property would change hands between a willing buyer and a willing seller, neither being under any compulsion to buy, sell, or transfer property or the right to use property, and both having reasonable knowledge of relevant facts.
Family	Includes an individual's spouse, ancestors, children, grandchildren, great grandchildren, siblings (whether by whole or half blood), and the spouses of children, grandchildren, great grandchildren, and siblings.
Foreign country	A country other than the United States, its territories and possessions, and the District of Columbia.
For-profit	A business entity whose activities are conducted or maintained to make a profit (e.g. revenues greater than expenses).
Foundation manager	Officers, directors, or trustees, or an individual having powers or responsibilities similar to those of a foundation's officers, directors, or trustees.
Fundraising	The organized activity of raising funds, whether by volunteers, employees, or paid independent contractors.
Gainfully employed	Employed or actively looking for work.
Gaming	The term gaming includes activities such as Bingo, Beano, lotteries, pull-tabs, pari-mutuel betting, Calcutta wagering, pickle jars, punch boards, tip boards, tip jars, certain video games, 21, raffles, keno, split-the-pot, and other games of chance.
Gross investment income	As defined in section 509, gross investment income means the gross amount of income from interest, dividends, payments with respect to securities loans, rents, and royalties, but not including any such income to the extent included in computing the tax imposed by section 511.
Gross receipts	For purposes of Part IX-A. Statement of Revenues and Expenses, gross receipts includes monies earned from activities related to your charitable or other section 501(c)(3) activities, such as selling admissions or merchandise, performing services, or furnishing facilities.
Handicapped	Persons with physical or mental disabilities with special needs for suitable housing, physical and mental health care, civic, cultural, and recreational activities, transportation, and an overall environment conducive to dignity and independence.

Hospital

Hospital or medical care includes the treatment of any physical or mental disability or condition, whether on an inpatient or outpatient basis. A hospital includes:

a. Hospitals and rehabilitation institutions, outpatient clinics, or community mental health or drug treatment centers if the principal purpose or function is the providing of medical or hospital care or medical education or research.

b. Medical research organizations, if the principal purpose or function is the continuous active conduct of medical research in conjunction with a hospital.

Independent contractors

Persons who are not treated as employees for employment tax purposes.

Influence legislation

The act of directly contacting or urging the public to contact members of a legislative body for the purpose of proposing, supporting, or opposing legislation. You are also attempting to influence legislation if you advocate the adoption or rejection of legislation.

Intellectual property

A type of property (distinct from real or personal property) which includes:

a. Patents (for inventions).

b. Copyrights (for literary and artistic works such as novels, poems, plays, films, musical works, drawings, paintings, photographs, sculptures, architectural designs, performances, recordings, film, and radio or television programs).

c. Trade names, trade marks, and service marks (for symbols, names, images, and designs).

d. Formulas, know-how, and trade secrets.

Joint ventures

A legal agreement in which the parties jointly undertake a transaction for mutual profit. Generally, each person contributes assets and shares risks. Like a partnership, joint ventures can involve any type of business transaction and the "persons" involved can be individuals, groups of individuals, companies, or corporations.

Limited liability company

A limited liability company (LLC) combines attributes of both corporations and partnerships (or, for one-person LLCs, sole proprietorships). The corporation's protection from personal liability for business debts and the pass-through tax structure of partnerships and sole proprietorships.

Low-income housing

Rental or ownership housing provided to persons based on financial need.

Mailing address

Address where you wish all correspondence to be sent.

Manage

Manage means to direct or administer.

Medical care

The treatment of any physical or mental disability or condition, whether on an inpatient or outpatient basis.

Medical research organization

An organization whose principal purpose or function is the continuous active conduct of medical research in conjunction with a hospital.

Net income (for Schedule D)

See adjusted net income.

Non-fixed payments

A non-fixed payment means a payment that depends on discretion. For example, a bonus of up to $100,000 that is based on an evaluation of performance by the governing board is a non-fixed payment because the governing body has discretion over whether the bonus is paid and the amount of the bonus.

Organizing document

The organizing document depends on the form of the organization. For a corporation, the document is the articles of incorporation. For a limited liability company (LLC), the document is the articles of organization. For an unincorporated association, the document is the articles of association or constitution. The organizing document of a trust is the trust agreement.

Political

You participate in a political campaign if you promote or oppose, through political literature, brochures, pamphlets, hosting or participating in events, etc., the candidacy of an individual for public office. Debates and nonpartisan voter education are not considered political.

Predecessor

An organization whose activities or assets were taken over by another organization.

Private foundations

Organizations that are exempt under section 501(c)(3) are private foundations unless they are: churches, schools, hospitals, governmental units, entities that undertake testing for public safety; organizations that have broad financial support from the general public; or organizations that support one or more other organizations that are themselves classified as public charities.

Private operating foundation

A type of private foundation that lacks general public support, but makes qualifying distributions directly for the active conduct of its educational, charitable, and religious purposes. "Directly for the active conduct" means that the distributions are used by the foundation itself to carry out the programs for which it is organized and operated. Grants made to assist other organizations or individuals are normally considered indirect.

Public charity

Organizations that are exempt under section 501(c)(3) and are not private foundations because they are: churches, schools, hospitals, governmental units, entities that undertake testing for public safety; organizations that have broad financial support from the general public; or organizations that support one or more other organizations that are themselves classified as public charities. Public charity status is a more favorable tax status than private foundation status.

Reasonable compensation

Reasonable compensation is the amount that would ordinarily be paid for like services by like organizations under like circumstances as of the date the compensation arrangement is made. Reasonable compensation is important because excessive benefits in the form of compensation to disqualified persons may result in the imposition of excise taxes and jeopardize the organization's tax-exempt status.

Related

The family or business relationships between persons.

Relationship

A relationship between you and the recipient organization includes the following situations:

a. You control the organization or it controls you through common officers, directors, or trustees, or through authority to approve budgets or expenditures.

b. You and the organization were created at approximately the same time and by the same persons.

c. You and the organization operate in a coordinated manner with respect to facilities, programs, employees, or other activities.

d. Persons who exercise substantial influence over you also exercise substantial influence over the other organization.

Revenue

Revenue means gross revenue amounts.

Revenue Procedure

An official statement of a procedure published in the IRS Cumulative Bulletin that either affects the rights or duties of taxpayers or other members of the public under the Internal Revenue Code and related statutes, treaties, and regulations or, although not necessarily affecting the rights and duties of the public, should be a matter of public knowledge.

Revenue Ruling

An official interpretation by the IRS of the Internal Revenue laws and related statutes, treaties, and regulations, that has been published in the Cumulative Bulletin. Revenue Rulings are issued only by the National Office and are published for the information and guidance of taxpayers, IRS officials, and others concerned.

SS-4

Application for Employer Identification Number.

School

A school is an educational organization whose primary function is the presentation of formal instruction and which normally maintains a regular faculty and curriculum and normally has a regularly enrolled body of pupils or students in attendance at the place where its educational activities are regularly carried on. A school may include a:

a. Primary, secondary, preparatory, or high school.

b. College or university.

c. Trade or technical school.

d. Nursery or preschool.

e. School that you operate as an activity, such as school that is operated as an activity of a museum, historical society, or church.

Similarly situated

Similarly situated organizations means tax-exempt or taxable organizations of a comparable size, purpose, and resources.

Substantial contributor

Any individual or organization that gave more than $5,000 to you from the date you were formed or other date that your exemption would be effective, to the end of the year in which the contributions were received. This total amount contributed must also be more than 2% of all the contributions you received. A creator of a trust is treated as a substantial contributor regardless of the amount contributed.

Successor

An organization that took over:

a. More than a negligible amount of the activities that were previously conducted by another organization;

b. Twenty-five percent or more of the fair market value of the net assets of another organization; or

c. Was established upon the conversion of an organization from for-profit to non-profit status.

Trust

A trust is an entity that may be formed by a trust agreement or declaration of trust. A trust may also be formed through a will.

Unincorporated association

An unincorporated association formed under state law must have at least two members who have signed a written document for a specifically defined purpose.

Unusual grants

Substantial contributions and bequests from disinterested persons that by their size adversely affect classification as a public charity. They are:

a. Unusual;

b. Unexpected; and

c. Received from an unrelated party.

Index

APPENDIX 2

CERTIFICATE OF INCORPORATION

OF

THE ______________________ FOUNDATION, INC.

The Undersigned, a natural person, for the purpose of organizing a corporation not for profit and without authority to issue capital stock under the provisions and subject to the requirements of the laws of the State of Delaware (particularly Chapter 1, Title 8 of the Delaware Code and the acts amendatory thereof and supplemental thereto, and known, identified, and referred to as the "General Corporation Law of the State of Delaware"), hereby certifies that:

FIRST: The name of the corporation (hereinafter called the "corporation") is THE ______________________________ FOUNDATION, INC.

SECOND: Its registered office in the State of Delaware is to be located at ________________________________Street, in the City of Wilmington, County of New Castle and its registered agent at such address is ___________________________________.

THIRD: The nature of the purposes to be conducted by the corporation is as follows:

-- providing support to [list specific charitable purposes] within the meaning of section 501(c)(3) of the Internal Revenue Code, or the corresponding section of any future Federal tax code;

-- providing support to programs, projects and organizations involved in [list additional specific charitable purposes] within the meaning of section 501(c)(3) of the Internal Revenue Code, or the corresponding section of any future Federal tax code;

-- providing support to [list additional specific charitable purposes] within the meaning of section 501(c)(3) of the Internal Revenue Code, or the corresponding section of any future Federal tax code; and

-- promoting charitable, religious, educational, and scientific purposes, including, for such purposes, the making of distributions to organizations that qualify as exempt organizations under section 501(c)(3) of the Internal Revenue Code, or the corresponding section of any future Federal tax code.

The Corporation is organized and operated exclusively for charitable, educational, religious, or scientific purposes within the meaning of section 501(c)(3) of the Internal Revenue Code, or the corresponding section of any future Federal tax code. Notwithstanding any other provision herein, the Corporation shall not carry on any other activities not permitted to be carried on

(a) by an organization exempt from Federal income tax under section 501(c)(3) of the Internal Revenue Code, or the corresponding section of any future Federal tax code or

(b) by an organization, contributions to which are deductible under section 170(c)(2) of the Internal Revenue Code, or the corresponding section of any future Federal tax code.

1) The Corporation will distribute its income for each tax year at such time and in such manner as not to become subject to the tax on undistributed income imposed by section 4942 of the Internal Revenue Code, or the corresponding section of any future Federal tax code.

2) The Corporation will not engage in any act of self-dealing as defined in section 4941(d) of the Internal Revenue Code, or the corresponding section of any future Federal tax code.

3) The Corporation will not retain any excess business holdings as defined in section 4943(c) of the Internal Revenue Code, or the corresponding section of any future Federal tax code.

4) The Corporation will not make any investments in such manner as to subject it to tax under section 4944 of the Internal Revenue Code, or the corresponding section of any future Federal tax code.

5) The Corporation will not make any taxable expenditures as defined in section 4945(d) of the Internal Revenue Code, or the corresponding section of any future Federal tax code.

The Corporation shall have the authority to exercise all of the powers conferred upon corporations organized not for profit and without authority to issue capital stock under the provisions of the General Corporation Law of the State of Delaware, provided, that the exercise of any such powers shall be in furtherance of any one or more of the aforesaid exempt purposes of the Corporation

FOURTH: The corporation is not to have authority to issue capital stock.

FIFTH: The name and the mailing address of the incorporator are as follows:

Name	Mailing Address

SIXTH: The duration of the corporation is to be perpetual.

SEVENTH: The personal liability of the directors of the corporation is hereby eliminated to the fullest extent permitted by paragraph (7) of subsection (b) of §102 of the General Corporation Law of the State of Delaware, as the same may be amended and supplemented.

<u>EIGHTH</u>: For the management of the business and for the conduct of the affairs of the corporation, and for the creation, definition, limitation, and regulation of the powers of the corporation and of its governing body and the member or members thereof, as the case may be, it is hereby provided:

1. After the original or other By-Laws of the corporation shall have been adopted, amended, or repealed, as the case may be, by the incorporator, the power to adopt, amend, or repeal the By-Laws of the corporation may be exercised by the Board of Directors of the corporation.

2. The activities and affairs of the corporation shall be managed by or under the direction of its governing body, which in this certificate of incorporation is referred to as a Board of Directors, although said Board may consist of only one member, and although the member or members of said governing body may be designated as a trustee or trustees, a manager or managers, a governor or governors, or otherwise under any provision of the By-Laws.

3. The number of directors constituting the initial whole Board of Directors shall be the number fixed in the original or initial By-Laws. Thereafter, the number of directors constituting the whole Board shall be fixed from time to time in the manner prescribed in the By-Laws.

4. A director shall have such qualifications as may be prescribed in the By-Laws. The initial Board of Directors shall be elected by the incorporator. Thereafter, each successive Board of Directors shall be elected as required by the By-Laws of the corporation.

5. Any person who is or was a director, officer, agent, or employee of the corporation or is or was serving, at the request of the corporation, as a director, officer, agent, or employee of another corporation, trust, or enterprise shall be entitled to be indemnified by the corporation upon the same terms, under the same conditions, and to the same extent as though he were a present or past director, officer, agent, or employee of a corporation of any type or kind organized under the General Corporation Law of the State of Delaware; provided that his conduct or action was in furtherance of, or in connection with, the exempt purposes of the corporation.

<u>NINTH</u>: From time to time, and in furtherance of the purposes for which the corporation is being organized, any of the provisions of this certificate of incorporation may be amended, altered, or repealed by the Board of Directors, and other provisions authorized by the laws of the State of Delaware at the time in force may be added or inserted in the manner and at the time prescribed by said laws.

<u>TENTH</u>: No part of the net earning of the corporation shall inure to the benefit of, or be distributable to its members, trustee, officers, or other private persons, except that the corporation shall be authorized and empowered to pay reasonable compensation for services

rendered and to make payments and distributions in furtherance of the purposes set forth in Article THIRD hereof. No substantial part of the activities of the corporation shall be the carrying on of propaganda, or otherwise attempting to influence legislation, and the corporation shall not participate in, or intervene in (including the publishing or distribution of statements) any political campaign on behalf of or in opposition to any candidate for public office. Notwithstanding any other provision of these articles, the corporation shall not carry on any other activities not permitted to be carried on (a) by a foundation exempt from federal income tax under section 501(c)(3) of the Internal Revenue Code or the corresponding section of any future federal tax code, or (b) by a corporation, contributions to which are deductible under section 170(c)(2) of the Internal Revenue Code, or the corresponding section of any future federal tax code.

ELEVENTH: Upon the dissolution of the corporation, assets shall be distributed for one or more exempt purposes within the meaning of section 501(c)(3) of the Internal Revenue Code or the corresponding section of any future federal tax code, or shall be distributed to the federal government, or to a state or local government, for public purposes. Any such assets not so disposed of shall be disposed of by a court of competent jurisdiction of the country in which the principal office of the corporation is then located, exclusively for such purposes or to such organization or organizations, as said court shall determine, which are organized and operated exclusively for such purposes.

IN WITNESS WHEREOF, the undersigned, being the incorporator herein before named, has executed, signed and acknowledged this Certificate of Incorporation this ___th day of __________, A.D., 20__.

____

____________, Incorporator

APPENDIX 3

CERTIFICATE OF INCORPORATION

OF

AMERICAN FRIENDS OF ………, INC.

The Undersigned, a natural person, for the purpose of organizing a corporation not for profit and without authority to issue capital stock under the provisions and subject to the requirements of the laws of the State of Delaware (particularly Chapter 1, Title 8 of the Delaware Code and the acts amendatory thereof and supplemental thereto, and known, identified, and referred to as the "General Corporation Law of the State of Delaware"), hereby certifies that:

FIRST: The name of the corporation (hereinafter called the "corporation") is AMERICAN FRIENDS OF …….., INC.

SECOND: Its registered office in the State of Delaware is to be located at ______________________________ in the City of Wilmington, County of New Castle, and its registered agent at such address is ___________________________.

THIRD: The nature of the purposes to be conducted by the corporation is as follows:

(a) The promotion of [list specific charitable purposes] in the United States and other countries of the world;

(b) The promotion of [list additional specific charitable purposes] in the United States and other countries of the world;

(c) The collaboration with and promotion of the activities of the [insert name of foreign charity] in furtherance of the foregoing activities in the United States and other countries of the world; and

(d) The promotion of charitable, religious, educational, and scientific purposes, including, for such purposes, the making of distributions to organizations that qualify as exempt organizations under section 501(c)(3) of the Internal Revenue Code, or the corresponding section of any future Federal tax code.

The Corporation is organized and operated exclusively for charitable, educational, religious, or scientific purposes within the meaning of section 501(c)(3) of the Internal Revenue Code, or the corresponding section of any future Federal tax code. Notwithstanding any other provision herein, the corporation shall not carry on any other activities not permitted to be carried on

(a) by an organization exempt from Federal income tax under section 501(c)(3) of the Internal Revenue Code, or the corresponding section of any future Federal tax code or

(b) by an organization, contributions to which are deductible under section 170(c)(2) of the Internal Revenue Code, or the corresponding section of any future Federal tax code.

The corporation shall have the authority to exercise all of the powers conferred upon corporations organized not for profit and without authority to issue capital stock under the provisions of the General Corporation Law of the State of Delaware, provided, that the exercise of any such powers shall be in furtherance of any one or more of the aforesaid exempt purposes of the corporation.

FOURTH: The corporation is not to have authority to issue capital stock.

FIFTH: The name and the mailing address of the incorporator are as follows:

Name	Mailing Address
______________	____________________

SIXTH: The duration of the corporation is to be perpetual.

SEVENTH: The personal liability of the directors of the corporation is hereby limited to the fullest extent permitted by paragraph (7) of subsection (b) of §102 of the General Corporation Law of the State of Delaware, as the same may be amended and supplemented.

EIGHTH: For the management of the business and for the conduct of the affairs of the corporation, and for the creation, definition, limitation, and regulation of the powers of the corporation and of its governing body and the member or members thereof, as the case may be, it is hereby provided:

1. After the original or other By-Laws of the corporation shall have been adopted, amended, or repealed, as the case may be, by the incorporator, the power to adopt, amend, or repeal the By-Laws of the corporation may be exercised by the Board of Directors of the corporation.

2. The activities and affairs of the corporation shall be managed by or under the direction of its governing body, which in this certificate of incorporation is referred to as a Board of Directors, although said Board may consist of only one member, and although the member or members of said governing body may be designated as a trustee or trustees, a manager

or managers, a governor or governors, or otherwise under any provision of the By-Laws.

3. The number of directors constituting the initial Board of Directors shall be the number fixed by the incorporator. Thereafter, the number of directors constituting the Board of Directors shall be fixed from time to time in the manner prescribed in the By-Laws.

4. A director shall have such qualifications as may be prescribed in the By-Laws. The initial Board of Directors shall be elected by the incorporator. Thereafter, each successive Board of Directors shall be elected as required by the By-Laws of the corporation.

5. Any person who is or was a director, officer, agent, or employee of the corporation or is or was serving, at the request of the corporation, as a director, officer, agent, or employee of another corporation, trust, or enterprise shall be entitled to be indemnified by the corporation upon the same terms, under the same conditions, and to the same extent as though he were a present or past director, officer, agent, or employee of a corporation of any type or kind organized under the General Corporation Law of the State of Delaware; provided that his conduct or action was in furtherance of, or in connection with, the exempt purposes of the corporation.

NINTH: From time to time, and in furtherance of the purposes for which the corporation is being organized, any of the provisions of this certificate of incorporation may be amended, altered, or repealed by the Board of Directors, and other provisions authorized by the laws of the State of Delaware at the time in force may be added or inserted in the manner and at the time prescribed by said laws.

TENTH: No part of the net earnings of the corporation shall inure to the benefit of, or be distributable to its directors, members, trustees, officers, or other private persons, except that the corporation shall be authorized and empowered to pay reasonable compensation for services rendered and to make payments and distributions in furtherance of the purposes set forth in Article THIRD hereof. No substantial part of the activities of the corporation shall be the carrying on of propaganda, or otherwise attempting to influence legislation, and the corporation shall not participate in, or intervene in (including the publishing or distribution of statements) any political campaign on behalf of or in opposition to any candidate for public office.

ELEVENTH: Upon the dissolution of the corporation, assets shall be distributed for one or more exempt purposes within the meaning of section 501(c)(3) of the Internal Revenue Code or the corresponding section of any future federal tax code, or shall be distributed to the federal government, or to a state or local government, for public purposes. Any such assets not so disposed of shall be disposed of by a court of competent jurisdiction of the country in which the principal office of the corporation is then located, exclusively for such purposes or to such organization or organizations, as said court shall determine, which are organized and operated exclusively for such purposes.

IN WITNESS WHEREOF, the undersigned, being the incorporator herein before named, has executed, signed and acknowledged this Certificate of Incorporation this ___ day of _____________, A.D., 20__.

____

______________________, Incorporator

APPENDIX 4

Appendix A: Sample Conflict of Interest Policy

Article I
Purpose

The purpose of the conflict of interest policy is to protect this tax-exempt organization's (Organization) interest when it is contemplating entering into a transaction or arrangement that might benefit the private interest of an officer or director of the Organization or might result in a possible excess benefit transaction. This policy is intended to supplement but not replace any applicable state and federal laws governing conflict of interest applicable to nonprofit and charitable organizations.

Article II
Definitions

1. Interested Person
Any director, principal officer, or member of a committee with governing board delegated powers, who has a direct or indirect financial interest, as defined below, is an interested person.

2. Financial Interest
A person has a financial interest if the person has, directly or indirectly, through business, investment, or family:

a. An ownership or investment interest in any entity with which the Organization has a transaction or arrangement, **b.** A compensation arrangement with the Organization or with any entity or individual with which the Organization has a transaction or arrangement, or
c. A potential ownership or investment interest in, or compensation arrangement with, any entity or individual with which the Organization is negotiating a transaction or arrangement.

Compensation includes direct and indirect remuneration as well as gifts or favors that are not insubstantial.

A financial interest is not necessarily a conflict of interest. Under Article III, Section 2, a person who has a financial interest may have a conflict of interest only if the appropriate governing board or committee decides that a conflict of interest exists.

Article III
Procedures

1. Duty to Disclose
In connection with any actual or possible conflict of interest, an interested person must disclose the existence of the financial interest and be given the opportunity to disclose all material facts to the directors and members of committees with governing board delegated powers considering the proposed transaction or arrangement.

2. Determining Whether a Conflict of Interest Exists
After disclosure of the financial interest and all material facts, and after any discussion with the interested person, he/she shall leave the governing board or committee meeting while the determination of a conflict of interest is discussed and voted upon. The remaining board or committee members shall decide if a conflict of interest exists.

3. Procedures for Addressing the Conflict of Interest
a. An interested person may make a presentation at the governing board or committee meeting, but after the presentation, he/she shall leave the meeting during the discussion of, and the vote on, the transaction or arrangement involving the possible conflict of interest.
b. The chairperson of the governing board or committee shall, if appropriate, appoint a disinterested person or committee to investigate alternatives to the proposed transaction or arrangement.
c. After exercising due diligence, the governing board or committee shall determine whether the Organization can obtain with reasonable efforts a more advantageous transaction or arrangement from a person or entity that would not give rise to a conflict of interest.

d. If a more advantageous transaction or arrangement is not reasonably possible under circumstances not producing a conflict of interest, the governing board or committee shall determine by a majority vote of the disinterested directors whether the transaction or arrangement is in the Organization's best interest, for its own benefit, and whether it is fair and reasonable. In conformity with the above determination it shall make its decision as to whether to enter into the transaction or arrangement.

4. Violations of the Conflicts of Interest Policy
a. If the governing board or committee has reasonable cause to believe a member has failed to disclose actual or possible conflicts of interest, it shall inform the member of the basis for such belief and afford the member an opportunity to explain the alleged failure to disclose.

b. If, after hearing the member's response and after making further investigation as warranted by the circumstances, the governing board or committee determines the member has failed to disclose an actual or possible conflict of interest, it shall take appropriate disciplinary and corrective action.

Article IV
Records of Proceedings

The minutes of the governing board and all committees with board delegated powers shall contain:

a. The names of the persons who disclosed or otherwise were found to have a financial interest in connection with an actual or possible conflict of interest, the nature of the financial interest, any action taken to determine whether a conflict of interest was present, and the governing board's or committee's decision as to whether a conflict of interest in fact existed.

b. The names of the persons who were present for discussions and votes relating to the transaction or arrangement, the content of the discussion, including any alternatives to the proposed transaction or arrangement, and a record of any votes taken in connection with the proceedings.

Article V
Compensation

a. A voting member of the governing board who receives compensation, directly or indirectly, from the Organization for services is precluded from voting on matters pertaining to that member's compensation.

b. A voting member of any committee whose jurisdiction includes compensation matters and who receives compensation, directly or indirectly, from the Organization for services is precluded from voting on matters pertaining to that member's compensation.

c. No voting member of the governing board or any committee whose jurisdiction includes compensation matters and who receives compensation, directly or indirectly, from the Organization, either individually or collectively, is prohibited from providing information to any committee regarding compensation.

Article VI
Annual Statements

Each director, principal officer and member of a committee with governing board delegated powers shall annually sign a statement which affirms such person:

a. Has received a copy of the conflicts of interest policy,

b. Has read and understands the policy,

c. Has agreed to comply with the policy, and

d. Understands the Organization is charitable and in order to maintain its federal tax exemption it must engage primarily in activities which accomplish one or more of its tax-exempt purposes.

Article VII
Periodic Reviews

To ensure the Organization operates in a manner consistent with charitable purposes and does not engage in activities that could jeopardize its tax-exempt status, periodic reviews shall be conducted. The periodic reviews shall, at a minimum, include the following subjects:

a. Whether compensation arrangements and benefits are reasonable, based on competent survey information, and the result of arm's length bargaining.

b. Whether partnerships, joint ventures, and arrangements with management organizations conform to the Organization's written policies, are properly recorded, reflect reasonable investment or payments for goods and services, further charitable purposes and do not result in inurement, impermissible private benefit or in an excess benefit transaction.

Article VIII
Use of Outside Experts

When conducting the periodic reviews as provided for in Article VII, the Organization may, but need not, use outside advisors. If outside experts are used, their use shall not relieve the governing board of its responsibility for ensuring periodic reviews are conducted.

Form **990-PF**

Department of the Treasury
Internal Revenue Service

Return of Private Foundation

or Section 4947(a)(1) Nonexempt Charitable Trust Treated as a Private Foundation

Note. The foundation may be able to use a copy of this return to satisfy state reporting requirements.

OMB No. 1545-0052

2008

For calendar year 2008, or tax year beginning , 2008, and ending , 20

G Check all that apply: ☐ Initial return ☐ Final return ☐ Amended return ☐ Address change ☐ Name change

Use the IRS label. Otherwise, print or type. See Specific Instructions.	Name of foundation		A Employer identification number
	Number and street (or P.O. box number if mail is not delivered to street address)	Room/suite	B Telephone number (see page 10 of the instructions) ( )
	City or town, state, and ZIP code		C If exemption application is pending, check here ▶ ☐
			D 1. Foreign organizations, check here . . ▶ ☐

H Check type of organization: ☐ Section 501(c)(3) exempt private foundation
☐ Section 4947(a)(1) nonexempt charitable trust ☐ Other taxable private foundation

2. Foreign organizations meeting the 85% test, check here and attach computation . ▶ ☐

I Fair market value of all assets at end of year *(from Part II, col. (c), line 16)* ▶ $

J Accounting method: ☐ Cash ☐ Accrual
☐ Other (specify)
(Part I, column (d) must be on cash basis.)

E If private foundation status was terminated under section 507(b)(1)(A), check here . ▶ ☐

F If the foundation is in a 60-month termination under section 507(b)(1)(B), check here . ▶ ☐

Part I **Analysis of Revenue and Expenses** *(The total of amounts in columns (b), (c), and (d) may not necessarily equal the amounts in column (a) (see page 11 of the instructions).)*

			(a) Revenue and expenses per books	(b) Net investment income	(c) Adjusted net income	(d) Disbursements for charitable purposes (cash basis only)
Revenue	1	Contributions, gifts, grants, etc., received (attach schedule)				
	2	Check ▶ ☐ if the foundation is **not** required to attach Sch. B				
	3	Interest on savings and temporary cash investments				
	4	Dividends and interest from securities				
	5a	Gross rents				
	b	Net rental income or (loss)				
	6a	Net gain or (loss) from sale of assets not on line 10				
	b	Gross sales price for all assets on line 6a				
	7	Capital gain net income (from Part IV, line 2) . .				
	8	Net short-term capital gain				
	9	Income modifications				
	10a	Gross sales less returns and allowances				
	b	Less: Cost of goods sold .				
	c	Gross profit or (loss) (attach schedule)				
	11	Other income (attach schedule)				
	12	**Total.** Add lines 1 through 11				
Operating and Administrative Expenses	13	Compensation of officers, directors, trustees, etc.				
	14	Other employee salaries and wages				
	15	Pension plans, employee benefits				
	16a	Legal fees (attach schedule)				
	b	Accounting fees (attach schedule)				
	c	Other professional fees (attach schedule) . . .				
	17	Interest				
	18	Taxes (attach schedule) (see page 14 of the instructions)				
	19	Depreciation (attach schedule) and depletion . .				
	20	Occupancy				
	21	Travel, conferences, and meetings				
	22	Printing and publications				
	23	Other expenses (attach schedule)				
	24	**Total operating and administrative expenses.** Add lines 13 through 23				
	25	Contributions, gifts, grants paid				
	26	**Total expenses and disbursements.** Add lines 24 and 25				
	27	Subtract line 26 from line 12:				
	a	**Excess of revenue over expenses and disbursements**				
	b	**Net investment income** (if negative, enter -0-)				
	c	**Adjusted net income** (if negative, enter -0-) . .				

For Privacy Act and Paperwork Reduction Act Notice, see page 30 of the instructions. Cat. No. 11289X Form **990-PF** (2008)

Form 990-PF (2008) Page **2**

Part II **Balance Sheets** Attached schedules and amounts in the description column should be for end-of-year amounts only. (See instructions.)

		Beginning of year	End of year	
		(a) Book Value	(b) Book Value	(c) Fair Market Value
Assets	1 Cash—non-interest-bearing			
	2 Savings and temporary cash investments			
	3 Accounts receivable ▶			
	Less: allowance for doubtful accounts ▶			
	4 Pledges receivable ▶			
	Less: allowance for doubtful accounts ▶			
	5 Grants receivable			
	6 Receivables due from officers, directors, trustees, and other disqualified persons (attach schedule) (see page 15 of the instructions)			
	7 Other notes and loans receivable (attach schedule) ▶			
	Less: allowance for doubtful accounts ▶			
	8 Inventories for sale or use			
	9 Prepaid expenses and deferred charges			
	10a Investments—U.S. and state government obligations (attach schedule)			
	b Investments—corporate stock (attach schedule)			
	c Investments—corporate bonds (attach schedule)			
	11 Investments—land, buildings, and equipment: basis ▶			
	Less: accumulated depreciation (attach schedule) ▶			
	12 Investments—mortgage loans			
	13 Investments—other (attach schedule)			
	14 Land, buildings, and equipment: basis ▶			
	Less: accumulated depreciation (attach schedule) ▶			
	15 Other assets (describe ▶)			
	16 **Total assets** (to be completed by all filers—see the instructions. Also, see page 1, item I)			
Liabilities	17 Accounts payable and accrued expenses			
	18 Grants payable			
	19 Deferred revenue			
	20 Loans from officers, directors, trustees, and other disqualified persons			
	21 Mortgages and other notes payable (attach schedule)			
	22 Other liabilities (describe ▶)			
	23 **Total liabilities** (add lines 17 through 22)			
Net Assets or Fund Balances	**Foundations that follow SFAS 117, check here ▶ ☐ and complete lines 24 through 26 and lines 30 and 31.**			
	24 Unrestricted			
	25 Temporarily restricted			
	26 Permanently restricted			
	Foundations that do not follow SFAS 117, check here ▶ ☐ and complete lines 27 through 31.			
	27 Capital stock, trust principal, or current funds			
	28 Paid-in or capital surplus, or land, bldg., and equipment fund			
	29 Retained earnings, accumulated income, endowment, or other funds			
	30 **Total net assets or fund balances** (see page 17 of the instructions)			
	31 **Total liabilities and net assets/fund balances** (see page 17 of the instructions)			

Part III **Analysis of Changes in Net Assets or Fund Balances**

1 Total net assets or fund balances at beginning of year—Part II, column (a), line 30 (must agree with end-of-year figure reported on prior year's return)	1	
2 Enter amount from Part I, line 27a	2	
3 Other increases not included in line 2 (itemize) ▶	3	
4 Add lines 1, 2, and 3	4	
5 Decreases not included in line 2 (itemize) ▶	5	
6 Total net assets or fund balances at end of year (line 4 minus line 5)—Part II, column (b), line 30	6	

Form **990-PF** (2008)

Form 990-PF (2008) Page **3**

Part IV Capital Gains and Losses for Tax on Investment Income

	(a) List and describe the kind(s) of property sold (e.g., real estate, 2-story brick warehouse; or common stock, 200 shs. MLC Co.)	(b) How acquired P—Purchase D—Donation	(c) Date acquired (mo., day, yr.)	(d) Date sold (mo., day, yr.)
1a				
b				
c				
d				
e				

	(e) Gross sales price	(f) Depreciation allowed (or allowable)	(g) Cost or other basis plus expense of sale	(h) Gain or (loss) (e) plus (f) minus (g)
a				
b				
c				
d				
e				

Complete only for assets showing gain in column (h) and owned by the foundation on 12/31/69

	(i) F.M.V. as of 12/31/69	(j) Adjusted basis as of 12/31/69	(k) Excess of col. (i) over col. (j), if any	(l) Gains (Col. (h) gain minus col. (k), but not less than -0-) **or** Losses (from col. (h))
a				
b				
c				
d				
e				

2 Capital gain net income or (net capital loss) { If gain, also enter in Part I, line 7 / If (loss), enter -0- in Part I, line 7 } **2**

3 Net short-term capital gain or (loss) as defined in sections 1222(5) and (6):
If gain, also enter in Part I, line 8, column (c) (see pages 13 and 17 of the instructions).
If (loss), enter -0- in Part I, line 8 . . . . **3**

Part V Qualification Under Section 4940(e) for Reduced Tax on Net Investment Income

(For optional use by domestic private foundations subject to the section 4940(a) tax on net investment income.)

If section 4940(d)(2) applies, leave this part blank.

Was the foundation liable for the section 4942 tax on the distributable amount of any year in the base period? ☐ Yes ☐ No
If "Yes," the foundation does not qualify under section 4940(e). Do not complete this part.

1 Enter the appropriate amount in each column for each year; see page 18 of the instructions before making any entries.

(a) Base period years Calendar year (or tax year beginning in)	(b) Adjusted qualifying distributions	(c) Net value of noncharitable-use assets	(d) Distribution ratio (col. (b) divided by col. (c))
2007			
2006			
2005			
2004			
2003			

2 **Total** of line 1, column (d)	2	
3 Average distribution ratio for the 5-year base period—divide the total on line 2 by 5, or by the number of years the foundation has been in existence if less than 5 years	3	
4 Enter the net value of noncharitable-use assets for 2008 from Part X, line 5	4	
5 Multiply line 4 by line 3	5	
6 Enter 1% of net investment income (1% of Part I, line 27b)	6	
7 Add lines 5 and 6	7	
8 Enter qualifying distributions from Part XII, line 4	8	

If line 8 is equal to or greater than line 7, check the box in Part VI, line 1b, and complete that part using a 1% tax rate. See the Part VI instructions on page 18.

Form **990-PF** (2008)

Form 990-PF (2008) Page 4

Part VI Excise Tax Based on Investment Income (Section 4940(a), 4940(b), 4940(e), or 4948—see page 18 of the instructions)

1a Exempt operating foundations described in section 4940(d)(2), check here ▶ ☐ and enter "N/A" on line 1. Date of ruling letter: .... **(attach copy of ruling letter if necessary—see instructions)**			
b Domestic foundations that meet the section 4940(e) requirements in Part V, check here ▶ ☐ and enter 1% of Part I, line 27b	1		
c All other domestic foundations enter 2% of line 27b. Exempt foreign organizations enter 4% of Part I, line 12, col. (b)			
2 Tax under section 511 (domestic section 4947(a)(1) trusts and taxable foundations only. Others enter -0-)	2		
3 Add lines 1 and 2	3		
4 Subtitle A (income) tax (domestic section 4947(a)(1) trusts and taxable foundations only. Others enter -0-)	4		
5 **Tax based on investment income.** Subtract line 4 from line 3. If zero or less, enter -0-	5		
6 Credits/Payments:			
a 2008 estimated tax payments and 2007 overpayment credited to 2008 — 6a			
b Exempt foreign organizations—tax withheld at source — 6b			
c Tax paid with application for extension of time to file (Form 8868) — 6c			
d Backup withholding erroneously withheld — 6d			
7 Total credits and payments. Add lines 6a through 6d	7		
8 Enter any **penalty** for underpayment of estimated tax. Check here ☐ if Form 2220 is attached	8		
9 **Tax due.** If the total of lines 5 and 8 is more than line 7, enter **amount owed** ▶	9		
10 **Overpayment.** If line 7 is more than the total of lines 5 and 8, enter the **amount overpaid** ▶	10		
11 Enter the amount of line 10 to be: **Credited to 2009 estimated tax** ▶ | **Refunded** ▶	11		

Part VII-A Statements Regarding Activities

		Yes	No
1a During the tax year, did the foundation attempt to influence any national, state, or local legislation or did it participate or intervene in any political campaign?	1a		
b Did it spend more than $100 during the year (either directly or indirectly) for political purposes (see page 19 of the instructions for definition)?	1b		
*If the answer is "Yes" to **1a** or **1b**, attach a detailed description of the activities and copies of any materials published or distributed by the foundation in connection with the activities.*			
c Did the foundation file **Form 1120-POL** for this year?	1c		
d Enter the amount (if any) of tax on political expenditures (section 4955) imposed during the year: **(1)** On the foundation. ▶ $ ________ **(2)** On foundation managers. ▶ $ ________			
e Enter the reimbursement (if any) paid by the foundation during the year for political expenditure tax imposed on foundation managers. ▶ $ ________			
2 Has the foundation engaged in any activities that have not previously been reported to the IRS? *If "Yes," attach a detailed description of the activities.*	2		
3 Has the foundation made any changes, not previously reported to the IRS, in its governing instrument, articles of incorporation, or bylaws, or other similar instruments? *If "Yes," attach a conformed copy of the changes*	3		
4a Did the foundation have unrelated business gross income of $1,000 or more during the year?	4a		
b If "Yes," has it filed a tax return on **Form 990-T** for this year?	4b		
5 Was there a liquidation, termination, dissolution, or substantial contraction during the year? *If "Yes," attach the statement required by General Instruction T.*	5		
6 Are the requirements of section 508(e) (relating to sections 4941 through 4945) satisfied either: • By language in the governing instrument, or • By state legislation that effectively amends the governing instrument so that no mandatory directions that conflict with the state law remain in the governing instrument?	6		
7 Did the foundation have at least $5,000 in assets at any time during the year? *If "Yes," complete Part II, col. (c), and Part XV.*	7		
8a Enter the states to which the foundation reports or with which it is registered (see page 19 of the instructions) ▶			
b If the answer is "Yes" to line 7, has the foundation furnished a copy of Form 990-PF to the Attorney General (or designate) of each state as required by *General Instruction G? If "No," attach explanation*	8b		
9 Is the foundation claiming status as a private operating foundation within the meaning of section 4942(j)(3) or 4942(j)(5) for calendar year 2008 or the taxable year beginning in 2008 (see instructions for Part XIV on page 27)? *If "Yes," complete Part XIV*	9		
10 Did any persons become substantial contributors during the tax year? *If "Yes," attach a schedule listing their names and addresses*	10		

Form **990-PF** (2008)

Form 990-PF (2008) Page **5**

Part VII-A Statements Regarding Activities *(continued)*

11 At any time during the year, did the foundation, directly or indirectly, own a controlled entity within the meaning of section 512(b)(13)? If "Yes," attach schedule (see page 20 of the instructions) **11**

12 Did the foundation acquire a direct or indirect interest in any applicable insurance contract before August 17, 2008? **12**

13 Did the foundation comply with the public inspection requirements for its annual returns and exemption application? **13**

Website address ▶ ....

14 The books are in care of ▶ .... Telephone no. ▶ ....

Located at ▶ .... ZIP+4 ▶ ....

15 Section 4947(a)(1) nonexempt charitable trusts filing Form 990-PF in lieu of **Form 1041**—Check here . . . . . . ▶ ☐
and enter the amount of tax-exempt interest received or accrued during the year . . . . . ▶ | **15** |

Part VII-B Statements Regarding Activities for Which Form 4720 May Be Required

File Form 4720 if any item is checked in the "Yes" column, unless an exception applies. | Yes | No

1a During the year did the foundation (either directly or indirectly):

(1) Engage in the sale or exchange, or leasing of property with a disqualified person? . ☐ **Yes** ☐ **No**

(2) Borrow money from, lend money to, or otherwise extend credit to (or accept it from) a disqualified person? . . . . ☐ **Yes** ☐ **No**

(3) Furnish goods, services, or facilities to (or accept them from) a disqualified person? . ☐ **Yes** ☐ **No**

(4) Pay compensation to, or pay or reimburse the expenses of, a disqualified person? . ☐ **Yes** ☐ **No**

(5) Transfer any income or assets to a disqualified person (or make any of either available for the benefit or use of a disqualified person)? . . . . ☐ **Yes** ☐ **No**

(6) Agree to pay money or property to a government official? (**Exception.** Check "No" if the foundation agreed to make a grant to or to employ the official for a period after termination of government service, if terminating within 90 days.) . . . . ☐ **Yes** ☐ **No**

b If any answer is "Yes" to 1a(1)–(6), did **any** of the acts fail to qualify under the exceptions described in Regulations section 53.4941(d)-3 or in a current notice regarding disaster assistance (see page 20 of the instructions)? . . **1b**

Organizations relying on a current notice regarding disaster assistance check here . . . . . . ▶ ☐

c Did the foundation engage in a prior year in any of the acts described in 1a, other than excepted acts, that were not corrected before the first day of the tax year beginning in 2008? **1c**

2 Taxes on failure to distribute income (section 4942) (does not apply for years the foundation was a private operating foundation defined in section 4942(j)(3) or 4942(j)(5)):

a At the end of tax year 2008, did the foundation have any undistributed income (lines 6d and 6e, Part XIII) for tax year(s) beginning before 2008? . . . . ☐ **Yes** ☐ **No**

If "Yes," list the years ▶ 20....., 20....., 20....., 20.....

b Are there any years listed in 2a for which the foundation is **not** applying the provisions of section 4942(a)(2) (relating to incorrect valuation of assets) to the year's undistributed income? (If applying section 4942(a)(2) to **all** years listed, answer "No" and attach statement—see page 20 of the instructions.) **2b**

c If the provisions of section 4942(a)(2) are being applied to **any** of the years listed in 2a, list the years here.
▶ 20...., 20...., 20...., 20.....

3a Did the foundation hold more than a 2% direct or indirect interest in any business enterprise at any time during the year? . . . . ☐ **Yes** ☐ **No**

b If "Yes," did it have excess business holdings in 2008 as a result of **(1)** any purchase by the foundation or disqualified persons after May 26, 1969; **(2)** the lapse of the 5-year period (or longer period approved by the Commissioner under section 4943(c)(7)) to dispose of holdings acquired by gift or bequest; or **(3)** the lapse of the 10-, 15-, or 20-year first phase holding period? *(Use Schedule C, Form 4720, to determine if the foundation had excess business holdings in 2008.)* **3b**

4a Did the foundation invest during the year any amount in a manner that would jeopardize its charitable purposes? **4a**

b Did the foundation make any investment in a prior year (but after December 31, 1969) that could jeopardize its charitable purpose that had not been removed from jeopardy before the first day of the tax year beginning in 2008? **4b**

Form **990-PF** (2008)

Form 990-PF (2008) Page **6**

Part VII-B Statements Regarding Activities for Which Form 4720 May Be Required *(continued)*

5a During the year did the foundation pay or incur any amount to:

(1) Carry on propaganda, or otherwise attempt to influence legislation (section 4945(e))? . ☐ **Yes** ☐ **No**

(2) Influence the outcome of any specific public election (see section 4955); or to carry on, directly or indirectly, any voter registration drive? . . . . ☐ **Yes** ☐ **No**

(3) Provide a grant to an individual for travel, study, or other similar purposes? . . . . ☐ **Yes** ☐ **No**

(4) Provide a grant to an organization other than a charitable, etc., organization described in section 509(a)(1), (2), or (3), or section 4940(d)(2)? (see page 22 of the instructions) . . . ☐ **Yes** ☐ **No**

(5) Provide for any purpose other than religious, charitable, scientific, literary, or educational purposes, or for the prevention of cruelty to children or animals? . ☐ **Yes** ☐ **No**

b If any answer is "Yes" to 5a(1)–(5), did **any** of the transactions fail to qualify under the exceptions described in Regulations section 53.4945 or in a current notice regarding disaster assistance (see page 22 of the instructions)? **5b**

Organizations relying on a current notice regarding disaster assistance check here . . . . . . ▶ ☐

c If the answer is "Yes" to question 5a(4), does the foundation claim exemption from the tax because it maintained expenditure responsibility for the grant? . . . . ☐ **Yes** ☐ **No**

If "Yes," attach the statement required by Regulations section 53.4945–5(d).

6a Did the foundation, during the year, receive any funds, directly or indirectly, to pay premiums on a personal benefit contract? . . . . ☐ **Yes** ☐ **No**

b Did the foundation, during the year, pay premiums, directly or indirectly, on a personal benefit contract? . . **6b**

If you answered "Yes" to 6b, also file Form 8870.

7a At any time during the tax year, was the foundation a party to a prohibited tax shelter transaction? . ☐ **Yes** ☐ **No**

b If yes, did the foundation receive any proceeds or have any net income attributable to the transaction? . . . **7b**

Part VIII Information About Officers, Directors, Trustees, Foundation Managers, Highly Paid Employees, and Contractors

1 List all officers, directors, trustees, foundation managers and their compensation (see page 22 of the instructions).

(a) Name and address	**(b)** Title, and average hours per week devoted to position	**(c)** Compensation **(If not paid, enter -0-)**	**(d)** Contributions to employee benefit plans and deferred compensation	**(e)** Expense account, other allowances

2 Compensation of five highest-paid employees (other than those included on line 1—see page 23 of the instructions). If none, enter "NONE."

(a) Name and address of each employee paid more than $50,000	**(b)** Title, and average hours per week devoted to position	**(c)** Compensation	**(d)** Contributions to employee benefit plans and deferred compensation	**(e)** Expense account, other allowances

Total number of other employees paid over $50,000 . . . . ▶

Form **990-PF** (2008)

Form 990-PF (2008) Page **7**

Part VIII **Information About Officers, Directors, Trustees, Foundation Managers, Highly Paid Employees, and Contractors** *(continued)*

3 Five highest-paid independent contractors for professional services (see page 23 of the instructions). If none, enter "NONE."

(a) Name and address of each person paid more than $50,000	**(b)** Type of service	**(c)** Compensation

Total number of others receiving over $50,000 for professional services . . . . ▶

Part IX-A **Summary of Direct Charitable Activities**

List the foundation's four largest direct charitable activities during the tax year. Include relevant statistical information such as the number of organizations and other beneficiaries served, conferences convened, research papers produced, etc.	Expenses
1	
2	
3	
4	

Part IX-B **Summary of Program-Related Investments** (see page 23 of the instructions)

Describe the two largest program-related investments made by the foundation during the tax year on lines 1 and 2.	Amount
1	
2	
All other program-related investments. See page 24 of the instructions. 3	
Total. Add lines 1 through 3 . . . . ▶	

Form **990-PF** (2008)

Form 990-PF (2008) Page **8**

Part X **Minimum Investment Return** (All domestic foundations must complete this part. Foreign foundations, see page 24 of the instructions.)

1	Fair market value of assets not used (or held for use) directly in carrying out charitable, etc., purposes:			
a	Average monthly fair market value of securities		1a	
b	Average of monthly cash balances		1b	
c	Fair market value of all other assets (see page 24 of the instructions)		1c	
d	**Total** (add lines 1a, b, and c)		1d	
e	Reduction claimed for blockage or other factors reported on lines 1a and 1c (attach detailed explanation)	1e		
2	Acquisition indebtedness applicable to line 1 assets		2	
3	Subtract line 2 from line 1d		3	
4	Cash deemed held for charitable activities. Enter 1½ % of line 3 (for greater amount, see page 25 of the instructions)		4	
5	**Net value of noncharitable-use assets.** Subtract line 4 from line 3. Enter here and on Part V, line 4		5	
6	**Minimum investment return.** Enter 5% of line 5		6	

Part XI **Distributable Amount** (see page 25 of the instructions) (Section 4942(j)(3) and (j)(5) private operating foundations and certain foreign organizations check here ▶ ☐ and do not complete this part.)

1	Minimum investment return from Part X, line 6		1	
2a	Tax on investment income for 2008 from Part VI, line 5	2a		
b	Income tax for 2008. (This does not include the tax from Part VI.)	2b		
c	Add lines 2a and 2b		2c	
3	Distributable amount before adjustments. Subtract line 2c from line 1		3	
4	Recoveries of amounts treated as qualifying distributions		4	
5	Add lines 3 and 4		5	
6	Deduction from distributable amount (see page 25 of the instructions)		6	
7	**Distributable amount** as adjusted. Subtract line 6 from line 5. Enter here and on Part XIII, line 1		7	

Part XII **Qualifying Distributions** (see page 25 of the instructions)

1	Amounts paid (including administrative expenses) to accomplish charitable, etc., purposes:		
a	Expenses, contributions, gifts, etc.—total from Part I, column (d), line 26	1a	
b	Program-related investments—total from Part IX-B	1b	
2	Amounts paid to acquire assets used (or held for use) directly in carrying out charitable, etc., purposes	2	
3	Amounts set aside for specific charitable projects that satisfy the:		
a	Suitability test (prior IRS approval required)	3a	
b	Cash distribution test (attach the required schedule)	3b	
4	**Qualifying distributions.** Add lines 1a through 3b. Enter here and on Part V, line 8, and Part XIII, line 4	4	
5	Foundations that qualify under section 4940(e) for the reduced rate of tax on net investment income. Enter 1% of Part I, line 27b (see page 26 of the instructions)	5	
6	**Adjusted qualifying distributions.** Subtract line 5 from line 4	6	

Note. The amount on line 6 will be used in Part V, column (b), in subsequent years when calculating whether the foundation qualifies for the section 4940(e) reduction of tax in those years.

Form **990-PF** (2008)

Form 990-PF (2008) Page 9

Part XIII Undistributed Income (see page 26 of the instructions)

		(a) Corpus	(b) Years prior to 2007	(c) 2007	(d) 2008
1	Distributable amount for 2008 from Part XI, line 7				
2	Undistributed income, if any, as of the end of 2007:				
a	Enter amount for 2007 only				
b	Total for prior years: 20____,20____,20____				
3	Excess distributions carryover, if any, to 2008:				
a	From 2003				
b	From 2004				
c	From 2005				
d	From 2006				
e	From 2007				
f	**Total** of lines 3a through e				
4	Qualifying distributions for 2008 from Part XII, line 4: ▶ $ __________				
a	Applied to 2007, but not more than line 2a				
b	Applied to undistributed income of prior years (Election required—see page 26 of the instructions)				
c	Treated as distributions out of corpus (Election required—see page 26 of the instructions)				
d	Applied to 2008 distributable amount				
e	Remaining amount distributed out of corpus				
5	Excess distributions carryover applied to 2008 *(If an amount appears in column (d), the same amount must be shown in column (a).)*				
6	**Enter the net total of each column as indicated below:**				
a	Corpus. Add lines 3f, 4c, and 4e. Subtract line 5				
b	Prior years' undistributed income. Subtract line 4b from line 2b				
c	Enter the amount of prior years' undistributed income for which a notice of deficiency has been issued, or on which the section 4942(a) tax has been previously assessed				
d	Subtract line 6c from line 6b. Taxable amount—see page 27 of the instructions				
e	Undistributed income for 2007. Subtract line 4a from line 2a. Taxable amount—see page 27 of the instructions				
f	Undistributed income for 2008. Subtract lines 4d and 5 from line 1. This amount must be distributed in 2009				
7	Amounts treated as distributions out of corpus to satisfy requirements imposed by section 170(b)(1)(F) or 4942(g)(3) (see page 27 of the instructions)				
8	Excess distributions carryover from 2003 not applied on line 5 or line 7 (see page 27 of the instructions)				
9	**Excess distributions carryover to 2009.** Subtract lines 7 and 8 from line 6a				
10	Analysis of line 9:				
a	Excess from 2004				
b	Excess from 2005				
c	Excess from 2006				
d	Excess from 2007				
e	Excess from 2008				

Form **990-PF** (2008)

Form 990-PF (2008) Page **10**

Part XIV **Private Operating Foundations** (see page 27 of the instructions and Part VII-A, question 9)

1a If the foundation has received a ruling or determination letter that it is a private operating foundation, and the ruling is effective for 2008, enter the date of the ruling . . . . ▶

b Check box to indicate whether the foundation is a private operating foundation described in section ☐ 4942(j)(3) or ☐ 4942(j)(5)

	Tax year	Prior 3 years			(e) Total
	(a) 2008	**(b)** 2007	**(c)** 2006	**(d)** 2005	
2a Enter the lesser of the adjusted net income from Part I or the minimum investment return from Part X for each year listed					
b 85% of line 2a					
c Qualifying distributions from Part XII, line 4 for each year listed . . .					
d Amounts included in line 2c not used directly for active conduct of exempt activities . .					
e Qualifying distributions made directly for active conduct of exempt activities. Subtract line 2d from line 2c . .					
3 Complete 3a, b, or c for the alternative test relied upon:					
a "Assets" alternative test—enter: (1) Value of all assets					
(2) Value of assets qualifying under section 4942(j)(3)(B)(i)					
b "Endowment" alternative test—enter ⅔ of minimum investment return shown in Part X, line 6 for each year listed . . .					
c "Support" alternative test—enter: (1) Total support other than gross investment income (interest, dividends, rents, payments on securities loans (section 512(a)(5)), or royalties) . . .					
(2) Support from general public and 5 or more exempt organizations as provided in section 4942(j)(3)(B)(iii) . . .					
(3) Largest amount of support from an exempt organization . . .					
(4) Gross investment income . .					

Part XV **Supplementary Information (Complete this part only if the foundation had $5,000 or more in assets at any time during the year—see page 27 of the instructions.)**

1 Information Regarding Foundation Managers:

a List any managers of the foundation who have contributed more than 2% of the total contributions received by the foundation before the close of any tax year (but only if they have contributed more than $5,000). (See section 507(d)(2).)

b List any managers of the foundation who own 10% or more of the stock of a corporation (or an equally large portion of the ownership of a partnership or other entity) of which the foundation has a 10% or greater interest.

2 Information Regarding Contribution, Grant, Gift, Loan, Scholarship, etc., Programs:

Check here ▶ ☐ if the foundation only makes contributions to preselected charitable organizations and does not accept unsolicited requests for funds. If the foundation makes gifts, grants, etc. (see page 28 of the instructions) to individuals or organizations under other conditions, complete items 2a, b, c, and d.

a The name, address, and telephone number of the person to whom applications should be addressed:

b The form in which applications should be submitted and information and materials they should include:

c Any submission deadlines:

d Any restrictions or limitations on awards, such as by geographical areas, charitable fields, kinds of institutions, or other factors:

Form **990-PF** (2008)

Form 990-PF (2008) Page **11**

Part XV Supplementary Information (continued)

3 Grants and Contributions Paid During the Year or Approved for Future Payment

Recipient Name and address (home or business)	If recipient is an individual, show any relationship to any foundation manager or substantial contributor	Foundation status of recipient	Purpose of grant or contribution	Amount
a *Paid during the year*				
Total . . . . ▶ **3a**				
b *Approved for future payment*				
Total . . . . ▶ **3b**				

Form **990-PF** (2008)

Form 990-PF (2008) Page **12**

Part XVI-A Analysis of Income-Producing Activities

Enter gross amounts unless otherwise indicated.	Unrelated business income		Excluded by section 512, 513, or 514		(e) Related or exempt function income (See page 28 of the instructions.)
	(a) Business code	(b) Amount	(c) Exclusion code	(d) Amount	
1 Program service revenue:					
a					
b					
c					
d					
e					
f					
g Fees and contracts from government agencies					
2 Membership dues and assessments					
3 Interest on savings and temporary cash investments					
4 Dividends and interest from securities					
5 Net rental income or (loss) from real estate:					
a Debt-financed property					
b Not debt-financed property					
6 Net rental income or (loss) from personal property					
7 Other investment income					
8 Gain or (loss) from sales of assets other than inventory					
9 Net income or (loss) from special events					
10 Gross profit or (loss) from sales of inventory					
11 Other revenue: a					
b					
c					
d					
e					
12 Subtotal. Add columns (b), (d), and (e)					

13 Total. Add line 12, columns (b), (d), and (e) . . . . 13 ____________

(See worksheet in line 13 instructions on page 28 to verify calculations.)

Part XVI-B Relationship of Activities to the Accomplishment of Exempt Purposes

Line No. ▼	Explain below how each activity for which income is reported in column (e) of Part XVI-A contributed importantly to the accomplishment of the foundation's exempt purposes (other than by providing funds for such purposes). (See page 28 of the instructions.)

Form **990-PF** (2008)

Form 990-PF (2008) Page **13**

Part XVII Information Regarding Transfers To and Transactions and Relationships With Noncharitable Exempt Organizations

			Yes	No
1	Did the organization directly or indirectly engage in any of the following with any other organization described in section 501(c) of the Code (other than section 501(c)(3) organizations) or in section 527, relating to political organizations?			
a	Transfers from the reporting foundation to a noncharitable exempt organization of:			
	(1) Cash	1a(1)		
	(2) Other assets	1a(2)		
b	Other transactions:			
	(1) Sales of assets to a noncharitable exempt organization	1b(1)		
	(2) Purchases of assets from a noncharitable exempt organization	1b(2)		
	(3) Rental of facilities, equipment, or other assets	1b(3)		
	(4) Reimbursement arrangements	1b(4)		
	(5) Loans or loan guarantees	1b(5)		
	(6) Performance of services or membership or fundraising solicitations	1b(6)		
c	Sharing of facilities, equipment, mailing lists, other assets, or paid employees	1c		

d If the answer to any of the above is "Yes," complete the following schedule. Column **(b)** should always show the fair market value of the goods, other assets, or services given by the reporting foundation. If the foundation received less than fair market value in any transaction or sharing arrangement, show in column **(d)** the value of the goods, other assets, or services received.

(a) Line no.	**(b)** Amount involved	**(c)** Name of noncharitable exempt organization	**(d)** Description of transfers, transactions, and sharing arrangements

2a Is the foundation directly or indirectly affiliated with, or related to, one or more tax-exempt organizations described in section 501(c) of the Code (other than section 501(c)(3)) or in section 527? ☐ Yes ☐ No

b If "Yes," complete the following schedule.

(a) Name of organization	**(b)** Type of organization	**(c)** Description of relationship

Sign Here

Under penalties of perjury, I declare that I have examined this return, including accompanying schedules and statements, and to the best of my knowledge and belief, it is true, correct, and complete. Declaration of preparer (other than taxpayer or fiduciary) is based on all information of which preparer has any knowledge.

▶ Signature of officer or trustee | Date | ▶ Title

Paid Preparer's Use Only

Preparer's signature ▶	Date	Check if self-employed ▶ ☐	Preparer's identifying number (see **Signature** on page 30 of the instructions)
Firm's name (or yours if self-employed), address, and ZIP code ▶		EIN ▶	
		Phone no. ( )	

2008

Department of the Treasury
Internal Revenue Service

Instructions for Form 990-PF

Return of Private Foundation or Section 4947(a)(1) Nonexempt Charitable Trust Treated as a Private Foundation

Section references are to the Internal Revenue Code unless otherwise noted.

Contents **Page**

Contents **Page**

What's New

If you are filing Form 990-PF because you no longer meet a public support test under sections 509(a)(1) and 170(b)(1)(A)(vi) or section 509(a)(2) and you have not previously filed Form 990-PF, write **PRIOR PC** in the top right corner of page 1 of your return. Before filing Form 990-PF for the first time, you may want to go to *www.irs.gov/eo* for the latest information and filing tips to confirm you are no longer a publicly supported organization.

Charitable trusts that became private foundations by virtue of section 1241(c) of the Pension Protection Act of 2006 must file Form 990-PF for taxable years beginning on or after January 1, 2008. Such organizations must file a **paper** Form 990-PF and write "**Notice 2008-6 status change** " at the top of Form 990-PF. See Notice 2008-6 for more information.

Photographs of Missing Children

The Internal Revenue Service is a proud partner with the National Center for Missing and Exploited Children. Photographs of missing children selected by the Center may appear in instructions on pages that would otherwise be blank. You can help bring these children home by looking at the photographs and calling 1-800-THE-LOST (1-800-843-5678) if you recognize a child.

Phone Help

If you have questions and/or need help completing this form, please call 1-877-829-5500. This toll-free telephone service is available Monday through Friday.

How To Get Forms and Publications

Internet

You can access the IRS website 24 hours a day, 7 days a week at *www.irs.gov* to:

- Download forms, instructions, and publications,
- Order IRS products online,
- See answers to frequently asked tax questions,
- Search publications online by topic or keyword,
- Send us comments or request help via email, or
- Sign up to receive local and national tax news by email.

DVD for tax products

You can order Publication 1796, IRS Tax Products DVD, and obtain:

- Current-year forms, instructions, and publications.
- Prior-year forms, instructions, and publications.

Cat. No. 11290Y

- Tax Map: an electronic research tool and finding aid.
- Tax Law frequently asked questions.
- Tax Topics from the IRS telephone response system.
- Internal Revenue Code – Title 26
- Fill-in, print, and save features for most tax forms.
- Internal Revenue Bulletins.
- Toll-free and email technical support.
- The DVD is released twice during the year.
- The first release will ship the beginning of January 2009.
- The final release will ship the beginning of March 2009.
- Purchase the DVD from National Technical Information Service (NTIS) at www.irs.gov/cdorders for $30 (no handling fee) or call 1-877-233-6767 toll free to purchase the DVD for $30 (plus a $6 handling fee).

By Phone and In Person

You can order forms and publications by calling 1-800-TAX-FORM (1-800-829-3676). You can also get most forms and publications at your local IRS office.

Use these electronic options to make filing and paying easier.

IRS E-Services Make Taxes Easier

Now more than ever before, businesses can enjoy the benefits of filing and paying their federal taxes electronically. Whether you rely on a tax professional or handle your own taxes, the IRS offers you convenient programs to make taxes easier.

- You can *e-file* your Form 990-PF; Form 940 and 941 employment tax returns; Form 1099 and other information returns. Visit *www.irs.gov/efile* for details.
- You can pay taxes online or by phone using the free Electronic Federal Tax Payment System (EFTPS). Visit *www.eftps.gov* or call 1-800-555-4477 for details. Electronic Funds Withdrawal (EFW) from a checking or savings account is also available to those who file electronically.

For the most up-to-date tax information, please visit us at *www.irs.gov/formspubs/index.html* and select Highlights of Recent Tax Changes under the Important changes section.

General Instructions

Purpose of form. Form 990-PF is used:
- To figure the tax based on investment income, and
- To report charitable distributions and activities.

Also, Form 990-PF serves as a substitute for the section 4947(a)(1) nonexempt charitable trust's income tax return, Form 1041, U.S. Income Tax Return for Estates and Trusts, when the trust has no taxable income.

A. Who Must File

Form 990-PF is an annual information return that must be filed by:
- Exempt private foundations (section 6033(a), (b), and (c)),
- Taxable private foundations (section 6033(d)),
- Organizations that agree to private foundation status and whose applications for exempt status are pending on the due date for filing Form 990-PF,
- Organizations that made an election under section 41(e)(6),
- Foundations that are making a section 507 termination, and
- Section 4947(a)(1) nonexempt charitable trusts that are treated as private foundations (section 6033(d)).

TIP *Include on the foundation's return the financial and other information of any disregarded entity owned by the foundation. See Regulations sections 301.7701-1 through 3 for information on the classification of certain business organizations including an eligible entity that is disregarded as an entity separate from its owner (disregarded entity).*

Other section 4947(a)(1) nonexempt charitable trusts. Section 4947(a)(1) nonexempt charitable trusts that are not treated as private foundations do not file Form 990-PF. However, they may need to file Form 990, Return of Organization Exempt From Income Tax, or Form 990-EZ, Short Form Return of Organization Exempt from Income Tax. With either of these forms, the trust must also file Schedule A (Form 990 or 990–EZ), Public Charity Status and Public Support. (See Form 990 and Form 990-EZ instructions.)

B. Which Parts To Complete

The parts of the form listed below do not apply to all filers. See *How to avoid filing an incomplete return* on this page for information on what to do if a part or an item does apply.
- Part I, column (c), applies only to private operating foundations and to nonoperating private foundations that have income from charitable activities.
- Part II, column (c), with the exception of line 16, applies only to organizations having at least $5,000 in assets per books at some time during the year. Line 16, column (c), applies to all filers.
- Part IV does not apply to foreign organizations.
- Parts V and VI do not apply to organizations making an election under section 41(e).
- Part X does not apply to foreign foundations that check box D2 on page 1 of Form 990-PF unless they claim status as a private operating foundation.
- Parts XI and XIII do not apply to foreign foundations that check box D2 on page 1 of Form 990-PF. However, check the box at the top of Part XI. Part XI does not apply to private operating foundations. Also, if the organization is a private operating foundation for any of the years shown in Part XIII, do not complete the portions that apply to those years.
- Part XIV applies only to private operating foundations.
- Part XV applies only to foundations having assets of $5,000 or more during the year. This part does not apply to certain foreign organizations.

How to avoid filing an incomplete return.
- Complete all applicable line items,
- Answer "Yes," "No," or "N/A" (not applicable) to each question on the return,
- Make an entry (including a zero when appropriate) on all total lines, and
- Enter "None" or "N/A" if an entire part does not apply.

Sequencing Chart To Complete the Form

You may find the following chart helpful. It limits jumping from one part of the form to another to compute an amount needed to complete an earlier part. If you complete the parts in the listed order, any information you may need from another part will already be entered.

Step	Part	Step	Part
1	IV	8	XII, lines 1–4
2	I & II	9	V & VI
3	Heading	10	XII, lines 5–6
4	III	11	XI
5	VII-A	12	XIII
6	VIII	13	VII-B
7	IX-A – X	14	XIV – XVII

C. Definitions

1. A private foundation is a domestic or foreign organization exempt from income tax under section 501(a); described in section 501(c)(3); and is other than an organization described in sections 509(a)(1) through (4).

In general, churches, hospitals, schools, and broadly publicly supported organizations are excluded from private foundation status by these sections. These organizations may be required to file Form 990 (or Form 990-EZ) instead of Form 990-PF.

2. A nonexempt charitable trust treated as a private foundation is a trust that is not exempt from tax under section 501(a) and all of the unexpired interests of which are devoted to religious, charitable, or other purposes described in section 170(c)(2)(B), and for which a deduction was allowed under a section of the Code listed in section 4947(a)(1).

3. A taxable private foundation is an organization that is no longer exempt under section 501(a) as an organization described in section 501(c)(3). Though it may operate as a taxable entity, it will continue to be treated as a private foundation until that status is terminated under section 507.

4. A private operating foundation is an organization that is described under section 4942(j)(3) or (5). It means any

private foundation that spends at least 85% of the smaller of its adjusted net income (figured in Part I) or its minimum investment return (figured in Part X) directly for the active conduct of the exempt purpose or functions for which the foundation is organized and operated and that also meets the assets test, the endowment test, or the support test (discussed in Part XIV).

5. A nonoperating private foundation is a private foundation that is not a private operating foundation.

6. A foundation manager is an officer, director, or trustee of a foundation, or an individual who has powers similar to those of officers, directors, or trustees. In the case of any act or failure to act, the term "foundation manager" may also include employees of the foundation who have the authority to act.

7. A disqualified person is:

a. A substantial contributor (see *instructions for Part VII-A, line 10,* on page 19);

b. A foundation manager;

c. A person who owns more than 20% of a corporation, partnership, trust, or unincorporated enterprise that is itself a substantial contributor;

d. A family member of an individual described in a, b, or c above; or

e. A corporation, partnership, trust, or estate in which persons described in a, b, c, or d above own a total beneficial interest of more than 35%.

f. For purposes of section 4941 (self-dealing), a disqualified person also includes certain government officials. (See section 4946(c) and the related regulations.)

g. For purposes of section 4943 (excess business holdings), a disqualified person also includes:

i. A private foundation that is effectively controlled (directly or indirectly) by the same persons who control the private foundation in question, or

ii. A private foundation to which substantially all of the contributions were made (directly or indirectly) by one or more of the persons described in a, b, and c above, or members of their families, within the meaning of section 4946(d).

8. An organization is controlled by a foundation or by one or more disqualified persons with respect to the foundation if any of these persons may, by combining their votes or positions of authority, require the organization to make an expenditure or prevent the organization from making an expenditure, regardless of the method of control. "Control" is determined regardless of how the foundation requires the contribution to be used.

D. Other Forms You May Need To File

- Form W-2, Wage and Tax Statement.
- Form W-3, Transmittal of Wage and Tax Statements.
- Form 940, Employer's Annual Federal Unemployment (FUTA) Tax Return.
- Form 941, Employer's Quarterly Federal Tax Return.

These forms are used to report social security, Medicare, and income taxes withheld by an employer and social security and Medicare taxes paid by an employer.

If income, social security, and Medicare taxes that must be withheld are not withheld or are not paid to the IRS, a trust fund recovery penalty may apply. The penalty is 100% of such unpaid taxes.

This penalty may be imposed on all persons (including volunteers, see below) whom the IRS determines to be responsible for collecting, accounting for, and paying over these taxes, and who willfully did not do so.

This penalty does not apply to any volunteer, unpaid member of any board of trustees or directors of a tax-exempt organization, if this member:

- Is solely serving in an honorary capacity,
- Does not participate in the day-to-day or financial activities of the organization, and
- Does not have actual knowledge of the failure to collect, account for, and pay over these taxes.

However, this exception does not apply if it results in no person being liable for the penalty.

Form 990-T, Exempt Organization Business Income Tax Return. Every organization exempt from income tax under section 501(a) that has total gross income of $1,000 or more from all trades or businesses that are unrelated to the organization's exempt purpose must file a return on Form 990-T. The form is also used by tax-exempt organizations to report other additional taxes including the additional tax figured in Part IV of Form 8621, Return by a Shareholder of a Passive Foreign Investment Company or Qualified Electing Fund.

Form 990-W, Estimated Tax on Unrelated Business Taxable Income for Tax-Exempt Organizations (and on Investment Income for Private Foundations). Use of this form is optional. It is provided only to aid you in determining your tax liability.

Form 1041, U.S. Income Tax Return for Estates and Trusts. Required of section 4947(a)(1) nonexempt charitable trusts that also file Form 990-PF. However, if the trust does not have any taxable income under the income tax provisions (subtitle A of the Code), it may use the filing of Form 990-PF to satisfy its Form 1041 filing requirement under section 6012. If this condition is met, check the box for question 15, Part VII-A, of Form 990-PF and do not file Form 1041.

Form 1041-ES, Estimated Income Tax for Estates and Trusts. Used to make estimated tax payments.

Form 1096, Annual Summary and Transmittal of U.S. Information Returns. Used to transmit Forms 1099, 1098, 5498, and W-2G to the IRS. Do not use it to transmit electronically.

Form 1098-C, Contributions of Motor Vehicles, Boats, and Airplanes. Information return for reporting contributions of qualified motor vehicles, boats, and airplanes from donors.

Forms 1099-INT, MISC, OID, and R. Information returns for reporting certain interest; miscellaneous income (for example, payments to providers of health and medical services, miscellaneous income payments, and nonemployee compensation); original issue discount; and distributions from retirement or profit-sharing plans, IRAs, SEPs or SIMPLEs, and insurance contracts.

Form 1120, U.S. Corporation Income Tax Return. Filed by nonexempt taxable private foundations that have taxable income under the income tax provisions (subtitle A of the Code). The Form 990-PF annual information return is also filed by these taxable foundations.

Form 1120-POL, U.S. Income Tax Return for Certain Political Organizations. Section 501(c) organizations must file Form 1120-POL if they are treated as having political organization taxable income under section 527(f)(1).

Form 1128, Application To Adopt, Change, or Retain a Tax Year. Form 1128 is used to request approval from the IRS to change a tax year or to adopt or retain a certain tax year.

Form 2220, Underpayment of Estimated Tax by Corporations. Form 2220 is used by corporations and trusts filing Form 990-PF to see if the foundation owes a penalty and to figure the amount of the penalty. Generally, the foundation is not required to file this form because the IRS can figure the amount of any penalty and bill the foundation for it. However, complete and attach Form 2220 even if the foundation does not owe the penalty if:

- The annualized income or the adjusted seasonal installment method is used, or
- The foundation is a "large organization," (see *General Instruction O*) computing its first required installment based on the prior year's tax.

If Form 2220 is attached, check the box on line 8, Part VI, on page 4 of Form 990-PF and enter the amount of any penalty on this line.

Form 4506, Request for Copy of Tax Return. Used by the organization or designated third party to get a complete copy of the organization's return.

Form 4506-A, Request for Public Inspection or Copy of Exempt or Political Organization IRS Form. Used to inspect or request a copy of an exempt or political organization's return, report, notice, or exemption application by the public or the organization.

Form 4720, Return of Certain Excise Taxes Under Chapters 41 and 42 of the Internal Revenue Code. Is primarily used to determine the excise taxes imposed on:

- Acts of self-dealing between private foundations and disqualified persons,
- Failure to distribute income,
- Excess business holdings,
- Investments that jeopardize the foundation's charitable purposes,
- Making political or other noncharitable expenditures, and
- Prohibited tax shelter transactions.

Form 5500, Annual Return/Report of Employee Benefit Plan. Is used to report information concerning employee benefit plans and Direct Filing Entities.

Form 8109, Federal Tax Deposit Coupon. Used by business entities to make federal tax deposits.

Form 8282, Donee Information Return. Required of the donee of "charitable deduction property" that sells, exchanges, or otherwise disposes of the property within 3 years after the date it received the property. Also required of any successor donee that disposes of charitable deduction property within 3 years after the date that the donor gave the property to the original donee. (It does not matter who gave the property to the successor donee. It may have been the original donee or another successor donee.) For successor donees, the form must be filed only for any property that was transferred by the original donee after July 5, 1988.

Form 8275, Disclosure Statement. Taxpayers and tax return preparers should attach this form to Form 990-PF to disclose items or positions (except those contrary to a regulation—see *Form 8275-R* below) that are not otherwise adequately disclosed on the tax return. The disclosure is made to avoid parts of the accuracy-related penalty imposed for disregard of rules or substantial understatement of tax. Form 8275 is also used for disclosures relating to preparer penalties for understatements due to unrealistic positions or for willful or reckless conduct.

Form 8275-R, Regulation Disclosure Statement. Use this form to disclose any item on a tax return for which a position has been taken that is contrary to Treasury regulations.

Form 8300, Report of Cash Payments Over $10,000 Received in a Trade or Business. Used to report cash amounts in excess of $10,000 that were received in a single transaction (or in two or more related transactions) in the course of a trade or business (as defined in section 162).

Form 8822, Change of Address. This form is used by taxpayers to notify the IRS of changes in individual and business mailing addresses.

Form 8886-T, Disclosure by Tax-Exempt Entity Regarding Prohibited Tax Shelter Transaction. This form is used by an exempt organization to disclose whether it was a party to a prohibited tax shelter transaction.

Form 8868, Application for Extension of Time To File an Exempt Organization Return. This form is used by an exempt organization to request an automatic 3-month extension of time to file its return and also to apply for an additional (not automatic) 3-month extension if the initial 3-month extension is not enough time.

Form 8870, Information Return for Transfers Associated With Certain Personal Benefit Contracts. Used to identify those personal benefit contracts for which funds were transferred to the organization, directly or indirectly, as well as the transferors and beneficiaries of those contracts.

Form 8899, Notice of Income from Donated Intellectual Property. Use this form to report income from qualified intellectual property.

Forms 8921 and 8922. These forms are used by an exempt organization to report its direct or indirect acquisition of certain insurance contracts.

E. Useful Publications

The following publications may be helpful in preparing Form 990-PF:

- Publication 525, Taxable and Nontaxable Income,
- Publication 583, Starting a Business and Keeping Records,
- Publication 598, Tax on Unrelated Business Income of Exempt Organizations,
- Publication 910, IRS Guide to Free Tax Services,
- Publication 1771, Charitable Contributions—Substantiation and Disclosure Requirements, and
- Publication 3833, Disaster Relief, Providing Assistance Through Charitable Organizations.

Publications and forms are available at no charge through IRS offices or by calling 1-800-TAX-FORM (1-800-829-3676).

F. Use of Form 990-PF To Satisfy State Reporting Requirements

Some states and local government units will accept a copy of Form 990-PF and required attachments instead of all or part of their own financial report forms.

If the organization plans to use Form 990-PF to satisfy state or local filing requirements, such as those from state charitable solicitation acts, note the following.

Determine state filing requirements. Consult the appropriate officials of all states and other jurisdictions in which the organization does business to determine their specific filing requirements. "Doing business" in a jurisdiction may include any of the following:

- Soliciting contributions or grants by mail or otherwise from individuals, businesses, or other charitable organizations,
- Conducting programs,
- Having employees within that jurisdiction, or
- Maintaining a checking account or owning or renting property there.

Monetary tests may differ. Some or all of the dollar limitations that apply to Form 990-PF when filed with the IRS may not apply when using Form 990-PF instead of state or local report forms. IRS dollar limitations that may not meet some state requirements are the $5,000 total assets minimum that requires completion of Part II, column (c), and Part XV; and the $50,000 minimum for listing the highest paid employees and for listing professional fees in Part VIII.

Additional information may be required. State and local filing requirements may require attaching to Form 990-PF one or more of the following:

- Additional financial statements, such as a complete analysis of functional expenses or a statement of changes in net assets,
- Notes to financial statements,
- Additional financial schedules,
- A report on the financial statements by an independent accountant, and
- Answers to additional questions and other information.

Each jurisdiction may require the additional material to be presented on forms they provide. The additional information does not have to be submitted with the Form 990-PF filed with the IRS.

If required information is not provided to a state, the organization may be asked by the state to provide it or to submit an amended return, even if the Form 990-PF is accepted by the IRS as complete.

Amended returns. If the organization submits supplemental information or files an amended Form 990-PF with the IRS, it must also include a copy of the information or amended return to any state with which it filed a copy of Form 990-PF.

Method of accounting. Many states require that all amounts be reported based on the accrual method of accounting.

Time for filing may differ. The time for filing Form 990-PF with the IRS may differ from the time for filing state reports.

G. Furnishing Copies of Form 990-PF to State Officials

The foundation managers must furnish a copy of the annual return Form 990-PF (and Form 4720 (if applicable)) to the attorney general of:

- Each state required to be listed in Part VII-A, line 8a,

• The state in which the foundation's principal office is located, and
• The state in which the foundation was incorporated or created.

A copy of the annual return must be sent to the attorney general at the same time the annual return is filed with the IRS.

Other requirements. If the attorney general or other appropriate state official of any state requests a copy of the annual return, the foundation managers must give them a copy of the annual return.

Exceptions. These rules do not apply to any foreign foundation which, from the date of its creation, has received at least 85% of its support (excluding gross investment income) from sources outside the United States. (See *General Instruction S* for other exceptions that affect this type of organization.)

Coordination with state reporting requirements. If the foundation managers submit a copy of Form 990-PF and Form 4720 (if applicable) to a state attorney general to satisfy a state reporting requirement, they do not have to furnish a second copy to that attorney general to comply with the Internal Revenue Code requirements discussed in this section.

If there is a state reporting requirement to file a copy of Form 990-PF with a state official other than the attorney general (for instance, the secretary of state), then the foundation managers must also send a copy of the Form 990-PF and Form 4720 (if applicable) to the attorney general of that state.

H. Accounting Period

• File the 2008 return for the calendar year 2008 or fiscal year beginning in 2008. If the return is for a fiscal year, fill in the tax year space at the top of the return.
• The return must be filed on the basis of the established annual accounting period of the organization. If the organization has no established accounting period, the return should be on the calendar-year basis.
• For initial or final returns or a change in accounting period, the 2008 form may also be used as the return for a short period (less than 12 months) ending November 30, 2009, or earlier.

In general, to change its accounting period, the organization must file Form 990-PF by the due date for the short period resulting from the change. At the top of this short period return, write "Change of Accounting Period."

If the organization changed its accounting period within the 10-calendar-year period that includes the beginning of the short period, and it had a Form 990-PF filing requirement at any time during that 10-year period, it must also attach a Form 1128 to the short-period return. See Rev. Proc. 85-58, 1985-2 C.B. 740.

I. Accounting Methods

Generally, you should report the financial information requested on the basis of the accounting method the foundation regularly uses to keep its books and records.

Exception. Complete Part I, column (d) on the cash receipts and disbursements method of accounting.

J. When, Where, and How To File

This return must be filed by the 15th day of the 5th month following the close of the foundation's accounting period. If the regular due date falls on a Saturday, Sunday, or legal holiday, file by the next business day. If the return is filed late, see *General Instruction M.*

In case of a complete liquidation, dissolution, or termination, file the return by the 15th day of the 5th month following complete liquidation, dissolution, or termination.

To file the return, mail or deliver it to:

Department of the Treasury

Internal Revenue Service Center

Ogden, UT 84201-0027

If the organization's principal business, office or agency is located in a foreign country or U.S. possession, the address for mailing the return is:

Internal Revenue Service Center

P.O. Box 409101

Ogden, UT 84409

Private delivery services. You can use certain private delivery services designated by the IRS to meet the "timely mailing as timely filing/paying" rule for tax returns and payments. These private delivery services include only the following.
• DHL Express (DHL): DHL "Same Day" Service, DHL Next Day 10:30 AM, DHL Next Day 12:00 PM, DHL Next Day 3:00 PM, and DHL 2nd Day Service.
• Federal Express (FedEx): FedEx Priority Overnight, FedEx Standard Overnight, FedEx 2Day, FedEx International Priority, FedEx International First.
• United Parcel Service (UPS): UPS Next Day Air, UPS Next Day Air Saver, UPS 2nd Day Air, UPS 2nd Day Air AM, UPS Worldwide Express Plus, and UPS Worldwide Express.

The private delivery service can tell you how to get written proof of the mailing date.

Electronic Filing

The foundation can file its Form 990-PF electronically. However, if the foundation files at least 250 returns during the calendar year, it must file Form 990-PF electronically. If the foundation must file a return electronically but does not, the organization is considered to have not filed its return. See Regulations section 301.6033-4 for more information. For additional information on the electronic filing requirement, visit *www.irs.gov/efile.*

TIP *The IRS may waive the requirements to file electronically in cases of undue hardship. For more information on filing a waiver, see Notice 2005-88, 2005-48 I.R.B. 1060, available at* www.irs.gov/irb/2005-48_IRB/index.html.

K. Extension of Time To File

A foundation uses Form 8868 to request an extension of time to file its return.

An automatic 3-month extension will be granted if you properly complete this form, file it, and pay any balance due by the due date for Form 990-PF.

If more time is needed, Form 8868 is also used to request an additional extension of up to 3 months. However, these extensions are not automatically granted. To obtain this additional extension of time to file, you must show reasonable cause for the additional time requested.

L. Amended Return

To change the organization's return for any year, file an amended return, including attachments, with the correct information. The amended return must provide all the information required by the form and instructions, not just the new or corrected information. Check the "Amended Return" box in G at the top of the return. See the *instructions for line 9 of Part VI* on page 19.

If the organization files an amended return to claim a refund of tax paid under section 4940 or 4948, it must file the amended return within 3 years after the date the original return was filed, or within 2 years from the date the tax was paid, whichever date is later.

State reporting requirements. See *Amended returns* under *General Instruction F.*

Need a copy of an old return or form? Use Form 4506 to obtain a copy of a previously filed return. You can obtain blank forms for prior years by calling 1-800-TAX-FORM (1-800-829-3676).

M. Penalty for Failure To File Timely, Completely, or Correctly

To avoid filing an incomplete return or having to respond to requests for missing information, see *General Instruction B.*

Against the organization. If an organization does not file timely and completely, or does not furnish the correct information, it must pay $20 for each day the failure continues ($100 a day if it is a large organization), unless it can show that the failure was due to reasonable cause. Those filing late (after the due date, including extensions) must attach an explanation to the return. The maximum penalty for each return will not exceed the smaller of $10,000 ($50,000 for a large organization) or 5% of the gross receipts of the organization for the year.

Large organization. A large organization is one that has gross receipts exceeding $1 million for the tax year.

Gross receipts. Gross receipts means the gross amount received during the foundation's annual accounting period from all sources without reduction for any costs or expenses.

To figure the foundation's gross receipts, start with Part I, line 12, column (a), then add to it lines 6b and 10b, then subtract line 6a from that amount.

Against the responsible person. The IRS will make written demand that the delinquent return be filed or the information furnished within a reasonable time after the mailing of the notice of the demand. The person failing to comply with the demand on or before the date specified will have to pay $10 for each day the failure continues, unless there is reasonable cause. The maximum penalty imposed on all persons for any one return is $5,000. If more than one person is liable for any failures, all such persons are jointly and severally liable for such failures (see section 6652(c)).

Other penalties. Because this return also satisfies the filing requirements of a tax return under section 6011 for the tax on investment income imposed by section 4940 (or 4948 if an exempt foreign organization), the penalties imposed by section 6651 for not filing a return (without reasonable cause) also apply.

There are also criminal penalties for willful failure to file and for filing fraudulent returns and statements. See sections 7203, 7206, and 7207.

N. Penalties for Not Paying Tax on Time

There is a penalty for not paying tax when due (section 6651). The penalty generally is 1/2 of 1% of the unpaid tax for each month or part of a month the tax remains unpaid, not to exceed 25% of the unpaid tax. If there was reasonable cause for not paying the tax on time, the penalty can be waived. However, interest is charged on any tax not paid on time, at the rate provided by section 6621.

Estimated tax penalty. The section 6655 penalty for failure to pay estimated tax applies to the tax on net investment income of domestic private foundations and section 4947(a)(1) nonexempt charitable trusts. The penalty also applies to any tax on unrelated business income of a private foundation. Generally, if a private foundation's tax liability is $500 or more and it did not make the required payments on time, then it is subject to the penalty.

For more details, see the discussion of Form 2220 in *General Instruction D.*

O. Figuring and Paying Estimated Tax

A domestic exempt private foundation, a domestic taxable private foundation, or a nonexempt charitable trust treated as a private foundation must make estimated tax payments for the excise tax based on investment income if it can expect its estimated tax (section 4940 tax minus allowable credits) to be $500 or more. The number of installment payments it must make under the depository method is determined at the time during the year that it first meets this requirement. For calendar-year taxpayers, the first deposit of estimated taxes for a year generally should be made by May 15 of the year.

Although Form 990-W is used primarily to compute the installment payments of unrelated business income tax, it is also used to determine the timing and amounts of installment payments of the section 4940 tax based on investment income. Compute separately any required deposits of excise tax based on investment income and unrelated business income tax.

To figure the estimated tax for the excise tax based on investment income, apply the rules of Part VI to your tax year 2009 estimated amounts for that part. Enter the tax you figured on line 10a of Form 990-W.

The Form 990-W line items and instructions for large organizations also apply to private foundations. For purposes of paying the estimated tax on net investment income, a "large organization" is one that had net investment income of $1 million or more for any of the 3 tax years immediately preceding the tax year involved.

Penalty. A foundation that does not pay the proper estimated tax when due may be subject to the estimated tax penalty for the period of the underpayment. (See sections 6655(b) and (d) and the Form 2220 instructions.)

Special Rules

Section 4947(a)(1) nonexempt charitable trusts. Form 1041-ES should be used to pay any estimated tax on income subject to tax under section 1. Form 1041-ES also contains the estimated tax rules for paying the tax on that income.

Taxable private foundations. Form 1120-W should be used to figure any estimated tax on income subject to tax under section 11. Form 1120-W contains the estimated tax rules for paying the tax on that income.

P. Tax Payment Methods for Domestic Private Foundations

Whether the foundation uses the depository method of tax payment or the special option for small foundations, it must pay the tax due (see Part VI) in full by the 15th day of the 5th month after the end of its tax year.

Depository Method of Tax Payment

Some foundations (described below) are required to electronically deposit all depository taxes, including their tax payments for the excise tax based on investment income.

Electronic Deposit Requirement

The foundation must make electronic deposits of all depository taxes (such as employment tax or the excise tax based on investment income) using the Electronic Federal Tax Payment System (EFTPS) in 2009 if:

- The total deposits of such taxes in 2007 were more than $200,000, or
- The foundation was required to use EFTPS in 2008.

If the foundation is required to use EFTPS and fails to do so, it may be subject to a 10% penalty. If the foundation is not required to use EFTPS, it may participate voluntarily. To enroll in or get more information about EFTPS, call 1-800-555-4477. To enroll online, visit *http://www.eftps.gov.*

Depositing on time. For deposits made by EFTPS to be on time, the foundation must initiate the transaction at least 1 business day before the date the deposit is due.

Deposits With Form 8109

If the foundation does not use EFTPS, deposit estimated tax payments and any balance due for the excise tax based on investment income with Form 8109, Federal Tax Deposit Coupon. If you do not have a preprinted Form 8109, use Form 8109-B to make deposits. You can get this form only by calling 1-800-829-4933. Be sure to have your employer identification number (EIN) ready when you call.

Do not send deposits directly to an IRS office; otherwise, the foundation may have to pay a penalty. Mail or deliver the completed Form 8109 with the payment to an authorized depositary, such as a commercial bank or other financial institution authorized to accept federal tax deposits.

Make checks or money orders payable to the depositary. To help ensure proper crediting, write the foundation's EIN, the tax period to which the deposit applies, and "Form 990-PF" on the check or money order. Be sure to darken the 990-PF box on the coupon. Records of these deposits will be sent to the IRS.

For more information on deposits, see the instructions in the coupon booklet (Form 8109) and Pub. 583, Starting a Business and Keeping Records.

Special Payment Option for Small Foundations

A private foundation may enclose a check or money order, payable to the United States Treasury, with the Form 990-PF or Form 8868, if it meets all of the following requirements:

1. The foundation must not be required to use EFTPS,
2. The tax based on investment income shown on line 5, Part VI of Form 990-PF is less than $500, and
3. If Form 8868 is used, the amount entered on line 3a of Part I or line 8a of Part II of Form 8868 must be less than $500 and it must be the full balance due.

Be sure to write "2008 Form 990-PF" and the foundation's name, address, and EIN on its check or money order.

CAUTION *Foreign organizations should see the* instructions for Part VI, line 9.

Q. Public Inspection Requirements

A private foundation must make its annual returns and exemption application available for public inspection.

CAUTION *Because Form 990-PF is disclosed to the public, do not report personal information about grantees or others that is not required and could be used for identity theft purposes, such as a social security number or bank account information.*

Definitions

Annual returns. Annual returns include an exact copy of the following documents as filed with the IRS:
- Form 990-PF, including all schedules, attachments, and supporting documents, and any amended return that is 3 or fewer years old from:

  1. The date the original return was filed or required to be filed, or
  2. The date the return was required to be filed.
- Form 990-T, if it was used to report any tax on unrelated business income.

Exemption application. An application for tax exemption includes (except as described, later):
- Any prescribed application form (such as Form 1023 or Form 1024),
- All documents and statements the IRS requires an applicant to file with the form,
- Any statement or other supporting document submitted in support of the application, and
- Any letter or other document issued by the IRS concerning the application.

An application for tax exemption does not include:
- Any application for tax exemption filed before July 15, 1987, unless the private foundation filing the application had a copy of the application on July 15, 1987, or
- Any material that is not available for public inspection under section 6104.

Who Must Make the Annual Returns and Exemption Application Available for Public Inspection?

The foundation's Form 990-PF, 990-T, and exemption application must be made available to the public by the foundation and the IRS.

How Does a Private Foundation Make Its Annual Returns and Exemption Application Available for Public Inspection?

A private foundation must make its annual returns and exemption application available in two ways:
- By office visitation, and
- By providing copies or making them widely available.

Public Inspection by Office Visitation

A private foundation must make its annual returns and exemption application available for public inspection without charge at its principal, regional, and district offices during regular business hours.

Conditions that may be set for public inspection at the office. A private foundation:
- May have an employee present,
- Must allow the individual conducting the inspection to take notes freely during the inspection, and
- Must allow an individual to make photocopies of documents at no charge but only if the individual brings photocopying equipment to the place of inspection.

Determining if a site is a regional or district office. A regional or district office is any office of a private foundation, other than its principal office, that has paid employees whose total number of paid hours a week are normally 120 hours or more. Include the hours worked by part-time (as well as full-time) employees in making that determination.

What sites are not considered a regional or district office. A site is not considered a regional or district office if:

1. The only services provided at the site further the foundation's exempt purposes (for example, day care, health care, or scientific or medical research), and
2. The site does not serve as an office for management staff, other than managers who are involved only in managing the exempt function activities at the site.

What if the private foundation does not maintain a permanent office? If the private foundation does not maintain a permanent office, it will comply with the public inspection by office visitation requirement by making the annual returns and exemption application available at a reasonable location of its choice. It must permit public inspection:
- Within a reasonable amount of time after receiving a request for inspection (normally, not more than 2 weeks), and
- At a reasonable time of day.

Optional method of complying. If a private foundation that does not have a permanent office wishes not to allow an inspection by office visitation, it may mail a copy of the requested documents instead of allowing an inspection. However, it must mail the documents within 2 weeks of receiving the request and may charge for copying and postage only if the requester consents to the charge.

Private foundations with a permanent office but limited or no hours. Even if a private foundation has a permanent office but no office hours or very limited hours during certain times of the year, it must still meet the office visitation requirement. To meet this requirement during those periods when office hours are limited or not available, follow the rules above under, *What if the private foundation does not maintain a permanent office?*

Public Inspection—Providing Copies

A private foundation must provide copies of its annual returns or exemption application to any individual who makes a request for a copy in person or in writing unless it makes these documents widely available.

In-person requests for document copies. A private foundation must provide copies to any individual who makes a request in person at the private foundation's principal, regional, or district offices during regular business hours on the same day that the individual makes the request.

Accepted delay in fulfilling an in-person request. If unusual circumstances exist and fulfilling a request on the same day places an unreasonable burden on the private foundation, it must provide copies by the earlier of:
- The next business day following the day that the unusual circumstances end, or
- The fifth business day after the date of the request.

Examples of unusual circumstances include:
- Receipt of a volume of requests (for document copies) that exceeds the private foundation's daily capacity to make copies,
- Requests received shortly before the end of regular business hours that require an extensive amount of copying, or
- Requests received on a day when the organization's managerial staff capable of fulfilling the request is conducting official duties (for instance, student registration or attending an off-site meeting or

convention) instead of its regular administrative duties.

Use of local agents for providing copies. A private foundation may use a local agent to handle in-person requests for document copies. If a private foundation uses a local agent, it must immediately provide the local agent's name, address, and telephone number to the requester.

The local agent must:

- Be located within reasonable proximity to the principal, regional, or district office where the individual makes the request, and
- Provide document copies within the same time frames as the private foundation.

Written requests for document copies. If a private foundation receives a written request for a copy of its annual returns or exemption application (or parts of these documents), it must give a copy to the requester. However, this rule only applies if the request:

- Is addressed to a private foundation's principal, regional, or district office,
- Is delivered to that address by mail, electronic mail (email), facsimile (fax), or a private delivery service approved by the IRS (see *Private delivery services* on page 5 for a list), and
- Gives the address to which the document copies should be sent.

How and when a written request is fulfilled.

- Requested document copies must be mailed within 30 days from the date the private foundation receives the request.
- Unless other evidence exists, a request or payment that is mailed is considered to be received by the private foundation 7 days after the postmark date.
- If an advance payment is required, copies must be provided within 30 days from the date payment is received.
- If the private foundation requires payment in advance and it receives a request without payment or with insufficient payment, it must notify the requester of the prepayment policy and the amount due within 7 days from the date it receives the request.
- A request that is transmitted to the private foundation by email or fax is considered received the day the request is transmitted successfully.
- Requested documents can be emailed instead of the traditional method of mailing if the requester consents to this method.

A document copy is considered as provided on the:

- Postmark date,
- Private delivery date,
- Registration date for certified or registered mail,
- Postmark date on the sender's receipt for certified or registered mail, or
- Day the email is successfully transmitted (if the requester agreed to this method).

Requests for parts of a document copy. A person can request all or any specific part or schedule of the annual returns or exemption application and the private foundation must fulfill their request for a copy.

Can an agent be used to provide copies? A private foundation can use an agent to provide document copies for the written requests it receives. However, the agent must provide the document copies under the same conditions that are imposed on the private foundation itself. Also, if an agent fails to provide the documents as required, the private foundation will continue to be subject to penalties.

Example. The ABC Foundation retained an agent to provide copies for all written requests for documents. However, ABC Foundation received a request for document copies before the agent did.

The deadline for providing a response is referenced by the date that the ABC Foundation received the request and not when the agent received it. If the agent received the request first, then a response would be referenced to the date that the agent received it.

Can a fee be charged for providing copies? A private foundation may charge a reasonable fee for providing copies. Also, it can require the fee to be paid before providing a copy of the requested document.

What is a reasonable fee? A fee is reasonable only if it is no more than the per-page copying fee charged by the IRS for providing copies, plus no more than the actual postage costs incurred to provide the copies.

What forms of payment must the private foundation accept? The form of payment depends on whether the request for copies is made in person or in writing.

Cash and money order must be accepted for in-person requests for document copies. The private foundation, if it wishes, may accept additional forms of payment.

Certified check, money order, and either personal check or credit card must be accepted for written requests for document copies. The private foundation, if it wishes, may accept additional forms of payment.

Other fee information. If a private foundation provides a requester with notice of a fee and the requester does not pay the fee within 30 days, it may ignore the request.

If a requester's check does not clear on deposit, it may ignore the request.

If a private foundation does not require prepayment and the requester does not prepay, the private foundation must receive consent from the requester if the copying and postage charge exceeds $20.

Private foundations subject to a harassment campaign. If the IRS determines that a private foundation is being harassed, it is not required to comply with any request for copies that it reasonably believes is part of the harassment campaign.

A group of requests for a private foundation's annual returns or exemption application is indicative of a harassment campaign if the requests are part of a single coordinated effort to disrupt the operations of the private foundation rather than to collect information about it.

See Regulations section 301.6104(d)-3 for more information.

Requests that may be disregarded without IRS approval. A private foundation may disregard any request for copies of all or part of any document beyond the first two received within any 30-day period or the first four received within any 1-year period from the same individual or the same address.

Making the Annual Returns and Exemption Application Widely Available

A private foundation does not have to provide copies of its annual returns and/or its exemption application if it makes these documents widely available. However, it must still allow public inspection by office visitation.

How does a private foundation make its annual returns and exemption application widely available? A private foundation's annual returns and/or exemption application is widely available if it meets all four of the following requirements:

1. The Internet posting requirement—This is met if:
   - The document is posted on a World Wide Web page that the private foundation establishes and maintains, or
   - The document is posted as part of a database of like documents of other tax-exempt organizations on a World Wide Web page established and maintained by another entity.
2. Additional posting information requirement—This is met if:
   - The World Wide Web page through which the document is available clearly informs readers that the document is available and provides instructions for downloading the document;
   - After it is downloaded and viewed, the web document exactly reproduces the image of the annual returns or exemption application as it was originally filed with the IRS, except for any information permitted by statute to be withheld from public disclosure; and
   - Any individual with access to the Internet can access, download, view, and print the document without special computer hardware or software required for that format (except software that is readily available to members of the public without payment of any fee) and without payment of a fee to the private foundation or to another entity maintaining the web page.
3. Reliability and accuracy requirements—To meet this, the entity

maintaining the World Wide Web page must:

- Have procedures for ensuring the reliability and accuracy of the document that it posts on the page;
- Take reasonable precautions to prevent alteration, destruction, or accidental loss of the document when posted on its page; and
- Correct or replace the document if a posted document is altered, destroyed, or lost.

4. Notice requirement—To meet this, a private foundation must notify any individual requesting a copy of its annual returns and/or exemption application where the documents are available (including the Internet address). If the request is made in person, the private foundation must notify the individual immediately. If the request is in writing, it must notify the individual within 7 days of receiving the request.

Penalties

A penalty may be imposed on any person who does not make the annual returns (including all required attachments to each return) or the exemption application available for public inspection according to the section 6104(d) rules discussed above. If more than one person fails to comply, each person is jointly and severally liable for the full amount of the penalty. The penalty amount is $20 for each day during which a failure occurs. The maximum penalty that may be imposed on all persons for any one annual return is $10,000. There is no maximum penalty amount for failure to make the exemption application available for public inspection.

Any person who willfully fails to comply with the section 6104(d) public inspection requirements is subject to an additional penalty of $5,000 (section 6685).

Requirements Placed on the IRS

A private foundation's Form 990-PF, 990-T, and approved exemption application may be inspected by the public at an IRS office for your area or at the IRS National Office in Washington, DC.

To request a copy or to inspect a Form 990-PF, 990-T, or an approved exemption application, complete Form 4506-A. Generally, there is a charge for photocopying.

Also, the IRS can provide a complete set of Forms 990-PF filed for a year on CD and/or DVD. A partial set of Forms 990-PF filed by state or by month is also available. Call 1-877-829-5500 or write to the address below for details.

Internal Revenue Service
RAIVS Unit MS:6716
Ogden, UT 84201

R. Disclosures Regarding Certain Information and Services Furnished

A section 501(c) organization that offers to sell or solicits money for specific information or a routine service to any individual that could be obtained by the individual from a Federal Government agency free or for a nominal charge must disclose that fact conspicuously when making such offer or solicitation.

Any organization that intentionally disregards this requirement will be subject to a penalty for each day the offers or solicitations are made. The penalty is the greater of $1,000 or 50% of the total cost of the offers and solicitations made on that day.

S. Organizations Organized or Created in a Foreign Country or U.S. Possession

If you apply any provision of any U.S. tax treaty to compute the foundation's taxable income, tax liability, or tax credits in a manner different from the 990-PF instructions, attach an explanation.

Regulations section 53.4948-1(b) states that sections 507, 508, and Chapter 42 (other than section 4948) do not apply to a foreign private foundation that from the date of its creation has received at least 85% of its support (as defined in section 509(d), other than section 509(d)(4)) from sources outside the United States.

Section 4948(a) imposes a 4% tax on the gross investment income from U.S. sources (such as income from dividends, interest, rents, payments received on securities loans (as defined in section 512(a)(5)), and royalties not reported on Form 990-T) of an exempt foreign private foundation. This tax replaces the section 4940 tax on the net investment income of a domestic private foundation. To pay any tax due, see the *instructions for Part VI, line 9.*

Taxable foreign private foundations and foreign section 4947(a)(1) nonexempt charitable trusts are not subject to the excise taxes under sections 4948(a) and 4940, but are subject to income tax under subtitle A of the Code.

Certain foreign foundations are not required to send copies of annual returns to state officials, or comply with the public inspection and notice requirements of annual returns. (See *General Instructions G* and *Q*.)

T. Liquidation, Dissolution, Termination, or Substantial Contraction

If there is a liquidation, dissolution, termination, or substantial contraction (defined below) of the organization, attach:

- A statement to the return explaining it,
- A certified copy of the liquidation plan, resolution, etc. (if any) and all amendments or supplements that were not previously filed,
- A schedule that lists the names and addresses of all recipients of assets, and
- An explanation of the nature and fair market value of the assets distributed to each recipient.

Additional requirements. For a complete corporate liquidation or trust termination, attach a statement as to whether a final distribution of assets was made and the date it was made (if applicable).

Also, an organization must indicate:

- That it has ceased to exist, check the "Final Return" box in G at the top of page 1 of the return, or
- Is terminating its private foundation status under section 507(b)(1)(B), see *General Instructions U* and *V*, or
- Is voluntarily terminating its private foundation status under section 507(a)(1) and owes a termination tax, send the notice (and tax payment, if applicable) required by Rev. Rul. 2003-13, 2003-4 I.R.B. 305, and Rev. Rul. 2002-28, 2002-20, I.R.B. 941 (2002-1 C.B., 941) to the Manager, Exempt Organizations Determinations, at the address given in *General Instruction U.*

Relief from public inspection requirements. If the organization has terminated its private foundation status under section 507(b)(1)(A), it does not have to comply with the notice and public inspection requirements of their return for the termination year.

Filing date. See *General Instruction J* for the filing date.

Definitions. The term substantial contraction includes any partial liquidation or any other significant disposition of assets. However, this does not include transfers for full and adequate consideration or distributions of current income.

A significant disposition of assets does not include any disposition for a tax year if:

1. The total of the dispositions for the tax year is less than 25% of the fair market value of the net assets of the organization at the beginning of the tax year, and
2. The total of the related dispositions made during prior tax years (if a disposition is part of a series of related dispositions made during these prior tax years) is less than 25% of the fair market value of the net assets of the organization at the beginning of the tax year in which any of the series of related dispositions was made.

The facts and circumstances of the particular case will determine whether a significant disposition has occurred through a series of related dispositions. Ordinarily, a distribution described in section 170(b)(1)(F)(ii) (relating to private foundations making qualifying distributions out of corpus equal to 100% of contributions received during the foundation's tax year) will not be taken into account as a significant disposition of assets. See Regulations section 1.170A-9(h)(2).

U. Filing Requirements During Section 507(b)(1)(B) Termination

Although an organization terminating its private foundation status under section 507(b)(1)(B) may be regarded as a public charity for certain purposes, it is considered a private foundation for filing requirement purposes and it must file an annual return on Form 990-PF. The return must be filed for each year in the 60-month termination period, if that period has not expired before the due date of the return.

Regulations under section 507(b)(1)(B)(iii) specify that within 90 days after the end of the termination period the organization must supply information to the IRS establishing that it has terminated its private foundation status and, therefore, qualifies as a public charity. Send the information to:

Internal Revenue Service

TE/GE –EO Determinations

P.O. Box 2508

Cincinnati, OH 45201

If information is furnished establishing a successful termination, then, for the final year of the termination period, the organization should comply with the filing requirements for the type of public charity it has become. See the Instructions for Form 990 and Schedule A (Form 990 or 990-EZ) for details on filing requirements. This applies even if the IRS has not confirmed that the organization has terminated its private foundation status by the time the return for the final year of the termination is due (or would be due if a return were required).

The organization will be allowed a reasonable period of time to file any private foundation returns required (for the last year of the termination period) but not previously filed if it is later determined that the organization did not terminate its private foundation status. Interest on any tax due will be charged from the original due date of the Form 990-PF, but penalties under sections 6651 and 6652 will not be assessed if the Form 990-PF is filed within the period allowed by the IRS.

V. Special Rules for Section 507(b)(1)(B) Terminations

If the organization is terminating its private foundation status under the 60-month provisions of section 507(b)(1)(B), special rules apply. (See *General Instructions T* and *U*.) Under these rules, the organization may file Form 990-PF without paying the tax based on investment income if it filed a consent under section 6501(c)(4) with its notification to the TE/GE Customer Account Services at the Cincinnati address given in *General Instruction U* of its intention to begin a section 507(b)(1)(B) termination. The consent provides that the period of limitation on the assessment of tax under Chapter 42, based on investment income for any tax year in the 60-month period, will not expire until at least 1 year after the period for assessing a deficiency for the last tax year in which the 60-month period would normally expire. Any foundation not paying the tax when it files Form 990-PF must attach a copy of the signed consent.

If the foundation did not file the consent, the tax must be paid in the normal manner as explained in *General Instructions O* and *P*. The organization may file a claim for refund after completing termination or during the termination period. The claim for refund must be filed on time and the organization must supply information establishing that it qualified as a public charity for the period for which it paid the tax.

W. Rounding, Currency, and Attachments

Rounding off to whole dollars. You may round off cents to whole dollars on your return and schedules. If you do round to whole dollars, you must round all amounts. To round, drop amounts under 50 cents and increase amounts from 50 to 99 cents to the next dollar. For example, $1.39 becomes $1 and $2.50 becomes $3.

If you have to add two or more amounts to figure the amount to enter on a line, include cents when adding the amounts and round off only the total.

Currency and language requirements. Report all amounts in U.S. dollars (state conversion rate used). Report all items in total, including amounts from both U.S. and non-U.S. sources. All information must be in English.

Attachments. Use the schedules on Form 990-PF. If you need more space, use attachments that are the same size as the printed forms.

On each attachment, write:

- "Form 990-PF,"
- The tax year,
- The corresponding schedule number or letter,
- The organization's name and EIN, and
- The information requested using the format and line sequence of the printed form.

Also, show totals on the printed forms.

Specific Instructions

Completing the Heading

The following instructions are keyed to items in the Form 990-PF heading.

Name and Address

If the organization operates under a name different from its legal name, give the legal name of the organization but identify its alternate name, after the legal name, by writing "aka"(also known as) and the alternate name of the organization. The address used must be that of the principal office of the foundation.

Include the suite, room, or other unit number after the street address. If the post office does not deliver mail to the street address and the organization has a P.O. box, show the box number instead of the street address.

A—Employer Identification Number

The organization should have only one employer identification number. If it has more than one number, notify the Internal Revenue Service Center at the address shown under *General Instruction J*. Explain what numbers the organization has, the name and address to which each number was assigned, and the address of the organization's principal office. The IRS will then advise which number to use.

B—Telephone Number

Enter a foundation telephone number (including the area code) that the public and government regulators may use to obtain information about the foundation's finances and activities. This information should be available at this telephone number during normal business hours. If the foundation does not have a telephone, enter a telephone number of a foundation official who can provide this information during normal business hours.

D2—Foreign Organizations

If the foreign organization meets the 85% test of Regulations section 53.4948-1(b), then:

- Check the box in D2 on page 1 of Form 990-PF,
- Check the box at the top of Part XI,
- Do not fill in Parts XI and XIII,
- Do not fill in Part X unless it is claiming status as a private operating foundation, and
- Attach the computation of the 85% test to Form 990-PF.

E—Section 507(b)(1)(A) Terminations

A private foundation that has terminated its status as such under section 507(b)(1)(A), by distributing all its net assets to one or more public charities without keeping any right, title, or interest in those assets, should check the box in E on page 1 of Form 990-PF. See *General Instructions Q* and *T*.

F—60-Month Termination Under Section 507(b)(1)(B)

Check the box in F on page 1 of Form 990-PF if the organization is terminating its private foundation status under the 60-month provisions of section 507(b)(1)(B) during the period covered by this return. To begin such a termination, a private foundation must have given advance notice to TE/GE at the Cincinnati address given on page 10 and provided the information outlined in Regulations section 1.507-2T(b)(3). See *General Instruction U* for information regarding filing requirements during a section 507(b)(1)(B) termination.

See *General Instruction V* for information regarding payment of the tax based on investment income (computed in Part VI) during a section 507(b)(1)(B) termination.

H—Type of Organization

Check the box for "Section 501(c)(3) exempt private foundation" if the foundation has a ruling or determination letter from the IRS in effect that recognizes its exemption from federal income tax as an organization described in section 501(c)(3) or if the organization's exemption application is pending with the IRS.

Check the "Section 4947(a)(1) nonexempt charitable trust" box if the trust is a nonexempt charitable trust treated as a private foundation. All others, check the "Other taxable private foundation" box.

I—Fair Market Value of All Assets

In block I on page 1 of Form 990-PF, enter the fair market value of all assets the foundation held at the end of the tax year.

TIP *This amount should be the same as the figure reported in Part II, column (c), line 16.*

Part I—Analysis of Revenue and Expenses

Column Instructions

The total of amounts in columns (b), (c), and (d) may not necessarily equal the amounts in column (a).

The amounts entered in column (a) and on line 5b must be analyzed in Part XVI-A.

Column (a)—Revenue and Expenses per Books

Enter in column (a) all items of revenue and expense shown in the books and records that increased or decreased the net assets of the organization. However, do not include the value of services donated to the foundation, or items such as the free use of equipment or facilities, in contributions received. Also, do not include any expenses used to compute capital gains and losses on lines 6, 7, and 8 or expenses included in cost of goods sold on line 10b.

Column (b)— Net Investment Income

All domestic private foundations (including section 4947(a)(1) nonexempt charitable trusts) are required to pay an excise tax each tax year on net investment income.

Exempt foreign foundations are subject to an excise tax on gross investment income from U.S. sources. These foreign organizations should complete lines 3, 4, 5, 11, 12, and 27b of column (b) and report only income derived from U.S. sources. No other income should be included. No expenses are allowed as deductions.

Definitions

Gross investment income. Gross investment income is the total amount of investment income that was received by a private foundation from all sources. However, it does not include any income subject to the unrelated business income tax. It includes interest, dividends, rents, payments with respect to securities loans (as defined in section 512(a)(5)), royalties received from assets devoted to charitable activities, income from notional principal contracts (as defined in Regulations section 1.863-7), annuities, substantially similar income from ordinary and routine investments, and income from similar sources. Therefore, interest received on a student loan is includible in the gross investment income of a private foundation making the loan.

Net investment income. Net investment income is the amount by which the sum of gross investment income and the capital gain net income exceeds the allowable deductions discussed later. Tax-exempt interest on governmental obligations and related expenses are excluded.

Investment income. Include in column (b) all or part of any amount from column (a) that applies to investment income. However, do not include in column (b) any income and related expenses reported on Form 990-T.

For example, investment income from debt-financed property unrelated to the organization's charitable purpose and certain rents (and related expenses) treated as unrelated trade or business income should be reported on Form 990-T. Income from debt-financed property that is not taxed under section 511 is taxed under section 4940. Thus, if the debt/basis percentage of a debt-financed property is 80%, only 80% of the gross income (and expenses) for that property is used to figure the section 511 tax on Form 990-T. The remaining 20% of the gross income (and expenses) of that property is used to figure the section 4940 tax on net investment income on Form 990-PF. (See Form 990-T and its instructions for more information.)

Investment expenses. Include in column (b) all ordinary and necessary expenses paid or incurred to produce or collect investment income from: interest, dividends, rents, amounts received from payments on securities loans (as defined in section 512(a)(5)), royalties, income from notional principal contracts, annuities, substantially similar income from ordinary and routine investments, and income from similar sources; or for the management, conservation, or maintenance of property held for the production of income that is taxable under section 4940.

If any of the expenses listed in column (a) are paid or incurred for both investment and charitable purposes, they must be allocated on a reasonable basis between the investment activities and the charitable activities so that only expenses from investment activities appear in column (b). Examples of allocation methods are given in the instructions for Part IX-A.

Limitation. The deduction for expenses paid or incurred in any tax year for producing gross investment income earned incident to a charitable function cannot be more than the amount of income earned from the function that is includible as gross investment income for the year.

For example, if rental income is incidentally realized in 2008 from historic buildings held open to the public, deductions for amounts paid or incurred in 2008 for the production of this income may not be more than the amount of rental income includible as gross investment income in column (b) for 2008.

Expenses related to tax-exempt interest. Do not include on lines 13–23 of column (b) any expenses paid or incurred that are allocable to tax-exempt interest that is excluded from lines 3 and 4.

Column (c)—Adjusted Net Income

TIP *Nonoperating private foundations should see item 1 under* Nonoperating private foundations, *later, to find out if they need to complete column (c).*

Private operating foundations. All organizations that claim status as private operating foundations under section 4942(j)(3) or (5) must complete all lines of column (c) that apply, according to the general rules for income and expenses that apply to this column, the specific line instructions for lines 3–27c, the Special rule, and Examples 1 and 2 below.

General rules. In general, adjusted net income is the amount of a private foundation's gross income that is more than the expenses of earning the income. The modifications and exclusions explained below are applied to gross income and expenses in figuring adjusted net income.

For income and expenses, include on each line of column (c) only that portion of the amount from column (a) that is applicable to the adjusted net income computation.

Income. For column (c), include income from charitable functions, investment activities, short-term capital gains from investments, amounts set aside, and unrelated trade or business activities. Do not include gifts, grants, or contributions, or long-term capital gains or losses.

Expenses. Deductible expenses include the part of a private foundation's operating expenses that is paid or incurred to produce or collect gross income reported on lines 3–11 of column (c). If only part of the property produces income includible in column (c), deductions such as interest, taxes, and rent must be divided between the charitable and noncharitable uses of the property. If the deductions for property used for a charitable, educational, or other similar purpose are more than the income from the property, the excess will not be allowed as a deduction but may be treated as a qualifying distribution in Part I, column (d). See Examples 1 and 2 below.

Special rule. The expenses attributable to each specific charitable activity, limited by the amount of income from the activity, must be reported in column (c) on lines 13–26. If the expenses of any charitable activity exceed the income generated by that activity, only the excess of these expenses over the income should be reported in column (d).

Examples.

1. A charitable activity generated $5,000 of income and $4,000 of expenses. Report all of the income and expenses in column (c) and none in column (d).
2. A charitable activity generated $5,000 of income and $6,000 of expenses. Report $5,000 of income and $5,000 of expenses in column (c) and the excess expenses of $1,000 in column (d).

Nonoperating private foundations. The following rules apply to nonoperating private foundations.

- If a nonoperating private foundation has no income from charitable activities that would be reportable on line 10 or line 11 of Part I, it does not have to make any entries in column (c).
- If a nonoperating private foundation has income from charitable activities, it must report that income only on lines 10 and/or 11 in column (c). These foundations do not need to report other kinds of income and expenses (such as investment income and expenses) in column (c).
- If a nonoperating private foundation has income that it reports on lines 10 and/ or 11, report any expenses relating to this income following the general rules and the special rule. See Examples 1 and 2 above.

Column (d)—Disbursements for Charitable Purposes

Expenses entered in column (d) relate to activities that constitute the charitable purpose of the foundation.

For amounts entered in column (d):

- Use the cash receipts and disbursements method of accounting no matter what accounting method is used in keeping the books of the foundation;
- Do not include any amount or part of an amount that is included in column (b) or (c);
- Include on lines 13–25 all expenses, including necessary and reasonable administrative expenses, paid by the foundation for religious, charitable, scientific, literary, educational, or other public purposes, or for the prevention of cruelty to children or animals;
- Include a distribution of property at the fair market value on the date the distribution was made; and
- Include only the part entered in column (a) that is allocable to the charitable purposes of the foundation.

Example. An educational seminar produced $1,000 in income that was reportable in columns (a) and (c). Expenses attributable to this charitable activity were $1,900. Only $1,000 of expense should be reported in column (c) and the remaining $900 in expense should be reported in column (d).

Qualifying distributions. Generally, gifts and grants to organizations described in section 501(c)(3), that have been determined to be publicly supported charities (for example, organizations that are not private foundations as defined in section 509(a)), are qualifying distributions only if the granting foundation does not control the public charity.

TIP *The total of the expenses and disbursements on line 26 is also entered on line 1a in Part XII to figure qualifying distributions.*

Alternative to completing lines 13–25. If you want to provide an analysis of disbursements that is more detailed than column (d), you may attach a schedule instead of completing lines 13–25. The schedule must include all the specific items of lines 13–25, and the total from the schedule must be entered in column (d), line 26.

Line Instructions

Line 1—Contributions, gifts, grants, etc., received. Enter the total of gross contributions, gifts, grants, and similar amounts received.

Schedule B (Form 990, 990-EZ, or 990-PF). If money, securities, or other property valued at $5,000 or more was received directly or indirectly from any one person during the year, complete Schedule B and attach it to the return. If the foundation is not required to complete Schedule B (no person contributed $5,000 or more), be sure to check the box on line 2.

To determine whether a person has contributed $5,000 or more, total only gifts of $1,000 or more from each person. Separate and independent gifts need not be totaled if less than $1,000. If a contribution is in the form of property, describe the property and include its fair market value.

The term "person" includes individuals, fiduciaries, partnerships, corporations, associations, trusts, and exempt organizations.

Split-interest trusts. Distributions from split-interest trusts should be entered on line 1 of column (a). They are a part of the amount on line 1.

Substantiation requirements. An organization must keep records, required by the regulations under section 170, for all its charitable contributions.

Generally, a donor making a charitable contribution of $250 or more will not be allowed a federal income tax deduction unless the donor obtains a written acknowledgment from the donee organization by the earlier of the date on which the donor files a tax return for the tax year in which the contribution was made or the due date, including extensions, for filing that return. However, see section 170(f)(8)(D) and Regulations section 1.170A-13(f) for exceptions to this rule.

The written acknowledgment the foundation provides to the donor must show:

1. The amount of cash contributed,
2. A description of any property contributed,
3. Whether the foundation provided any goods or services to the donor, and
4. A description and a good-faith estimate of the value of any goods or services the foundation gave in return for the contribution, unless:

a. The goods and services have insubstantial value, or

b. A statement is included that these goods and services consist solely of intangible religious benefits.

Generally, if a charitable organization solicits or receives a contribution of more than $75 for which it gives the donor something in return (a quid pro quo contribution), the organization must inform the donor, by written statement, that the amount of the contribution deductible for federal income tax purposes is limited to the amount by which the contribution exceeds the value of the goods or services received by the donor. The written statement must also provide the donor with a good-faith estimate of the value of goods or services given in return for the contribution.

Penalties. An organization that does not make the required disclosure for each quid pro quo contribution will incur a penalty of $10 for each failure, not to exceed $5,000 for a particular fundraising event or mailing, unless it can show reasonable cause for not providing the disclosure.

For more information. See Regulations section 1.170A-13 for more information on charitable recordkeeping and substantiation requirements.

Line 2. Check this box if the foundation is not required to attach Schedule B.

Line 3—Interest on savings and temporary cash investments.

In column (a). Enter the total amount of interest income from investments of the type reportable in Balance Sheets, Part II, line 2. These include savings or other interest-bearing accounts and temporary cash investments, such as money market funds, commercial paper, certificates of deposit, and U.S. Treasury bills or other government obligations that mature in less than 1 year.

In column (b). Enter the amount of interest income shown in column (a). Do not include interest on tax-exempt government obligations.

In column (c). Enter the amount of interest income shown in column (a). Include interest on tax-exempt government obligations.

Line 4—Dividends and interest from securities.

In column (a). Enter the amount of dividend and interest income from securities (stocks and bonds) of the type reportable in Balance Sheets, Part II, line 10. Include amounts received from payments on securities loans, as defined in section 512(a)(5). Do not include any capital gain dividends reportable on line 6. Report income from program-related investments on line 11. For debt instruments with an original issue discount, report the original issue discount ratably over the life of the bond on line 4. See section 1272 for more information.

In column (b). Enter the amount of dividend and interest income, and payments on securities loans from column (a). Do not include interest on tax-exempt government obligations.

In column (c). Enter the amount of dividends and interest income, and payments on securities loans from column (a). Include interest on tax-exempt government obligations.

Line 5a—Gross rents.

In column (a). Enter the gross rental income for the year from investment property reportable on line 11 of Part II.

In columns (b) and (c). Enter the gross rental income from column (a).

Line 5b—Net rental income or (loss). Figure the net rental income or (loss) for the year and enter that amount on the entry line to the left of column (a).

Report rents from other sources on line 11, Other income. Enter any expenses attributable to the rental income reported on line 5, such as interest and depreciation, on lines 13–23.

Line 6a—Net gain or (loss) from sale of assets. Enter the net gain or (loss) per books from all asset sales not included on line 10.

For assets sold and not included in Part IV, attach a schedule showing:
- Date acquired,
- Manner of acquisition,
- Gross sales price,
- Cost, other basis, or value at time of acquisition (if donated) and which of these methods was used,
- Date sold,
- To whom sold,
- Expense of sale and cost of improvements made subsequent to acquisition, and
- Depreciation since acquisition (if depreciable property).

Line 6b—Gross sales price for all assets on line 6a. Enter the gross sales price from all asset sales whose net gain or loss was reported on line 6a.

Line 7—Capital gain net income. Enter the capital gain net income from Part IV, line 2. See *Part IV instructions.*

Line 8—Net short-term capital gain.

TIP *Only private operating foundations report their short-term capital gains on line 8.*

Include only net short-term capital gain for the year (assets sold or exchanged that were held not more than 1 year). Do not include a net long-term capital gain or a net loss in column (c).

Do not include on line 8 a net gain from the sale or exchange of depreciable property, or land used in a trade or business (section 1231) and held for more than 1 year. However, include a net loss from such property on line 23 as an Other expense.

In general, foundations may carry to line 8 the net short-term capital gain reported on Part IV, line 3. However, if the foundation had any short-term capital gain from sales of debt-financed property, add it to the amount reported on Part IV, line 3, to figure the amount to include on line 8. For the definition of "debt-financed property," see the Instructions for Form 990-T.

Line 9—Income modifications. Include on this line:

1. Amounts received or accrued as repayments of amounts taken into account as qualifying distributions;
2. Amounts received or accrued from the sale or other disposition of property to the extent that the acquisition of the property was considered a qualifying distribution for any tax year;
3. Any amount set aside for a specific project (see explanation in the instructions for Part XII) that was not necessary for the purposes for which it was set aside;
4. Income received from an estate, but only if the estate was considered terminated for income tax purposes due to a prolonged administration period; and
5. Amounts treated in an earlier tax year as qualifying distributions to:

- A nonoperating private foundation, if the amounts were not redistributed by the grantee organization by the close of its tax year following the year in which it received the funds, or
- An organization controlled by the distributing foundation or a disqualified person if the amounts were not redistributed by the grantee organization by the close of its tax year following the year in which it received the funds.

Lines 10a, b, c— Gross profit from sales of inventory. Enter the gross sales (less returns and allowances), cost of goods sold, and gross profit or (loss) from the sale of all inventory items, including those sold in the course of special events and activities. These inventory items are the ones the organization either makes to sell to others or buys for resale.

Do not report any sales or exchanges of investments on line 10.

Do not include any profit or (loss) from the sale of capital items such as securities, land, buildings, or equipment on line 10. Enter these amounts on line 6a.

Do not include any business expenses such as salaries, taxes, rent, etc., on line 10. Include them on lines 13–23.

Attach a schedule showing the following items: Gross sales, Cost of goods sold, Gross profit or (loss). These items should be classified according to type of inventory sold (such as books, tapes, other educational or religious material, etc.). The totals from the schedule should agree with the entries on lines 10a–10c.

In column (c), enter the gross profit or (loss) from sales of inventory shown in column (a), line 10c.

Line 11—Other income. Enter the total of all the foundation's other income for the year. Attach a schedule that gives a description and the amount of the income. Include all income not reported on lines 1 through 10c. Also, see the *instructions for Part XVI-A, line 11.*

Include imputed interest on certain deferred payments figured under section 483 and any investment income not reportable on lines 3 through 5, including income from program-related investments (defined in the instructions for Part IX-B).

Do not include unrealized gains and losses on investments carried at market value. Report those as fund balance or net asset adjustments in Part III.

In column (b). Enter the amount of investment income included in line 11, column (a). Include dividends, interest, rents, and royalties derived from assets devoted to charitable activities, such as interest on student loans.

In column (c). Include all other items includible in adjusted net income not covered elsewhere in column (c).

Line 12—Total. In column (b). Domestic organizations should enter the total of lines 3–11. Exempt foreign organizations, enter the total of lines 3, 4, 5, and 11 only.

Line 13—Compensation of officers, directors, trustees, etc.

In column (a). Enter the total compensation for the year of all officers, directors, and trustees. If none was paid, enter zero. Complete line 1 of Part VIII to show the compensation of officers, directors, trustees, and foundation managers.

In columns (b), (c), and (d). Enter the portion of the compensation included in column (a) that is applicable to the column. For example, in column (c) enter the portion of the compensation included in column (a) that was paid or incurred to produce or collect income included in column (c).

Line 14—Other employee salaries and wages. Enter the salaries and wages of all employees other than those included on line 13.

Line 15—Contributions to employee pension plans and other benefits. Enter the employer's share of the contributions the organization paid to qualified and nonqualified pension plans and the employer's share of contributions to employee benefit programs (such as insurance, health, and welfare programs) that are not an incidental part of a pension plan. Complete the return/report of the Form 5500 series appropriate for the organization's plan. (See the Instructions for Form 5500 for information about employee welfare benefit plans required to file that form.)

Also include the amount of federal, state, and local payroll taxes for the year, but only those that are imposed on the organization as an employer. This includes the employer's share of social security and Medicare taxes, FUTA tax, state unemployment compensation tax, and other state and local payroll taxes. Do not include taxes withheld from employees' salaries and paid over to the various governmental units (such as federal and state income taxes and the employee's share of social security and Medicare taxes).

Lines 16a, b, and c—Legal, accounting, and other professional fees. On the appropriate line(s), enter the amount of legal, accounting, auditing, and other professional fees (such as fees for fundraising or investment services) charged by outside firms and individuals who are not employees of the foundation.

Attach a schedule for lines 16a, b, and c. Show the type of service and amount of expense for each. If the same person provided more than one of these services, include an allocation of those expenses.

Report any fines, penalties, or judgments imposed against the foundation as a result of legal proceedings on line 23, Other expenses.

Line 18—Taxes. Attach a schedule listing the type and amount of each tax reported on line 18. Do not enter any taxes included on line 15.

In column (a). Enter the taxes paid (or accrued) during the year. Include all types of taxes recorded on the books, including real estate tax not reported on line 20; the tax on investment income; and any income tax.

In column (b). Enter only those taxes included in column (a) that are related to investment income taxable under section 4940. Do not include the section 4940 tax paid or incurred on net investment income or the section 511 tax on unrelated business income. Sales taxes may not be deducted separately, but must be treated as a part of the cost of acquired property, or as a reduction of the amount realized on disposition of the property.

In column (c). Enter only those taxes included in column (a) that relate to income included in column (c). Do not include any excise tax paid or incurred on the net investment income (as shown in Part VI), or any tax reported on Form 990-T.

In column (d). Do not include any excise tax paid on investment income (as reported in Part VI of this return or the equivalent part of a return for prior years) unless the organization is claiming status as a private operating foundation and completes Part XIV.

Line 19—Depreciation and depletion.

In column (a). Enter the expense recorded in the books for the year.

For depreciation, attach a schedule showing:

- A description of the property,
- The date acquired,
- The cost or other basis (exclude any land),
- The depreciation allowed or allowable in prior years,
- The method of computation,
- The rate (%) or life (years), and
- The depreciation this year.

On a separate line on the schedule, show the amount of depreciation included in cost of goods sold and not included on line 19.

In columns (b) and (c). A deduction for depreciation is allowed only for property used in the production of income reported in the column, and only using the straight line method of computing depreciation. A deduction for depletion is allowed but must be figured only using the cost depletion method.

The basis used in figuring depreciation and depletion is the basis determined under normal basis rules, without regard to the special rules for using the fair market value on December 31, 1969, that relate only to gain or loss on dispositions for purposes of the tax on net investment income.

Line 20—Occupancy. Enter the amount paid or incurred for the use of office space or other facilities. If the space is rented or leased, enter the amount of rent. If the space is owned, enter the amount of mortgage interest, real estate taxes, and similar expenses, but not depreciation (reportable on line 19). In either case, include the amount for utilities and related expenses (for example, heat, lights, water, power, telephone, sewer, trash removal, outside janitorial services, and similar services). Do not include any salaries of the organization's own employees that are reportable on line 15.

Line 21—Travel, conferences, and meetings. Enter the expenses for officers, employees, or others during the year for travel, attending conferences, meetings, etc. Include transportation (including fares, mileage allowance, or automobile expenses), meals and lodging, and related costs whether paid on the basis of a per diem allowance or actual expenses incurred. Do not include any compensation paid to those who participate.

In column (b). Only 50% of the expense for business meals, etc., paid or incurred in connection with travel, meetings, etc., relating to the production of investment income may be deducted in figuring net investment income (section 274(n)).

In column (c). Enter the total amount of expenses paid or incurred by officers, employees, or others for travel, conferences, meetings, etc., related to income included in column (c).

Line 22—Printing and publications. Enter the expenses for printing or publishing and distributing any newsletters, magazines, etc. Also include the cost of subscriptions to, or purchases of, magazines, newspapers, etc.

Line 23—Other expenses. Enter all other expenses for the year. Include all expenses not reported on lines 13–22. Attach a schedule showing the type and amount of each expense.

If a deduction is claimed for amortization, attach a schedule showing:

- Description of the amortized expenses;
- Date acquired, completed, or expended;
- Amount amortized;
- Deduction for prior years;
- Amortization period (number of months);
- Current-year amortization; and
- Total amount of amortization.

In column (c). In addition to the applicable portion of expenses from column (a), include any net loss from the sale or exchange of land or depreciable property that was held for more than 1 year and used in a trade or business.

A deduction for amortization is allowed but only for assets used for the production of income reported in column (c).

Line 25—Contributions, gifts, grants paid.

In column (a). Enter the total of all contributions, gifts, grants, and similar amounts paid (or accrued) for the year.

List each contribution, gift, grant, etc., in Part XV, or attach a schedule of the items included on line 25 and list:

1. Each class of activity,
2. A separate total for each activity,
3. Name and address of donee,
4. Relationship of donee if related by:

a. Blood,
b. Marriage,
c. Adoption, or
d. Employment (including children of employees) to any disqualified person (see *General Instruction C* for definitions), and

5. The organizational status of donee (for instance, public charity—an organization described in section 509(a)(1), (2), or (3)).

You do not have to give the name of any indigent person who received one or more gifts or grants from the foundation unless that individual is a disqualified person or one who received a total of more than $1,000 from the foundation during the year.

Activities should be classified according to purpose and in greater detail than merely classifying them as charitable, educational, religious, or scientific activities. For example, use identification such as: payments for nursing service, for fellowships, or for assistance to indigent families.

Foundations may include, as a single entry on the schedule, the total of amounts paid as grants for which the foundation exercised expenditure responsibility. Attach a separate report for each grant.

When the fair market value of the property at the time of disbursement is the measure of a contribution, the schedule must also show:

- A description of the contributed property,
- The book value of the contributed property,
- The method used to determine the book value,
- The method used to determine the fair market value, and
- The date of the gift.

TIP *The difference between fair market value and book value should be shown in the books of account and as a net asset adjustment in* Part III.

In column (d). Enter on line 25 all contributions, gifts, and grants the foundation paid during the year.

- Do not include contributions to organizations controlled by the foundation or by a disqualified person (see *General Instruction C* for definitions). Do not include contributions to nonoperating private foundations unless the donees are exempt from tax under section 501(c)(3), they redistribute the contributions, and they maintain sufficient evidence of redistributions according to the regulations under section 4942(g).
- Do not include contributions paid from a nonoperating private foundation to a Type III supporting organization (as defined under section 4943(f)(5)) that is not a functionally integrated Type III supporting organization (as defined under section 4943(f)(5)(B)). See Notice 2006-109, 2006-51 I.R.B. 1121, available at *www.irs.gov/irb/2006-51_IRB/index.html.*
- Do not include contributions paid from a nonoperating private foundation to any supporting organization if a disqualified person of the private foundation controls the supporting organization or any of its supported organizations. See Notice 2006-109.
- Do not reduce the amount of grants paid in the current year by the amount of grants paid in a prior year that was returned or recovered in the current year. Report those repayments in column (c), line 9, and in Part XI, line 4.
- Do not include any payments of set-asides (see *instructions for Part XII, line 3*) taken into account as qualifying distributions in the current year or any prior year. All set-asides are included in qualifying distributions (Part XII, line 3) in the year of the set-aside, regardless of when paid.
- Do not include current year write-offs of prior years' program-related investments. All program-related investments are included in qualifying distributions (Part XII, line 1b) in the year the investment is made.
- Do not include any payments that are not qualifying distributions as defined in section 4942(g)(1).

Net Amounts

Line 27a—Excess of revenue over expenses. Subtract line 26, column (a), from line 12, column (a). Enter the result. Generally, the amount shown in column (a) on this line is also the amount by which net assets (or fund balances) have increased or decreased for the year. See the instructions for *Part III, Analysis of Changes in Net Assets or Fund Balances.*

Line 27b—Net investment income. Domestic organizations, subtract line 26 from line 12. Enter the result. Exempt foreign organizations, enter the amount shown on line 12. However, if the organization is a domestic organization and line 26 is more than line 12 (such as expenses exceed income), enter zero (not a negative amount).

Line 27c—Adjusted net income. Subtract line 26, column (c) from line 12, column (c) and enter the result.

Part II—Balance Sheets

For column (b), show the book value at the end of the year. For column (c), show the fair market value at the end of the year. Attached schedules must show the end-of-year value for each asset listed in columns (b) and (c).

- Foundations whose books of account included total assets of $5,000 or more at any time during the year must complete all of columns (a), (b), and (c).
- Foundations with less than $5,000 of total assets per books at all times during the year must complete all of columns (a) and (b), and only line 16 of column (c).

Line 1—Cash—Non-interest-bearing. Enter the amount of cash on deposit in checking accounts, deposits in transit, change funds, petty cash funds, or any other non-interest-bearing account. Do not include advances to employees or officers or refundable deposits paid to suppliers or others.

Line 2—Savings and temporary cash investments. Enter the total of cash in savings or other interest-bearing accounts and temporary cash investments, such as money market funds, commercial paper, certificates of deposit, and U.S. Treasury bills or other governmental obligations that mature in less than 1 year.

Line 3—Accounts receivable. On the dashed lines to the left of column (a), enter the year-end figures for total accounts receivable and allowance for doubtful accounts from the sale of goods and/or the performance of services. In columns (a), (b), and (c), enter net amounts (total accounts receivable reduced by the corresponding allowance for doubtful accounts). Claims against vendors or refundable deposits with suppliers or others may be reported here if not significant in amount. (Otherwise, report them on line 15, Other assets.) Any receivables due from officers, directors, trustees, foundation managers, or other disqualified persons must be reported on line 6. Report receivables (including loans and advances) due from other employees on line 15.

Line 4—Pledges receivable. On the dashed lines to the left of column (a), enter the year-end figures for total pledges receivable and allowance for doubtful accounts (pledges estimated to be uncollectible). In columns (a), (b), and (c), enter net amounts (total pledges receivable reduced by the corresponding allowance for doubtful accounts).

Line 5—Grants receivable. Enter the total grants receivable from governmental agencies, foundations, and other organizations as of the beginning and end of the year.

Line 6—Receivables due from officers, directors, trustees, and other disqualified persons. Enter here (and on an attached schedule described below) all receivables due from officers, directors, trustees, foundation managers, and other disqualified persons and all secured and unsecured loans (including advances) to such persons. Disqualified person is defined in *General Instruction C.*

Attached schedules. (a) On the required schedule, report each loan separately, even if more than one loan was made to the same person, or the same terms apply to all loans made.

Salary advances and other advances for the personal use and benefit of the recipient and receivables subject to special terms or arising from transactions not functionally related to the foundation's charitable purposes must be reported as separate loans for each officer, director, etc.

(b) Receivables that are subject to the same terms and conditions (including credit limits and rate of interest) as receivables due from the general public from an activity functionally related to the foundation's charitable purposes may be reported as a single total for all the officers, directors, etc. Travel advances made for official business of the organization may also be reported as a single total.

For each outstanding loan or other receivable that must be reported separately, the attached schedule should show the following information (preferably in columnar form):

1. Borrower's name and title,
2. Original amount,
3. Balance due,
4. Date of note,
5. Maturity date,
6. Repayment terms,
7. Interest rate,
8. Security provided by the borrower,
9. Purpose of the loan, and
10. Description and fair market value of the consideration furnished by the lender (for example, cash—$1,000; or 100 shares of XYZ, Inc., common stock—$9,000).

The above detail is not required for receivables or travel advances that may be reported as a single total (see *(b)* above); however, report and identify those totals separately on the attachment.

Line 7—Other notes and loans receivable. On the dashed lines to the left of column (a), enter the combined total year-end figures for notes receivable and loans receivable and the allowance for doubtful accounts.

Notes receivable. In columns (a), (b), and (c), enter the amount of all notes receivable not listed on line 6 and not acquired as investments. Attach a schedule similar to the one for line 6. The schedule should also identify the relationship of the borrower to any officer, director, trustee, foundation manager, or other disqualified person.

For a note receivable from any section 501(c)(3) organization, list only the name of the borrower and the balance due on the required schedule.

Loans receivable. In columns (a), (b), and (c), enter the gross amount of loans receivable, minus the allowance for doubtful accounts, from the normal activities of the filing organization (such as scholarship loans). An itemized list of these loans is not required, but attach a schedule showing the total amount of each type of outstanding loan. Report loans to officers, directors, trustees, foundation managers, or other disqualified persons on line 6 and loans to other employees on line 15.

Line 8—Inventories for sale or use. Enter the amount of materials, goods, and supplies purchased or manufactured by the organization and held for sale or use in some future period.

Line 9—Prepaid expenses and deferred charges. Enter the amount of short-term and long-term prepayments of expenses attributable to one or more future accounting periods. Examples include prepayments of rent, insurance, and pension costs, and expenses incurred in connection with a solicitation campaign to be conducted in a future accounting period.

Lines 10a, b, and c—Investments—government obligations, corporate stocks and bonds. Enter the book value (which may be market value) of these investments.

Attach a schedule that lists each security held at the end of the year and shows whether the security is listed at cost (including the value recorded at the time of receipt in the case of donated securities) or end-of-year market value. Do not include amounts shown on line 2. Governmental obligations reported on line 10a are those that mature in 1 year or more. Debt securities of the U.S. Government may be reported as a single total rather than itemized. Obligations of state and municipal governments may also be reported as a lump-sum total. Do not combine U.S. Government obligations with state and municipal obligations on this schedule.

Line 11—Investments—land, buildings, and equipment. On the dashed lines to the left of column (a), enter the year-end book value (cost or other basis) and accumulated depreciation of all land, buildings, and equipment held for investment purposes, such as rental properties. In columns (a) and (b), enter the book value of all land, buildings, and equipment held for investment less accumulated depreciation. In column (c), enter the fair market value of these assets. Attach a schedule listing these investment fixed assets held at the end of the year and showing, for each item or category listed, the cost or other basis, accumulated depreciation, and book value.

Line 12—Investments—mortgage loans. Enter the amount of mortgage loans receivable held as investments but do not include program-related investments (see *instructions for line 15*).

Line 13—Investments—other. Enter the amount of all other investment holdings not reported on lines 10 through 12. Attach a schedule listing and describing each of these investments held at the end of the year. Show the book value for each and indicate whether the investment is listed at cost or end-of-year market value. Do not include program-related investments (see *instructions for line 15*).

Line 14—Land, buildings, and equipment. On the dashed lines to the left of column (a), enter the year-end book value (cost or other basis) and accumulated depreciation of all land, buildings, and equipment owned by the organization and not held for investment. In columns (a) and (b), enter the book value of all land, buildings, and equipment not held for investment less accumulated depreciation. In column (c), enter the fair market value of these assets. Include any property, plant, and equipment owned and used by the organization to conduct its charitable activities. Attach a schedule listing these fixed assets held at the end of the year and showing the cost or other basis, accumulated depreciation, and book value of each item or category listed.

Line 15—Other assets. List and show the book value of each category of assets not reportable on lines 1 through 14. Attach a separate schedule if more space is needed.

One type of asset reportable on line 15 is program-related investments. These are investments made primarily to accomplish a charitable purpose of the filing organization rather than to produce income.

Line 16—Total assets. All filers must complete line 16 of columns (a), (b), and (c). These entries represent the totals of lines 1 through 15 of each column. However, foundations that have assets of less than $5,000 per books at all times during the year need not complete lines 1 through 15 of column (c).

TIP *The column (c) amount is also entered on the entry space for I on page 1.*

Line 17—Accounts payable and accrued expenses. Enter the total of accounts payable to suppliers and others and accrued expenses, such as salaries payable, accrued payroll taxes, and interest payable.

Line 18—Grants payable. Enter the unpaid portion of grants and awards that the organization has made a commitment to pay other organizations or individuals, whether or not the commitments have been communicated to the grantees.

Line 19—Deferred revenue. Include revenue that the organization has received but not yet earned as of the balance sheet date under its method of accounting.

Line 20—Loans from officers, directors, trustees, and other disqualified persons. Enter the unpaid balance of loans received from officers, directors, trustees, and other disqualified persons. For loans outstanding at the end of the year, attach a schedule that shows (for each loan) the name and title of the lender and the information listed in items 2 through 10 of the *instructions for line 6* above.

Line 21—Mortgages and other notes payable. Enter the amount of mortgages and other notes payable at the beginning and end of the year. Attach a schedule showing, as of the end of the year, the total amount of all mortgages payable and, for each nonmortgage note payable, the name of the lender and the other information specified in items 2 through 10 of the *instructions for line 6*. The schedule should also identify the relationship of the lender to any officer, director, trustee, foundation manager, or other disqualified person.

Line 22—Other liabilities. List and show the amount of each liability not reportable on lines 17 through 21. Attach a separate schedule if more space is needed.

Lines 24 Through 30—Net Assets or Fund Balances

Foundations that follow SFAS 117. If the foundation follows SFAS 117, check the box above line 24. Classify and report net assets in three groups—unrestricted, temporarily restricted, and permanently restricted—based on the existence or absence of donor-imposed restrictions and the nature of those restrictions. Show the sum of the three classes of net assets on line 30. On line 31, add the amounts on lines 23 and 30 to show total liabilities and net assets. This figure should be the same as the figure for Total assets on line 16.

Line 24—Unrestricted. Enter the balances per books of the unrestricted class of net assets. Unrestricted net assets are neither permanently restricted nor temporarily restricted by donor-imposed stipulations. All funds without donor-imposed restrictions must be classified as unrestricted, regardless of the existence of any board designations or appropriations.

Line 25—Temporarily restricted. Enter the balances per books of the temporarily restricted class of net assets. Donors' temporary restrictions may require that resources be used in a later period or after a specified date (time restrictions), or that resources be used for a specified purpose (purpose restrictions), or both.

Line 26—Permanently restricted. Enter the total of the balances for the permanently restricted class of net assets. Permanently restricted net assets are (a) assets, such as land or works of art, donated with stipulations that they be used for a specified purpose, be preserved, and not be sold or (b) assets donated with stipulations that they be invested to provide a permanent source of income. The latter result from gifts and bequests that create permanent endowment funds.

Foundations that do not follow SFAS 117. If the foundation does not follow SFAS 117, check the box above line 27 and report account balances on lines 27 through 29. Report net assets or fund balances on line 30. Also complete line 31 to report the sum of the total liabilities and net assets/fund balances.

Line 27—Capital stock, trust principal, or current funds. For corporations, enter the balance per books for capital stock accounts. Show par or stated value (or for stock with no par or stated value, total amount received upon issuance) of all classes of stock issued and, as yet, uncancelled. For trusts, enter the amount in the trust principal or corpus account. For foundations continuing to use the fund method of accounting, enter the fund balances for the foundation's current restricted and unrestricted funds.

Line 28—Paid-in or capital surplus, or land, building, and equipment fund. Enter the balance per books for all paid-in capital in excess of par or stated value for all stock issued and uncancelled. If stockholders or others gave donations that the organization records as paid-in capital, include them here. Report any current-year donations you included on line 28 in Part I, line 1. The fund balance for the land, building, and equipment fund would be entered here.

Line 29—Retained earnings, accumulated income, endowment, or other funds. For corporations, enter the balance in the retained earnings, or similar account, minus the cost of any corporate treasury stock. For trusts, enter the balance per books in the accumulated income or similar account. For foundations using fund accounting, enter the total of the fund balances for the permanent and term endowment funds as well as balances of any other funds not reported on lines 27 and 28.

Line 30—Total net assets or fund balances. For foundations that follow SFAS 117, enter the total of lines 24 through 26. For all other foundations, enter the total of lines 27 through 29. Enter the beginning-of-year figure in column (a) on line 1, Part III. The end-of-year figure in column (b) must agree with the figure in Part III, line 6.

Line 31—Total liabilities and net assets/fund balances. Enter the total of lines 23 and 30. This amount must equal the amount for total assets reported on line 16 for both the beginning and end of the year.

Part III—Analysis of Changes in Net Assets or Fund Balances

Generally, the excess of revenue over expenses accounts for the difference between the net assets at the beginning and end of the year.

On line 2, Part III, re-enter the figure from Part I, line 27(a), column (a).

On lines 3 and 5, list any changes in net assets that were not caused by the receipts or expenses shown in Part I, column (a). For example, if a foundation follows FASB Statement No. 12 and shows an asset in the ending balance sheet at a higher value than in the beginning balance sheet because of an increased market value (after a larger decrease in a prior year), include the increase in Part III, line 3.

If the organization uses a stepped-up basis to determine gains on sales of assets included in Part I, column (a), then include the amount of step-up in basis in Part III. If you entered a contribution, gift, or grant of property valued at fair market value on line 25 of Part I, column (a), the difference between fair market value and book value should be shown in the books of account and as a net asset adjustment in Part III.

Part IV—Capital Gains and Losses for Tax on Investment Income

Use Part IV to figure the amount of net capital gain to report on lines 7 and 8 of Part I.

- Part IV does not apply to foreign organizations.
- Nonoperating private foundations may not have to figure their short-term capital gain or loss on line 3. See the rules for *Nonoperating private foundations* on page 12.

Reportable gains and losses. Capital gains or losses include gains or losses from the sale or other disposition of property that:

- Is used for a charitable purpose,
- Is held for investment, or
- Is used in the production of income. Do not include the gain or loss that is included in figuring the foundation's unrelated business taxable income.

However, do not include gains or losses for any portion of property if:

- The property was used for 1 year or more in furthering the foundation's exempt purpose or function, and
- Immediately following the use, is exchanged for property of like kind that is to be used primarily in furthering the foundation's exempt purpose or function. Rules similar to the rules of section 1031 relating to exchange of property held for productive use or investment apply. See *Gross Investment Income* on page 11.

Basis. The basis for determining gain from the sale or other disposition of property is the larger of:

1. The fair market value of the property on December 31, 1969, plus or minus all adjustments after December 31, 1969, and before the date of disposition, if the foundation held the property on that date and continuously after that date until disposition, or
2. The basis of the property on the date of disposition under normal basis rules (actual basis). See Code sections 1011–1021.

The rules that generally apply to property dispositions reported in this part are:

- Section 1011, Adjusted basis for determining gain or loss;

- Section 1012, Basis of property-cost;
- Section 1014, Basis of property acquired from a decedent;
- Section 1015, Basis of property acquired by gifts and transfers in trust; and
- Section 1016, Adjustments to basis.

To figure a loss, basis on the date of disposition is determined under normal basis rules.

Losses. If the disposition of investment property results in a loss, that loss may be subtracted from capital gains realized from the disposition of property during the same tax year but only to the extent of the gains. If losses are more than gains, the excess may not be subtracted from gross investment income, nor may the losses be carried back or forward to other tax years.

Reporting Transactions on Part IV

Publicly traded securities. For sales of publicly traded securities through a broker, enter the description "publicly traded securities" on line 1, column (a). Leave columns (b), (c), and (d) blank. Total the gross sales price, the cost or other basis, and the expense of sale on all such securities sold. Report these lump-sum figures in columns (e) through (l), as appropriate. You must maintain detailed records of each transaction in your books and records.

Publicly traded securities are securities that are listed and regularly traded on an over-the-counter market or an established exchange in which market quotations are published or otherwise readily available. Securities include:
- Common and preferred stock,
- Bonds (including governmental obligations), and
- Mutual fund shares.

Other gains and losses. For sales of anything other than publicly traded securities sold, each transaction must be listed and reported separately, completing all appropriate columns in Part IV.

Part V—Qualification Under Section 4940(e) for Reduced Tax on Net Investment Income

This part is used by domestic private foundations (exempt and taxable) to determine whether they qualify for the reduced 1% tax under section 4940(e) on net investment income rather than the 2% tax on net investment income under section 4940(a).

Do not complete Part V if this is the organization's first year. A private foundation cannot qualify under section 4940(e) for its first year of existence, nor can a former public charity qualify for the first year it is treated as a private foundation.

A separate computation must be made for each year in which the foundation wants to qualify for the reduced tax.

Line 1, column (b). Enter the amount of adjusted qualifying distributions made for each year shown. The amounts in column (b) are taken from Part XII, line 6 of the Form 990-PF for 2003–2007.

Line 1, column (c). Enter the net value of noncharitable-use assets for each year. The amounts in column (c) are taken from Part X, line 5, for 2003–2007.

Part VI—Excise Tax Based on Investment Income (Section 4940(a), 4940(b), 4940(e), or 4948)

General Rules

Domestic exempt private foundations. These foundations are subject to a 2% tax on net investment income under section 4940(a). However, certain exempt operating foundations described in section 4940(d)(2) may not owe any tax, and certain private foundations that meet the requirements of section 4940(e) may qualify for a reduced tax of 1% (see the *Part V instructions*).

Exception. The section 4940 tax does not apply to an organization making an election under section 41(e)(6). Enter "N/A" in Part VI.

Domestic taxable private foundations and section 4947(a)(1) nonexempt charitable trusts. These organizations are subject to a modified 2% tax on net investment income under section 4940(b). (See *Part V and its instructions* to find out if they meet the requirements of section 4940(e) that allows them to use a modified 1% tax on net investment income.) However, they must first compute the tax under section 4940(a) as if that tax applied to them.

Foreign organizations. Under section 4948, exempt foreign private foundations are subject to a 4% tax on their gross investment income derived from U.S. sources.

Taxable foreign private foundations that filed Form 1040NR, U.S. Nonresident Alien Income Tax Return, or Form 1120-F, U.S. Income Tax Return of a Foreign Corporation, enter "N/A" in Part VI.

Estimated tax. Domestic exempt and taxable private foundations and section 4947(a)(1) nonexempt charitable trusts may have to make estimated tax payments for the excise tax based on investment income. See *General Instruction O* for more information.

Tax Computation

CAUTION *Line 1a only applies to domestic exempt operating foundations that are described in section 4940(d)(2) and that have a ruling letter from the IRS establishing exempt operating foundation status. If your organization does not have this letter, skip line 1a.*

Line 1a. A domestic exempt private foundation that qualifies as an exempt operating foundation under section 4940(d)(2) is not liable for any tax on net investment income on this return.

If your organization qualifies, check the box and enter the date of the ruling letter on line 1a and enter "N/A" on line 1. Leave the rest of Part VI blank. For the first year, the organization must attach a copy of the ruling letter establishing exempt operating foundation status. As long as the organization retains this status, write the date of the ruling letter in the space on line 1a. If the organization no longer qualifies under section 4940(d)(2), leave the date line blank and compute the section 4940 tax in the normal manner.

Qualification. To qualify as an exempt operating foundation for a tax year, an organization must meet the following requirements of section 4940(d)(2).
- It is an operating foundation described in section 4942(j)(3).
- It has been publicly supported for at least 10 tax years or was a private operating foundation on January 1, 1983, or for its last tax year ending before January 1, 1983.
- Its governing body, at all times during the tax year, consists of individuals less than 25% of whom are disqualified individuals, and is broadly representative of the general public.
- It has no officer who was a disqualified individual at any time during the tax year.

Line 2—Section 511 tax. Under section 4940(b), a domestic section 4947(a)(1) nonexempt charitable trust or taxable private foundation must add to the tax figured under section 4940(a) (on line 1) the tax which would have been imposed under section 511 for the tax year if it had been exempt from tax under section 501(a). If the domestic section 4947(a)(1) nonexempt charitable trust or taxable private foundation has unrelated business taxable income that would have been subject to the tax imposed by section 511, the computation of tax must be shown in an attachment. Form 990-T may be used as the attachment. All other filers, enter zero.

Line 4—Subtitle A tax. Domestic section 4947(a)(1) nonexempt charitable trusts and taxable private foundations, enter the amount of subtitle A (income) tax for the year reported on Form 1041 or Form 1120. All other filers, enter zero.

Line 5—Tax based on investment income. Subtract line 4 from line 3 and enter the difference (but not less than zero) on line 5. Any overpayment entered on line 10 that is the result of a negative amount shown on line 5 will not be refunded. Unless the organization is a domestic section 4947(a)(1) nonexempt charitable trust or taxable private foundation, the amount on line 5 is the same as on line 1.

Line 6a. Enter the amount of 2008 estimated tax payments, and any 2007 overpayment of taxes that the organization specified on its 2007 return to be credited toward payment of 2008 estimated taxes.

CAUTION *Line 6a applies only to domestic foundations.*

Trust payments treated as beneficiary payments. A trust may treat any part of estimated taxes it paid as taxes paid by the beneficiary. If the filing organization was a beneficiary that received the benefit of such a payment from a trust, include the amount on line 6a of Part VI, and write, "Includes section 643(g) payment." See section 643(g) for more information about estimated tax payments treated as paid by a beneficiary.

Line 6b. Exempt foreign foundations must enter the amount of tax withheld at the source.

Line 6d. Enter the amount of any backup withholding erroneously withheld. Recipients of interest or dividend payments must generally certify their correct tax identification number to the bank or other payer on Form W-9, Request for Taxpayer Identification Number and Certification. If the payer does not get this information, it must withhold part of the payments as "backup withholding." If the organization files Form 990-PF and was subject to erroneous backup withholding because the payer did not realize the payee was an exempt organization and not subject to this withholding, the organization can claim credit for the amount withheld.

CAUTION *Do not claim erroneous backup withholding on line 6d if you claim it on Form 990-T.*

Line 8—Penalty. Enter any penalty for underpayment of estimated tax shown on Form 2220. Form 2220 is used by both corporations and trusts.

Line 9—Tax due. Domestic foundations should see *General Instruction P.*

All foreign organizations should enclose a check or money order (in U.S. funds), made payable to the United States Treasury, with Form 990-PF.

Amended return. If you are amending Part VI, be sure to combine any tax due that was paid with the original return (or any overpayment credited or refunded) in the total for line 7. On the dotted line to the left of the line 7 entry space, write "Tax Paid w/ O.R." and the amount paid. If you had an overpayment, write "O.R. Overpayment" and the amount credited or refunded in brackets.

If you file more than one amended return, attach a schedule listing the tax due amounts that were paid and overpayment amounts that were credited or refunded. Write "See Attachment" on the dotted line and enter the net amount in the entry space for line 7.

Part VII-A—Statements Regarding Activities

Each question in this section must be answered "Yes," "No," or "N/A" (not applicable).

Line 1. "Political purposes" include, but are not limited to: directly or indirectly accepting contributions or making payments to influence the selection, nomination, election, or appointment of any individual to any federal, state, or local public office or office in a political organization, or the election of presidential or vice presidential electors, whether or not the individual or electors are actually selected, nominated, elected, or appointed.

Line 3. A "conformed copy" of an organizational document is one that agrees with the original document and all its amendments. If copies are not signed, attach a written declaration signed by an officer authorized to sign for the organization, certifying that they are complete and accurate copies of the original documents.

Note. If you are filing electronically, send a conformed copy of the changes to the IRS at the address listed in *General Instruction U.*

Line 6. For a private foundation to be exempt from income tax, its governing instrument must include provisions that require it to act or refrain from acting so as not to engage in an act of self-dealing (section 4941), or subject the foundation to the taxes imposed by sections 4942 (failure to distribute income), 4943 (excess business holdings), 4944 (investments which jeopardize charitable purpose), and 4945 (taxable expenditures). A private foundation may satisfy these section 508(e) requirements either by express language in its governing instrument or by application of state law that imposes the above requirements on the foundation or treats these requirements as being contained in the governing instrument. If an organization claims it satisfies the requirements of section 508(e) by operation of state law, the provisions of state law must effectively impose the section 508(e) requirements on the organization. See Rev. Rul. 75-38, 1975-1 C.B. 161, for a list of states with legislation that satisfies the requirements of section 508(e).

However, if the state law does not apply to a governing instrument that contains mandatory directions conflicting with any of its requirements and the organization has such mandatory directions in its governing instrument, then the organization has not satisfied the requirements of section 508(e) by the operation of that legislation.

Line 8a. In the space provided list all states:

1. To which the organization reports in any way about its organization, assets, or activities, and
2. With which the organization has registered (or which it has otherwise notified in any manner) that it intends to be, or is, a charitable organization or that it is, or intends to be, a holder of property devoted to a charitable purpose.

Attach a separate list if you need more space.

Line 9. If the organization claims status as a private operating foundation for 2008 and, in fact, meets the private operating foundation requirements for that year (as reflected in Part XIV), any excess distributions carryover from 2007 or prior years may not be carried over to 2008 or any year after 2008 even if it does not meet the private operating foundation requirements. See the *instructions for Part XIII.*

Line 10—Substantial contributors. If you answer "Yes," attach a schedule listing the names and addresses of all persons who became substantial contributors during the year.

The term "substantial contributor" means any person whose contributions or bequests during the current tax year and prior tax years total more than $5,000 and are more than 2% of the total contributions and bequests received by the foundation from its creation through the close of its tax year. In the case of a trust, the term "substantial contributor" also means the creator of the trust (section 507(d)(2)(A)).

The term "person" includes individuals, trusts, estates, partnerships, associations, corporations, and other exempt organizations.

Each contribution or bequest must be valued at fair market value on the date it was received.

Any person who is a substantial contributor on any date will remain a substantial contributor for all later periods.

However, a person will cease to be a substantial contributor with respect to any private foundation if:

1. The person, and all related persons, made no contributions to the foundation during the 10-year period ending with the close of the taxable year;
2. The person, or any related person, was never the foundation's manager during this 10-year period; and
3. The aggregate contributions made by the person, and related persons, are determined by the IRS to be insignificant compared to the aggregate amount of contributions to the foundation by any other person and the appreciated value of contributions held by the foundation.

The term "related person" includes any other person who would be a disqualified person because of a relationship with the substantial contributor (section 4946). When the substantial contributor is a corporation, the term also includes any officer or director of the corporation. The term "substantial contributor" does not include public charities (organizations described in section 509(a)(1), (2), or (3)).

Line 11. Answer "Yes" if at any time during the tax year the foundation owned a controlled entity. A controlled entity is an entity in which the foundation owns more than 50% of the:

1. Stock (by vote or value) in a corporation,
2. Interest (of profit or capital) in a partnership, or
3. Beneficial interest of any other entity.

The foundation must apply section 318 in determining its ownership of stock in a corporation and use similar principles in determining its ownership interests in other entities.

The foundation must attach the applicable schedules described below:

1. If the foundation answered "Yes" to line 11, and
2. If at any time during the tax year, the foundation made any loans or transfers to a controlled entity, or
3. If at any time during the tax year, the foundation received any transfers of funds or payments (received or accrued) from a controlled entity, including, but not limited to, interest, annuities, royalties, rents, dividends, fees, or other payments for services, contributions to capital, and loans.

Attached schedule for transfers to controlled entities. If at any time during the tax year, the foundation made any loans or transfers to a corporation, partnership, or other entity, which it controlled within the meaning of section 512(b)(13), attach a schedule using the format provided in the sample schedule below. In column (c), describe each loan or transfer. In column (d), enter the amount for each loan or transfer to each controlled entity.

Attached schedule for transfers from controlled entities. If at any time during the tax year, the foundation received any transfers of funds or payments from a controlled entity within the meaning of section 512(b)(13), attach a schedule using the format provided in the sample schedule below. In column (c), describe each transfer or payment received, including payment of interest, annuities, royalties, rents, dividends, fees or other payments for services, contributions to capital, and loans. In column (d), enter the amount of each loan or transfer to each controlled entity.

Line 12—Interest in insurance contracts. Answer "Yes" if after August 17, 2006, but before August 17, 2008, the foundation directly or indirectly acquired any applicable insurance contract that is a part of a structured transaction involving a pool of such contracts. If you answer "Yes," complete Forms 8921 and 8922.

An applicable insurance contract is any life insurance, annuity, or endowment contract in which an applicable exempt organization and a person other than an applicable exempt organization have directly or indirectly held an interest in the contract (whether or not at the same time). However, an applicable insurance contract does not include any life insurance, annuity, or endowment contract if:

1. All persons directly or indirectly holding any interest in the contract (other than applicable exempt organizations) have an insurable interest in the insured under the contract independent of any interest of an applicable exempt organization in the contract, or
2. The sole interest in the contract of an applicable exempt organization or each person other than an applicable exempt organization is as a named beneficiary, or
3. The sole interest in the contract of each person other than an applicable exempt organization is:

a. As a beneficiary of a trust holding an interest in the contract, but only if the person's designation as such beneficiary was made without consideration and solely on a gratuitous basis, or

b. As a trustee who holds an interest in the contract in a fiduciary capacity solely for the benefit of applicable organizations or persons described above in 1, 2, or 3a. An applicable organization is the foundation and any organization to which contributions are deductible for income tax, estate tax, or gift tax purposes and Indian tribal governments.

Line 13—Public inspection requirements and website address. All domestic private foundations (including section 4947(a)(1) nonexempt charitable trusts treated as private foundations) are subject to the public inspection requirements. See *General Instruction Q* for information on making the foundation's annual returns and exemption application available for public inspection.

Enter the foundation's website address if the foundation has a website. Otherwise, enter "N/A."

Line 15—Section 4947(a)(1) trusts. Section 4947(a)(1) nonexempt charitable trusts that file Form 990-PF instead of Form 1041 must complete this line. The trust should include exempt-interest dividends received from a mutual fund or other regulated investment company as well as tax-exempt interest received directly.

Part VII-B—Activities for Which Form 4720 May Be Required

The purpose of these questions is to determine if there is any initial excise tax due under sections 170(f)(10), 4941–4945, 4955, 4958, 4966, and 4967. If the answer is "Yes" to question 1b, 1c, 2b, 3b, 4a, 4b, 5b, 6b, or 7b, complete and file Form 4720, unless an exception applies.

Line 1—Self-dealing. The activities listed in 1a(1)–(6) are considered self-dealing under section 4941 unless one of the exceptions applies. See *www.irs.gov/charities/foundations/article/0,,1d=137679,00.html.*

The terms "disqualified person" and "foundation manager" are defined in *General Instruction C.*

Line 1b. If you answered "Yes" to any of the questions in 1a, you should answer "Yes" to 1b unless all of the acts engaged in were "excepted" acts. Excepted acts are described in Regulations sections 53.4941(d)-3 and 4 or appear in Notices published in the Internal Revenue Bulletin relating to disaster assistance.

Line 2b—Taxes on failure to distribute income. If you answer "No" to question 2b, attach a statement explaining:

- All the facts regarding the incorrect valuation of assets, and
- The actions taken (or planned) to comply with section 4942(a)(2)(B), (C), and (D) and the related regulations.

Line 3a. A private foundation is not treated as having excess business holdings in any enterprise if, together with related foundations, it owns 2% or less of the voting stock and 2% or less in value of all outstanding shares of all classes of stock. (See "*disqualified person*" under *General Instruction C.*) A similar exception applies to a beneficial or profits interest in any business enterprise that is a trust or partnership.

For more information about excess business holdings, see the instructions for Form 4720.

Line 4—Taxes on investments that jeopardize charitable purposes. In general, an investment that jeopardizes any of the charitable purposes of a private foundation is one for which a foundation manager did not exercise ordinary business care to provide for the long-and short-term financial needs of the foundation in carrying out its charitable purposes. For more details, see the regulations under section 4944.

Line 5—Taxes on taxable expenditures and political expenditures. In general, payments made for the activities described on lines 5a(1)–(5) are taxable expenditures. Go to *www.irs.gov/charities/foundations/article/0,,id=137250,00.html.*

Except as discussed below, a grant by a private foundation to a public charity is not a taxable expenditure if the private foundation does not earmark the grant for any of the activities described in lines 5a(1)–(5), and there is no oral or written agreement by which the grantor foundation may cause the grantee to engage in any such prohibited activity or to select the grant recipient.

Grants made to exempt operating foundations (as defined in section 4940(d)(2) and the instructions to Part VI) are not subject to the expenditure responsibility provisions of section 4945.

Line 11—Example A
Schedule of Information Regarding Transfers To a Controlled Entity

	(A) Name and address of each controlled entity	(B) Employer Identification Number	(C) Description of transfer	(D) Amount of transfer
a				
b				
c				
d				
e				
Total				

Line 11—Example B
Schedule of Information Regarding Transfers From a Controlled Entity

	(A) Name and address of each controlled entity	(B) Employer Identification Number	(C) Description of transfer	(D) Amount of transfer
a				
b				
c				
d				
e				
Total				

A grant from a nonoperating foundation may be a taxable expenditure if made to a Type III supporting organization (as defined in 4943(f)(5)) that is not a functionally integrated supporting organization (as defined in 4943(f)(5)(B)). Check "Yes" on Line 5a(4) if you made such a grant. See Notice 2006-109 for more information.

A grant from a nonoperating foundation may be a taxable expenditure if made to any other supporting organization (including a functionally integrated Type III), if a disqualified person of the private foundation controls the supporting organization or any of its supported organizations. Check "Yes" on Line 5a(4) if you made such a grant. See Notice 2006-109 for more information.

Under section 4955, a section 501(c)(3) organization must pay an excise tax for any amount paid or incurred on behalf of or opposing any candidate for public office. The organization must pay an additional excise tax if it does not correct the expenditure timely.

A manager of a section 501(c)(3) organization who knowingly agrees to a political expenditure must pay an excise tax unless the agreement is not willful and there is reasonable cause. A manager who does not agree to a correction of the political expenditure may have to pay an additional excise tax.

A section 501(c)(3) organization will lose its exempt status if it engages in political activity.

A political expenditure that is treated as an expenditure under section 4955 is not treated as a taxable expenditure under section 4945.

For purposes of the section 4955 tax, when an organization promotes a candidate for public office (or is used or controlled by a candidate or prospective candidate), amounts paid or incurred for the following purposes are political expenditures:

- Remuneration to the individual (or candidate or prospective candidate) for speeches or other services,
- Travel expenses of the individual,
- Expenses of conducting polls, surveys, or other studies, or preparing papers or other material for use by the individual,
- Expenses of advertising, publicity, and fundraising for such individual, and
- Any other expense that has the primary effect of promoting public recognition or otherwise primarily accruing to the benefit of the individual.

See the regulations under section 4945 for more information.

Line 5b. If you answered "Yes" to any of the questions in 5a, you should answer "Yes" to 5b unless all of the transactions engaged in were "excepted" transactions. Excepted transactions are described in Regulations section 53.4945 and appear in Notices published in the Internal Revenue Bulletin relating to disaster assistance. For example, see IRS Publication 3833, Disaster Relief.

Line 6b. Check "Yes" if, in connection with any transfer of funds to a private foundation, the foundation directly or indirectly pays premiums on any personal benefit contract, or there is an understanding or expectation that any person will directly or indirectly pay these premiums.

Report the premiums it paid and the premiums paid by others, but treated as paid by the private foundation, on Form 8870 and pay the excise tax (which is equal to premiums paid) on Form 4720.

For more information, see Form 8870 and Notice 2000-24, 2000-17 I.R.B. 952 (Notice 2000-24, 2000-1 C.B. 952).

Line 7a. Answer "Yes" if the foundation was a party to a prohibited tax shelter transaction ("PTST") as described in section 4965(e) at any time during the tax year.

Prohibited tax shelter transaction. In general, prohibited tax shelter transaction means any listed transaction and any prohibited reportable transaction.

Listed transaction. A listed transaction, within the meaning of Code section 6707A(c)(2), is a transaction that is the same as, or substantially similar to, any transaction that has been specifically identified by the Secretary in published guidance as a tax avoidance transaction for purposes of Code section 6011.

Prohibited reportable transaction. Prohibited reportable transaction means any confidential transaction or any transaction with contractual protection (as defined under regulations prescribed by the Secretary) (see Regulations section 1.6011-4(b)(3) and (4)) which is a reportable transaction (as defined in section 6707A(c)(1)).

If the answer to this question **is "Yes,"** the foundation **must also** file Form 8886-T.

Line 7b. Answer "Yes" if the foundation answered "Yes" to 7a and it had net income or received proceeds attributable to the PTST during the tax year.

If the foundation answers "Yes" to both Lines 7a and 7b, it may be required to file Form 4720 and pay tax with respect to each PTST. The foundation's managers also may be required to file Form 4720 and pay tax with respect to the relevant PTSTs.

Part VIII—Information About Officers, Directors, Trustees, Foundation Managers, Highly Paid Employees, and Contractors

Line 1—List of officers, directors, trustees, etc. List the names, addresses, and other information requested for those who were officers, directors, and trustees (or any person who had responsibilities or powers similar to those of officers, directors, or trustees) of the foundation at any time during the year. Each must be listed whether or not they receive any compensation from the foundation. Give the address at which officers, etc., prefer the Internal Revenue Service to contact them.

Also include on this list any officers or directors (or any person who had responsibilities or powers similar to those of officers or directors) of a disregarded entity owned by the foundation who are not officers, directors, etc., of the foundation.

If the foundation (or disregarded entity) pays any other person, such as a management services company, for the services provided by any of the foundation's officers, directors, or trustees (or any person who had responsibilities or powers similar to those of officers, directors, or trustees), report the compensation and other items on Part VIII as if you had paid the officers, etc., directly. Also, see Announcement 2001-33, 2001-17 I.R.B. 1137, 2001-1 C.B. 1137.

Show all forms of compensation earned by each listed officer, etc. In addition to completing Part VIII, if you want to explain the compensation of one or more officers, directors, and trustees, you may provide an attachment describing the person's entire 2000 compensation package.

Enter zero in columns (c), (d), and (e) if no compensation was paid. Attach a schedule if more space is needed.

Column (b). A numerical estimate of the average hours per week devoted to the position is required for the answer to be considered complete.

CAUTION *Phrases such as "as needed" or "as required" are unacceptable entries for column (b).*

Column (c). Enter salary, fees, bonuses, and severance payments received by each person listed. Include current year payments of amounts reported or reportable as deferred compensation in any prior year.

Column (d). Include all forms of deferred compensation and future severance payments (whether or not funded or vested, and whether or not the deferred compensation plan is a qualified plan under section 401(a)). Include payments to welfare benefit plans (employee welfare benefit plans covered by Part I of Title 1 of ERISA, providing benefits such as medical, dental, life insurance, apprenticeship and training, scholarship funds, severance pay, disability, etc.) on behalf of the officers, etc. Reasonable estimates may be used if precise cost figures are not readily available.

Unless the amounts are reported in column (c), report, as deferred compensation in column (d), salaries and other compensation earned during the period covered by the return, but not yet paid by the date the foundation files its return.

Column (e). Enter both taxable and nontaxable fringe benefits, expense account and other allowances (other than de minimis fringe benefits described in section 132(e)). See Publication 525, Taxable and Nontaxable Income, for more information. Examples of allowances include amounts for which the recipient did not account to the organization or allowances that were more than the payee spent on serving the organization. Include payments made in connection with indemnification arrangements, the value of the personal use of housing, automobiles, or other assets owned or leased by the organization (or provided for the organization's use without charge).

Line 2—Compensation of five highest-paid employees. Fill in the information requested for the five employees (if any) of the foundation (or disregarded entity that the foundation owns) who received the greatest amount of annual compensation over $50,000. Do not include employees listed on line 1. Also enter the total number of other employees who received more than $50,000 in annual compensation.

Show each listed employee's entire compensation package for the period covered by the return. Include all forms of compensation that each listed employee received in return for his or her services. See the *line 1 instructions* for more details on includible compensation.

Line 3—Five highest-paid independent contractors for professional services. Fill in the information requested for the five highest-paid independent contractors (if any), whether individuals or professional service corporations or associations, to whom the organization paid more than $50,000 for the year to perform personal services of a professional nature for the organization (for example, attorneys, accountants, and doctors). Also show the total number of all other independent contractors who received more than $50,000 for the year for performing professional services.

Part IX-A—Summary of Direct Charitable Activities

List the foundation's four largest programs as measured by the direct and indirect expenses attributable to each that consist of the direct active conduct of charitable activities. Whether any expenditure is for the direct active conduct of a charitable activity is determined, generally, by the definitions and special rules of section 4942(j)(3) and the related regulations, which define a private operating foundation.

Except for significant involvement grant programs, described below, do not include in Part IX-A any grants or expenses attributable to administering grant programs, such as reviewing grant applications, interviewing or testing applicants, selecting grantees, and reviewing reports relating to the use of the grant funds.

Include scholarships, grants, or other payments to individuals as part of an active program in which the foundation maintains some significant involvement. Related administrative expenses should also be included. Examples of active programs and definitions of the term "significant involvement" are provided in Regulations sections 53.4942(b)-1(b)(2) and 53.4942(b)-1(d).

Do not include any program-related investments (reportable in Part IX-B) in the description and expense totals, but be sure to include qualified set-asides for direct charitable activities, reported on line 3 of Part XII. Also, include in Part IX-A amounts paid or set aside to acquire assets used in the direct active conduct of charitable activities.

Expenditures for direct charitable activities include, among others, amounts paid or set aside to:

1. Acquire or maintain the operating assets of a museum, library, or historic site or to operate the facility;
2. Provide goods, shelter, or clothing to indigent or disaster victims if the foundation maintains some significant involvement in the activity rather than merely making grants to the recipients;
3. Conduct educational conferences and seminars;
4. Operate a home for the elderly or disabled;
5. Conduct scientific, historic, public policy, or other research with significance beyond the foundation's grant program that does not constitute a prohibited attempt to influence legislation;
6. Publish and disseminate the results of such research, reports of educational conferences, or similar educational material;
7. Support the service of foundation staff on boards or advisory committees of other charitable organizations or on public commissions or task forces;
8. Provide technical advice or assistance to a governmental body, a governmental committee, or subdivision of either, in response to a written request by the governmental body, committee, or subdivision;
9. Conduct performing arts performances; or
10. Provide technical assistance to grantees and other charitable organizations. This assistance must have significance beyond the purposes of the grants made to the grantees and must not consist merely of monitoring or advising the grantees in their use of the grant funds. Technical assistance involves the furnishing of expert advice and related assistance regarding, for example:

a. Compliance with governmental regulations,
b. Reducing operating costs or increasing program accomplishments,
c. Fundraising methods, and
d. Maintaining complete and accurate financial records.

Report both direct and indirect expenses in the expense totals. Direct expenses are those that can be specifically identified as connected with a particular activity. These include, among others, compensation and travel expenses of employees and officers directly engaged in an activity, the cost of materials and supplies utilized in conducting the activity, and fees paid to outside firms and individuals in connection with a specific activity.

Indirect (overhead) expenses are those that are not specifically identified as connected with a particular activity but that relate to the direct costs incurred in conducting the activity. Examples of indirect expenses include:

- Occupancy expenses;
- Supervisory and clerical compensation;
- Repair, rental, and maintenance of equipment;
- Expenses of other departments or cost centers (such as accounting, personnel, and payroll departments or units) that service the department or function that incurs the direct expenses of conducting an activity; and
- Other applicable general and administrative expenses, including the compensation of top management, to the extent reasonably allocable to a particular activity.

No specific method of allocation is required. The method used, however, must be reasonable and must be used consistently.

Examples of acceptable allocation methods include:

- Compensation that is allocated on a time basis,
- Employee benefits that are allocated on the basis of direct salary expenses,
- Travel, conference, and meeting expenses that are charged directly to the activity that incurred the expense,
- Occupancy expenses that are allocated on a space-utilized basis, and
- Other indirect expenses that are allocated on the basis of direct salary expenses or total direct expenses.

Part IX-B—Summary of Program-Related Investments

Program-related investment. Section 4944(c) and corresponding regulations define a program-related investment as one that is made primarily to accomplish a charitable purpose of the foundation and no substantial purpose of which is to produce investment income or a capital gain from the sale of the investment. Examples of program-related investments include educational loans to individuals and low-interest loans to other section 501(c)(3) organizations.

General instructions. Include only those investments that were reported in

Part XII, line 1b, for the current year. Do not include any investments made in any prior year even if they were still held by the foundation at the end of 2008.

Investments consisting of loans to individuals (such as educational loans) are not required to be listed separately but may be grouped with other program-related investments of the same type. Loans to other section 501(c)(3) organizations and all other types of program-related investments must be listed separately on lines 1 through 3 or on an attachment.

Lines 1 and 2. List the two largest program-related investments made by the foundation in 2008, whether or not the investments were still held by the foundation at the end of the year.

Line 3. Combine all other program-related investments and enter the total on the line 3 Amount column. List the individual investments or groups of investments included (attach a schedule if necessary).

TIP *The total of lines 1 through 3 in the Amount column must equal the amount reported on line 1b of Part XII.*

Part X—Minimum Investment Return

Who must complete this section? All domestic foundations must complete Part X.

Foreign foundations that checked box D2 on page 1 do not have to complete Part X unless claiming status as a private operating foundation.

Private operating foundations, described in sections 4942(j)(3) or 4942(j)(5), must complete Part X in order to complete Part XIV.

Overview. A private foundation that is not a private operating foundation must pay out, as qualifying distributions, its minimum investment return. This is generally 5% of the total fair market value of its noncharitable assets, subject to further adjustments as explained in the instructions for Part XI. The amount of this minimum investment return is figured in Part X and is used in Part XI to figure the amount that is required to be paid out (the distributable amount).

Minimum investment return. In figuring the minimum investment return, include only those assets that are not actually used or held for use by the organization for a charitable, educational, or other similar function that contributed to the charitable status of the foundation. Cash on hand and on deposit is considered used or held for use for charitable purposes only to the extent of the reasonable cash balances reported in Part X, line 4. See the *instructions for lines 1b and 4* below.

Assets that are held for the production of income or for investment are not considered to be used directly for charitable functions even though the income from the assets is used for the charitable functions. It is a factual question whether an asset is held for the production of income or for investment rather than used or held for use directly by the foundation for charitable purposes.

For example, an office building that is used to provide offices for employees engaged in managing endowment funds for the foundation is not considered an asset used for charitable purposes.

Dual-use property. When property is used both for charitable and other purposes, the property is considered used entirely for charitable purposes if 95% or more of its total use is for that purpose. If less than 95% of its total use is for charitable purposes, a reasonable allocation must be made between charitable and noncharitable use.

Excluded property. Certain assets are excluded entirely from the computation of the minimum investment return. These include pledges of grants and contributions to be received in the future and future interests in estates and trusts.

Line 1a—Average monthly fair market value of securities. If market quotations are readily available, a foundation may use any reasonable method to determine the average monthly fair market value of securities such as common and preferred stock, bonds, and mutual fund shares, as long as that method is consistently used. For example, a value for a particular month might be determined by the closing price on the first or last trading days of the month or an average of the closing prices on the first and last trading days of the month. Market quotations are considered readily available if a security is any of the following:

- Listed on the New York or American Stock Exchange or any city or regional exchange in which quotations appear on a daily basis, including foreign securities listed on a recognized foreign national or regional exchange,
- Regularly traded in the national or regional over-the-counter market for which published quotations are available, or
- Locally traded, for which quotations can be readily obtained from established brokerage firms.

If securities are held in trust for, or on behalf of, a foundation by a bank or other financial institution that values those securities periodically using a computer pricing system, a foundation may use that system to determine the value of the securities. The system must be acceptable to the IRS for federal estate tax purposes.

The foundation may reduce the fair market value of securities only to the extent that it can establish that the securities could only be liquidated in a reasonable period of time at a price less than the fair market value because of:

- The size of the block of the securities,
- The fact that the securities held are securities in a closely held corporation, or
- The fact that the sale of the securities would result in a forced or distress sale.

Any reduction in value allowed under these provisions may not be more than 10% of the fair market value (determined without regard to any reduction in value).

Also, see Regulations sections 53.4942(a)-2(c)(4)(i)(b), (c), and (iv)(a).

Line 1b—Average of monthly cash balances. Compute cash balances on a monthly basis by averaging the amount of cash on hand on the first and last days of each month. Include all cash balances and amounts that may be used for charitable purposes (see line 4 below) or set aside and taken as a qualifying distribution (see *Part XII*).

Line 1c—Fair market value of all other assets. The fair market value of assets other than securities is determined annually except as described below. The valuation may be made by private foundation employees or by any other person even if that person is a disqualified person. If the IRS accepts the valuation, it is valid only for the tax year for which it is made. A new valuation is required for the next tax year.

5-year valuation. A written, certified, and independent appraisal of the fair market value of any real estate, including any improvements, may be determined on a 5-year basis by a qualified person.

The qualified person may not be a disqualified person (see *General Instruction C*) with respect to the private foundation or an employee of the foundation.

Commonly accepted valuation methods must be used in making the appraisal. A valuation based on acceptable methods of valuing property for federal estate tax purposes will be considered acceptable.

The appraisal must include a closing statement that, in the appraiser's opinion, the appraised assets were valued according to valuation principles regularly employed in making appraisals of such property, using all reasonable valuation methods. The foundation must keep a copy of the independent appraisal for its records. If a valuation is reasonable, the foundation may use it for the tax year for which the valuation is made and for each of the 4 following tax years.

Any valuation of real estate by a certified independent appraisal may be replaced during the 5-year period by a subsequent 5-year certified independent appraisal or by an annual valuation as described above. The most recent valuation should be used to compute the foundation's minimum investment return.

If the valuation is made according to the above rules, the IRS will continue to accept it during the 5-year period for which it applies even if the actual fair market value of the property changes during the period.

Valuation date. An asset required to be valued annually may be valued as of any day in the private foundation's tax year, provided the foundation values the asset as of that date in all tax years. However, a valuation of real estate determined on a 5-year basis by a certified, independent appraisal may be made as of any day in the first tax year of the foundation to which the valuation applies.

Assets held for less than a tax year. To determine the value of an asset held less than 1 tax year, divide the number of days the foundation held the asset by the number of days in the tax year. Multiply the result by the fair market value of the asset.

Line 1e—Reduction claimed for blockage or other factors. If the fair market value of any securities, real estate holdings, or other assets reported on lines 1a and 1c reflects a blockage discount, marketability discount, or other reduction from full fair market value because of the size of the asset holding or any other factor, enter on line 1e the aggregate amount of the discounts claimed. Attach an explanation that includes the following information for each asset or group of assets involved:

1. A description of the asset or asset group (for example, 20,000 shares of XYZ, Inc., common stock),
2. For securities, the percentage of the total issued and outstanding securities of the same class that is represented by the foundation's holding,
3. The fair market value of the asset or asset group before any claimed blockage discount or other reduction,
4. The amount of the discount claimed, and
5. A statement that explains why the claimed discount is appropriate in valuing the asset or group of assets for section 4942 purposes.

In the case of securities, there are certain limitations on the size of the reduction in value that can be claimed. See the *instructions for Part X, line 1a.*

Line 2—Acquisition indebtedness. Enter the total acquisition indebtedness that applies to assets included on line 1. For details, see section 514(c)(1).

Line 4—Cash deemed held for charitable activities. Foundations may exclude from the assets used in the minimum investment return computation the reasonable cash balances necessary to cover current administrative expenses and other normal and current disbursements directly connected with the charitable, educational, or other similar activities. The amount of cash that may be excluded is generally 1½% of the fair market value of all assets (minus any acquisition indebtedness) as computed in Part X, line 3. However, if under the facts and circumstances an amount larger than the deemed amount is necessary to pay expenses and disbursements, then you may enter the larger amount instead of 1½% of the fair market value on line 4. If you use a larger amount, attach an explanation.

Line 6—Short tax periods. If the foundation's tax period is less than 12 months, determine the applicable percentage by dividing the number of days in the short tax period by 365 (or 366 in a leap year). Multiply the result by 5%. Then multiply the modified percentage by the amount on line 5 and enter the result on line 6.

Part XI—Distributable Amount

If the organization is claiming status as a private operating foundation described in section 4942(j)(3) or (j)(5) or if it is a foreign foundation that checked box D2 on page 1, check the box in the heading for Part XI. You do not need to complete this part. See the *Part XIV instructions* for more details on private operating foundations.

Section 4942(j)(5) foundations are classified as private operating foundations for purposes of section 4942 only if they meet the requirements of Regulations section 53.4942(b)-1(a)(2).

The distributable amount for 2008 is the amount that the foundation must distribute by the end of 2009 as qualifying distributions to avoid the 30% tax on the undistributed portion.

Line 4. Enter the total of recoveries of amounts treated as qualifying distributions for any year under section 4942(g). Include recoveries of part or all (as applicable) of grants previously made; proceeds from the sale or other disposition of property whose cost was treated as a qualifying distribution when the property was acquired; and any amount set aside under section 4942(g) to the extent it is determined that this amount is not necessary for the purposes of the set-aside.

Line 6—Deduction from distributable amount. If the foundation was organized before May 27, 1969, and its governing instrument or any other instrument continues to require the accumulation of income after a judicial proceeding to reform the instrument has terminated, then the amount of the income required to be accumulated must be subtracted from the distributable amount beginning with the first tax year after the tax year in which the judicial proceeding was terminated. (See the *instructions for Part VII-A, line 6.*)

Part XII—Qualifying Distributions

"Qualifying distributions" are amounts spent or set aside for religious, educational, or similar charitable purposes. The total amount of qualifying distributions for any year is used to reduce the distributable amount for specified years to arrive at the undistributed income (if any) for those years.

Line 1a—Expenses, contributions, gifts, etc. Enter the amount from Part I, column (d), line 26. However, if the borrowed funds election applies, add the total of the repayments during the year to the amount from Part I, column (d), line 26, and enter it on line 1a.

Borrowed funds. If the foundation borrowed money in a tax year beginning before January 1, 1970, or later borrows money under a written commitment binding on December 31, 1969, the foundation may elect to treat any repayments of the loan principal after December 31, 1969, as qualifying distributions at the time of repayment, rather than at the earlier time that the borrowed funds were actually distributed, only if:

1. The money is used to make expenditures for a charitable or similar purpose, and
2. Repayment on the loan did not start until a year beginning after 1969.

On these loans, deduct any interest payment from gross income to compute adjusted net income in the year paid.

Election. To make this election, attach a statement to Form 990-PF for the first tax year beginning after 1969 in which a repayment of loan principal is made and for each tax year after that in which any repayment of loan principal is made. The statement should show:

- The lender's name and address,
- The amount borrowed,
- The specific use of the borrowed funds, and
- The private foundation's election to treat repayments of loan principal as qualifying distributions.

Line 1b—Program-related investments. Enter the total of the "Amount" column from Part IX-B. See the *Part IX-B instructions* for the definition of program-related investments.

Line 3—Amounts set aside. Amounts set aside may be treated as qualifying distributions only if the private foundation establishes to the satisfaction of the IRS that the amount will be paid for the specific project within 60 months from the date of the first set-aside and meets 1 or 2 below.

1. The project can be better accomplished by a set-aside than by the immediate payment of funds (suitability test), or
2. The private foundation meets the requirements of section 4942(g)(2)(B)(ii) (cash distribution test).

Set-aside under item 1. For any set-aside under 1 above, the private foundation must apply for IRS approval by the end of the tax year in which the amount is set aside. Send the application for approval to the:

Internal Revenue Service

TE/GE EO - Determinations

P.O. Box 2508

Cincinnati, OH 45201

The application for approval must give all of the following information:

- The nature and purposes of the specific project and the amount of the set-aside for which approval is requested,
- The amounts and approximate dates of any planned additions to the set-aside after its initial establishment,
- The reasons why the project can be better accomplished by the set-aside than by the immediate payment of funds,
- A detailed description of the project, including estimated costs, sources of any future funds expected to be used for completion of the project, and the location(s) (general or specific) of any physical facilities to be acquired or constructed as part of the project, and
- A statement of an appropriate foundation manager that the amounts set aside will actually be paid for the specific project within a specified period of time ending within 60 months after the date of the first set-aside; or a statement explaining why the period for paying the amount set aside should be extended and indicating the extension of time requested. (Include in this statement the reason why the proposed project could not be divided into two or more projects covering periods of no more than 60 months each.)

Set-aside under item 2. For any set-aside under 2 above, the private foundation must attach a schedule to its annual information return showing how the requirements are met. A schedule is required for the year of the set-aside and for each subsequent year until the set-aside amount has been distributed. See Regulations section 53.4942(a)-3(b)(7)(ii) for specific requirements.

Line 5—Reduced tax on investment income under section 4940(e). If the organization does not qualify for the 1% tax under section 4940(e), enter zero. See *Parts V and VI of the instructions.*

Part XIII—Undistributed Income

If you checked box D2 on page 1, do not fill in this part.

If the organization is a private operating foundation for any of the years shown in Part XIII, do not complete the portions of Part XIII that apply to those years. If there are excess qualifying distributions for any tax year, do not carry them over to a year in which the organization is a private operating foundation or to any later year. For example, if a foundation made excess qualifying distributions in 2006 and became a private operating foundation in 2008, the excess qualifying distributions from 2006 could be applied against the distributable amount for 2007 but not to any year after 2007.

The purpose of this part is to enable the foundation to comply with the rules for applying its qualifying distributions for the year 2008. In applying the qualifying distributions, there are three basic steps.

1. Reduce any undistributed income for 2007 (but not below zero).
2. The organization may use any part or all remaining qualifying distributions for 2008 to satisfy elections. For example, if undistributed income remained for any year before 2007, it could be reduced to zero or, if the foundation wished, the distributions could be treated as distributions out of corpus.
3. If no elections are involved, apply remaining qualifying distributions to the 2008 distributable amount on line 4d. If the remaining qualifying distributions are greater than the 2008 distributable amount, the excess is treated as a distribution out of corpus on line 4e.

If for any reason the 2008 qualifying distributions do not reduce any 2007 undistributed income to zero, the amount not distributed is subject to a 30% tax. If the 2007 income remains undistributed at the end of 2009, it could be subject again to the 30% tax. Also, see section 4942(b) for the circumstances under which a second-tier tax could be imposed.

Line 1—Distributable amount. Enter the distributable amount for 2008 from Part XI, line 7.

Line 2—Undistributed income. Enter the distributable amount for 2007 and amounts for earlier years that remained undistributed at the beginning of the 2008 tax year.

Line 2b. Enter the amount of undistributed income for years before 2007.

Line 3—Excess distributions carryover to 2008. If the foundation has made excess distributions out of corpus in prior years, which have not been applied in any year, enter the amount for each year. Do not enter an amount for a particular year if the organization was a private operating foundation for any later year.

Lines 3a through 3e. Enter the amount of any excess distribution made on the line for each year listed. Do not include any amount that was applied against the distributable amount of an earlier year or that was already used to meet pass-through distribution requirements. (See the instructions for line 7.)

Line 3f. This amount can be applied in 2008.

Line 4—Qualifying distributions. Enter the total amount of qualifying distributions made in 2008 from Part XII, line 4. The total of the amounts applied on lines 4a through 4e is equal to the qualifying distributions made in 2008.

Line 4a. The qualifying distributions for 2008 are first used to reduce any undistributed income remaining from 2007. Enter only enough of the 2008 qualifying distributions to reduce the 2007 undistributed income to zero.

Lines 4b and 4c. If there are any 2008 qualifying distributions remaining after reducing the 2007 undistributed income to zero, one or more elections can be made under Regulations section 53.4942(a)-3(d)(2) to apply all or part of the remaining qualifying distributions to any undistributed income remaining from years before 2007 or to apply to corpus.

Elections. To make these elections, the organization must file a statement with the IRS or attach a statement, as described in the above regulations section, to Form 990-PF. An election made by filing a separate statement with the IRS must be made within the year for which the election is made. Otherwise, attach a statement to the Form 990-PF filed for the year the election was made.

Where to enter. If the organization elected to apply all or part of the remaining amount to the undistributed income remaining from years before 2007, enter the amount on line 4b.

If the organization elected to treat those qualifying distributions as a distribution out of corpus, enter the amount on line 4c.

CAUTION *Entering an amount on line 4b or 4c without submitting the required statement is not considered a valid election.*

Line 4d. Treat as a distribution of the distributable amount for 2008 any qualifying distributions for 2008 that remain after reducing the 2007 undistributed income to zero and after electing to treat any part of the remaining distributions as a distribution out of corpus or as a distribution of a prior year's undistributed income. Enter only enough of the remaining 2008 qualifying distributions to reduce the 2008 distributable amount to zero.

Line 4e. Any 2008 qualifying distributions remaining after reducing the 2008 distributable amount to zero should be treated as an excess distribution out of corpus. This amount may be carried over and applied to later years.

Line 5—Excess qualifying distributions carryover applied to 2008. Enter any excess qualifying distributions from line 3, which were applied to 2008, in both the Corpus column and the 2008 column. Apply the oldest excess qualifying distributions first. Thus, the organization will apply any excess qualifying distributions carried forward from 2003 before those from later years.

Line 6a. Add lines 3f, 4c, and 4e. Subtract line 5 from the total. Enter the net total in the Corpus column.

Line 6c. Enter only the undistributed income from 2006 and prior years for which either a notice of deficiency under section 6212(a) has been mailed for the section 4942(a) first-tier tax, or on which the first-tier tax has been assessed because the organization filed a Form 4720 for a tax year that began before 2007.

Lines 6d and 6e. These amounts are taxable under the provisions of section 4942(a), except for any part that is due solely to improper valuation of assets to which the provisions of section 4942(a)(2) are being applied (see *Part VII-B, line 2b*). Report the taxable amount on Form 4720. If the exception applies, attach an explanation.

Line 6f. In the 2008 column, enter the amount by which line 1 is more than the total of lines 4d and 5. This is the undistributed income for 2008. The organization must distribute the amount shown by the end of its 2009 tax year so that it will not be liable for the tax on undistributed income.

Line 7—Distributions out of corpus for 2008 pass-through distributions.

1. If the foundation is the donee and receives a contribution from another private foundation, the donor foundation may treat the contribution as a qualifying distribution only if the donee foundation makes a distribution equal to the full amount of the contribution and the distribution is a qualifying distribution that is treated as a distribution of corpus. The donee foundation must, no later than the close of the first tax year after the tax year in which it receives the contributions, distribute an amount equal in value to the contributions received in the prior tax year and have no remaining undistributed income for the prior year. For example, if private foundation X received $1,000 in tax year 2007 from foundation Y, foundation X would have to distribute the $1,000 as a qualifying distribution out of corpus by the end of 2008 and have no remaining undistributed income for 2007.

2. If a private foundation receives a contribution from an individual or a corporation and the individual is seeking the 50% contribution base limit on deductions for the tax year (or the individual or corporation is not applying the limit imposed on deductions for contributions to the foundation of capital gain property), the foundation must comply with certain distribution requirements.

By the 15th day of the 3rd month after the end of the tax year in which the foundation received the contributions, the donee foundation must distribute as qualifying distributions out of corpus:

a. An amount equal to 100% of all contributions received during the year in order for the individual contributor to receive the benefit of the 50% limit on deductions, and

b. Distribute all contributions of property only so that the individual or corporation making the contribution is not subject to the section 170(e)(1)(B)(ii) limitations.

If the organization is applying excess distributions from prior years (for instance, any part of the amount in Part XIII, line 3f) to satisfy the distribution requirements of section 170(b)(1)(F) or 4942(g)(3), it must make the election under Regulations section 53.4942(a)-3(c)(2). Also, see Regulations section 1.170A-9(h)(2).

Enter on line 7 the total distributions out of corpus made to satisfy the restrictions on amounts received from donors described above.

Line 8—Outdated excess distributions carryover. Because of the 5-year carryover limitation under section 4942(i)(2), the organization must reduce any excess distributions carryover by any amounts from 2003 that were not applied in 2008.

Line 9—Excess distributions carryover to 2009. Enter the amount by which line 6a is more than the total of lines 7 and 8. This is the amount the organization may apply to 2009 and following years. Line 9 can never be less than zero.

Line 10—Analysis of line 9. In the space provided for each year, enter the amount of excess distributions carryover from that year that has not been applied as of the end of the 2008 tax year. If there is an amount on the line for 2004, it must be applied by the end of the 2009 tax year since the 5-year carryover period for 2004 ends in 2009.

Part XIV—Private Operating Foundations

All organizations that claim status as private operating foundations under section 4942(j)(3) or (5) for 2008 must complete Part XIV.

Certain elderly care facilities (section 4942(j)(5)). For purposes of section 4942 only, certain elderly care facilities may be classified as private operating foundations. To be so classified, they must be operated and maintained for the principal purpose explained in section 4942(j)(5) and also meet the endowment test described below.

If the foundation is a section 4942(j)(5) organization, complete only lines 1a, 1b, 2c, 2d, 2e, and 3b. Enter "N/A" on all other lines in the Total column for Part XIV.

Private operating foundation (section 4942(j)(3)). The term "private operating foundation" means any private foundation that spends at least 85% of the smaller of its adjusted net income or its minimum investment return directly for the active conduct of the exempt purpose or functions for which the foundation is organized and operated (the Income Test) and that also meets one of the three tests below.

1. Assets test. 65% or more of the foundation's assets are devoted directly to those activities or functionally related businesses, or both. Or 65% or more of the foundation's assets are stock of a corporation that is controlled by the foundation, and substantially all of the assets of the corporation are devoted to those activities or functionally related businesses.

2. Endowment test. The foundation normally makes qualifying distributions directly for the active conduct of the exempt purpose or functions for which it is organized and operated in an amount that is two-thirds or more of its minimum investment return.

3. Support test. The foundation normally receives 85% or more of its support (other than gross investment income as defined in section 509(e)) from the public and from five or more exempt organizations that are not described in section 4946(a)(1)(H) with respect to each other or the recipient foundation. Not more than 25% of the support (other than gross investment income) normally may be received from any one of the exempt organizations and not more than one-half of the support normally may be received from gross investment income.

See regulations under section 4942 for the meaning of "directly for the active conduct" of exempt activities for purposes of these tests.

Complying with these tests. A foundation may meet the income test and either the assets, endowment, or support test by satisfying the tests for any 3 years during a 4-year period consisting of the tax year in question and the 3 immediately preceding tax years. It may also meet the tests based on the total of all related amounts of income or assets held, received, or distributed during that 4-year period. A foundation may not use one method for satisfying the income test and another for satisfying one of the three alternative tests. Thus, if a foundation meets the income test on the 3-out-of-4-year basis for a particular tax year, it may not use the 4-year aggregation method for meeting one of the three alternative tests for that same year.

In completing line 3c(3) of Part XIV under the aggregation method, the largest amount of support from an exempt organization will be based on the total amount received for the 4-year period from any one exempt organization.

A new private foundation must use the aggregation method to satisfy the tests for its first tax year in order to be treated as a private operating foundation from the beginning of that year. It must continue to use the aggregation method for its 2nd and 3rd tax years to maintain its status for those years.

Part XV—Supplementary Information

Complete this part only if the foundation had assets of $5,000 or more at any time during the year. This part does not apply to a foreign foundation that during its entire period of existence received substantially all (85% or more) of its support (other than gross investment income) from sources outside the United States.

Line 2. In the space provided (or in an attachment, if necessary), furnish the required information about the organization's grant, scholarship, fellowship, loan, etc., programs. In addition to restrictions or limitations on awards by geographical areas, charitable fields, and kinds of recipients, indicate any specific dollar limitations or other restrictions applicable to each type of award the organization makes. This information benefits the grant seeker and the foundation. The grant seekers will be aware of the grant eligibility requirements and the foundation should receive only applications that adhere to these grant application requirements.

If the foundation only makes contributions to preselected charitable organizations and does not accept unsolicited applications for funds, check the box on line 2.

Line 3. If necessary, attach a schedule for lines 3a and 3b that lists separately amounts given to individuals and amounts given to organizations.

Purpose of grant or contribution. Entries under this column should reflect the grant's or contribution's purpose and should be in greater detail than merely classifying them as charitable, educational, religious, or scientific activities.

For example, use an identification such as payments:
- For nursing service,
- For fellowships, or
- For assistance to indigent families.

CAUTION *Entries such as "grant" or "contribution" under the column titled Purpose of grant or contribution are unacceptable.*

Line 3a—Paid during year. List all contributions, grants, etc., actually paid during the year, including grants or contributions that are not qualifying distributions under section 4942(g). Include current year payments of set-asides treated as qualifying distributions in the current tax year or any prior year.

Line 3b—Approved for future payment. List all contributions, grants, etc., approved during the year but not paid by the end of the year, including the unpaid portion of any current year set-aside.

CAUTION *Because Form 990-PF is disclosed to the public, do not report personal information about grantees that is not required and could be used for identity theft purposes, such as a social security number, taxpayer identification number, or bank account information. See General Instruction Q for more information about public inspection and disclosure requirements.*

Part XVI-A—Analysis of Income-Producing Activities

In Part XVI-A, analyze revenue items that are also entered in Part I, column (a), lines 3–11, and on line 5b. Contributions reported on line 1 of Part I are not entered in Part XVI-A. For information on unrelated business income, see the Instructions for Form 990-T and Pub. 598.

Columns (a) and (c). In column (a), enter a 6-digit business code, from the list in the Instructions for Form 990-T, to identify any income reported in column (b). In column (c), enter an exclusion code, from the list on page 31, to identify any income reported in column (d). If more than one exclusion code is applicable to a particular revenue item, select the lowest numbered exclusion code that applies. Also, if nontaxable revenues from several sources are reportable on the same line in column (d), use the exclusion code that applies to the largest revenue source.

Columns (b), (d), and (e). For amounts reported in Part XVI-A on lines 1–11, enter in column (b) any income earned that is unrelated business income (see section 512). In column (d), enter any income earned that is excluded from the computation of unrelated business taxable income by Code section 512, 513, or 514. In column (e), enter any related or exempt function income; that is, any income earned that is related to the organization's purpose or function which constitutes the basis for the organization's exemption.

Also enter in column (e) any income specifically excluded from gross income other than by Code section 512, 513, or 514, such as interest on state and local bonds that is excluded from tax by section 103. You must explain in Part XVI-B any amount shown in column (e).

Comparing Part XVI-A with Part I. The sum of the amounts entered on each line of lines 1–11 of columns (b), (d), and (e) of Part XVI-A should equal corresponding amounts entered on lines 3–11 of Part I, column (a), and on line 5b as shown below:

Amounts in Part XVI-A on line . . .	Correspond to Amounts in Part I, column (a), line . . .
1a–g	11
2	11
3	3
4	4
5 and 6	5b (description column)
7	11
8	6
9	11 minus any special event expenses included on lines 13 through 23 of Part I, column (a)
10	10c
11a–e	11

Line 1—Program service revenue. On lines 1a–g, list each revenue-producing program service activity of the organization. For each program service activity listed, enter the gross revenue earned for each activity, as well as identifying business and exclusion codes, in the appropriate columns. For line 1g, enter amounts that are payments for services rendered to governmental units. Do not include governmental grants that are reportable on line 1 of Part I.

Report the total of lines 1a–g on line 11 of Part I, along with any other income reportable on line 11.

Program services are mainly those activities that the reporting organization was created to conduct and that, along with any activities begun later, form the basis of the organization's current exemption from tax.

Program services can also include the organization's unrelated trade or business activities. Program service revenue also includes income from program-related investments (such as interest earned on scholarship loans) as defined in the *instructions for Part IX-B.*

Line 11. On lines 11a–e, list each "Other revenue" activity not reported on lines 1 through 10. Report the sum of the amounts entered for lines 11a–e, columns (b), (d), and (e), on line 11, Part I.

Line 13. On line 13, enter the total of columns (b), (d), and (e) of line 12.

You may use the following worksheet to verify your calculations.

Line 13,	Part XVI-A	_____
Minus:	Line 5b, Part I . . . . **Note:** *If line 5b, Part I, reflects a loss, add that amount here instead of subtracting.*	_____
Plus:	Line 1, Part I	_____
Plus:	Line 5a, Part I	_____
Plus:	Expenses of special events deducted in computing line 9 of Part XVI-A	_____
Equal:	Line 12, column (a), of Part I	_____

Part XVI-B—Relationship of Activities to the Accomplishment of Exempt Purposes

To explain how each amount in column (e) of Part XVI-A was related or exempt function income, show the line number of the amount in column (e) and give a brief description of how each activity reported in column (e) contributed importantly to the accomplishment of the organization's exempt purposes (other than by providing funds for such purposes). Activities that generate exempt-function income are activities that form the basis of the organization's exemption from tax.

Also, explain any income entered in column (e) that is specifically excluded from gross income other than by Code section 512, 513, or 514. If no amount is entered in column (e), do not complete Part XVI-B.

Example. M, a performing arts association, is primarily supported by endowment funds. It raises revenue by charging admissions to its performances. These performances are the primary means by which the organization accomplishes its cultural and educational purposes.

M reported admissions income in column (e) of Part XVI-A and explained in Part XVI-B that these performances are the primary means by which it accomplishes its cultural and educational purposes.

Because M also reported interest from state bonds in column (e) of Part XVI-A, M explained in Part XVI-B that such interest was excluded from gross income by Code section 103.

Part XVII—Information Regarding Transfers To and Transactions and Relationships With Noncharitable Exempt Organizations

Part XVII is used to report direct and indirect transfers to (line 1a) and direct and indirect transactions with (line 1b) and relationships with (line 2) any other noncharitable exempt organization. A "noncharitable exempt organization" is an organization exempt under section 501(c) (that is not exempt under section 501(c)(3)), or a political organization described in section 527.

For purposes of these instructions, the section 501(c)(3) organization completing Part XVII is referred to as the "reporting organization."

A noncharitable exempt organization is "related to or affiliated with" the reporting organization if either:

• The two organizations share some element of common control, or
• A historic and continuing relationship exists between the two organizations.

A noncharitable exempt organization is unrelated to the reporting organization if:

• The two organizations share no element of common control, and
• A historic and continuing relationship does not exist between the two organizations.

An "element of common control" is present when one or more of the officers, directors, or trustees of one organization are elected or appointed by the officers, directors, trustees, or members of the other. An element of common control is also present when more than 25% of the officers, directors, or trustees of one organization serve as officers, directors, or trustees of the other organization.

A "historic and continuing relationship" exists when two organizations participate in a joint effort to achieve one or more common purposes on a continuous or recurring basis rather than on the basis of one or more isolated transactions or activities. Such a relationship also exists when two organizations share facilities, equipment, or paid personnel during the year, regardless of the length of time the arrangement is in effect.

Line 1—Reporting of certain transfers and transactions. Generally, report on line 1 any transfer to or transaction with a noncharitable exempt organization even if the transfer or transaction constitutes the only connection with the noncharitable exempt organization.

Related organizations. If the noncharitable exempt organization is related to or affiliated with the reporting organization, report all direct and indirect transfers and transactions except for contributions and grants it received.

Unrelated organizations. All transfers to an unrelated noncharitable exempt organization must be reported on line 1a. All transactions between the reporting organization and an unrelated noncharitable exempt organization must be shown on line 1b unless they meet the exception in the specific instructions for line 1b.

Line 1a—Transfers. Answer "Yes" to lines 1a(1) and 1a(2) if the reporting organization made any direct or indirect transfers of any value to a noncharitable exempt organization.

A "transfer" is any transaction or arrangement whereby one organization transfers something of value (cash, other assets, services, use of property, etc.) to another organization without receiving something of more than nominal value in return. Contributions, gifts, and grants are examples of transfers.

If the only transfers between the two organizations were contributions and grants made by the noncharitable exempt organization to the reporting organization, answer "No."

Line 1b—Other transactions. Answer "Yes" for any transaction described on line 1b(1)–(6), regardless of its amount, if it is with a related or affiliated organization.

Unrelated organizations. Answer "Yes" for any transaction between the reporting organization and an unrelated noncharitable exempt organization, regardless of its amount, if the reporting organization received less than adequate consideration. There is adequate consideration when the fair market value of the goods and other assets or services furnished by the reporting organization is not more than the fair market value of the goods and other assets or services received from the unrelated noncharitable exempt organization. The exception described below does not apply to transactions for less than adequate consideration.

Answer "Yes" for any transaction between the reporting organization and an unrelated noncharitable exempt organization if the "amount involved" is more than $500. The "amount involved" is the fair market value of the goods, services, or other assets furnished by the reporting organization.

Exception. If a transaction with an unrelated noncharitable exempt organization was for adequate consideration and the amount involved was $500 or less, answer "No" for that transaction.

Line 1b(3). Answer "Yes" for transactions in which the reporting organization was either the lessor or the lessee.

Line 1b(4). Answer "Yes" if either organization reimbursed expenses incurred by the other.

Line 1b(5). Answer "Yes" if either organization made loans to the other or if the reporting organization guaranteed the other's loans.

Line 1b(6). Answer "Yes" if either organization performed services or membership or fundraising solicitations for the other.

Line 1c. Complete line 1c regardless of whether the noncharitable exempt organization is related to or closely affiliated with the reporting organization. For purposes of this line, "facilities" includes office space and any other land, building, or structure whether owned or leased by, or provided free of charge to, the reporting organization or the noncharitable exempt organization.

Line 1d. Use this schedule to describe the transfers and transactions for which "Yes" was entered on lines 1a–c above. You must describe each transfer or transaction for which the answer was "Yes." You may combine all of the cash transfers (line 1a(1)) to each organization into a single entry. Otherwise, make a separate entry for each transfer or transaction.

Column (a). For each entry, enter the line number from line 1a–c. For example, if the answer was "Yes" to line 1b(3), enter "b(3)" in column (a).

Column (d). If you need more space, write "see attached" in column (d) and use an attached sheet for the description. If making more than one entry on line 1d, specify on the attached sheet which transfer or transaction you are describing.

Line 2—Reporting of certain relationships. Enter on line 2 each noncharitable exempt organization that the reporting organization is related to or affiliated with, as defined above. If the control factor or the historic and continuing relationship factor (or both) is present at any time during the year, identify the organization on line 2 even if neither factor is present at the end of the year.

Do not enter unrelated noncharitable exempt organizations on line 2 even if transfers to or transactions with those organizations were entered on line 1. For example, if a one-time transfer to an unrelated noncharitable exempt organization was entered on line 1a(2), do not enter the organization on line 2.

Column (b). Enter the exempt category of the organization; for example, "501(c)(4)."

Column (c). In most cases, a simple description, such as "common directors" or "auxiliary of reporting organization" will be sufficient. If you need more space, write "see attached" in column (c) and use an attached sheet to describe the relationship. If you are entering more than one organization on line 2, identify which organization you are describing on the attached sheet.

Signature

The return must be signed by the president, vice president, treasurer, assistant treasurer, chief accounting officer, or other corporate officer (such as tax officer) who is authorized to sign. A receiver, trustee, or assignee must sign any return that he or she is required to file for a corporation. If the return is filed for a trust, it must be signed by the authorized trustee or trustees. Sign and date the form and fill in the signer's title.

If an officer or employee of the organization prepares the return, the Paid Preparer's space should remain blank. If someone prepares the return without charge, that person should not sign the return.

Generally, anyone who is paid to prepare the organization's tax return must sign the return and fill in the Paid Preparer's Use Only area.

If you have questions about whether a preparer is required to sign the return, please contact an IRS office.

The paid preparer must complete the required preparer information and:

- Sign it in the space provided for the preparer's signature (a facsimile signature is acceptable), and
- Give the organization a copy of the return in addition to the copy to be filed with the IRS.

If the box for question 15 of Part VII-A is checked (section 4947(a)(1) nonexempt charitable trust filing Form 990-PF instead of Form 1041), the paid preparer must also enter his or her social security number or, if applicable, PTIN and employer identification number in the spaces provided. Otherwise, do not enter the preparer's social security or employer identification number.

CAUTION ***Caution.*** *The IRS is not authorized to redact the paid preparer's SSN if such SSN is entered on the paid preparer's block. Because Form 990-PF is a publicly disclosable document, any information entered on this block will be publicly disclosed (see General Instruction Q). Accordingly, any paid preparer whose identifying number must be listed on Form 990-PF may wish to apply for and obtain a PTIN using Form W-7P, Application for Preparer Tax Indentification Number.*

Privacy Act and Paperwork Reduction Act Notice. We ask for the information on this form to carry out the Internal Revenue laws of the United States. You are required to give us the information. We need it to ensure that you are complying with these laws and to allow us to figure and collect the right amount of tax. Section 6109 requires return preparers to provide their identifying numbers on the return.

You are not required to provide the information requested on a form that is subject to the Paperwork Reduction Act unless the form displays a valid OMB control number. Books or records relating to a form or its instructions must be retained as long as their contents may become material in the administration of any Internal Revenue law. The rules governing the confidentiality of Form 990-PF are covered in Code section 6104.

The time needed to complete and file this form will vary depending on individual circumstances. The estimated average time is:

Recordkeeping	140 hr., 37 min.
Learning about the law or the form	28 hr., 15 min.
Preparing the form	33 hr., 39 min.
Copying, assembling, and sending the form to the IRS	32 min.

If you have comments concerning the accuracy of these time estimates or suggestions for making this form simpler, we would be happy to hear from you. You can write to the Internal Revenue Service, Tax Products Coordinating Committee, SE:W:CAR:MP:T:T:SP, 1111 Constitution Ave. NW, IR-6526, Washington, DC 20224. Do not send the tax form to this address. Instead, see *When, Where, and How To File* on page 5.

Exclusion Codes

General Exceptions

01— Income from an activity that is not regularly carried on (section 512(a)(1))

02— Income from an activity in which labor is a material income-producing factor and substantially all (at least 85%) of the work is performed with unpaid labor (section 513(a)(1))

03— Section 501(c)(3) organization— Income from an activity carried on primarily for the convenience of the organization's members, students, patients, visitors, officers, or employees (hospital parking lot or museum cafeteria, for example) (section 513(a)(2))

04— Section 501(c)(4) local association of employees organized before May 27, 1969— Income from the sale of work-related clothes or equipment and items normally sold through vending machines; food dispensing facilities; or snack bars for the convenience of association members at their usual places of employment (section 513(a)(2))

05— Income from the sale of merchandise, substantially all of which (at least 85%) was donated to the organization (section 513(a)(3))

Specific Exceptions

06— Section 501(c)(3), (4), or (5) organization conducting an agricultural or educational fair or exposition— Qualified public entertainment activity income (section 513(d)(2))

07— Section 501(c)(3), (4), (5), or (6) organization—Qualified convention and trade show activity income (section 513(d)(3))

08— Income from hospital services described in section 513(e)

09— Income from noncommercial bingo games that do not violate state or local law (section 513(f))

10— Income from games of chance conducted by an organization in North Dakota (section 311 of the Deficit Reduction Act of 1984, as amended)

11— Section 501(c)(12) organization— Qualified pole rental income (section 513(g)) and/or member income (described in section 501(c)(12)(H))

12— Income from the distribution of low-cost articles in connection with the solicitation of charitable contributions (section 513(h))

13— Income from the exchange or rental of membership or donor list with an organization eligible to receive charitable contributions by a section 501(c)(3) organization; by a war veterans' organization; or an auxiliary unit or society of, or trust or foundation for, a war veterans' post or organization (section 513(h))

Modifications and Exclusions

14— Dividends, interest, payments with respect to securities loans, annuities, income from notional principal contracts, other substantially similar income from ordinary and routine investments, and loan commitment fees, excluded by section 512(b)(1)

15— Royalty income excluded by section 512(b)(2)

16— Real property rental income that does not depend on the income or profits derived by the person leasing the property and is excluded by section 512 (b)(3)

17— Rent from personal property leased with real property and incidental (10% or less) in relation to the combined income from the real and personal property (section 512(b)(3))

18— Gain or loss from the sale of investments and other non-inventory property and from certain property acquired from financial institutions that are in conservatorship or receivership (sections 512(b)(5) and (16)(A))

19— Gain or loss from the lapse or termination of options to buy or sell securities or real property, and on options and from the forfeiture of good-faith deposits for the purchase, sale, or lease of investment real estate (section 512(b)(5))

20— Income from research for the United States; its agencies or instrumentalities; or any state or political subdivision (section 512(b)(7))

21— Income from research conducted by a college, university, or hospital (section 512(b)(8))

22— Income from research conducted by an organization whose primary activity is conducting fundamental research, the results of which are freely available to the general public (section 512(b)(9))

23— Income from services provided under license issued by a federal regulatory agency and conducted by a religious order or school operated by a religious order, but only if the trade or business has been carried on by the organization since before May 27, 1959 (section 512 (b)(15))

Foreign Organizations

24— Foreign organizations only—Income from a trade or business NOT conducted in the United States and NOT derived from United States sources (patrons) (section 512(a)(2))

Social Clubs and VEBAs

25— Section 501(c)(7), (9), or (17) organization—Non-exempt function income set aside for a charitable, etc., purpose specified in section 170(c)(4) (section 512(a)(3)(B)(i))

26— Section 501(c)(7), (9), or (17) organization—Proceeds from the sale of exempt function property that was or will be timely reinvested in similar property (section 512(a)(3)(D))

27— Section 501(c)(9) or (17) organization— Nonfunction income set aside for the payment of life, sick, accident, or other benefits (section 512(a)(3)(B)(ii))

Veterans' Organizations

28— Section 501(c)(19) organization— Payments for life, sick, accident, or health insurance for members or their dependents that are set aside for the payment of such insurance benefits or for a charitable, etc., purpose specified in section 170(c)(4) (section 512(a)(4))

29— Section 501(c)(19) organization— Income from an insurance set-aside (see code 28 above) that is set aside for payment of insurance benefits or for a charitable, etc., purpose specified in section 170(c)(4) (Regs. 1.512(a)–4(b)(2))

Debt-Financed Income

30— Income exempt from debt-financed (section 514) provisions because at least 85% of the use of the property is for the organization's exempt purposes. (**Note:** *This code is only for income from the 15% or less non-exempt purpose use.*) (section 514(b)(1)(A))

31— Gross income from mortgaged property used in research activities described in section 512(b)(7), (8), or (9) (section 514(b)(1)(C))

32— Gross income from mortgaged property used in any activity described in section 513(a)(1), (2), or (3) (section 514(b)(1)(D))

33— Income from mortgaged property (neighborhood land) acquired for exempt purpose use within 10 years (section 514(b)(3))

34— Income from mortgaged property acquired by bequest or devise (applies to income received within 10 years from the date of acquisition) (section 514(c)(2)(B))

35— Income from mortgaged property acquired by gift where the mortgage was placed on the property more than 5 years previously and the property was held by the donor for more than 5 years (applies to income received within 10 years from the date of gift (section 514(c)(2)(B))

36— Income from property received in return for the obligation to pay an annuity described in section 514(c)(5)

37— Income from mortgaged property that provides housing to low and moderate income persons, to the extent the mortgage is insured by the Federal Housing Administration (section 514(c)(6)). (**Note:** *In many cases, this would be exempt function income reportable in column (e). It would not be so in the case of a section 501(c)(5) or (6) organization, for example, that acquired the housing as an investment or as a charitable activity.*)

38— Income from mortgaged real property owned by: a school described in section 170(b)(1)(A)(ii); a section 509(a)(3) affiliated support organization of such a school; a section 501(c)(25) organization; or by a partnership in which any of the above organizations owns an interest if the requirements of section 514(c)(9)(B)(vi) are met (section 514(c)(9))

Special Rules

39— Section 501(c)(5) organization—Farm income used to finance the operation and maintenance of a retirement home, hospital, or similar facility operated by the organization for its members on property adjacent to the farm land (section 1951(b)(8)(B) of Public Law 94-455)

40— Annual dues, not exceeding $139 (subject to inflation), paid to a section 501(c)(5) agricultural or horticultural organization (section 512(d))

Trade or Business

41— Gross income from an unrelated activity that is regularly carried on but, in light of continuous losses sustained over a number of tax periods, cannot be regarded as being conducted with the motive to make a profit (not a trade or business)

Other

42— Receipt of qualified sponsorship payments described in section 513(i)

43— Exclusion of any gain or loss from the qualified sale, exchange, or other disposition of any qualifying brownfield property (section 512(b)(19))

Index

Form **4720**

Department of the Treasury
Internal Revenue Service

Return of Certain Excise Taxes Under Chapters 41 and 42 of the Internal Revenue Code

(Sections 170(f)(10), 664(c)(2), 4911, 4912, 4941, 4942, 4943, 4944, 4945, 4955, 4958, 4965, 4966, and 4967)

▶ See separate instructions.

OMB No. 1545-0052

2008

For calendar year 2008 or other tax year beginning , 2008, and ending , 20

Name of organization or entity

Employer identification number

Number, street, and room or suite no. (or P.O. box if mail is not delivered to street address)

City or town, state, and ZIP code

Check box for type of annual return:
☐ Form 990 ☐ Form 990-EZ
☐ Form 990-PF
☐ Form 5227

		Yes	No
A	Is the organization a foreign private foundation within the meaning of section 4948(b)?		
B	Has corrective action been taken on any taxable event that resulted in Chapter 42 taxes being reported on this form? (Enter "N/A" if not applicable)		

If "Yes," attach a detailed description and documentation of the corrective action taken and, if applicable, enter the fair market value of any property recovered as a result of the correction ▶ $ ______ . If "No," (i.e., any uncorrected acts, or transactions), attach an explanation (see page 4 of the instructions).

Part I Taxes on Organization (Sections 170(f)(10), 664(c)(2), 4911(a), 4912(a), 4942(a), 4943(a), 4944(a)(1), 4945(a)(1), 4955(a)(1), 4965(a)(1), and 4966(a)(1))

1	Tax on undistributed income—Schedule B, line 4	1	
2	Tax on excess business holdings—Schedule C, line 7	2	
3	Tax on investments that jeopardize charitable purpose—Schedule D, Part I, column (e)	3	
4	Tax on taxable expenditures—Schedule E, Part I, column (g)	4	
5	Tax on political expenditures—Schedule F, Part I, column (e)	5	
6	Tax on excess lobbying expenditures—Schedule G, line 4	6	
7	Tax on disqualifying lobbying expenditures—Schedule H, Part I, column (e)	7	
8	Tax on premiums paid on personal benefit contracts	8	
9	Tax on being a party to prohibited tax shelter transactions—Schedule J, Part I, column (h)	9	
10	Tax on taxable distributions—Schedule K, Part I, column (f)	10	
11	Tax on a charitable remainder trust's unrelated business taxable income. Attach schedule	11	
12	**Total** (add lines 1–11)	12	

Part II-A Taxes on Managers, Self-Dealers, Disqualified Persons, Donors, Donor Advisors, and Related Persons (Sections 4912(b), 4941(a), 4944(a)(2), 4945(a)(2), 4955(a)(2), 4958(a), 4965(a)(2), 4966(a)(2), and 4967(a))

	(a) Name and address of person subject to tax	(b) Taxpayer identification number
a		
b		
c		
d		

	(c) Tax on self-dealing—Schedule A, Part II, col. (d), and Part III, col. (d)	(d) Tax on investments that jeopardize charitable purpose—Schedule D, Part II, col. (d)	(e) Tax on taxable expenditures—Schedule E, Part II, col. (d)	(f) Tax on political expenditures—Schedule F, Part II, col. (d)
a				
b				
c				
d				
Total				

	(g) Tax on disqualifying lobbying expenditures—Schedule H, Part II, col. (d)	(h) Tax on excess benefit transactions—Schedule I, Part II, col. (d), and Part III, col. (d)	(i) Tax on being a party to prohibited tax shelter transactions—Schedule J, Part II, col. (d)	(j) Tax on taxable distributions—Schedule K, Part II, col. (d)
a				
b				
c				
d				
Total				

	(k) Tax on prohibited benefits—Sch L, Part II, col. (d), and Part III, col. (d)	(l) Total—Add cols. (c) through (k)
a		
b		
c		
d		
Total		

For Privacy Act and Paperwork Reduction Act Notice, see page 15 of the instructions. Cat. No. 13021D Form **4720** (2008)

Form 4720 (2008) Page 2

Part II-B **Summary of Taxes** (See **Tax Payments** on page 3 of the instructions.)

1	Enter the taxes listed in Part II-A, column (l), that apply to managers, self-dealers, disqualified persons, donors, donor advisors, and related persons who sign this form. If all sign, enter the total amount from Part II-A, column (l)	1	
2	**Total tax.** Add Part I, line 12, and Part II-B, line 1. (Make check(s) or money order(s) payable to the United States Treasury.)	2	

SCHEDULE A—Initial Taxes on Self-Dealing (Section 4941)

Part I **Acts of Self-Dealing and Tax Computation**

(a) Act number	(b) Date of act	(c) Description of act
1		
2		
3		
4		
5		

(d) Question number from Form 990-PF, Part VII-B, or Form 5227, Part VI-B, applicable to the act	(e) Amount involved in act	(f) Initial tax on self-dealing (10% of col. (e))	(g) Tax on foundation managers (if applicable) (lesser of $20,000 or 5% of col. (e))

Part II **Summary of Tax Liability of Self-Dealers and Proration of Payments**

(a) Names of self-dealers liable for tax	(b) Act no. from Part I, col. (a)	(c) Tax from Part I, col. (f), or prorated amount	(d) Self-dealer's total tax liability (add amounts in col. (c)) (see page 6 of the instructions)

Part III **Summary of Tax Liability of Foundation Managers and Proration of Payments**

(a) Names of foundation managers liable for tax	(b) Act no. from Part I, col. (a)	(c) Tax from Part I, col. (g), or prorated amount	(d) Manager's total tax liability (add amounts in col. (c)) (see page 6 of the instructions)

SCHEDULE B—Initial Tax on Undistributed Income (Section 4942)

1	Undistributed income for years before 2007 (from Form 990-PF for 2008, Part XIII, line 6d)	1	
2	Undistributed income for 2007 (from Form 990-PF for 2008, Part XIII, line 6e)	2	
3	Total undistributed income at end of current tax year beginning in 2008 and subject to tax under section 4942 (add lines 1 and 2)	3	
4	**Tax**—Enter 30% of line 3 here and on page 1, Part I, line 1	4	

Form **4720** (2008)

Form 4720 (2008) Page 3

SCHEDULE C—Initial Tax on Excess Business Holdings (Section 4943)

Business Holdings and Computation of Tax

If you have taxable excess holdings in more than one business enterprise, attach a separate schedule for each enterprise. Refer to the instructions on page 7 for each line item before making any entries.

Name and address of business enterprise

Employer identification number . . . . ▶

Form of enterprise (corporation, partnership, trust, joint venture, sole proprietorship, etc.) . ▶

		(a) Voting stock (profits interest or beneficial interest)	(b) Value	(c) Nonvoting stock (capital interest)
1 Foundation holdings in business enterprise .	1	%	%	
2 Permitted holdings in business enterprise .	2	%	%	
3 Value of excess holdings in business enterprise	3			
4 Value of excess holdings disposed of within 90 days; or, other value of excess holdings not subject to section 4943 tax (attach explanation)	4			
5 Taxable excess holdings in business enterprise—line 3 minus line 4	5			
6 Tax—Enter 10% of line 5	6			
7 **Total tax**—Add amounts on line 6, columns (a), (b), and (c); enter total here and on page 1, Part I, line 2	7			

SCHEDULE D—Initial Taxes on Investments That Jeopardize Charitable Purpose (Section 4944)

Part I Investments and Tax Computation

(a) Investment number	(b) Date of investment	(c) Description of investment	(d) Amount of investment	(e) Initial tax on foundation (10% of col. (d))	(f) Initial tax on foundation managers (if applicable)—(lesser of $10,000 or 10% of col. (d))
1					
2					
3					
4					
5					
Total—column (e). Enter here and on page 1, Part I, line 3					
Total—column (f). Enter total (or prorated amount) here and in Part II, column (c), below . . .					

Part II Summary of Tax Liability of Foundation Managers and Proration of Payments

(a) Names of foundation managers liable for tax	(b) Investment no. from Part I, col. (a)	(c) Tax from Part I, col. (f), or prorated amount	(d) Manager's total tax liability (add amounts in col. (c)) (see page 10 of the instructions)

Form **4720** (2008)

Form 4720 (2008) Page 4

SCHEDULE E—Initial Taxes on Taxable Expenditures (Section 4945)

Part I Expenditures and Computation of Tax

(a) Item number	(b) Amount	(c) Date paid or incurred	(d) Name and address of recipient	(e) Description of expenditure and purposes for which made
1				
2				
3				
4				
5				

(f) Question number from Form 990-PF, Part VII-B, or Form 5227, Part VI-B, applicable to the expenditure	(g) Initial tax imposed on foundation (20% of col. (b))	(h) Initial tax imposed on foundation managers (if applicable)—(lesser of $10,000 or 5% of col. (b))
Total—column (g). Enter here and on page 1, Part I, line 4		
Total—column (h). Enter total (or prorated amount) here and in Part II, column (c), below		

Part II Summary of Tax Liability of Foundation Managers and Proration of Payments

(a) Names of foundation managers liable for tax	(b) Item no. from Part I, col. (a)	(c) Tax from Part I, col. (h), or prorated amount	(d) Manager's total tax liability (add amounts in col. (c)) (see page 10 of the instructions)

SCHEDULE F—Initial Taxes on Political Expenditures (Section 4955)

Part I Expenditures and Computation of Tax

(a) Item number	(b) Amount	(c) Date paid or incurred	(d) Description of political expenditure	(e) Initial tax imposed on organization or foundation (10% of col. (b))	(f) Initial tax imposed on managers (if applicable) (lesser of $5,000 or 2½% of col. (b))
1					
2					
3					
4					
5					
Total—column (e). Enter here and on page 1, Part I, line 5					
Total—column (f). Enter total (or prorated amount) here and in Part II, column (c), below					

Part II Summary of Tax Liability of Organization Managers or Foundation Managers and Proration of Payments

(a) Names of organization managers or foundation managers liable for tax	(b) Item no. from Part I, col. (a)	(c) Tax from Part I, col. (f), or prorated amount	(d) Manager's total tax liability (add amounts in col. (c)) (see page 11 of the instructions)

Form 4720 (2008)

SCHEDULE G—Tax on Excess Lobbying Expenditures (Section 4911)

1	Excess of grassroots expenditures over grassroots nontaxable amount (from Schedule C (Form 990 or 990-EZ), Part II-A, column (b), line 1h). (See page 11 of the instructions before making entry.)	1	
2	Excess of lobbying expenditures over lobbying nontaxable amount (from Schedule C (Form 990 or 990-EZ), Part II-A, column (b), line 1i). (See page 11 of the instructions before making entry.)	2	
3	Taxable lobbying expenditures—enter the larger of line 1 or line 2	3	
4	**Tax**—Enter 25% of line 3 here and on page 1, Part I, line 6	4	

SCHEDULE H—Taxes on Disqualifying Lobbying Expenditures (Section 4912)

Part I Expenditures and Computation of Tax

(a) Item number	(b) Amount	(c) Date paid or incurred	(d) Description of lobbying expenditures	(e) Tax imposed on organization (5% of col. (b))	(f) Tax imposed on organization managers (if applicable)—(5% of col. (b))
1					
2					
3					
4					
5					
Total—column (e). Enter here and on page 1, Part I, line 7					
Total—column (f). Enter total (or prorated amount) here and in Part II, column (c), below					

Part II Summary of Tax Liability of Organization Managers and Proration of Payments

(a) Names of organization managers liable for tax	(b) Item no. from Part I, col. (a)	(c) Tax from Part I, col. (f), or prorated amount	(d) Manager's total tax liability (add amounts in col. (c)) (see page 11 of the instructions)

SCHEDULE I—Initial Taxes on Excess Benefit Transactions (Section 4958)

Part I Excess Benefit Transactions and Tax Computation

(a) Transaction number	(b) Date of transaction	(c) Description of transaction
1		
2		
3		
4		
5		

(d) Amount of excess benefit	(e) Initial tax on disqualified persons (25% of col. (d))	(f) Tax on organization managers (if applicable) (lesser of $20,000 or 10% of col. (d))

Form 4720 (2008) Page 6

SCHEDULE I—Initial Taxes on Excess Benefit Transactions (Section 4958) *Continued*

Part II Summary of Tax Liability of Disqualified Persons and Proration of Payments

(a) Names of disqualified persons liable for tax	(b) Trans. no. from Part I, col. (a)	(c) Tax from Part I, col. (e), or prorated amount	(d) Disqualified person's total tax liability (add amounts in col. (c)) (see page 13 of the instructions)

Part III Summary of Tax Liability of 501(c)(3) & (4) Organization Managers and Proration of Payments

(a) Names of 501(c)(3) & (4) organization managers liable for tax	(b) Trans. no. from Part I, col. (a)	(c) Tax from Part I, col. (f), or prorated amount	(d) Manager's total tax liability (add amounts in col. (c)) (see page 13 of the instructions)

SCHEDULE J—Taxes on Being a Party to Prohibited Tax Shelter Transactions (Section 4965)

Part I Prohibited Tax Shelter Transactions (PTST) and Tax Imposed on the Tax-Exempt Entity (see page 13 of the instructions)

(a) Transaction number	(b) Transaction date	(c) Type of transaction 1—Listed 2—Subsequently listed 3—Confidential 4—Contractual protection	(d) Description of transaction
1			
2			
3			
4			
5			

(e) Did the tax-exempt entity know or have reason to know this transaction was a PTST when it became a party to the trans.? Answer **Yes** or **No**	(f) Net income attributable to the PTST	(g) 75% of proceeds attributable to the PTST	(h) Tax imposed on the tax-exempt entity (see page 14 of the instructions)
Total—column (h). Enter here and on page 1, Part I, line 9			

Form **4720** (2008)

Part II **Tax Imposed on Entity Managers** (Section 4965) *Continued*

(a) Name of entity manager	(b) Transaction number from Part I, col. (a)	(c) Tax—enter $20,000 for each transaction listed in col. (b) for each manager in col. (a)	(d) Manager's total tax liability (add amounts in col. (c))

SCHEDULE K—Taxes on Taxable Distributions of Sponsoring Organizations Maintaining Donor Advised Funds (Section 4966). See page 14 of the instructions.

Part I **Taxable Distributions and Tax Computation**

(a) Item number	(b) Name of sponsoring organization and donor advised fund	(c) Description of distribution
1		
2		
3		
4		

(d) Date of distribution	(e) Amount of distribution	(f) Tax imposed on organization (20% of col. (e))	(g) Tax on fund managers (lesser of 5% of col. (e) or $10,000)
Total—column (f). Enter here and on page 1, Part I, line 10			
Total—column (g). Enter total (or prorated amount) here and in Part II, column (c), below			

Part II **Summary of Tax Liability of Fund Managers and Proration of Payments**

(a) Name of fund managers liable for tax	(b) Item no. from Part I, col. (a)	(c) Tax from Part I, col. (g) or prorated amount	(d) Manager's total tax liability (add amounts in col. (c)) (see instructions)

Form 4720 (2008) Page 8

SCHEDULE L—Taxes on Prohibited Benefits Distributed From Donor Advised Funds (Section 4967).
See page 14 of the instructions.

Part I Prohibited Benefits and Tax Computation

(a) Item number	(b) Date of prohibited benefit	(c) Description of benefit
1		
2		
3		
4		
5		

(d) Amount of prohibited benefit	(e) Tax on prohibited benefit (125% of col. (d)) (see instructions)	(f) Tax on fund managers (if applicable) (lesser of 10% of col. (d) or $10,000) (see instructions)

Part II Summary of Tax Liability of Donors, Donor Advisors, Related Persons and Proration of Payments

(a) Names of donors, donor advisor, or related persons liable for tax	(b) Item no. from Part I, col. (a)	(c) Tax from Part I, col. (e) or prorated amount	(d) Donor, donor advisor, or related persons total tax liability (add amounts in col. (c)) (see instructions)

Part III Tax Liability of Fund Managers and Proration of Payments

(a) Names of fund managers liable for tax	(b) Item no. from Part I, col. (a)	(c) Tax from Part I, col. (f) or prorated amount	(d) Fund managers total tax liability (add amounts in col. (c)) (see instructions)

Form **4720** (2008)

Sign Here

Under penalties of perjury, I declare that I have examined this return, including accompanying schedules and statements, and to the best of my knowledge and belief it is true, correct, and complete. Declaration of preparer (other than taxpayer) is based on all information of which preparer has any knowledge.

Signature of officer or trustee	Title	Date

Signature (and organization or entity name if applicable) of manager, self-dealer, disqualified person, donor, donor advisor, or related person	Date

Signature (and organization or entity name if applicable) of manager, self-dealer, disqualified person, donor, donor advisor, or related person	Date

Signature (and organization or entity name if applicable) of manager, self-dealer, disqualified person, donor, donor advisor, or related person	Date

Signature (and organization or entity name if applicable) of manager, self-dealer, disqualified person, donor, donor advisor, or related person	Date

Paid Preparer's Use Only

Preparer's signature	Date	Check if self-employed ☐	Preparer's SSN or PTIN
Firm's name (or yours if self-employed), address, and ZIP code		EIN	
		Phone no. ( )	

2008

Department of the Treasury
Internal Revenue Service

Instructions for Form 4720

Return of Certain Excise Taxes Under Chapters 41 and 42 of the Internal Revenue Code (Sections 170(f)(10), 664(c)(2), 4911, 4912, 4941, 4942, 4943, 4944, 4945, 4955, 4958, 4965, 4966, and 4967)

Section references are to the Internal Revenue Code unless otherwise noted.

Contents **Page**

Contents **Page**

What's New

We revised the *Signature* area of Form 4720 to include a paid preparer's section. The Small Business and Work Opportunity Act of 2007 extends the application of return preparer penalties to preparers of tax returns which includes Form 4720.

Reminders

For the most up-to-date tax information, please visit us at *www.irs.gov/formspubs/index.html* and select Highlights of Recent Tax Changes under the Important changes section.

Phone Help

If you have questions and/or need help completing this form, please call 1-877-829-5500. This toll-free telephone service is available Monday through Friday.

Photographs of Missing Children

The Internal Revenue Service is a proud partner with the National Center for Missing and Exploited Children. Photographs of missing children selected by the Center may appear in instructions on pages that would otherwise be blank. You can help bring these children home by looking at the photographs and calling 1-800-THE-LOST (1-800-843-5678) if you recognize a child.

How To Get Forms and Publications

Internet. You can access the IRS website 24 hours a day, 7 days a week, at *www.irs.gov* to:

- Download forms, instructions, and publications.
- Order IRS products online.
- Research your tax questions online.
- Search publications online by topic or keyword.
- Sign up to receive local and national tax news by email.

DVD for tax products. You can order Publication 1796, IRS Tax Products DVD, and obtain:

- Current-year forms, instructions, and publications.
- Prior-year forms, instructions, and publications.
- Tax Map: an electronic research tool and finding aid.
- Tax Law frequently asked questions.
- Tax Topics from the IRS telephone response system.
- Internal Revenue Code—Title 26
- Fill-in, print, and save features for most tax forms.
- Internal Revenue Bulletins.
- Toll-free and email technical support.
- The DVD is released twice during the year.
  —The first release will ship the beginning of January 2009.
  —The final release will ship the beginning of March 2009.

Purchase the DVD from National Technical Information Service (NTIS) at *www.irs.gov/cdorders* for $30 (no handling fee) or call 1-877-233-6767 toll free to purchase the DVD for $30 (plus a $6 handling fee). The price is discounted to $25 for orders placed prior to December 1, 2008.

By phone and in person. You can order forms and publications by calling 1-800-TAX-FORMS (1-800-829-3676). You can also get most forms and publications at your local IRS office.

IRS E-Services Make Taxes Easier

Now more than ever before, businesses can enjoy the benefits of filing and paying their federal taxes electronically. Whether you rely on a tax professional or handle your own taxes, the IRS offers you convenient programs to make taxes easier. Use these electronic options to make filing and paying easier.

Cat. No. 13023Z

- You can *e-file* your Form 990 or Form 990-PF; Form 940 and 941 employment tax returns; Forms 1099; and other information returns. Visit *www.irs.gov/efile* for details.
- You can pay taxes online or by phone using the free Electronic Federal Tax Payment System (EFTPS). Visit *www.eftps.gov* or call 1-800-555-4477 for details. Electronic Funds Withdrawal (EFW) from a checking or savings account also is available to those who file electronically.

General Instructions

Purpose of Form

Use Form 4720 to figure and pay:

- The initial taxes on private foundations and self-dealers, under sections 4941 through 4945 for self-dealing, failure to distribute income, excess business holdings, investments that jeopardize charitable purpose, and taxable expenditures;
- The initial tax on certain supporting organizations and donor advised funds for excess business holdings under section 4943;
- The section 4911 tax on excess lobbying expenditures by public charities that have elected to be subject to section 501(h) regarding expenditures to influence legislation. (Private foundations and section 4947(a) trusts are not eligible to make this election.);
- The section 4912 tax on excess lobbying expenditures that result in loss of section 501(c)(3) tax-exempt status;
- The section 4955 tax imposed on any amount paid or incurred by a section 501(c)(3) organization that participates or intervenes in any political campaign on behalf of, or in opposition to, any candidate for public office;
- The section 4958 initial taxes on disqualified persons and organization managers of section 501(c)(3) (except private foundations) and section 501(c)(4) organizations that engage in excess benefit transactions;
- The section 4965 taxes related to prohibited tax shelter transactions;
- The section 4966 taxes on taxable distributions by sponsoring organizations maintaining donor advised funds;
- The section 4967 taxes on distribution of prohibited benefits from donor advised funds;
- The section 170(f)(10) tax on any premiums paid on a personal benefit contract in connection with a transfer to an organization or charitable remainder trust for which a charitable deduction is not allowed to the transferor; and
- The section 664(c)(2) tax on the unrelated business taxable income of a charitable remainder trust.

Who Must File

Private foundations and section 4947(a) trusts. Generally, Form 4720 must be filed by all organizations, including foreign organizations, that answered "Yes" to question 1b, 1c, 2b, 3b, 4a, 4b, 5b, 6b, or 7b in Part VII-B of Form 990-PF; or "Yes" to question 75b, 75c, 77b, 78a, 78b, 79b, or 80b in Part VI-B, and item G on page 1, of Form 5227. A trust described in section 4947(a)(2) is considered a private foundation insofar as it is subject to Chapter 42 provisions.

Public charities making excess lobbying expenditures. Public charities that made the election under section 501(h) and owe tax on excess lobbying expenditures as figured on Schedule C (Form 990 or 990-EZ), Part II-A, must file Form 4720 to report the liability and pay the tax (Schedule G).

Certain organizations (and possibly their managers) whose section 501(c)(3) status is revoked because of excess lobbying activities are subject to a 5% excise tax on their lobbying expenditures.

Organizations making political expenditures. All section 501(c)(3) organizations that make a political expenditure must file Form 4720 to report the liability and pay the tax. Organization managers may report any first tier tax they owe on Schedule F of Form 4720. (See *Schedule F* instructions for the definition of political expenditures.)

Charitable organizations that make certain premium payments on personal benefit contracts. Form 4720 must be filed by any organization described in section 170(c) or section 664(d) that answered "Yes" to question 7f in Part V of Form 990, question 6b in Part VII-B of Form 990-PF, question 80b in Part VI-B of Form 5227, or that otherwise paid premiums on a personal benefit contract in connection with a transfer to an organization for which a charitable deduction was not allowed to the transferor.

Sponsoring organizations maintaining donor advised funds. All section 170(c) organizations (excluding private foundations and government organizations referred to in sections 170(c)(1) and 170(c)(2)(A)) that maintain one or more donor advised funds must file Form 4720 to report the liability and pay the tax owed on any taxable distributions under section 4966 (Schedule K).

Certain tax-exempt entities that are a party to a prohibited tax shelter transaction (PTST). Certain tax-exempt entities must file Form 4720 to report the liability and pay the tax due under section 4965(a)(1). This requirement applies to entities described in section 501(c), 501(d), or 170(c) (other than the United States) or an Indian tribal government (within the meaning of section 7701(a)(40)).

TIP *Any entity described in section 4965(c) that is a party to a PTST must file Form 8886-T.*

Managers, self-dealers, disqualified persons, donors, donor advisors, and related persons. If you are a manager, self-dealer, disqualified person, donor, donor advisor, or related person who owes tax under Chapter 41 or 42, including entity managers under section 4965, and you have the same tax year (or accounting year, as applicable) of the entity, you may report the tax you owe on the Form 4720 filed by the entity. Managers, self-dealers, and disqualified persons who do this are responsible for the parts that relate to taxes they owe and should include their own check or money order, payable to the United States Treasury, with the return.

Managers, self-dealers, disqualified persons, donors, donor advisors, and related persons who owe tax under Chapter 41 or 42, including entity managers under section 4965, and do not have the same tax year (or accounting year, as applicable) or do not sign the return of the entity, must file a separate return on Form 4720 showing the tax owed and the name of the entity for which you owe tax. If you file a separate Form 4720, enter your tax year at the top of the form. Enter your name, address, and taxpayer identification number in Part II-A. Complete all the information the form requires, to the extent possible, that applies to your liability.

TIP *Managers of tax favored retirement plans, individual retirement arrangements, and savings arrangements described in sections 401(a), 403(a), 403(b), 529, 457(b), 408(a), 220(d), 408(b), 530, or 223(d) must report and pay tax due under section 4965(a)(2) on Form 5330.*

Charitable Remainder Trusts. All charitable remainder trusts described in section 664 that have unrelated business taxable income for the tax year must file Form 4720 to report the liability and pay the tax due. Unrelated business taxable income is figured under section 512 and is determined as if Part III of subchapter F applies to such trusts.

Where To File

If you are located in	Then use the following address
The United States	Department of the Treasury Internal Revenue Service Center Ogden, UT 84201-0027
A foreign country or a U.S. possession	Internal Revenue Service Center P.O. Box 409101 Ogden, UT 84409

When To File

Part I taxes. File Form 4720 by the due date (not including extensions) for filing the organization's Form 990-PF, Form 990, Form 990-EZ, or Form 5227. If you are not required to file any of these forms, file Form 4720 by the 15th day of the 5th month after the entity's accounting period ends.

If the regular due date falls on a Saturday, Sunday, or legal holiday, file by the next business day.

Affiliated group member. For members of an affiliated group of organizations that have different tax years, and who are filing Form 4720 to report tax under section 4911, the tax year of the affiliated group is the calendar year, unless all members of the group elect under Regulations section 56.4911-7(e)(5) to make a member's year the group's tax year.

Part II taxes. If you are a manager, self-dealer, disqualified person, donor, donor advisor, or related person, owing taxes under Chapter 41 or 42 and filing a separate Form 4720, and your tax year ends on the same date as the organization, you must file by the due date for filing Form 990-PF, Form 5227, Form 990, or Form 990-EZ of the organization for which you owe tax. If your tax year ends on a date different from that of the organization, or your organization is not required to file a Form 990, Form 990-EZ, Form 990-PF, or Form 5227, you must file a Form 4720 by the 15th day of the 5th month after your tax year ends.

If the regular due date falls on a Saturday, Sunday, or legal holiday, file by the next business day.

Extension

If you cannot file Form 4720 by the due date, you may request an automatic 3-month extension of time to file by using Form 8868, Application for Extension of Time To File an Exempt Organization Return. The automatic 3-month extension will be granted if you properly complete this form, file it, and pay any balance due by the due date for Form 4720.

Form 8868 is also used to request an additional extension of time to file; however, these extensions are not automatically granted.

Name, Address, etc.

The name, address, and employer identification number of the organization or entity should be the same as shown on Form 990-PF, Form 5227, Form 990, Form 990-EZ, and Schedule A (Form 990 or 990-EZ). If you are a self-dealer, donor, donor advisor, related person, disqualified person, or manager filing a separate Form 4720, enter your name, address, and taxpayer identification number in Part II-A.

Include the suite, room, or other unit number after the street address.

If the Post Office does not deliver mail to the street address, show the P.O. box number instead of the street address.

If you want a third party (such as an accountant or an attorney) to receive mail for the foundation or charity, enter on the street address line "C/O" followed by the third party's name and street address or P.O. box.

Signature and Verification

If you are a manager, self-dealer, disqualified person, donor, donor advisor, or related person, you should sign only in the spaces that apply, whether you use the return of the foundation or organization as your return, or file separately.

If you are signing on behalf of the foundation or organization and also because of personal tax liability, you must sign twice. You sign:

1. On behalf of the foundation or organization, and
2. For your own personal tax liability.

For a corporation (or an association), the form may be signed by one of the following: president, vice president, treasurer, assistant treasurer, chief accounting officer, or other corporate officer (such as tax officer).

For a partnership, the form may be signed by a partner or partners authorized to sign the partnership return.

If the return is filed on behalf of a trust, the authorized trustee(s) must sign it.

A receiver, trustee, or assignee required to file any return on behalf of an individual, a trust, estate, partnership, association, company, or corporation must sign the Form 4720 filed for these taxpayers.

Also, a person with a valid power of attorney may sign for the organization, foundation, manager, self-dealer, donor, donor advisor, or related person. Include a copy of the power of attorney with the return.

Paid Preparer

Generally, anyone who is paid to prepare a tax return must sign the return and fill in the blanks in the *Paid Preparer's Use Only* area of the return.

The person required to sign the return must:
- Complete the required preparer information,
- Sign it in the space provided for the preparer's signature (a facsimilie signature is acceptable), and
- Give you a copy of the return for your records.

Attachments

If you need more space, attach separate sheets showing the same information in the same order as on the printed form. Show the totals on the printed form.

Enter the organization's name and EIN on each sheet. Use sheets that are the same size as the form and indicate clearly the line of the printed form to which the information relates.

Organizations Organized or Created in a Foreign Country or U.S. Possession

Report all amounts in U.S. currency (state conversion rate used) and give information in English. Report items in total, including amounts and transactions from both inside and outside the United States.

Sections 4941 through 4945 and section 4955 do not apply to foreign private foundations that receive substantially all of their support (other than gross investment income) from sources outside the United States. These organizations must complete this form and file it in the same manner as other private foundations. However, these organizations, as well as foundation managers and self-dealers, do not have to pay any tax that would otherwise be due on this return.

Tax Payments

Managers, self-dealers, disqualified persons, donors, donor advisors, and related persons, paying tax on the organization's Form 4720 must pay with

Form 4720 Instructions -3-

the return the tax that applies to them as shown in Part II-A, page 1. Managers, self-dealers, disqualified persons, donors, donor advisors, and related persons, who file separate Forms 4720 must pay the applicable tax with their separate returns. When managers do not sign the organization's Form 4720 to report their own tax liability, the amount of tax they owe should not be entered in Part II-B, line 1.

Payment by a private foundation of any taxes owed by the foundation managers or self-dealers will result in additional taxes under the self-dealing and taxable expenditure provisions. Managers and self-dealers should pay taxes imposed on them with their own check or money order.

Disqualified persons and entity managers should pay taxes on excess benefit transactions that are imposed on them with their own check or money order. Any reimbursement of a disqualified person's tax liability from excess benefit transactions by the organization will be treated as an excess benefit transaction subject to the tax unless the organization included the reimbursement in the disqualified person's compensation and the disqualified person's total compensation was reasonable. See the instructions for Schedule I on page 12 for information on excess benefit transactions.

Rounding Off to Whole Dollars

You may round off cents to whole dollars on your return and schedules. If you do round to whole dollars, you must round all amounts. To round, drop amounts under 50 cents and increase amounts from 50 to 99 cents to the next dollar. For example, $1.39 becomes $1 and $2.50 becomes $3.

If you have to add two or more amounts to figure the amount to enter on a line, include cents when adding the amounts and round off only the total.

Penalties and Interest

There are penalties for failure to file or to pay tax. There are also penalties for willful failure to file, supply information or pay tax, and for filing fraudulent returns and statements, that apply to public charities, private foundations, managers, donors, donor advisors, related persons, and self-dealers who are required to file this return. See sections 6651, 7203, 7206, and 7207. Also, see section 6684 for penalties that relate to tax liability under Chapter 42.

Interest at the underpayment rate established under section 6621 is charged for any unpaid tax. The interest on underpayments is in addition to any penalties.

Abatement

See section 4962 for rules on abatement, refund, or relief from payment of first tier taxes under sections 4942 through 4945, 4955, 4958, 4966, and 4967. To request abatement, refund, or relief under section 4962, write "Request for Abatement Under Section 4962" in the top margin of Form 4720, page 1.

Initial Tax Liability

If you pay an initial tax on self-dealing or on investments that jeopardize charitable purpose (figured on Schedules A and D of Form 4720, respectively) for tax year 2008, the payment may not satisfy the entire tax liability for an act of self-dealing or a jeopardy investment. (For the definition of self-dealing, see the instructions for Schedule A of this form; for the definition of jeopardy investment, see the instructions for Schedule D of this form.) Paying the tax and filing a Form 4720 are required for each year or part of a year in the taxable period that applies to the act or investment. Generally, the taxable period begins with the date of the act or investment and ends with the date corrective action is completed, a notice of deficiency is mailed, or the tax is assessed, whichever comes first.

Similar rules apply for the initial tax liability resulting from failing to distribute income (Schedule B) and from acquiring excess business holdings (Schedule C). Thus, the initial tax liability for those taxes continues to accrue until the date a notice of deficiency is mailed, the violation is corrected, or the tax is assessed, whichever comes first.

Completing the Schedules

Before completing any of the schedules in this return, read the applicable instructions. If any completed schedule shows taxes owed, enter them on page 1 of this return.

The instructions for Schedules A through L describe acts or transactions subject to tax under Chapter 42. Also, go to *www.irs.gov/charities/foundations/index.html* for a list of exceptions that eliminate any tax liability that would otherwise be shown on Schedules A and E. Do not complete Schedules A and E if exceptions apply to all the acts or transactions. In general, question A on page 1 and Schedules A, B, C, D, and E do not apply to public charities. However, Schedule C does apply to some public charities including donor advised funds and certain supporting organizations that are treated as private foundations for purposes of section 4943. See the instructions for Schedule C for a description of the public charities to which section 4943 applies.

Before completing Schedule C, determine whether the organization or donor advised fund has excess holdings in any business enterprise. If the organization or donor advised fund has holdings subject to the tax on excess business holdings, complete Schedule C for each enterprise.

Before completing Schedule D, determine whether the investment was program related. If not, complete Schedule D for each investment for which you answered "Yes" to Form 990-PF, Part VII-B, question 4a or b, or Form 5227, Part VI-B, question 78a or b.

Specific Instructions for Page 1

Question B. To avoid additional taxes and penalties under sections 4941 through 4945, 4955, and 4958, and in some cases further initial taxes on the foundation, organization, and related persons, a foundation, organization, disqualified person, or manager must correct the taxable event within the correction period. The taxable event is the act, failure to act, or transaction that resulted in the liability for initial taxes under these provisions.

Generally, the correction period begins on the date the event occurs and ends 90 days after the mailing date of a notice of deficiency, under section 6212, in connection with the second tier tax imposed on that taxable event. That time is extended by:

- Any period in which a deficiency cannot be assessed under section 6213(a) because a petition to the Tax Court for redetermination of the deficiency is pending, not extended by any supplemental proceeding by the Tax Court under section 4961(b), regarding whether correction was made, and
- Any other period the IRS determines is reasonable and necessary to correct the taxable event.

The taxable event will be treated as occurring:

- For the tax on failure to distribute income, on the first day of the tax year for which there was a failure to distribute income,
- For the tax on excess business holdings, on the first day on which there were excess business holdings, or

• In any other case, on the date the event occurred.

Generally, the term "correction" has the following meanings.

1. Section 4941 (Schedule A)—Undoing the transaction to the extent possible, but in any case placing the private foundation in a financial position not worse than that in which it would be if the disqualified person were dealing under the highest fiduciary standards.

2. Section 4942 (Schedule B)—Making sufficient qualifying distributions to compensate for deficient qualifying distributions for a prior tax year.

3. Section 4943 (Schedule C)—Action that results in the foundation no longer having excess business holdings in a business enterprise.

4. Section 4944 (Schedule D)—An investment is considered to be removed from jeopardy when the investment is sold or otherwise disposed of, and the proceeds of such sale or other disposition are not investments that jeopardize the carrying out of the foundation's exempt purposes.

5. Section 4945 (Schedule E)—

a. Recovering part or all of the expenditure to the extent recovery is possible, and where full recovery is not possible, such additional corrective action as is prescribed by regulations, or

b. Obtaining or making the report in question for a case that fails to comply with section 4945(h)(2) or (3) (expenditure responsibility).

6. Section 4955 (Schedule F)—Recovering part or all of the expenditure to the extent recovery is possible, establishment of safeguards to prevent future political expenditures, and where full recovery is not possible, such additional corrective action as is prescribed by the regulations.

7. Section 4958 (Schedule I)—Undoing the excess benefit to the extent possible and taking any additional measures necessary to place the organization in a financial position not worse than that in which it would be if the disqualified person had been dealing under the highest fiduciary standards.

If, when the return is filed, the foundation, entity, managers, self-dealers, disqualified persons, donors, donor advisors, or related persons have corrected any acts or transactions resulting in liability for tax under Chapter 42, answer "Yes" to question B and give the following information separately for each correction:

• Schedule and item number of the act or transaction that has been corrected,
• A description of the act or transaction that resulted in the tax,
• A detailed description of the correction made,
• The amount of any political expenditure recovered,
• Description of safeguards to prevent future political expenditures, and
• The date of correction.

For any acts or transactions the foundation, entity, managers, self-dealers, disqualified persons, donors, donor advisors, or related persons have not corrected, give the following information separately for each act:

• Schedule and item number of the act or transaction that has not been corrected,
• A description of the act or transaction, and
• A detailed explanation of why correction has not been made and what steps are being taken to make the correction.

If you are correcting deficient distributions under section 4942 where an election under section 4942(h)(2) was filed with the IRS, provide a copy of the election. See the instructions for Form 990-PF, Part XIII, lines 4b and 4c for more information.

Part I

Line 8

TIP *If the organization has an entry on this line, it must also file Form 8870.*

Enter the total of all premiums paid by the organization on any personal benefit contract if the payment of premiums is in connection with a transfer for which a deduction is not allowed under section 170(f)(10)(A). Also, if there is an understanding or expectation that any person will directly or indirectly pay any premium on a personal benefit contract for the transferor, include those premium payments in the amount entered on this line.

A personal benefit contract is (to the transferor) any life insurance, annuity, or endowment contract that benefits directly or indirectly the transferor, a member of the transferor's family, or any other person designated by the transferor (other than an organization described in section 170(c)).

For more information, see Notice 2000-24, which is on page 952 of Internal Revenue Bulletin 2000-17 at *www.irs.gov/pub/irs-irbs/irb00-17.pdf.*

Line 11

Enter the charitable remainder trust's unrelated business taxable income on line 11. Charitable remainder trusts must attach a schedule that shows how their unrelated business taxable income was computed. The excise tax imposed on a charitable remainder trust is equal to the trust's unrelated business taxable income.

Attached schedule. Charitable remainder trusts may use Form 990-T as the attached schedule. If the trust uses Form 990-T as the attached schedule, complete Form 990-T as follows:

1. Write "ATTACHMENT TO FORM 4720" at the top of page 1.

2. Enter the trust's name under "Name of organization" and complete item D and E at the top of page 1.

3. Complete Parts I and II. If a line does not apply, leave it blank.

4. Complete any of the Schedules on Form 990-T or other forms or attach a schedule as required by any line on which an entry is made for Parts I and II. Also, attach any schedule as may be required on any Schedule on Form 990-T or other form that you are required to complete. However, if Schedule D (Form 1041) is required, do not complete Part V of Schedule D (Form 1041).

5. Enter the amount from line 34 of Form 990-T on Part I, line 11 of Form 4720. Do not complete Parts III-V or the signature area of Form 990-T.

If you do not complete a Form 990-T as the attached schedule, then attach a schedule with the same information as Form 990-T and its Schedules (as discussed above) including all the information that must be attached to Form 990-T and its Schedules, such as other forms and attachments. Be sure to enter the amount shown as unrelated business taxable income on Part I, line 11 of Form 4720.

Part II-A

Columns (a) and (b). List the names, addresses, and taxpayer identification numbers of all persons who owe tax in connection with the foundation or organization, whether as managers, self-dealers, disqualified persons, donors, donor advisors, or related persons, as shown in Schedules A, D, E, F, H, I, J, K, and L.

Column (c). For each person listed in column (a), enter the sum of:

1. Taxes that person owes as a self-dealer, from Schedule A, Part II, column (d), and

2. Tax for acts of self-dealing in which the individual participated as a manager, from Schedule A, Part III, column (d).

Column (d). Enter for each person listed in column (a) the tax on jeopardy investments from Schedule D, Part II, column (d), that the individual took part in as a foundation manager.

Column (e). Enter for each person listed in column (a) the tax on taxable expenditures from Schedule E, Part II, column (d), that the individual took part in as a foundation manager.

Column (f). Enter for each person listed in column (a) the tax on political expenditures from Schedule F, Part II, column (d), that the individual took part in as an organization or foundation manager.

Column (g). Enter for each person listed in column (a) the tax on disqualifying lobbying expenditures from Schedule H, Part II, column (d), that the individual took part in as an organization manager.

Column (h). For each person listed in column (a), enter the sum of:

1. Taxes that person owes as a disqualified person, from Schedule I, Part II, column (d), and
2. Tax on excess benefit transactions in which the organization manager participated knowing that the transaction was improper, from Schedule I, Part III, column (d).

Column (i). Enter for each person listed in column (a) the tax on the entity manager who approved or otherwise caused the entity to be a party to a prohibited tax shelter transaction from Schedule J, Part II, column (d).

Column (j). Enter for each person listed in column (a) the tax on taxable distributions from sponsoring organizations maintaining donor advised funds from Schedule K, Part II, column (d) that the individual took part in as a manager.

Column (k). For each person listed in column (a), enter the:

1. Tax imposed on a donor, donor advisor, or related person, from Schedule L, Part II, column (d), and
2. Tax on each fund manager who agreed to the making of a distribution of a prohibited benefit from Schedule L, Part III, column (d) that the individual took part in as a manager.

Liability for tax. A person's liability for tax as a manager, self-dealer, disqualified person, donor, donor advisor, or related person, under sections 4912, 4941, 4944, 4945, 4955, 4958, 4966, and 4967 is joint and several. Therefore, if more than one person owes tax on an act as a manager, self-dealer, disqualified person, donor, donor advisor, or related person, they may apportion the tax among themselves. However, when all managers, self-dealers, donors, donor advisors, related persons, or disqualified persons who are liable for tax on a particular transaction under sections 4912, 4941, 4944, 4945, 4955, 4958, 4966, or 4967 pay less than the total tax due on that transaction, then the IRS may charge the amount owed to one or more of them regardless of the tax apportionment shown on this return.

Schedule A—Initial Taxes on Self-Dealing (Section 4941)

General Instructions

Requirement. All organizations that answered "Yes" to question 1b or 1c in Part VII-B of Form 990-PF, or "Yes" to question 75b or 75c in Part VI-B of Form 5227, must complete Schedule A. Complete Parts I, II, and III of Schedule A only in connection with acts that are subject to the tax on self-dealing.

Paying the tax and filing a Form 4720 is required for each year or part of a year in the taxable period that applies to the act of self-dealing. Generally, the taxable period begins with the date on which the self-dealing occurs and ends on the earliest of:

- The date a notice of deficiency is mailed under section 6212, in connection with the initial tax imposed on the self-dealer,
- The date the initial tax on the self-dealer is assessed, or
- The date correction of the act of self-dealing is completed.

Self-dealing. Self-dealing includes any direct or indirect:

- Sale, exchange, or leasing of property between a private foundation and a disqualified person (see *definitions* in Form 990-PF instructions),
- Lending of money or other extension of credit between a private foundation and a disqualified person,
- Furnishing of goods, services, or facilities between a private foundation and a disqualified person,
- Payment of compensation (or payment or reimbursement of expenses) by a private foundation to a disqualified person,
- Transfer to, or use by or for the benefit of, a disqualified person of the income or assets of a private foundation, and
- Agreement by a private foundation to make any payment of money or other property to a government official (go to *www.irs.gov/charities/foundations/article/0,,id=137679,00.html* for more information), other than an agreement to employ or make a grant to that individual for any period after the end of government service if that individual will be ending government service within a 90-day period.

Exceptions to self-dealing. Go to *http://www.irs.gov/irm/part7/ch12s12.html* for a description of acts that are not considered self-dealing.

Initial taxes on self-dealer. An initial tax of 10% of the amount involved is charged for each act of self-dealing between a disqualified person and a private foundation for each year or part of a year in the taxable period. Any disqualified person (other than a foundation manager acting only as such) who takes part in the act of self-dealing must pay the tax.

Initial taxes on foundation managers. When a tax is imposed on a foundation manager for an act of self-dealing, the tax will be 5% of the amount involved in the act of self-dealing for each year or part of a year in the taxable period. However, the total tax imposed for all years in the taxable period is limited to $20,000 for each act of self-dealing. The tax is imposed on any foundation manager who took part in the act knowing that it was self-dealing except those foundation managers whose participation was not willful and was due to reasonable cause. Any foundation manager who took part in the act of self-dealing must pay the tax.

Specific Instructions

Part I. List each act of self-dealing in Part I. Enter in column (d) the number designation from Form 990-PF, Part VII-B, question 1a, or Form 5227, Part VI-B, question 75a, that applies to the act. For example, "1a(1)" or "1a(4)."

Part II. Enter in column (a) the names of all disqualified persons who took part in the acts of self-dealing listed in Part I. If more than one disqualified person took part in an act of self-dealing, each is individually liable for the entire tax in connection with the act. But the disqualified persons who are liable for the tax may prorate the payment among themselves. Enter in column (c) the tax to be paid by each disqualified person.

Carry the total amount in column (d) for each self-dealer to page 1, Part II-A, column (c).

Part III. Enter in column (a) the names of all foundation managers who took part in the acts of self-dealing listed in Part I, and who knew that they were acts of self-dealing (except for foundation managers whose participation was not willful and was due to reasonable cause).

If more than one foundation manager took part in the act of self-dealing, knowing that it was such an act, and participation was willful and not due to reasonable cause, each is individually liable for the entire tax in connection with the act. But the foundation managers liable for the tax may prorate the payment among themselves. Enter in column (c) the tax to be paid by each foundation manager.

Carry the total amount in column (d) for each foundation manager to page 1, Part II-A, column (c).

Schedule B—Initial Tax on Undistributed Income (Section 4942)

Complete Schedule B if you answered "Yes" to Form 990-PF, Part VII-B, question 2b.

An initial excise tax of 30% is imposed on a private foundation's undistributed income on the first day of the second or any succeeding tax year after the tax year in connection with which income remains undistributed.

Use the 2008 Form 4720 to report the initial tax on undistributed income for tax years beginning in 2007 or earlier that remains undistributed at the end of the foundation's current tax year beginning in 2008. The initial tax will not apply to a private foundation's undistributed income:

- For any tax year it is an operating foundation (as defined in section 4942(j)(3) and related regulations or in section 4942(j)(5)), or
- To the extent it did not distribute an amount solely because of an incorrect valuation of assets, provided the foundation satisfies the requirements of section 4942(a)(2), or
- For any year for which the initial tax was previously assessed or a notice of deficiency was issued.

Do not complete Schedule B for any year for which any of the above provisions apply to the undistributed income.

Schedule C—Initial Tax on Excess Business Holdings (Section 4943)

General Instructions

Private foundations are generally not permitted to hold more than a 20% interest in an unrelated business enterprise. They may be subject to an excise tax on the amount of any excess holdings. For purposes of section 4943, donor advised funds and certain supporting organizations are considered private foundations. For more information on the applicability of Schedule C to such organizations, see *General rules on the permitted holdings of donor advised funds and certain supporting organizations in a business enterprise* on page 9.

Requirement. If you answered "Yes" to Form 990-PF, Part VII-B, question 3b; Form 990, Part V, question 8; or Form 5227, Part VI-B, question 77b, or otherwise had excess business holdings, complete a Schedule C for each business enterprise in which the foundation had excess business holdings for its tax year beginning in 2008.

Taxes. A private foundation that has excess holdings in a business enterprise may become liable for an excise tax based on the amount of holdings. The initial tax is 10% of the value of the excess holdings and is imposed on the last day of each tax year that ends during the taxable period. The excess holdings are determined on the day during the tax year when they were the largest.

If the foundation keeps the excess business holdings after the initial tax has been imposed, it becomes liable for an additional tax of 200% of the remaining excess business holdings unless it disposes of them within the taxable period. However, if the foundation disposes of its excess business holdings during the correction period, the additional tax will not be assessed or, if assessed, will be abated and if collected, will be credited or refunded. For information on the correction period, go to *http://www.irs.gov/irm/part7/ch12s14.html#d0e114882.*

Business enterprise. In general, this means the active conduct of a trade or business, including any activity regularly conducted to produce income from selling goods or performing services, that is an unrelated trade or business described in section 513.

The term "business enterprise" does not include a functionally related business as defined in section 4942(j)(4). In addition, business holdings do not include program-related investments (such as investments in small businesses in economically depressed areas or in corporations to assist in neighborhood renovations) as defined in section 4944(c) and related regulations. Also, business enterprise does not include a trade or business at least 95% of the gross income of which comes from passive sources. Log on to *http://www.irs.gov/irm/part7/ch12s14.html#d0e114882.*

Excess business holdings. Excess business holdings is the amount of stock or other interest in a business enterprise that the foundation would have to dispose of to a person other than a disqualified person in order for the foundation's remaining holdings in the enterprise to be permitted holdings (section 4943(c)(1)). Go to *http://www.irs.gov/irm/part7/ch12s14.html#d0e114882* for more information.

Sole proprietorships. In general, a private foundation may not have any permitted holdings in a business enterprise that is a sole proprietorship. For exceptions, go to *http://www.irs.gov/irm/part7/ch12s14.html#d0e114882.* For a definition of sole proprietorship, see Regulations section 53.4943-10(e).

Corporate voting stock. This stock entitles a person to vote for the election of directors. Treasury stock and stock that is authorized but unissued is not voting stock for these purposes. See Regulations sections 53.4943-3(b)(1)(ii) and 53.4943-3(b)(2)(ii).

For a partnership (including a limited partnership) or joint venture, the term "profits interest" should be substituted for "voting stock." For any unincorporated business enterprise that is not a partnership, joint venture, or sole proprietorship, the term "beneficial interest" should be substituted for "voting stock." See Regulations section 53.4943-3(c).

Nonvoting stock. Corporate equity interests that do not have voting power should be classified as nonvoting stock. Evidences of indebtedness (including convertible indebtedness), warrants, and other options or rights to acquire stock should not be considered equity interests. See Regulations section 53.4943-3(b)(2).

For a partnership (including a limited partnership) or joint venture, the term "capital interest" should be substituted for "nonvoting stock." For any unincorporated business that is not a partnership, joint venture, or sole proprietorship, references to nonvoting stock do not apply for computation of permitted holdings. See Regulations section 53.4943-3(c)(4).

Attribution of business holdings. In determining the holdings in a business enterprise of either a private foundation or a disqualified person, any stock or other interest owned directly or indirectly by or for a corporation, partnership, estate, or trust is considered owned proportionately by or for its shareholders, partners, or beneficiaries. In general, this rule does not apply to certain income interests or remainder interests of a private foundation in a split-interest trust described in section 4947(a)(2). See Regulations section 53.4943-8.

Taxable period. The taxable period begins on the first day the foundation has excess business holdings and ends on the earliest of:

• The mailing date of a notice of deficiency, under section 6212, in connection with the initial tax on excess business holdings related to those holdings,
• The date the excess is eliminated, or
• The date the initial tax on excess business holdings related to those holdings is assessed.

When a notice of deficiency is not mailed because the restrictions on assessment and collection are waived or because the deficiency is paid, the date of filing the waiver or the date of paying the tax, respectively, will be treated as the end of the taxable period. See Regulations section 53.4943-9.

Exceptions to Tax on Excess Business Holdings

2% De minimis rule. A private foundation will not be treated as having excess business holdings in any enterprise in which it, together with related foundations as described in the instructions for Form 990-PF (under the definition for "disqualified person" in the *General Instructions*) owns not more than 2% of the voting stock and not more than 2% in value of all outstanding shares of all classes of stock.

Disposition of excess business holdings within 90 days. Generally, when a private foundation acquires excess business holdings other than as a result of purchase by the foundation (such as an acquisition by a disqualified person), the foundation will not be taxed on those excess holdings if it disposes of enough of them so that it no longer has an excess. To avoid the tax, the disposition must take place within 90 days from the date the foundation knew, or had reason to know, of the event that caused it to have excess business holdings. That 90-day period will be extended to include the period during which federal or state securities laws prevent the foundation from disposing of those excess business holdings. See Regulations section 53.4943-2(a).

General rules on the permitted holdings of a private foundation in a business enterprise. No excess business holdings tax is imposed (a) if a private foundation and all disqualified persons together hold no more than 20% of the voting stock of a business enterprise or (b) on nonvoting stock, if all disqualified persons together do not own more than 20% of the voting stock of the business enterprise.

If the private foundation and all disqualified persons together do not own more than 35% of the enterprise's voting stock, and effective control is in one or more persons who are not disqualified persons in connection with the foundation, then 35% may be substituted for 20% wherever it appears in the preceding paragraph. See sections 4943(c)(2) and 4943(c)(3).

If a private foundation and all disqualified persons together had holdings in a business enterprise of more than 20% of the voting stock on May 26, 1969, substitute that percentage for 20% and for 35% (if the holding is greater than 35%), using the principles of section 4943(c)(4) that apply. However, the percentage substituted may not be more than 50%.

The percentage substituted under the preceding paragraph is (a) subject to reductions and limitations (see sections 4943(c)(4)(A)(ii) and 4943(c)(4)(D)) and (b) applicable, both in connection with the voting stock and, separately, in connection with the value of all outstanding shares of all classes of stock (see section 4943(c)(4)(A)(iii)).

Interests held by a private foundation (other than donor advised funds and supporting organizations) on May 26, 1969. For private foundations, other than donor advised funds and supporting organizations considered to be private foundations for purposes of section 4943, that had business holdings on May 26, 1969 (or holdings acquired by trust or will as described below), that were more than the current limits permit, there are transitional rules that permit the foundation to dispose of the excess over time without being subject to the tax on excess business holdings.

During the first phase, no excess business holdings tax was imposed on a private foundation for interests held since May 26, 1969, if the foundation had excess holdings on that date. The first phase is:

• A 20-year period beginning on May 26, 1969, if on that date the foundation and all disqualified persons held more than a 95% voting interest in the enterprise (the 20-year first phase expired on May 25, 1989);
• A 15-year period beginning on May 26, 1969, if on that date the foundation and all disqualified persons together had more than a 75% voting stock interest (or more than a 75% profits or beneficial interest of any unincorporated business), or more than a 75% interest in the value of all outstanding shares of all classes of stock (or more than a 75% capital interest of a partnership or joint venture) in the enterprise (the 15-year first phase expired on May 25, 1984); and
• A 10-year period beginning on May 26, 1969, in all other cases in which the foundation had excess business holdings on May 26, 1969. The 10-year first phase expired on May 25, 1979.

During the second phase (the 15-year period after the first phase), if the foundation's disqualified persons hold more than 2% of the enterprise's voting stock, the foundation will be liable for tax if the foundation holds more than 25% of the voting stock or if the foundation and its disqualified persons together hold more than 50% of the voting stock.

However, during the second phase, if a foundation's disqualified persons purchase voting stock in a business enterprise after July 18, 1984, causing the combined holdings of the disqualified persons to exceed 2% of the enterprise's voting stock, the foundation has 5 years to reduce its holdings in the enterprise to below its second phase limit before the increase will be treated as held by the foundation. See sections 4943(c)(4)(D) and 4943(c)(6).

The first-phase periods may be suspended pending the outcome of any judicial proceeding the private foundation brings regarding reform or other procedure to excuse it from compliance with its governing instrument or similar instrument in effect on May 26, 1969. See section 4943(c)(4)(C) and Regulations section 53.4943-4.

Holdings acquired by trust or will. Holdings acquired under the terms of a trust that was irrevocable on May 26, 1969, or under the terms of a will executed by that date, are treated as held by the foundation on May 26, 1969, except that the 15- and 10-year periods of the first phase for the holdings start on the date of distribution under the trust or will instead of on May 26, 1969. See section 4943(c)(5) and Regulations section 53.4943-5. See section 4943(d)(1) and Regulations section 53.4943-8 for rules relating to constructive holdings held in a corporation, partnership, estate, or trust for the benefit of the foundation.

Gifts or bequests of business holdings. Except as provided in the exception regarding *Holdings acquired by trust or will* (discussed above), there is a special rule for private foundations that have excess business holdings as a result of a change in holdings after May 26,1969. This rule applies if the change is other than by purchase by the foundation or by disqualified persons (such as through gift or bequest) and the additional holdings result in the foundation having excess business holdings. In that case, the foundation has 5 years to reduce these holdings or those of its disqualified persons to permissible levels to avoid the tax. See section 4943(c)(6) and Regulations section 53.4943-6.

A private foundation that received an unusually large gift or bequest of business holdings after 1969, and that has made a diligent effort to dispose of excess business holdings, may apply for an additional 5-year period to reduce its holdings to permissible levels if certain conditions are met. See section 4943(c)(7).

General rules on the permitted holdings of donor advised funds and certain supporting organizations in a business enterprise. Rules similar to those described above for interests held by private foundations on May 26, 1969, will be applied to determine if donor advised funds or certain supporting organizations with interests as of August 17, 2006, have any excess business holdings. However, the date of August 17, 2006, will be substituted for May 26, 1969.

Donor advised fund. In general, a donor advised fund is a fund or account separately identified by reference to contributions of a donor or donors that is owned and controlled by a sponsoring organization and for which the donor has or expects to have advisory privileges concerning the distribution or investment of the funds. See *Schedule K* for further details.

Sponsoring organization. A sponsoring organization is any section170(c) organization other than governmental entities (described in section 170(c)(1) and (2)(A)) that is not a private foundation as defined in section 509(a)(3) that maintains one or more donor advised funds.

Supporting organizations. Only certain supporting organizations are subject to the excess business holdings tax under section 4943. These include (1) Type III supporting organizations that are not functionally integrated and (2) Type II supporting organizations that accept any gift or contribution from a person who by himself or in connection with a related party controls the supported organization that the Type II supporting organization supports. (See the 2008 Instructions for Schedule A (Form 990 or 990-EZ), Part I, question 11, for help in determining the type of your supporting organization.)

Readjustments, distributions, or changes in relative value of different classes of stock. See Regulations section 53.4943-4(d)(10) for special rules whereby increases in the percentage of value of holdings in a corporation that result solely from changes in the relative values of different classes of stock will not result in excess business holdings.

See Regulations section 53.4943-6(d) for rules on treatment of increases in holdings due to readjustments, distributions, or redemptions.

See Regulations section 53.4943-7 for special rules for readjustments involving grandfathered holdings.

Exceptions from self-dealing taxes on certain dispositions of excess business holdings. Section 101(l)(2)(B) of the Tax Reform Act of 1969 provides for a limited exception from self-dealing taxes for private foundations that dispose of certain excess business holdings to disqualified persons, as long as the sales price equals or is more than fair market value.

The excess business holdings involved are interests that are subject to the section 4941 transitional rules for May 26, 1969, holdings. These interests would also be subject to the excess business holdings tax if they were not reduced by the required amount.

Specific Instructions

Complete columns (a) and (b) of Schedule C if sections 4943(c)(4), 4943(c)(3) (using the principles of 4943(c)(4)), or 4943(c)(5) apply.

Complete column (a) and column (c) (if applicable) if sections 4943(c)(2) or 4943(c)(3) (using the principles of 4943(c)(2)) apply.

Complete Schedule C for that day during the tax year when the foundation's excess holdings in the enterprise were largest.

Line 1. Enter in column (a) the percentage of voting stock the foundation holds in the business enterprise.

If the foundation is using the rules or principles for determining present holdings under section 4943(c)(4)(A) or (D) (or rules similar to that for donor advised funds and certain supporting organizations), enter in column (b) the percentage of value the foundation holds in all outstanding shares of all classes of stock.

Do not include in either column (a) or (b) stock treated as held by disqualified persons:
• Under section 4943(c)(6) or Regulations sections 53.4943-6 and 53.4943-10(d), or
• During the first phase if the first phase is still in effect (see Regulations sections 53.4943-4(a), (b), and (c)).

Line 2. If the foundation is using the rules or principles for determining present holdings under section 4943(c)(4) (or rules similar to that for donor advised funds and certain supporting organizations), refer to that section and Regulations section 53.4943-4(d) to determine which entries to record in columns (a) and (b). Enter in column (a) the excess of the substituted combined voting level over the disqualified person voting level. Enter in column (b) the excess of the substituted combined value level over the disqualified person value level.

If the foundation is using the rules or principles for determining permitted holdings under section 4943(c)(2), refer to that section to determine which entries to record in column (a). Enter in column (a) the percentage, using the general rule (section 4943(c)(2)(A)) or the 35% rule (see section 4943(c)(2)(B)), if applicable, of permitted holdings the foundation may have in the enterprise's voting stock. If the foundation determines the permitted holdings under section 4943(c)(2)(B), attach a statement showing effective control by a third party.

Line 3. Enter the value of any stock, interest, etc., in the business enterprise that the foundation is required to dispose of so the foundation's holdings in the enterprise are permitted. See section 4943 and related regulations.

A private foundation using the section 4943(c)(4) rules, or a donor advised fund or supporting organization using rules similar to that, has excess holdings if line 1 is more than line 2 in either column (a) or column (b). Do not include in column (b) the value of any voting stock included in column (a).

A private foundation using the section 4943(c)(2) rules has excess holdings if line 1 is more than line 2 in column (a) or if the private foundation holds nonvoting stock and all disqualified persons together own more than 20% (or 35%, if applicable) of the enterprise's voting stock, interest, etc. In the latter case, enter in column (c) the value of all nonvoting stock the foundation holds.

Line 4. Enter the value of excess holdings disposed of under the 90-day rule in Regulations section 53.4943-2(a)(1)(ii). If other conditions preclude imposition of tax on excess business holdings, include the value of the nontaxable amount on this line and attach an explanation.

Schedule D—Initial Taxes on Investments That Jeopardize Charitable Purpose (Section 4944)

General Instructions

Requirement. Complete Schedule D if you answered "Yes" to Form 990-PF, Part VII-B, question 4a or b, or Form 5227, Part VI-B, question 78a or b. Report each investment separately. Paying tax and filing a Form 4720 are required for each year or part of a year in the taxable period that applies to the investments that jeopardize the foundation's charitable purpose. Generally, the taxable period begins with the date of the investment and ends with the date corrective action is completed, a notice of deficiency is mailed, or the initial tax is assessed, whichever comes first. Therefore, in addition to investments made in 2008, include all investments subject to tax that were made before 2008 if those investments were not removed from jeopardy before 2008 and the initial tax was not assessed before 2008.

Taxable investments. An investment to be taxed on this schedule is an investment by a private foundation that jeopardizes the carrying out of its exempt purposes (for example, if it is determined that the foundation managers, in making the investment, did not exercise ordinary business care and prudence, under prevailing facts and circumstances, in providing for the long- and short-term financial needs of the foundation to carry out its exempt purposes). See Regulations section 53.4944-1(a)(2). An investment is not taxed on this schedule if it is a program-related investment; that is, one whose primary purpose is one or more of those described in section 170(c)(2)(B) (religious, charitable, educational, etc.). A significant purpose of such an investment cannot be the production of income or the appreciation of property. See section 4944(c) and Regulations section 53.4944-3.

Initial taxes on foundation. The initial tax is 10% of the amount invested for each year or part of a year in the taxable period.

Initial taxes on foundation managers. When a tax is imposed on a jeopardy investment of the foundation, the tax will be 10% of the investment for each year or part of a year in the taxable period, up to $10,000 for any one investment. It is imposed on all foundation managers who took part in the act, knowing that it was such an act, except for foundation managers whose participation was not willful and was due to reasonable cause. Any foundation manager who took part in making the investment must pay the tax.

Specific Instructions

Part I. Complete this part for all taxable investments.

Part II. Enter in column (a) the names of all foundation managers who took part in making the investments listed in Part I. See *Initial taxes on foundation managers* above.

If more than one foundation manager is listed in column (a), each is individually liable for the entire amount of tax in connection with the investment. However, the foundation managers who are liable for the tax may prorate payment among themselves. Enter in column (c) the tax each foundation manager will pay.

Carry the total amount in column (d) for each foundation manager to page 1, Part II-A, column (d).

Schedule E—Initial Taxes on Taxable Expenditures (Section 4945)

General Instructions

Requirement. Complete Schedule E if you answered "Yes" to Form 990-PF, Part VII-B, question 5b, or Form 5227, Part VI-B, question 79b. Complete Parts I and II of Schedule E only for expenditures that are subject to tax.

Note. Also, see *Schedule F, Initial Taxes on Political Expenditures.*

Taxable expenditures. With certain exceptions, this means any amount a private foundation pays or incurs:

1. To carry on propaganda or otherwise influence any legislation through:

a. An attempt to influence general public opinion or any segment of it, and

b. Communication with any member or employee of a legislative body, or with any other government official or employee who may take part in formulating legislation;

2. To influence the outcome of any specific public election, or to conduct, directly or indirectly, any voter registration drive;

3. As a grant to an individual for travel, study, or other purposes;

4. As a grant to an organization not described in section 509(a)(1), (2), or (3) or that is not an exempt operating foundation (as defined in section 4940(d)(2)). This includes grants to:

a. Type I, Type II, and Type III functionally integrated supporting organizations (as described in section 4942(g)(4)(B)) if a disqualified person of the foundation controls such supporting organization or the supported organizations of such supporting organizations, and

b. Type III supporting organizations (as described in section 4943(f)(5)(B)) that are not functionally integrated with its supported organizations; or

5. For any purpose other than religious, charitable, scientific, literary, educational, or public purposes, or the prevention of cruelty to children or animals.

Exceptions. Section 4945(d)(4)(B) provides an exception to taxable expenditures that applies to certain grants to organizations when the granting foundation exercises expenditure responsibility described in section 4945(h). Additional information on special rules and exceptions to the definition of taxable expenditures given above can be found at *http://www.irs.gov/irm/part7/ch12s16.html.*

Initial tax on foundation. An initial tax of 20% is imposed on each taxable expenditure of the foundation.

Initial tax on foundation managers. When a tax is imposed on a taxable expenditure of the foundation, a tax of 5% of the expenditure will be imposed on any foundation manager who agreed to the expenditure and who knew that it was a taxable expenditure. Foundation managers whose participation was not willful and was due to reasonable cause are not liable for the tax. Any foundation manager who took part in the expenditure and is liable for the tax must pay the tax. The maximum total amount of tax on all foundation managers for any one taxable expenditure is $10,000. If more than one foundation manager is liable for tax on a taxable expenditure, all those foundation managers are jointly and severally liable for the tax.

Specific Instructions

Part I. Complete this part for all taxable expenditures. Enter in column (f) the number designation from Form 990-PF, Part VII-B, question 5a, or Form 5227, Part VI-B, question 79a, that applies to the act; for example, "5a(1)."

Part II. Enter in column (a) the names of all foundation managers who agreed to make the taxable expenditure. See *Initial tax on foundation managers* above. If more than one foundation manager is listed in column (a), each is individually liable for the entire tax in connection with the expenditure. However, the foundation managers who are liable for the tax may prorate the payment among themselves. Enter in column (c) the tax each foundation manager will pay.

Carry the total amount in column (d) for each foundation manager to page 1, Part II-A, column (e).

Schedule F—Initial Taxes on Political Expenditures (Section 4955)

General Instructions

Requirement. Complete Schedule F if you answered "Yes" to question 5a(2) and 5b of Form 990-PF, Part VII-B. Complete Schedule F if you entered an amount on line 2 of Schedule C (Form 990 or 990-EZ), Part 1-A. Complete Schedule F if you are otherwise a section 501(c)(3) organization that made a political expenditure.

Political expenditures. These include any amount paid or incurred by a section 501(c)(3) organization that participates or intervenes in (including the publication or distribution of statements) any political campaign on behalf of, or in opposition to, any candidate for public office. The tax is imposed even if the political expenditure gives rise to a revocation of the organization's section 501(c)(3) status.

These taxes apply in the case of both public charities and private foundations. When tax is imposed under this provision in the case of a private foundation, however, the expenditure in question will not be treated as a taxable expenditure under section 4945.

For an organization formed primarily to promote the candidacy or prospective candidacy of an individual for public office (or that is effectively controlled by a candidate or prospective candidate and is used primarily for such purposes), amounts paid or incurred for any of the following purposes are deemed political expenditures:

- Remuneration to the candidate or prospective candidate for speeches or other services;
- Travel expenses of the individual;
- Expenses of conducting polls, surveys, or other studies, or preparing papers or other material for use by the individual;
- Expenses of advertising, publicity, and fundraising for such individual; and
- Any other expense which has the primary effect of promoting public recognition or otherwise primarily accruing to the benefit of the individual.

Initial tax on organization or foundation. The initial tax on the organization or foundation is 10% of the amount involved.

Initial tax on organization managers or foundation managers. An initial tax of 2½% of the amount involved (up to $5,000 of tax on any one expenditure) is imposed on any manager who agrees to an expenditure, knowing that it is a political expenditure, unless the agreement is not willful and is due to reasonable cause.

Any manager who agreed to the expenditure must pay the tax.

Specific Instructions

Part I. Complete this part for all political expenditures.

Part II. Enter in column (a) the names of all managers who took part in making the political expenditures listed in Part I. See *Initial tax on organization managers or foundation managers* above.

If more than one manager is listed in column (a), each is individually liable for the entire amount of tax on the expenditure. However, the managers who are liable for the tax may prorate payment among themselves. Enter in column (c) the tax each manager will pay.

Carry the total amount in column (d) for each manager to page 1, Part II-A, column (f).

Schedule G—Tax on Excess Lobbying Expenditures (Section 4911)

Requirement. Schedule G must be completed by eligible section 501(c)(3) organizations that elected to be subject to the limitations on lobbying expenditures under section 501(h) and that made excess lobbying expenditures as defined in section 4911(b).

Except as noted below, follow the line instructions on Schedule G.

Affiliated groups. If you are a nonelecting member of an affiliated group, you are not required to file Form 4720.

If you are an electing member of an affiliated group and are filing a separate return, enter on line 1 the amount from Schedule C (Form 990 or 990-EZ), Part II-A, column (a), line 1h. Enter on line 2 the amount from Schedule C (Form 990 or 990-EZ), Part II-A, column (a), line 1i.

If you are an electing member of an affiliated group and are included in a group return, enter on line 1 your share of the excess grassroot lobbying expenditures of the affiliated group, and on line 2 your share of the excess lobbying expenditures of the affiliated group. Take these amounts from the schedule of excess lobbying expenditures that must be attached to Schedule C (Form 990 or 990-EZ). See the instructions for Schedule C (Form 990 or 990-EZ), Part II-A, for a discussion of the lobbying provisions, including how to figure the taxable amount.

Schedule H—Taxes on Disqualifying Lobbying Expenditures (Section 4912)

General Instructions

Requirement. Schedule H must be completed by certain organizations whose section 501(c)(3) status is revoked because of excess lobbying activities.

Exceptions. These taxes are not imposed on a private foundation (whose lobbying expenditures may be subject to the tax on taxable expenditures). These taxes also are not imposed on any organization for which a section 501(h) election was in effect at the time of the lobbying expenditures or that was not eligible to make a section 501(h) election.

Tax on organization. A tax of 5% of the lobbying expenditures is imposed on the organization whose section 501(c)(3) status is revoked because of excess lobbying activities.

Tax on organization managers. A tax of 5% of the lobbying expenditures is also imposed on any manager who willfully and without reasonable cause consented to the lobbying expenditures, knowing that they would likely result in the organization no longer qualifying under section 501(c)(3).

There is no limit on the amount of this tax that may be imposed against either the organization or its managers. Any organization manager who agreed to the expenditure must pay the tax.

Specific Instructions

Part I. Complete this part for all disqualifying lobbying expenditures.

Part II. Enter in column (a) the names of all organization managers who took part in making disqualifying lobbying expenditures listed in Part I. See *Tax on organization managers* above.

If more than one organization manager is listed in column (a), each is individually liable for the entire amount of tax in connection with the expenditure. However, the managers who are liable for the tax may prorate payment among themselves. Enter in column (c) the tax each manager will pay.

Carry the total amount in column (d) for each organization manager to page 1, Part II-A, column (g).

Schedule I—Initial Taxes on Excess Benefit Transactions (Section 4958)

General Instructions

Requirement. Complete Schedule I for any *Excess benefit transaction* in which an *Applicable organization* provides an *Excess benefit* to a *Disqualified person.* These terms are discussed below.

Applicable organization. In general, an applicable organization is any section 501(c)(3) (except a private foundation) or any 501(c)(4) organization.

Also, an applicable organization includes any organization that was a 501(c)(3) (except a private foundation) or 501(c)(4) organization at any time during a five-year period ending on the date of an excess benefit transaction (the lookback period).

Initial taxes. Excise taxes are imposed under section 4958 on each excess benefit transaction. If a manager receives an excess benefit from an excess benefit transaction, the manager may be liable for the tax on disqualified persons and the tax on the organization manager. See *Abatement* on page 4 for information on abatement, refund, or relief from this tax.

Tax on disqualified persons. The tax is 25% of the excess benefit and is paid by any disqualified person who improperly benefited from the excess benefit transaction.

Tax on organization managers. If tax is imposed on a disqualified person for any excess benefit transaction, then tax is also imposed on any manager who knowingly participated in the excess benefit transaction. The tax is 10% of the excess, not to exceed $20,000 for each transaction.

Additional tax on the disqualified person. If the initial tax is imposed on an excess benefit transaction and the transaction is not corrected within the taxable period, then any disqualified person involved shall be liable for an additional tax equal to 200% of the excess benefit.

This additional tax is abated (refunded if collected) if the excess benefit transaction is corrected within the correction period (defined in *Question B,* under *Specific Instructions for Page 1* on page 4).

Taxable period. Taxable period means the period beginning with the date on which the excess benefit transaction occurs and ending on the earlier of:

1. The date a notice of deficiency was mailed to the disqualified person for the initial tax on the excess benefit transaction, or
2. The date on which the initial tax on the excess benefit transaction for the disqualified person is assessed.

Excess benefit transaction. An excess benefit transaction is any transaction in which:

1. An excess benefit is provided by the organization, directly or indirectly to, or for the use of, any disqualified person, or
2. The amount of any economic benefit provided to, or for the use of, a disqualified person is determined in whole or in part by the revenues of the organization and violates the private inurement prohibition rules (to the extent provided in regulations).

CAUTION *Until final regulations are issued regarding the special rules for revenue sharing transactions described in 2 above, these transactions will only be subject to section 4958 liability under the general rule described in 1 above.*

Supporting organization transactions occurring after July 25, 2006. For any supporting organization, as defined in section 509(a)(3), any grant, loan, compensation, or other similar payment provided to a substantial contributor (defined later), family member, or 35% controlled entity will be considered an excess benefit transaction. The amount of the excess benefit is the amount of such grant, loan, compensation, or other similar payment. Also, any loan provided to a disqualified person that is not an organization described in section 509(a)(1), (2), or (4) or a supported organization of the supporting organization exempt under section 501(c)(4), (5), (6) and described in the last sentence of section 509(a) is considered an excess benefit transaction.

Donor advised fund transactions occurring after August 17, 2006. Any grant, loan, compensation, or other similar payment from any donor advised fund to a donor, family member, or 35% controlled entity is an excess benefit transaction. The amount of the excess benefit is the amount of such grant, loan, compensation, or other similar payment.

Excess benefit. Excess benefit means the excess of the economic benefit received from the applicable organization over the consideration given (including services) by a disqualified person.

However, an economic benefit will not be treated as compensation for services unless the applicable organization clearly indicates its intent to treat the economic benefit (when paid) as compensation for a disqualified person's services. See Regulations section 53.4958-4(c) for more information.

Exception. Generally, section 4958 does not apply to any fixed payment made to a person under an initial contract. See Regulations section 53.4958-4(a)(3) for details.

Special rule. The initial and additional taxes of this section do not apply if the transaction described in 1 under *Excess benefit transaction,* was pursuant to a written contract in effect on September 13, 1995, and at all times after that date until the time that the transaction occurs.

However, if a written contract is materially modified, it is treated as a new contract entered into as of the date of the material modification. A material modification includes amending the contract to extend its term or to increase the compensation payable to a disqualified person.

Disqualified person. For purposes of this Schedule I, a disqualified person means:

1. Any person (at any time during the 5-year period ending on the date of the transaction) in a position to exercise substantial influence over the affairs of the organization,
2. A family member of an individual described in 1, 2, or 3, and
3. A 35% controlled entity.

Family members. Family members of an individual (described in 1 above) include a disqualified person's spouse, ancestors, children, grandchildren, great grandchildren, and brothers and sisters (whether by whole- or half-blood). It also includes the spouse of the children, grandchildren, great grandchildren, brothers, or sisters (whether by whole- or half-blood).

35% controlled entity. The term 35% controlled entity means:

- A corporation in which a person described in 1 through 5 under *Disqualified person* owns more than

35% of the total combined voting power,
• A partnership in which such persons own more than 35% of the profits interest, or
• A trust or estate in which such persons own more than 35% of the beneficial interest.

In determining the holdings of a business enterprise, any stock or other interest owned directly or indirectly shall apply.

For donor advised funds, sponsoring organizations, and certain supporting organization transactions occurring after August 17, 2006. The following persons will be considered disqualified persons along with certain family members and 35% controlled entities associated with them:

• Donors of donor advised funds,
• Investment advisors of sponsoring organizations; and
• Disqualified persons of a section 509(a)(3) supporting organization for the organizations that organization supports.

For certain supporting organization transactions occurring after July 25, 2006. Substantial contributors to supporting organizations will also be considered disqualified persons along with their family members and 35% controlled entities.

Donor advised fund. See the *Schedule K* instructions for a definition of donor advised fund.

Investment advisor. Investment advisor means for any sponsoring organization, any person compensated by such organization (but not an employee of such organization) for managing the investment of, or providing investment advice for assets maintained in donor advised funds maintained by such sponsoring organization.

Sponsoring organization. See the *Schedule K instructions* for a definition of sponsoring organization.

Substantial contributor. In general, a substantial contributor means any person who contributed or bequeathed an aggregate of more than $5,000 to the organization, if that amount is more than 2% of the total contributions and bequests received by the organization before the end of the tax year of the organization in which the contribution or bequest is received by the organization from such person. A substantial contributor includes the grantor of a trust.

Specific Instructions

Part I. List each excess benefit transaction in Part I, column (c). Enter the date of the transaction in column (b) and the amount of the excess benefit in column (d). Compute the tax on the excess benefit for disqualified persons and enter it in column (e). Compute any tax on the excess benefit for organization managers and enter the amount in column (f).

For organization managers, the tax is the lesser of 10% of the excess benefit or $20,000. This tax is computed on each transaction.

Part II. Enter in column (a) the names of all disqualified persons who took part in the excess benefit transactions. If more than one disqualified person took part in an excess benefit transaction, each is individually liable for the entire tax on the transaction. But the disqualified persons who are liable for the tax may prorate the payment among themselves. Enter in column (c) the tax to be paid by each disqualified person.

Carry the total amount in column (d) for each disqualified person to page 1, Part II-A, column (h).

Part III. Enter in column (a) the names of all managers who knowingly took part in the excess benefit transactions listed in Part I. If more than one manager knowingly took part in an excess benefit transaction, each is individually liable for the entire tax in connection with the transaction. But the managers liable for the tax may prorate the payment among themselves. Enter in column (c) the tax to be paid by each organization manager.

Carry the total amount in column (d) for each manager to page 1, Part II-A, column (h).

Schedule J—Taxes on Being a Party to Prohibited Tax Shelter Transactions (Section 4965)

General Instructions

Requirement.

1. Complete Schedule J if you are an entity described in section 501(c), 501(d), or 170(c) (other than the United States) or an Indian tribal government (within the meaning of section 7701(a)(40)) and you received proceeds from or have net income attributable to a prohibited tax shelter transaction (PTST).

2. Complete Schedule J if you are an entity manager of such an entity who approved the entity as (or otherwise caused the entity to be) a party to a PTST at any time during the tax year and who knew (or had reason to know) that the transaction is a PTST.

See the following guidance and any future guidance for details.
• Notice 2006-65, 2006-31 I.R.B. 102
• Notice 2007-18, 2007-9 I.R.B. 608
• T.D. 9334, 2007-34 I.R.B. 382
• T.D. 9335, 2007-34 I.R.B. 380

TIP *Managers of tax favored retirement plans, individual retirement arrangements, and savings arrangements described in sections 401(a), 403(a), 403(b), 529, 457(b), 408(a), 220(d), 408(b), 530, or 223(d) must report and pay tax due under 4965(a)(2) on Form 5330.*

Prohibited tax shelter transaction. In general, a prohibited tax shelter transaction means any listed transaction (including a subsequently listed transaction) and any prohibited reportable transaction.

Listed transaction. A listed transaction includes any transaction that is the same as or substantially similar to one of the types of transactions that the IRS has determined to be a tax avoidance transaction. These transactions are identified by notice, regulation, or other form of published guidance as a listed transaction. For existing guidance see:
• Notice 2004-67, 2004-41 I.R.B. 600
• Notice 2005-13, 2005-9 I.R.B. 630.
• Notice 2007-57, 2007-29 I.R.B. 87

For updates to this list go to the IRS web page at *www.irs.gov/businesses/corporations* and click on Abusive Tax Shelters and Transactions. The listed transactions in the above notices and rulings will also be periodically updated in future issues of the Internal Revenue Bulletin.

Subsequently listed transaction A subsequently listed transaction is a transaction that is identified in published guidance as a listed transaction after the entity has entered into the transaction and that was not a confidential transaction or transaction with contractual protection at the time the entity entered into the transaction.

Prohibited reportable transaction. A prohibited reportable transaction is any confidential transaction or any transaction with contractual protection that is a reportable transaction. See Regulations sections 1.6011-4(b)(3) and (4), and the Instructions for Form 8886-T, Disclosure by Tax-Exempt Entity Regarding Prohibited Tax Shelter Transaction for more information.

Allocation of net income and proceeds to a tax year. The net income and proceeds attributable to a prohibited tax shelter transaction must be allocated to a particular tax year in a manner consistent with the entity's established method of accounting for federal income tax purposes. If an entity has not established a method of accounting for federal income tax purposes, the entity must use the cash receipts and disbursements method to determine the amount and timing of net income and proceeds attributable to a prohibited tax shelter transaction.

If an entity has an established method of accounting other than the cash method, the entity may use the cash method to determine the amount of the net income and proceeds attributable to a prohibited tax shelter transaction.

Specific Instructions

Part I. Complete this part for each transaction if during the tax year, the entity received proceeds from or has net income attributable to a PTST.

Figure the tax for each transaction as follows:

- If column (e) was answered "Yes," then enter the larger of the column (f) or column (g) amount in column (h).
- If column e was answered "No," then multiply the larger of the amount in column (f) or column (g) by 35% (.35) and enter the result in column (h).

After the tax has been figured for all PTSTs entered on Schedule J, then total column (h) and enter the amount on the Total line and on line 9 of Part I, page 1.

Part II. Enter in column (a) the names of all entity managers who approved the entity as (or otherwise caused the entity to be) a party to a PTST at any time during the tax year and who knew or had reason to know that the transaction is a PTST.

Carry the total amount in column (d) for each manager to page 1, Part II-A, column (i).

Schedule K—Taxes on Taxable Distributions of Sponsoring Organizations Maintaining Donor Advised Funds (Section 4966)

General Instructions

Requirement. Complete Schedule K if you answered "Yes" to question 9a in Part V of Form 990, or if you are a fund manager of a sponsoring organization who agreed to the making of a taxable distribution knowing that it was a taxable distribution. Report each taxable distribution separately. These terms are discussed below.

Taxable distribution. A taxable distribution is any distribution from a donor advised fund to any natural person or to any other person if:

1. the distribution is for any purpose other than one specified in section 170(c)(2)(B), or
2. the sponsoring organization maintaining the donor advised fund does not exercise expenditure responsibility with respect to such distribution in accordance with section 4945(h).

However, a taxable distribution does not include a distribution from a donor advised fund to:

1. any organization described in section 170(b)(1)(A) (other than a disqualified supporting organization),
2. the sponsoring organization of such donor advised fund, or
3. any other donor advised fund.

Sponsoring organization. A sponsoring organization is a section 170(c) organization that is not a government organization (as referred to in section 170(c)(1) and (2)(A)) or a private foundation and maintains one or more donor advised funds.

Donor advised fund. A donor advised fund is a fund or account:

1. Which is separately identified by reference to contributions of a donor or donors,
2. Which is owned and controlled by a sponsoring organization, and
3. For which the donor (or any person appointed or designated by the donor) has or expects to have advisory privileges concerning the distribution or investment of the funds held in the donor advised funds or accounts because of the donor's status as a donor.

Exception. A donor advised fund does not include:

1. A fund or account that makes distributions only to a single identified organization or governmental entity, or
2. Any fund or account for a person described in **3** above that gives advice about which individuals receive grants for travel, study, or similar purposes, if;

a. The person's advisory privileges are performed exclusively by such person in their capacity as a committee member of which all the committee members are appointed by the sponsoring organization.

b. No combination of persons with advisory privileges, described in **3** above, or persons related to those in **3** above, directly or indirectly control the committee, or

c. All grants from the fund or account are awarded on an objective and nondiscriminatory basis according to a procedure approved in advance by the board of directors of the sponsoring organization. The procedure must be designed to ensure that all grants meet the requirements of section 4945(g)(1), (2), or (3).

Tax on sponsoring organization. A tax of 20% of the amount of each taxable distribution is imposed on the sponsoring organization.

Tax on fund manager. If a tax is imposed on a taxable distribution of the sponsoring organization, a tax of 5% of the distribution will be imposed on any fund manager who agreed to the distribution knowing that it was a taxable distribution. Any fund manager who took part in the distribution and is liable for the tax must pay the tax. The maximum amount of tax on all fund managers for any one taxable distribution is $10,000. If more than one fund manager is liable for tax on a taxable distribution, all such managers are jointly and severally liable for the tax.

Specific Instructions

Part I. Complete this part for all taxable distributions.

Part II. Enter in column (a) the names of all fund managers who agreed to make the taxable distribution. If more than one fund manager is listed in column (a) for one distribution, each is individually liable for the entire tax in connection with that distribution. However, the fund managers who are liable for the tax may prorate the payment among themselves. Enter in column (c) the tax each manager will pay for each distribution for which such manager owes a tax.

Carry the total amount in column (d) for each fund manager to page 1, Part II-A, column (j).

Schedule L—Taxes on Prohibited Benefits Distributed From Donor Advised Funds (Section 4967)

General Instructions

Requirement. All sponsoring organizations of donor advised funds that answered "Yes" to Form 990, Part V, line 9b, or that otherwise distributed prohibited benefits under section 4967, must complete Schedule L. Report each taxable distribution separately. Complete Parts I, II, and III of Schedule L only in connection with distributions made by a sponsoring organization from a donor advised fund which results in a prohibited benefit. (See instructions to Schedule K for definitions of the terms sponsoring organization and donor advised fund).

Prohibited benefit. If any donor, donor advisor, or related party advises the sponsoring organization about making a distribution which results in a donor, donor advisor, or related party receiving (either directly or indirectly) a more than incidental benefit, then such benefit is a prohibited benefit.

Donor advisor. A donor advisor is any person appointed or designated by a donor to advise a sponsoring organization on the distribution or investment of amounts held in the donor's fund or account.

Related party. A related party includes any family member or 35% controlled entity. See the *General Instructions for Schedule I* for a definition of those terms.

Tax on donor, donor advisor, or related person. A tax of 125% of the benefit resulting from the distribution is imposed on both the party who advised as to the distribution (which might be a donor, donor advisor or related party) and the party who received such benefit (which might be a donor, donor advisor, or related party). The advisor and the party who received the benefit are jointly and severally liable for the tax.

Tax on fund managers. If a tax is imposed on a prohibited benefit received by a donor, donor advisor, or related person, a tax of 10% of the amount of the prohibited benefit is imposed on any fund manager who agreed to the distribution knowing that it would confer a prohibited benefit. Any fund manager who took part in the distribution and is liable for the tax must pay the tax. The maximum amount of tax on all fund managers for any one taxable distribution is $10,000. If more than one fund manager is liable for tax on a taxable distribution, all such managers are jointly and severally liable for the tax.

Exception. If a person engaged in an excess benefit transaction and received a prohibited benefit for the same transaction, the person is taxed under section 4958, and no tax is imposed under section 4967 for a prohibited benefit.

Specific Instructions

Part I. Complete this part for all prohibited benefits.

Part II. Enter in column (a) the names of all donors, donor advisors, and related persons who received a prohibited benefit. If more than one donor, donor advisor, or related person is listed in column (a) for one distribution, each is individually liable for the entire tax for that distribution. However, the donors, donor advisors, or related persons who are liable for the tax may prorate the payment among themselves. Enter in column (c) the tax each manager will pay for each distribution for which such manager owes a tax.

Carry the total amount in column (d) for each donor, donor advisor, or related person to page 1, Part II-A, column (k).

Part III. Enter in column (a) the names of all fund managers who agreed to make the distribution conferring the prohibited benefit. If more than one fund manager is listed in column (a) for one distribution, each is individually liable for the entire tax for that distribution. However, the fund managers who are liable for the tax may prorate the payment among themselves. Enter in column (c) the tax each manager will pay for each distribution for which such manager owes a tax.

Carry the total amount in column (d) for each fund manager to page 1, Part II-A, column (k).

Privacy Act and Paperwork Reduction Act Notice.
We ask for the information on this form to carry out the Internal Revenue laws of the United States. We need it to ensure that you are complying with these laws and to allow us to figure and collect the right amount of tax. Certain individuals who owe tax under Chapter 41 or 42 of the Internal Revenue Code, and who do not sign the Form 4720 of the foundation or organization, must file a separate Form 4720 showing the tax owed and the name of the foundation or organization for which they owe tax. Sections 6001 and 6011 of the Internal Revenue Code require you to provide the requested information if the tax applies to you. Section 6109 requires signing individuals and paid preparers to provide their identifying number.

Routine uses of this information include disclosing it to the Department of Justice for civil and criminal litigation and to other federal agencies, as provided by law. We may disclose the information to cities, states, the District of Columbia, and U.S. Commonwealths or possessions to administer their laws. If you do not file this information, you may be subject to interest, penalties, and/or criminal prosecution.

We may also disclose this information to other countries under a tax treaty, to federal and state agencies to enforce federal nontax criminal laws, or to federal law enforcement and intelligence agencies to combat terrorism.

You are not required to provide the information requested on a form that is subject to the Paperwork Reduction Act unless the form displays a valid OMB control number. Books or records relating to a form or its instructions must be retained as long as their contents may become material in the administration of any Internal Revenue law. Generally, tax returns and return information are confidential, as required by section 6103.

The time needed to complete and file this form will vary depending on individual circumstances. The estimated average time is:

Recordkeeping	39 hr., 55 min.
Learning about the law or the form	16 hr., 30 min.
Preparing the form . . .	23 hr., 22 min.
Copying, assembling, and sending the form to the IRS	1 hr., 36 min.

If you have comments concerning the accuracy of these time estimates or suggestions for making this form simpler, we would be happy to hear from you. You can write to the Internal Revenue Service, Tax Products Coordinating Committee, SE:W:CAR:MP:T:T:SP, 1111 Constitution Ave. NW, IR-6526, Washington, DC 20224. Do not send the tax form to this address. Instead, see *Where To File* on page 3.

Rev. Proc. 92-94, 1992-1 C.B. 507

SECTION 1. PURPOSE

Private foundations generally want their grants to foreign grantees to be treated as qualifying distributions for purposes of section 4942 of the Internal Revenue Code rather than as taxable expenditures for purposes of section 4945 of the Code. This treatment is assured if the foreign grantee has a ruling or determination letter classifying it as a public charity within the meaning of section 509(a)(1), (2), or (3), or a private operating foundation under section 4942(j)(3) of the Code. If a foreign grantee does not have such a ruling or determination letter, the Foundation Excise Tax Regulations set forth requirements that must be satisfied in order to assure that the grant will be considered a qualifying distribution.

In response to requests from private foundations, this revenue procedure provides a simplified procedure that private foundations (including nonexempt charitable trusts) may follow in making "reasonable judgments" and "good faith determinations" under sections 53.4945-6(c)-(2)(ii), 53.4942(a)-3(a)(6) and 53.4945-5(a)(5) of the Foundation Excise Tax Regulations. If the requirements of this revenue procedure are met, a grant to a foreign grantee will be treated as a grant to an organization that is described in section 501(c)(3) or section 4947(a)(1) of the Internal Revenue Code, and, that is either a public charity within the meaning of section 509(a)(1), (2), or (3), or a private operating foundation under section 4942(j)(3) of the Code.

SEC. 2. BACKGROUND

.01 Section 53.4945-6(c)(2)(ii) of the regulations applies to a private foundation (grantor) making a grant for certain purposes to a foreign organization (grantee) that does not have a ruling or determination letter recognizing it as an organization described in section 501(c)(3) of the Code. ("Certain purposes" are those described in section 170(c)(2)(B) except for any transfer of assets pursuant to any liquidation, merger, redemption, recapitalization, or other adjustment, organization, or reorganization described in section 507(b)-(2).) The grantor may treat such a grant as a grant to an organization described in section 501(c)(3) (other than section 509(a)(4)) if, in the reasonable judgment of the foundation manager, the grantee is an organization described in section 501(c)(3) (other than section 509(a)(4)).

.02 Sections 53.4942(a)-3(a)(6) and 53.4945-5(a)(5) of the regulations apply to a distribution (or grant) for the purposes described in section 170(c)-(2)(B) of the Code to a foreign organization that has not received a ruling or determination letter that it is a public charity described in section 509(a)(1), (2), or (3), or an operating foundation described in section 4942(j)(3). In this case, the grant will be treated as a grant to a public charity (for purposes of both sections 4942 and 4945) or to an operating foundation (for purposes of section 4942 only) if the grantor has made a "good faith determination" that the grantee is described in section 509(a)-(1), (2), or (3), or section 4942(j)(3).

.03 Under sections 53.4942(a)-3(a)(6) and 53.4945-5(a)(5) of the regulations, a "good faith determination" may be based on an affidavit of the grantee or an opinion of counsel of either the grantor or the grantee. The affidavit or opinion of counsel must give enough facts about the grantee's operations and support to enable the Internal Revenue Service to determine that the grantee would likely qualify as an organization described in section 509(a)(1), (2), or (3), or section 4942(j)(3) of the Code.

.04 Thus, under the regulations, a foundation that wishes to have a grant treated as a grant to a public charity must complete two steps. First, the foundation manager of the grantor must make a "reasonable judgment" that the grantee is an organization described in section 501(c)-(3) (other than section 509(a)(4)). Second, the grantor must make a good faith determination, based on an affidavit of the grantee or an opinion of counsel of either the grantor or the grantee, that the grantee is described in section 509(a)(1), (2), or (3), or section 4942(j)(3).

SEC. 3. SCOPE

This revenue procedure applies to a grant made for purposes set out in section 170(c)(2)(B) of the Code, (except for any transfer of assets pursuant to any liquidation, merger, redemption, recapitalization, or other adjustment, organization, or reorganization described in section 507(b)(2)), if the grant is made by a domestic private foundation to a foreign organization that does not have an Internal Revenue Service ruling letter recognizing its exemption under section 501(c)(3), or classifying it as a public charity under section 509(a)(1), (2), or (3), or as a private operating foundation under section 4942(j)(3).

SEC. 4. PROCEDURE

.01 A private foundation will be deemed to have satisfied the requirements of sections 53.4945-6(c)(2)(ii), 53.4942(a)-3(a)(6), and 53.4945-5(a)-(5) of the regulations if (1) a grant is not a transfer of assets pursuant to any liquidation, merger, redemption, recapitalization, or other adjustment, organization, or reorganization described in section 507(b)(2) of the Code, and (2) the grantor bases its "reasonable judgment" and "good faith determination" (as described in the regulations) on a "currently qualified" affidavit prepared by the grantee for the grantor or another grantor that contains the information set out in Sec. 5., below. The original affidavit, or a photocopy of the original affidavit, must be retained by the grantor and made available to the Service upon request. Whether an affidavit is "currently qualified" is discussed in .02 through .06, below. If, however, the grantor possesses information that suggests the affidavit may not be reliable, it must consider that information in determining whether the affidavit is currently qualified.

.02 An affidavit will be considered currently qualified as long as the facts it contains are up to date, as provided in either .03 or .04, below, and as long as the relevant substantive requirements of sections 501(c)(3) and 4947(a)(1) of the Code and sections 509(a)(1), (2), or (3) or section 4942(j)(3) remain unchanged.

.03 The facts in an affidavit will be considered up to date if those facts reflect the grantee organization's latest complete accounting year or the affidavit is updated to reflect the grantee organization's current data as described in .04 below.

.04 Where a grantee's status under sections 501(c)(3) and 4947(a)(1), 509(a)(1), (2), or (3) or section 4942(j)(3) of the Code does not depend on financial support, which can change from year to year, an affidavit need be updated only by asking the grantee to amend the description of any facts in the original affidavit that have changed. If the facts have not changed, an attested statement by the grantee to that effect is enough to update an affidavit. Where a grantee's status under section 509(a)(1), (2), or (3) or section 4942(j)(3) depends on financial support, the affidavit must be updated by asking the grantee to provide an attested statement containing enough financial data to establish that it continues to meet the requirements of the applicable Code section.

.05 The information required by .04, above, is not necessarily financial data from the grantee's latest accounting year. For example, financial data from years 1985, 1986, 1987, and 1988 are enough to establish that an organization is "publicly supported" within the meaning of section 509(a)(2) of the Code for years 1989 and 1990 if the granting foundation is not responsible for a substantial and material change in the grantee organization's sources of support in years 1989 and 1990. See section 1.509(a)-3(c)(1) of the regulations. A grantor will not be considered responsible for a substantial and material change in the grantee's sources of financial support as long as:

(1) The grantee's affidavit is "currently qualified" within the meaning of .04, above;

(2) The grantor neither has learned that the Internal Revenue Service is challenging the validity of the grantee's affidavit, nor has reason to doubt that the affidavit remains valid; and

(3) The grantee is not controlled directly or indirectly by the grantor. A grantee is controlled by the grantor if the grantor and disqualified persons (defined in section 4946(a)(1)(A) through (G) of the Code) with respect to the grantor, by aggregating their votes or positions of authority, may require the grantee to perform any act that significantly affects its operations or may prevent the grantee from performing such an act.

.06 Private foundations are permitted but not required to use the procedures described above in making grants to foreign organizations. The two-step procedure referred to in Section 2.04, above, is still the general mechanism for meeting the requirements of sections 53.4945-(c)(2)(ii) 53.4942(a)-3(a)(6) and 53.4945-5(a)(5) of the regulations.

SEC. 5. AFFIDAVIT REQUIREMENTS

.01 An affidavit must be written in English and contain the substantive information set out below. However, the affidavit need not strictly follow the form set forth below. An English translation must be provided for any supporting documents that are not written in English. The affidavit must be attested to by a principal officer of the grantee organization.

.02 Affidavits for grantee organizations described in section 170(b)(1)(A)(vi) of the Code must include a financial schedule as described in .04(11), below. Grantee organizations described in section 509(a)(2) must provide comparable information.

.03 Any grantee that claims to be a school described in section 170(b)(1)(A)(ii) of the Code must provide the statement set out in .03(12), concerning whether it operates pursuant to a racially nondiscriminatory policy as to students. Section 170(b)(1)(A)(ii) describes "an educational organization which normally maintains a regular faculty and curriculum and normally has a regularly enrolled body of pupils or students in attendance at the place where its educational activities are regularly carried on." In addition, the affidavit must explain any basis for the grantee school's failure to comply with one or more of the provisions of Rev.Proc. 75-50, 1975-2 C.B. 587.

.04 The affidavit must contain a declaration to the following effect: "The undersigned, to assist grant-making foundations in the United States of America determine whether [name of grantee organization] (the grantee organization) is the equivalent of a public charity described in section 509(a)(1), (2) or (3) of the United States Internal Revenue Code or a private operating foundation described in section 4942(j)(3) of the Code, makes the following statement:

"(1) I am the [title of principal officer] of the grantee organization.

"(2) The grantee organization was created by [identify statute, charter, or other document] in [year], and is operated exclusively for [check applicable box or boxes]:

[ ] charitable
[ ] religious
[ ] scientific
[ ] literary
[ ] educational
[ ] fostering national or international amateur sports competition, or
[ ] prevention of cruelty to children or animals purposes under the laws of [the country in which the grantee organization was formed].

"(3) The activities of the grantee organization have included [describe past and current activities and operations] and will include [describe future activities and operations].

"(4) Copies of the charter, by-laws, and other documents pursuant to which the grantee organization is governed are attached.

"(5) The laws and customs applicable to the grantee organization do not permit any of its income or assets to be distributed to, or applied for the benefit of, a private person or non-charitable organization other than pursuant to the conduct of the grantee organization's charitable activities, or as payment of reasonable compensation for services rendered or as payment representing the fair market value of property which the grantee organization has purchased.

"(6) The grantee organization has no shareholders or members who have a proprietary interest in the income or assets of the organization.

"(7) In the event that the grantee organization were to be liquidated or dissolved, under the laws and customs applicable, or under the governing instruments, all its assets would be distributed to another not-for-profit organization for charitable, religious, scientific, literary, or educational purposes, or to a government instrumentality. A copy of the relevant statutory law or provisions in the governing instruments controlling the distribution of the organization's assets on liquidation is attached.

"(8) The laws and customs applicable to the grantee organization do not permit the organization, other than as an insubstantial part of its activities,

(A) to engage in activities that are not for religious, charitable, scientific, literary, or educational purposes; or

(B) to attempt to influence legislation, by propaganda or otherwise.

"(9) The laws and customs applicable to the grantee organization do not permit the organization directly or indirectly to participate or intervene in any political campaign on behalf of, or in opposition to, any candidate for public office.

"(10) The grantee organization is not controlled by or operated in connection with any organization other than as follows [describe]:

"(11) (The following is required only if the grantee organization's status under sections 501(c)(3) and 4947(a)(1), 509(a)(1), (2), or (3) or section 4942(j)(3) of the Code depends on its financial support.) A schedule of support for the four most recently completed taxable years is attached showing (for each year and in total)

(A) Gifts, grants, and contributions received;

(B) Membership fees received;

(C) Gross receipts from admissions, merchandise sold or services performed, or furnishing of facilities in any activity that is not a business unrelated to the organization's exempt purposes;

(D) Gross income from interest, dividends, rents, and royalties;

(E) Net income from business activities that are unrelated to the organization's exempt purposes;

(F) The value of services or facilities furnished by a governmental unit without charge;

(G) The total of lines (A) through (F);

(H) Line (G) minus line (C);

(I) Two percent of line (H);

(J) A schedule of contributions for each donor whose support for the four-year period was greater than the amount on line (1) (a major donor), and showing the amount by which each major donor's total contributions exceeded the amount on line (1) (excess contributions);

(K) The sum of all major donors' excess contributions;

(L) The four-year total for line (H) minus the four-year totals of lines (D), (E), and (K) (the amount of public support);

(M) Line (L) divided by the four-year total for line (H) (the percentage of the organization's support that is public support).

"(12) (The following is required only if the grantee is not a public charity described in section 509(a)(1), (2), or (3) of the Code but claims to be an operating foundation described in section 4942(j)(3) of the Code.) A schedule showing that the organization satisfies (i) the income test of section 53.4942(b)-1(a) of the regulations and (ii) one of the alternative tests described in section 53.4942(b)-2.

"(13) (The following is required only if the grantee is a school described in section 170 of the Code.) The grantee organization is an organization described in section 170(b)(1)(A)(ii) of the Code that has adopted and operates pursuant to a racially nondiscriminatory policy as to students, as set forth in Rev.Rul. 71-447, 1971-2 C.B. 230, and Rev.Rul. 75-231, 1975-1 C.B. 158, and as implemented in Rev.Proc. 75-50, 1975-2 C.B. 587."

DRAFTING INFORMATION

The principal author of this revenue procedure is Thomas J. Miller of the Exempt Organizations Technical Division. For further information regarding this revenue procedure contact Mr. Miller on (202) 622-7867 (not a toll-free number).

APPENDIX 8

U.S. Department of the Treasury Anti-Terrorist Financing Guidelines: Voluntary Best Practices for U.S.-Based Charities[1]

Table of Contents

---

[1] This document is a revised version of the original *Anti-Terrorist Financing Guidelines: Voluntary Best Practices for U.S.-Based Charities* released by the U.S. Department of the Treasury in November 2002. This revised version incorporates comments received in response to the issuance of the draft revised Guidelines released for public comment in December 2005.

These Guidelines are designed to assist charities that attempt in good faith to protect themselves from terrorist abuse and are not intended to address the problem of organizations that use the cover of charitable work, whether real or perceived, to provide support to terrorist groups or fronts operating on behalf of terrorist groups. Non-adherence to these Guidelines, in and of itself, does not constitute a violation of existing U.S. law. Conversely, adherence to these Guidelines does not excuse any person (individual or entity) from compliance with any local, state, or federal law or regulation, nor does it release any person from or constitute a legal defense against any civil or criminal liability for violating any such law or regulation. In particular, adherence to these Guidelines shall not be construed to preclude any criminal charge, civil fine, or other action by Treasury or the Department of Justice against persons who engage in prohibited transactions with persons designated pursuant to the Antiterrorism and Effective Death Penalty Act of 1996, as amended, or with those that are designated under the criteria defining prohibited persons in the relevant Executive orders issued pursuant to statute, such as the International Emergency Economic Powers Act, as amended. Please see Footnote 12 for an explanation of the master list of Specially Designated Nationals (the "SDN List"), which includes all such designated persons. These Guidelines are also separate and apart from requirements that apply to charitable organizations under the Internal Revenue Code ("IRC").

I. Introduction

Upon issuance of Executive Order 13224, President George W. Bush directed the U.S. Department of the Treasury ("Treasury") to work with other elements of the federal government and the international community to develop a comprehensive and sustained campaign against the sources and conduits of terrorist financing. Investigations have revealed terrorist abuse of charitable organizations, both in the United States and worldwide, to raise and move funds, provide logistical support, encourage terrorist recruitment or otherwise cultivate support for terrorist organizations and operations. This abuse threatens to undermine donor confidence and jeopardizes the integrity of the charitable sector, whose services are indispensable to both national and world communities.

In response to this threat, Treasury first released the *Anti-Terrorist Financing Guidelines: Voluntary Best Practices for U.S.-Based Charities* ("Guidelines") in November 2002. In December 2005, based on extensive review and comment by public and private sector interested parties, Treasury revised and released the Guidelines in draft form for further public comment. Based on the comments received, Treasury has further amended the Guidelines to improve their utility to the charitable sector in adopting practices that can better protect it from terrorists and their support networks.

The Guidelines are designed to enhance awareness in the donor and charitable communities of the kinds of practices that charities may adopt to reduce the risk of terrorist financing or abuse. These Guidelines are voluntary and do not create, supersede, or modify current or future legal requirements applicable to U.S. persons, including U.S. non-profit institutions. Adherence to these guidelines does not constitute a legal defense against any civil or criminal liability for violating any local, state, or federal law or regulations. In addition, these Guidelines do not represent an exhaustive or comprehensive compilation of best practices. Many charities, through their extensive experience and expertise in delivering international aid, have already developed effective internal controls and practices that lessen the risk of terrorist financing or abuse. In view of this fact, Treasury does not want charities to abandon proven internal controls and practices. Rather, the Guidelines are intended to assist charities in developing, re-evaluating, or strengthening a risk-based approach to guard against the threat of diversion of charitable funds or exploitation of charitable activity by terrorist organizations and their support networks.

In addition, these Guidelines are intended to assist charities in understanding and facilitating compliance with preexisting U.S. legal requirements related to combating terrorist financing, which include, but are not limited to, various sanctions programs administered by the Office of Foreign Assets Control ("OFAC"). These preexisting legal requirements are clearly marked in the text of the Guidelines.

The risk-based nature of these Guidelines reflects Treasury's recognition that a "one-size-fits-all" approach is untenable and inappropriate due to the diversity of the charitable sector and its operations. Accordingly, certain aspects of the Guidelines will not be applicable to every charity, charitable activity, or circumstance. Moreover, Treasury acknowledges that certain exigent circumstances (such as catastrophic disasters) may make application of the Guidelines difficult. In such cases, charities should maintain a risk-based approach that includes all prudent and reasonable measures that are feasible under the circumstances. Charities and donors are encouraged to consult these Guidelines when considering protective measures to prevent infiltration, exploitation, or abuse by terrorists. Although adherence to these Guidelines does not guarantee protection from terrorist abuse, effective internal controls which incorporate the principles and practices set forth in these Guidelines can prevent the diversion of charitable resources from their proper uses, as well as identify situations involving terrorist financing or abuse.

Treasury recognizes the vital importance of the charitable community in providing essential services around the world. Treasury also understands the difficulty of providing assistance to those in need, often in remote and inaccessible regions, and applauds the efforts of the charitable community to meet such needs. The goal of these Guidelines is to facilitate legitimate charitable efforts and protect the integrity of the charitable sector and good faith donors by offering the sector ways to prevent terrorist organizations from exploiting charitable activities for their own benefit.

II. Fundamental Principles of Good Charitable Practice

A. Charities are independent entities and are not part of the U.S. Government. Like all U.S. persons, charitable organizations must comply with the laws of the United States, which include, but are not limited to, all OFAC-administered sanctions programs.[2]

---

[2] OFAC sanctions programs include those relating to particular countries or regimes (country-based programs), as well as those relating to groups, individuals, or entities engaged in specific activities (list-based programs). Sanctions programs normally: (i) prohibit U.S. persons from engaging in certain transactions, such as trade in goods and services and financial transactions, and/or (ii) require U.S. persons to block the assets and property of persons designated under the relevant Executive order or law. The particular prohibitions and/or obligations of U.S. persons vary by program. OFAC can issue licenses to U.S. persons to engage in transactions that would otherwise be prohibited, if there is a policy-permissible reason to do so, and if permitted by statute. Further information on how to apply for specific licenses is available at http://www.treas.gov/offices/enforcement/ofac/faq/index.shtml#license.

For further information on OFAC-administered sanctions programs and general licensing under these programs, please see http://www.treas.gov/offices/enforcement/ofac.

OFAC guidelines for non-governmental organizations wishing to undertake humanitarian activities in sanctioned countries are available at http://www.treas.gov/offices/enforcement/ofac/regulations/ngo_reg.pdf.

Other helpful guidance materials for charities relating to protection from terrorist abuse may be found at http://www.treas.gov/offices/enforcement/key-issues/protecting/index.shtml.

The United States relies on a wide array of federal criminal statutes in fighting the threat of terrorist financing. Charities should be particularly aware that in its efforts against the financing of terrorism, the U.S. relies on, among others, the federal statutes that prohibit:

- the financing of terrorism (18 U.S.C. § 2339C),
- providing material support or resources to terrorists (18 U.S.C. § 2339A), and
- providing material support or resources to designated terrorist organizations (18 U.S.C. § 2339B).

In that effort, the U.S. also particularly relies upon the federal statutes which criminalize:

B. Charitable organizations are encouraged to adopt practices in addition to those required by law that provide additional assurances that all assets[3] are used exclusively for charitable or other legitimate purposes.[4]

C. Individuals acting in a fiduciary capacity for any charitable organization should exercise due care in the performance of their responsibilities, consistent with applicable common law as well as local, state, and federal statutes and regulations.

D. Governance, fiscal and programmatic responsibility and accountability are essential components of charitable work and must be reflected at every level of a charitable organization and its operations.

III. Governance Accountability and Transparency

A. Governing Instruments: Charitable organizations should operate in accordance with governing instruments, *e.g.*, charter, articles of incorporation, bylaws, *etc.* The governing instruments should:

1. delineate the charity's basic goal(s) and purpose(s);

2. define the structure of the charity, including the composition of its governing body, how such body is selected and replaced, and the authority and responsibilities of the body;

3. set forth requirements concerning financial reporting, accountability, and practices for solicitation and distribution of funds; and

4. state that the charity shall comply with all applicable local, state, and federal laws and regulations.

B. Independent Oversight: It is important for charitable organizations to have independent oversight of charitable operations, and each charitable organization should determine what oversight structure best suits that organization and will provide for unbiased scrutiny of its operations. The following provisions set forth

---

- the laundering of monetary instruments (18 U.S.C. § 1956), and
- engaging in monetary transactions in property derived from specified unlawful activity (18 U.S.C. § 1957).

[3] An asset is any item of value, including, but not limited to, services, resources, business, equitable holdings, real estate, stocks, bonds, mutual funds, currency, certificates of deposit, bank accounts, trust funds, and the property and investments placed therein.

[4] A charitable organization may never use charitable assets for illegal purposes; however, a charitable organization may accrue unrelated business taxable income in the course of legitimately doing business as a charitable organization. Even though an organization is recognized as tax exempt, it still may be liable for tax on its unrelated business taxable income.

basic principles for the creation of a transparent and accountable oversight body (the "governing board").

1. Members of the governing board ordinarily should not have an active role in the day-to-day management of the charitable organization.[5] The charity should establish a conflict of interest policy for both members of the governing board and employees. That policy should establish procedures to be followed if a member of the governing board or employee has a conflict of interest or a perceived conflict of interest relating to the management or operations of the charity.

2. The governing board should be responsible for the charitable organization's compliance with relevant laws, its finances and accounting practices and for the adoption, implementation, and oversight of practices, including financial recordkeeping that will safeguard charitable assets effectively.

3. The governing board should maintain records of its decisions.

4. Charities should maintain and make publicly available a current list of members of the governing board, their salaries and their affiliation with any subsidiary or affiliate of the charitable organization.

5. While fully respecting individual privacy rights, charities should maintain records of additional identifying information about the members of the governing board, such as available home, email and URL addresses, social security number, citizenship, *etc.*

6. While fully respecting individual privacy rights, charities should maintain records of identifying information for the members of the governing boards of any subsidiaries or affiliates[6] receiving funds from them.

7. When served with process or when other appropriate authorization exists, charities should produce requested records maintained in accordance with these Guidelines to the appropriate regulatory/supervisory and law enforcement authorities in a timely fashion.

C. Key Employees[7]

---

[5] Certain charitable organizations, such as houses of worship, certain trusts, and corporations sole, may not be able to apply this practice due to their varying organizational and operational structures.

[6] Subsidiaries or affiliates are organizations that are subject to the general supervision or control of a parent or central organization.

[7] Key employees include not only highly compensated employees but employees who have responsibilities, powers, or influence similar to those of officials, directors, or trustees. Key employees also include chief management and administrative officials of a charitable organization, including those involved in the disbursement of funds.

1. Charities should maintain and make publicly available a current list of their five highest paid or most influential employees (the key employees) and the salaries and direct or indirect benefits they receive.

2. While fully respecting individual privacy rights, charities should maintain records containing identifying information (such as available home, email and URL addresses, social security or other identification number – *e.g.*, taxpayer identification number, national identity, or passport number – citizenship, *etc.*) about their key, non-U.S. employees working abroad. Such information should be similar to that maintained by charities in the normal course of operations about all U.S. employees, wherever employed, and foreign employees working in the United States.

3. While fully respecting individual privacy rights, charities should maintain records containing identifying information for the key employees of any subsidiaries or affiliates receiving funds from them.

IV. Financial Accountability and Transparency

A. The charity should have a budget, adopted in advance on an annual basis and approved and overseen by the governing board.

B. The governing board should appoint one individual to serve as the financial/accounting officer who should be responsible for day-to-day control over the charity's assets.

C. If the charity's total annual gross income exceeds $250,000,[8] the governing board should select an independent certified public accounting firm to audit the finances of the charity and to issue a publicly available, audited financial statement on an annual basis.

D. Solicitations for Funds

1. The charity should clearly state its goals for and purposes of soliciting funds so that anyone examining the charity's disbursement of funds can determine whether the charity is adhering to those goals.

2. Solicitations for donations should accurately and transparently tell donors how and where their donations are going to be expended.

3. The charity should substantiate on request that solicitations and

[8] The $250,000 figure is drawn from the June 2005 final report to Congress of the Panel on the Nonprofit Sector, convened by Independent Sector. This report, which offers a comprehensive approach to improving oversight and governance of charitable organizations, recommends independent financial audits for charities that have more than $250,000 in total annual revenue. This report is available at http://www.nonprofitpanel.org/final/.

informational materials, distributed by any means, are accurate, truthful, and not misleading, in whole or in part.

4. The charity should fully, immediately, and publicly disclose if it makes a determination that circumstances justify applying funds for a charitable purpose different from the purpose for which such funds were contributed or solicited.

E. Receipt and Disbursement of Funds

1. The charity should account for all funds received and disbursed in accordance with generally accepted accounting principles and the requirements of the Internal Revenue Code. The charity should maintain records of the salaries it pays and the expenses it incurs (domestically and internationally).

2. The charity should include in its accounting of all charitable disbursements the name of each grantee,[9] the amount disbursed, the date, and form of payment for each disbursement.

3. The charity, after recording, should promptly deposit all received funds into an account maintained by the charity at a financial institution. In particular, all currency donated should be promptly deposited into the charity's financial institution account.

4. The charity should make disbursements by check or wire transfer rather than in currency whenever such financial arrangements are reasonably available. Where these financial services do not exist or other exigencies require making disbursements in currency (as in the case of humanitarian assistance provided in rural areas of many developing countries, or in remote areas afflicted by natural disasters), the charity should disburse the currency in the smallest increments sufficient to meet immediate and short-term needs or specific projects/initiatives rather than in large sums intended to cover needs over an extended time frame, and it should exercise oversight regarding the use of the currency for the intended charitable purposes, including keeping detailed internal records of such currency disbursements.

F. Mechanisms for Public Disclosure of Distribution of Resources and Services

[9] The term "grantee," as it is used throughout these Guidelines, means an immediate grantee of charitable resources or services. To the extent reasonably practicable, charitable organizations should also apply or ensure the existence of applicable safeguards (as described in Sections III, IV, V, and VI) in any downstream sub-grantees or recipients to protect charitable resources from exploitation by terrorists, terrorist organizations, or terrorist supporters. Charities should not enter into a relationship with a grantee where any doubts exist about the grantee's ability to ensure safe delivery of charitable resources independent of influence by or association with any terrorist organization.

1. The charity should maintain and make publicly available a current list of any branches, subsidiaries, and/or affiliates that receive resources and/or services from the charity.

2. The charity should make publicly available or provide to any member of the general public, upon request, an annual report. The annual report should describe the charity's purpose(s), programs, activities, tax exempt status, the structure and responsibility of the governing board of the charity, and financial information.

3. The charity should make publicly available or provide to any member of the general public, upon request, complete annual financial statements, including a summary of the results of the charity's most recent audit. The financial statements should present the overall financial condition of the charity and its financial activities in accordance with generally accepted accounting principles and reporting practices.

V. Programmatic Verification

A. Supplying Resources

When supplying charitable *resources* (monetary and in-kind contributions), fiscal responsibility on the part of a charity should include:

1. determining that the potential grantee of monetary or in-kind contributions has the ability to both accomplish the charitable purpose of the grant and protect the resources from diversion to non-charitable purposes or exploitation by terrorist organizations and/or their support networks;

2. reducing the terms of the grant to a written agreement signed by both the charity and the grantee;

3. ongoing monitoring of the grantee and the activities funded under the grant for the term of the grant; and

4. correcting any misuse of resources by the grantee and terminating the relationship should misuse continue.

B. Supplying Services

When supplying charitable *services*, fiscal responsibility on the part of a charity should include:

1. appropriate measures to reduce the risk that its assets would be used for non-charitable purposes or exploitation by terrorist organizations and/or their support networks; and

2. sufficient auditing or accounting controls to trace services or commodities between delivery by the charity and/or service provider and use by the grantee.

C. Programmatic Review

The charity should review the programmatic and financial operations of each grantee as follows:

1. The charity should require periodic reports from grantees on their operational activities and their use of the disbursed funds;

2. The charity should require grantees to take reasonable steps to ensure that funds provided by the charity are neither distributed to terrorists or their support networks nor used for activities that support terrorism or terrorist organizations. Periodically, a grantee should apprise the charity of the steps it has taken to meet this goal; and

3. The charity should perform routine, on-site audits of grantees to the extent reasonable – consistent with the size of the disbursement, the cost of the audit, and the risks of diversion or abuse of charitable resources – to ensure that the grantee has taken adequate measures to protect its charitable resources from diversion to, or abuse or influence by, terrorists or their support networks.

VI. Anti-Terrorist Financing Best Practices

Charities should consider taking the following steps before distributing any charitable funds (and in-kind contributions). As explained in Section I, these suggested steps are voluntary. The purpose of these steps is to enable charities to better protect themselves from the risk of terrorist abuse and to facilitate compliance with U.S. laws, statutes, and regulations, with which all U.S. persons, including U.S. charities, must comply. Depending upon the risk profile of an individual charitable organization, adopting all of these steps may not be applicable or appropriate. When taking these steps, charities should apply a risk-based approach, particularly with respect to engagement with foreign grantees due to the increased risks associated with overseas charitable activity.

A. The charity should collect the following basic information about grantees:

1. The grantee's name in English, in the language of origin, and any acronym or other names used to identify the grantee;[10]

[10] Charities should also be mindful of the possibility that a grantee may have changed its name or transformed its organizational structure to avoid being associated with prior questionable activity. If a charity has any reason to believe that the grantee is operating under a different identity or has used a different name in the past, the charity should undertake reasonable efforts to uncover any such prior identity or name.

2. The jurisdictions in which a grantee maintains a physical presence;

3. Any reasonably available historical information about the grantee that assures the charity of the grantee's identity and integrity, including: (i) the jurisdiction in which a grantee organization is incorporated or formed; (ii) copies of incorporating or other governing instruments; (iii) information on the individuals who formed and operate the organization; and (iv) information relating to the grantee's operating history;

4. The available postal, email and URL addresses and phone number of each place of business of a grantee;

5. A statement of the principal purpose of the grantee, including a detailed report of the grantee's projects and goals;

6. The names and available postal, email and URL addresses of individuals, entities, or organizations to which the grantee currently provides or proposes to provide funding, services, or material support, to the extent reasonably discoverable;

7. The names and available postal, email and URL addresses of any subcontracting organizations utilized by the grantee;

8. Copies of any public filings or releases made by the grantee, including the most recent official registry documents, annual reports, and annual filings with the pertinent government, as applicable; and

9. The grantee's sources of income, such as official grants, private endowments, and commercial activities.

B. The charity should conduct basic vetting of grantees as follows:

1. The charity should conduct a reasonable search of publicly available information to determine whether the grantee is suspected of activity relating to terrorism, including terrorist financing or other support. Charities should not enter into a relationship with a grantee where any terrorist-related suspicions exist;[11]

[11] List-checking alone (as described throughout this section) does not guarantee the safe and secure delivery of charitable funds and services in high-risk areas. For this reason, the Guidelines encourage charities to employ all reasonably available resources both when determining the level of risk in a particular charitable operation and when engaging in appropriate vetting procedures. One example of publicly available information of which charities should be aware is the Terrorist Exclusion List (the "TEL"). The TEL was created pursuant to the USA PATRIOT Act, which authorizes the Secretary of State to designate organizations or groups for inclusion on the TEL in consultation with or upon the request of the Attorney General. Inclusion on the TEL allows the U.S. Government to exclude or deport aliens who provide material assistance to, or solicit assistance for, designated TEL organizations. Although many of the organizations included on the TEL are also included on the Office of Foreign Assets Control ("OFAC") SDN List, several TEL organizations are not listed on the SDN List because of the different purposes and legal criteria associated with these lists.

2. The charity should assure itself that grantees do not appear on OFAC's master list of Specially Designated Nationals (the "SDN List"), maintained on OFAC's website at www.treas.gov/offices/enforcement/ofac/sdn/,[12] and are not otherwise subject to OFAC sanctions.[13]

3. With respect to key employees, members of the governing board, or other senior management at a grantee's principal place of business, and for key employees at the grantee's other business locations, the charity should, to the extent reasonable, obtain the full name in English, in the language of origin, and any acronym or other names used; nationality; citizenship;

TEL designations do not trigger any legal obligations for U.S. persons; however, the TEL does provide charities with additional terrorist-related information that may assist charities in making well-informed decisions on how best to protect themselves from terrorist abuse or association. For further information regarding the TEL, including access to the list containing all TEL designees, please refer to the U.S. Department of State's website at http://www.state.gov/s/ct/rls/fs/2004/32678.htm.

[12] The master SDN List is an integrated listing of designated parties with whom U.S. persons are prohibited from providing services or conducting transactions and whose assets are blocked. OFAC's designations are available in a variety of formats and can easily be broken down into subsets of the master list by program, by country of residency, individuals vs. entities, and other variations for appropriate use in a charity's risk-based approach. Each charity should determine which OFAC listings align with the specific risks the charity faces in its operations and should check grantees accordingly.

OFAC routinely updates information on its targets, including persons designated under country-based and list-based economic sanctions programs, such as individuals and entities designated under the various Executive orders and statutes aimed at terrorism. OFAC offers a free email subscription service that enables subscribers to keep current with these updates. With respect to terrorism-related OFAC sanctions programs, SDN listings include persons designated under Executive Order 13224, Executive Order 12947, or the Antiterrorism and Effective Death Penalty Act of 1996, as amended; such persons are called "Specially Designated Global Terrorists" or "SDGTs", "Specially Designated Terrorists" or "SDTs", or "Foreign Terrorist Organizations" or "FTOs", respectively. SDN listings also include parties subject to OFAC sanctions pursuant to other list-based programs (such as counter-WMD proliferation and counter-narcotics) and country-based programs.

In addition to checking appropriate SDN listings, charities should consult OFAC's website for other information relating to sanctioned activities or countries that may implicate their operations.

[13] As discussed in Footnote 12, the SDN List is an integrated list of individuals, organizations, and entities that the U.S. Government has designated pursuant to both country-based and list-based OFAC administered sanctions programs. U.S. persons, including U.S.-based charities, are prohibited from dealing with any of the parties included on the SDN List. A charity wishing to engage in activity in a country subject to economic sanctions should contact OFAC directly about any authorizations necessary to engage in such activity. Although the SDN List includes persons meeting the criteria established in the authorities or Executive orders that define certain OFAC sanctions programs, transactions with actors not named on the SDN List may nevertheless violate U.S. sanctions due to interests of designated parties in such transactions or prohibitions owing to country-based OFAC administered sanctions programs. For example, if a charity engages in a particular transaction with a party not on the SDN List that involves the property or interests in property of a designated actor, the transaction may be subject to OFAC sanctions. This underscores the importance of charities knowing their grantees and monitoring their programs and transactions through the use of appropriate due diligence measures. Therefore, while the SDN List is a critically important compliance tool that can assist charities in meeting their legal obligations under the variety of sanctions programs that OFAC administers, it should only form one part of a charitable organization's broader risk-based approach to protect against the risks of terrorist abuse.

current country of residence; and place and date of birth. The charity should assure itself that none of these individuals is subject to OFAC sanctions.

4. Charities should be aware that other nations may have their own lists of designated terrorist-related individuals, entities, or organizations pursuant to national obligations arising from United Nations Security Council Resolution 1373 (2001).[14]

5. With respect to the key employees, members of the governing board, or other senior management described in the preceding paragraph, the charity should also consider consulting publicly available information to ensure that such parties are not reasonably suspected of activity relating to terrorism, including terrorist financing or other support; and

6. As a pre-condition to the issuance of a charitable grant, the charity should require grantees to certify that they are in compliance with all laws, statutes, and regulations restricting U.S. persons from dealing with any individuals, entities, or groups subject to OFAC sanctions, or, in the case of foreign grantees, that they do not deal with any individuals, entities, or groups subject to OFAC sanctions or any other persons known to the foreign grantee to support terrorism or to have violated OFAC sanctions.

C. The charity should conduct basic vetting of its own key employees as follows:

1. The charity should conduct a reasonable search of publicly available information to determine whether any of its key employees is suspected of activity relating to terrorism, including terrorist financing or other support. Charities should not employ a person where any terrorist-related suspicions exist; and

[14] Under United Nations Security Council Resolution 1373 (2001) (UNSCR 1373), UN Member States must generally freeze without delay the funds and other financial assets or economic resources of persons financing or otherwise supporting terrorist activity or terrorist-related individuals, entities, or organizations. In addition, UN Member States must generally prohibit their nationals from engaging in transactions with such parties. In order to implement these obligations under UNSCR 1373, each UN member state should, as a practical matter, develop its own list of parties sanctioned under the criteria of UNSCR 1373. For example, the SDN List incorporates those parties designated by the United States pursuant to its national obligations under UNSCR 1373.

The Guidelines do not legitimize or endorse the UNSCR 1373 lists adopted by foreign jurisdictions. Rather, this information is intended to assist charities in developing their own risk-based programs based upon a full understanding of the law in those jurisdictions in which they may operate. Charities operating in a foreign jurisdiction may choose to take the additional precautionary measures of determining whether that jurisdiction maintains a national list under UNSCR 1373 and screening the identities of grantee organizations (including their directors and key employees) against any such list. Such precautionary measures may protect charities from potential sanctions or other consequences to which they might be subject from foreign jurisdictions as a result of engaging in transactions with individuals, entities, or organizations deemed to be financing or otherwise supportive of terrorist activity under the laws of those jurisdictions.

2. The charity should assure itself that none of its key employees is subject to OFAC sanctions or have violated OFAC sanctions.

D. Should a charity's vetting practices lead to a finding that any of its own key employees, any of its grantees, or any of the key employees, members of the governing board, or other senior management of its grantees is suspected of activity relating to terrorism, including terrorist financing or other support, there are a number of available mechanisms and resources that a charity may utilize:

1. If the charity believes there is a match between the name of one of the individuals or organizations listed above and a name on the SDN List, the charity should take appropriate due diligence steps to ascertain whether the match is valid. These steps and further guidance are available on OFAC's Web site at http://www.treas.gov/offices/enforcement/ofac/faq/answer.shtml#hotline; and

2. The charity should provide information on any suspicious activity relating to terrorism, including terrorist financing or other support, which does not directly involve an OFAC match, through a referral form available on Treasury's Web site at http://www.treas.gov/offices/enforcement/key-issues/protecting/index.shtml. In addition, the Federal Bureau of Investigation maintains local field offices to which charities should provide such suspicious information. A list of the locations and phone numbers of the FBI's field offices is available at http://www.fbi.gov/contact/fo/fo.htm.

ANNEX TO GUIDELINES

The risk of terrorist abuse facing charitable organizations is ongoing and significant and cannot be measured from the important but relatively narrow perspective of terrorist diversion of charitable funds to support terrorist acts. Rather, terrorist abuse also includes the exploitation of charitable services and activities to radicalize vulnerable populations and cultivate support for terrorist organizations and activities. As reported through a wide range of media sources, terrorist organizations deliberately establish, infiltrate, or otherwise exploit charitable organizations to build terrorist support networks.[15] Recent developments – such as the exploitation by Lashkar e Tayyiba (a.k.a. Jamaat-ud-Dawa) and other terrorist entities/charitable fronts of relief efforts following the October 2005 earthquake in South Asia, the critical role of Hamas-associated charities in building popular support in the Palestinian territories for the terrorist organization, and Hezbollah's substantial control of charitable distribution networks in southern Lebanon – demonstrate the ongoing intent and effectiveness of terrorist organizations in exploiting charitable organizations and relief efforts.

Treasury, together with other Departments across the U.S. Government, is continuing to combat such terrorist abuse of the charitable sector by: (i) administratively sanctioning terrorist-related charities and charitable officials through terrorist financing designations; (ii) contributing financial information and investigative resources and expertise to advance criminal investigations and prosecutions of charities and charitable officials providing material support for designated terrorist organizations or activities; (iii) facilitating international action to address these abuses; and (iv) conducting comprehensive outreach to the charitable sector to raise awareness of terrorist exploitation and the steps charities can take protect themselves from such abuse.

U.S. designations of charities and charitable officials demonstrate the breadth of the problem of terrorist infiltration and exploitation of the charitable sector. To date, the United States has designated forty-three charities worldwide and twenty-nine associated individuals for their support of terrorist organizations and operations. These seventy-two charities and individuals

---

[15] *See, e.g.*, Matthew Levitt, HAMAS: Politics, Charity and Terrorism in the Service of Jihad; New Haven, CT: Yale Univ. Press, 2006 (documenting the logistical and financial support Hamas charities provide for the group's political and terrorist activities); Heather Timmons, *British Study Charitable Organizations for Links to Plot*, N.Y. TIMES, Aug. 25, 2006 (describing the risks inherent in delivering charitable aid and resources to high-risk areas where terrorist organizations are known to operate); Robert F. Worth & Hassan M. Fattah, *Relief Agencies Find Hezbollah Hard to Avoid*, N.Y. TIMES, Aug. 23, 2006 (describing Hezbollah's efforts to cultivate support by controlling the provision of charitable resources and services across southern Lebanon); Laila Bokhair, *Political Struggle Over Earthquake Victims*, Norwegian Defense Research Establishment, Nov. 23, 2005 (documenting terrorist organizations such as Lashkar-e-Taiba and Jaish-e-Mohammed efforts to provide humanitarian aid to affected areas in the months following the earthquake in South Asia); Christopher Kremmer, *Charities Linked to Extremists Lead Quake Relief*, Age, Nov. 21, 2005 (reporting that in addition to providing relief in South Asia, terrorist organizations are recruiting and indoctrinating orphan children in their extensive network of orphanages); Evan Kohlmann, *The Role of Islamic Charities in International Terrorist Recruitment and Financing* (2006), Danish Institute for International Studies: available at http://www.diis.dk/graphics/Publications/WP2006/DIIS%20WP%202006-7.web.pdf (tracing the historical link between charitable organizations and terrorist activities from the Soviet-Afghan war through to the present); BBC News, *Faith, hate and charity: Transcript*, BBC One, Recorded from Transmission, July 30, 2006 (reporting on one of Britain's leading Islamic charities, Interpal, and illustrating Interpal's use of a network of charities in Gaza and the West Bank to support and fund Hamas, a terrorist organization designated by the U.S. Government and the European Union).

comprise over fifteen percent of all U.S.-designated terrorist supporters or financiers, indicating the primary importance of charities as a critical means of support for terrorist organizations and activities. Treasury maintains a summary of all designated charities, including unclassified background information summarizing the basis of each designation, to assist the donor and charitable communities in identifying those charities associated with terrorist financing and support. Further information and press releases relating to these designations are available on the Treasury Web site at http://www.treas.gov/offices/enforcement/key-issues/protecting/charities_exec-orders.shtml.

In addition to these ongoing efforts by Treasury and the U.S. Government, other countries and organizations from around the world have recognized and helped curb abuse of the charitable sector by terrorist organizations. The Financial Action Task Force (FATF) – the premier inter-governmental organization responsible for developing and promoting global policies to combat money laundering and terrorist financing – has studied the problem of terrorist financing and abuse across the charitable sector globally and has published typologies of such abuse. The FATF has also published Best Practices for Non-Profit Organizations and more recently issued interpretive guidance strengthening the international standard for combating terrorist abuse of non-profit organizations. Additionally, FATF style regional bodies (FSRBs) such as the Asia Pacific Group (APG), Eurasian Group (EAG) and the Middle East and North Africa Financial Action Task Force (MENA FATF) are developing typologies and studies on the active threat of terrorist financing and support through charities that operate within their regions.[16] These organizations and their member countries are implementing measures to actively combat this threat through the development and application of supervisory, investigative, and financial authorities to identify and dismantle charities engaged in terrorist financing or support. Many of these documents, which underscore the threat that terrorist organizations and operations pose to the charitable sector, are available on the Treasury Web site at http://www.treas.gov/offices/enforcement/key-issues/protecting/index.shtml.

Treasury continually engages in outreach and updates its Web site to communicate useful information regarding: (i) the ongoing risks of terrorist abuse in the charitable sector; (ii) ongoing U.S. and other governmental efforts to mitigate these risks and combat terrorist abuse, and (iii) steps the sector can take to protect against such abuse. Treasury's Guidelines represent one essential component and product of the ongoing outreach that Treasury is conducting with the charitable sector to empower and protect the sector from terrorist abuse. Another example of available resources is Treasury's December 2005 advisory paper, which provides information to charities delivering relief in areas affected by the 2005 South Asia earthquake by detailing typologies of terrorist abuse of charities and reports on activity by militant and terrorist groups in those areas. This paper also shows, through media reports, the extent to which terrorist organizations pose a risk to charities trying to deliver aid in unstable areas, where terrorist

[16] The efforts of the MENA FATF are particularly exemplary of international efforts to combat terrorist abuse of charities. MENA FATF Member States have issued a best practices paper, based on the FATF's international standard for combating terrorist abuse of the non-profit sector, tailored to the specific religious, social, and economic values of the region. The comprehensive framework, crafted by the MENA FATF, outlines legislative, regulatory, and procedural measures to ensure that the charitable sector is not misused or abused by terrorist financiers. The MENA FATF charities best practices paper is an indispensable tool for the Middle East and North Africa region in helping to protect against terrorist abuse of charities by offering guidance to promote transparency and accountability in the charitable sector.

organizations themselves and/or their charitable fronts are often engaged in delivering relief as an effective recruitment mechanism in building broader support for their organizations.

Treasury will continue its outreach and informational efforts as part of its larger mission to combat terrorist financing and safeguard the charitable sector from terrorist abuse.

Form **3520**

Department of the Treasury
Internal Revenue Service

Annual Return To Report Transactions With Foreign Trusts and Receipt of Certain Foreign Gifts

▶ See separate instructions.

OMB No. 1545-0159

2008

Note: *All information must be in English. Show all amounts in U.S. dollars. File a* ***separate*** *Form 3520 for* ***each*** *foreign trust.*

For calendar year 2008, or tax year beginning , 2008, ending , 20

A Check appropriate boxes: ☐ Initial return ☐ Final return ☐ Amended return

B Check box that applies to person filing return: ☐ Individual ☐ Partnership ☐ Corporation ☐ Trust ☐ Executor

Check all applicable boxes:

☐ **(a)** You are a U.S. transferor who, directly or indirectly, transferred money or other property during the current tax year to a foreign trust, **(b)** You held an outstanding obligation of a related foreign trust (or a person related to the trust) issued during the current tax year, that you reported as a "qualified obligation" (defined in the instructions) during the current tax year, or **(c)** You are the executor of the estate of a U.S. decedent and (1) the decedent made a transfer to a foreign trust by reason of death, (2) the decedent was treated as the owner of any portion of a foreign trust immediately prior to death, or (3) the decedent's estate included any portion of the assets of a foreign trust. See the instructions for Part I.

☐ You are a U.S. owner of all or any portion of a foreign trust at any time during the tax year. See the instructions for Part II.

☐ **(a)** You are a U.S. person who, during the current tax year, received a distribution from a foreign trust, or **(b)** You are a U.S. person and you are also a grantor or beneficiary of a foreign trust that has made a loan of cash or marketable securities directly or indirectly to you during the current tax year that you reported as a "qualified obligation" (defined in the instructions) during the current tax year. See the instructions for Part III.

☐ You are a U.S. person who, during the current tax year, received certain gifts or bequests from a foreign person. See the instructions for Part IV.

Service Center where U.S. person's income tax return is filed ▶

1a Name of person(s) filing return (see instructions)			**b** Identification number
c Number, street, and room or suite no. (if a P.O. box, see instructions)			**d** Spouse's identification number
e City or town	**f** State or province	**g** ZIP or postal code	**h** Country
2a Name of foreign trust (if applicable)			**b** Employer identification number (if any)
c Number, street, and room or suite no. (if a P.O. box, see instructions)			
d City or town	**e** State or province	**f** ZIP or postal code	**g** Country

3 Did the foreign trust appoint a U.S. agent (defined in the instructions) who can provide the IRS with all relevant trust information? . . . . ☐ **Yes** ☐ **No**
If "Yes," complete lines 3a through 3g.

3a Name of U.S. agent			**b** Identification number (if any)
c Number, street, and room or suite no. (if a P.O. box, see instructions)			
d City or town	**e** State or province	**f** ZIP or postal code	**g** Country
4a Name of U.S. decedent (see instr.)	**b** Address		**c** TIN of decedent
d Date of death			**e** EIN of estate

f Check applicable box:
☐ U.S. decedent made transfer to a foreign trust by reason of death.
☐ U.S. decedent treated as owner of foreign trust immediately prior to death.
☐ Assets of foreign trust were included in estate of U.S. decedent.

Under penalties of perjury, I declare that I have examined this return, including any accompanying reports, schedules, or statements, and to the best of my knowledge and belief, it is true, correct, and complete.

▶ Signature Title Date

▶ Preparer's signature Preparer's SSN or PTIN Date

For Privacy Act and Paperwork Reduction Act Notice, see instructions. Cat. No. 19594V Form **3520** (2008)

Form 3520 (2008) Page **2**

Part I Transfers by U.S. Persons to a Foreign Trust During the Current Tax Year (see instructions)

5a Name of trust creator (if different from line 1a)	b Address	c Identification number (if any)

6a Country code of country where trust was created	b Country code of country whose law governs the trust	c Date trust was created

7a Will any person (other than the U.S. transferor or the foreign trust) be treated as the owner of the transferred assets after the transfer? ☐ Yes ☐ No

b

(i) Name of other foreign trust owners, if any	(ii) Address	(iii) Country of residence	(iv) Identification number, if any	(v) Relevant code section

8 Was the transfer a completed gift or bequest? If "Yes," see instructions . . . . ☐ Yes ☐ No

9a Now or in the future, can any part of the income or corpus of the trust benefit any U.S. beneficiary? . . . ☐ Yes ☐ No

b If "No," could the trust be revised or amended to benefit a U.S. beneficiary? . . . . ☐ Yes ☐ No

10 Will you continue to be treated as the owner of the transferred asset(s) after the transfer? . . . . ☐ Yes ☐ No

Schedule A—Obligations of a Related Trust (see instructions)

11a During the current tax year, did you transfer property (including cash) to a related foreign trust in exchange for an obligation of the trust or an obligation of a person related to the trust? See instructions . . . . ☐ Yes ☐ No
If "Yes," complete the rest of Schedule A, as applicable. If "No," go to Schedule B.

b Were any of the obligations you received (with respect to a transfer described in 11a above) qualified obligations? ☐ Yes ☐ No
If "Yes," complete the rest of Schedule A with respect to each qualified obligation.
If "No," go to Schedule B and, when completing columns (a) through (i) of line 13 with respect to each nonqualified obligation, enter "-0-" in column (h).

(i) Date of transfer giving rise to obligation	(ii) Maximum term	(iii) Yield to maturity	(iv) FMV of obligation

12 With respect to each qualified obligation you reported on line 11b: Do you agree to extend the period of assessment of any income or transfer tax attributable to the transfer, and any consequential income tax changes for each year that the obligation is outstanding, to a date 3 years after the maturity date of the obligation? . . . . . . ☐ Yes ☐ No
Note: *Generally, you must answer "Yes," if you checked "Yes" to the question on line 11b.*

Schedule B—Gratuitous Transfers (see instructions)

13 During the current tax year, did you make any transfers (directly or indirectly) to the trust and receive less than FMV, or no consideration at all, for the property transferred? . . . . ☐ Yes ☐ No
If "Yes," complete columns (a) through (i) below and the rest of Schedule B, as applicable.
If "No," go to Schedule C.

(a) Date of transfer	(b) Description of property transferred	(c) FMV of property transferred	(d) U.S. adjusted basis of property transferred	(e) Gain recognized at time of transfer	(f) Excess, if any, of column (c) over the sum of columns (d) and (e)	(g) Description of property received, if any	(h) FMV of property received	(i) Excess of column (c) over column (h)
Totals ▶					$			$

14 You are required to attach a copy of each sale or loan document entered into in connection with a transfer reported on line 13. If these documents have been attached to a Form 3520 filed within the previous 3 years, attach only relevant updates.

Are you attaching a copy of:	Yes	No	Attached Previously	Year Attached
a Sale document?	☐	☐	☐	
b Loan document?	☐	☐	☐	
c Subsequent variances to original sale or loan documents?	☐	☐	☐	

Form **3520** (2008)

Form 3520 (2008) Page **3**

Part I **Schedule B—Gratuitous Transfers** *(Continued)*

Note: *Complete lines 15 through 18 only if you answered "No" to line 3.*

15 (a) Name of beneficiary	(b) Address of beneficiary	(c) U.S. beneficiary? Yes	No	(d) Identification number, if any

16 (a) Name of trustee	(b) Address of trustee	(c) Identification number, if any

17 (a) Name of other persons with trust powers	(b) Address of other persons with trust powers	(c) Description of powers	(d) Identification number, if any

18 If you checked "No" on line 3 (or did not complete lines 3a through 3g), you are required to attach a copy of all trust documents as indicated below. If these documents have been attached to a Form 3520-A filed within the previous 3 years, attach only relevant updates.

Are you attaching a copy of:	**Yes**	**No**	**Attached Previously**	**Year Attached**
a Summary of all written and oral agreements and understandings relating to the trust?	☐	☐	☐	
b The trust instrument?	☐	☐	☐	
c Memoranda or letters of wishes?	☐	☐	☐	
d Subsequent variances to original trust documents?	☐	☐	☐	
e Trust financial statements?	☐	☐	☐	
f Other trust documents?	☐	☐	☐	

Schedule C—Qualified Obligations Outstanding in the Current Tax Year (see instructions)

19 Did you, at any time during the tax year, hold an outstanding obligation of a related foreign trust (or a person related to the trust) that you reported as a "qualified obligation" in the current tax year? ☐ **Yes** ☐ **No**
If "Yes," complete columns (a) through (e) below.

(a) Date of original obligation	(b) Tax year qualified obligation first reported	(c) Amount of principal payments made during the tax year	(d) Amount of interest payments made during the tax year	(e) Does the obligation still meet the criteria for a qualified obligation? Yes	No

Form **3520** (2008)

Form 3520 (2008) Page **4**

Part II U.S. Owner of a Foreign Trust (see instructions)

20

(a) Name of other foreign trust owners, if any	(b) Address	(c) Country of residence	(d) Identification number, if any	(e) Relevant code section

21

(a) Country code of country where foreign trust was created	(b) Country code of country whose law governs the foreign trust	(c) Date foreign trust was created

22 Did the foreign trust file Form 3520-A for the current year? . . . ☐ **Yes** ☐ **No**

If "Yes," attach the Foreign Grantor Trust Owner Statement you received from the foreign trust.

If "No," to the best of your ability, complete and attach a substitute Form 3520-A for the foreign trust.

See instructions for information on penalties.

23 Enter the gross value of the portion of the foreign trust that you are treated as owning . . . ▶ $

Part III Distributions to a U.S. Person From a Foreign Trust During the Current Tax Year (see instructions)

24 Cash amounts or FMV of property received, directly or indirectly, during the current tax year, from the foreign trust (exclude loans included on line 25).

(a) Date of distribution	(b) Description of property received	(c) FMV of property received (determined on date of distribution)	(d) Description of property transferred, if any	(e) FMV of property transferred	(f) Excess of column (c) over column (e)
Totals . . . ▶					$

25 During the current tax year, did you (or a person related to you) receive a loan from a related foreign trust (including an extension of credit upon the purchase of property from the trust)? . . . ☐ **Yes** ☐ **No**

If "Yes," complete columns (a) through (g) below for each such loan.

Note: *The FMV of an obligation (column (f)) is -0- unless it is a "qualified obligation."*

(a) FMV of loan proceeds	(b) Date of original loan transaction	(c) Maximum term of repayment of obligation	(d) Interest rate of obligation	(e) Is the obligation a "qualified obligation?"		(f) FMV of obligation	(g) Amount treated as distribution from the trust (subtract column (f) from column (a))
				Yes	No		
Total . . . ▶							$

26 With respect to each obligation you reported as a "qualified obligation" on line 25: Do you agree to extend the period of assessment of any income or transfer tax attributable to the transaction, and any consequential income tax changes for each year that the obligation is outstanding, to a date 3 years after the maturity date of the obligation? . . . ☐ **Yes** ☐ **No**

Note: *Generally, you must answer "Yes" if you checked "Yes" in column (e) of line 25.*

27 Total distributions received during the current tax year. Add line 24, column (f), and line 25, column (g). . ▶ $

28 Did the trust, at any time during the tax year, hold an outstanding obligation of yours (or a person related to you) that you reported as a "qualified obligation" in the current tax year? . . . ☐ **Yes** ☐ **No**

If "Yes," complete columns (a) through (e) below for each obligation.

(a) Date of original loan transaction	(b) Tax year qualified obligation first reported	(c) Amount of principal payments made during the tax year	(d) Amount of interest payments made during the tax year	(e) Does the loan still meet the criteria of a qualified obligation?	
				Yes	No

Form **3520** (2008)

Form 3520 (2008) Page 5

Part III Distributions to a U.S. Person From a Foreign Trust During the Current Tax Year *(Continued)*

29 Did you receive a Foreign Grantor Trust Beneficiary Statement from the foreign trust with respect to a distribution? ☐ Yes ☐ No
If "Yes," attach the statement and do not complete the remainder of Part III with respect to that distribution.
If "No," complete Schedule A with respect to that distribution. Also complete Schedule C if you enter an amount greater than zero on line 37.

30 Did you receive a Foreign Nongrantor Trust Beneficiary Statement from the foreign trust with respect to a distribution? ☐ Yes ☐ No
If "Yes," attach the statement and complete either Schedule A or Schedule B below (see instructions). Also complete Schedule C if you enter an amount greater than zero on line 37 or line 41.
If "No," complete Schedule A with respect to that distribution. Also complete Schedule C if you enter an amount greater than zero on line 37.

Schedule A—Default Calculation of Trust Distributions (see instructions)

31	Enter amount from line 27	
32	Number of years the trust has been a foreign trust (see instructions) ▶ ______	
33	Enter total distributions received from the foreign trust during the 3 preceding tax years (or during the number of years the trust has been a foreign trust, if fewer than 3)	
34	Multiply line 33 by 1.25	
35	Average distribution. Divide line 34 by 3 (or the number of years the trust has been a foreign trust, if fewer than 3) and enter the result	
36	Amount treated as ordinary income earned in the current year. Enter the smaller of line 31 or line 35	
37	Amount treated as accumulation distribution. Subtract line 36 from line 31. If -0-, do not complete the rest of Part III	
38	Applicable number of years of trust. Divide line 32 by 2 and enter the result here ▶	

Schedule B—Actual Calculation of Trust Distributions (see instructions)

39	Enter amount from line 27	
40	Amount treated as ordinary income in the current tax year	
41	Amount treated as accumulation distribution. If -0-, do not complete Schedule C, Part III	
42	Amount treated as capital gains in the current tax year	
43	Amount treated as distribution from trust corpus	
44	Enter any other distributed amount received from the foreign trust not included on lines 40, 41, 42, and 43 (attach explanation)	
45	Amount of foreign trust's aggregate undistributed net income	
46	Amount of foreign trust's weighted undistributed net income	
47	Applicable number of years of trust. Divide line 46 by line 45 and enter the result here ▶	

Schedule C—Calculation of Interest Charge (see instructions)

48	Enter accumulation distribution from line 37 or 41, as applicable	
49	Enter tax on total accumulation distribution from line 28 of Form 4970	
50	Enter applicable number of years of foreign trust from line 38 or 47, as applicable (round to nearest half-year) ▶ ______	
51	Combined interest rate imposed on the total accumulation distribution (see instructions)	
52	Interest charge. Multiply the amount on line 49 by the combined interest rate on line 51	
53	Tax attributable to accumulation distributions. Add lines 49 and 52. Enter here and as "additional tax" on your income tax return	

Form **3520** (2008)

Form 3520 (2008) Page **6**

Part IV **U.S. Recipients of Gifts or Bequests Received During the Current Tax Year From Foreign Persons** (see instructions)

54 During the current tax year, did you receive more than $100,000 that you treated as gifts or bequests from a nonresident alien or a foreign estate? See instructions for special rules regarding related donors and gifts or bequests from "covered expatriates" . . . . ☐ **Yes** ☐ **No**

If "Yes," complete columns (a) through (c) with respect to each such gift or bequest in excess of $5,000. If more space is needed, attach schedule.

(a) Date of gift or bequest	(b) Description of property received	(c) FMV of property received
Total . . . . ▶		$

55 During the current tax year, did you receive more than $13,561 that you treated as gifts from a foreign corporation or a foreign partnership? See instructions regarding related donors . . . . ☐ **Yes** ☐ **No**

If "Yes," complete columns (a) through (g) with respect to each such gift. If more space is needed, attach schedule.

(a) Date of gift	(b) Name of donor	(c) Address of donor	(d) Identification number, if any

(e) Check the box that applies to the foreign donor		(f) Description of property received	(g) FMV of property received
Corporation	Partnership		

56 Do you have any reason to believe that the foreign donor, in making any gift or bequest described in lines 54 and 55, was acting as a nominee or intermediary for any other person? If "Yes," see instructions . . . . ☐ **Yes** ☐ **No**

57 During the current tax year, did you receive a "covered gift or bequest" (as defined in section 2801(e)) of more than $12,000 from a "covered expatriate" (as defined in section 877A(g)(1)) (see instructions)? . . . . ☐ **Yes** ☐ **No**

If "Yes," complete and file Form 708, U.S. Return of Tax for Gifts and Bequests Received From Expatriates.

Form **3520** (2008)

2008

Department of the Treasury
Internal Revenue Service

Instructions for Form 3520

Annual Return To Report Transactions With Foreign Trusts and Receipt of Certain Foreign Gifts

Section references are to the Internal Revenue Code unless otherwise noted.

What's New

Line 57 of the form is new. U.S. persons who receive a covered gift or bequest of more than $12,000 from a covered expatriate are subject to a new tax under section 2801. See the instructions for line 57 for details.

General Instructions

Purpose of Form

U.S. persons (and executors of estates of U.S. decedents) file Form 3520 to report:
- Certain transactions with foreign trusts and
- Receipt of certain large gifts or bequests from certain foreign persons.

A separate Form 3520 must be filed for transactions with **each** foreign trust.

Who Must File

File Form 3520 if:

1. You are the responsible party for reporting a reportable event that occurred during the current tax year, or you held an outstanding obligation of a related foreign trust (or a person related to the trust) that you treated as a qualified obligation during the current tax year. Responsible party, reportable event, and qualified obligation are defined on pages 3 and 4.

Complete the identifying information on page 1 of the form and the relevant portions of Part I. See the instructions for Part I.

2. You are a U.S. person who, during the current tax year, is treated as the owner of any part of the assets of a foreign trust under the grantor trust rules.

Complete the identifying information on page 1 of the form and Part II. See the instructions for Part II.

3. You are a U.S. person who received (directly or indirectly) a distribution from a foreign trust during the current tax year **or** a related foreign trust held an outstanding obligation issued by you (or a person related to you) that you treated as a qualified obligation (defined on page 3) during the current tax year.

Complete the identifying information on page 1 of the form and Part III. See the instructions for Part III.

4. You are a U.S. person who, during the current tax year, received either:

a. More than $100,000 from a nonresident alien individual or a foreign estate (including foreign persons related to that nonresident alien individual or foreign estate) that you treated as gifts or bequests; or

b. More than $13,561 from foreign corporations or foreign partnerships (including foreign persons related to such foreign corporations or foreign partnerships) that you treated as gifts.

Complete the identifying information on page 1 of the form and Part IV. See the instructions for Part IV.

Note. You may also be required to file Form TD F 90-22.1, Report of Foreign Bank and Financial Accounts.

Exceptions To Filing

Form 3520 does not have to be filed to report the following transactions.
- Transfers to foreign trusts described in sections 402(b), 404(a)(4), or 404A.
- Most fair market value (FMV) transfers by a U.S. person to a foreign trust. However, some FMV transfers must nevertheless be reported on Form 3520 (e.g., transfers in exchange for obligations that are treated as qualified obligations, transfers of appreciated property to a foreign trust for which the U.S. transferor does not immediately recognize all of the gain on the property transferred, transfers involving a U.S. transferor that is related to the foreign trust). See Section III of Notice 97-34, 1997-25 I.R.B. 22.
- Transfers to foreign trusts that have a current determination letter from the IRS recognizing their status as exempt from income taxation under section 501(c)(3).
- Transfers to, ownership of, and distributions from a Canadian registered retirement savings plan (RRSP) or a Canadian registered retirement income fund (RRIF), where the U.S. citizen or resident alien holding an interest in such RRSP or RRIF is eligible to file Form 8891, U.S. Information Return for Beneficiaries of Certain Canadian Registered Retirement Plans, with respect to the RRSP or RRIF.
- Distributions from foreign trusts that are taxable as compensation for services rendered (within the meaning of section 672(f)(2)(B) and its regulations), so long as the recipient reports the distribution as compensation income on its applicable federal income tax return.
- Distributions from foreign trusts to domestic trusts that have a current determination letter from the IRS recognizing their status as exempt from income taxation under section 501(c)(3).
- Domestic trusts that become foreign trusts to the extent the trust is treated as owned by a foreign person, after application of section 672(f).

Joint Returns

Two transferors or grantors of the same foreign trust, or two U.S. beneficiaries of the same foreign trust, may file a joint Form 3520, but only if they file a joint income tax return.

Additional Reporting Information

For more information on foreign trust reporting, including abusive foreign trust schemes, go to the IRS website at *www.irs.gov.*

Cat. No. 23068I

When and Where To File

In general, Form 3520 is due on the date that your income tax return is due, including extensions. In the case of a Form 3520 filed with respect to a U.S. decedent, Form 3520 is due on the date that the estate tax return is due (or would be due if the estate were required to file a return), including extensions. Send Form 3520 to the Internal Revenue Service Center, P.O. Box 409101, Ogden, UT 84409.

Form 3520 must have all required attachments to be considered complete.

Note. If a complete Form 3520 is not filed by the due date, including extensions, the time for assessment of any tax imposed with respect to any event or period to which the information required to be reported in Parts I through III of such Form 3520 relates, will not expire before the date that is 3 years after the date on which the required information is reported. See section 6501(c)(8).

Who Must Sign

If the return is filed by:

- An individual or a fiduciary, it must be signed and dated by that individual or fiduciary.
- A partnership, it must be signed and dated by a general partner or limited liability company member.
- A corporation, it must be signed and dated by the president, vice president, treasurer, assistant treasurer, chief accounting officer, or any other corporate officer (such as a tax officer) who is authorized to sign.

The paid preparer must complete the required preparer information and:

- Sign the return in the space provided for the preparer's signature.
- Give a copy of the return to the filer.

Inconsistent Treatment of Items

The U.S. beneficiary and U.S. owner's tax return must be consistent with the Form 3520-A, Annual Information Return of Foreign Trust With a U.S. Owner, filed by the foreign trust unless you report the inconsistency to the IRS. If you are treating items on your tax return differently from the way the foreign trust treated them on its return, file Form 8082, Notice of Inconsistent Treatment or Administrative Adjustment Request (AAR). See Form 8082 for more details.

Penalties

A penalty generally applies if Form 3520 is not timely filed or if the information is incomplete or incorrect. Generally, the penalty is:

- 35% of the gross value of any property transferred to a foreign trust for failure by a U.S. transferor to report the transfer,
- 35% of the gross value of the distributions received from a foreign trust for failure by a U.S. person to report receipt of the distribution, or
- 5% of the amount of certain foreign gifts for each month for which the failure to report continues (not to exceed a total of 25%). See section 6039F(c).

If a foreign trust has a U.S. owner and the trust fails to file the required annual reports on trust activities and income, the U.S. owner is subject to a penalty equal to 5% of the gross value of the portion of the trust's assets treated as owned by the U.S. person (the gross reportable amount). See Form 3520-A.

Additional penalties may be imposed if noncompliance continues after the IRS mails a notice of failure to comply with required reporting. However, this penalty may not exceed the gross reportable amount. Also, penalties will only be imposed to the extent that the transaction is not reported. For example, if a U.S. person transfers property worth $1 million to a foreign trust but only reports $400,000 of that amount, penalties could only be imposed on the unreported $600,000.

For more information, see section 6677.

Reasonable cause. No penalties will be imposed if the taxpayer can demonstrate that the failure to comply was due to reasonable cause and not willful neglect.

Note. The fact that a foreign country would impose penalties for disclosing the required information is not reasonable cause. Similarly, reluctance on the part of a foreign fiduciary or provisions in the trust instrument that prevent the disclosure of required information is not reasonable cause.

Definitions

Distribution

A distribution is any gratuitous transfer of money or other property from a trust, whether or not the trust is treated as owned by another person under the grantor trust rules, and without regard to whether the recipient is designated as a beneficiary by the terms of the trust. A distribution includes the receipt of trust corpus and the receipt of a gift or bequest described in section 663(a).

A distribution also includes constructive transfers from a trust. For example, if charges you make on a credit card are paid by a foreign trust or guaranteed or secured by the assets of a foreign trust, the amount charged will be treated as a distribution to you by the foreign trust. Similarly, if you write checks on a foreign trust's bank account, the amount will be treated as a distribution.

Also, if you receive a payment from a foreign trust in exchange for property transferred to the trust or services rendered to the trust, and the FMV of the payment received exceeds the FMV of the property transferred or services rendered, the excess will be treated as a distribution to you.

Examples

1. If you sell stock with an FMV of $100 to a foreign trust and receive $150 in exchange, you have received a distribution of $50.
2. If you receive $100 from the trust for services performed by you for the trust, and the services have an FMV of $20, you have received a distribution of $80.

See the instructions for Part III, line 25, on page 7, for another example of a distribution from a foreign trust.

Foreign Trust and Domestic Trust

A foreign trust is any trust other than a domestic trust.

A domestic trust is any trust if:

1. A court within the United States is able to exercise primary supervision over the administration of the trust; and
2. One or more U.S. persons have the authority to control all substantial decisions of the trust.

Grantor

A grantor includes any person who creates a trust or directly or indirectly makes a gratuitous transfer of cash or other property to a trust. A grantor includes any person treated as the owner of any part of a foreign trust's assets under sections 671 through 679, excluding section 678.

Note. If a partnership or corporation makes a gratuitous transfer to a trust, the partners or shareholders are generally treated as the grantors of the trust, unless the partnership or corporation made the transfer for a business purpose of the partnership or corporation.

If a trust makes a gratuitous transfer to another trust, the grantor of the transferor trust is treated as the grantor of the transferee trust, except that if a person with a general power of appointment over the transferor trust exercises that power in favor of another trust, such person is treated as the grantor of the transferee trust, even if the grantor of the transferor trust is treated as the owner of the transferor trust.

Grantor Trust

A grantor trust is any trust to the extent that the assets of the trust are treated as owned by a person other than the trust. See the grantor trust rules in sections 671 through 679. A part of the trust may be treated as a grantor trust to the extent that only a portion of the trust assets are owned by a person other than the trust.

Gratuitous Transfer

A gratuitous transfer to a foreign trust is any transfer to the trust other than (a) a transfer for FMV or (b) a distribution to the trust with respect to an interest held by the trust (i) in an entity other than a trust (e.g., a corporation or a partnership) or (ii) in an investment trust described in Regulations section 301.7701-4(c), a liquidating trust described in Regulations section 301.7701-4(d), or an environmental remediation trust described in Regulations section 301.7701-4(e).

A transfer of property to a trust may be considered a gratuitous transfer without regard to whether the transfer is a gift for gift tax purposes (see Chapter 12 of Subtitle B of the Code).

For purposes of this determination, if a U.S. person contributes property to a trust in exchange for any type of interest in the trust, such interest in the trust will be disregarded in determining whether FMV has been received. In addition, a U.S. person will not be treated as making a transfer for FMV merely because the transferor is deemed to recognize gain on the transaction.

If you transfer property to a foreign trust in exchange for an obligation of the trust (or a person related to the trust), it will be a gratuitous transfer unless the obligation is a qualified obligation. Obligation and qualified obligation are defined below.

Gross Reportable Amount

Gross reportable amount is:

- The gross value of property involved in the creation of a foreign trust or the transfer of property to a foreign trust (including a transfer by reason of death);
- The gross value of any portion of a foreign trust treated as owned by a U.S. person under the grantor trust rules or any part of a foreign trust that is included in the gross estate of a U.S. citizen or resident;
- The gross value of assets deemed transferred at the time a domestic trust to which a U.S. citizen or resident previously transferred property becomes a foreign trust, provided such U.S. citizen or resident is alive at the time the trust becomes a foreign trust (see section 679(a)(5)); or
- The gross amount of distributions received from a foreign trust.

Gross Value

Gross value is the FMV of property as determined under section 2031 and its regulations as if the owner had died on the valuation date. Although formal appraisals are not generally required, you should keep contemporaneous records of how you arrived at your good faith estimate.

Guarantee

A guarantee:

- Includes any arrangement under which a person, directly or indirectly, assures, on a conditional or unconditional basis, the payment of another's obligation;
- Encompasses any form of credit support, and includes a commitment to make a capital contribution to the debtor or otherwise maintain its financial viability; or
- Includes an arrangement reflected in a "comfort letter," regardless of whether the arrangement gives rise to a legally enforceable obligation. If an arrangement is contingent upon the occurrence of an event, in determining whether the arrangement is a guarantee, you must assume that the event has occurred.

Nongrantor Trust

A nongrantor trust is any trust to the extent that the assets of the trust are not treated as owned by a person other than the trust. Thus, a nongrantor trust is treated as a taxable entity. A trust may be treated as a nongrantor trust with respect to only a portion of the trust assets. See *Grantor Trust* above.

Obligation

An obligation includes any bond, note, debenture, certificate, bill receivable, account receivable, note receivable, open account, or other evidence of indebtedness, and, to the extent not previously described, any annuity contract.

Owner

An owner of a foreign trust is the person that is treated as owning any of the assets of a foreign trust under the grantor trust rules.

Property

Property means any property, whether tangible or intangible, including cash.

Qualified Obligation

A qualified obligation, for purposes of this form, is any obligation only if:

1. The obligation is reduced to writing by an express written agreement;
2. The term of the obligation does not exceed 5 years (including options to renew and rollovers) and it is repaid within the 5-year term;
3. All payments on the obligation are denominated in U.S. dollars;
4. The yield to maturity of the obligation is not less than 100% of the applicable federal rate under section 1274(d) for the day on which the obligation is issued and not greater than 130% of the applicable federal rate;
5. The U.S. person agrees to extend the period for assessment of any income or transfer tax attributable to the transfer and any consequential income tax changes for each year that the obligation is outstanding, to a date not earlier than 3 years after the maturity date of the obligation, unless the maturity date of the obligation does not extend beyond the end of the U.S. person's tax year and is paid within such period (this is done on Part I, Schedule A, and Part III, as applicable); and
6. The U.S. person reports the status of the obligation, including principal and interest payments, on Part I, Schedule C, and Part III, as applicable, for each year that the obligation is outstanding.

Related Person

A related person generally includes any person who is related to you for purposes of section 267 and 707(b). This includes, but is not limited to:

- A member of your family—your brothers and sisters, half-brothers and half-sisters, spouse, ancestors (parents, grandparents, etc.), lineal descendants (children, grandchildren, etc.), and the spouses of any of these persons.
- A corporation in which you, directly or indirectly, own more than 50% in value of the outstanding stock.

See section 643(i)(2)(B) and the regulations under sections 267 and 707(b).

Person related to a foreign trust. A person is related to a foreign trust if such person, without regard to the transfer at issue, is a grantor of the trust, a beneficiary of the trust, or is related to any grantor or beneficiary of the trust. See the definition of related person on page 3.

Reportable Event

A reportable event includes:

1. The creation of a foreign trust by a U.S. person.
2. The transfer of any money or property, directly or indirectly, to a foreign trust by a U.S. person, including a transfer by reason of death. This includes transfers that are deemed to have occurred under sections 679(a)(4) and (5).
3. The death of a citizen or resident of the United States if:
   - The decedent was treated as the owner of any portion of a foreign trust under the grantor trust rules or
   - Any portion of a foreign trust was included in the gross estate of the decedent.

Responsible Party

Responsible party means:

- The grantor in the case of the creation of an inter vivos trust,
- The transferor, in the case of a reportable event (defined above) other than a transfer by reason of death, or
- The executor of the decedent's estate in any other case (whether or not the executor is a U.S. person).

U.S. Agent

A U.S. agent is a U.S. person (defined below) that has a binding contract with a foreign trust that allows the U.S. person to act as the trust's authorized U.S. agent in applying sections 7602, 7603, and 7604 with respect to:

- Any request by the IRS to examine records or produce testimony related to the proper U.S. tax treatment of amounts distributed, or required to be taken into account under the grantor trust rules, with respect to a foreign trust; or
- Any summons by the IRS for such records or testimony.

A U.S. grantor, a U.S. beneficiary, or a domestic corporation controlled by the grantor or beneficiary may act as a U.S. agent. However, you may not treat the foreign trust as having a U.S. agent unless you enter the name, address, and taxpayer identification number of the U.S. agent on lines 3a through 3g. See *Identification numbers* on page 5.

If the person identified as the U.S. agent does not produce records or testimony when requested or summoned by the IRS, the IRS may redetermine the tax consequences of your transactions with the trust and impose appropriate penalties under section 6677.

The agency relationship must be established by the time the U.S. person files Form 3520 for the relevant tax year and must continue as long as the statute of limitations remains open for the relevant tax year. If the agent resigns or liquidates, or its responsibility as an agent of the trust is terminated, see Section IV(B) of Notice 97-34.

U.S. Beneficiary

A U.S. beneficiary generally includes any U.S. person that could possibly benefit (directly or indirectly) from the trust (including an amended trust) at any time, whether or not the person is named in the trust instrument as a beneficiary and whether or not the person can receive a distribution from the trust in the current year. In addition, a U.S. beneficiary includes:

- A foreign corporation that is a controlled foreign corporation (as defined in section 957(a)),
- A foreign partnership if a U.S. person is a partner of the partnership, and
- A foreign estate or trust if the estate or trust has a U.S. beneficiary.

A foreign trust will be treated as having a U.S. beneficiary unless the terms of the trust instrument specifically prohibit any distribution of income or corpus to a U.S. person at any time, even after the death of the U.S. transferor, and the trust cannot be amended or revised to allow such a distribution.

U.S. Person

A U.S. person is:

- A citizen or resident alien of the United States (see Pub. 519, U.S. Tax Guide for Aliens, for guidance on determining resident alien status),
- A domestic partnership,
- A domestic corporation,
- Any estate (other than a foreign estate, within the meaning of section 7701(a)(31)(A)), and
- Any domestic trust (defined on page 2).

U.S. Transferor

A U.S. transferor is any U.S. person who:

1. Creates or settles a foreign trust.
2. Directly or indirectly transfers money or property to a foreign trust. This includes a U.S. citizen or resident who has made a deemed transfer under section 679(a)(4) or a U.S. resident who has made a deemed transfer under section 679(a)(5).
3. Makes a sale to a foreign trust if the sale was at other than arm's-length terms or was to a related foreign trust, or makes (or guarantees) a loan to a related foreign trust.
4. Is the executor of the estate of a U.S. person and:

a. The decedent made a testamentary transfer (a transfer by reason of death) to a foreign trust,

b. Immediately prior to death, the decedent was treated as the owner of any portion of a foreign trust under the grantor trust rules, or

c. Any portion of a foreign trust's assets were included in the estate of the decedent.

Generally, the person defined as the transferor is the responsible party (defined above) who must ensure that required information be provided or pay appropriate penalties.

Specific Instructions

Period Covered

File the 2008 return for calendar year 2008 and fiscal years that begin in 2008 and end in 2009. For a fiscal year, fill in the tax year space at the top of the form.

Item A—Initial Return, Final Return, Amended Return

Initial return. If this is the first return you are filing concerning the foreign trust identified, check the "Initial return" box.

Final return. If no further returns for transactions with the foreign trust are required, check the "Final return" box.

Example. If you annually filed Part II, Form 3520, because you were the owner of the trust for U.S. income tax purposes and the trust has terminated within the tax year, that year's return would be a final return with respect to that foreign trust.

Amended return. If this Form 3520 is filed to amend a Form 3520 that you previously filed, check the "Amended return" box.

Identifying Information

Service Center. Generally, enter the name of the Service Center where you file your income tax return. However, if you are an executor filing a Form 3520 with respect to a U.S. decedent, provide both the name of the Service Center where the decedent's final income tax return will be filed, and the name of the Service Center where the estate tax return will be filed. Please enter the information as follows. First enter the name of the Service Center where the decedent's final income tax return will be filed. Then enter the name of the Service Center where the estate tax return will be filed, followed by "(estate tax return)."

If your income tax return is filed electronically, enter "e-filed."

Identification numbers. Use social security numbers or individual taxpayer identification numbers to identify individuals. Use employer identification numbers to identify estates, trusts, partnerships, and corporations.

CAUTION *Do not enter a preparer tax identification number (PTIN) in any entry space on Form 3520 other than the entry space for "Preparer's SSN or PTIN" at the bottom of page 1 of the form.*

Address. Include the suite, room, or other unit number after the street address. If the post office does not deliver mail to the street address and the U.S. person has a P.O. box, show the box number instead.

Foreign address. Do **not** abbreviate the country name.

Line 1. This line identifies the person that is filing Form 3520. If you and your spouse are both making transfers to the same trust and you file joint returns, you may file only one Form 3520. Put the names and taxpayer identification numbers in the same order as they appear on your Form 1040.

Line 4. If you are the executor of the estate of a U.S. citizen or resident, you must provide information about the decedent on lines 4a through 4e. You must also check the applicable box on line 4f to indicate which of the following applies: the U.S. decedent made a transfer to a foreign trust by reason of death, the U.S. decedent was treated as the owner of a portion of a foreign trust immediately prior to death, or the estate of the U.S. decedent included assets of a foreign trust.

Part I—Transfers by U.S. Persons to a Foreign Trust During the Current Tax Year

Complete Part I for information on a reportable event (defined on page 4).

Note. Although the basic reporting requirements for Form 3520 are contained in section 6048 (and are clarified by Notice 97-34), the reporting requirements have been clarified by the regulations under sections 679 and 684. Accordingly, the regulations under sections 679 and 684 should be referred to for additional clarification for transfers that are required to be reported in Part I of Form 3520.

Line 5. If you are not the trust creator, enter the name of the person that created or originally settled the foreign trust.

Line 6. See the list of country codes on pages 11, 12, and 13. If the country is not included in the list, enter "OC" for "other country" and enter the country's name.

Lines 7, 8, and 10. If you are reporting multiple transfers to a single foreign trust and the answers to lines 7, 8, or 10 are different for various transfers, complete a separate line for each transfer on duplicate copies of the relevant pages of the form.

Line 7a. If "Yes," you must comply with the reporting requirements that would apply to a direct transfer to that other person. For example, if that other person is a foreign partnership, you must comply with the reporting requirements for transfers to foreign partnerships (see Form 8865, Return of U.S. Persons With Respect to Certain Foreign Partnerships).

Line 8. If the transfer was a completed gift (see Regulations section 25.2511-2) or bequest, you may have to file Form 706, United States Estate (and Generation-Skipping Transfer) Tax Return, or Form 709, United States Gift (and Generation-Skipping Transfer) Tax Return.

Line 9. See definition of U.S. beneficiary on page 4.

Line 10. If you are treated as the owner of any portion of the foreign trust under the grantor trust rules, answer "Yes" to this question and complete Part II.

Schedule A—Obligations of a Related Trust

Line 11a. The FMV of an obligation of the trust (or an obligation of another person related to the trust) that you receive in exchange for the transferred property equals zero, unless the obligation meets the requirements of a qualified obligation. See page 3 for the definitions of obligation and qualified obligation. See page 4 for the definition of person related to a foreign trust.

Lines 12 and 26. If you answered "Yes" to the question on line 11b (line 25, column (e)) with respect to any obligation, you generally must answer "Yes" to the question on line 12 (line 26). By so doing, you agree to extend the period of assessment of any income or transfer tax attributable to the transfer and any consequential income tax changes for each year that the obligation is outstanding. This form will be deemed to be agreed upon and executed by the IRS for purposes of Regulations section 301.6501(c)-1(d).

If you answer "No" to the question on line 12 (line 26), you generally may not treat an obligation as a qualified obligation on line 11b (line 25, column (e)). The one exception to this is if the maturity date of the obligation does not extend beyond the end of your tax year for which you are reporting and such obligation is paid within that tax year.

Schedule B—Gratuitous Transfers

Complete the applicable portions of Schedule B with respect to all reportable events (defined on page 4) that took place during the current tax year.

Line 13

- In your description, indicate whether the property is tangible or intangible.
- You may aggregate transfers of cash during the year on a single line of line 13.

• If there is not enough space on the form, please attach a statement.
• For transfers reported on attachments, you must enter "Attachment" on one of the lines in column (b), and enter the total amount of transfers reported on the attachment on line 13, columns (c), (d), (e), (f), (h), and (i).

Note. Penalties may be imposed for failure to report all required information. See *Penalties* on page 2.

Line 13, column (e). Only include gain that is immediately recognized at the time of the transfer.

Note. For any transfer by a U.S. person to a foreign nongrantor trust after August 4, 1997, the transfer is treated as a sale or exchange and the transferor must recognize as a gain the excess of the FMV of the transferred property over its adjusted basis. Although the gain is not recognized on Form 3520, it must be reported on the appropriate form or schedule of the transferor's income tax return. See section 684.

Line 13, column (f). Generally, if the reported transaction is a sale, you should report the gain on the appropriate form or schedule of your income tax return.

Line 15. Enter the name, address, whether the person is a U.S. beneficiary (defined on page 4), and taxpayer identification number, if any, of all reportable beneficiaries. Include specified beneficiaries, classes of discretionary beneficiaries, and names or classes of any beneficiaries that could be named as additional beneficiaries. If there is not enough space on the form, please attach a statement.

Line 17. Enter the name, address, and taxpayer identification number (if any) of any person, other than those listed on line 16, that has significant powers over the trust (e.g., "protectors," "enforcers," any person that must approve trustee decisions or otherwise direct trustees, any person with a power of appointment, any person with powers to remove or appoint trustees, etc.). Include a description of each person's powers. If there is not enough space, attach a statement.

Line 18. If you checked "No" on line 3 (or you did not complete lines 3a through 3g) attach:
• A summary of the terms of the trust that includes a summary of any oral agreements or understandings you have with the trustee, whether or not legally enforceable.
• A copy of all trust documents (and any revisions), including the trust instrument, any memoranda of wishes prepared by the trustees summarizing the settlor's wishes, any letter of wishes prepared by the settlor summarizing his or her wishes, and any similar documents.
• A copy of the trust's financial statements, including a balance sheet and an income statement similar to those shown on Form 3520-A. These financial statements must reasonably reflect the trust's accumulated income under U.S. income tax principles. For example, the statements must not treat capital gains as additions to trust corpus.

Schedule C—Qualified Obligations Outstanding in the Current Tax Year

Line 19. Provide information on the status of outstanding obligations of the foreign trust (or person related to the foreign trust) that you reported as a qualified obligation in the current tax year. This information is required in order to retain the obligation's status as a qualified obligation. If relevant, attach a statement describing any changes in the terms of the qualified obligation.

If the obligation fails to retain the status of a qualified obligation, you will be treated as having made a gratuitous transfer to the foreign trust, which must be reported on Schedule B, Part I. See Section III(C)(2) of Notice 97-34.

Part II—U.S. Owner of a Foreign Trust

Complete Part II if you are considered the owner of any assets of a foreign trust under the grantor trust rules during the tax year. You are required to enter a taxpayer identification number for such foreign trust on line 2b.

Line 20. Enter information regarding any person other than yourself who is considered the owner of any portion of the trust under the grantor trust rules. Also, enter in column (e) the specific Code section that causes that person to be considered an owner for U.S. income tax purposes. See the grantor trust rules under sections 671 through 679.

Line 21. See the list of country codes on pages 11, 12, and 13. If the country is not included in the list, enter "OC" for "other country" and the country's name.

Line 22. If "Yes," the copy of the Foreign Grantor Trust Owner Statement (page 3 of Form 3520-A) should show the amount of the foreign trust's income that is attributable to you for U.S. income tax purposes. See Section IV of Notice 97-34.

If "No," you may be liable for a penalty of 5% of the trust assets that you are treated as owning, plus additional penalties for continuing failure to file after notice by the IRS. See section 6677. Also see *Penalties* on page 2.

Line 23. Enter the FMV of the trust assets that you are treated as owning. Include all assets at FMV as of the end of the tax year. For this purpose, disregard all liabilities. The trust should send you this information in connection with its Form 3520-A. If you did not receive such information (line 9 of the Foreign Grantor Trust Owner Statement) from the trust, complete line 23 to the best of your ability. At a minimum, include the value of all assets that you have transferred to the trust. Also use Form 8082 to notify the IRS that you did not receive a Foreign Grantor Trust Owner Statement. However, filing Form 8082 does not relieve you of any penalties that may be imposed under section 6677. See *Penalties* on page 2.

Part III—Distributions to a U.S. Person From a Foreign Trust During the Current Tax Year

If you received an amount from a portion of a foreign trust of which you are treated as the owner and you have correctly reported any information required on Part II and the trust has filed a Form 3520-A with the IRS, do not separately disclose distributions again in Part III. If you received an amount from a foreign trust that would require a report under both Parts III and IV (gifts and bequests) of Form 3520, report the amount only in Part III.

Line 24. Report any cash or other property that you received (actually or constructively, directly or indirectly) during the current tax year, from a foreign trust, whether or not taxable, unless the amount is a loan to you from the trust that must be reported on line 25. For example, if you are a partner in a partnership that receives a distribution from a foreign trust, you must report your allocable share of such payment as an indirect distribution from the trust.

Line 24, column (c). The filer is permitted to enter the basis of the property in the hands of the beneficiary (as determined under section 643(e)(1)), if lower than the FMV of the property, but only if the taxpayer is not required to complete Schedule A (lines 31 through 38) due to lack of documentation. For these purposes, lack of documentation refers to a situation in which the filer checked "No" on line 29 or 30 because (a) the beneficiary did not receive a Foreign Grantor Trust Beneficiary Statement or a Foreign Nongrantor Trust Beneficiary Statement from the trust or (b) such statement did not contain all six of the items specified under the instructions for line 29 or line 30 below.

Line 25. If you, or a person related to you, received a loan from a related foreign trust, it will be treated as a distribution to you unless the obligation you issued in exchange is a qualified obligation.

For this purpose, a loan to you by an unrelated third party that is guaranteed by a foreign trust is generally treated as a loan from the trust.

Line 25, column (e). Answer "Yes" if your obligation given in exchange for the loan is a qualified obligation (defined on page 3).

Line 26. See *Lines 12 and 26* on page 5.

Line 27. Penalties may be imposed for failure to accurately report all distributions received during the current tax year. See *Penalties* on page 2.

Line 28. Provide information on the status of any outstanding obligation to the foreign trust that you reported as a qualified obligation in the current tax year. This information is required in order to retain the obligation's status as a qualified obligation. If relevant, attach a statement describing any changes to the terms of the qualified obligation. If the obligation fails to retain the status of a qualified obligation, you will be treated as having received a distribution from the foreign trust, which must be reported as such on line 25. See Section V(A) of Notice 97-34.

Lines 29 and 30. If any of the six items required for the Foreign Grantor Trust Beneficiary Statement (see *Line 29* below) or for the Foreign Nongrantor Trust Beneficiary Statement (see *Line 30* below) is missing, you must check "No" on line 29 or line 30, as applicable.

Also, if you answer "Yes" to line 29 or line 30, and the foreign trust or U.S. agent does not produce records or testimony when requested or summoned by the IRS, the IRS may redetermine the tax consequences of your transactions with the trust and impose appropriate penalties under section 6677.

Line 29. If "Yes," attach the Foreign Grantor Trust Beneficiary Statement (page 4 of Form 3520-A) from the foreign trust and do not complete the rest of Part III with respect to the distribution. If a U.S. beneficiary receives a complete Foreign Grantor Trust Beneficiary Statement with respect to a distribution during the tax year, the beneficiary should treat the distribution for income tax purposes as if it came directly from the owner. For example, if the distribution is a gift, the beneficiary should not include the distribution in gross income.

In addition to basic identifying information (i.e., name, address, TIN, etc.) about the foreign trust and its trustee, this statement must contain these items:

1. The first and last day of the tax year of the foreign trust to which this statement applies.
2. An explanation of the facts necessary to establish that the foreign trust should be treated for U.S. tax purposes as owned by another person. (The explanation should identify the Code section that treats the trust as owned by another person.)
3. A statement identifying whether the owner of the trust is an individual, corporation, or partnership.
4. A description of property (including cash) distributed or deemed distributed to the U.S. person during the tax year, and the FMV of the property distributed.
5. A statement that the trust will permit either the IRS or the U.S. beneficiary to inspect and copy the trust's permanent books of account, records, and such other documents that are necessary to establish that the trust should be treated for U.S. tax purposes as owned by another person. This statement is not necessary if the trust has appointed a U.S. agent.
6. A statement as to whether the foreign trust has appointed a U.S. agent (defined on page 4). If the trust has a U.S. agent, include the name, address, and taxpayer identification number of the agent.

Line 30. If "Yes," attach the Foreign Nongrantor Trust Beneficiary Statement from the foreign trust. A Foreign Nongrantor Trust Beneficiary Statement must include the following items:

1. An explanation of the appropriate U.S. tax treatment of any distribution or deemed distribution for U.S. tax purposes, or sufficient information to enable the U.S. beneficiary to establish the appropriate treatment of any distribution or deemed distribution for U.S. tax purposes.
2. A statement identifying whether any grantor of the trust is a partnership or a foreign corporation. If so, attach an explanation of the relevant facts.
3. A statement that the trust will permit either the IRS or the U.S. beneficiary to inspect and copy the trust's permanent books of account, records, and such other documents that are necessary to establish the appropriate treatment of any distribution or deemed distribution for U.S. tax purposes. This statement is not necessary if the trust has appointed a U.S. agent.
4. The Foreign Nongrantor Trust Beneficiary Statement must also include items 1, 4, and 6, as listed for line 29 above as well as basic identifying information (e.g., name, address, TIN, etc.) about the foreign trust and its trustee.

Schedule A—Default Calculation of Trust Distributions

If you answered "Yes" to line 30, you may complete either Schedule A or Schedule B. Generally, however, if you complete Schedule A in the current year (or did so in the prior years), you must continue to complete Schedule A for all future years, even if you are able to answer "Yes" to line 30 in that future year. (The only exception to this consistency rule is that you may use Schedule B in the year that a trust terminates, but only if you are able to answer "Yes" to line 30 in the year of termination.)

Line 32. To the best of your knowledge, state the number of years the trust has been in existence as a foreign trust and attach an explanation of your basis for this statement. Consider any portion of a year to be a complete year. If this is the first year that the trust has been a foreign trust, do not complete the rest of Part III (you do not have an accumulation distribution).

Line 33. Enter the total amount of distributions that you received during the 3 preceding tax years (or the number of years the trust has been a foreign trust, if less than 3). For example, if a trust distributed $50 in year 1, $120 in year 2, and $150 in year 3, the amount reported on line 33 would be $320 ($50 + $120 + $150).

Line 35. Divide line 34 by 3 (or the number of years the trust has been a foreign trust if fewer than 3). Consider any portion of a year to be a complete year. For example, a foreign trust created on July 1, 2006, would be treated on a 2008 calendar year return as having 2 preceding years (2006 and 2007). In this case, you would calculate the amount on line 35 by dividing line 34 by 2. Do not disregard tax years in which no distributions were made. The IRS will consider your proof of these prior distributions as adequate records to demonstrate that any distribution up to the amount on line 31 is not an accumulation distribution in the current tax year.

Line 36. Enter this amount as ordinary income on your tax return. Report this amount on the appropriate schedule of your tax return (e.g., Schedule E (Form 1040), Part III).

Note. If there is an amount on line 37, you must also complete line 38 and *Schedule C — Calculation of Interest Charge*, to determine the amount of any interest charge you may owe.

Schedule B—Actual Calculation of Trust Distributions

You may only use Schedule B if:

- You answered "Yes" to line 30,
- You attach a copy of the Foreign Nongrantor Trust Beneficiary Statement to this return, and
- You have never before used Schedule A for this foreign trust or this foreign trust terminated during the tax year.

Line 40. Enter the amount received by you from the foreign trust that is treated as ordinary income of the trust in the current tax year. Ordinary income is all income that is not capital gains. Report this amount on the appropriate schedule of your tax return (e.g., Schedule E (Form 1040), Part III).

Line 42. Enter the amount received by you from the foreign trust that is treated as capital gain income of that trust in the current tax year. Report this amount on the appropriate schedule of your tax return (e.g., Schedule D (Form 1040)).

Line 45. Enter the foreign trust's aggregate undistributed net income (UNI). For example, assume that a trust was created in 2002 and has made no distributions prior to 2008. Assume the trust's ordinary income was $0 in 2007, $60 in 2006, $124 in 2005, $87 in 2004, $54 in 2003, and $25 in 2002. Thus, for 2008, the trust's UNI would be $350. If the trust earned $100 and distributed $200 during 2008 (so that $100 was distributed from accumulated earnings), the trust's 2009 aggregate UNI would be $250 ($350 + $100 - $200).

Line 46. Enter the foreign trust's weighted undistributed net income (weighted UNI). The trust's weighted UNI is its accumulated income that has not been distributed, weighted by the years that it has accumulated income. To calculate weighted UNI, multiply the undistributed income from each of the trust's years by the number of years since that year, and then add each year's result. Using the example from line 45, the trust's weighted UNI in 2008 would be $1,260, calculated as follows:

Year	No. of years since that year	UNI from each year	Weighted UNI
2007	1	$ 0	$ 0
2006	2	60	120
2005	3	124	372
2004	4	87	348
2003	5	54	270
2002	6	25	150
TOTAL		$350	$1,260

To calculate the trust's weighted UNI for the following year (2009), the trust could update this calculation, or the weighted UNI shown on line 46 of the 2008 Form 3520 could simply be updated using the following steps:

1. Begin with the 2008 weighted UNI.
2. Add UNI at the beginning of 2008.
3. Add trust earnings in 2008.
4. Subtract trust distributions in 2008.
5. Subtract weighted trust accumulation distributions in 2008. (Weighted trust accumulation distributions are the trust accumulation distributions in 2008 multiplied by the applicable number of years from 2008.)

Using the examples above, the trust's 2009 weighted UNI would be $1,150, calculated as follows.

2008 weighted UNI	$1,260
UNI at beginning of 2008	+ 350
Trust earnings in 2008	+ 100
Trust distributions in 2008	- 200
Weighted trust accumulation distributions in 2008 ($100 X 3.6)	- 360
2009 weighted UNI	$1,150

Line 47. Calculate the trust's applicable number of years by dividing line 46 by line 45. Using the examples in the instructions for lines 45 and 46, the trust's applicable number of years would be 3.6 in 2008 (1,260/350) and 4.6 in 2009 (1,150/250).

Note. Include as many decimal places as there are digits in the UNI on line 45 (e.g., using the example in the instructions for line 45, include three decimal places).

Schedule C—Calculation of Interest Charge

Complete Schedule C if you entered an amount on line 37 or line 41.

Line 49. Include the amount from line 48 of this form on line 1, Form 4970. Then compute the tax on the total accumulation distribution using lines 1 through 28 of Form 4970. Enter on line 49 the tax from line 28 of Form 4970, Tax on Accumulation Distribution of Trusts.

Note. Use Form 4970 as a worksheet and attach it to Form 3520.

Line 51. Interest accumulates on the tax (line 49) for the period beginning on the date that is the applicable number of years (as rounded on line 50) prior to the applicable date and ending on the applicable date. For purposes of making this interest calculation, the applicable date is the date that is mid-year through the tax year for which reporting is made (e.g., in the case of a 2008 calendar year taxpayer, the applicable date would be June 30, 2008). Alternatively, if you received only a single distribution during the tax year that is treated as an accumulation distribution, you may use the date of that distribution as the applicable date.

For portions of the interest accumulation period that are prior to 1996 (and after 1976), interest accumulates at a simple rate of 6% annually, without compounding. For portions of the interest accumulation period that are after 1995, interest is compounded daily at the rate imposed on underpayments of tax under section 6621(a)(2). This compounded interest for periods after 1995 is imposed not only on the tax, but also on the total simple interest attributable to pre-1996 periods.

If you are a 2008 calendar year taxpayer and you use June 30, 2008, as the applicable date for calculating interest, use the table below to determine the combined interest rate and enter it on line 51. If you are not a 2008 calendar year taxpayer or you choose to use the actual date of the distribution as the applicable date, calculate the combined interest rate using the above principles and enter it on line 51.

Table of Combined Interest Rate Imposed on the Total Accumulation Distribution

Look up the applicable number of years of the foreign trust that you entered on line 50. Read across to find the combined interest rate to enter on line 51. Use this table only if you are a 2008 calendar year taxpayer and are using June 30, 2008, as the applicable date.

Applicable number of years of trust (from line 50)	Combined interest rate (enter on line 51)
1	0.0753
1.5	0.1189
2	0.1649
2.5	0.2060
3	0.2462
3.5	0.2807
4	0.3100
4.5	0.3396
5	0.3704
5.5	0.4048
6	0.4479
6.5	0.4916
7	0.5452
7.5	0.6117
8	0.6863
8.5	0.7591
9	0.8314
9.5	0.9009
10	0.9791
10.5	1.0642
11	1.1600
11.5	1.2586
12	1.3631
12.5	1.4652
13	1.5391
13.5	1.6131
14	1.6870
14.5	1.7610
15	1.8349
15.5	1.9089
16	1.9828
16.5	2.0568
17	2.1308
17.5	2.2047
18	2.2787
18.5	2.3526
19	2.4266
19.5	2.5005
20	2.5745
20.5	2.6484
21	2.7224
21.5	2.7963
22	2.8703
22.5	2.9443
23	3.0182
23.5	3.0922
24	3.1661
24.5	3.2401
25	3.3140
25.5	3.3880
26	3.4619
26.5	3.5359
27	3.6098
27.5	3.6838
28	3.7578
28.5	3.8317
29	3.9057
29.5	3.9796
30	4.0536
30.5	4.1275
31	4.2015
All Years Greater than 31	4.2754

(**Note.** Interest charges began in 1977.)

Line 53. Report this amount as additional tax (ADT) on the appropriate line of your income tax return (e.g., for Form 1040 filers, include this amount as part of the total for line 61 of your 2008 Form 1040 and enter "ADT" to the left of the line 61 entry space).

Part IV—U.S. Recipients of Gifts or Bequests Received During the Current Tax Year From Foreign Persons

Note. Penalties may be imposed for failure to report gifts that should be reported. See *Penalties* on page 2.

A gift to a U.S. person does not include any amount paid for qualified tuition or medical payments made on behalf of the U.S. person.

If a foreign trust makes a distribution to a U.S. beneficiary, the beneficiary must report the amount as a distribution in Part III, rather than as a gift in Part IV.

Contributions of property by foreign persons to domestic or foreign trusts that have U.S. beneficiaries are not reportable by those beneficiaries in Part IV unless they are treated as receiving the contribution in the year of the transfer (e.g., the beneficiary is an owner of that portion of the trust under section 678).

A domestic trust that is not treated as owned by another person is required to report the receipt of a contribution to the trust from a foreign person as a gift in Part IV.

A domestic trust that is treated as owned by a foreign person is not required to report the receipt of a contribution to the trust from a foreign person. However, a U.S. person should report the receipt of a distribution from such a trust as a gift from a foreign person in Part IV.

Line 54. To calculate the threshold amount ($100,000), you must aggregate gifts from different foreign nonresident aliens and foreign estates if you know (or have reason to know) that those persons are related to each other (see definition of related person on page 3) or one is acting as a nominee or intermediary for the other. For example, if you receive a gift of $75,000 from nonresident alien individual A and a gift of $40,000 from nonresident alien individual B, and you know that A and B are related, you must answer "Yes" and complete columns (a) through (c) for each gift.

If you answered "Yes" to the question on line 54 and none of the gifts or bequests received exceeds $5,000, do not complete columns (a) through (c) of line 54. Instead, enter in column (b) of the first line: "No gifts or bequests exceed $5,000."

Note. Include gifts or bequests from a "covered expatriate" (as defined in section 877A(g)(1)) when calculating the $100,000 threshold amount.

Line 55. Answer "Yes" if you received aggregate amounts in excess of $13,561 during the current tax year that you treated as gifts from foreign corporations or foreign partnerships (or any persons that you know (or have reason to know) are related to such foreign corporations or foreign partnerships).

For example, if you, a calendar-year taxpayer during 2008, received $6,000 from foreign corporation X that you treated as a gift, and $8,000 that you received from nonresident alien A that you treated as a gift, and you know that X is wholly owned by A, you must complete columns (a) through (g) for each gift.

Note. Gifts from foreign corporations or foreign partnerships are subject to recharacterization by the IRS under section 672(f)(4).

Line 56. If you answered "Yes" to the question on line 56 and the ultimate donor on whose behalf the reporting donor is acting is a foreign corporation or foreign partnership, attach an explanation including the ultimate foreign donor's name, address, identification number (if any), and status as a corporation or partnership.

If the ultimate donor is a foreign trust, treat the amount received as a distribution from a foreign trust and complete Part III.

Line 57. Answer "Yes" if, during the current tax year, you received a "covered gift or bequest" (as defined in section 2801(e)) of more than $12,000 from a "covered expatriate" (as defined in section 877A(g)(1)).

Important. Answer "Yes" only in the case of "covered gifts and bequests" received on or after June 17, 2008 from transferors (or from the estates of transferors) whose expatriation date is on or after June 17, 2008.

Note. If you answer "Yes" to the question on line 57, complete and file Form 708. Presently, the IRS is developing this form. When available, this form will be posted at *www.irs.gov.* If Form 708 is not available at the time you file your income tax return, attach a separate statement to your income tax return which shows your computation of the section 2801 tax.

Privacy Act and Paperwork Reduction Act Notice. We ask for the information on this form to carry out the Internal Revenue laws of the United States. You are required to give us the information. We need it to ensure that you are complying with these laws and to allow us to figure and collect the right amount of tax.

Our authority to ask for information is sections 6001, 6011, and 6012(a) and their regulations, which require you to file a return or statement with us for any tax for which you are liable. Your response is mandatory under these sections. Section 6109 requires filers and return preparers to provide their identification numbers. This is so we know who you are, and can process your return and other papers. You must fill in all parts of the tax form that apply to you.

You are not required to provide the information requested on a form that is subject to the Paperwork Reduction Act unless the form displays a valid OMB control number. Books or records relating to a form or its instructions must be retained as long as their contents may become material in the administration of any Internal Revenue law. Generally, tax returns and return information are confidential, as required by section 6103. However, section 6103 allows or requires the Internal Revenue Service to disclose or give the information shown on your tax return to others as described in the Code. For example, we may disclose your tax information to the Department of Justice to enforce the tax laws, both civil and criminal, and to cities, states, the District of Columbia, and U.S. commonwealths or possessions to carry out their tax laws. We may also disclose this information to other countries under a tax treaty, to federal and state agencies to enforce federal nontax criminal laws, or to federal law enforcement and intelligence agencies to combat terrorism. Failure to provide this information, or providing false information, may subject you to fines or penalties.

Please keep this notice with your records. It may help you if we ask you for other information. If you have any questions about the rules for filing and giving information, please call or visit any Internal Revenue Service office.

The time needed to complete and file this form and related schedules will vary depending on individual circumstances. The estimated burden for individual taxpayers filing this form is approved under OMB control number 1545-0074 and is included in the estimates shown in the instructions for their individual income tax return. The estimated burden for all other taxpayers who file this form is shown below.

Recordkeeping	42 hr., 48 min.
Learning about the law or the form	4 hr., 50 min.
Preparing the form	6 hr., 40 min.
Sending the form to the IRS	16 min.

If you have comments concerning the accuracy of these time estimates or suggestions for making this form simpler, we would be happy to hear from you. You can write to the Internal Revenue Service, Tax Products Coordinating Committee, SE:W:CAR:MP:T:T:SP, 1111 Constitution Ave. NW, IR-6526, Washington, DC 20224. Do not send the tax form to this office. Instead, see *When and Where To File* on page 2.

Country Codes

Enter on lines 6a and 6b and line 21, columns (a) and (b), the codes from the list below.

Country	Country Code
Afghanistan	AF
Akrotiri	AX
Albania	AL
Algeria	AG
American Samoa	AQ
Andorra	AN
Angola	AO
Anguilla	AV
Antarctica	AY
Antigua and Barbuda	AC
Argentina	AR
Armenia	AM
Aruba	AA
Ashmore and Cartier Islands	AT
Australia	AS
Austria	AU
Azerbaijan	AJ
Bahamas	BF
Bahrain	BA
Baker Island	FQ
Bangladesh	BG
Barbados	BB
Belarus	BO
Belgium	BE
Belize	BH
Benin	BN
Bermuda	BD
Bhutan	BT
Bolivia	BL
Bosnia-Herzegovina	BK
Botswana	BC
Bouvet Island	BV
Brazil	BR
British Indian Ocean Territory	IO
Brunei	BX
Bulgaria	BU
Burkina Faso	UV
Burma	BM
Burundi	BY

Country	Country Code
Cambodia	CB
Cameroon	CM
Canada	CA
Cape Verde	CV
Cayman Islands	CJ
Central African Republic	CT
Chad	CD
Chile	CI
China, People's Republic of (including Inner Mongolia, Tibet and Manchuria)	CH
Christmas Island	KT
Clipperton Island	IP
Cocos (Keeling) Islands	CK
Colombia	CO
Comoros	CN
Congo (Brazzaville)	CF
Congo, Democratic Republic of (Kinshasa)	CG
Cook Islands	CW
Coral Sea Islands	CR
Costa Rica	CS
Cote d'Ivoire (Ivory Coast)	IV
Croatia	HR
Cuba	CU
Cyprus	CY
Czech Republic	EZ
Denmark	DA
Dhekelia	DX
Djibouti	DJ
Dominica	DO
Dominican Republic	DR
East Timor	TT
Ecuador	EC
Egypt	EG
El Salvador	ES
Equatorial Guinea	EK
Eritrea	ER
Estonia	EN
Ethiopia	ET
Falkland Islands (Islas Malvinas)	FK

Country	Country Code
Faroe Islands	FO
Fiji	FJ
Finland	FI
France	FR
French Polynesia	FP
French Southern & Antarctic Lands	FS
Gabon	GB
Gambia	GA
Georgia	GG
Germany	GM
Ghana	GH
Gibraltar	GI
Greece	GR
Greenland	GL
Grenada	GJ
Guadeloupe	GP
Guam	GQ
Guatemala	GT
Guernsey	GK
Guinea	GV
Guinea-Bissau	PU
Guyana	GY
Haiti	HA
Heard Island and McDonald Islands	HM
Holy See	VT
Honduras	HO
Hong Kong	HK
Howland Island	HQ
Hungary	HU
Iceland	IC
India	IN
Indonesia	ID
Iran	IR
Iraq	IZ
Ireland	EI
Isle of Man	IM
Israel	IS
Italy	IT
Jamaica	JM
Jan Mayen	JN
Japan	JA
Jarvis Island	DQ
Jersey	JE

-11-

Country	Country Code
Johnston Atoll	JQ
Jordan	JO
Kazakhstan	KZ
Kenya	KE
Kingman Reef	KQ
Kiribati	KR
Korea, North	KN
Korea, South	KS
Kosovo, Republic of	KV
Kuwait	KU
Kyrgyzstan	KG
Laos	LA
Latvia	LG
Lebanon	LE
Lesotho	LT
Liberia	LI
Libya	LY
Liechtenstein	LS
Lithuania	LH
Luxembourg	LU
Macau	MC
Macedonia	MK
Madagascar	MA
Malawi	MI
Malaysia	MY
Maldives	MV
Mali	ML
Malta	MT
Marshall Islands	RM
Martinique	MB
Mauritania	MR
Mauritus	MP
Mayotte	MF
Mexico	MX
Micronesia, Federated States of	FM
Midway Islands	MQ
Moldova	MD
Monaco	MN
Mongolia	MG
Montenegro	MJ
Montserrat	MH
Morocco	MO
Mozambique	MZ

Country	Country Code
Namibia	WA
Nauru	NR
Navassa Island	BQ
Nepal	NP
Netherlands	NL
Netherlands Antilles	NT
New Caledonia	NC
New Zealand	NZ
Nicaragua	NU
Niger	NG
Nigeria	NI
Niue	NE
Norfolk Island	NF
Northern Mariana Island	CQ
Norway	NO
Oman	MU
Pakistan	PK
Palau	PS
Palmyra Atoll	LQ
Panama	PM
Papua New Guinea	PP
Paracel Island	PF
Paraguay	PA
Peru	PE
Philippines	RP
Pitcairn Islands	PC
Poland	PL
Portugal	PO
Puerto Rico	RQ
Qatar	QA
Reunion	RE
Romania	RO
Russia	RS
Rwanda	RW
Samoa	WS
San Marino	SM
Sao Tome and Principe	TP
Saudi Arabia	SA
Senegal	SG
Serbia	RB
Seychelles	SE
Sierra Leone	SL
Singapore	SN

Country	Country Code
Slovakia	LO
Slovenia	SI
Solomon Islands	BP
Somalia	SO
South Africa	SF
South Georgia and South Sandwich Islands	SX
Spain	SP
Spratly Islands	PG
Sri Lanka	CE
St. Barthelemy	TB
St. Helena	SH
St. Kitts and Nevis	SC
St. Lucia	ST
St. Martin	RN
St. Pierre and Miquelon	SB
St. Vincent and The Grenadines	VC
Sudan	SU
Suriname	NS
Svalbard	SV
Swaziland	WZ
Sweden	SW
Switzerland	SZ
Syria	SY
Tajikistan	TI
Tanzania	TZ
Thailand	TH
Timor-Leste	TT
Togo	TO
Tokelau	TL
Tonga	TN
Trinidad and Tobago	TD
Tunisia	TS
Turkey	TU
Turkmenistan	TX
Turks and Caicos Islands	TK
Tuvalu	TV
Uganda	UG
Ukraine	UP
United Arab Emirates	AE
United Kingdom	UK

Country	Country Code
United States	US
Uruguay	UY
Uzbekistan	UZ
Vanuatu	NH
Venezuela	VE

Country	Country Code
Vietnam	VM
Virgin Islands	VI
Virgin Islands, U.S.	VQ
Wake Island	WQ
Wallis and Futuna	WF

Country	Country Code
Western Sahara	WI
Yemen	YM
Zambia	ZA
Zimbabwe	ZI
Other Countries	OC

Form **W-8EXP**
(Rev. February 2006)
Department of the Treasury
Internal Revenue Service

Certificate of Foreign Government or Other Foreign Organization for United States Tax Withholding

(For use by foreign governments, international organizations, foreign central banks of issue, foreign tax-exempt organizations, foreign private foundations, and governments of U.S. possessions.)

▶ Section references are to the Internal Revenue Code. ▶ See separate instructions.

▶ Give this form to the withholding agent or payer. Do not send to the IRS

OMB No. 1545-1621

Do not use this form for:	**Instead, use Form:**
• Any foreign government or other foreign organization that is not claiming the applicability of section(s) 115(2), 501(c), 892, 895, or 1443(b).	W-8BEN or W-8ECI
• A beneficial owner solely claiming foreign status or treaty benefits	W-8BEN
• A foreign partnership or a foreign trust	W-8BEN or W-8IMY
• A person claimimg that income is effectively connected with the conduct of a trade or business in the United States	W-8ECI
• A person acting as an intermediary	W-8IMY

Part I Identification of Beneficial Owner (See instructions before completing this part.)

1 Name of organization

2 Country of incorporation or organization

3 Type of entity ☐ Foreign government ☐ Government of a U.S. possession ☐ International organization ☐ Foreign central bank of issue (not wholly owned by the foreign sovereign) ☐ Foreign tax-exempt organization ☐ Foreign private foundation

4 Permanent address (street, apt. or suite no., or rural route). **Do not use a P.O. box.**

City or town, state or province. Include postal code where appropriate.

Country (do not abbreviate)

5 Mailing address (if different from above)

City or town, state or province. Include postal or ZIP code where appropriate.

Country (do not abbreviate)

6 U.S. taxpayer identification number, if required (see instructions)

7 Foreign tax identifying number, if any (optional)

8 Reference number(s) (see instructions)

Part II Qualification Statement

9 For a foreign government:

a ☐ I certify that the entity identified in Part I is a foreign government within the meaning of section 892 and the payments are within the scope of the exemption granted by section 892.

Check box 9b or box 9c, whichever applies:

b ☐ The entity identified in Part I is an integral part of the government of ....

c ☐ The entity identified in Part I is a controlled entity of the government of ....

10 For an international organization:

☐ I certify that:

- The entity identified in Part I is an international organization within the meaning of section 7701(a)(18) **and**
- The payments are within the scope of the exemption granted by section 892.

11 For a foreign central bank of issue (not wholly owned by the foreign sovereign):

☐ I certify that:

- The entity identified in Part I is a foreign central bank of issue,
- The entity identified in Part I does not hold obligations or bank deposits to which this form relates for use in connection with the conduct of a commercial banking function or other commercial activity, **and**
- The payments are within the scope of the exemption granted by section 895.

(Part II and required certification continued on page 2)

For Paperwork Reduction Act Notice, see separate instructions. Cat. No. 25401F Form **W-8EXP** (Rev. 2-2006)

Form W-8EXP (Rev. 2-2006) Page **2**

Part II **Qualification Statement** *(continued)*

12 For a foreign tax-exempt organization, including foreign private foundations:

If any of the income to which this certification relates constitutes income includible under section 512 in computing the entity's unrelated business taxable income, attach a statement identifying the amounts.

Check either box 12a or box 12b:

a ☐ I certify that the entity identified in Part I has been issued a determination letter by the IRS dated .... that is currently in effect and that concludes that it is an exempt organization described in section 501(c).

b ☐ I have attached to this form an opinion from U.S. counsel concluding that the entity identified in Part I is described in section 501(c).

For section 501(c)(3) organizations only, check either box 12c or box 12d:

c ☐ If the determination letter or opinion of counsel concludes that the entity identified in Part I is described in section 501(c)(3), I certify that the organization is not a private foundation described in section 509. I have attached an affidavit of the organization setting forth sufficient facts for the IRS to determine that the organization is not a private foundation because it meets one of the exceptions described in section 509(a)(1), (2), (3), or (4).

d ☐ If the determination letter or opinion of counsel concludes that the entity identified in Part I is described in section 501(c)(3), I certify that the organization is a private foundation described in section 509.

13 For a government of a U.S. possession:

☐ I certify that the entity identified in Part I is a government of a possession of the United States, or is a political subdivision thereof, and is claiming the exemption granted by section 115(2).

Part III **Certification**

Under penalties of perjury, I declare that I have examined the information on this form and to the best of my knowledge and belief it is true, correct, and complete. I further certify under penalties of perjury that:

- The organization for which I am signing is the beneficial owner of the income to which this form relates,
- The beneficial owner is not a U.S. person,
- For a beneficial owner that is a controlled entity of a foreign sovereign (other than a central bank of issue wholly owned by a foreign sovereign), the beneficial owner is not engaged in commercial activities within or outside the United States, **and**
- For a beneficial owner that is a central bank of issue wholly owned by a foreign sovereign, the beneficial owner is not engaged in commercial activities within the United States.

Furthermore, I authorize this form to be provided to any withholding agent that has control, receipt, or custody of the income of which I am the beneficial owner or any withholding agent that can disburse or make payments of the income of which I am the beneficial owner.

Sign Here ....

Signature of authorized official | Date (MM-DD-YYYY) | Capacity in which acting

Instructions for Form W-8EXP

Department of the Treasury
Internal Revenue Service

(Rev. February 2006)

Certificate of Foreign Government or Other Foreign Organization for United States Tax Withholding

General Instructions

Section references are to the Internal Revenue Code unless otherwise noted.

Note. For definitions of terms used throughout these instructions, see Definitions on pages 2 and 3.

Purpose of form. Foreign persons are subject to U.S. tax at a 30% rate on income they receive from U.S. sources that consists of interest (including certain original issue discount (OID)), dividends, rents, premiums, annuities, compensation for, or in expectation of, services performed, or other fixed or determinable annual or periodical gains, profits, or income. This tax is imposed on the gross amount paid and is generally collected by withholding under section 1441 or 1442 on that amount. A payment is considered to have been made whether it is made directly to the beneficial owner or to another person for the benefit of the beneficial owner.

Foreign persons are also subject to tax at graduated rates on income they earn that is considered effectively connected with a U.S. trade or business. If a foreign person invests in a partnership that conducts a U.S. trade or business, the foreign person is considered to be engaged in a U.S. trade or business. The partnership is required to withhold tax under section 1446 on the foreign person's distributive share of the partnership's effectively connected taxable income.

If you receive certain types of income, you must provide Form W-8EXP to:

- Establish that you are not a U.S. person,
- Claim that you are the beneficial owner of the income for which Form W-8EXP is given, and
- Claim a reduced rate of, or exemption from, withholding as a foreign government, international organization, foreign central bank of issue, foreign tax-exempt organization, foreign private foundation, or government of a U.S. possession.

In general, payments to a foreign government (including a foreign central bank of issue wholly-owned by a foreign sovereign) from investments in the United States in stocks, bonds, other domestic securities, financial instruments held in the execution of governmental financial or monetary policy, and interest on deposits in banks in the United States are exempt from tax under section 892 and exempt from withholding under sections 1441 and 1442. Payments other than those described above, including income derived in the U.S. from the conduct of a commercial activity, income received from a controlled commercial entity (including gain from the disposition of any interest in a controlled commercial entity), and income received by a controlled commercial entity, do not qualify for exemption from tax under section 892 or exemption from withholding under sections 1441 and 1442. See Temporary Regulations section 1.892-3T. In addition, certain distributions to a foreign government from a real estate investment trust (REIT) may not be eligible for relief from withholding and may be subject to withholding at 35% of the gain realized. For the definition of "commercial activities," see Temporary Regulations section 1.892-4T.

Amounts allocable to a foreign person from a partnership's trade or business in the United States are considered derived from a commercial activity in the United States. The partnership's net effectively connected taxable income is subject to withholding under section 1446.

In general, payments to an international organization from investment in the United States in stocks, bonds and other domestic securities, interest on deposits in banks in the United States, and payments from any other source within the United States are exempt from tax under section 892 and exempt from withholding under sections 1441 and 1442. See Temporary Regulations section 1.892-6T. Payments to a foreign central bank of issue (whether or not wholly owned by a foreign sovereign) or to the Bank for International Settlements from obligations of the United States or of any agency or instrumentality thereof, or from interest on deposits with persons carrying on the banking business, are also generally exempt from tax under section 895 and exempt from withholding under sections 1441 and 1442. In addition, payments to a foreign central bank of issue from bankers' acceptances are exempt from tax under section 871(i)(2)(C) and exempt from withholding under sections 1441 and 1442. Effectively connected income or gain from a partnership conducting a trade or business in the United States may be subject to withholding under section 1446.

Payments to a foreign tax-exempt organization of certain types of U.S. source income are also generally exempt from tax and exempt from withholding. Gross investment income of a foreign private foundation, however, is subject to withholding under section 1443(b) at a rate of 4%. Effectively connected income or gain from a partnership conducting a trade or business in the United States may be subject to withholding under section 1446.

Payments to a government of a possession of the United States are generally exempt from tax and withholding under section 115(2).

To establish eligibility for exemption from 30% tax and withholding, a foreign government, international organization, foreign central bank of issue, foreign tax-exempt organization, foreign private foundation, or government of a U.S. possession must provide a Form W-8EXP to a withholding agent or payer with all

Cat. No. 25903G

necessary documentation. The withholding agent or payer of the income may rely on a properly completed Form W-8EXP to treat the payment, credit, or allocation associated with the Form W-8EXP as being made to a foreign government, international organization, foreign central bank of issue, foreign tax-exempt organization, foreign private foundation, or government of a U.S. possession exempt from withholding at the 30% rate (or, where appropriate, subject to withholding at a 4% rate).

Provide Form W-8EXP to the withholding agent or payer before income is paid, credited, or allocated to you. Failure by a beneficial owner to provide a Form W-8EXP when requested may lead to withholding at the 30% rate, the backup withholding rate, or the rate applicable under section 1446.

Additional information. For additional information and instructions for the withholding agent, see the Instructions for the Requester of Forms W-8BEN, W-8ECI, W-8EXP, and W-8IMY.

Who must file. You must give Form W-8EXP to the withholding agent or payer if you are a foreign government, international organization, foreign central bank of issue, foreign tax-exempt organization, foreign private foundation, or government of a U.S. possession. Submit Form W-8EXP whether or not you are claiming a reduced rate of, or exemption from, U.S. tax withholding.

Do not use Form W-8EXP if:

- You are not a foreign government, international organization, foreign central bank of issue, foreign tax-exempt organization, foreign private foundation, or government of a U.S. possession claiming the applicability of section 115(2), 501(c), 892, 895, or 1443(b). Instead, provide Form W-8BEN, Certificate of Foreign Status of Beneficial Owner for United States Tax Withholding, or Form W-8ECI, Certificate of Foreign Person's Claim That Income Is Effectively Connected With the Conduct of a Trade or Business in the United States. For example, if you are a foreign tax-exempt organization claiming a benefit under an income tax treaty, provide Form W-8BEN.
- You are receiving income that is effectively connected with the conduct of a trade or business in the United States. Instead, provide Form W-8ECI.
- You are a tax-exempt organization receiving unrelated business taxable income subject to withholding under section 1443(a). Instead, provide Form W-8BEN or Form W-8ECI for this portion of your income.
- You are a foreign partnership, a foreign simple trust, or a foreign grantor trust. Instead, provide Form W-8ECI or Form W-8IMY, Certificate of Foreign Intermediary, Foreign Flow-Through Entity, or Certain U.S. Branches for United States Tax Withholding. However, a foreign grantor trust is required to provide documentation of its grantor or other owner for purposes of section 1446. See Regulations section 1.1446-1.
- You are acting as an intermediary (that is, acting not for your own account, but for the account of others as an agent, nominee, or custodian). Instead, provide Form W-8IMY.

Giving Form W-8EXP to the withholding agent. Do not send Form W-8EXP to the IRS. Instead, give it to the person who is requesting it from you. Generally, this person will be the one from whom you receive the payment, who credits your account, or a partnership that allocates income to you. Generally, a separate Form W-8EXP must be given to each withholding agent.

Give Form W-8EXP to the person requesting it before the payment is made, credited, or allocated to you or your account. If you do not provide this form, the withholding agent may have to withhold tax at the 30% rate, the backup withholding rate, or the rate applicable under section 1446. If you receive more than one type of income from a single withholding agent, the withholding agent may require you to submit a Form W-8EXP for each different type of income.

Change in circumstances. If a change in circumstances makes any information on the Form W-8EXP you have submitted incorrect, you must notify the withholding agent within 30 days of the change in circumstances and you must file a new Form W-8EXP or other appropriate form.

Expiration of Form W-8EXP. Generally, a Form W-8EXP filed without a U.S. taxpayer identification number (TIN) will remain in effect for a period starting on the date the form is signed and ending on the last day of the third succeeding calendar year. However, in the case of an integral part of a foreign government (within the meaning of Temporary Regulations section 1.892-2T(a)(2)) or a foreign central bank of issue, a Form W-8EXP filed without a U.S. TIN will remain in effect until a change in circumstances makes any of the information on the form incorrect. A Form W-8EXP furnished with a U.S. TIN will remain in effect until a change in circumstances makes any information on the form incorrect provided that the withholding agent reports on Form 1042-S, Foreign Person's U.S. Source Income Subject to Withholding, at least one payment annually to the beneficial owner.

Definitions

Beneficial owner. For payments other than those for which a reduced rate of withholding is claimed under an income tax treaty, the beneficial owner of income is generally the person who is required under U.S. tax principles to include the income in gross income on a tax return. A person is not a beneficial owner of income, however, to the extent that person is receiving the income as a nominee, agent, or custodian, or to the extent the person is a conduit whose participation in a transaction is disregarded. In the case of amounts paid that do not constitute income, beneficial ownership is determined as if the payment were income.

Foreign partnerships, foreign simple trusts, and foreign grantor trusts are not the beneficial owners of income paid to the partnership or trust. The beneficial owners of income paid to a foreign partnership are generally the partners in the partnership, provided that the partner is not itself a partnership, foreign simple or grantor trust, nominee or other agent. The beneficial owners of income paid to a foreign simple trust (that is, a foreign trust that is described in section 651(a)) are generally the beneficiaries of the trust, if the beneficiary is not a foreign partnership, foreign simple or grantor trust, nominee or other agent. The beneficial owners of a foreign grantor trust (that is, a foreign trust to the extent that all or a portion of the income of the trust is treated as owned by the grantor or another person under sections 671 through 679) are the persons treated as the owners of the trust. The beneficial owners of income paid to a foreign complex trust (that is, a foreign trust that is not a foreign simple trust or foreign grantor trust) is the trust itself.

The beneficial owner of income paid to a foreign estate is the estate itself.

These beneficial owner rules apply primarily for purposes of withholding under sections 1441 and 1442. The rules also generally apply for purposes of section 1446, with a few exceptions. See Regulations section 1.1446-1 for instances where the documentation requirements of sections 1441 and 1442 differ from section 1446.

Foreign person. A foreign person includes a nonresident alien individual, foreign corporation, foreign partnership, foreign trust, foreign estate, foreign government, international organization, foreign central bank of issue, foreign tax-exempt organization, foreign private foundation, or government of a U.S. possession, and any other person that is not a U.S. person. It also includes a foreign branch or office of a U.S. financial institution or U.S. clearing organization if the foreign branch is a qualified intermediary. Generally, a payment to a U.S. branch of a foreign person is a payment to a foreign person.

Foreign government. A foreign government includes only the integral parts or controlled entities of a foreign sovereign as defined in Temporary Regulations section 1.892-2T.

An integral part of a foreign sovereign, in general, is any person, body of persons, organization, agency, bureau, fund, instrumentality, or other body, however designated, that constitutes a governing authority of a foreign country. The net earnings of the governing authority must be credited to its own account or to other accounts of the foreign sovereign, with no portion benefiting any private person.

A controlled entity of a foreign sovereign is an entity that is separate in form from the foreign sovereign or otherwise constitutes a separate juridical entity only if:
- It is wholly owned and controlled by the foreign sovereign directly or indirectly through one or more controlled entities.
- It is organized under the laws of the foreign sovereign by which it is owned.
- Its net earnings are credited to its own account or to other accounts of the foreign sovereign, with no portion of its income benefiting any private person.
- Its assets vest in the foreign sovereign upon dissolution.

A controlled entity also includes a pension trust defined in Temporary Regulations section 1.892-2T(c) and may include a foreign central bank of issue to the extent that it is wholly owned by a foreign sovereign.

A foreign government must provide Form W-8EXP to establish eligibility for exemption from withholding for payments exempt from tax under section 892.

International organization. An international organization is any public international organization entitled to enjoy privileges, exemptions, and immunities as an international organization under the International Organizations Immunities Act (22 U.S.C. 288-288(f)). In general, to qualify as an international organization, the United States must participate in the organization pursuant to a treaty or under the authority of an Act of Congress authorizing such participation.

Amounts exempt from tax under section 892. Only a foreign government or an international organization as defined above qualifies for exemption from taxation under section 892. Section 892 generally excludes from gross income and exempts from U.S. taxation income a foreign government receives from investments in the United States in stocks, bonds, or other domestic securities; financial instruments held in the execution of governmental financial or monetary policy; and interest on deposits in banks in the United States of monies belonging to the foreign government. Income of a foreign government from any of the following sources is not exempt from U.S. taxation.
- The conduct of any commercial activity.
- A controlled commercial entity.
- The disposition of any interest in a controlled commercial entity.

For the definition of "commercial activity," see Temporary Regulations section 1.892-4T.

Section 892 also generally excludes from gross income and exempts from U.S. taxation income of an international organization received from investments in the United States in stocks, bonds, or other domestic securities and interest on deposits in banks in the United States of monies belonging to the international organization or from any other source within the United States.

Controlled commercial entity. A controlled commercial entity is an entity engaged in commercial activities (whether within or outside the United States) if the foreign government holds:
- Any interest in the entity that is 50% or more of the total of all interests in the entity, or
- A sufficient interest or any other interest in the entity which provides the foreign government with effective practical control of the entity.

An entity includes a corporation, a partnership, a trust (including a pension trust) and an estate. A partnership's commercial activities are attributable to its general and limited partners for purposes of section 892. The partnership's activities will result in the partnership having to withhold tax under section 1446 on the effectively connected taxable income allocable to a foreign government partner.

Note. A foreign central bank of issue will be treated as a controlled commercial entity only if it engages in commercial activities within the United States.

Foreign central bank of issue. A foreign central bank of issue is a bank that is by law or government sanction the principal authority, other than the government itself, to issue instruments intended to circulate as currency. Such a bank is generally the custodian of the banking reserves of the country under whose law it is organized. For purposes of section 895, the Bank of International Settlements is treated as though it were a foreign central bank of issue.

A foreign central bank of issue must provide Form W-8EXP to establish eligibility for exemption from withholding for payments exempt from tax under either section 892 or section 895.

Amounts exempt from tax under section 895. Section 895 generally excludes from gross income and exempts from U.S. taxation income a foreign central bank of issue receives from obligations of the United States (or of any agency or instrumentality thereof) or from interest on deposits with persons carrying on the banking business unless such obligations or deposits are held for, or used in connection with, the conduct of commercial banking functions or other commercial activities of the foreign central bank of issue.

Amounts subject to withholding. Generally, an amount subject to withholding under section 1441 or 1442 is an amount from sources within the United States that is fixed or determinable annual or periodical (FDAP) income. FDAP income is all income included in gross income, including interest (as well as original issue discount (OID)), dividends, rents, royalties, and compensation. FDAP income does not include most gains from the sale of property (including market discount and option premiums).

Income is subject to withholding under section 1446 if the income is effectively connected with a partnership's trade or business in the United States and is allocable to a foreign person.

Withholding agent. Any person, U.S. or foreign, that has control, receipt, or custody of an amount subject to withholding or who can disburse or make payments of an amount subject to withholding is a withholding agent. The withholding agent may be an individual, corporation, partnership, trust, association, or any other entity including (but not limited to) any foreign intermediary, foreign partnership, and U.S. branches of certain foreign banks and insurance companies. Generally, the person who pays (or causes to be paid) an amount subject to withholding to the foreign person (or to its agent) must withhold.

Specific Instructions

Part I

Before completing Part I, complete the Worksheet for Foreign Governments, International Organizations, and Foreign Central Banks of Issue on page 6 to determine whether amounts received are or will be exempt from U.S. tax under section 892 or 895 and exempt from withholding under sections 1441 and 1442. Use the results of this worksheet to check the appropriate box in Part II. Do not give the worksheet to the withholding agent. Instead, keep it for your records.

Line 1. Enter the full name of the organization.

Line 2. Enter the country under the laws of which the foreign government or other foreign organization was created, incorporated, organized, or governed.

Line 3. Check the one box that applies. A foreign central bank of issue (wholly owned by a foreign sovereign) should check the "Foreign government" box.

Line 4. The permanent address of a foreign government, international organization, or foreign central bank of issue is where it maintains its principal office. For all other organizations, the permanent address is the address in the country where the organization claims to be a resident for tax purposes. Do not show the address of a financial institution, a post office box, or an address used solely for mailing purposes.

Line 5. Enter the mailing address only if it is different from the address shown on line 4.

Line 6. A U.S. taxpayer identification number (TIN) means an employer identification number (EIN). A U.S. TIN is generally required if you are claiming an exemption or reduced rate of withholding based solely on your claim of tax-exempt status under section 501(c) or private foundation status. Use Form SS-4, Application for Employer Identification Number, to obtain an EIN.

Line 7. If the country of residence for tax purposes has issued the organization a tax identifying number, enter it here.

Line 8. This line may be used by the filer of Form W-8EXP or by the withholding agent to whom it is provided to include any referencing information that is useful to the withholding agent in carrying out its obligations. A filer may use line 8 to include the name and number of the account for which the filer is providing the form.

Part II

Line 9. Check box 9a and box 9b or box 9c, whichever applies. Enter the name of the foreign sovereign's country on line 9b (if the entity is an integral part of a foreign government) or on line 9c (if the entity is a controlled entity). A central bank of issue (wholly owned by a foreign sovereign) should check box 9c.

Line 10. Check this box if you are an international organization. By checking this box, you are certifying to all the statements made in line 10.

Line 11. Check this box if you are a foreign central bank of issue not wholly owned by a foreign sovereign. By checking this box, you are certifying to all the statements made in line 11.

Line 12. Check the appropriate box if you are a foreign tax-exempt organization.

CAUTION: If you are a foreign tax-exempt organization, you must attach a statement setting forth any income that is includible under section 512 in computing your unrelated business taxable income.

Box 12a. Check this box if you have been issued a determination letter by the IRS. Enter the date of the IRS determination letter.

Box 12b. Check this box if you do not have an IRS determination letter, but are providing an opinion of U.S. counsel concluding that you are an organization described in section 501(c).

Box 12c. If you are a section 501(c)(3) organization, check this box if you are not a private foundation. You must attach to the withholding certificate an affidavit setting forth sufficient facts concerning your operations and support to enable the IRS to determine that you would be likely to qualify as an organization described in section 509(a)(1), (2), (3), or (4). See Rev. Proc. 92-94, 1992-2 C.B. 507, section 4, for information on affidavit preparation of foreign equivalents of domestic public charities.

Box 12d. Check this box if you are a section 501(c)(3) organization and you are a private foundation described in section 509.

Line 13. Check this box if you are a government of a U.S. possession. By checking this box you are certifying to the statements made in line 13.

Part III

Form W-8EXP must be signed and dated by an authorized official of the foreign government, international organization, foreign central bank of issue, foreign tax-exempt organization, foreign private foundation, or government of a U.S. possession, as appropriate.

Paperwork Reduction Act Notice. We ask for the information on this form to carry out the Internal Revenue laws of the United States. You are required to provide the information. We need it to ensure that you are complying with these laws and to allow us to figure and collect the right amount of tax.

You are not required to provide the information requested on a form that is subject to the Paperwork Reduction Act unless the form displays a valid OMB control number. Books or records relating to a form or its instructions must be retained as long as their contents may become material in the administration of any Internal Revenue law. Generally, tax returns and return information are confidential, as required by section 6103.

The time needed to complete and file this form will vary depending on individual circumstances. The estimated average time is: **Recordkeeping,** 7 hr., 10 min.; **Learning about the law or the form,** 5 hr., 28 min.; **Preparing and sending the form to IRS,** 5 hr., 49 min.

If you have comments concerning the accuracy of these time estimates or suggestions for making this form simpler, we would be happy to hear from you. You can email us at *taxforms@irs.gov. Please put "Forms Comment" on the subject line. Or you can write to Internal Revenue Service, Tax Products Coordinating Committee, SE:W:CAR:MP:T:T:SP, 1111 Constitution Ave. NW, IR-6406, Washington, DC 20224. Do not send Form W-8EXP to this office. Instead, give it to your withholding agent.

WORKSHEET FOR FOREIGN GOVERNMENTS, INTERNATIONAL ORGANIZATIONS, AND FOREIGN CENTRAL BANKS OF ISSUE

(Do not give to the withholding agent. Keep for your records.)

Complete this worksheet to determine whether amounts received are or will be exempt from United States tax under section 892 or section 895 and exempt from withholding under sections 1441 and 1442.

- Foreign governments and foreign central banks of issue, start with question **1.**
- International organizations, go directly to question **6.**

FOREIGN GOVERNMENT	**Yes**	**No**
1 a Is the foreign government an integral part of a foreign sovereign (see **Definitions**)? (If "Yes," go to question **4**. If "No," answer question **1b**.)		
b Is the foreign government a controlled entity of a foreign sovereign (see **Definitions**)? (If "Yes," answer question **2a**. If "No," go to question **7a**.)		
2 a Is the controlled entity a foreign central bank of issue (see **Definitions**)? (If "Yes," answer question **2b**. If "No," go to question **3**.)		
b Is the foreign central bank of issue engaged in commercial activities within the United States? (If "Yes," answer question **7a**. If "No," go to question **4**.)		
3 Is the controlled entity engaged in commercial activities anywhere in the world? (If "Yes," income is **not** exempt from tax under section 892 and may be subject to withholding. **Do not** complete Form W-8EXP for such income. Instead, complete Form W-8BEN or W-8ECI. If "No," answer question **4**.)		
4 Does the foreign government or foreign central bank of issue (wholly owned by the foreign sovereign) receive income directly or indirectly from any controlled commercial entities or income derived from the disposition of any interest in a controlled commercial entity (see **Definitions**)? (If "Yes," income is **not** exempt from tax under section 892 and may be subject to withholding. **Do not** complete Form W-8EXP for such income. Instead, complete Form W-8BEN or W-8ECI. If "No," answer question **5**.)		
5 Is any of the income received by the foreign government or foreign central bank of issue (wholly owned by the foreign sovereign) from sources other than investments in the United States in stocks, bonds, other domestic securities (as defined in Temporary Regulations section 1.892-3T(a)(3)), financial instruments held in the execution of governmental financial or monetary policy (as defined in Temporary Regulations section 1.892-3T(a)(4) and (a)(5)), or interest on deposits in banks in the United States? (If "Yes," income is **not** exempt from tax under section 892 and may be subject to withholding. **Do not** complete Form W-8EXP for such income. Instead, complete Form W-8BEN or W-8ECI. If "No," check the appropriate box on **line 9** of Form W-8EXP.)		

INTERNATIONAL ORGANIZATION	**Yes**	**No**
6 Is the international organization an organization in which the United States participates pursuant to any treaty or under an Act of Congress authorizing such participation and to which the President of the United States has issued an Executive Order entitling the organization to enjoy the privileges, exemptions, and immunities provided under the International Organization Immunities Act (22 U.S.C. 288, 288e, 288f)? (If "Yes," check the box on **line 10** of Form W-8EXP. If "No," income may be subject to withholding. **Do not** complete this form for such income. Instead, complete Form W-8BEN or W-8ECI.)		

FOREIGN CENTRAL BANK OF ISSUE	**Yes**	**No**
7 a Is the entity, whether wholly or partially owned by the foreign sovereign, a foreign central bank of issue? (If "Yes," answer question **7b**. If "No," income is **not** exempt from tax under section 895 and may be subject to withholding. **Do not** complete Form W-8EXP for such income. Instead, complete Form W-8BEN or W-8ECI.)		
b Is the income received by the foreign central bank of issue from sources other than obligations of the United States (or any agency or instrumentality thereof) or from interest on deposits with persons carrying on the banking business? (If "Yes," income is **not** exempt from tax under section 895 and may be subject to withholding. **Do not** complete Form W-8EXP for such income. Instead, complete Form W-8BEN or W-8ECI. If "No," answer question **7c**.)		
c Are the obligations of the United States (or any agency or instrumentality thereof) or bank deposits owned by the foreign central bank of issue held for, or used in connection with, the conduct of commercial banking functions or other commercial activities by the foreign central bank of issue? (If "Yes," income is **not** exempt from tax under section 895 and may be subject to withholding. **Do not** complete Form W-8EXP for such income. Instead, complete Form W-8BEN or W-8ECI. If "No," check the box on **line 11** of Form W-8EXP.)		

APPENDIX 11

DATE:

DECLARATION OF TRUST

constituting

THE ABC FOUNDATION

A BERMUDA CHARITABLE TRUST

THE ABC FOUNDATION

Table of contents

9. Borrowing
10. Reserves
11. Delegation
12. Custodians and nominees
13. Power to appoint a chairman and other officers and to employ staff and pay for services
14. Regulations
15. Bank accounts
16. Power to pay for audit
17. Receipts
18. Power to insure
19. Indemnity insurance
20. Trustee liability
21. Professional charging clause
22. Costs
23. Change of name
24. Power of variation
25. Power to wind up charity
26. Committee of Trust Advisors

Schedule

DECLARATION OF TRUST

THIS DECLARATION OF TRUST is made the __________ day of , 20__ by THE ________________________ TRUST COMPANY LIMITED, a company incorporated under the laws of Bermuda and having its registered office at ____________________________________, Hamilton, Bermuda (the "Original Trustee").

RECITALS

(A) The Trustee has agreed to make this Declaration of Trust, and has received the property specified in the Schedule to be held by it on the trusts specified below. It intends to accept donations, subscriptions, covenants, sponsorships, legacies and other gifts to be held on the same trusts.

(B) This trust shall be irrevocable.

PART 1—OPERATIVE PROVISIONS

1 Title

The charity constituted by this Deed shall be called **THE ABC FOUNDATION** or such other name as the Trustee may from time to time determine in accordance with the power contained in this Deed.

2 Definitions and construction

In this Deed, where the context admits, the following definitions and rules of construction shall apply.

2.1 The **'Charity'** shall mean the charity constituted by this Deed.

2.2 The **'Committee'** shall mean the Committee of Trust Advisors as constituted in Part 2, clause 26 of this Deed.

2.3 The **'Trust Fund'** shall mean:

(a) the property specified in the Schedule;

(b) all money, investments or other property paid or transferred by any person to, or so as to be under the control of, and in either case, accepted by the Trustee;

(c) all accumulations (if any) of income; and

(d) the money, investments and property from time to time representing the above.

2.4 **'charitable'** means charitable according to the law of Bermuda.

2.5 The **'Commission'** shall mean the Charity Commissioners for Bermuda.

2.6 The expression **'the Trustee'** shall, where the context admits, include the Original Trustee or other trustee or trustees for the time being of this Trust.

2.7 Words denoting the singular shall include the plural and vice versa.

2.8 Words denoting any gender shall include both the other genders.

2.9 References to any statutory provision shall include any statutory modification or re-enactment of such provision.

2.10 The table of contents and clause headings are included for reference only and shall not affect the interpretation of this Deed.

3 Objects

3.1 The Trustee shall hold the capital and income of the Trust Fund upon trust to apply the income and all or such part or parts of the capital, at such times and in such manner, as the Trustee may in its discretion think fit for:

(a) ____;

(b) ____; and

(c) the benefit of such other exclusively charitable objects and purposes in any part of the world as the Trustee may in its discretion think fit PROVIDED THAT no donations or other distributions shall be made to any "United States person" within the meaning of the Internal Revenue Code of the United States of America (the "Code") (or to any other person that would cause the Charity to have a "United States beneficiary" within the meaning of Section 679 of the Code).

3.2 The Trustee shall not apply any part of the Trust Fund directly in relief of public funds, but may apply the whole or any part of the Trust Fund in supplementing public funds.

3.3 The Trustee may, in its discretion, instead of applying the income of the Charity in any year, accumulate all or any part of such income at compound interest by investing the same, and the resulting income, in any authorised investments and shall hold the same as an accretion to and as part of the capital of the Charity, without prejudice to their right to apply the whole or any part of such accumulated income in any subsequent year as if the same were income of the Charity arising in the then current year.

4 Conduct of charity and general management powers

The Trustee shall conduct the affairs of the Charity in such manner as it may consider appropriate, and may make such arrangements in relation to the administration of the Charity as it considers advisable.

5 Accounts, reports and returns

The Trustees shall maintain financial records, and prepare and submit accounts and returns, in accordance with the requirements of the Charities Act 1978.

6 Exercise of trustees' powers and discretions

6.1 The Trustee shall, in addition and without prejudice to clause 4 and all statutory powers, have the powers and immunities set out in Part 2 of this Deed.

6.2 No power or discretion conferred on the Trustee shall be exercised except in furtherance of the charitable objects. No portion of the Trust Fund shall be distributed as a private inurement or benefit in contravention of the objects of the charity as set forth in clause 3 hereof.

7 Appointment of new trustees

7.1 A new trustee or new trustees may be appointed at any time (either by way of replacement or addition) by the Committee but so that the total number of Trustees shall at no time exceed five PROVIDED ALWAYS THAT a majority of the Trustees shall be persons who are not "related or subordinate parties" within the meaning of Sections 672(c) and 674(c) of the Code to any member of the Committee.

7.2 A trustee may be appointed or discharged by a resolution of a meeting of the Committee, provided that a memorandum declaring such appointment or discharge shall be signed as a deed, either at the meeting by the person presiding, or in some other manner directed by the meeting, and attested by two other persons present at the meeting.

8 Meetings

8.1 The Trustees shall hold at least one meeting in each calendar year.

8.2 One half of the number (for the time being) of the Trustees will form a quorum at any meeting.

8.3 Trustees shall attend meetings in person unless the Trustees shall agree another appropriate means of communication between those taking part.

9 Voting

9.1 Save in exercise of the powers in clauses 24 (to vary the terms of this Deed) and 25 (to wind up the Charity) and set out in Part 2 of this Deed, which shall be exercisable only by unanimous decision of the Trustees, a decision of the majority of the Trustees present and voting at any duly constituted meeting shall be valid and binding on all the Trustees.

9.2 Any of the Trustees who shall dissent from such a decision shall nevertheless concur in executing or signing any document or doing any act necessary for giving effect to such decision without being responsible for any resulting loss.

10 Written resolutions

A resolution in writing signed by all the Trustees shall be as valid as a resolution passed at a meeting.

11 Ratification

The Trustees may implement decisions reached by them informally, provided that such decisions are ratified at the next or subsequent meeting of the Trustees.

12 Notices

Notices to be given to the Trustees shall be in writing and shall be sufficiently given if delivered to any one of the Trustees either personally, or sent by registered post to the usual or last known address of such Trustee.

13 Trustee benefit

13.1 Subject to the provisions of clause 19 (power to take out trustee indemnity insurance) and clause 21 (professional trustees' charging) in Part 2 of this Deed, no Trustee may

(a) receive any benefit in money or kind from the Charity (other than reasonable out of pocket expenses); or

(b) have a financial interest in the supply of goods or services to the Charity; or

(c) acquire or hold any interest in property of the Charity (except in order to hold it as Trustee of the Charity).

13.2 Notwithstanding the provisions of sub-clause 13.1, the Trustees shall not, nor shall any of them, be accountable for any remuneration or other benefit received by the Trustees, or any of them (whether as director, auditor or other officer or otherwise), from any company in which shares, stock, debentures or other securities are for the time being held by the Trustees as trustees, except to the extent (if any) to which such remuneration or other benefit is received by the Trustees or any of them by reason of such shares, stock, debentures or other securities being in the name of the Trustees or held on their behalf. None of the Trustees shall concur in exercising any voting rights in respect of any shares, stock, debentures or other securities comprised in the Trust Fund in such a way that a personal benefit is thereby secured to the Trustees or any of them.

14 Construction

14.1 In making this Declaration, it is the intention of the Trustee that the Charity be organized and operated as an organization described in sections 501(c)(3) and 2522 (a)(2) of the Code.

14.2 In making this Declaration, it is the intention of the Trustee that the Charity be created as a non-grantor trust and so characterized for purposes of the Code.

PART 2—ADMINISTRATIVE PROVISIONS

1 General

1.1 The Trustees shall have power to do all such lawful acts or things as shall further the attainment of the objects of the Charity.

1.2 Subject to such restrictions as may be imposed by law, or such consents as may be required by law, the Trustees shall have all the powers of an absolute beneficial owner in relation to the management and administration of the Trust Fund.

2 Publicity

The Trustees may print, publish, circulate, and broadcast or cause to be printed, published, circulated or broadcast (whether gratuitously or not) any newspapers, periodicals, magazines, books, pamphlets, leaflets and any programmes or other publicity material of any kind that may be deemed desirable for the promotion of the objects of the Charity or for the informing of contributors and others of the needs and progress of the Charity.

3 Collaboration

The Trustees may act in collaboration with any person, body, institution or authority.

4 Assistance to and support of other charities

The Trustees may make contributions, as they may think fit, towards, or otherwise to assist (and whether out of capital or income), the objects or expenses of any charitable trust, institution or body having objects similar to those declared in this Deed.

5 Appeals, acceptance of gifts, etc

5.1 The Trustees may accept any devises, gifts, subscriptions (whether or not under Deed of Covenant), donations or bequests of land, money, securities or other real or personal property, offered or made for the objects of the Charity, and utilise or employ the same (whether in its original form or converted into another appropriate form of investment as the Trustees shall think fit) for such objects.

5.2 The Trustees may take such lawful steps, by personal or written appeals (whether periodical or occasional), public meetings, or otherwise, as may from time to time be deemed expedient for the purpose of procuring contributions to the Charity in the form of donations, annual subscriptions, covenants or in any other form whatever.

5.3 The Trustees may accept any funds or donations on any special trusts or conditions within the objects of the Charity, so that each fund or donation so accepted shall be held, subject to the trusts or conditions on which it is transferred or given, and may undertake any special trust or trusts falling within the objects of the Charity, and may hold and apply any particular or designated funds upon and subject to any such special trust or trusts.

6 Investment power

The Trustees may apply any money to be invested in the purchase of or at interest upon the security of such shares, stocks, funds, securities, land, buildings, chattels or other investments or property of whatever nature and wherever situate, and whether involving liabilities or producing income or not, as it think fit, so that it shall have the same powers to apply money to be invested as if they were an absolute beneficial owner.

7 Trustees' responsibility as shareholder

The Trustees shall not be bound to interfere in the management or conduct of the business of any company the shares or securities of which comprise the whole or any part of the Trust Fund. Where the Trustees' holding of such shares is sufficient to confer voting control of the company concerned, the Trustees shall nevertheless from time to time obtain such information from the company as would be made available to a non-executive director, to satisfy themselves (so far as may be possible from such information) that the affairs of the company are being properly managed and, in the absence of any notice to the contrary, the Trustees shall be at liberty to leave the conduct of their business (including the payment or non-payment of dividends) wholly to the directors.

8 Powers in relation to land

8.1 Subject to such restrictions imposed on them, and with such consents as may be required by law, the Trustees shall have all the powers of an absolute beneficial owner in relation to the disposition, development and improvement of any land comprised in the Trust Fund.

8.2 The Trustees shall not be bound to maintain any building or other structure on land comprised in the Trust Fund or to preserve or repair any chattels comprised in the Trust Fund.

8.3 The Trustees may transfer land comprised in the Trust Fund to such other charitable body or bodies, having objects the same as or similar to the Charity, on such terms as the Trustees shall in their discretion think fit.

9 Borrowing

Subject to such restrictions imposed on them, and such consents as may be required by law, the Trustees may borrow on the security of all or any part of the Trust Fund or otherwise for any purpose.

10 Reserves

The Trustees shall have power to establish funds for particular purposes or to maintain reserves.

11 Delegation

11.1 The Trustees may delegate such of their powers of management and administration as the Trustees may from time to time decide to committees, consisting of not less than one of their number and such other persons as the Trustees may appoint, and may make regulations for the conduct of such committees and from time to time amend regulations. All acts and proceedings of any such committee shall be reported as soon as possible to the Trustees and no such committee shall incur expenditure on behalf of the Charity except in accordance with a budget that has been approved by the Trustees.

11.2 The Trustees may delegate, upon such terms and at such reasonable remuneration as the Trustees may think fit, to any person who is, in the opinion of the Trustees, qualified for that purpose, the management of any land comprised in the Trust Fund. All acts and proceedings of any such person must be reported to the Trustees as soon as possible.

11.3 The Trustees may delegate, upon such terms and at such reasonable remuneration as the Trustees may think fit, to professional investment managers (the **'Managers'**) the exercise of all or any of their powers of investment on condition that:

(a) the Managers shall be persons who are entitled to carry on investment business under the provisions of any Financial Services legislation from time to time in force within Bermuda;

(b) the delegated powers shall be exercisable only within clear policy guidelines drawn up in advance by the Trustees and within the powers of investment conferred by this Deed;

(c) the Managers shall be under a duty to report promptly to the Trustees any exercise of the delegated powers, and in particular to report every transaction carried out by the Managers to the Trustees within 14 days, and to report on the performance of investments managed by them at least every three months;

(d) the Trustees shall be entitled at any time and without notice to review, alter or determine the delegation or their terms;

(e) the Trustees shall be bound to review the arrangements for delegation at intervals not (in the absence of special reasons) exceeding 12 months, but so that any failure by the Trustees to undertake such reviews within the period of 12 months shall not invalidate the delegation;

(f) the Trustees shall be liable for any failure to take reasonable care in choosing the Managers, fixing or enforcing the terms upon which the Managers are employed, requiring the remedying of any breaches of those terms and otherwise supervising the Managers, but otherwise shall not be liable for the acts and defaults of the Managers.

12 Custodians and nominees

12.1 The Trustees may hold all or any part of the Trust Fund in the name of any corporation or any other person (being, if individuals, at least two in number, whether or not including one or more of the Trustees) as nominee for the Trustees and on such terms as the Trustees think fit.

12.2 The Trustees shall have power to appoint as custodian trustee any corporation empowered so to act, upon such terms as it shall think fit, and may transfer the whole or any part of the Trust Fund to or so as to be under the control of such custodian trustee, provided that the remuneration payable to such corporation shall in no case exceed what is provided for in sub-clause 21.3.

13 Power to employ staff and pay for services, appoint a chairman and officers, etc

13.1 The Trustees may:

(a) employ any person or firm, not being a trustee, to manage or assist in managing the grant-making activities of the Charity or the day-to-day running of the Charity or the Trust Fund; and

(b) employ a secretary and other such officials or staff, not being a trustee, as the Trustees may in their discretion from time to time determine;

And in either case upon such terms and at such remuneration as the Trustees think fit.

13.2 The Trustees may from time to time:

(a) appoint one of their number to be the Chairman of Trustees (the **'Chairman'**) for the time being;

(b) authorise the Chairman, between meetings of the Trustees, to act on their behalf and to report such actions at the next or any subsequent meeting; and

(c) appoint the Chairman to be an ex officio member of any committee set up by the Trustees under their powers under this Deed;

PROVIDED ALWAYS that the Trustees reserve the right at any time to remove the Chairman from the office of Chairman.

13.3 The Trustees may from time to time:

(a) appoint any one or more from among their number to be officers of the Charity (the **'Officers'**) to act in such capacity and with such title as the Trustees deem expedient for a fixed period or for the time being;

(b) authorise the Officers to act on their behalf in any matter or to undertake or be responsible for any activity of the Charity and to report such actions at the next or any subsequent meeting of the Trustees; and

(c) appoint any one or more of the Officers to be an ex officio member of any committee set up by the Trustees under their powers under this Deed;

PROVIDED ALWAYS that the Trustees reserve the right at any time and from time to time to remove the Officers (or any one or more of them) from their office.

14 Regulations

The Trustees may make regulations for the management of the Charity and for the conduct of the business of the Trustees and may, from time to time, amend such regulations.

15 Bank accounts

15.1 The Trustees may open and maintain in the name of the Charity, or in such other name as the Trustees may think fit, bank accounts at such banks as the Trustees may from time to time decide, and at any time may pay any money forming part of the Trust Fund or its income to the credit of any such account or place the same on deposit with any bank.

15.2 The Trustees may from time to time make such arrangements as it shall think fit for the operation of any bank account in the name of the Charity or under the control of the Trustees.

16 Power to pay for audit

The Trustees may arrange for the accounts of the Charity to be audited annually by a qualified accountant at the expense of the Trust Fund even if not so required by law.

17 Receipts

When making grants of any funds to any charitable organisation or charitable institution, the Trustees may accept as a good discharge in respect of any such funds the receipt of the treasurer, secretary or other authorised officer for the time being of such charitable organisation or charitable institution.

18 Power to insure

The Trustees may insure any fund raising activities of the Charity and all or any part of the Trust Fund against any risk, for any amount and on such terms as it think fit.

19 Indemnity insurance

19.1 The Trustees may pay out of the Trust Fund the cost of any premium in respect of insurance or indemnity (notwithstanding the Trustees' interest in such insurance or indemnity) to cover all personal liabilities which may be incurred by the Trustees, or any of them, in connection with the Charity or its fund raising activities. No Trustee shall be accountable for any money paid to a Trustee under the terms of any such insurance or indemnity unless such Trustee shall otherwise have been fully indemnified in respect of the liability to which such payment relates.

19.2 Any such insurance or indemnity shall not extend to any claim by a Trustee arising from any act or omission which the Trustee in question commits, either knowing it to be a breach of trust, or breach of duty, or in reckless disregard of whether it was a breach of trust or breach of duty or not.

20 Trustees liability

In the professed execution of these trusts and powers, no Trustee, being an individual shall be liable for any loss to the Trust Fund arising by reason of any improper investment made in good faith (so long as he shall have sought professional advice before making such investment), or for the negligence or fraud of any agent employed by him, or by any other Trustee in good faith, although the employment of such agent was not strictly necessary or expedient (provided reasonable supervision shall have been exercised), or by reason of any mistake or omission made in good faith by any Trustee or by reason of any other matter or thing except the deliberate, reckless or negligent breach of an equitable duty on the part of the Trustee who is sought to be made liable.

21 Professional charging clause

21.1 Subject to sub-clause 21.2 any Trustee, being a person who possesses specialist skill or knowledge, shall be entitled to charge and be paid all usual professional or other charges for work done by him, or his firm, when instructed by his co-Trustees so to act in that capacity on behalf of the Charity.

21.2 At no time shall a majority of the Trustees benefit under the provisions of sub-clause 22.1 and a Trustee shall withdraw from any meeting of the Trustees while his or her own instruction or remuneration, or that of his or her firm, is being discussed.

21.3 Any Trustee, being a corporation appointed to act as a custodian trustee, may act on its published terms and conditions in force from time to time, provided that this shall not authorise payment for any act done or services rendered by any director or other officer of such corporation in a personal capacity.

22 Costs

22.1 The Trustees shall have power to pay out of the capital or income of the Trust Fund all costs of and incidental to:

(a) the creation of the Charity; and

(b) the management and administration of the same, including the costs of appeals for funds, expenses and fees for fund raising and the services of financial consultants, professional managers and advisers in connection with any such appeal.

22.2 Subject to clauses 13 of Part 1 of this Deed (Trustee benefit clause) and 21 of Part 2 of this Deed (professional charging clause), no Trustee shall receive any such remuneration.

23 Change of name

Subject to the prior written approval of the Commission (if required), the Trustees may at any time or times alter the name of the Charity by deed.

24 Power of variation

24.1 Subject to the provisions of sub-clause 24.2, the Trustees shall have power to vary this Deed in any particular by any deed which shall be expressed to be supplemental to this Deed. From and after the date of any such supplemental deed, this Deed shall be read and construed as if the provisions of such supplemental deed were incorporated in this Deed.

24.2 (a) No such variation shall be made that shall cause the trusts declared by this Deed to cease to be charitable; and

(b) no variation shall be made to clauses 3 (objects), 13 (Trustee benefit), 20 (Trustees' indemnity insurance), 21 (Trustees' charging clause) or 26 (winding-up of charity) without the prior written approval of the Commission (if required by law).

25 Power to wind up charity

If at any time the Trustees are of the opinion that the purposes of the Charity can no longer be effectively carried out by them or can be more effectively carried out by others, it shall wind up the Charity. After discharging the debts of the Charity out of the Trust Fund, the Trustees shall transfer the remainder of the Trust Fund to such other charitable body or bodies, having objects the same as or similar to the Charity, in such proportions and on such terms as the Trustees shall in their discretion decide.

26 Committee of Trust Advisors

26.1 A Committee of Trust Advisors is hereby constituted to provide advice to the Trustees as the Committee deems it appropriate to give. The Committee shall have any and all powers provided to it hereunder, and should the Committee deem it desirable for any reason otherwise to diminish their powers, it shall promptly notify the Trustees in writing.

26.2 The Committee shall be comprised of no more than five (5) members and no fewer than one member. The first Chairman of the Committee shall be irrevocably appointed by the Original Trustee and shall hold office until such time as he shall respectively die, resign or become incapacitated. The remaining members of the Committee shall be appointed by the Chairman.

26.3 The first Chairman may appoint a first Vice-Chairman to serve for a term to be designated by the First Chairman, which Vice-Chairman shall also be designated as successor Chairman to serve in that capacity in the event that the first Chairman shall resign or for any reason cease or be unable to act as first Chairman. The first Chairman may, if he so chooses, appoint and designate subsequent Vice Chairmen and successor Chairmen. Subsequent Vice-Chairmen and other members shall be appointed by the then-acting Chairman so far as such action is not precluded by the above and shall serve for a term designated by him. Subsequent Chairmen so far as not precluded from the above may designate a successor Chairman. The Vice-Chairman may also serve as successor Chairman. All appointments and designations shall be made by an instrument in writing duly signed and acknowledged by the persons so making the appointment of designation and delivered to the Trustees. In the event that a successor Chairman has not been designated and the Chairman ceases or is unable or unwilling to act as Chairman, then the then-acting Vice-Chairman shall succeed to the position of Chairman. The person appointing a first Vice-Chairman, successor Chairman and subsequent Vice-Chairman shall have the power to terminate any such appointment.

26.4 For so long as the first Chairman shall serve in that position, all actions taken and advice rendered by the Committee shall require his approval only. Thereafter, all actions taken and advice rendered by the Committee shall require the written approval of a majority of the members (should there be more than one) either in the form of approval of the Minutes of meetings or unanimous consent to actions by proxy or otherwise. Approvals signed in counterpart shall be as valid as if signed on the same document.

26.5 In the event that the office of Chairman shall become vacant and no successor shall be named in accordance with clause 26.2 or 26.3, the Committee shall appoint one of its members to be Chairman who shall serve as such until he shall die, resign, or become incapacitated. If at any time there shall be no Chairman acting hereunder for a period of ninety (90) days, then the Trustees are empowered to appoint a successor Chairman to act hereunder.

26.6 A Trustee who in the opinion of the Committee is in any way interested otherwise than as a Trustee in any trust business proposed to be transacted at any meeting of the Trustees or who is otherwise subject or likely to be subject to any such extraneous constraint or influence as would in the opinion of the Committee preclude him from transacting any such trust business or exercising or refraining from exercising any power or discretion conferred upon him by this Settlement (whether alone or jointly with any others) or for any other reason determined in the sole discretion of the Committee shall not be entitled to participate in any such trust business or vote in regard to any decision to be made in connection therewith and may be removed as a Trustee as the Committee may direct. In the case of removal, the decision of the Committee shall be approved by the other Trustees not being removed, and the Committee may thereafter appoint a successor Trustee who must be an independent trustee. A certificate in writing signed by the Chairman of the Committee to the effect that the contents thereof represent the opinion of the Committee shall be conclusive evidence thereof, and neither the Trustees nor any other person entitled or interested or claiming to be entitled or interested under the trusts, powers and provisions contained in this Settlement shall be concerned or entitled to inquire into or question the propriety or validity of such opinion or the reasons therefor.

IN WITNESS WHEREOF the Original Trustee has hereunto set its hand and seal to be hereunto affixed as of the date and year first above written.

THE COMMON SEAL OF ________________ TRUST COMPANY LIMITED
was hereunto affixed in the presence of:

____

Bermuda Charitable Trust Template 080819

APPOINTMENT OF FIRST CHAIRMAN

OF THE

COMMITTEE OF TRUST ADVISORS

OF

THE ABC FOUNDATION

The Trustee of the ABC Foundation hereby appoints ________________ as the first Chairman of the Committee of Trust Advisors, effective immediately.

Date: ________________________ ______________________________

Duly Authorized Trustee

The COMMON SEAL of _____________)
TRUST COMPANY LIMITED)
was affixed in the presence of:)

____

APPENDIX 12

XYZ FOUNDATION

This irrevocable trust agreement made and entered into by and between ____________________, herein referred to as Settlor" and _____________ of _________________ and _____________________________________ of __________________________, herein referred to as "Trustees," on this __th day of _____________, 20__.

ARTICLE I

NAME

This trust shall be known as the XYZ FOUNDATION.

ARTICLE 11

TRUST PROPERTY

The trust property shall consist of any and all property listed on SCHEDULE A attached hereto and made a part hereof, and the Settlor hereby transfers and agrees to do all acts necessary to complete the transfer of such property to the Trustees.

The Settlor reserves the right to add property to the trust.

The Trustees may receive and accept property, whether real, personal, or mixed, by way of gift, bequest, legacy or devise, from any person, firm, trust, or corporation, to be held, administered, and disposed of in accordance with and pursuant to the provisions of this trust; but no gift, bequest, legacy or devise of any such property shall be received and accepted if it is conditioned or limited in such manner as to require the disposition of the income or its principal to any person or organization other than a "Charitable Organization" or for other than "Charitable Purposes" within the meaning of such terms as defined in Article VI of this trust, or as shall in the opinion of the Trustees, jeopardize either (i) the United States federal income tax exemption of this trust pursuant to Section 501(c)(3) of the United States Internal Revenue Code of 1986, as now in force or afterwards amended (such Code as may be amended from time to time and any successor provisions thereto shall be referred to herein as "Code"); (ii) the status of this trust as an organization described in Section 2055(a) of the Code at the time of the Settlor's death; or (iii) the status of this trust as an institution entitled to be treated as a charity under applicable ______________ law, as now in force or afterwards amended (such law as may be amended from time to time and any successor provisions thereto shall be referred to herein as "______________ Law).

All of the property listed in SCHEDULE A and all property subsequently coming into the possession of the Trustees shall be held in trust according to the terms and conditions hereinafter set forth.

ARTICLE III

ACCEPTANCE OF TRUST

The Trustees hereby accept all of the trust property listed in SCHEDULE A attached hereto, and all other property coming into the possession of the Trustees, and Trustees agree to administer and distribute the trust property and the income therefrom according to the terms and conditions hereinafter set forth.

ARTICLE IV

AMENDMENT, ALTERNATION OR REVOCATION

(a) This trust is irrevocable. This trust agreement may be amended at any time by a written document signed by the Settlor prior to issuance of a ruling or determination letter by the United States Internal Revenue Service recognizing that the trust is exempt under the Code ("IRS Tax Exempt Status Determination") and accepted by the Trustees, or after Settlor's death, by a written document signed by the Trustees and consented to, in writing, by the Advisory Committee in accordance with the requirements of Article XI; provided, however, that no such amendment made after issuance of an IRS Tax Exempt Status Determination shall be inconsistent with Sections 501(c)(3) or 2055(a) of the Code or any applicable provisions of the ______________ Law (unless in the case of amendments inconsistent with any applicable provisions of the ______________ Law such amendments are made pursuant to the exercise of the power given to the Trustees by Article IX(c)). An amendment to this Article IV (or any amendment to it) shall be valid only if and to the extent that such amendment further restricts the Settlor's and/or the Trustees' amending power. All documents or instruments amending this trust shall be noted upon or kept attached to the executed original (or executed counterpart) of this trust agreement held by the Trustees.

(b) The Settlor authorizes and empowers, but does not direct, the Trustees to form one or more corporations, at any time, to contain within its or their name the words "XYZ Foundation Limited" (or a name similar thereto) to carry out the purposes and exercise the powers provided by this agreement. Upon the organization of such corporation(s), the Trustees are authorized and empowered to transfer to the corporation(s) all or a portion of the property and income held by the trust. Any such corporation(s) shall be organized in ______________ or such other jurisdiction(s) as the Trustees shall determine and operated in a manner consistent with Sections 501(c)(3) and 2055(c) of the Code and all applicable provisions of ______________ Law. In addition, the Settlor authorizes and empowers, but does not direct, the

Trustees at any time, to transfer all or a portion of the trust property and income to, merge, consolidate, combine, or otherwise join with such Charitable Organizations (within the meaning of Article VI(b)) as the Settlor has or may hereafter create or organize during his lifetime or at death; provided, however for that any such Charitable Organization is organized and operated for Charitable Purposes within the meaning of Article VI(c).

ARTICLE V

TERM, PERIOD FOR COMMENCING OPERATIONS; TIME FOR FILING FOR TAX EXEMPTION

(a) This trust, including any successor, unless the trust shall have sooner terminated in accordance with Article IV, shall continue forever, provided, however, that at any time after twenty-five (25) years after the date of the Settlor's death, the Trustees may terminate this trust with the written consent of the Advisory Committee in accordance with the requirements of Article XI. On such termination, the trust property and income as then constituted shall be distributed to or for the use of such Charitable Organizations, in such amounts and for such Charitable Purposes as the Trustees shall then select and determine.

(b) For purposes of complying with _____________ Law, it is hereby stated that this trust in all events shall commence operations prior to the greater of 21 years after the death of the Settlor [insert appropriate language in compliance with applicable Rule against Perpetuities] as the Trustees may determine is required under any applicable _____________ Law.

(c) It is anticipated that this trust may file an application to be recognized as an exempt organization under United States tax law and that this filing might be made at a time when the Settlor's family's interest in Optimay Corporation is less than twenty (20) percent.

ARTICLE VI

CHARITABLE PURPOSES

(a) (1) The principal and income of all property received and accepted by the Trustees to be administered under this trust shall be held in trust by it, and the Trustees may make payments or distributions from income or principal, or both, to or for the use of such Charitable Organizations, within the meaning of that tern as defined in paragraph (b) of this Article, in such amounts and for such Charitable Purposes of the trust as the Trustees shall from time to time select and determine; and the Trustees may make payments or distributions from income or principal, or both, directly for such Charitable Purposes, within the meaning of that term as defined in paragraph (c), in such amounts as the Trustees shall from time to time select and determine without making use of any other Charitable Organization. The Trustees may also make payments or distributions of all or any part of the income or principal to states, territories, or possessions of the United States, any political subdivision of any of the foregoing, or to the United States or the District of Columbia but only for Charitable Purposes within the meaning of that term as defined in paragraph (c). No part of the net earnings of this trust shall inure or be payable to or for the benefit of any private shareholder or individual and no substantial part of the activities of this trust shall be the carrying on of propaganda, or otherwise attempting, to influence legislation in any jurisdiction. No part of the activities of this trust in any jurisdiction shall be the participation in, or intervention in (including the publishing or distributing of statements) any political campaign on behalf of any candidate for public office.

(2) The trust shall distribute its income for each taxable year at such time and in such manner as not to become subject to the tax on undistributed income imposed by Section 4942 of the Code.

(3) The trust shall not engage in any act of self-dealing as defined in Section 4941(d) of the Code.

(4) The trust shall not retain any excess business holdings as defined in Section 4943(c) of theCode which would subject the trust to tax under Section 4943 of the Code.

(5) The trust shall not make any investments in such manner as to subject it to tax under Section 4944 of the Code.

(6) The trust shall not make any taxable expenditures as defined in Section 4945(d) of the Code.

(7) Notwithstanding any other provisions of this trust agreement, the trust shall not conduct or carry on any activities not permitted to be conducted or carried on by an organization exempt under Section 501(c)(3) of the Code and its regulations as they now exist or as they may hereafter be amended, or by an organization to which bequests, legacies, devises, or transfers are deductible under Section 2055(a) of such Code and its regulations as they now exist or as they may hereafter be amended.

(b) In this trust agreement and in any amendments to it, references to "Charitable Organizations" or "Charitable Organization" mean corporations, trusts, funds, foundations, or community chests created or organized and operated exclusively for Charitable Purposes, no part of the net earnings of which inures or is payable to or for the benefit of any private shareholder or individual, and no substantial part of the activities of which is carrying on propaganda, or otherwise attempting, to influence legislation, and which do not participate in or intervene in (including the publishing or distributing of statements) any political campaign on behalf of any candidate for public office. It is intended that the organization(s) described in this paragraph (b) shall be entitled to exemption from United States federal income tax under Section 501(c)(3) of the Code and shall be organization(s) to which bequests, legacies, devises or transfers are deductible for United States federal estate tax purposes under Section 2055(a) of such Code. Such organization(s) may include registered charities in ______________, as defined in applicable ______________ Law.

(c) In this trust agreement and in any amendments to it, the term "Charitable Purposes" shall be limited to and shall include only religious, charitable, scientific, literary, or educational purposes within the meaning of those terms as used in Sections 501(c)(3) and 2055(a) of the Code and _____________ Law.

(d) The trust shall maintain a substantial and genuine connection with _____________ as defined in _____________ Law for the purposes of safeguarding the status of the Trust as a _____________ qualified charity.

(e) For as long as this trust shall be a _____________ qualified charity the Trustees shall distribute in priority and before any other payment or distribution pursuant to subparagraph Article (a)(1) of this Article, whether out of income or out of principal, the sum of US$1,000 (One Thousand U.S. Dollars) per annum for such one or more Charitable Purposes which in the opinion of the Trustees shall be beneficial to the communities or inhabitants of _____________ and upon this trust ceasing to be a _____________ qualified charity the Trustees may make such distribution as it deems appropriate and the absolute entitlement conferred by this subparagraph (e) shall cease. This provision shall not take effect until such time as this trust disposes of some or all of the Optimay Corporation shares transferred to it upon its establishment.

ARTICLE VII

DEATH TAX CLAIMS

The principal and income of this trust shall not be subject to claim for any taxing jurisdiction's estate, inheritance or succession taxes or duties which may be assessed against the estate of the Settlor or due because of the Settlor's death provided that the Settlor, at the date of his death, is not a resident or domiciliary of _____________ and no assets included in his estate are located in _____________.

ARTICLE VIII

TRUSTEES' POWERS

Except as limited by Article VI hereof, the Trustees shall have all the usual powers conferred by law upon Trustees in every jurisdiction in which the Trustees may act. Subject to Article VI and in extension and not in limitation of law and statutory powers of Trustees and other powers granted in this agreement, the Trustees shall have the following additional powers:

(a) To invest and reinvest the principal and income of the trust in such property, real, personal, or mixed, and in such manner as it shall deem proper, and from time to time to change investments as it shall deem advisable; to invest in or retain any stocks, shares, bonds, notes, obligations, or personal or real property (including without limitation any interests in or obligations of any corporation, association business trust, investment trust, common trust fund, or investment company) although some or all of the property so acquired or retained is of a kind or size which but for this express authority would not be considered proper and although all of the trust funds are invested in the securities of one company. No principal or income, however, shall be loaned, directly or indirectly, to any Trustees or to anyone else, corporate or otherwise, who has at any time made a contribution to this trust, nor to anyone except on the basis of an adequate interest charge and with adequate security.

(b) To sell, lease, or exchange any personal, mixed, or real property, at public auction or by private contract, for such consideration and on such terms as to credit or otherwise, and to make such contracts and enter into such undertakings relating to the trust property, as it considers advisable, whether or not such leases or contracts may extend beyond the duration of the trust.

(c) To borrow money for such periods, at such rates of interest, and upon such terms as the Trustees considers advisable, and as security for such loans to mortgage or pledge any real or personal property with or without power of sale; to acquire or hold any real or personal property, subject to any mortgage or pledge on or of property acquired or held by this trust.

(d) To execute and deliver deeds, assignments, transfers, mortgages, pledges, leases, covenants, contracts, promissory notes, releases, and other instruments, sealed or unsealed, incident to any transaction in which it engages.

(e) To vote, to give proxies to participate in the reorganization, merger or consolidation of any concern, or in the sale, lease, disposition, or distribution of its assets; to join with other security holders in acting through a committee, depository, voting trustees, or otherwise, and in this connection to delegate authority to such committee, depository, or trustees and to deposit securities with them or transfer securities to them; to pay assessments levied on securities or to exercise subscription rights in respect of securities.

(f) To employ a bank or trust company as custodian of any funds or securities and to delegate to it such powers as it deems appropriate; to hold trust property without indication of fiduciary capacity but only in the name of a registered nominee, provided the trust property is at all times identified as such on the books of the trust; to keep any or all of the trust property or funds in any place or places in the world; to employ clerks, accountants, investment counsel, investment agents, and any special services, and to pay the reasonable compensation and expenses of all such services in addition to the compensation of the Trustees and the Advisory Committee.

The Trustees' powers are exercisable solely in their fiduciary capacity consistent with and in furtherance of the Charitable Purposes of this trust as specified in Article VI and not otherwise. In this trust agreement and in any amendment to it, references to "Trustees" means the one or more trustees, whether original or successor, for the time being in office. Any person may rely upon a copy, certified by a notary public or an officer of a court, of the executed original (or executed counterpart) of this trust agreement held by the Trustees, and of any of the notations on it and writings attached to it, as fully as he might rely on the original documents themselves. Any such person may rely fully upon any statements of facts certified by anyone who appears from such documents or from such certified copy to be a trustee under this trust agreement. No one dealing with the Trustees need inquire concerning the validity of anything the Trustees purport to do. No one dealing with the Trustees needs to see the application of anything paid or transferred to or upon the order of the Trustees or the trust.

ARTICLE IX

GOVERNING LAW; SITUS OF ADMINISTRATION POWER TO CREATE SEPARATE TRUSTS-, POWER TO CHANGE GOVERNING LAW AND/OR SITUS OF ADMINISTRATION

(a) This trust is established under the laws of _____________ (unless either a different law is selected, or a change of place of management and control of the trust property and income is made, by the Trustees under paragraph (b) of this Article) and the rights of all parties and the construction and effect of each provision hereof, subject only as herein appears, shall be subject to the exclusive jurisdiction of and construed only according to the said laws of _____________ which, subject as aforesaid, shall be the forum for the administration hereof. Notwithstanding the foregoing, this trust and the provisions hereof shall be construed in a manner consistent with (i) the Charitable Purposes and limitations as set forth in Article VI hereof and (ii) the Code provisions referenced in this trust agreement. It is the Settlor's intention that this trust shall be qualified as an organization described in Section 2055(a) of such Code at the time of his death and at all other relevant times so as to ensure that all bequests, legacies, devises and transfers to this trust received by it on account of Settlor's death, if any, shall be deductible for United States federal estate tax purposes under Section 2055(a) of such Code.

(b) Subject as hereinabove provided in Articles IV, V, VI, and VII the Trustees may pay or transfer any trust property and income to the Trustees of any trust (whether or not governed by the law of _____________), the charitable purposes of which are the same as those of this trust. The receipt of a recipient Trustees shall be a complete and absolute discharge to the Trustees paying or transferring for such payment or transfer and all and any liability of the latter Trustees in relation to the money property or investments so paid or transferred shall thereupon cease.

(c) The Trustees may by any deed revocable or irrevocable declare that this trust shall from the date of such declaration take effect in accordance with the laws of any other place in any part of the world or have the administration of this trust including the situs of the trust property and income removed to any other place in any other part of the world with full effects regarding the jurisdiction and the forum for the administration and with the rights for the Trustees to make in its absolute discretion such alterations in the trust provisions as it considers necessary to secure that this trust be rendered as valid and effective under the laws of the country named in such declaration as it is under the laws of _____________, PROVIDED THAT no such deed shall take effect unless and until a copy thereof shall have been endorsed on or annexed to this trust agreement and that no such alteration be inconsistent, in any material respect, with the Charitable Purposes and limitations of Article VI hereof

ARTICLE X

ADDITIONAL TRUSTEES PROVISIONS

(a) Number of Trustees.

The number of Trustees shall be not less than one and not more than three at least one of whom shall be resident in ______________ so long as this trust is governed by the laws of ______________.

(b) Meetings of Trustees.

The Trustees shall meet together for the conduct of trust business and otherwise regulate their meetings in such manner as they shall in heir absolute discretion think fit.

(c) Calling of Meetings of Trustees.

Any Trustees or the Chairman of the Advisory Committee shall be entitled to convene a meeting of the Trustees by giving to the other Trustees and to the Chairman of the Advisory Committee seven days notice in writing thereof specifying the date, time and place at which such meeting is to be held and the business to be transacted thereat.

(d) Conduct of Meetings of Trustees.

If within half an hour from the time appointed for the holding of the meeting any two or more Trustees (if more than one trustees is then serving) shall be present, the trustees present shall constitute a quorum. The Trustees present shall elect one of their number to be the Chairman of the meeting and shall proceed to business. Decisions taken and business transacted at such meeting shall be valid for all the purposes of this trust agreement and shall be binding on any dissenting Trustee and any Trustee absent from the meeting.

(e) Conduct of Meeting Attended By One Trustee.

If within half an hour from the time appointed for the holding of the meeting one Trustee only shall be present, such Trustee shall constitute the meeting and the Chairman thereof and shall proceed to business. Decisions taken and business transacted by such Trustee shall be valid for all the purposes of this trust agreement and shall be binding on any Trustees absent from the meeting.

(f) Representative of Corporate Trustees.

A Trustee which is a corporation may by resolution of its directors or other governing body authorize such individual as it thinks fit to act as its representative at any meeting of the Trustees and any person so authorized shall be entitled to exercise the same powers on behalf of the corporation which he represents as the corporation could have exercised if it were an individual.

(g) Voting of Trustees.

Decisions of the Trustees shall be taken by majority vote. In the event of an equality of votes, the trustee acting as Chairman shall have a casting vote. A declaration by the Chairman that a particular resolution proposed has been carried or lost and an entry to that effect in the minutes of the meeting signed by the Chairman shall be conclusive evidence thereof and no Charitable Organization or other person entitled or interested or claiming to be entitled or interested under the trusts powers and provisions contained in this trust agreement shall be concerned or entitled to inquire into or question the proprietary or validity of the passing or otherwise of such resolution.

(h) Minutes of Meetings.

The Trustees shall keep minutes of their meetings and such minutes if signed by the Chairman shall be conclusive evidence of the proceedings thereof and of any decisions taken at the meeting to which the minutes relate and no Charitable Organization or other person entitled or interested or claiming to be entitled or interested under the trusts powers and provisions contained in this trust agreement shall be concerned or entitled to inquire into or question the propriety or validity of any such proceedings or decision.

(i) Resolutions at Meetings.

A resolution in writing signed by or on behalf of all the Trustees for the time being hereof shall be as valid and effective as a resolution passed at a meeting of the Trustees duly convened and held and may consist of one or more documents signed as aforesaid.

(j) Removal and Appointment of Trustees.

(1) The Settlor shall have the right, during his lifetime, to terminate the appointment of any Trustee or any member of the Advisory Committee, with or without cause.

(2) A Trustee who, in the opinion of the Advisory Committee, is in any way interested otherwise than as a trustee in any trust business proposed to be transacted at any meeting of the Trustees or who is otherwise subject or likely to be subject to any such extraneous constraint or influence as would in the opinion of the Advisory Committee preclude them from transacting any such trust business or exercising or refraining from exercising any power or discretion conferred upon him by this trust agreement whether alone or jointly with any other or others solely in the best interests of this trust or any Charitable Organization or other person entitled or interested under the trusts powers and provisions in this trust agreement contained shall not be entitled to participate in any such trust business or vote in regard to any decision to be made in connection therewith and may be removed as a Trustee as the Advisory Committee may direct or by the Settlor as provided by the preceding subparagraph (1) hereof. In the case of removal of any Trustee by the Advisory Committee, the decision of the Advisory Committee shall be approved by the other Trustees not being removed. In the case of removal of any Trustee by the Advisory Committee or by the Settlor as aforesaid, then the Advisory Committee may thereafter appoint a successor Trustee who must be an independent trustee. A certificate in writing signed by the Chairman of the Advisory Committee to the effect that the contents thereof represent the opinion of the Advisory Committee shall be conclusive evidence thereof and neither the Trustees nor any Charitable Organization nor other person entitled or interested or claiming to be entitled or interested under the trusts powers and provisions in this trust agreement contained shall be concerned or entitled to inquire into or question the propriety or validity of such opinion or the reasons therefor PROVIDED THAT nothing herein shall in any way preclude any Trustee excluded hereunder from participation in any trust business or from voting in connection therewith from executing any deed or document whether alone or jointly with the other Trustees or from otherwise giving effect to any decision of the other Trustees or shall in any way invalidate the execution of any deed or document by the Trustee whether by the Trustee itself or by a duly appointed attorney.

(k) Trustees to Act Without Interference But With Advice of The Committee.

Notwithstanding anything to the contrary in this trust agreement expressed or implied, the Advisory Committee shall in no circumstances transact any trust business, make any decisions, or exercise or refrain from exercising any powers or discretions to be transacted, made or exercised under this trust agreement by the Trustees or, subject as hereinabove provided in Article X(j) hereof, in any way participate or interfere in the transaction of any such business making or in any such decisions or the exercise or otherwise of any such discretion PROVIDED THAT the Trustees shall be entitled at all times to consider and have regard to the advice of the Advisory Committee in transacting trust business, making decisions, or exercising or refraining from exercising powers and discretions as aforesaid.

ARTICLE XI

ADVISORY COMMITTEE

(a) Constitution.

An Advisory Committee (the "Committee") is hereby constituted to provide advice to the Trustees as the Committee deems it appropriate to give and such consent to the Trustees as this trust agreement may require. The Committee shall have any and all powers provided to it hereunder. Should the Committee deem it desirable for any reason to otherwise diminish its powers it shall promptly notify the Trustees in writing.

(b) Membership.

The Advisory Committee shall be comprised of no fewer than one and no more than three members. The original members of the Committee shall be [the Settlor] and one or two other individuals that may be selected by him and shall hold office until such time as they shall respectively die, resign or be removed as provided in this Article XI or Article X(j)(1). The first Chairman shall be [the Settlor] who shall serve as such until he shall die, resign or be removed from office as hereinafter provided in this Article XI.

(c) Vice-Chairman And Successor Chairman.

(1) During his lifetime, the first Chairman shall have the sole and absolute right to select and appoint the Vice-Chairman of the Committee and his successor Chairman. The successor Chairman need not be a member of the Committee at the time of his designation and appointment, but shall be an individual who meets the qualifications set out at paragraph (f) of this Article. The Vice-Chairman shall have such duties and serve for such term as determined by the first Chairman. All designations and appointments by the first Chairman may be made by will or a written instrument duly signed and acknowledged by him and delivered to the Trustees.

(2) Upon the death of the first Chairman, or should the first Chairman become unable or unwilling to act as Chairman, then his successor Chairman shall be the individual duly designated and appointed by the first Chairman as provided by the preceding subparagraph. In the event that a successor Chairman has not been so designated and the first Chairman ceases or is unable or unwilling to act as Chairman, then the then-acting Vice-Chairman shall succeed to the position of Chairman and should the Vice-Chairman cease or be unable to serve in the capacity of Chairman, then the Trustees are empowered and directed to appoint one of the remaining members of the Committee to act as a successor Chairman hereunder for a term of no more than three (3) years. Thereafter, any other successor Chairman shall be designated and appointed by the Trustees from the members of the Committee, on a rotating basis and for such term as the Trustees shall determine. The person(s) appointing a first Vice-Chairman, successor Chairman, and subsequent Vice-Chairman shall have the power to terminate any such appointment.

(d) Voting.

For so long as the first Chairman shall serve in that position all actions taken and advice rendered by the Committee shall require his approval only. Thereafter, except as hereinbelow specifically provided otherwise, all actions taken and advice rendered by the Committee shall require the written approval of a majority of the members should there be more than one either in the form of approval of the minutes of meetings, unanimous consent to actions by proxy or otherwise. Approvals signed in counterpart shall be as valid as if signed on the same document. After the first Chairman's death, resignation or removal from office as provided in this Article XI, the following Committee actions shall require the written approval of at least two (2) of the members of the Committee (or if less than two (2) members of the Committee are then serving or entitled to vote hereunder, such actions will require the unanimous written approval of such members).

(1) Any written consent to any amendment to this trust agreement by the Trustees;

(2) Removal of any Trustee and appointment of its successor;

(3) Removal of any member of the Committee (in which even, the member who is the subject of removal shall not vote with respect to the same);

(4) Designation and appointment of a new member of the Committee; and

(5) Diminution of the powers of the Committee as provided herein.

(c) Removal for Incapacity of Chairman Or Vice-Chairman Or Members.

If the Chairman or Vice-Chairman of the Committee or any member thereof shall in the opinion of the Committee (as determined pursuant to paragraph (d) of this Article) be unable or unwilling to act as such, the Committee, by notice in writing to the Trustees and such non-acting member, may remove him from office. In so removing a Chairman, Vice-Chairman or Committee Member from office, the Committee may consider any relevant evidence, including medical evidence. No member of the Committee, Charitable Organization or any other person entitled or interested or claiming to be entitled or interested under the trusts powers and provisions in this trust agreement shall be in any way concerned or entitled to inquire into or question the removal by the Committee of any such Chairman, Vice-Chairman or member. Upon such removal, the Committee shall designate and appoint a successor member of the Committee and shall notify the Trustees, in writing, of the appointment of any such successor.

(f) Qualifications for Members of the Committee.

Any successor member of the Committee must satisfy the following requirements: Such successor must be at least twenty-one (21) years of age.

No member of the Committee, other than the first Chairman, shall be permitted to serve as such after reaching seventy-five (75) years of age and shall be automatically treated as removed from such membership upon the earlier of (i) December 31 of the year in which such member attains such age; or (ii) the designation and appointment of such member's successor as provided herein. Such retiring member and the remaining members of the Committee shall designate and appoint such retiring member's successor in accordance with the provisions of this Article.

(g) Compensation of Committee.

The members of the Committee shall be entitled to reasonable compensation for their services rendered as such and for reimbursement of their out-of-pocket expenses reasonably incurred in connection with such services. Such compensation and reimbursement shall be paid out of the trust property or income.

ARTICLE XII

RECORDS AND ACCOUNTING

The Trustees shall keep accurate accounts of its Trusteeship and, after Settlor's death, shall have them audited annually by a firm of certified public accountants or chartered accountants of good repute to be selected by the Trustees and the expenses of such audit shall be paid either out of the capital or income of this trust as the Trustees may decide to be appropriate. It is intended that such accounting and audit shall comply with the requirements of ______________ Law. All records and accounts shall be open to inspection by the Committee.

ARTICLE XIII

COMPENSATION OF TRUSTEES; AUTHORIZATION TO ACT IN OTHER CAPACITIES; POWER TO OBTAIN RELEASES AND INDEMNITIES

(a) Compensation of Trustees.

A Trustee of this trust shall be entitled to be reasonably remunerated, and reimbursed and indemnified for expenditures as follows:

(1) On the basis of any agreement entered into by correspondence or otherwise between such person or corporation and the Settlor on or before the appointment of such person or corporation as Trustees and in default of any such express agreement then;

(2) On the basis of the terms and conditions as to the acceptance of Trusteeship and remuneration chargeable therefor published by such person or corporation and current at the date of the appointment of such person or corporation as Trustees and in default of any such published terms and conditions then;

(3) On the basis of a reasonable recompense to trust business transacted, time expended, and acts and things done by such person or corporation including time expended and acts and things done on behalf of such person or corporation by any partner of any such person or by any corporation subsidiary to or associated with any such corporation and also;

4) To be reimbursed for any expenditure properly incurred in the transaction of trust business, in the execution or administration of the said trust or in the exercise of the said powers and discretions;

(5) To deduct and retain from any money from time to time under the control of the Trustees and included in or forming part of the trust property or income or subject to any trust created under the powers and discretions in this trust agreement contained a sum equal to the amount of any such remuneration and expenditure as aforesaid then due and owing; and

(6) To be indemnified out of the trust property or income or out of any money investments or property for the time being subject to any trust created under the powers and discretions contained in this trust agreement in respect of any expenditure properly incurred as mentioned in subparagraph (a) (iv) of this Article.

(b) Corporate Trustees.

A corporation being a successor or substituted Trustees hereof may transact in its own office on behalf of the trust any business which by its constitution it is authorized to undertake upon the same terms as would for the time being be made with an ordinary customer and may retain on current or deposit account or advance at interest all moneys necessary or convenient to be retained or advanced in connection with the trust premises.

(c) Indemnification of Trustees and the Advisory Committee.

Except as otherwise required by law, no Trustee nor any member of the Advisory Committee shall be responsible or liable for the acts or omissions of any other of the Trustees or the members of the Committee or of any predecessor or of a custodian, agent, depository or counsel selected with reasonable care. Except as otherwise required by law, no Trustees nor any member of the Committee shall be liable for any acts or omissions in connection with the subject matter hereof except in the case of such Trustees' or such Committee member's fraud negligence or intentional or willful disregard of the provisions hereof. Except as limited in this paragraph (c), the Trustees and the members of the Committee shall be indemnified out of the trust property or income for all reasonable costs, damages, legal fees, expenses and liabilities, which in good faith, and without fault in its or their part, the Trustees or the Committee members may incur or sustain in connection with its or their performance under this agreement.

ARTICLE XIV

THIRD-PARTIES

Any person may rely upon a copy, certified by a notary public or an officer of a court, of the executed original (or executed counterpart) of this trust agreement held by the Trustees, and of any of the notations on it and writings attached to it, as fully as he might rely on the original documents themselves. Any such person may rely fully upon any statements of fact certified by anyone who appears from such documents or from such certified copy to be a trustee under this trust agreement. No one dealing with the Trustees need inquire concerning the validity of anything the Trustees purport to do. No one dealing with the Trustees needs to see the application of anything paid or transferred to or upon the order of the Trustees or the trust.

ARTICLE XV

SETTLOR EXCLUSION

Notwithstanding anything to the contrary hereinbefore contained no discretion or power by this trust conferred on the Trustees shall be exercised and no provision of this trust shall operate so as to cause any part of the income or principal of the trust fund to become payable to or applicable for the benefit of the Settlor or any spouse of the Settlor or any person who shall contribute to the trust fund or the spouse of any such person.

ARTICLE XVI

NOTICE TO TRUSTEES

Communications, correspondence, directions, notices, consents, designations, appointments, statements, releases, or other documents to be delivered to the Trustees may be delivered to _______________ at the address set forth in SCHEDULE B hereto or such other address as the Trustees or any successor thereto shall designate in writing to the Committee.

IN WITNESS WHEREOF, the Settlor and the Trustees have executed this Agreement as of the date first-above written.

SETTLOR:

____

TRUSTEE:

____

TRUSTEE:

____

Generic Charitable Trust Template 080819

APPENDIX 13

DATE:

DECLARATION OF TRUST

constituting

THE ____________________ INTERNATIONAL FOUNDATION CHARITABLE TRUST

A BERMUDA PURPOSE TRUST

THE _____________ INTERNATIONAL FOUNDATION CHARITABLE TRUST

Table of contents

DECLARATION OF TRUST

THIS DECLARATION OF TRUST is made the 28th day of December, 2006 by ________________________________TRUST COMPANY LTD., a licensed trust company incorporated under the laws of Bermuda and having its principal office at _____________________, Hamilton, Bermuda (the “Original Trustee”).

RECITALS

(A) The Trustee has agreed to make this Declaration of Trust, and has received the property specified in the Schedule to be held by it on the trusts specified below. It intends to accept donations, subscriptions, covenants, sponsorships, legacies and other gifts to be held on the same trusts.

(B) The Settlor intends hereby to create a purpose trust within the meaning of the Trusts (Special Provisions) Act 1989 as amended in the manner hereinafter appearing.

(C) This trust shall be irrevocable.

PART 1—OPERATIVE PROVISIONS

1 Title

The charity constituted by this Deed shall be called **THE ____________ INTERNATIONAL FOUNDATION CHARITABLE TRUST** or such other name as the Trustee may from time to time determine in accordance with the power contained in this Deed.

2 Definitions and construction

In this Deed, where the context admits, the following definitions and rules of construction shall apply.

2.1 The "Act" means the Trusts (Special Revisions) Act 1989 as amended.

2.2 The **‘Charity’** shall mean the charity constituted by this Deed.

2.3 The **‘Committee’** shall mean the Committee of Trust Advisors as constituted in Part 2, clause 27 of this Deed.

2.4 The **‘Trust Fund’** shall mean:

(a) the property specified in the Schedule;

(b) all money, investments or other property paid or transferred by any person to, or so as to be under the control of, and in either case, accepted by the Trustee;

(c) all accumulations (if any) of income; and

(d) the money, investments and property from time to time representing the above.

2.5 The '**Code**' shall mean the Internal Revenue Code 1986 of the United States of America as amended and any successor statue to such code.

2.6 **'Charitable'** means charitable according to the law of Bermuda and within the meaning of Section 501(c)(3) of the Code.

2.7 The **'Commission'** shall mean the Charity Commissioners for Bermuda.

2.8 The "**Enforcer**" means Jonathon R. Moore or such other person or persons who is or are appointed by or pursuant to clause 29 as an enforcer for purposes of the Act.

2.9 The **'Grant Advisory Committee'** shall mean the Grant Advisory Committee as constituted in Part 2, clause 28 of this Deed.

2.10 The "Purposes" means the purposes described in clause 3.

2.11 The expression '**the Trustees**' shall, where the context admits, include the trustee or trustees for the time being of this Trust and where a trustee is a corporation, the provisions relating to individual trustees shall apply *mutatis mutandis* to a corporate trustee.

2.12 Words denoting the singular shall include the plural and vice versa.

2.13 Words denoting any gender shall include both the other genders.

2.14 References to any statutory provision shall include any statutory modification or re-enactment of such provision.

2.15 The table of contents and clause headings are included for reference only and shall not affect the interpretation of this Deed.

3 Purposes

3.1 The Trustee shall hold the capital and income of the Trust Fund upon trust to apply the income and all or such part or parts of the capital, at such times and in such manner, as the Trustee may in its discretion think fit for:

(a) the advancement of [insert specific purpose] in the world;

(b) the advancement of [insert additional specific purpose] in the world;

(c) the benefit of such other exclusively charitable religious, cultural, educational, and scientific objects and purposes including, for such purposes, the making of distributions to organizations and institutions described in section 501(c)(3) of the Code in the world as the Trustee may in its discretion think fit

PROVIDED THAT no donations or other distributions shall be made to any "United States person" within the meaning of the Code (or to any other person that would cause the Charity to have a "United States beneficiary" within the meaning of Section 679 of the Code). In accomplishing the foregoing objects, the Trustee may engage in research; the dissemination and distribution of its results through seminars, publications or otherwise; the promotion of techniques, equipment and methodologies; and the licensing of the foregoing, either directly or through new or existing organizations, whether such organizations be organized for profit, non-profit or charitable purposes.

3.2 The Trustee shall not apply any part of the Trust Fund directly in relief of public funds, but may apply the whole or any part of the Trust Fund in supplementing public funds.

3.3 The Trustee may, in its discretion, instead of applying the income of the Charity in any year, accumulate all or any part of such income at compound interest by investing the same, and the resulting income, in any authorised investments and shall hold the same as an accretion to and as part of the capital of the Charity, without prejudice to their right to apply the whole or any part of such accumulated income in any subsequent year as if the same were income of the Charity arising in the then current year.

3.4 In exercising its discretion to apply assets of the Trust Fund to the foregoing objects, the Trustee may consider any recommendations made to the Trustees by the Grant Advisory Committee. Any such recommendations made by the Grant Advisory Committee shall be only advisory in nature and the Trustee shall not be bound in any way to accept the same.

3.5 Notwithstanding any other provision herein, the Charity shall not carry on any other activities not permitted to be carried on by an organization exempt from United States Federal income tax under section 501(c)(3) of the Code or the corresponding section of any future United States Federal tax code.

4 Conduct of charity and general management powers

The Trustee shall conduct the affairs of the Charity in such manner as it may consider appropriate, and may make such arrangements in relation to the administration of the Charity as it considers advisable.

5 Accounts, reports and returns

The Trustees shall maintain financial records, and prepare and submit accounts and returns, in accordance with the requirements of the Charities Act 1978. The Trustees shall enter the details of this Trust as required by the Act on a register kept for that purpose by the Trustees.

6 Exercise of trustees' powers and discretions

6.1 The Trustee shall, in addition and without prejudice to clause 4 and all statutory powers, have the powers and immunities set out in Part 2 of this Deed.

6.2 No power or discretion conferred on the Trustee shall be exercised except in furtherance of the charitable objects. No portion of the Trust Fund shall be distributed as a private inurement or benefit in contravention of the objects of the Charity as set forth in clause 3 hereof.

6.3 No part of the income or principal of the Charity shall inure to the benefit of, or be distributable to the Trustees or other private persons, except that the Charity shall be authorized and empowered to pay reasonable compensation for services rendered and to make payments and distributions in furtherance of the purposes set forth in Part 1, clause 3 of this Deed. No substantial part of the activities of the Charity shall be the carrying on of propaganda, or otherwise attempting to influence legislation, and the Charity shall not participate in, or intervene in (including the publishing or distribution of statements) any political campaign on behalf of or in opposition to any candidate for public office. Notwithstanding any other provision of these articles, the Charity shall not carry on any other activities not permitted to be carried on an organization exempt from United States Federal income tax under section 501(c)(3) of the Code or the corresponding section of any future United States Federal tax code.

7 **Appointment of new trustees**

7.1 A new trustee or new trustees may be appointed at any time (either by way of replacement or addition) by the Committee but so that the total number of Trustees shall at no time exceed three PROVIDED ALWAYS THAT a majority of the Trustees shall be persons who are not "related or subordinate parties" within the meaning of Sections 672(c) and 674(c) of the Code to any member of the Committee or the Grant Advisory Committee.

7.2 A trustee may be appointed or discharged by a resolution of a meeting of the Committee, provided that a memorandum declaring such appointment or discharge shall be signed as a deed, either at the meeting by the person presiding, or in some other manner directed by the meeting, and attested by two other persons present at the meeting. Any Trustee which is discharged or resigns shall be provided an indemnity by the remaining and/or new trustee(s) in a form satisfactory to the discharged trustee.

7.3 Any person may be appointed a trustee of this Trust whether resident or incorporated (as the case may be) within or outside the jurisdiction of the Proper Law of this Trust PROVIDED THAT so long as the Proper Law shall be the law of Bermuda any sole Trustee hereof or at least one of the Trustees shall be a designated person within the meaning given to that expression by the Act.

8 **Meetings**

8.1 The Trustees shall hold at least one meeting in each calendar year.

8.2 One half of the number (for the time being) of the Trustees will form a quorum at any meeting.

8.3 Trustees shall attend meetings in person unless the Trustees shall agree another appropriate means of communication between those taking part.

9 **Voting**

9.1 Save in exercise of the powers in clauses 25 (to vary the terms of this Deed) and 26 (to wind up the Charity) and set out in Part 2 of this Deed, which shall be exercisable only by unanimous decision of the Trustees, a decision of the majority of the Trustees present and voting at any duly constituted meeting shall be valid and binding on all the Trustees.

9.2 Any of the Trustees who shall dissent from such a decision shall nevertheless concur in executing or signing any document or doing any act necessary for giving effect to such decision without being responsible for any resulting loss.

10 Written resolutions

A resolution in writing signed by all the Trustees shall be as valid as a resolution passed at a meeting.

11 Ratification

The Trustees may implement decisions reached by them informally, provided that such decisions are ratified at the next or subsequent meeting of the Trustees.

12 Notices

Notices to be given to the Trustees shall be in writing and shall be sufficiently given if delivered to any one of the Trustees either personally, or sent via courier to the usual or last known address of such Trustee.

13 Trustee benefit

13.1 Subject to the provisions of clause 20 (power to take out trustee indemnity insurance) and clause 22 (professional trustees' charging) in Part 2 of this Deed, no Trustee may

(a) receive any benefit in money or kind from the Charity (other than reasonable out of pocket expenses); or

(b) have a financial interest in the supply of goods or services to the Charity; or

(c) acquire or hold any interest in property of the Charity (except in order to hold it as Trustee of the Charity).

13.2 Notwithstanding the provisions of sub-clause 13.1, the Trustees shall not, nor shall any of them, be accountable for any remuneration or other benefit received by the Trustees, or any of them (whether as director, auditor or other officer or otherwise), from any company in which shares, stock, debentures or other securities are for the time being held by the Trustees as trustees, except to the extent (if any) to which such remuneration or other benefit is received by the Trustees or any of them by reason of such shares, stock, debentures or other securities being in the name of the Trustees or held on their behalf. None of the Trustees shall concur in exercising any voting rights in respect of any shares, stock, debentures or other securities comprised in the Trust Fund in such a way that a personal benefit is thereby secured to the Trustees or any of them.

14 Construction

14.1 In making this Declaration, it is the intention of the Trustee that the Charity be organized and operated as an organization described in sections 501(c)(3) and 2522 (a)(2) of the Code.

14.2 In making this Declaration, it is the intention of the Trustee that the Charity be created as a non-grantor trust and so characterized for purposes of the Code.

PART 2—ADMINISTRATIVE PROVISIONS

General charitable trust administrative powers

Table of contents

1 General

1.1 The Trustees shall have power to do all such lawful acts or things as shall further the attainment of the Objects.

1.2 Subject to such restrictions as may be imposed by law, or such consents as may be required by law, the Trustees shall have all the powers of an absolute beneficial owner in relation to the management and administration of the Trust Fund.

1.3 This Trust is established under and in accordance with the laws of Bermuda and the rights of all parties and the construction and effect of each and every provision hereof shall be subject to the exclusive jurisdiction and construed and regulated only according to the laws of Bermuda which shall be the forum for the administration hereof SAVE THAT notwithstanding the foregoing provisions of this clause, the Trustee shall have the power under Clause 25.4 hereof to select a different jurisdiction.

2 Dissemination of information

The Trustees may:

2.1 promote research and publish the useful results of such research;

2.2 commission, promote, publish, distribute and sell facsimiles, photographs, models and publications of every description;

2.3 provide, promote, sponsor and organise lectures, discussions, exhibitions and other like events.

3 Use of Charity's facilities

3.1 Subject to sub-clause 3.2, the Trustees may make available all or any of the facilities of any property vested in the Trustees, or in which they have an interest, for such functions or to such bodies or individuals as the Trustees shall in their discretion think fit.

3.2 In exercising their powers pursuant to sub-clause 3.1, the Trustees shall ensure

(a) a proper fee at full market value shall be charged where the purposes for which the facilities are being made available do not fall within the Objects;

(b) the provision of such facilities shall not interfere with the Objects; and

(c) such facilities shall not be required at the time for the purposes of the Charity.

4 Collaboration

The Trustees may act in collaboration with any person, body, institution or authority.

5 Assistance to and support of other charities

The Trustees may make contributions, as they may think fit, towards, or otherwise assist (and whether out of capital or income), any charitable trust, institution or body having objects similar to the Objects PROVIDED THAT any such charitable trust, institution or body shall not be a "United States person" within the meaning of the Code and shall not permit donations or other distributions to be made to any "United States person" within the meaning of the Code (or to any other person that would cause such charitable trust, institution or body to have a "United States beneficiary" within the meaning of Section 679 of the Code).

6 Appeals, etc

The Trustees may appeal for and accept donations, subscriptions, legacies or other payments to be held on trust for the purposes of the Charity.

7 Investment power

The Trustees may apply any money to be invested in the purchase of or at interest upon the security of such shares, stocks, funds, securities, land, buildings, chattels or other investments or property of whatever nature and wherever situate, and whether involving liabilities or producing income or not, as they think fit, so that they shall have the same powers to apply money to be invested as if they were an absolute beneficial owner.

8 Trustees' responsibility as shareholder

The Trustees shall not be bound to interfere in the management or conduct of the business of any company the shares or securities of which comprise the whole or any part of the Trust Fund. Where the Trustees' holding of such shares is sufficient to confer voting control of the company concerned, the Trustees shall nevertheless from time to time obtain such information from the company as would be made available to a non-executive director, to satisfy themselves (so far as may be possible from such information) that the affairs of the company are being properly managed and, in the absence of any notice to the contrary, the Trustees shall be at liberty to leave the conduct of its business (including the payment or non-payment of dividends) wholly to the directors.

9 Powers in relation to land

9.1 Subject to such restrictions imposed on them, and with such consents as may be required by law, the Trustees shall have all the powers of an absolute beneficial owner in relation to the disposition, development and improvement of any land comprised in the Trust Fund.

9.2 The Trustees shall not be bound to maintain any building or other structure on land comprised in the Trust Fund or to preserve or repair any chattels comprised in the Trust Fund.

9.3 The Trustees may transfer land comprised in the Trust Fund to such other charitable body or bodies, having objects the same as or similar to the Objects, on such terms as the Trustees shall in their discretion think fit PROVIDED THAT any such charitable body shall not be a "United States person" within the meaning of the Code and shall not permit donations or other distributions to be made to any "United States person" within the meaning of the Code (or to any other person that would cause such charitable body to have a "United States beneficiary" within the meaning of Section 679 of the Code).

10 Borrowing

Subject to such restrictions imposed on them, and such consents as may be required by law, the Trustees may borrow on the security of all or any part of the Trust Fund or otherwise for any purpose.

11 Reserves

The Trustees shall have power to establish funds for particular purposes or to maintain reserves.

12 Delegation

12.1 The Trustees may delegate such of their powers of management and administration as the Trustees may from time to time decide to committees, consisting of not less than one of their number and such other persons as the Trustees may appoint, and may make regulations for the conduct of such committees and from time to time amend regulations. All acts and proceedings of any such committee shall be reported as soon as possible to the Trustees and no such committee shall incur expenditure on behalf of the Charity except in accordance with a budget which has been approved by the Trustees.

12.2 The Trustees may delegate, upon such terms and at such reasonable remuneration as the Trustees may think fit, to any person who is, in the opinion of the Trustees, qualified for that purpose, the management of any land comprised in the Trust Fund. All acts and proceedings of any such person must be reported to the Trustees as soon as possible.

12.3 The Trustees may delegate, upon such terms and at such reasonable remuneration as the Trustees may think fit, to professional investment managers (the 'Managers') the exercise of all or any of their powers of investment on condition that:

(a) such delegation shall be by an agreement which is made or evidenced in writing;
(b) the delegated powers shall be exercisable only within clear policy guidelines drawn up in advance by the Trustees and within the powers of investment conferred by this Deed;
(c) the Managers shall be under a duty to report promptly to the Trustees any exercise of the delegated powers, and in particular to report every transaction carried out by the Managers to the Trustees within 14 days, and to report on the performance of investments managed by them at least every three months;
(d) the Trustees shall be entitled at any time and without notice to review, alter or determine the delegation or its terms;
(e) the Trustees shall be bound to review the arrangements for delegation at intervals not (in the absence of special reasons) exceeding 12 months, but so that any failure by the Trustees to undertake such reviews within the period of 12 months shall not invalidate the delegation;
(f) the Trustees shall be liable for any failure to take reasonable care in choosing the Managers, fixing or enforcing the terms upon which the Managers are employed, requiring the remedying of any breaches of those terms and otherwise supervising the Managers, but otherwise shall not be liable for the acts and defaults of the Managers.

13 Custodians and nominees

13.1 The Trustees may hold all or any part of the Trust Fund in the name of any corporation or any other person (being, if individuals, at least two in number (whether or not including one or more of the Trustees)) as nominee for the trustees on such terms as the Trustees think fit.

13.2 The Trustees shall have power to appoint as custodian trustee any corporation empowered so to act, upon such terms as they shall think fit, and may transfer the whole or any part of the Trust Fund to or so as to be under the control of such custodian trustee, provided that the remuneration payable to such corporation shall in no case exceed what is provided for in sub-clause 22.3.

13.3 In exercising the powers conferred by sub-clauses 13.1 and 13.2 the Trustees shall comply with any guidance published by the Charity Commission from time to time.

14 Power to employ staff and pay for services

The Trustees may

14.1 Employ any person or firm, not being a trustee, to manage or assist in managing the day-to-day running of the Trust Fund; and

14.2 Employ a secretary and such other officials or staff, not being a trustee, as the Trustees may in their discretion from time to time determine; in either case upon such terms and at such remuneration as the Trustees think fit.

15 Regulations

The Trustees may make regulations for the management of the Charity and for the conduct of the business of the Trustees and may, from time to time, amend such regulations.

16 Bank accounts

16.1 The Trustees may open and maintain in the name of the Charity, or in such other name as the Trustees may think fit, bank accounts at such banks as the Trustees may from time to time decide, and at any time may pay any money forming part of the Trust Fund or its income to the credit of any such account or place the same on deposit with any bank.

16.2 Subject to sub-clause 16.3, the Trustees may from time to time make such arrangements as they shall think fit for the operation of any bank account in the name of the Charity or under the control of the Trustees.

16.3 All cheques and orders for payment of money from any bank account in the name of the Charity or under the control of the Trustees shall be signed by at least two trustees.

17 Power to pay for audit

The Trustees may arrange for the accounts of the Charity to be audited annually by a qualified accountant at the expense of the Trust Fund even if not so required by law.

18 Receipts

When making grants of any funds to any charitable organisation or charitable institution, the Trustees may accept as a good discharge in respect of any such funds the receipt of the treasurer, secretary or other authorised officer for the time being of such charitable organisation or charitable institution.

19 Power to insure

The Trustees may insure all or any part of the Trust Fund against any risk, for any amount and on such terms as they think fit.

20 Indemnity insurance

20.1 The Trustees may pay out of the Trust Fund the cost of any premium in respect of insurance or indemnity (notwithstanding the Trustees' interest in such insurance or indemnity) to cover all personal liabilities which may be incurred by the Trustees, or any of them, in connection with the Charity. No Trustee shall be accountable for any money paid to such Trustee under the terms of any such insurance or indemnity unless the Trustee shall otherwise have been fully indemnified in respect of the liability to which such payment relates.

20.2 Any such insurance or indemnity shall not extend to any claim by a Trustee arising from any act or omission which the Trustee in question commits, either knowing it to be a breach of trust, or breach of duty, or in reckless disregard of whether it was a breach of trust or breach of duty or not.

21 Trustee liability

No trustee shall be liable for any loss to the Trust Fund except as a result of the gross negligence, willful misconduct or fraud of such trustee arising by reason of

21.1 any unauthorised investment made in good faith (so long as he shall have sought professional advice before making such investment);

21.2 the negligence or fraud of any agent employed by such trustee or any of the Trustees in good faith, although the employment of such agent was not strictly necessary or expedient (provided reasonable supervision shall have been exercised); or

21.3 any other act or omission made in good faith by such trustee or any of the Trustees.

22 Professional charging clause

22.1 Subject to sub-clause 22.2 any trustee, being a person who possesses specialist skill or knowledge, shall be entitled to charge and be paid all usual professional or other charges for work done by him, or his firm, when instructed by his co-trustees so to act in that capacity on behalf of the Charity.

22.2 At no time shall a majority of the individual Trustees benefit under the provisions of sub-clause 22.1 and a trustee shall withdraw from any meeting of the Trustees while his own instruction or remuneration, or that of his firm, is being discussed

22.3 Any trustee, being a corporation appointed to act as a trustee or custodian trustee, may act on its published terms and conditions in force from time to time.

23 Costs

The Trustees may pay out of the capital or income of the Trust Fund all costs of and incidental to the creation of the Charity.

24 Change of name

The Trustees may alter the name of the Charity by deed.

25 Power of variation

25.1 Subject to the provisions of sub-clauses 25.2 and 25.3, the Trustees shall have power to vary this Deed in any particular by deed which shall be expressed to be supplemental to this Deed. From and after the date of any such deed, this Deed shall be read and construed as if the provisions of such deed were incorporated in this Deed.

25.2 No variation shall be made that shall cause the trusts declared by this Deed to cease to be charitable.

25.3 No variation shall be made that shall cause the trusts declared by this Deed to be or to become or to be treated as "grantor trusts" under the provisions of Chapter 1, Subchapter J, Part I, Subpart E of the Code or that shall cause such trusts to be includable in the "gross estate" of any member of the Committee or of the Grant Advisory Committee within the meaning of Section 2031 of the Code.

25.4 The trustee may by any deed, revocable or irrevocable, declare that this Trust shall from the date of such declaration take effect in accordance with the law of any other place in any part of the world or have the administration of this Trust, including the situs of the Trust Fund, removed to any other place in any other part of the world with full effect regarding the jurisdiction and the forum for the administration and with the right for the Trustee to make in its absolute discretion such alterations in the Trust provisions as it may consider necessary to secure that this Trust be rendered as valid and effective under the laws of the country named in such declaration as it is under the laws of Bermuda, PROVIDED THAT no such deed shall take effect unless and until a copy thereof shall have been endorsed on or annexed to this Declaration, and PROVIDED FURTHER THAT the provisions of sub-clauses 7.1 and 7.2 of Part 1 and of clause 27 of Part 2 shall not be varied without the prior written consent of the Committee.

26 Power to wind up Charity

If at any time the Trustees are of the opinion that the purposes of the Charity can no longer be effectively carried out by them or can be more effectively carried out by others, they shall wind up the Charity. After discharging the debts of the Charity out of the Trust Fund, the Trustees shall transfer the remainder of the Trust Fund to such other charitable body or bodies, having objects the same as or similar to the Objects, in such proportions and on such terms as the Trustees shall in their discretion decide PROVIDED THAT any such chartable body shall not be a "United States person" within the meaning of the Code and shall not permit donations or other distributions to be made to any "United States person" within the meaning of the Code (or to any other person that would cause such charitable body to have a "United States beneficiary" within the meaning of Section 679 of the Code). For avoidance of doubt, upon the winding up and termination of the Charity, the Trust Fund shall be distributed for one or more exempt purposes within the meaning of section 501(c)(3) of the Code or the corresponding section of any future United States Federal Tax code. Any such assets not so disposed of shall be disposed of by a court of competent jurisdiction of the country in which the principal office of the Charity is then located, exclusively for such purposes or to such organization or organizations, as said court shall determine, which are organized and operated exclusively for such purposes.

27 Committee of Trust Advisors

27.1 A Committee of Trust Advisors is hereby constituted to provide advice to the Trustees as the Committee deems it appropriate to give. The Committee shall have any and all powers provided to it hereunder, and should the Committee deem it desirable for any reason otherwise to diminish its powers, it shall promptly notify the Trustees in writing.

27.2 The Committee shall be comprised of no more than five (5) members and no fewer than one member. The first Chairman of the Committee shall be irrevocably appointed by the Original Trustee and shall hold office until such time as he shall respectively die, resign or become incapacitated. The remaining members of the Committee shall be appointed by the Chairman.

27.3 The first Chairman may appoint a first Vice-Chairman to serve for a term to be designated by the First Chairman, which Vice-Chairman shall also be designated as successor Chairman to serve in that capacity in the event that the first Chairman shall resign or for any reason cease or be unable to act as first Chairman. The first Chairman may, if he so chooses, appoint and designate subsequent Vice Chairmen and successor Chairmen. Subsequent Vice-Chairmen and other members shall be appointed by the then-acting Chairman so far as such action is not precluded by the above and shall serve for a term designated by him. Subsequent Chairmen so far as not precluded from the above may designate a successor Chairman. The Vice-Chairman may also serve as successor Chairman. All appointments and designations shall be made by an instrument in writing duly signed and acknowledged by the persons so making the appointment of designation and delivered to the Trustees. In the event that a successor Chairman has not been designated and the Chairman ceases or is unable or unwilling to act as Chairman, then the then-acting Vice-Chairman shall succeed to the position of Chairman. The person appointing a first Vice-Chairman, successor Chairman and subsequent Vice-Chairman shall have the power to terminate any such appointment.

27.4 For so long as the first Chairman shall serve in that position, all actions taken and advice rendered by the Committee shall require his approval only. Thereafter, all actions taken and advice rendered by the Committee shall require the written approval of a majority of the members (should there be more than one) either in the form of approval of the Minutes of meetings or unanimous consent to actions by proxy or otherwise. Approvals signed in counterpart shall be as valid as if signed on the same document.

27.5 In the event that the office of Chairman shall become vacant and no successor shall be named in accordance with clause 27.2 or 27.3, the Committee shall appoint one of its members to be Chairman who shall serve as such until he shall die, resign, or become incapacitated. If at any time there shall be no Chairman acting hereunder for a period of ninety (90) days, then the Trustees are empowered to appoint a successor Chairman to act hereunder.

27.6 A Trustee who in the opinion of the Committee is in any way interested otherwise than as a Trustee in any trust business proposed to be transacted at any meeting of the Trustees or who is otherwise subject or likely to be subject to any such extraneous constraint or influence as would in the opinion of the Committee preclude him from transacting any such trust business or exercising or refraining from exercising any power or discretion conferred upon him by this Deed (whether alone or jointly with any others) or for any other reason determined in the sole discretion of the Committee shall not be entitled to participate in any such trust business or vote in regard to any decision to be made in connection therewith and may be removed as a Trustee as the Committee may direct. In the case of removal, the decision of the Committee shall be approved by the other Trustees not being removed, and the Committee may thereafter appoint a successor Trustee who must be an independent trustee. A certificate in writing signed by the Chairman of the Committee to the effect that the contents thereof represent the opinion of the Committee shall be conclusive evidence thereof, and neither the Trustees nor any other person entitled or interested or claiming to be entitled or interested under the trusts, powers and provisions contained in this Settlement shall be concerned or entitled to inquire into or question the propriety or validity of such opinion or the reasons therefor.

28 Grant Advisory Committee

A Grant Advisory Committee is hereby constituted to provide advice to the Trustees on matters relating to distributions, grants and other expenditures for the purpose of the Objects set forth in Part 1, clause 3 of the deed.

28.2 The Grant Advisory Committee shall be comprised of no more than seven (7) members and no fewer than one member. The first Chairman of the Committee shall be irrevocably appointed by the Original Trustee and shall hold office until such time as he shall respectively die, resign or become incapacitated. The remaining members of the Committee shall be appointed by the Chairman.

28.3 The Grant Advisory Committee shall seek to establish a set of basic policies that govern its actions. It shall develop ideas and opportunities to maximize the impact of any distributions the Charity may make relative to the amount of resources distributed. From time to time it may receive, examine and evaluate applications from third parties seeking grants from the Charity, within the guidelines and policies it has established.

28.4 Advice given to the Trustees by the Grant Advisory Committee shall be in the nature of suggestions and recommendations, and no advice given by the Grant Advisory Committee shall be seen as limiting or constraining the discretion granted to the Trustees under this Deed.

28.5 The Grant Advisory Committee shall evaluate the effectiveness of any distributions made by the Trustees for the purpose of enhancing the effectiveness of any future grants and distributions.

29 **The Enforcer**

29.1 The Enforcer is hereby appointed as the person entitled to enforce this Trust for the purposes of Section 12(B)(1) of the Act. The Enforcer shall also have the powers and discharge the duties respectively conferred or imposed upon him by the provisions of this Declaration.

29.2 Any person for the time being appointed as an Enforcer may, subject as hereinafter provided, resign as such at any time for such reasons as may appear to him to be sufficient and without any necessity for obtaining authorization from the Court and such resignation shall be by instrument in writing, delivered by him to the Trustees and after the expiration of thirty (30) days from the date of such notice, or such shorter period as may be agreed in writing between him and the Trustees, that person shall thereafter cease to be an Enforcer, provided that, where that person is the sole Enforcer, his resignation shall not be effective unless and until the Committee shall have appointed another person to be the Enforcer in his place.

29.3 Any person for the time being appointed as an Enforcer shall immediately cease to be such if he becomes physically or mentally incapacitated or is otherwise unable to carry out his duties as an Enforcer or (being a company) is dissolved.

29.4 If at any time there is no Enforcer, the Committee shall appoint as the Enforcer any person who is not a Trustee or a director, officer or employee of a corporate Trustee or of any affiliate of such a Trustee.

29.5 All appointments made pursuant to this Clause 29 shall be in writing, signed by the person making the appointment and by the person being appointed signifying his acceptance thereof, and shall become effective upon delivery to the Trustees.

29.6 Any action of the Enforcer pursuant to any provision of this Declaration shall be evidenced by a written instrument signed by the Enforcer and the Trustees shall be conclusively entitled to rely upon any such instrument received by them from the Enforcer and believed by them to be genuine and shall act and be fully protected in acting in accordance therewith.

29.7 The Enforcer shall not owe any fiduciary or similar duty towards and shall not be accountable to any person or to the Trustees for any act of omission or commission of the Enforcer in relation to the powers given to the Enforcer by this Declaration to the intent that the Enforcer, in the absence of fraud, dishonesty or willful misconduct, shall be free from any liability whatsoever in relation to such powers.

29.8 The Enforcer shall be wholly indemnified and held harmless out of the Trust Fund from any losses, damages or judgment debts arising out of any action or suit in a court of law based upon or in connection with the powers conferred upon the Enforcer under this Declaration.

29.9 For the avoidance of doubt, it is hereby expressly declared that the powers by this Declaration vested in the Enforcer shall not be construed as fiduciary or similar in powers, but as personal general powers.

IN WITNESS WHEREOF the Original Trustee has hereunto set its hand and seal to be hereunto affixed as of the date and year first above written.

THE COMMON SEAL OF ____________________ TRUST COMPANY LTD.
was hereunto affixed in the presence of:

____

Index